Contributions to Economics

The series *Contributions to Economics* provides an outlet for innovative research in all areas of economics. Books published in the series are primarily monographs and multiple author works that present new research results on a clearly defined topic, but contributed volumes and conference proceedings are also considered. All books are published in print and ebook and disseminated and promoted globally. The series and the volumes published in it are indexed by Scopus and ISI (selected volumes).

Moritz Kappler

Western Multinational Corporations in Latin America

Conflating Capitalisms and Institutional Dynamics of Inter-systemic Actor Exchange

Springer

Moritz Kappler
German University of Administrative Sciences
Speyer, Rheinland-Pfalz, Germany

ISSN 1431-1933 ISSN 2197-7178 (electronic)
Contributions to Economics
ISBN 978-3-030-93804-8 ISBN 978-3-030-93805-5 (eBook)
https://doi.org/10.1007/978-3-030-93805-5

This Springer imprint is published by the registered company Springer Nature Switzerland AG
The registered company address is: Gewerbestrasse 11, 6330 Cham, Switzerland

To my family and the invaluable contributors across the continents, I would like to say thank you. I will remain true to my promise to try to do the same as you have done—to keep up the spirit of support, kindness, and curiosity.

Most importantly, I would like to express my deepest appreciation for two women with a sharp mind and above all a huge heart. Thank you, Jasmin, my love, and Rahel, my friend and colleague.

About this Book

This book contributes to the debate on multinational corporations (MNCs) and their impact on developing countries. It does so by proposing an analytical shift towards understanding development as a matter of institutional (dys-)functionality rather than one of aggregate (monetary) measures. Consequently, MNCs' contribution to development is seen as relating to the institutional change which they cause. To grasp direction and quality of institutional change caused by alien-to-the-system MNCs' foreign subsidiaries, the new analytical framework Conflating Capitalisms is developed. It approaches MNCs' foreign subsidiaries—being situated in a constant state of institutional duality—as being a source of institutional (behavioral) contradiction. They are, therefore, seen as being a potential source of institutional change in the host country, through actor-centered channels of reversed isomorphic pressures and institutional entrepreneurship. The empirical case referred to is that of Western MNCs, which operate wholly owned subsidiaries in Latin America. A sequential mixed-method design is applied with, first, a large-scale elite survey on behavioral patterns among corporate decision-makers in MNCs' home and host countries. In-depth statistical analysis finds strong evidence for behavioral contradiction, with MNCs' foreign subsidiaries partly behaving according to what is deemed appropriate in their country of origin. The strongest impact here is on the subsidiaries' educational practices. Second, the conduct of German dual vocational training (DVT) by German MNCs in Brazil and the impact on the Brazilian institutional setting is investigated qualitatively and compared with the case of Mexico. Conducting semi-structured interviews with local DVT decision-makers, evidence is found that strongly supports the notion of actor-induced institutional change, though its strength depends on local receptiveness in a complex multi-level context. Unprecedented findings of further interest are made across qualitative and quantitative studies on, first, MNCs' subsidiaries themselves compensating for missing complementary institutions when enacting alien-to-the-system practices and, second, the potentially successful institutionalization of complex coordinated educational practices in Latin American hierarchical market economies.

Contents

About the Author

Moritz Kappler is a senior researcher with the European Union's Horizon 2020 TiGRE project and teaches political economy. He holds a Ph.D. and has international working experience as researcher and advisor in top-level institutions in Europe, Latin America, and North America. Major research interests are trust in cooperative regimes and institutional dynamics in socio-economic organization and their impact on development.

List of Abbreviations

ACI	Actor-centered Institutionalism
AHK	Auslandshandelskammer
BDA	Bundesvereinigung der Deutschen Arbeitgeberverbände
BIA	Bilateral Investment Agreement
BIBB	Bundesinstitut für Berufsbildung
CAMEXA	AHK Mexiko
CEPAL	Comisión Económica para América Latina y el Caribe
CC	Comparative Capitalism
CG	Corporate Governance
CIA	Comparative Institutional Advantage
CME	Coordinated Market Economy
CONALEP	Colegio Nacional de Educación Profesional Técnica
CoO	Country of Origin
COPARMEX	La Confederación Patronal de la República Mexicana
DIHK	Deutscher Industrie- und Handelskammertag
DV	Dependent Variable
DVT	Dual Vocational Training
ECLAC	Economic Commission for Latin America and the Caribbean
ER	Employee Relations
EV	Education and Vocational Training
FDI	Foreign Direct Investment
GDP	Gross Domestic Product
GDPR	General Data Protection Regulation
GIZ	Deutsche Gesellschaft für Internationale Zusammenarbeit
HME	Hierarchical Market Economy
HR	Human Relations
HQ	Headquarters
IAD	Institutional Analysis and Development Framework
IF	Inter-firm Relations
ISI	Import Substituting Industrialization
IR	Industrial Relations

IDB	Inter-American Development Bank
ILO	International Labour Organization
IV	Independent Variable
LCR	Local Content Requirement
LME	Liberal Market Economy
JV	Joint Venture
MMFD	Modelo Mexicano de Formación Dual
MNC	Multinational Corporation
NBS	National Business Systems
NME	Network Market Economy
OECD	Organisation for Economic Cooperation and Development
PPP	Purchasing Power Parity
SENAC	Serviço Nacional de Aprendizagem Comercial
SENAI	Serviço Nacional de Aprendizagem Industrial
SEP	Secretaría de Educación Pública
SoO	System of Origin
SSP	Social Systems of Production
TRIM	Trade-Related Investment Measures
UN	United Nations
UNCTAD	United Nations Conference on Trade and Development
USD	United States Dollar
VET	Vocational Education and Training
VoC	Varieties of Capitalism
WOS	Wholly Owned Subsidiary
WTO	World Trade Organization

List of Figures

List of Tables

Chapter 1
Introduction

> Face reality. Be honest about what is happening to the majority of people .. . . the benefits of development, so long promised over the past fifty years, have not come about for most people. Nor are they going to. (de Rivero, 2001, p. 216)

In his quote above, de Rivero[1] indicates that for most of the so-called developing countries, developmental efforts have not led to inclusive socioeconomic development. His statement seems to apply in certain ways, especially in the case of Latin America. Despite general growth of aggregate economic measurements such as the gross domestic product (GDP),[2] certain important development indicators lag behind remarkably. Of particular importance in Latin America are unmatched high levels of income inequality and overall very low levels of education and productivity, which are the major development barriers in today's Latin America. Following this line of argumentation, the developmental progress expressed in GDP made over the past few decades seems to be of an exclusive nature in Latin America and does not benefit the wider society.

Along these lines, this work attempts to understand development not purely as a function of GDP and, consequently, to approach the nexus between multinational corporations (MNCs) and developing countries as a phenomenon beyond the former's contribution to local GDP. To grasp the roots of ongoing underdevelopment and to consider the role of MNCs' foreign subsidiaries in the host country, this work proposes an analytical shift from development understood as a matter of GDP toward understanding development as a matter of institutional (dys-)functionality. For the case of Latin America, this work borrows from the literature on the hierarchical market economy (HME) and perceives major local political economies as being ensnared in an institutionally constituted "low-skill trap" that hampers

[1] Oswaldo de Rivero is a former Peruvian statesman and United Nations and World Trade Organization official.

[2] "GDP is the final value of the goods and services produced within the geographic boundaries of a country during a specified period of time, normally a year" (The Economic Times, 2020, budget).

M. Kappler, *Western Multinational Corporations in Latin America*, Contributions to Economics, https://doi.org/10.1007/978-3-030-93805-5_1

socioeconomic development. In line with Schneider (2013, p. 16), such a low-skill trap is characterized by its incapability to generate more "...skilled, productive, and well-paid jobs," which would generate both productivity and a broader well-earning middle class.

Consequently, the primary objective of this work is to contribute to a better understanding of MNCs and their role in the context of the low-skill trap and the (dysfunctional) institutional setting that reproduces the developmental deadlock. Accordingly, it attempts to capture MNCs' contribution to development as a matter caused by institutional change.

To do so, this work incorporates a wider range of related economic and sociological strands, in particular the Varieties of Capitalism approach and its advancements into Latin America, and develops the new analytical framework called Conflating Capitalisms. Put briefly, Conflating Capitalisms is equipped with a sensitive understanding of structure and agency and assumes that institutional contradiction is a major source of institutional change. MNCs' subsidiaries, being situated in a constant state of institutional duality, and responding to home and host country sets of isomorphic pressures, are considered a source of such contradiction. Following these lines, Conflating Capitalisms makes it possible to scrutinize, first, the specific behavior shown by foreign subsidiaries of MNCs and, second, the impact of potential alien-to-the-system behavior on the host country's institutional setting and the low-skill trap which this setting creates.

Applying the newly developed framework, institutional contradiction and potential actor-induced change are subjected to in-depth empirical scrutiny using the case of MNCs from France, Germany, the USA, and the UK that operate wholly owned subsidiaries (WOS) in the Latin American countries of Argentina, Brazil, Chile, and Colombia. All these are archetypes of different types of capitalism. A sequential mixed-method design is applied in order to first scrutinize behavioral patterns. A larger-scale expert survey among corporate decision-makers in both home and host countries is carried out, and in-depth statistical analysis is applied to the data collected. Strong evidence is found that, indeed, foreign subsidiaries behave partly according to what is deemed appropriate in their country of origin, with the strongest impact on the subsidiaries' educational practices. Second, the conduct of German dual vocational training (DVT) in Brazil and the impact on the Brazilian institutional setting are investigated qualitatively compared with the case of Mexico, using data gained through semi-structured interviews with local DVT decision-makers. Evidence is found that strongly supports the notion of actor-induced institutional change, though its strength depends on local receptiveness in a multi-level context.

Two "by-findings" also add depth to the surrounding debate. First, evidence is found across both quantitative and qualitative studies on institutional complementarity in the context of alien-to-the-system action, particularly, with the subsidiary itself compensating for absent supportive institutions. Second, enriching literature on institutional change and development, this work emphasizes the potential institutionalization of hitherto neglected coordinated practices in unsupportive environments and, thereby, adds depth to the developmental debate in hierarchical market economies.

A better understanding of MNCs' foreign subsidiaries as potential sources of local contradiction and the subsequent dynamics of institutional contestation and potential actor-induced change is, above all, desirable for two general reasons. First, scholars and practitioners rely heavily on outcome criteria such as GDP and run the risk of disregarding the aforementioned detachment of GDP from socioeconomic development. In the vast majority of the scholarly debate around development approaches, the MNC–development nexus is approached by treating GDP as the dependent variable of choice that is to be maximized. Confirming the identified differences between financial aggregate indicators and the living conditions of the wider society, the four Latin American economies of specific interest serve as archetypal examples whose developmental trajectories may best be described as "economic growth without development." Remarkably, following, for example, the World Bank taxonomy that relies on GDP per capita, Chile belongs to the high-income and Argentina, Colombia, and Brazil to the upper middle-income economies (The World Bank, 2018). Along these lines, the four countries of interest belong to the highest two levels possible in development thinking. At the same time, trajectories of various socioeconomic indicators tell a rather frustrating story. Relating to socioeconomic indicators such as productivity, youth unemployment, and equality, the same apparently strongly developed countries belong to the worst performing countries globally. Accordingly, such disregard can have largely negative consequences and is fortified by theory's penetrative power into local economic policy. A better understanding of development and the consideration of the constituting institutional system can contribute to providing decision-makers with a more solid foundation upon which to act.

Second, in line with GDP as the dependent variable of choice, analogously large parts of the corresponding literature express MNCs as the explanatory variable as a quantity of monetary units (in US Dollar (USD)). The assumption of MNCs as featureless flows of USD depicts the highest degree of abstraction possible and obscures their multifaceted nature and may deprive scholars and practitioners of a more nuanced treatment. The largest part of current economic literature body expects MNCs either to blend in passively with national institutions of the host country or to generally show US-like characteristics (liberal markets) regarding their strategic interests and behavior. The inherent "disembedding" of MNCs from their (social) surroundings neglects large parts of literature on different types of socioeconomic organization. This limited understanding prevents the analysis of potentially differing effects on host countries and leads to a narrow set of opportunities for policy makers. A more nuanced perception of MNCs is of special importance to Latin American countries, where large parts of decisions are made within the internal corporate hierarchies. The relevance of gaining a better understanding about the role of MNCs in developing countries is strengthened by MNCs being a major pillar of today's globalized economy. In brief, according to the United Nations (UNCTAD, 2010; United Nations, 2018) there are more than 82,000 MNCs operating worldwide, employing over 77 million people in more than 800,000 international subsidiaries (Bartram et al., 2015). Relating to Latin America, MNCs account for between 30 and 40 percent of the 500 largest companies and, therefore, are a major local actor (Schneider, 2013).

This book is structured as follows. Chapter 2 depicts the point of departure for this work. It analyzes the related economic approaches in respect of their capability to deal with the detachment of GDP trajectory from socioeconomic development. This chapter points out the drawbacks to be overcome and the assets to be included in theory development. Building upon knowledge gained and borrowing from actor-centered institutionalism, the general logic of investigation is constructed and the major necessary building blocks for the analytical framework of Conflating Capitalisms are derived. Chapter 3 discusses in depth the MNC as a unique actor in the universe of institutions and broadens the analytical perspective by introducing differently organized capitalist systems, largely based on the Varieties of Capitalism (VoC) approach. In order to include the Latin American countries of interest into analysis and to understand local developmental distortions as a matter of the institutional setting, this chapter introduces and further develops the approach of hierarchical market economies (HME). Firmly grounded in a comprehensive understanding of the MNC and the different types of institutional settings, Chap. 4 elaborates on a broader understanding of structure and agency and makes it possible to grasp the institutional dynamics that occur when system-crossing MNCs and local institutions interact. Most importantly, this chapter contributes to understanding how behavioral contradiction in the host country may be caused by MNCs, by overcoming rigidity of institutions and narrow postulates of actors' assumed rationality. In so doing, among other things, organizational fields and the concept of institutional duality are introduced and adjusted to the purpose of this work. Capturing contradiction, Chap. 4 further develops channels of actor-induced institutional change to grasp the impact of contradictory behavior on the local institutional setting of the host country.

After having established contradiction and actor-induced institutional change as the analytical points of interest, Chap. 4 ends with the assembly of Conflating Capitalisms. The following chapters apply the newly developed framework to the empirical case of Western MNCs in Latin America. As such, Chap. 5 introduces the case study in detail and verifies the fit of the countries as archetypal representatives of their specific home institutional system. Chapter 6 conducts a quantitative analysis of MNCs' specific conduct of socioeconomic interaction in the host country and allows behavioral contradiction shown by MNCs to be captured. The chapter describes the creation and carrying out of a survey made for this purpose, among decision-makers both in MNCs' subsidiaries in Latin America and in the headquarters of the countries of origin. It applies in-depth statistical analyses to newly collected data at the micro-interaction level. Chapter 6 concludes with a discussion of findings made and links them to the wider scholarly debate. Having gained a genuine understanding of contradictions shown by MNCs, Chap. 7 investigates a special case of MNCs' contradictions in the host countries (in the context of education and vocational training) and scrutinizes potential actor-induced institutional change in the Latin American host countries. Here, Conflating Capitalisms is applied to the cases of Brazil and Mexico (the latter serves as a reference case of alleged best practice) using a qualitative content analysis. At the end of Chap. 7, the two cases are compared and findings discussed and embedded in the wider debate. Finally, Chap. 8 briefly summarizes this work, indicates certain limitations, and proposes future opportunities for related research.

References

Bartram, T., Boyle, B., Stanton, P., Burgess, J., & McDonnell, A. (2015). Multinational companies and industrial relations: A research agenda for the 21st century. *Journal of Industrial Relations, 57(2)*, 127–145.

de Rivero, O. (2001). *The myth of development: Nony-viable economies of the 21st century*. Zed Books.

Schneider, B. R. (2013). *Hierarchical capitalism in Latin America: Business, labor, and the challenges of equitable development*. Cambridge University Press.

The World Bank. (2018). iccmoot.com. Retrieved from http://iccmoot.com/wp-content/uploads/2017/07/World-Bank-List-of-Economies.pdf

The World Bank. (2020). *Chapter 6: Ease of doing business score and ease of doing business ranking*. Retrieved from https://openknowledge.worldbank.org/bitstream/handle/10986/32436/9781464814402_Ch06.pdf

UNCTAD. (2010). World Investment Report 2010. https://unctad.org/system/files/official-document/wir2010_en.pdf

United Nations. (2018, December 15). *Economic Analysis & Policy Division*. Retrieved from https://www.un.org/development/desa/dpad/least-developed-country-category.html

Chapter 2
Point of Departure

In order to put the theoretical development on a solid foundation, this chapter scrutinizes the nexus between MNCs and developing countries in existing literature and contests it with empirical data, in particular with the Latin American case. The objective is to dismantle the predominant schools of thought and to identify potential shortcomings, to find valid points of departure, and to extract substantial knowledge upon which to build. After reviewing the existing related literature body, the overarching logic of this work's investigation is introduced and building blocks for further theory development are derived.

2.1 The Empirical and the Theoretical Puzzle

The ubiquitous presence of multinational corporations (MNCs) and the overwhelming magnitude of foreign direct investment (FDI) all over the world are undisputed among professionals and scholars across the disciplines. Equally beyond dispute is the decisive role FDI plays as a constituent part of essentially every single national economy. What certainly is under dispute are the following questions that are inherently connected to one another. First, how to approach the role of MNCs/FDI in host countries. Second, do the applied approaches cope with developmental issues in reality? In an attempt to answer the abovementioned questions, this chapter aims to understand the developmental situation in Latin America, to break up mainstream economic theoretical approaches, and to understand the relationship between the former and the latter. The anticipated answer in summary is that treating MNCs as homogeneous capital flows in an environment where economic exchange is either assumed to be free of charge or practicable only through impersonal markets makes it difficult for most of the orthodox theories to capture some of the major economic distortions in developing countries.

However, this work is by no means meant to disqualify existing literature and it recognizes the merits of mostly macro-level investigation on economic growth and

M. Kappler, *Western Multinational Corporations in Latin America*, Contributions to Economics, https://doi.org/10.1007/978-3-030-93805-5_2

various spillover effects on domestic firms. However, there are certain severe constraints on development that need alternative perspectives that take into account the embeddedness of MNCs in idiosyncratic political economies.

To better understand the *status quo* in MNC-related investigations, this chapter is structured as follows: first, it introduces the role of MNCs and FDI in Latin America and their increasing importance since the early 1990s. In further course, the trajectory of FDI and GDP and its ability to translate into socioeconomic development is put under scrutiny. Second, it dismantles mainstream economic theory and its ability to acknowledge certain realities in developing (Latin American) countries. As indicated above, major theoretical strands do not seem to entirely grasp certain systemic developmental distortions.

2.1.1 The Empirical Puzzle

In general, MNCs are a major pillar of today's globalized economy. According to the United Nations (UNCTAD, 2010), there are more than 82,000 MNCs operating worldwide, employing over 77 million people in more than 800,000 international subsidiaries (Bartram et al., 2015). Moreover, over one-third of total world trade is accounted for by MNCs. In the recent past, this development has specifically been propelled by the intensifying economic interaction between developed and developing countries. Despite relatively volatile and decreasing aggregate FDI flows worldwide in recent years due to high geopolitical risks, flows to developing countries have increased constantly and totaled 671 billion USD in 2014 (UNCTAD, 2018b). The relation, particularly, between FDI and Latin America revived and gained unprecedented magnitudes in the early 1990s and can be described by two developments.

First, in the wake of the failure of import substitution industrialization that led the major Latin American countries into a ubiquitous debt crisis and the subsequent *decada perdida* in the 1980s, from the early 1990s onward these political economies underwent an unprecedented transformation (Boris, 2009). The Latin American sentiment that protectionist policies—mostly import substitution industrialization—had failed to stimulate development and distrust in domestic governmental agencies, combined with the International Monetary Fund's and the World Bank's structural adjustment programs (Bacha & Feinberg, 1985; Dasgupta, 1997; Glassman & Carmody, 2001), led to pushing for deregulation, integration into the world economy, liberalization of labor relations, retreat of the formerly interventionist state, and privatization of state-owned enterprises (Boris, 2009; Dijkstra, 2000; Iqbal et al., 2016). Second, mostly Western investors were happy to enter Latin American open markets. Latin America's upcoming emerging economies promised cheap production facilities and growth opportunities for MNCs that were eager to escape stagnating and crises-torn home countries (Khanna et al., 2010). This two-sided development led to today's situation in which MNCs are pivotal actors in the Latin American landscape. Today, MNCs account for between 30 and 40 percent of the 500 largest companies in the region (Schneider, 2013). FDI[1] has become an integral part of Latin American economies. In the period between 1990 and 2015, according to UNCTAD data, the FDI inward stock of Argentina increased tenfold, those of Brazil and Chile increased 13-fold, and that of Colombian increased by 43 times (UNCTAD, 2016a, b). Despite the relative decrease of FDI inflow in Latin America in the past few years due to the fading natural resources boom,[2] FDI stock (2.3 trillion USD) as a percentage of GDP remains among the highest in the world and has a larger footprint in the region than ever before (ECLAC, 2015). In comparison with other developing regions, Latin America comes up with an FDI stock as a percentage of GDP of about 37.4 percent in 2017 (UNCTAD, 2018a, b) and, thus, has the highest value. Regarding the individual countries of interest, Chile ranks top with a value of 109.6 percent, followed by Colombia 58.8 percent, Brazil 36.4 percent, and Argentina 12.2 percent. As a reference, on an average developing countries level, FDI stock as a percentage of GDP amounts to 33.6 percent. FDI/MNCs by its sheer magnitude—beyond its functions of providing capital and technology—takes an outstanding and constituting role in the Latin American economic landscape. A closer scrutiny aiming at a better understanding of MNCs' nature in developing countries should be of high interest.

From a pure economic growth perspective, in very brief, without going into detail for now, as Fig. 2.1 shows, there has been a generally positive development of GDP per capita since the early 1990s with a relatively sharp decrease between 1998 and 2003 caused by various national crises. The upsurge after 2003 is commonly attributed to, inter alia, cheap external finance, deferred investments (due to the crises), positive development of commodity prices,[3] and FDI.

Accordingly, this brief excursion into FDI and general growth of GDP shows that, referring to the countries under scrutiny, there is no lack either in the amount of inward FDI or in GDP growth. At first sight, one is tempted to evaluate the development trajectory as a success. However, beyond these indicators, the evaluation of development becomes blurred. As the mere growth of GDP is hardly an end in itself, one has to ask how that increase of GDP materializes in socioeconomic improvements, such as a higher degree of equity, productivity, education, and so on. It is exactly this point where developmental questions and severe problems, especially in Latin America, arise, since economic growth does not lead

[1] FDI is not to be confused with MNCs. FDI also includes other investment types, such as portfolio investments. However, every MNC is FDI and, thus, the amount of FDI proxies the relative importance of MNCs to a certain degree.

[2] It should be noted here that major parts of the decline of FDI can be found concentrated in the primary sector, in which investors have been discouraged to invest by falling commodity prices after its peak in 2011/12. In contrast, manufacturing grew throughout the entire phase and the service sector decreased only slightly (ECLAC, 2018).

[3] There are certain scholars who closely link the trajectory of GDP with the one of oil price. This argument is valid to a certain degree, since the oil price began to surge in 2002, reached its peak in 2008, and began to decrease in 2014. This trajectory shows significant similarities with the trajectory of the overall GDP (The Financial Times, 2017).

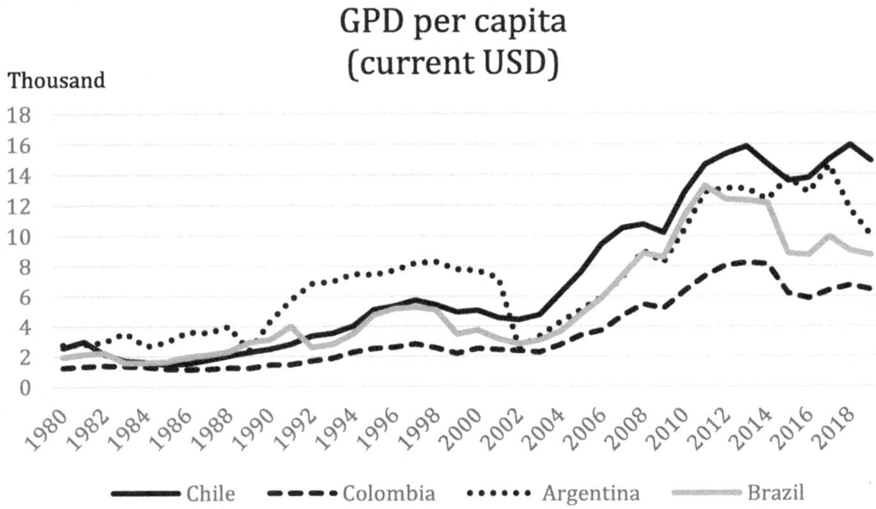

Fig. 2.1 GDP per capita. Source: From the author, based on the World Bank (2019)

automatically via the trickle-down effect to a widening middle class, better education, better jobs, etc. (Busch, 2010, p. 9).

Despite roughly 30 million people having been pulled out of extreme poverty all over Latin America within the time frame considered, social inequality remains at unmatched high levels. Confirming this, Boris (2009) recognizes growing societal tensions, as the growth of GDP and the increasing quantity of overall jobs have not increased, for example, the level of education, nor did they lead to a large number of high-skilled jobs or increased productivity. Boris' detection of polarizing societal effects is supported by the trajectory of the GINI coefficient in Latin America. World Bank data indicates that since the first measurements in the early and mid-1980s, social inequality—which in Latin America has always been among the highest in the world—has been stagnant and remains one of the major characteristics of Latin American political economies. Whereas Brazil and Chile have slightly improved, Argentina and Colombia have remained static or even worsened (World Bank, 2017a). Ranked globally, Brazil, Chile, and Colombia take—in a negative sense—leading positions and can be found among the 20 most unequal countries (Central Intelligence Agency, 2019). Excluding Sub-Saharan Africa, Colombia and Brazil are among the three most unequal countries. With an unchanged value since 1986, Argentina is an exception and is ranked at 57. In the current debate on inequality, there is a high consensus that a large degree of inequality is an obstacle to sustainable development. Inequality indicates that there is actually no equality of opportunity and that economic wealth is rather inherited than earned by one's own efforts (Corak, 2013). This discourages individual efforts and adversely affects social outcomes and social cohesion (Jencks, 2002). Empirical studies support this and show that it is in Chile where, for lower social classes, investments in education are de facto negatively correlated with professional success and money earned throughout the entire career. Supporting the general importance of inequality, recent OECD investigations highlight the relatedness of inequality and the negative consequences on economic growth on the one hand and the positive correlation between more equality and the faster pace and longer durability of growth on the other hand (OECD, 2014). Other scholars empirically verified the negative consequences of high inequality on, among other things, health and education and political and economic stability (ILO, 2015), which are without any doubt key to long-term prosperity.

Along these lines, the trajectory of real wage growth in Latin America and the Caribbean is the most stagnant one globally. In the time frame from 2008 to 2013, on average, real wages have grown by one percent annually. In comparison to Asia (six percent per year), Eastern Europe, and Central Asia (five percent per year), Latin America clearly lags behind. According to IMF calculations, in the time period between the early 1980s and the early 2000s and compared to the other regions of the world, Latin America has performed worst in overall productivity growth. Between 1990 and 2005, Brazil stagnated in terms of labor productivity and Colombia even recorded a net loss. In the same time frame, Chile and Argentina improved slightly (IMF, 2007). The average growth of total factor productivity from 1961 to 2008 was 0.3 percent per year and, thus, not even one-seventh of the growth in East Asia with 2.2 percent per year (Schneider, 2013). To put it even more clearly, according to calculations of the International Monetary Fund (IMF), Latin American countries have performed worst in productivity growth compared to all other developing regions in the world (IMF, 2007).

In terms of education, the picture looks similar. Even though education coverage has improved significantly, the quality of education remains a major challenge in Latin America. The Programme for International Student Assessment (PISA) evaluates Chile as the best Latin American performer, performing ten percent lower than the world average. Brazil, Argentina, and Colombia can be found locked among the worst performing ten percent among all countries (OECD, 2013). This trend is confirmed across all levels of education and can equally be verified regarding the quality of university education. The educational area certainly is key to more sustainable and equitable development, since the resulting skills and human capital can be interpreted as a vector connecting the key challenges of productivity, innovation, inequality, and social exclusion (Salazar-Xirinachs, 2015).

It is these contradictions between economic growth, huge numbers of inward FDI, and stagnant socioeconomic development that raise questions. Since the beginning of liberalization and privatization efforts in the early 1990s, Latin America had on average a moderate growth of GDP and continuous and considerable inflows of FDI. Above that, the sheer amount of employment and the coverage of education have increased significantly. The latter achievements in particular can partially be seen as a success. However, the absence of the expected trickle-down effect on, for example, the general skill level, innovativeness, equity, and productivity makes development an exclusive endeavor. In reality, exclusiveness provides two major problems. First, development does not reach the majority of Latin Americans and expected socioeconomic effects fail to materialize. Apart from exclusivity that can be condemned because of normative assumptions, this exclusivity leads to limitations in the overall growth of a domestic market. A widening middle class can be assumed key to a strong domestic market. Second, leaving behind the majority of people is a major source of social tensions. The Latin American history is rich in examples of how social tensions directly trigger political and economic instability (Boris, 2009); stability, certainly, is the sine qua non for sustainable development.

The purpose of this section was to detect the major problems and their inherent contradictions regarding Latin American development in general. Even though the actual topic of this chapter is about the role of MNCs, it is of utmost importance to see what the problems actually are and, thus, indicate how one should approach impact evaluation. In the following part, theories around FDI/MNCs and their ability to cope with the mentioned contradictions are being investigated. Doing so, this work dismantles theories' assumptions and attempts to see to what degree theory is capable of capturing Latin American reality.

2.1.2 The Theoretical Puzzle

The previous section has detected some of the major developmental contradictions existing in contemporary Latin America. Based on knowledge of these distortions, the subsequent section investigates the predominantly deployed economic development theories—here cautiously labeled orthodox and institutional economics schools of thought—and examines their inherent capability to cope with the problems discussed above. In doing so, this chapter attempts to break up the various related approaches, to identify shortcomings, to find valid points of departure, and to extract substantial knowledge upon which to build.

Orthodox Theories and FDI

In very brief and consciously oversimplified terms, large parts of economic literature translate development with a delta caused in performance indicators at the macro-level and, accordingly, mostly approach welfare as a matter of GDP growth (Agarwal & Atri, 2015; Whalley & Weisbrod, 2012; Almfraji et al., 2014; Borensztein et al., 1998; De Mello, 1999; Mankiw & Taylor, 2018). It is basic welfare economics literature that guides developmental thinking with the rationale of maximizing resource allocation efficiency through the functioning of unobstructed free market forces. As such, across the sub-disciplines, emphasis is put on the importance and benefits of (increased) competition, a free price system, and—if at all—a night-watchman state to cope with market failures. Any market distortion—according to market-oriented theory—would be accompanied by a net loss in general welfare (deadweight loss).

Following these lines, orthodox economic thinking approaches the matter of MNCs and development mostly positively. The "new players" in the local game are supposed to increase the economy's capital stock and to lead to higher productivity that finally culminates in growing GDP levels (Buckley et al., 2006; Hejazi &

Pauly, 2003; Solow, 1956; Kokko, 1996). Substantive development is understood, among other things, as improved skill level, employment, and equity, and, generally, a decline in poverty is assumed to follow automatically from GDP growth "trickling down" to the wider society (Jafar, 2015; Schneider, 2013; Kaulihowa & Adjasi, 2018).

However, even within the FDI/MNC–GDP nexus, empirical studies at the macro-level have always shown a major dissent regarding the impact of FDI also on economic growth and certain spillover effects (Balasubramanyam et al., 1996; Choe, 2003; Hansen & Rand, 2006; Kaulihowa & Adjasi, 2018; Kemp, 1961; Olofsdotter, 1998; Schneider, 2013). Investigating the expected trickle-down effect in developing countries, affirming the empirical puzzle discussed above, the effect of FDI becomes even fuzzier, with changes in FDI being disconnected from socioeconomic indicators (Jafar, 2015). Accordingly, recognizing a pattern in extant empirical work, it is mostly developing countries that seem to lack the capacity to transform economic growth into substantive development (Schneider, 2013, p. 73). Following this, one can cautiously conclude that the peculiarities within a system (a country's political economy) play a significant role regarding developmental success or failure. As such, sticking to the macro-level and aggregate indicators, one can assume major obstacles within an economy being below the radar of orthodox economic thinking, making it poorly equipped to understand the empirical puzzle, and depriving policy makers of a more nuanced handling of MNCs.

Making an alternative perspective even more relevant, orthodox thinking largely informs practitioners' understanding of development. As such, among others, there are the development powerhouses the World Bank and the International Monetary Fund (IMF) whose lead indicators for development[4] imply that the higher the national income per capita, the higher the developmental status of a country (Nielsen, 2011; The World Bank, 2011). The World Bank, for example, uses four categories based exclusively on gross national income (GNI)[5] per capita that are low-income countries with 995 USD or less, lower middle-income countries with a GNI per capita between 996 USD and 3945 USD, upper middle-income countries with a value between 3946 USD and 12,195 USD, and high-income countries with more than 12,196 USD GNI per capita (The World Bank, 2011). In line with the understanding of development as a matter of size, national policy makers—for decades—have been largely preoccupied with the rather binary question to either open (liberalize) or protect the local market, instead of considering the systemic functioning of the political economy. Relating to FDI and MNCs, this led to a rather dichotomous "yes or no" attitude when discussing FDI. As a consequence, policy

---

[4]The World Bank states on its website that "Classification by income does not necessarily reflect development status." (The World Bank, 2011). However, de facto the World Bank's taxonomy has gained major currency and is widely accepted as a development indicator.

[5]GNI is the entirety of domestic and foreign output generated by all residents of a country.

making follows orthodox economic thinking and the rationale of "growing the pie,"[6] meaning the promotion of FDI mostly without considering the systemic inability to develop substantively. As a confirmation of this, the UNCTAD (2016a, b)—reporting about annual changes in national investment policies—indicates that in Latin America from 2001 and 2015, 1202 regulatory changes geared toward investment liberalization and FDI promotion were implemented, and only 271 geared toward restriction and regulation.

In summary, the orthodox economic approach seems to reach its limits when GDP growth—as discussed before—does not lead to socioeconomic development, particularly, in Latin America as an archetypal example for economic growth without development. According to the World Bank taxonomy, Chile belongs to the high-income and Argentina, Colombia, and Brazil to the upper middle-income economies (The World Bank, 2018); i.e., the four countries belong to the upper two levels possible in development thinking. At the same time, the expected trickle-down effect fails to materialize, and, thus, trajectories of various socioeconomic indicators tell a rather frustrating and largely contradictory story.

(New) Institutional Economics and FDI

A theoretical body that incorporates an economy's distinct design found its way into the field of development economics more than two decades ago. Since the mid-1990s and North's (1992) incorporation of the concept of institutions into development, the debate seems to be more fine-tuned. The recognition of institutions and, thus, also imperfect markets clearly goes beyond the perception of orthodox thinkers. Accepting imperfect markets necessarily assumes the abandonment of instrumental rationality and the subsequent notion of economies as institution-free areas (1992). It is now widely acknowledged that "institutions matter" for understanding the very differing performances of economies (Aoki, 2010). However, the orthodox assumptions are still in a hegemonic position.

First of all, this section gives a very brief and consciously oversimplified outline of institutions in the context of institutional economics. Chapter 3 further elaborates institutions and their inherent dynamics. According to North, institutions are the "rules of the game." This set of rules includes formal and informal ones and it is generally followed by the actors (North, 1991). Ostrom further suggests that institutions, universally speaking, reduce uncertainty among actors about the behavior of other actors. By that, increased certainty allows actors to make credible commitment to one another. In more detail, institutions are supposed to provide capacities to (a) exchange information, (b) monitor behavior, and (c) sanction in case of defection (Ostrom, 1990).

The actual causality between institutions and economic performance may briefly be summarized as follows: the better the institutions work, the less the costs of transaction (the costs that arise by transacting due to costly information, monitoring

---

[6]Proponents of "growing the pie" argue that before wealth can be distributed among society, it first needs to be generated. As such, emphasis is put on making the economy larger and, inherently, the above-discussed trickle-down effect is assumed to follow automatically.

and enforcement of agreements), the more successful the functioning of the whole economy. Since the institutional setting is by no means guaranteed to be efficient, this causality holds up in a reverse negative perspective as well. Thus, a malfunctioning economy may have its major distortions within the distinct arrangement of institutions. Logically, an improvement of the institutional setting may lead to an improvement of overall economic efficiency.

Putting institutions in the center of interest, they are meant to be the indicator of choice for structural development. Consequentially, approaching development from an institutional perspective, it is not about immediate effects on economic growth, but it is rather a matter of the longer-term structural composition of an economy. This way, development is being approached with an indirect causality that assumes institutional development leading to higher institutional quality that again leads to sustainable overall development.

After this short introduction into the logic of institutional economics, the following section investigates the applicability of this approach to properly scrutinizing the role of MNCs/FDI in host countries. Even though institutions have been recognized as a major source of a well-functioning economy and comparative advantage (Acemoglu et al., 2005; Dutt & Traca, 2010), institutional economics within the wider field of FDI was merely a servant of orthodox economics. Affected by the orthodox thinking discussed above and the assumed inherent positive correlation between FDI and, above all, economic growth, the institutional setting has most often been treated as an asset that attracts FDI (Daude & Stein, 2007; Kersan-Skabic, 2013) and not as a potential source of distortions. Consequentially, the vast majority of empirical studies investigate which institutional design is able to attract most FDI. This FDI-oriented approach is supported by the general sentiment (see liberalization tendency above) in, particularly, Latin American countries that successful development policy directly correlates with the quantity of inward FDI generated.

The direction of causality has been reversed recently by various exceptions such as Demir (2016), Dang (2013), and Long et al. (2015). Within the scope of institutional economics, they investigate how FDI may impact on institutional development in certain countries. For now, it is not too important if FDI is evaluated as good or bad or somewhere in between. To understand the fit of theory with the empirical puzzle above, it is of major interest what the assumptions are that lead to their conclusions. As such, the following section examines the perception of (researchable) institutions and the choice of indicators, the perception of developmental success, and the treatment of FDI.

According to North and Ostrom's broad introduction of institutions above, it is difficult to see any problem with them. However, the broad application of the concept of institutions in today's economics needs some further elaboration. It was David Hamilton (1962) who first recognized and criticized the overarching meaning of institutions. Detecting a blurred understanding, he talks about institutionalism as an "...inquiry on some vague thing called institutions" (1962, p. 309). In the case of institutional economics, this paper detects a gap between the said and the done, between theory and empirical application. Assertions on the limited applicability of "best practice" institutions on the one hand and the suggested one-size-fits-all institutional arrangements on the other hand seem to have been contradictory ever since the initial notions of North in his seminal work, *The New Institutional Economics and Development* (1992). To put it in his words "…transferring the formal political and economic rules of successful western market economies to third world and eastern European economies is not a sufficient condition for good economic performance" (1992, p. 7). In the same paper, he argues that "The second economic revolution created an economic world characterized by impersonal markets and all the attendant characteristics of the latter game theoretic conditions" (1992, p. 5). Whereas the first statement indicates potential different organization of economies, in the second one he generalizes economies per se as being characterized by impersonal markets. However, it is the second assertion that informed the perception of which institutions to consider, in both the scholarly debate and among practitioners. The universal approach on economies as generally impersonal markets and the perception of institutions needed to "…permit anonymous, impersonal exchange…" (1992, p. 4) narrow down the scope of institutions tremendously. Impersonal markets need institutions that facilitate cooperative solutions in anonymous and impersonal game theoretic situations. Consequentially, property rights, the rule of law, and the suitable enforcement mechanisms have been chosen as the most important institutions (Ménard & Shirley, 2014). Since the mentioned seminal works, the major focus on market-improving institutions has remained unchanged. More than two decades later, most scholars in the field of institutional economics have agreed on the major institutional indicators to be considered (Bruinshoofd, 2016; Fabro & Aixalá, 2013; IMF, 2003; Yildirim & Gökalp, 2016). The indicators that lead institutional investigation, including the research of Demir, Dang, and Long, comprise most often the six "World Bank Governance Indicators"[7] and the 11 "World Bank's Ease of Doing Business Index"[8] (World Bank, 2017b). Taking a closer look at the individual indicators, the most heavily weighted indicators by far deal with a market-friendly regulatory environment and the protection of property rights. Using this set of indicators to make statements about a country's institutions clearly continues in a Northian fashion and the perception of impersonal markets is the object of interest. Accordingly, the institutional economics' rather vague concept of institutions and development may be summarized as "different institutions can lead to different results," but it is only the right (market) institutions that lead to a right result.

The impact of FDI on institutions is evaluated by the degree of institutional change as caused by the change of quantity of FDI inflows. FDI contributes positively if its increased quantity leads to institutional development (increase of

[7]The World Bank Governance Indicators include the following indicators: Political Stability and Lack of Violence, Regulatory Quality, Rule of Law, Government Effectiveness, Voice and Accountability, and Control of Corruption.

[8]The World Bank Ease of Doing Business Index includes the following indicators: starting a business, dealing with construction permits, getting electricity, registering property, getting credit, protecting minority investors, paying taxes, trading across borders, enforcing contracts, and resolving insolvency.

the World Bank Governance Indicators and the Ease of Doing Business Index) and, thus, to a higher perceived institutional quality. The same logic holds up vice versa, and therefore, the inherent desire is convergence of the indices measurements. Deviation (institutional divergence) from these ideals is generally seen as undesirable. Countries are labeled as more developed and in possession of high-quality institutions by fulfilling the World Bank's expectations of a functioning "impersonal market." Institutions that support transactions within the boundaries of impersonal markets are desired. This approach is applied in an unchanged fashion to all countries; examples are China (Long et al., 2015), Vietnam (Dang, 2013), the "North" and the "South" (Demir, 2016), Western Balkan countries (Pere, 2015), and Latin America (Sawyer, 2010). In so doing, North's statement referring to the problematic use of blueprint institutions is neglected. It is North's second statement on the omnipresence of impersonal markets that continues to shape the debate about institutional development. This paper strongly disagrees with this perception of impersonal markets as the only way economies work.

Since the World Bank's indices do not include indicators that directly measure substantive socioeconomic development as described in the section on the empirical puzzle, the litmus test is as follows. Since the development of institutions is again—even if mostly treated like one—not an end in itself, one has to investigate how a higher institutional quality impacts on long-term socioeconomic indicators. Change of institutions should also lead to a change of socioeconomic development indicators. If that is not the case—just like with orthodox theories—that would clearly call these approaches into question. This feedback loop has very rarely been under investigation and has not yet delivered reliable findings. On the contrary, if at all, the final developmental contribution of a higher institutional quality is most often measured in terms of changes in GDP (Bruinshoofd, 2016). By that, similar problems arise concerning the institutional economics' validity on development as to the one of the orthodox theories.

As such, this work dissents with literature on institutional economics, in particular, regarding the translation of development into the functioning of impersonal markets rather than substantive socioeconomic improvement. By the assumption of "impersonal markets" as a single possible mode of economic organization, this research neglects the wealth of literature in different coordination of economic activities—i.e., transactions (Hall & Soskice, 2001; Jackson, 2010; Thelen, 2001). This is a major point of critique, since this work recognizes the danger of putting, for example, network economies—such as Japan—in the straitjacket of transparent market enabling institutions. Following this line of thought, one may expect a perceived increase in institutional quality (according to World Bank data) even damaging economies by undermining idiosyncratic institutional characteristics. Accordingly, even though this work accepts the notion of the market as one important institution in all market economies, exclusive attention on the market is certainly an inherent problem and makes it very difficult to comprehensively evaluate the impact of FDI on development within political economies with other dominant modes of economic organization.

Of utmost importance for this work, institutional economics' negation of alternative institutional arrangements inevitably leads to the negation of differing actors in different institutional settings. As such, treating MNCs as a featureless flow of USD (or any other currency) aligned in interests and behavior does not allow us to perceive MNCs as potential drivers of institutional change and, thus, depicts the second major point of criticism. As a consequence of the potential multifacetedness of institutional appearance, this work endorses a similarly nuanced approach to actors and their behavior. To translate it into the language of institutional economics, allowing for institutional variety, one analytically allows for various games each with distinct rules. Since actors wisely choose their play according to the surrounding institutions, the choice of play will change in accordance with the change of rules, when playing a different game. This means that behavior (choice of play) most likely shows different patterns in different institutional environments. The recognition of MNCs as a homogeneous bulk and its passive role in institution building was permitted only if assuming, first, MNCs blending in entirely with local institutions, second as sheer rules takers, or, third, as generally aligned in interests and behavior. This work dissents from the three potential justifications for such generic approaches and will discuss it further throughout the subsequent chapters.

2.1.3 Discussion and Overcoming Drawbacks

Breaking up the two major strands of economic thinking, against the backdrop of certain contradictory developmental distortions, has led to the recognition of certain merits to build upon and showed some shortcomings that require further theory development.

Existing economic theory serves as a model in numerous ways. The research setting in its most general structure remains unchanged, i.e., the nexus between MNCs and impact on a host country. Institutional economics provides the investigation's rationale that "institutions matter" (North, 1992) for the socioeconomic performance of an economy, since they structure economic activity (Hodgson, 2006; Knight, 1992). In line with economic theory, the interaction between various actors in order to solve coordination problems is acknowledged as the central unit of analysis. Following Coase who interprets any transaction that does not take place as a failure to gain "...the greater production that would flow from specialization..." (1992, p. 7), most general, performance of an economy is understood as a function of number and quality of interactions. Since institutions are decisive for exactly these interactions and the subsequent success or failure in solving coordination problems, causes for economic distortions may be found in the institutional setting. Accordingly, this work aims at understanding development as a systemic endeavor rather than one of sheer size, i.e., quantity of USD.

Roughly applying the structure of existing economic thinking, there are certain points that need further development to cope with the work's requirements. In summary, regarding orthodox economics, this work does not share the exclusive reliance on, for example, GDP as a dependent variable, nor the assumptions of automatism and of institutional free exchange. Furthermore, the notion of blueprint economies, the omnipresence of liberal markets, and the passive role of a homogeneous bulk of MNCs run into danger of camouflaging inherent systemic distortions. Certainly, the institutional economics school of thought leads to a more nuanced understanding, though deprives itself by its exclusive interest in institutions as supporting market mechanisms and the continuing perception of MNCs as a passive mass. Institutional economics' consequent assumption of a generally desirable development of institutions in a certain (market) direction neglects the variety of economic modes of organization and does not cope with idiosyncratic distortions in, for example, developing countries. Again, merits of mainstream economic thinking are by no means to be generally disqualified. However, this special research setting involving the complex nature of interchanging elements between distinct types of institutional settings requires a more fine-tuned approach and a vital supplement to existing academia.

Since orthodox economic theory and the existing literature body on MNCs in developing countries do not allow for such a nuanced analysis, it is a major challenge to develop a framework that is capable, first, of capturing the variety of institutional environments and, second, of investigating the dynamics that occur when actors from one institutional environment move to and act in another one. The need to better understand MNCs and the dynamics they cause in foreign political economies is especially urgent in the developing country context in which MNCs take a very important role.

This work aims at taking the debate around MNCs and host countries one step further by overcoming the major analytical shortcomings detected. In order to do so, theoretical standpoints need to be extended, adjusted, merged, and, most generally, further developed. In a nutshell, this work develops and applies a tailored framework that considers the non-identical *Gestalt* of MNCs across different institutional contexts, spatially idiosyncratic systemic (institutional) distortions in developing countries, and the interplay of the two in host countries. It hereby departs from the existing body of literature by incorporating the following points into theory:

- Treating development as a systemic matter rather than one of sheer volume of GDP. Targeting the institutional setting itself, and not the quantity of USD, allows one to grasp the actual rules of the game and enhancement of the "game's" quality may be within reach.
- Allowing institutional diversity and, thus, overcoming the exclusive and often limited reliance on market transactions as the only way of conducting economic activity. In so doing, research may leave behind one-size-fits-all approaches that sometimes fail to cope with national idiosyncrasies.
- Giving MNCs an active role and embedding them into their social context. Acknowledging the (paradoxical) reciprocal relationship between actors (MNCs) and institutions seems to be fruitful especially in developing countries. In line with the centrality of interaction, it is exactly the specific behavior of economic actors with peculiar habits, interest, and strategies that sometimes lead

to systemic dysfunctions and stagnant—sometimes even retrograde—development. Along these lines, it is of major interest to better understand the interplay between behavior and institutions.

As such, large parts of economic understanding, as this chapter indicates, run the risk of missing peculiar systemic distortions that may be more suitable to characterizing a developing country and can be interpreted—to translate it into Northian language—as the attempt to inflate a malfunctioning "game" rather than to make the rules work. Aiming at making development a matter of (dys-)functioning institutional settings and, thus, tackling developmental problems at their (institutional) roots, the next chapter outlines subsequent steps.

2.2 Setup for Further Theory Development

This chapter introduces the logic and idea behind the investigation and discusses actor-centered approaches on behavior and institutions. Deriving the process of investigation, raising specific questions, and obtaining major building blocks of an MNC-centered approach will serve as agenda for further theory development. Particular concepts that will be under discussion throughout Chaps. 3 and 4 will be anticipated. They are—for this chapter—used in a superficial manner (using the reader's common sense and the knowledge built so far in this work) to facilitate the comprehension of the work's rationale and to embed the individual subchapters into the research's overarching rationale. This chapter, first, elaborates the logic of the investigation in the context of MNCs and developing countries and raises major questions that require new and alternative approaches. Second, discussing the importance of MNCs, the building blocks that are required to develop an MNC-centered approach on institutional settings in the host country are derived.

2.2.1 Logic of this Investigation and Research Questions

Figure 2.2 depicts the logic of this research in an oversimplified manner. A, B, and C represent political economies with distinct predominant (institutional) systemic principles; each one is highlighted in a different color. The notion of different systems clearly departs from institutional economics' exclusive focus on impersonal markets and will be further developed in the subsequent chapters. To put it in the words of institutional economics, one may say that within distinct nations different games are played. For now, it suffices to acknowledge that different systems may exist; theoretical development will take place in Chap. 3.

As indicated above, the performance of a political economy is understood as being conditioned by the quality and quantity of interactions between economic actors, meaning the capability to solve coordination problems. However, it is

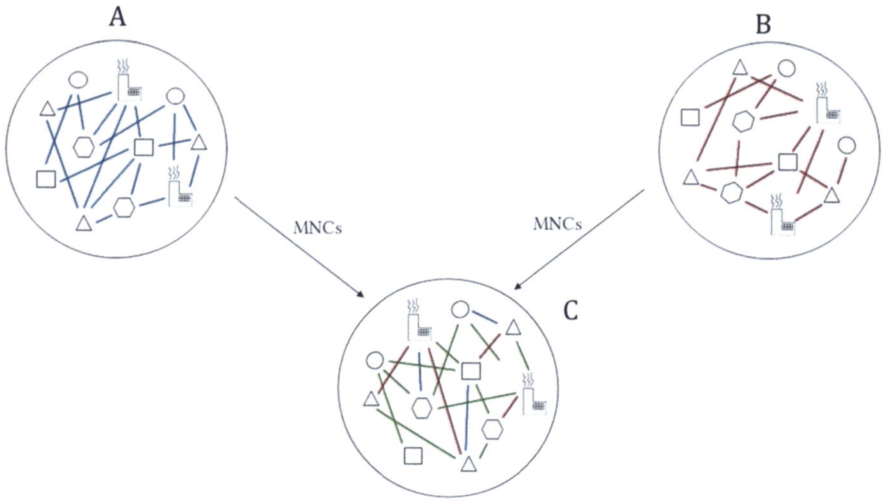

Fig. 2.2 Logic of investigation. Source: From the author

important to understand that the different systemic principles implied in Fig. 2.2 by different colors indicate that different political economies induce different predominant ways of solving coordination problems and, thus, generate different characteristics of an interaction. Within this work, solving coordination problems according to a specific rationale is understood as behavior. Economic actors therefore behave differently in A, in B, and in C. Here, behavior is defined as the choice of specific action/ways to interact and the reliance on distinct logics to solve coordination problems.[9]

In the next step, companies within A and B turn into MNCs by deciding to engage in international business by establishing subsidiaries in C (see arrows in Fig. 2.2). It is exactly this "transplantation" of constituting elements from one system into another and the subsequent dynamics in the host country that lie at the heart of this work. Its overarching objective is to contribute to the better understanding of potential inter-systemic behavioral conflicts within C and, if existent, the dynamics that may occur in C. To cope with these objectives, the first question raised is:

1. How do subsidiaries from parent companies in A and B behave in C?

   Alternative questions, aiming at the same issue, could be: On which specific kind of coordination principle do they rely? Which game do they play? On which rules do they rely? Which practice is chosen? Considering that actors from A and

[9]For example, Seo and Creed (2002) distinguish action from behavior insofar as the former reproduces the status quo and the latter changes it. Such a distinction is not made within this work. "Whereas human behavior contributes to the automatic reproduction of social arrangements, action entails a particular type of human behavior, involving conscious and purposeful departures from institutionalized social patterns" (2002, p. 230).

B act differently in their home countries than they are supposed to do in C, there are various potential answers that range from entire adjustment to C up to entire reliance on the parent company's coordination principle endemic to A or B. The characteristics of behavior may cause certain dynamics in C. Accordingly, the second question raised is:

2. How does behavior from subsidiaries with parent companies in A and B impact on the distinct system of C?

   Potential dynamics caused by behavior of alien elements in C depend on behavioral characteristics. According to the range of behavior, the consequences can also be illustrated by their extremes. Assuming subsidiaries' reliance on home country principles from A and B, they would behave other than "normal" local actors in C. A subsidiary playing C's game relying on A's and B's rules would generate a misfit and could potentially lead to behavioral conflicts that arise when alien (subsidiary) actors interact with local ones. Such a conflict may challenge the existing principle and could lead to adaptations of the local game. Assuming the other behavioral pole, that is the subsidiary from A and B's entire adjustment to C, could certainly result in a consolidation of C's status quo.

   Both change and consolidation can be perceived within a spectrum from good to bad. It depends on, first, the quality of the existing game and its capability to provide a "decent life" (ILO, 2019), and, second, the direction of change and consolidation relating to the game's status quo. In terms of consolidation, the notion of direction is meant as either strengthening something good or bad. Translating the normatively loaded "good" and "bad" into a more technical language, good means something desirable, as it is deemed to improve the working of the system. Similarly, bad means something undesirable, as it is deemed to worsen the system. Referring to potential changes, a good change means something that counters distortions that hamper a nation from providing a decent life. In contrast, bad could mean a change that counters economic characteristics that work well. Consolidation as a result of assimilation within C may also be recognized as either good or bad. In this context, good means the further consolidation of economic characteristics that contribute to the functioning of C's economy and, analogously, the bad stands for a potential consolidation of economic distortions.

Figure 2.3 summarizes the process triggered by the specific behavior of alien elements (here a WOS) in a foreign environment. The chronology and interconnectedness of behavior, dynamics, and quality is structured schematically.

These cautious attempts to hypothesize on the behavior of subsidiaries in C and potential effects on the host country will be sharpened and further developed in the upcoming chapters. Furthermore, assuming different systems that induce distinct behavior when solving coordination problems entirely considers the alternative concept of developing countries. It allows consideration of idiosyncrasies regarding both the structure and potential inherent distortions. The treatment of MNCs as constituting actors and political economies as distinct systems allows investigation of the specific rules of a distinct game.

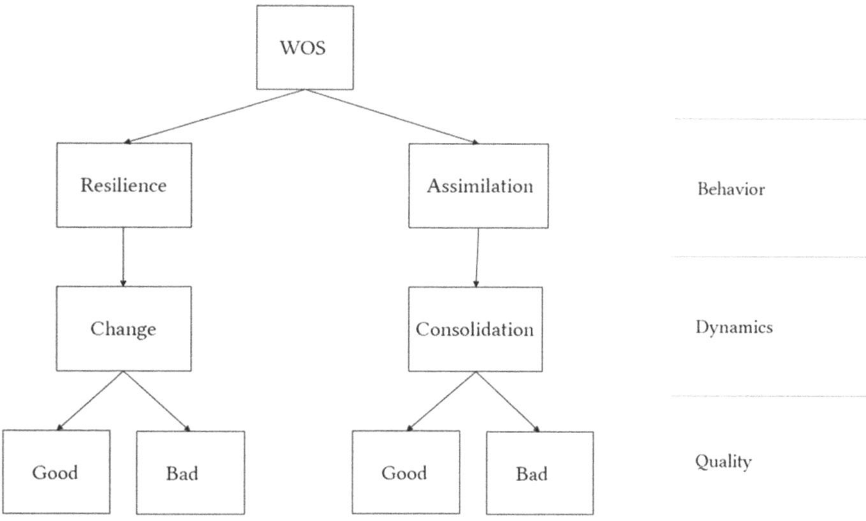

Fig. 2.3 WOS' behavior in C, dynamics, and quality of impact. Source: From the author

The aforementioned notions of behavior, dynamics, and quality are blurred and may differ from case to case. In order to make reasonable hypotheses on these concepts and their manifestations, it is important to not generalize or make assumptions about specific cases without in-depth knowledge. A prior thorough analysis is needed to understand several processes that build upon one another. Setting the theoretical agenda for such an analysis and the subsequent research, the following sections will, first, indicate the importance of MNCs, and second, elaborate the most important building blocks required for an actor-centered approach that may provide answers to the aforementioned questions and clearness on the hitherto made presumptions.

2.2.2 *Bringing the MNC Back In*

The hegemony of mainstream economics has led to the notion of companies as entities assumed "...to form naturally, and optimally, in response to market signals" (Schneider, 2013, p. 6) and, hence, made MNCs empirically a mere flow of featureless currency. As such, the organic understanding of companies and the perception of companies as an active research object has merely been present in recent scholarship.[10] Nonetheless, the company itself is not a new player in developmental

[10] One could, however, say that, as an exception, Chinese (occasionally also generally the BRIICS states) policy making and the assumed state capitalism clearly focuses on the design of companies, for example, see Kowalski et al. (2013).

thinking; it was, however, removed from both economic thinking and policy making decades ago. Until the 1960s and 1970s, the question of what kinds of companies are desired has been a top priority when discussing development (Pargendler, 2012; Schneider, 2013). National level economic policy has long been actively involved in both promoting certain forms of companies and managing MNCs and state-owned enterprises themselves.

This work's approach goes back to the tradition of political economy and uses the company's (MNC's) point of view. As the remainder of this work will show, Alexander (1990) is most likely right in arguing that the analysis of structure—as it is done, for example, by institutional economics—without reference to actors is incomplete, as it was an investigation on actors' behavior without reference to the surrounding structures. Pancaldi's emphasis on the interrelated relationship of actors and institutions on "eye's level" "…institutions use actors as much as they are used by actors" (2012, p. 7) illustrates the polar attitude represented by a smaller fraction of public policy researchers. Agreeing with Alexander and conditionally with Pancaldi, this work grants the actor an active role within the game. This analytical inclusion of active actors seems to be especially important and justified in the developing country context. As will be shown, there are both empirical and theoretical considerations that motivate the approach around MNCs.

MNCs, as a matter of sheer size (see Sect. 2.1.1), are the most important economic actors on a global base. The footprint of MNCs in the global economy is now larger than it has ever been before. With ongoing liberalization, global integration of political economies around the globe, the extensive building of global value chains combined with saturating home markets, and unprecedented growth opportunities overseas, there seems to be no reason to expect a downward trend relating to cross-border MNC activity. On the contrary, companies from developing countries also strengthen their engagement in the global economy and become major economic players themselves and, thus, further accelerate and intensify FDI (Alden & Davies, 2006; Fleury et al., 2010; Guillén & García-Canal, 2009). An approach that puts MNCs in the most prominent role enables one to deal with this global phenomenon rather than to either praise it as a "panacea" or reject it as the "evil." A more fine-tuned understanding of MNCs and potentially new instruments to improve socioeconomic interaction can be conducive for a wide audience including, economists, managers, and policy makers.

The sections before have already cautiously introduced the notion of potential divergent patterns of MNCs according to, for example, their form of appearance and the "system of origin." The potential existence of different behavior within the group of MNCs is of utmost importance since it breaks with the assumptions of homogeneity among actors. Considering differences in MNCs and, thus, also assuming divergence from sheer market-led actors, giving companies the position as the mainstay of an entire political economy not only serves the nature of the investigation at hand, but also copes with some developments in reality. For example, in the Latin American context, FDI is theoretically still mostly connected to inflows from the USA. However, this one-sided understanding does not take reality into account. FDI is inflowing from all parts of the world and the European Union replaced the

USA as the major investor in Latin America. This dispersion regarding the country of origin, in combination with the notion of systemic differences above, urgently requires a behavioral approach on MNCs.

The incorporation of MNCs into a systemic approach on behavior and development allows recognition of companies as what they are, entities with the primary tasks of competing, surviving, and growing. As MNCs are not development agencies, one cannot expect managers to align their economic activities according to their impact on development. It is the behavior and strategies chosen in the exercise of their actual duties interacting with others that finally impact on the (socio)economic performance and the institutional setting. By that, the impact of MNCs' behavior on development may be entirely unintended. Considering a for-profit company's rationale, systemic explanations of behavior and development may help to better understand the entire MNC–host country nexus.

In general, the companies may be an important endogenous agent of change. North recognizes the capability of "powerful" actors to shape "...the direction of long-run economic change." (1992, p. 3). Without any doubt, MNCs in Latin America are among the actors that command power. In the same vein, Hall and Thelen (2009) recognize various agents of adjustment but clearly see—apart from governments—companies as pivotal since "...shifts in firm strategy can erode the viability of some institutions and strengthen others"[11] (2009, p. 16). This assumed role as agent of change in conjunction with potential divergent behavior of MNCs and idiosyncratic interests certainly make the MNCs a unique and impactful object of study.

This need of actor-centrism, unfortunately, encounters a literature body that most often succumbs to the "deterministic temptation of institutionalism" (Radaelli et al., 2012). As already indicated in the discussion on the theoretical puzzle and in more detail later on, related schools of institutionalism most often see institutions as, first, changeable exclusively exogenously and, second, as (fully) determining actors. In order to build the framework suitable for the inter-systemic exchange of companies and to include the "real actors" (Scharpf, 1997) into the analysis of the game, this section consults a conceptual duo that depicts the very exception within institutional thought for guidance:

- Actor-centered Institutionalism by Mayntz and Scharpf (1995) and Scharpf (1997, 2000).
- Institutional Analysis and Development Framework by Ostrom (2005, 2010a, b).

The objective of the following section is to dismantle commonalities and differences of these actor-centered approaches in order to derive major building blocks for this work's conceptual framework. As such, the subsequent discussion, for now,

[11] Hall and Thelen (2009) use wage bargaining in Sweden as an example that shows the direct consequence of employers' strategic choices on the stand and fall of centralized bargaining agreements (2009, p. 15).

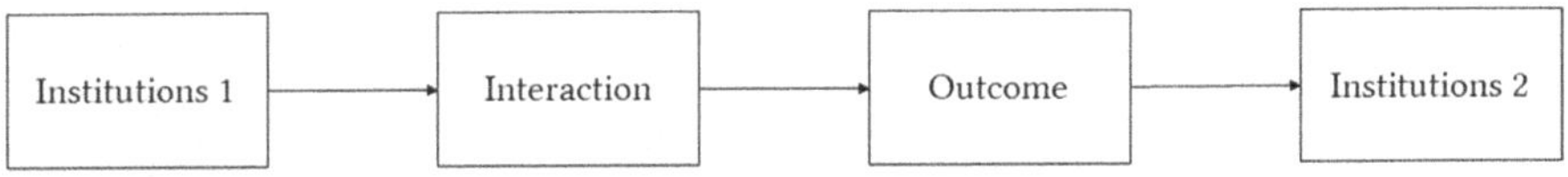

Fig. 2.4 Basic idea of actor-centered approaches. Source: From the author

consciously remains at the surface of the two approaches and digs only as deep as necessary to understand general patterns.

Neither of the two approaches can be found in the context of MNCs; however, they offer some valuable grounding. The concepts under scrutiny are to be found in public policy, emphasizing the potential of political actors to shape their environment (Mayntz & Scharpf, 1995; McGinnis, 2011; Pancaldi, 2012; Ostrom, 2005, 2010a, b; Scharpf, 1997, 2000). These concepts qualify as models since they share certain characteristics that comply with this work's requirements. They put the actor right at the center of interest, recognizing it as a constitutive and active element of a political economy. As such, institutions are treated as both independent and dependent variables. Following this line of thought, institutions are understood as not entirely determining actors' behavior and that also allows actors to determine (to a certain degree) institutions. In an oversimplified manner, Fig. 2.4 depicts the intertwined relation between institutions and actors. "Institutions 1" as a starting point depict the initial institutional setting. They do not fully determine but partially steer actors' behavior when interacting. Granting actors leeway for behavioral divergence from the one induced by "Institutions 1" may result in an (new) idiosyncratic behavior when interacting with others. Depending on the outcome of the interactions, the new practice may become institutionalized and, thus, institutions change and appear as "Institutions 2."

The two approaches have some major commonalities and differences that, partly, complement each other and contribute to the better understanding of the mechanics of actor-centered approaches. Allowing idiosyncratic actions and, in line with ACI and IAD, different trajectories of institutional development, it is reasonable to expect systemic differences and, thus, institutional diversity. McGinnis (2011, p. 171) introduces the notion and importance of an agent of change as follows: "Since institutional processes necessarily require the concerted action of many individuals, an especially critical function is filled by those entrepreneurs who offer appealing new visions or innovative practical solutions to governance problems." Even though McGinnis targets official policy makers as public entrepreneurs, his statement may indicate the potential impact of alien-to-the-system companies in developing countries that may introduce new "unfitting" practices.

Despite different wording, both ACI and IAD share several basic assumptions. As indicated above, the two frameworks perceive a circular relationship between institutions and actors through their interaction and specific outcome. Social phenomena, such as a system's performance, are described as the outcome of such interactions (Blomquist & deLeon, 2011; Mayntz & Scharpf, 1995; McGinnis, 2011; Ostrom, 2005, 2010a, b, 2011; Scharpf, 1997; Van Lieshout, 2008). As a consequence, problems can be found within the "game" and are caused by interactions that produce a negative (undesired) output. Since it is institutions that shape the interaction, one may reasonably argue that in both frameworks, (societal) problems indeed manifest themselves in interaction, but the origin of the problem lies within the institutional setting that structures the action situation, though, being firmly rooted in dysfunctional institutional arrangements. Hence, the IAD shares the notion of ACI of relying on the observable action of actors as the proximate cause and the institutional setting as the remote cause.

Both approaches—despite having different labels for it—mainly build upon a rather comprehensive actor constellation that introduces the concept of interaction in which multiple interdependent actors interact in an idiosyncratic environment (Mayntz & Scharpf, 1995). An actor constellation is roughly constituted by specific participating actors, the institutional setting, particular interaction mode, actors' orientations, etc.

The observable unit of analysis is the action situation in which actors need to decide on how to (inter-)act (McGinnis, 2011; Ostrom, 2005, 2011). The action situation lies at the heart of both the IAD and the ACI and is the crucial stage where rules work, actors meet and interact, make decisions, and generate a certain outcome. Ostrom defines the action situation as "...the social space where participants with diverse preferences interact, exchange goods and services, solve problems, dominate one another, or fight" (Ostrom, 2005, p. 14) and further states that the performance of an entire system can be judged by scrutinizing individual interactions and subsequent outcomes. Based on the understanding of the game and the demarcation of specific researchable interactions, one can, first, scrutinize the specific "input" factors that structure the action situation and attempt to improve the factors, so that the interaction may be able to produce a better output. Second, one can examine changes within the action situation, i.e., changes within the institutional environment over time.

The feedback loop is to be understood as the impact of action situations on subsequent actions situations through changing input factors. Both frameworks account for interactions' feedback on the institutional setting. The ACI and IAD view the feedback process within the specific frame structured by the underlying perception of institutions. Most roughly, the ACI referring to institutions as the regulatory framework allows change to happen when (written) regulation is changed (Woll & Jacquot, 2010; Mayntz & Scharpf, 1995; Scharpf, 1997; Treib, 2003).[12] IAD also includes this official channel of change and additionally, considering both informal and formal rules, allows for further feedback transmitted, for example, through habitualized patterns of behavior. Furthermore, IAD introduces the notion of rules in form, emphasizing that only the rules that really exert force count. In conclusion, both IAD and ACI—as one could expect from public policy frameworks—mostly focus on the regulation context referring to institutions, change, and the specific actors.

[12] Mayntz and Scharpf (1995) criticize the predominant conception of institutions (including norms and cognitive and symbolic elements) as too vague as to establish a ceteris paribus institutional environment that allows the analysis of potentially momentous actor behavior as a discrete variable.

Considering a certain degree of agency, the actor itself, its preferences, capabilities, and orientations become a decisive part of analysis explaining parts of specific behavior. In particular, it is ACI that grants actors space for agency due to actor-specific characteristics, whereas leeway in IAD is constituted by actors' rather strict pursuit of bounded rationalism (Mayntz & Scharpf, 1995; Pancaldi, 2012).

ACI, in line with its origins in public policy, further offers four general principle of action coordination (modes of interaction) that are unilateral action, negotiated agreements, majority vote, and hierarchical determination (Scharpf, 1997; van Lieshout, 2008). Summarizing behavior into subunits and assigning predominant modes to particular institutional arrangements help to systematically conduct research. Furthermore, IAD's introduction of evaluative criteria helps to estimate change dynamics, since it enables the recognition of whether a specific output may be perceived as desirable or not and, thus, allows us to hypothesize effect sizes of change accordingly.

Since ACI and IAD do not consider MNCs as actors and mostly scrutinize policy issues, all these building blocks discussed need to be theoretically developed for the endeavor at hand. Applying the knowledge gained from this section to the research questions developed above, the objective is to understand the actor constellations, to grasp the institutional roots of the problem, and to analyze the action situation (behavior) and the feedback loop (impact).

In order to do so, following IAD and ACI, it is the sine qua non to understand the game as comprehensive as possible. Deconstructing a game from the actor's perspective, the following building blocks shall be elaborated on for the specific requirements of this work:

- Who plays the game?
  - Actor
  - Preferences and capabilities
- What game is being played? What is the actor constellation?
  - Institutions (Input)
  - Modes of interaction
  - Interactions of interest
  - Potential output
  - Evaluative criteria
- Transcending borders—What does it take to cope with MNCs?
  - Relationship between institutions and actors
  - Feedback channels
  - Impact

As a preliminary conclusion, this work aims at offering a tailor-made and integrative approach that helps understanding the MNC as both being shaped by and as shaper of its idiosyncratic environment. The building blocks derived guide the subsequent theoretical development. Local phenomena, the actor and the game that can be approached through an isolated system perspective, will be elaborated throughout Chap. 3. Chapter 4 will explore and develop theory in order to cope with the dynamics that occur when actors move across the borders of distinct systems.

References

Acemoglu, D., Johnson, S., & Robinson, J. A. (2005). Institutions as the fundamental cause of long-run growth. In I. P. Aghion & S. Durlauf (Eds.), *Handbook of economic growth* (pp. 385–472). Elsevier.

Agarwal, M., & Atri, P. (2015). Foreign direct investment and poverty reduction: India in regional context. In *Research and information system for developing countries discussion paper.*

Alden, C., & Davies, M. (2006). A profile of the operations of Chinese multinationals in Africa. *South African Journal of International Affairs, 13*, 83–96.

Alexander, J. C. (1990, June). *Commentary: Structure, value, action* (pp. 339–345). American Sociological Association.

Almfraji, M. A., Almsafir, M. K., & Yao, I. (2014). Economic growth and foreign direct investment inflows: The case of Qatar. *Procedia-Social and Behavioral Science, 109*, 1040–1045.

Aoki, M. (2010). *Corporations in evolving dinversity*. Oxford Universtiy Press.

Bacha, E., & Feinberg, R. (1985). The World bank and structural adjustment in Latin America. In *Texto para discussão, No. 100, Pontifícia Universidade Católica doRio de Janeiro (PUC-Rio)*, pp. 2–28.

Balasubramanyam, V. N., Salisu, M., & Sapsford, D. (1996). Foreign direct investment and growth in EP and IS countries. *The Economic Journal, 106*, 92–105.

Bartram, T., Boyle, B., Stanton, P., Burgess, J., & McDonnell, A. (2015). Multinational companies and industrial relations: A research agenda for the 21st century. *Journal of Industrial Relations, 57*(2), 127–145.

Blomquist, W., & deLeon, P. (2011). The design and promise of the institutional analysis and development framework. *The Policy Studies Journal, 39*(1), 1–6.

Borensztein, E., De Gregoria, J., & Lee, J. (1998). How does foreign direct investment affect economic growth? *Journal of International Economics, 45*(1), 115–135.

Boris, D. (2009). *Lateinamerikas Politische Ökonomie: Aufbruch aus historischen Abhängigkeiten im 21. Jahrhundert*. VSA Verlag.

Bruinshoofd, A. (2016). *Institutional quality and economic performance*. Rabo Research/Economic Research.

Buckley, P. J., Clegg, J., & Wang, C. (2006). Inward foreign direct investment and host country productivty: Evidence from China electronics industry. *Transnational Corporations, 15*(1), 13–37.

Busch, K. (2010). *World economic crisis and the welfare state: Possible solutions to reduce economic and social imbalances in the world economy, Europe and Germany*. Friedrich Ebert Stiftung.

Central Intelligence Agency. (2019, January 10). *The World Factbook*. Retrieved from https://www.cia.gov/library/publications/the-world-factbook/rankorder/2172rank.html

Choe, J. I. (2003). Do foreign direct investment and gross domestic investment promote economic growth? *Review of Development Economics, 2003*, 44–57.

Coase, R. H. (1992). The institutional structure of production. *University of Chicago Law Occasional Paper, 28*, 1–16.

Corak, M. (2013). Income inequality, equality of opportunity, and intergenerational mobility. *Journal of Economic Perspectives, 27*(3), 79–102.

Dang, D. A. (2013). How foreign direct investment promote institutional quality: Evidence from Vietnam. *Journal of Comparative Economics, 41*, 1054–1072.

Dasgupta, B. (1997). SAP: Issues and conditionalities: A global review. *Economic and Political Weekly, 1997*, 1091–1104.
Daude, C., & Stein, E. (2007, November). The quality of institutions and foreign direct investment. *Economics & Politics, 19*, 317–344.
De Mello, L. R. (1999). Foreign direct investment-led growth: Evidence from time series and panel data. *Oxford Economic Papers, 51*, 133–151.
Demir, F. (2016). Effects of FDI flows on institutional development: Does it matter where the investors are from? *World Development, 78*, 341–359.
Dijkstra, A. G. (2000). Trade liberalization and industrial development on Latin America. *World Development, 28*, 1567–1582.
Dutt, P., & Traca, D. (2010). With whom do you trade? Defensive innovation and the skill-bias. *Canadian Journal of Economics, 43*(4), 1198–1221.
ECLAC. (2018, April). *repositotio.cepal.org*. Retrieved from https://repositorio.cepal.org/bitstream/handle/11362/43423/1/S1800258_en.pdf
Economic Commission for Latin America and the Caribbean (ECLAC). (2015). *Foreign direct investment in Latin America and the Caribbean*. LC/G.2641-P.
Fabro, G., & Aixalá, J. (2013). Do the models of institutional quality differ according to the income level of the countries? The case of the low-income countries. *Review of Public Economics, 206*, 11–26.
Fleury, A., Leme Fleury, M. T., & Glufke Reis, G. (2010). El camino se hace al andar: La trayectoria des la multinacionales brasilenas. *Universia Business Review, 25*, 34–55.
Glassman, J., & Carmody, P. (2001). Structural adjustment in East and Southeast Asia: Lessons learned from Latin America. *Geoforum, 32*, 77–90.
Guillén, M. F., & García-Canal, E. (2009, March). The American model of the multinational firm and the "new" multinationals from emerging economies. *Academy of Management Perspectives, 23*(2), 23–35.
Hall, P. A., & Soskice, D. (2001). *Varieties of capitalism: The institutional foundations of comparative advantage*. Oxford University Press.
Hall, P. A., & Thelen, K. (2009). Institutional change in varieties of capitalism. *Socio-Economic Review, 7*, 7–34.
Hamilton, D. (1962, July). Why is institutional economics not institutional? *The American Journal of Economics and Sociology, 21*, 309–317.
Hansen, H., & Rand, J. (2006). On the causal links between FDI and growth in developing countries. *The World Economy, 29*, 21–41.
Hejazi, W., & Pauly, P. (2003). Motivations for FDI and domestic capital formation. *Journal of International Business Studies, 34*, 282–289.
Hodgson, G. M. (2006, March). What are institutions? *Journal of Economic Issues, XL*(1), 1–25.
ILO. (2015). *Global wage report 2014/15: Wages and income inequality*. International Labour Office.
ILO. (2019, April 6). *Decent work*. Retrieved from https://www.ilo.org/global/topics/decent-work/lang%2D%2Den/index.htm
IMF. (2003). *World economic outlook: Growth and institutions*. International Monetary Fund.
IMF. (2007). imf.org. Retrieved May 31, 2017, from Latin America: Productivity Is Lagging https://www.imf.org/external/pubs/ft/weo/2007/01/c2/FIG 2_7.pdf
Iqbal, B. A., Rahman, M. N., & Hassan, M. (2016). MNCs and their role and contribution in Latin American countries. *Transnational Corporations Review, 8*(2), 151–164.
Jackson, G. (2010). Actors and institutions. In G. Morgan, J. L. Campbell, C. Crouch, O. K. Pedersen, & R. Whitley (Eds.), *The Oxford handbook of comparative institutional analysis* (pp. 63–87). Oxford University Press.
Jafar, B. (2015). *Why trickle-down economics won't eliminate poverty*. Retrieved from World Economic Forum https://www.weforum.org/agenda/2015/10/why-trickle-down-economics-wont-eliminate-poverty/?utm_source=Cambridge%20Judge%20Business%20School&utm_medium=email&utm_campaign=6342300_Media%20summary%2030%20October%202015&dm_i=HVY,3RXR0,EFFS53,DLMYN,1
Jencks, C. (2002). Does inequality matter? *Daedalus, 131*(1), 49–65.

Kaulihowa, T., & Adjasi, C. (2018). FDI and welfare dynamics in Africa. *Thunderbird International Business Review, 60*(3), 313–328.

Kemp, M. (1961). Foreign investment and national advantage. *Economic Record, 28*, 56–62.

Kersan-Skabic, I. (2013). *Institutional development as a determinant of FDI attractiveness in Southeast Europe.*

Khanna, T., Palepu, K., & Bullock, R. J. (2010). *Winning in emerging markets: A road map for strategy and execution.* Harvard Business Press Book.

Knight, J. (1992). *Institutions and social conflict.* Cambridge University Press.

Kokko, A. (1996). Productivity spillovers from competition between local firms and foreign affiliates. *Journal of International Development, 8*, 517–530.

Kowalski, P., Brüge, M., Sztajerowska, M., & Egeland, M. (2013). *State-owned enterprises: Trade effects and policy implications.* Retrieved from ECD Trade Policy Papers, No. 147, OECD Publishing. https://doi.org/10.1787/5k4869ckqk7l-en

Long, C., Yang, J., & Zhang, J. (2015). Institutional impact of foreign direct investment in China. *World Development, 66*, 31–48.

Mankiw, N. G., & Taylor, M. P. (2018). *Grundzüge der Volkswirtschaftslehre*. Schäffer-Poeschel Verlag Stuttgart.

Mayntz, R., & Scharpf, F. W. (1995). Der Ansatz des akteurzentrierten Institutionalismus. In R. Mayntz & F. W. Scharpf (Eds.), *Gesellschaftliche Selbstregelung und politische Steuerung* (pp. 39–73). Campus Verlag.

McGinnis, M. D. (2011). An introduction to IAD and the language of the Ostrom workshop: A simple guide to a complex framework for the analysis of institutions and their development. *Policy Studies Journal, 39*(1), 169–183.

Ménard, C., & Shirley, M. M. (2014). The contribution of Douglass North to New institutional economics. In S. Galani & I. Sened (Eds.), *Institutions, property rights and economic growth: The legacy of Douglass North* (pp. 11–29). Cambridge University Press.

Nielsen, L. (2011). *Classifications of countries based on their level of development: How it is done and how it could be done.* International Monetary Fund.

North, D. C. (1991). Institutions. *Journal of Economic Perspectives, 5*(1), 97–112.

North, D. C. (1992). Institutions and economic theory. *The American Economist, 36*(1), 3–6.

OECD. (2013). *PISA 2012 Ergebnisse im Fokus: Was 15-Jährige wissen und wie sie dieses Wissen einsetzen können.* .

OECD. (2014). *All on board: Making inclusive growth happen.* .

Olofsdotter, K. (1998). Foreign direct investment, country capabilities and economic growth. *Weltwirtschaftliches Archiv, 134*(3), 534–547.

Ostrom, E. (1990). *Governing the commons: The evolution of institutions for collective action.* Cambridge University Press.

Ostrom, E. (2005). *Understanding institutional diversity*. Princeton University Press.

Ostrom, E. (2010a). Analyzing collective action. *International Association of Agricultural Economist, 41*, 155–166.

Ostrom, E. (2010b). Institutional analysis and development: Elements of the framework in historical perspective. In C. Crothers (Ed.), *Historical developments and theoretical approaches in sociology* (Vol. II, pp. 261–288). Eolss Publishers.

Ostrom, E. (2011). Background on the institutional analysis and development framework. *The Policy Studies Journal, 39*, 7–27.

Pancaldi, F. (2012, September). The turn to real actors: Achievements and challenges for actor-centered institutionalism in the comparative political economy. *La Metodologia dei Giovani Politologi in Italia*, pp. 1–28.

Pargendler, M. (2012). The unintended consequences of state ownership. *Theoretical Inquiries in Law,13*(2), 503–523. Retrieved from Social Science Research Network.

Pere, E. (2015). The impact of good governance in the economic development of Western Balkan countries. *European Journal of Government and Economics, 4(1)*, 25–45.

Radaelli, C., Dente, B., & Dossi, S. (2012). Recasting institutionalism: Institutional analysis and public policy. *European Political Science, 11*, 1–14.
Salazar-Xirinachs, J. M. (2015, May 7). *weforum.org*. Retrieved May 31, 2017, from World Economic Forum https://www.weforum.org/agenda/2015/05/6-ways-latin-america-can-close-its-skills-gap/
Sawyer, W. C. (2010). Institutional quality and economic growth in Latin America. *Global Economy Journal, 10*(4), 1850214.
Scharpf, F. W. (1997). *Games real actors play: Actor-centered institutionalism in policy research*. Westview Press.
Scharpf, F. (2000). Institutions in comparative policy research. *Comparative Political Studies, 33*(6–7), 762–790.
Schneider, B. R. (2013). *Hierarchical capitalism in Latin America: Business, labor, and the challenges of equitable development*. Cambridge University Press.
Seo, M.-G., & Creed, D. W. (2002). Institutional contradictions, praxis, and institutional change: A Dialectical perspective. *The Academy of Management Review, 27*(2), 222–247.
Solow, R. M. (1956). A contribution to the theory of economic growth. *Quarterly Journal of Economics, 70*, 65–94.
The Financial Times. (2017, May). fDi Intelligence from the Financial Times Ltd. https://www.fdimarkets.com/
The World Bank. (2011). worldbank.org. Retrieved from http://web.worldbank.org/WBSITE/EXTERNAL/DATASTATISTIC/0,,contentMDK:20420458~menuPK:64909257~pagePK:64909151~piPK:64909148~theSitePK:6950074,00.html
The World Bank. (2018). iccmoot.com. Retrieved from http://iccmoot.com/wp-content/uploads/2017/07/World-Bank-List-of-Economies.pdf
The World Bank. (2019). *World Bank Statistics*. Retrieved from https://data.worldbank.org/indicator/SI.POV.GINI?end=2017&locations=DE-GB-US-FR-OE&start=1995&view=chart
Thelen, K. (2001). Varieties of labor politics in the developed democracies. In P. A. Hall & D. Soskice (Eds.), *Varieties of capitalism: The institutional foundations of comparative advantage* (pp. 71–103). Oxford University Press.
Treib, O. (2003). Die Umsetzung von EU-Richtlinien im Zeichen der Parteipolitik: Eine akteurzentrierte Antwort auf die Misfit-These. *Politische Vierteljahresschrift, 44*(4), 506–528.
UNCTAD. (2010). World Investment Report 2010. https://unctad.org/system/files/official-document/wir2010_en.pdf
UNCTAD. (2016a). unctad.org. Retrieved May 30, 2017, from World Investment Report 2016: Annex Tables http://unctad.org/en/Pages/DIAE/World%20Investment%20Report/Annex-Tables.aspx
UNCTAD. (2016b). *World investment report 2016*. United Nations Publications.
UNCTAD. (2018a, November). *United Nations Confrence on Trade and Development*. Retrieved from https://unctad.org/en/Pages/DIAE/World%20Investment%20Report/Country-Fact-Sheets.aspx
UNCTAD. (2018b). *World investment report 2018*. United Nations.
van Lieshout, H. A. (2008). *Different hands. Markets for intermediate skills in Germany, the U.S. and the Netherlands.*
Whalley, J., & Weisbrod, A. (2012). The contribution of Chinese FDI to Africa's pre crisis growth surge. *Global Economy Journal, 12*(4), 1–28.
Woll, C., & Jacquot, S. (2010). Using Europe: Strategic action in multi-level politics. *Comparative European Politics*, 110–126.
World Bank. (2017a, May). worldbank.org. Retrieved May 30, 2017, from http://data.worldbank.org/indicator/NY.GDP.PCAP.CD?end=2015&locations=AR-CO-BR-CL&start=1985
World Bank. (2017b). doingbusiness.org. Retrieved June 2, 2017, from About doing business: Doing business 2017 http://www.doingbusiness.org/~/media/WBG/DoingBusiness/Documents/Annual-Reports/English/DB17-Chapters/DB17-About-Doing-Business.pdf
Yildirim, A., & Gökalp, M. F. (2016). Institutions and economic performace: A review on the developing countries. *Procedia Economics and Finance, 38*, 347–359.

Chapter 3
Actor Specificities and the Types of Socio-economic Organization

Before genuinely moving to the dynamics of inter-systemic exchange, the constituent elements of the actor constellation(s) are developed within the context of the endeavor at hand. On that account, Sect. 3.1 theoretically discusses the nature and organizational peculiarities of the MNC as a unique actor that is physically present in various countries. Second, Sect. 3.2 gives an overview of the different "games" being played relying on the Comparative Capitalism (CC) literature. Most prominently, it introduces in detail Hall and Soskice's (2001) Varieties of Capitalism (VoC) approach and discusses associated points of critique and succeeding extensions. Various modes of economic organization and their underlying institutional settings are discussed, shedding light on institutional diversity and systemic functioning. Extending the VoC framework onto the "Global South," Sect. 3.3 introduces various VoC extensions and discusses—most prominently—Schneider's (2013) hierarchical market economy (HME) for Latin America and brings it in line with the conventional VoC approach. Understanding and further developing Schneider's HME allows for an analytical shift inasmuch as development, specifically socioeconomic distortions in, for example, Latin America, can be reasonably approached through institutional analysis.

3.1 Understanding the MNC

As discussed above, a proper understanding of the actor under scrutiny is strongly needed to better comprehend behavioral dynamics and the specific relationship between action and institutions. Accordingly, before digging deeper into MNCs' position within a unique social context and peculiarities of institutional dynamics in Chap. 4, this chapter introduces a rather technical understanding of the border-crossing actor. Most importantly, first, the MNC cannot be treated like a traditional firm and, second, the MNC is not to be understood as a developmental agency. On that account specifics on MNCs' nature, organizational structures, and, among

M. Kappler, *Western Multinational Corporations in Latin America*, Contributions to Economics, https://doi.org/10.1007/978-3-030-93805-5_3

others, issues of ownership need to be further explained to reasonably approach the MNC as both tension field and potential agent of change in host countries.

The general perception of an MNC is quite vague and definitions are ambiguous. Whereas some scholars, for example, define a corporation as multinational when generating more than 25 percent of revenue from out-of-home-country activities (The Law Dictionary, 2019), this work keeps to a more precise definition. According to scholars investigating FDI,[1] the distinguishing characteristic of an MNC is the direct investment made abroad and is defined accordingly "...as a firm that owns and controls activities in two or more different countries" (Buckley & Casson, 2009, p. 2). However, this first approximation only serves as rough guidance and needs further explanation. Despite being merely a label, certain characteristics such as control and ownership are decisive for this work. To better grasp the nature of FDI, the following section embeds the MNC within the corresponding literature body.

MNCs have been part of a vivid debate ever since the mid-1970s' seminal works of, inter alia, Buckley and Casson (1976), Hymer (1976), and Dunning (1979). The actual motivation of MNC theory is, first, mostly in a tradition building upon Coase's (internalization) theory of the firm (1937), to explain their existence (Buckley & Casson, 1976, 2010; Rugman & Verbeke, 2008), second, to understand the determinants and the strategy of the international division of labor (Blomström & Lipsey, 1989, 1991; Buckley & Casson, 2010; Dunning, 2009; Gulati et al., 2002; Porter, 1990)—following a Smithsonian tradition (Smith, 1776)—and third, to comprehend MNCs' different forms and organizational structures (Buckley & Casson, 2010; Dunning, 1979; Wach, 2014).

Since of utmost importance for this work, mostly referring to the latter strand of literature, the notion of different forms of foreign business activity directly provides information about resource commitment, dependence, control, and technology risk (Osland et al., 2001). Resource commitment can be understood as the dedicated assets (intangible, such as managerial skills, and tangible, such as machines and money) that cannot be used for other activities without causing costs. Control—according to Osland et al. (2001)—is the ability and willingness to influence operations, systems, decisions, and methods in the host country through intra-organizational channels. Also important for this work, the dependence of a subsidiary on a specific company follows the trajectory of ownership intensity and, thus, the one of control. Technology risk is defined as the likelihood that an MNCs' knowledge (intangible or tangible) will be transferred to a local company unintentionally (Osland et al., 2001). In addition, the form of foreign business gives certain information about the stage of the company's internationalization process, which again provides information on experience, market knowledge, and commitment within the foreign country (Johanson & Vahlne, 2009). These

[1] The concept of multinational is not to be confused with the one of Ghoshal and Bartlett discussing different forms of corporate organization as a response to the needs of local adaptation and financial pressure (Ghoshal & Westney, 1993).

characteristics may be decisive when investigating transfer of practices from the home to the host country through intra-organizational channels.

To better understand the concept of MNCs, the following section embeds the underlying concept of FDI in the context of a company's internationalization process and discusses alternative forms of foreign market entry. These forms vary with the aforementioned resource commitment, control, dependence, and risk.

Simply put, Welch and Luostarinen (1988) define internationalization as the process of a company's increasing entanglement in international business (Root, 1994; Wach, 2014). In order to participate in international business, a company can draw on various modes of participation, better known as entry strategies to foreign markets. Most basically, one can distinguish between three categories of international engagement, which are exporting, contractual, and investment modes (FAO, 2019; Osland et al., 2001; Wach, 2014). Each category in itself is a field of distinguished scholarship; however, since particular interest is put on the investment modes, very brief notions of exporting and contractual modes are sufficient for the purpose of this work.

The simplest entry strategy is one of exporting, that is, selling goods (and services) produced in one country into another (FAO, 2019). By this, exporting differs from other modes since it is the only one in which the final or intermediate product is manufactured outside of the actual target country (Osland et al., 2001). In line with companies' rationale of profit-making, exporting can be seen as the first logical step of internationalization when facing saturated domestic markets, surplus production, and growth opportunities abroad (Blomström & Lipsey, 1989; Pope, 2002; Wach, 2014). Selling abroad can be conducted either indirectly through independent export intermediaries from within the parent company's home country or directly through foreign distributors such as external agents or the company's own representative offices. Generally, exporting is associated with very low entry costs, low staffing requirements, low technology risk, and low financial risk on the one hand and with relatively low profitability, dependence on intermediaries (when external), high transport costs, and a relatively low degree of control on the other hand (Wach, 2014).

Contractual modes, also called non-equity modes, such as licensing, leasing, franchising, and management service contracts allow a company to transfer specific capabilities to host country ventures without the necessity of prior equity investments (Dunning et al., 2007; Erramilli et al., 2002; Sherman, 2011). Licensing, as an example, is a contractual mode of market entry with one or more partner companies in the host country. A company using licensing (the licensor) goes abroad inasmuch as it transfers the right to use its property such as patents, brand name, business methods, and technology to another company in the host country. In return, the licensor receives a licensing fee or a royalty. Contractual modes are associated with medium financial risk, low entry costs, and possibility of rapid foreign expansion but comes with the downside of, inter alia, relatively low profitability, low control, high technological risk, and the inability to gain experience abroad (Wach, 2014).

The internationalization mode of particular interest for this work is the investment mode. It is the most complex one and requires the largest commitment within international business. It entails direct investments and refers to the situation when a company invests in a constant and physical presence in markets abroad. Hence, it is FDI that makes a company an MNC. An MNC engages in FDI and, thus, owns and controls economic activities in more than one country (Dunning, 1993, p. 3). Pries (2000) introduces the notion of a "company of companies" that involves corporate headquarters in the country of origin and subsidiaries in host countries, which together form a joint organization. In line with Dunning, the single most important characteristic of FDI is that the MNC undertakes this effort with the purpose of exercising direct control over the subsidiary (Buckley & Casson, 2010; Buckley & Pearce, 1979; UNCTAD, 2017). Along the same lines, Kogut defines the MNC as "...the product of foreign direct investment that is defined as the effective control of operations in a country by foreign owners" (Kogut, 2001, p. 10197). Following the importance of control, it is important to distinguish FDI from portfolio investment. Ever since Hymer (1976), it is recognized that capital flows (portfolio investment) should not be mixed up with FDI. It is not the exertion of control, but the objective to levy the highest interest rates possible that motivates the flow of portfolio investments. Usually, such capital flows may be invested in bonds or in equity shares that are too insignificant to approve control (Kogut, 2001; Roy et al., 2017).

An MNC investing directly abroad has to take two major decisions, one on the ownership structure and one to either build or buy. Referring to the ownership structure, it needs to decide between two investment entry modes that both provide an ownership claim of the investing company on a foreign subsidiary in the host country but differ in the degree of ownership and, accordingly, also in the degree of control. Most basically these are either a joint venture[2] or a WOS. Joint ventures involve at least two organizations that agree to share access to key resources, technology, knowledge, rights, etc. to supplement each other's needs. On a more formal basis, they—most often an MNC and a local partner—share ownership, risks, rewards, and management of the newly formed company in the host country (Chao et al., 2014; Osland et al., 2001). Joint ventures are subject to critique because of the ambiguity of control, potential conflicts with the partner, medium technology risk, and high entry costs. On the other side, there are potential benefits such as synergy effects, shared risk, and access to sometimes closed markets. Having a joint venture subsidiary abroad can provide a wide range of ownership claims including minority interests, joint control (50:50), and majority interests.

WOS are entities in host countries in which the parent company (MNC) has full ownership and sole responsibility for the conduct of business activities and its management (Chang et al., 2013; Osland et al., 2001). WOS depend exclusively on the resources of its parent company and demonstrate the entity that is most dependent on one source of knowledge, technology, finance, etc. This specific relation between a parent company and WOS leads to certain characteristics. WOS are attractive since they offer the highest degree of control without any need for

[2]Regarding JVs, there are various sub-modes. For more details, see Yan and Luo (2015) and Luo (2007).

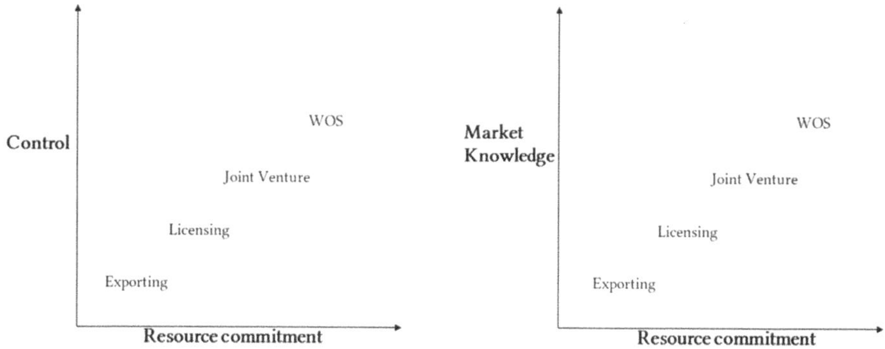

Fig. 3.1 Control, knowledge, and resource commitment. Source: From the author, based on Osland et al. (2001); Forsgren and Johanson (2010)

finding a consensus with other stakeholders. Along the same lines, WOS come up with the lowest technology risk and the potentially highest profitability both for the same reasons that is being alone, which again means no need for sharing profits nor is there any danger of partners breaching their agreement. On the downside, entry costs and general resource commitment are the highest among all potential entry strategies. Establishing one's own entity and conducting all necessary steps required to build up a company and to keep it running is complex and costly (Osland et al., 2001; Wach, 2014).

The other consideration as to whether to build or buy a subsidiary abroad is of further interest: within the category of investment modes, a company needs to decide whether to make either a greenfield or a brownfield investment. The concept of greenfield investments includes investing from the beginning and starting a new plant by creating a new facility in the host country. Brownfield investments are made when establishing a foreign subsidiary by taking over an already existing firm (Blomström et al., 2000, Wach, 2014). Generally, international business literature does not differ between greenfield and brownfield investments when discussing characteristics of commitment, control, and risk. However, following Osland et al.'s definition of control as the ability to influence the subsidiary's operations and decisions, one could reasonably argue that it may be easier to implement a desired setup by establishing a new organization rather than changing an existing one.

Summing up the discussion, particularly, on control and costs (commitment) above, on the left side of Fig. 3.1, the positive relation between resource commitment and control is shown. WOS clearly stands out for the highest commitment of resources in the foreign market, remunerated by the highest possible level of control exercisable by the parent company.

Alongside with the aforementioned notions of control by Kogut and Osland et al., when establishing a WOS a parent company can be assumed to be most capable of implementing operations and systems and of taking decisions according to their conception within an entity in a foreign country. Keeping resource commitment on the abscissa and replacing control with financial risk, the trajectory remains unchanged, grounding in the straightforward rationale: the more invested a company, the higher the potential loss. Putting technology risk on the ordinate, the trajectory changes into an inversed U-curve. Both exporting and WOS in its original form are conducted by one company solely and, thus, the risk of unintentionally transferring knowledge to a local company is very low. Technology risk peaks when conducting contractual agreements and joint ventures with another company that may cause a breach of specific agreements (Osland et al., 2001). Following this line of thought, every partner—even though providing complementary resources—poses a certain additional risk.

On the right side of Fig. 3.1, the relation between commitment (costs) and market knowledge is shown, well known from the context of the Uppsala internationalization model (Johanson & Vahlne, 1977, 2009). The Uppsala model perceives the internationalization process as experiential and evolutionary in nature, which is built upon the intertwined relation between learning and commitment. Accordingly, based on market knowledge, a company selects a suitable commitment strategy. As Fig. 3.1 shows, a company that knows little about the market tends to invest less in the foreign market/country. However, being engaged in the market, a company learns continuously and, thus, accumulates higher market knowledge. As a consequence, the commitment strategy will be adjusted to the increased knowledge over time. According to Johanson and Vahlne (1977, 2009), these strategic cycles usually begin with ad hoc exporting and potentially end with the establishment of WOS. This so-called establishment chain is further being strengthened by the concept of psychic distance, which makes it more difficult to understand foreign markets and, consequently, also to accumulate market knowledge. The concept of psychic distance stems from, among others, Hymer's notion of liability of foreignness (1976). According to the liability of foreignness, a foreign investor needs to come up with firm-specific advantages that more than offset this liability (the burden of being foreign and not knowing about the local market) (Johanson & Vahlne, 2009). Following these lines, the larger the psychic distance from a foreign market—keeping the investment mode stable and reasonable—the larger the liability a company has to bear or the clearer the firm-specific advantages need to be to offset the liability.

Applying the Uppsala model in conjunction with Hymer's liability of foreignness, one can draw two conclusions. First, MNCs establishing WOS in foreign markets are assumed to have quite a lot of knowledge about the local markets. Second, the further the psychic distance between markets (political economies), the more complex it is to accumulate market knowledge, since it deviates from the home context. In combination, despite a large psychic distance, if a company establishes a WOS in a foreign country, it is assumed to have enough knowledge about the foreign market.

Figure 3.2 summarizes the sequence of decisions a company faces when thinking about going abroad. All internationalization modes discussed above are potential outcomes of a set of different decisions that build upon each other. The first decision to either go abroad or not is the point of departure and will be followed by deciding

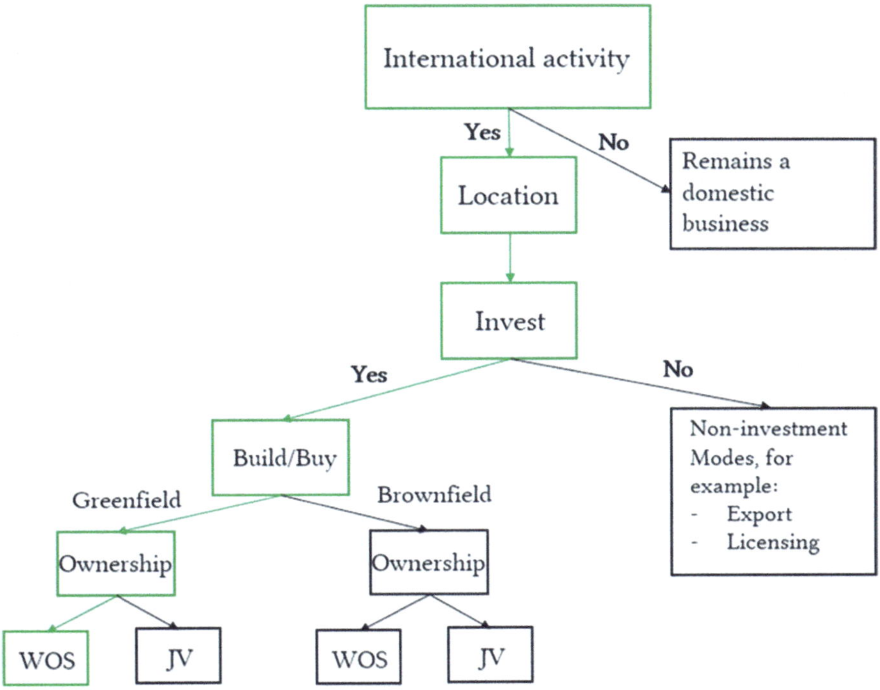

Fig. 3.2 Internationalization decision tree. Source: From the author, based on Nitsch (1999)

whether to invest directly in the foreign country or to rely on non-equity entry strategies such as exporting or licensing. If a company decides to engage in a foreign market through FDI, a company can either build a new plant from the "green field" or merge or acquire an already existing one (brownfield investment). Relating to both paths chosen, the final decision takes place within the context of the ownership structure and leads to either a joint venture with at least one partner or a WOS.

As the green highlighted path in Fig. 3.2 indicates, this work exclusively scrutinizes WOS that were built through greenfield investments. Since it is the investigation's overarching objective to detect and scrutinize potential patterns of MNCs' behavior relating to the corresponding country of origin, the entry strategy that promises the purest and clearest connection to the parent company within the home country has been chosen. As elaborated above, relating to WOS, the parent company's potential to exercise control is the highest among all possible market entry strategies. In line with this unmatched degree of control, the parent company should be capable of influencing operations, systems, decisions, and methods of the foreign subsidiary according to its perception through intra-organizational channels. Since the parent company comes up with complete ownership of and sole responsibility for the subsidiary, the foreign entity is entirely dependent on one company. This dependence may strengthen the parent company's leverage over the subsidiary abroad. Furthermore, being strongly committed to a foreign market makes the parent company subject to the highest financial risk possible. Together with the Uppsala model and the assumed self-enforcing relation between knowledge and commitment, one can assume a company is well aware of foreign market peculiarities when deciding to directly invest in WOS. In addition, this work focuses exclusively on WOS established through greenfield investments, since it is assumed that building something new facilitates the implementation of one's own perceptions when comparing it to buying an already existing entity.

The following section attempts to build a bridge between the rather technical view on MNCs and the meaning of control and commitment for the remainder of this work. In so doing, MNCs' potential role as a (foreign) societal actor in the host country is anticipated. The differences between the various entry modes and the clear demarcation from portfolio investments suggest that an MNC is more than just an import flow of capital. However, as is shown in Chap. 2, the notion of capital flows is exactly the way mainstream economics treats MNCs. In line with this chapter on control, commitment, risk, and knowledge, it is Hymer's notion of foreign liability (1976) that hints at the special nature of MNCs. Explaining MNCs' existence abroad despite having the burden of foreign liability, MNCs must have a competitive advantage that more than offsets this disadvantage in comparison to local competitors. According to Kogut (2001), this advantage is inevitably the same one that the company has built on in the home market. In line with that, one can reasonably argue that the MNC most likely expands into a foreign market using what it has experienced and learned in the home country. Following this line of argument, Kogut proposes an alternative, less technical definition of MNCs. Investigating the internationalization process of a company, he emphasizes the expanding company's role as "...the mechanism by which organizational practices are transferred and replicated..." (Kogut, 2001, p. 10197). One can therefore conclude that the MNC may transfer home country practices to the subsidiary abroad. Further supporting this view, applying standardized practices and organizational forms worldwide is supposed to leverage synergies and to increase corporate efficiency (Ghoshal & Bartlett, 1990; Kogut, 2001). Both definitions of MNCs, the more technical ones by Dunning and Osland et al. above and the rather sociological one by Kogut, seem to be complementary in the context of control and transfer of practices for two reasons: first, a higher degree of control facilitates the transfer of practices and, second, the transfer of practices, de facto, is an instrument of exercising control.

This chapter defined FDI and the subsequent concept of the MNC and introduced the various entry strategies that are available to a company when engaging in international business. Most generally, these are exporting, contractual, and investment modes. Investigating the three modes and its subunits according to their corresponding degree of control, commitment, risk, and market knowledge led to the recognition of WOS as the entry strategy that provides the highest control, accompanied by the highest commitment and the highest risk. Additionally, accompanying risk and commitment, the Uppsala model suggests that companies establishing WOS should be well aware of foreign market peculiarities. Since this work's main objective is to scrutinize potential patterns of MNCs' behavior relating to the corresponding country of origin, this chapter elaborated on the subject of analysis that offers the potentially purest impact of a clearly traceable parent company, which is the WOS established through greenfield investments. In conclusion, the combination of the rather technical definitions of MNCs as an instrument to exercise control on entities in foreign countries (Buckley & Casson, 2009; Dunning, 1993) with Hymer's (1976) notion of foreign liability and Kogut's (2001) emphasis on MNCs as mechanism to replicate practices in its subsidiaries anticipates the potential conflicting role of MNCs as a unique societal actor, being potentially (partially) steered by an entity in another country.

3.2 Understanding the Game(s) Beyond Impersonal Markets

At first sight, the application of CC literature on dynamics of change is counterintuitive since its bread and butter is the explication of stability. However, as a first step, an understanding of the status quo of the systems at an isolated systemic level is required to elaborate on dynamics of inter-systemic exchange at a meso-level where various systems come into conflict with one another that follow in Chap. 4. Hence, following the building blocks derived in Sect. 3.2.2, this chapter is exclusively interested in understanding the spatially isolated "pure game(s)" (respectively the actor constellation and action situations) being played in countries A, B, and C. To grasp the logic of the game(s) and to acknowledge the "...differences in the social organization of private economic activity..."(Jackson & Deeg, 2006, p. 11), the issues of institutions, interaction, and output are approached within the frames set in Sect. 3.2.2. Accordingly, the approach of choice should be able to capture institutional variety beyond markets and to give information on potentially differing behavior of economic actors. Given the research subject as being MNCs, the company as actor should be given the most prominent role within the political economy. Therefore, "eyes," domains, interaction, etc. should be selected appropriately. Additionally, the entire theoretical body serves only inasmuch as it is able to connect institutions with the socioeconomic outcomes already addressed above. Along these lines, to contribute to the understanding of micro-behavioral patterns of WOS in host countries that connect to macroeconomic outcomes, the game being played should be able to be tested on a relatively large scale.

The game itself has already been part of this work's discussion; however, its functioning beyond "playing the market" has not yet been under scrutiny. On that account, this chapter introduces the school of CC and further elaborates on it for the use of this work. This chapter is of particular importance since it represents the status quo (ante) of the "games" of which one should be aware as it serves as the initial stage for theoretical development and empirical analyses.

In brief, CC depicts the scholarly debate on the distinctiveness of spatially separated institutional settings and the subsequent varying coordination (governance) principles, including both market and nonmarket ones. Querying the hegemony of the market, Hollingsworth and Boyer (1997), among others, emphasize the existence of alternative coordination mechanisms and report various examples that show market coordination as not leading to the best outcome possible. Along the same lines, various scholars such as Hall and Soskice (2001) bring in an understanding of institutional equifinality, meaning that different coordination principles can generate equal levels of prosperity. Accordingly, they doubt Fukuyama's (1992) postulated "end of history" and the inherent unquestioned victory of free-market capitalism and the neoliberal global convergence hypotheses trusting entirely in self-adjusting market mechanisms (Schröder, 2014). Moving within the boundaries of capitalism, though, all different forms of political economies include the market as the governance mechanism. Nonetheless, since capitalist nations have developed idiosyncratically, CC recognizes that the role of the market and the reliance on alternative coordination mechanisms vary significantly between nation-states (Crouch & Streeck, 1997; Deeg & Jackson, 2007; Hall & Soskice, 2001).

As such, institutional typologies proposed by CC serve to roughly categorize institutional settings and subsequent expectable behavior. With the proposed less deterministic view—compared to orthodox economics—comes the limited ability to precisely predict an individual's behavior as a consequence of being embedded in a specific set of institutions. Applying Ostrom (2005, 2010a, b, 2011) to nationally differing institutional settings in a metaphorical manner: "In a well-ordered human enterprise, some behaviors are rarely observed because individuals following rules do not normally engage in that activity in the given setting." Hence, under the umbrella of a specific set of institutions, individuals tend to rely on a distinct set of behavior. However, such a set of behavior may be relatively broad and different individuals may behave substantially differently when facing the same situation. Bottom line: CC does not presume to predict individual behavior, but shows significant differences targeting the masses. Thus, the general goal is to detect broad behavioral patterns of interaction.

To improve the understanding of the individual games at the isolated systemic level, this chapter is structured as follows. First, introducing CC's general idea and dismantling the different strands enables the detection of the approach that best suits the endeavor at hand. On that account, CC approaches to national business systems (NBS), social systems of production (SSP), and the varieties of capitalism (VoC) will be introduced, analyzed, and compared relating to the fit with this work. Second, VoC as the CC approach of choice serves as a basis for further theory development and, therefore, will significantly shape the newly developed conceptual framework and the subsequent empirical study. On that account, the VoC approach is discussed in detail and the corresponding understanding of institutions is introduced, alongside with the concepts of, among others, institutional complementarity and comparative institutional arbitrage. Finally, a brief reflectional section discusses critique on VoC's fit, in particular, with developing countries and proposes to widen the scope and to incorporate certain advancements in the wider VoC literature body.

3.2.1 Comparative Capitalism

National disparities in economic performance and competitiveness in specific sectors have attracted scholarly attention ever since the 1980s. The vanishing of socialism on a global level, the subsequent capitalist hegemony, and Japan's and Germany's outstanding economic performance in manufacturing and exporting have propelled the intra-capitalist quest for the best "recipe" for governing the economy. The 1990s and 2000s (at least until the financial crisis in 2008) were characterized by a mostly unquestioned predominance of liberal market-oriented policy and CC lost currency. However, as Walker et al. (2014, p. 494) state, ". . .the exuberance of liberal market economies..." and the subsequent crash led to a renewed interest in alternative forms of capitalist organization.

One of CC's central messages is that the assumption of "one best way" of economic organization—irrespective of time and space—most likely will be limited when approaching different political economies (Sayer, 2000). Contrary to the theoretical bodies analyzed in the section on the theoretical puzzle that assume convergence of institutions and of economic performances across countries following a (market) model of best practice, CC literature asserts continuing divergence among countries characterized by different institutional settings that induce a specific logic of economic activity. Querying the sense of one-size-fits-all blueprints as proposed by orthodox economics, CC implies that ". . .common pressures may be refracted through different sets of institutions, leading to different sorts of problems and calling forth distinct solutions" (Jackson & Deeg, 2006, p. 6).

In general terms, CC is introduced by Walker et al. (2014) as the scholarship investigating the relationship between distinct national institutional settings and patterns in firm practices. Deeg and Jackson (2007) refer to CC as a set of approaches aiming at understanding the institutional foundations of general differences between national forms of business organization. The fit with the actor-centered approaches of ACI and IAD in Sect. 3.2.2 is supported by Jackson (2010) who depicts CC's major added value as the improvement of understanding actors and actor constellations. In order to gain an understanding of institutional variety and differing coordination principles, it is the task of this first section to establish some common knowledge regarding the multifaceted nature of political economies.

Commonalities and Critique

The next part of this chapter briefly introduces the related body of literature. In so doing, it tests which analytical framework within this body best suits the objectives of the framework in progress. All strands of CC share major concerns on the existence and functioning of different forms of capitalism, their economic performance, and (mostly) constant institutional divergence across nations despite facing similar pressures within a globalized and economically integrated world (Deeg & Jackson, 2007). Borrowing from Jackson and Deeg (2006, p. 11), five analytical premises are detected that can be interpreted as the foundation of CC literature. The subsequent introduction of the five common foundations of CC may be simplified and certainly leaves out facets of ongoing and partly vigorous intra-CC discussions.

However, the general introduction and connection to the work at hand suffices for obtaining an understanding of the variety of games being played.

First, economic action is a special case of social action. In order to make action work, coordination among economic actors is needed. On that account, distinct institutional arrangements create a specific logic of economic action that actors generally follow (Aoki, 2010). As a consequence, interaction is embedded within specific social contexts and shaped by distinct institutions (Granovetter, 1985; Powell & DiMaggio, 1991). Following this logic, institutions are most often treated as the independent variable determining—to a certain degree—the mode of governance, actor strategies, and corporate choices (Jackson & Deeg, 2006). As such, CC literature opens up alternative perspectives on coordination mechanisms for economic activity. Second, the utmost interest of CC lies in understanding the effects of institutional variation on, among others, firm strategy, macroeconomic performance, and national distributional consequences (Jackson & Deeg, 2006). Institutional commonalities and differences cause distinct actor behavior and, thus, cause specific performance outcomes.

Third, institutions do relate to each other and are therefore interdependent. Well known within the CC literature is the concept of institutional complementarity, which suggests that two institutions are complementary if the presence of one institution increases the returns of the other (Aoki, 2001; Nölke, 2013). The expectation of increasing returns consequently leads to mutually beneficial results and may also lead to mutually reinforcing behavioral patterns. On a systemic level, institutions are interdependent, meaning that different institutional domains within the same nation are supposed to follow a similar logic and generate a coherent national overall institutional configuration that creates a specific logic (or institutional coordination principle) of economic action. Jackson and Deeg (2008) exposes the central meaning of institutional complementarity as making piecemeal institutional change very unlikely to happen and, thus, as providing stability. Assuming an efficient system with complete complementarity, change would cause inefficiency since synergetic effects from formerly complementary institutions would no longer become operative. Along the same lines, Amable (2003) states that the understanding of complementarities is limited, but the sheer existence of different stable institutional settings can be interpreted as an indicator for their very existence. In general, institutional complementarity is supposed to be positively related to socio-economic performance and sociopolitical stability. A lack of complementarity therefore most likely has negative effects on the aforementioned aspects. Empirical investigations within highly industrialized Western political economies support this hypothesized relation (Amable et al., 2011; Hall & Gingerich, 2009).

Fourth, certain institutional configurations offer distinct support that urges actors to conduct specific economic activity more efficiently (Aoki, 2010). CC's notion of comparative institutional advantage on a national level explains ongoing institutional divergence between nations and further emphasizes the idea of equifinality inasmuch as differently organized economies—through specifically supported economic activity—can generate equal levels of success. By following certain strategic patterns and conducting idiosyncratic activities (thus producing specific goods), firms within distinct forms of capitalism are said to exploit the locally given institutional endowment to obtain a competitive advantage (Hall & Gingerich, 2009; Amable, 2003). This phenomenon explains varying and rather stable patterns of specialization across nations (Storz et al., 2013).

As interim conclusion, social embeddedness, institutional complementarity, and comparative advantage help to explain the existence of idiosyncratic institutional settings and ongoing capitalist divergence and mostly contribute to understanding institutional stability. Logically and of utmost importance for this work, institutional stability leads to relatively consistent strategical and behavioral patterns. Following these concepts, there is only little—if at all—space for institutional change. Nonetheless, the postulated institutional differences across countries have somehow evolved over time and themselves are proof for change.

Coping with the very existence of institutional differences, the fifth general agreement in the CC literature is that change will largely be incremental and highly depends on prior developments. This relatively rigid concept of institutional path dependence combined with the idea that "history matters," in a broad sense, means that structures built in the past highly influence decisions today (Storz et al., 2013). Postulating ongoing (and even reinforcing) diversity, CC leaves space for change only inasmuch as it is on path: within the boundaries of a certain type of capitalism but not across types of capitalism. However, CC in a traditional sense mostly considers a path, if consequently followed, as leading to success. As already introduced above, especially in the context of dysfunctional systems, the steps taken in the past have shaped a path that most likely leads to, if at all, very limited success. Incorporating the possibility of a "wrong path" may open doors for off-path change. Nevertheless, following the original logic of Hall and Soskice (2001) one may find only limited space for actor-induced change. Considering VoC's concept of "history matters" in conjunction with the perception of history as the set of action in the past, though, indicates the potentially impactful role actors may have on formal and informal institutions.

Complementarity, embeddedness, and institutional advantages that all evolved alongside a specific path make off-path changes a rather futile endeavor. Accordingly, fundamental change—understood as being against the existing institutional logic—can be explained—most often—only by exogenous shocks. In general, as indicated above, the poor account of change within CC literature is recognized as its biggest weakness. Briefly summarizing, CC's strengths mentioned above, indeed, allow an understanding of national institutional varieties, differing behavior and systemic stability. However, CC's premises run the risk of neglecting certain aspects and explanations of stability bear the price of being relatively static and sometimes over-deterministic. CC in general is criticized for being limited in explaining the more dynamic aspects of institutional development and heterogeneity (Deeg & Jackson, 2007; Streeck, 2009). Problems with explaining institutional genesis, its evolutionary trajectory, and changes are perceived as a general weakness of CC (Crouch et al., 2005; Jackson & Deeg, 2006; Storz et al., 2013). Since it is this work's very prime interest to investigate dynamics when different forms of capitalism interchange, this work aims at using CC's inherent strengths and attempts to equip it with a broader theoretical grounding in order to overcome its major weaknesses. Nevertheless, as indicated above, CC serves well for understanding the single games and the underlying actor constellations at the national level. The meso-level with the inherent query on what happens when various games conflate and the general elaboration of a more dynamic approach on change will be part of Chap. 4.

Different Strands

Besides CC's commonalities, there are various strands that show significant disagreement relating to the question on how to conceptualize capitalist diversity. Whereas—as indicated above—CC in general shares major analytical presumptions, its inherent strands differ, among others, regarding the selected dimensions, the ordering principles, the conceptions of how institutions relate to actor behavior, and the level of abstraction chosen. Deeg and Jackson (2007) identify three major approaches on how to approach the game(s) being played. CC's strands of literature that will be under closer scrutiny are the Varieties of Capitalism approach (VoC), the National Business System approach (NBS), and the Social Systems of Production approach (SSP). Each approach contributes differently, serves for specific scientific endeavors, and comes up with distinct limitations. It is the task of the subsequent section to see which approach fits best to the work at hand. For the sake of transparency, it needs to be mentioned that the selection of strands and the assignment of authors to specific strands are certainly—to a certain degree—based on subjectivity. Furthermore, drawn conclusions build upon only a fraction of literature available. Thus, the following section is by no means meant to be exhaustive. However, the taxonomy proposed by Deeg and Jackson covers the most important aspects and suits well for reasonably developing the argumentation.

Table 3.1 indicates the essence comparing the various strands of CC for this work. The indicators listed are supposed to help identify the approach best suitable for conducting the endeavor at hand.

The typologies used are more than mere labels. They vary relating to its content and number and reveal information about ordering principles (dominant interaction modes), levels of abstraction, and statistical testability. Regarding the sheer number of typologies, one recognizes significant differences, since it ranges from two to the number of cases studied. Whereas the VoC approach aims at assigning all countries to two archetypal "grand principles" of economic coordination, SSP orientates itself on as Hollingsworth and Boyer name it, "…a complex two-dimensional taxonomy… (1997, p. 8)" and tend to treat each national case as unique. Roughly relying on the dimensions "action motive"—distinguishing between self-interest and obligation—and "power relations"—distinguishing between horizontal (equally powerful actors) and vertical (hierarchical) power distribution—SSP copes with the perceived higher complexity by relying on "thick descriptions"[3] for each case

[3]The term "thick description" stems from Ryle and Geertz. The latter used the term for describing the working of cultures by just noting behavior, but by also including specifics of the context, connected with meanings and subjective perceptions of the actors. It aims at making action more embedded and more transparent for outsiders (Redding, 2005).

Table 3.1 Comparing CC

	VoC	SSP	NBS
Typologies	Liberal and coordinated (polar constellation)	Every case unique	Fragmented, coordinated, industrial district, compartmentalized, state-organized, and highly coordinated
Level of abstraction	High	Low	Moderate (multi variety)
Inter-typology relation	Polar	Diffuse	Diffuse
Statistical testability	High	Very low	Low
Actor of interest	Firm	Multi-actor	Multi-actor
Observability of change and divergent behavior	Very low	Relatively low	Low
Interpretability of change and divergent behavior	Very low	Low	Low
Level of investigation	Nation	Region, sector	Nation

Source: From the author, based on Jackson and Deeg (2006), Schröder (2014), Hollingsworth and Boyer (1997), Amblard et al. (2001), Paunescu and Schneider (2012), Hall and Soskice (2001), Sayer (2000), and Storz et al. (2013)

(Jackson & Deeg, 2006).[4] NBS, as a middle ground, comes up with a multi-variety approach including six distinct typologies. In the same vein, VoC assigns the two grand principles according to a rather fixed set of reasonably observable institutions, whereas SSP focuses more on social norms and a relatively diffuse "logics of appropriateness" (Jackson & Deeg, 2006, p. 24).

Relating to the decision on the number of typologies, the inherent trade-off, as Jackson and Deeg (2006, p. 21) name it, between "parsimony and complexity," is quite consequential. Since each nation comes up with a—to a certain degree—idiosyncratically evolved culture, linguistic environment, legal system, norms, social prescriptions, etc., within CC it is pretty much the consensus that there are no two countries that are exactly identical. Even finding a most-similar case, there will be substantial differences. As a consequence, assigning various cases to a group is always reductionist in nature and comes at the cost of losing information about its (unique) constituting elements. Hence, the number of typologies indicates the specific level of abstraction applied. Applying the rule of diminishing abstraction (Lindenberg, 1992; Amblard et al., 2001), one may say that on a range from an abstract to a complete depiction of reality—within CC literature—the VoC approach can be found rather on the abstract side and the SSP rather on the complete one. Beyond the sheer number of typologies, an outstandingly important but most often

[4]For the sake of completeness, Hollingsworth and Boyer (1997) propose a general taxonomy involving six modes of coordination, which are markets, hierarchy, communities, state, networks, and associations. However, following this general taxonomy, they split up the typologies into more than 20 sub-typologies, i.e., the number of cases studied.

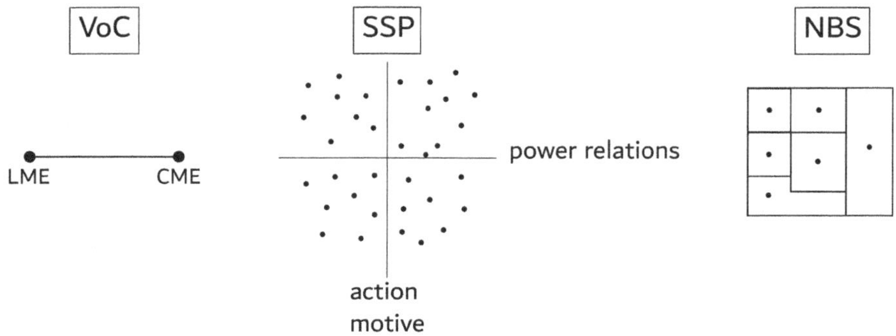

Fig. 3.3 Relation between CC's typologies. Source: From the author

neglected attribute is the relation between typologies. Figure 3.3 schematically highlights the inter-typological relationships of CC's approaches.

Whereas there is general agreement that at one end of the ordering principle spectrum countries are clustered as market-oriented economies, the other end—the non-liberal range of the spectrum—causes more inconsistency across the approaches. VoC offers a two-dimensional approach which puts the typologies (two archetypal representatives of specific ordering principles that are market and coordination) at the opposite ends of the possible spectrum. Logically, relying on VoC, for example, being more market-oriented always comes with being less coordinated and vice versa. NBS' introduction of six principles makes such reasoning hardly possible. Finally, SSP does not offer clear typological borders and hence impedes relating the various typologies logically. Typologies' relationships crucially inform the potential of conducting specific investigations. Generating a high degree of internal validity, SSP and NBS are very limited regarding further statistical endeavors. On the other hand, VoC's dichotomous approach includes less case-specific information but comes with the crucial advantage of providing testable hypotheses and allowing for statistical analyses, which allows the improvement of external validity (Hall & Gingerich, 2009; Jackson & Deeg, 2006; Martinelli, 1998; Paunescu & Schneider, 2004, 2012).

Along with the level of abstraction the capability of coping with changes varies significantly. Using the VoC approach's bipolar ordering principles makes systemic shifts almost impossible. Complete shifts to the polar category are rather unlikely to happen and smaller changes (not changing the entire system) within one principle run the risk of being slurred by comprehensive and rather insensitive categories of either market-oriented or coordinated (Schröder, 2014; Streeck, 2009). Furthermore, the discussion on where to draw the line between the two principles, i.e., from when can a political economy be called coordinated or liberal, gives no final answer. NBS and SSP are capable of observing changes more sensitively. Opposite to VoC's static notion of ordering principles, SSP offers the opportunity of a "free-floating" categorization alongside its two dimensions. Changes can therefore be observed more sensitively and are less restricted by overarching labels (Jackson & Deeg, 2006; Hollingsworth et al., 1994).

VoC's polar relation of its ordering principles is possible by, among others, using exclusively the "firm's eye" (Hall & Soskice, 2001). VoC gives the firm the central role since, according to Hall and Soskice, it takes the vector position within a capitalist economy. A vector position is characterized by its centrality, connected to the entirety of other (economic) actors; this will be discussed in more detail in the upcoming chapters. Which strategy (liberal or coordinated) to choose finally depends on the firm minimizing transaction costs. NBS and SSP also include other actors and give, inter alia, the state, its structure, the civil society, and social justice in general a more crucial role (Martinelli, 1998). Here, a sometimes-dominant state actively shapes the business system by, for example, formal regulation and the degree to which the state is positively inclined or antagonistic to specific influential actors (Redding, 2005; Whitley, 1998). Beyond that, regarding SSP, for example, Hollingsworth includes firm-to-state and state-to-state relations in the investigation and emphasizes that the state itself may be, for example, an important producer (Hollingsworth & Boyer, 1997; Sayer, 2000). State intervention relating to its degree and quality is taken into account by VoC—if at all—as a rather passive actor responsible for the context in which action choices are made (Hall & Soskice, 2001; Jackson & Deeg, 2006; Redding, 2005).

CC's strands also differ regarding the level on which investigation can take place. The underlying question is where variation for coordinating economic actors may best be captured. Whereas there is general agreement that the level of the nation-state serves well, various SSP-related scholars also open up perspectives on other levels including the sectoral, the regional (within nations), the national, the transnational, and the global level (Crouch et al., 2009; Herrigel, 1996; Hollingsworth & Boyer, 1997). It, thus, offers theoretical grounding for different levels and for multilevel research in the context of potential dependence and influence between the levels. Exemplary, such as a multilevel approach, may be especially beneficial for scrutinizing transnational integration projects such as the European Union. VoC offers analytical grounding exclusively for the national-state level.

Discussion

CC literature generally seems to be a good starting point for developing an understanding of the isolated games being played and their inherent institutional status quo (ante). In so doing, it overcomes certain deficiencies of the theories discussed in the section on the theoretical puzzle. First, political economies are not generally meant to converge toward a market-enabling environment. CC indicates that institutions may take different shapes across—most often—the borders of countries. Stable institutional settings may provide an alternative coordination mechanism beyond the pure reliance on markets and hierarchies. CC allows one to perceive and understand the variety of games being played besides playing the market. Second, following the existence of various institutional logics, one can assume that the behavior of actors changes accordingly. This notion of the "...non-identical nature of actors across different institutional contexts" (Jackson, 2010) allows actors to act differently, according to the institutional environment. Third, combining a wider sociological perspective with economic reasoning, the final aim is still to improve the general understanding of the relation between institutional settings and (socio)-economic output.

With regard to the choice of a suitable analytical framework, comparing the various strands, one recognizes that there are some good but no perfect approaches upon which to build. For this reason, one faces several analytical trade-offs. The overarching objective is to find a model that is as complete (complex) as necessary but as abstract (simple) as possible.

In contrast to the VoC approach, SSP and NBS with reservations stand out for their high internal validity and, thus, seem to be best capable when approaching single cases by thick descriptions. However, as it turns out, in the context of this work, the strength of Hall and Soskice's approach lies in its generally perceived weakness of analytical dualism. The prime objective of this work is to investigate potential behavioral patterns that Western WOS show in Latin America. On that account, the bipolar inter-typological relation of VoC is the only one that supports large-scale empirical comparisons and is capable of creating testable hypotheses. Nonetheless, the decision in favor of VoC and the level of abstraction necessary to see institutional diversity through a dichotomous lens bears the cost of losing some case-specific information.

Each different level of investigation contributes specifically to illuminating different issues. This work's focus on institutional settings as demarcated by the borders of nation states is consequential. Whereas SSP allows for multilevel studies, the bread and butter of VoC is a comparison on the nation-state level. Thus, VoC offers the analytical approach best concerted for this work.

Relating to this investigation's actor of interest, VoC is clearly ahead since it offers the complete firm package. Hall and Soskice (2001) revive the "firm's eye" and offer a firm-tailored approach on national political economies. This orientation complies very well with the requirements of this work's MNC-based investigation. Inherent in VoC established firm-related institutional domains, economic interactions, and socioeconomic output best suit the logic of the research discussed in Sect. 3.2.2. The state has—apart from constituting parts of the institutional surrounding—a rather passive role. Using the firm's eye is supposed to be complementary to, for example, state-centered approaches, and to further illuminate the crucial and recently rather neglected perspective of the company.

Since this work is very much interested in dynamics of exchange, behavioral patterns of adaption and institutional change, CC generally reaches some limitations. However, even within CC, VoC, indeed, stands out with a very low degree of observability of change and divergent behavior. This rather static approach with only two very extensive categories, certainly, is disadvantageous. On the other hand, change within VoC can be better interpreted because it can only happen one-dimensionally. Every kind of change away from one pole can be understood as a development toward the other one. Nonetheless, in order to empirically observe and analyze change, all the three strands need further development.

In conclusion, VoC comes closest to the requirements set above. However, a best match is not to be equated with total conformity. It offers a firm grounding for further theoretical development, since it offers an institutionalist firm-centered package on the national level, which allows for sophisticated statistical analyses. This relatively high degree of external validity comes at the price of sacrificing some case-specific information. However, as will be seen in the upcoming chapters, VoC is complete (complex) enough to contribute positively to the debate of socioeconomic development. Furthermore, VoC certainly has an inherent weakness when referring to institutional change and divergent behavior that needs further elaboration, so this will be done in Chap. 4. Nevertheless, if behavior and change can be made observable, potential change and deviation can be interpreted more easily on the bipolar axis between coordinated and liberal.

The following chapter will introduce the VoC approach in detail and introduces, among others, institutional domains, interactions of interest, and potential outputs. This will be the foundation for developing and operationalizing the concepts in the empirical study.

3.2.2 Varieties of Capitalism: Diversity of Games

As the previous chapter shows, within CC literature, Hall and Soskice's (2001) approach fits best with the requirements of this work. Approaching the diversity of games relying on VoC offers a sound economic and institutional micro foundation with a broad understanding of capitalist institutions (Nölke, 2013). Hall and Soskice (2001) compare forms of capitalism as production regimes and focus on the perspective of micro-agents such as firms, employees, shareholders, and stakeholders. VoC's central postulate is that political economies can be described by idiosyncratic general principles on which firms mainly rely to solve coordination problems. VoC has gained a canonical status, especially referring to its concepts of institutional complementarity, comparative institutional advantage and its explanations for continuing institutional divergence, and different forms of innovation. However, most important for this work—at this stage—is to understand the actual (diverse) economic interaction as a special case of embedded social action whose conduct varies over space and time. Accordingly, the interaction (as core of the action situation) itself will be the core of this chapter.

The VoC approach scrutinizes aggregate socioeconomic outcome by relying on micro-agent interactions and their surrounding institutions. Socioeconomic outcome on the level of entire political economies thus depends on a very large number of single interactions and on the institutions that "govern" them. To investigate interactions, VoC puts the firm at the center of scrutiny and uses a relational view to understand the interactions with other relevant actors. Perceiving the firm in an organic manner, its capabilities and success ultimately depend on the quality of the relations it establishes within the firm (employees) and outside the firm (suppliers, education facilities, clients, associations, unions, governments, etc.). The quality of relations directly correlates with the firm' capacity to effectively solve coordination problems with the abovementioned economic actors (Hall & Soskice, 2001, p. 6).

To conclude, VoC follows a straightforward multilevel line of reasoning founded at the micro level. The quality of an interaction—in the first place—decides whether or not it contributes positively to the firm's success. The firm is described by its relations and its success depends on the quality and quantity of the interactions conducted. The entirety of firms' successes determines the overall performance of the entire political economy. Depending on the subject matter (here the political economy), one can shorten the reasoning by skipping the aggregate firm performance so that the single interaction effectively determines the performance of an entire country. Interesting and important for the empirical study later on, since the successes of the interactions of both the firm and of the entire country are supposed to be commutated, vested interests of managers and policy makers should be equally aligned. Hence, what serves a firm should also serve the people and the entire political economy, and vice versa.

VoC is highly beneficial for the endeavor at hand since it facilitates the investigation of the main subject matter, i.e., the interaction between economic actors. VoC helps to understand in more detail the building blocks set out in Sect. 3.2.2 by explaining the game(s) being played and further elaborating on the diversity of participating actors. VoC elaborates on the most important elements when approaching a political economy institutionally on the micro-level. Focusing on the interaction, VoC introduces the constituent elements of a political economy from the firm's perspective, which are:

- Other economic agents to act with
- The institutional surroundings (institutional domains) that govern interaction
- Interactions of interest
- Behavioral choices
- Potential performance outcomes

Hence, within the scope of this work, VoC complies with Jackson (2010), Ostrom (2005, 2011), and Mayntz and Scharpf (1995), as well as the requirements set in Sect. 3.2.2, since it improves the understanding and puts flesh on the bones of the previously discussed actor constellations and, thus, contributes significantly to the setup of Conflating Capitalisms. By indicating which institutions may matter and how they influence firms' behavior (specific choice when situated in an action situation), VoC allows integrating firm behavior into the analysis of the entire political economy (Hall & Soskice, 2001, p. 14). According to VoC, though, the direction of causality remains pretty stable inasmuch as behavior is assumed to automatically follow the institutional surroundings. Figure 3.4 depicts a simplified visual interpretation of the VoC approach. The economy can be seen as a mesh of an ongoing and very huge number of interactions (depicted by straight lines). Right in the center, the company finds itself in a vector position, interacting in all economic realms with all other economic agents. Each interaction between the firm and another actor can either work well, work sufficiently, or may not work at all, whereby the quality of the interaction decreases from the left to the right.

Following this line of thought, here the "(inter)action situation" describes a situation in which economic agents interact with each other to solve a coordination

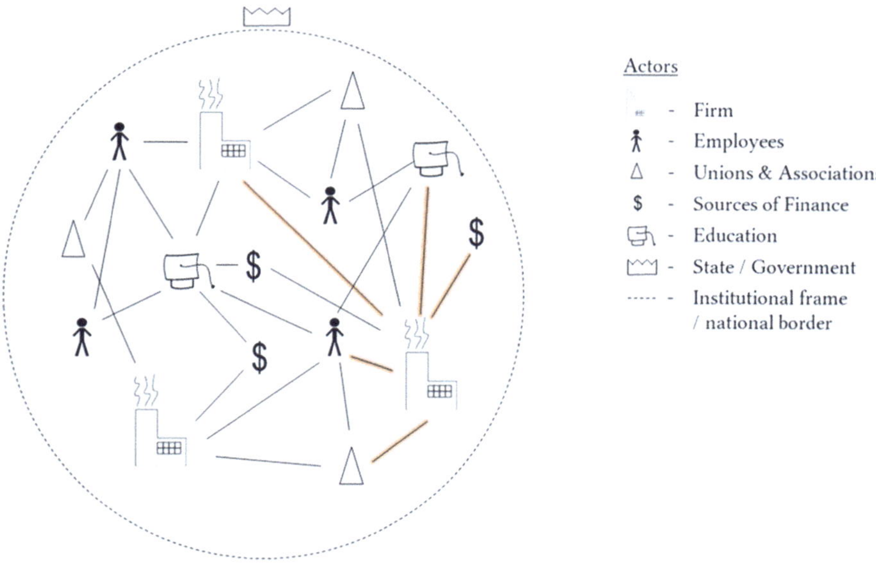

Fig. 3.4 An institutionalist approach to the political economy. Source: From the author

problem in an institutional environment delimited range (Jackson & Deeg, 2006, p. 22). In VoC, a coordination problem surges between economic actors such as companies, employees, unions, associations, clients, education facilities, and governments. Oversimplified, examples of coordination problems may be (1) a company and a bank that negotiate a loan or (2) a company and a potential employee that negotiate a job and so on. Each coordination problem that is not solved properly depicts a potential economic activity that has not been materialized. An unsolved coordination problem leads to, following the brief examples, one unemployed person (and therefore also a company with one less suitable worker) and a company without sufficient funds to e.g. buy machinery (and therefore also a bank with one less "sold" service).

Accordingly, the non-occurrence of the interaction depicts the worst-case scenario for both the firm and the political economy. Hence, apart from the occurrence of an interaction, its specific conduct is of utmost importance. As already indicated above, quantity and quality of interactions are supposed to be decisive for an economy's overall performance. In line with the entire political economy as the dependent variable, VoC investigates institutional diversity at the national level. As Fig. 3.4 indicates, the dashed line delimits the institutional context under scrutiny. All actors and interactions within this context are subject to the same institutional pressures. The focus on national political economies is justified by Hall and Soskice, since the institutional structure that shapes in particular the domains of labor market regulation, education and training, and corporate governance depends on regulatory systems that are the responsibility of the nation state (Hall & Soskice, 2001, p. 4).

In line with institutional economics literature discussed in in the section on the theoretical puzzle, the VoC approach shares the Northian understanding of institutions as "the rules of the game" (North, 1992, p. 5) structuring actors' behavior. Thus, Hall and Soskice (2001) define institutions "...as a set of rules, formal and informal, that actors generally follow, whether for normative, cognitive, or material reasons...." It also shares the idea of the bounded-rational actor that conducts interaction in a manner to maximize utility by minimizing transaction costs. Along these lines, emphasizing the notion of rational, strategic behavior, rational actors are supposed to implicitly or explicitly agree on the mode of interaction that promises the lowest transaction costs, i.e., the one implied by the surrounding institutions. Aligned action regarding the choice of behavior, that is, the choice of the underlying coordination principle, promises interaction at the best conditions. Thus, the more the behavior and interest of participating actors converge, the more successful the transaction will be. Jackson and Deeg describe the joint agreement as the output of institutions that exert a societal effect and create a "...particular contextual "logic" or rationality of economic action..." (2006, p. 12). As such, divergent behavior from the one generally induced would be disadvantageous. VoC's underlying conception of man will be contested and further developed relating to the requirements of this investigation in Chap. 4.

However, VoC clearly differentiates itself from, for example, institutional economics by allowing for cross-national differences in institutional settings, which are supposed to have historically evolved in a path-dependent manner. Coherently, and of particular importance to this work, different institutional settings lead to different behavior of agents conducting interactions and, thus, solving coordination problems. In so doing, VoC introduces, first, a multifaceted understanding of institutions and behavior and, second, a shift away from institutional economics' exclusive reliance on institutions as enabler of impersonal markets.

The relationship between institutions and actors' behavior is key to understanding the concept of stable and successful varieties of institutional settings. According to Hall and Soskice (2001), in prior literature, institutions can generally affect actors' behavior either as socializing agencies (norms and attitudes), via power conferred to specific actors (coercion through formal sanctions), and through sanctions and incentives. Additionally, and clearly going beyond other approaches, VoC introduces the concept of strategic interaction (Hall & Soskice, 2001, p. 5). According to Hall and Soskice, strategic interaction is central to the behavior of economic actors and, consequentially, also to the aggregate economic and political outcomes. It is these strategic interactions that describe the pursuit of multiple actors (each of them) to advance their distinct interests in a (bounded)-rational way (Scharpf, 1997). Strategic interaction (pursuing interactions with the lowest transaction costs possible and overcoming principal-agent problems) allows actors to find equilibrious solutions to coordination problems, in an institutional environment delimited range (Jackson & Deeg, 2006, p. 22). In order to deal with the detected concept of strategic interaction, Hall and Soskice expand the understanding of institutions. Building upon Ostrom's introduction of institutions (1990)—as supporting information exchange, monitoring, and sanctioning—Hall and Soskice add analytical depth to the analysis by adding institutions that provide capacities for deliberation. The proposition is that successful solving of coordination problems requires actors to reach agreements and to engage in collective discussion (Hall & Soskice, 2001, p. 11). Deliberation supports strategic coordination in three ways. First, it improves extensive information sharing beyond the thin level of common knowledge including the same language and the knowledge about the potential payoffs, which are the necessary commonalities for impersonal market exchange. Sharing information about interests, beliefs, and motivations builds an increased level of common knowledge, improves confidence in the counterpart's behavior, and decreases uncertainty. Second, deliberation allows establishing risks and gains that accompany cooperation and consequently their equitable distribution among the participating actors. Third, intensive communication and consultation is likely to improve handling of unknown challenges. In summary, institutions that support deliberation equip actors with the capacity to approach coordination problems differently than would be the case by relying on, for example, Ostrom's more narrowly defined institutional tasks.

Considering national idiosyncrasies, the VoC approach categorizes the entire political economy according to the distinct manner of solving coordination problems. The broadened understanding of institutional tasks allows the investigation of interactions beyond the reliance on markets and hierarchies and to add a potential relationship between economic actors. Beyond markets and hierarchies, Hall and Soskice add coordination to the taxonomy that relies on strategic action that aims at securing "...cooperative outcomes among the actors using a range of institutional devices that underpin credible commitments" (2001, p. 14). Hall and Soskice assert that for each interaction, one can approach coordination problems by relying on either markets or nonmarket relationships. Accordingly, political economies can be assigned to two ideal types (coordination principles) that are the liberal market economy (LME) and the coordinated market economy (CME). The former resembles the economy as perceived by orthodox economics and tends to rely on arm's-length exchange and inherent price signals, whereas the latter tends to rely on collaboration and strategic planning through relational contracting, network monitoring, etc. LMEs will find their equilibrium outcomes of firm behavior determined by supply and demand and CME will find it as a result of strategic interaction. Hall and Soskice conceptualize these ideal types of market economies in a Weberian sense inasmuch as VoC emphasizes that the theoretical model will inevitably be different from the empirical ones. Thus, only the ideal types rely exclusively on one manner to approach coordination problems. VoC acknowledges the importance of markets and coordination in both sorts of market economies (Hall & Soskice, 2001; Hall & Gingerich, 2009). However, above all, Hall and Soskice stress the systemic variation across economies regarding the reliance on nonmarket institutions to solve coordination problems. In CMEs "...economic behavior is strategically coordinated to a larger extent through nonmarket mechanisms..." than in LMEs (Jackson & Deeg, 2006, p. 22). Moreover, they acknowledge various hybrid forms. However, it is the institutional setting that is supportive for either market relations or strategic interaction and, thus, urges actors to solve coordination problems in a specific way.

Even though actors have the "free" choice, Hall and Soskice expect firms to "...gravitate toward the mode of coordination for which there is institutional support" (Hall & Soskice, 2001, p. 9). In this context, it is worth mentioning that there is no a priori valuation of institutional settings. Emphasizing the concept of equifinality, the two settings lead to different corporate strategies that can result in the same economic performance (Hall & Gingerich, 2004, 2009).

Nonetheless, according to VoC, institutional variation can cause differences in economic performance. Hall and Soskice, in line with the notions of complementarity, path dependence, embeddedness, etc., perceive institutions as not being under control of current actors. Thus, structure does (usually) not follow (corporate) strategy (Hall & Soskice, 2001). On that account, institutions—in line with North—can be interpreted as constraints on behavior. However, Hall and Soskice generally agree with Streeck's notion of "beneficial constraints" (2009) inasmuch a given set of institutions offers distinct opportunities, that is, institutional devices, which firms can use to solve coordination problems. In order to fully exploit the given opportunities, Hall and Soskice expect either liberal or coordinated coordination as successful and fully backed by distinct institutional surrounding. Deviation from these two pure forms of coordination—such as various hybrid forms—is generally perceived as bringing worsening overall performance (Hall & Gingerich, 2004, 2009; Hall & Soskice, 2001; Schröder, 2014).[5]

Institutional Domains

As indicated in Fig. 3.4 by the five orange highlighted straight lines, the VoC approach proposes five institutional domains in which firms have important relationships and interact with other economic actors. Relations of interest can be both outside the company (banks, other companies, unions, etc.) and inside the company (employees).

According to VoC the political economy of a country is built upon the shoulders of firms' activity. Using the firm's eye, activity is conducted—respectively coordination problems are solved—in five major institutional domains (Hall & Soskice, 2001). The central problem, thus, is the coordination problem and the firm's objective is to solve it as smoothly as possible. The success or failure of coordination leads to severe impacts for both firms and entire economies. One may label the result of coordination as successful, not successful, and failure (non-appearance of economic transaction); of which the latter depicts the worst case according to Williamson (1995).

Firms engage with other actors to raise finance (corporate governance), to bargain over working conditions and wages (industrial relations), to ensure a suitably skilled workforce (education and training), to access technology and other inputs (through inter-firm relations), and to ensure compliance and collaboration of the workforce

[5] Empirical studies, however, are not able to finally back this hypothesis. Schröder (2014), for example, analyzes the degree of being either coordinated or liberal with regard to GDP. While he backs Hall and Soskice's thesis of equifinality, he cannot find evidence that the degree of being either coordinated or liberal within the groups is decisive for economic success.

(employee relations) (Hall & Gingerich, 2009). Following Hall and Soskice's holistic approach, none of the domains is considered as dominant, that is to say as more important in determining the overall system than others (Höpner, 2009).[6]

The following section introduces VoC's institutional domains relating to its overarching content, model-like interaction modes via both the market and strategical action, active actors, and potential impacts on both the firm and the entire economy. Regarding the latter, since domains are interconnected, outcomes in one domain may lead to complex dynamics. Hence, an outcome in one domain may trigger changes in another that are difficult to foresee. Furthermore, as indicated above in the discussion on CC's different strands and the inherent level of abstraction applied, VoC comes up with a rather fixed set of reasonably observable institutions. The thereby improved manageability comes at the cost of grasping only a section of the domains. Each domain's label stands for a wide and distinguished scholarship and certainly scholars from within these areas will find reasonable limitations within the necessarily narrowed VoC approach. However, Hall and Soskice (2001)—and later on many others—developed domains that represent the issue sufficiently well for improving the understanding regarding the topics raised by this work. Each domain will be put under more detailed and empirical scrutiny in Chaps. 6 and 7 when applied to quantitative and qualitative analyses.

Industrial Relations (IR)

One of the basic coordination problems within every capitalist economy is to reasonably bring together the ones that own means of production (employer) and others that own manpower (employees). Neither capital nor labor alone is able to conduct productive operations. Not before the latter utilizes and processes the former a value is added that can be marketed. As one of a few major principles, this value (that should exceed production costs) needs to be distributed among the stakeholders—in monetary terms—as either company profit (employer contribution) or wage (employee contribution). Since costs, prices, and values are subject to change, a mechanism is necessary to partition the right shares (Schröder, 2014). The distribution of value added is conducted within—according to VoC—the institutional domain of industrial relations. At a rather general level, it comprises bargaining over wages and conditions of work between firms, their labor force, organizations that represent labor (unions), and other employers (associations) (Hall & Soskice, 2001, p. 7).

As an example, an archetypal firm in a CME comes up with and invests reasonably in a high-skilled labor force that is granted an extensive amount of autonomy in order to deliberate with others continuously improving the product or service being marketed. On that account, CME companies are vulnerable to poaching and "holding up." The term "poaching" describes the situation in which skilled workers are

[6] For some exceptions, see Thelen (2001), Amable (2003), Hollingsworth and Boyer (1997), and Nölke and Perry (2007) that focus on industrial relations (wage–labor nexus) and the financial domain (especially referring to financialization) as the most crucial dimensions inasmuch to determine the entire system's logic.

enticed away by a "free-riding" company that itself does not invest in the development of the workforce' skills (Jackson & Deeg, 2006). Furthermore, a high degree of employees' autonomy may lead to workers being reluctant to further hand all information available to the management in order to back up demands. Hence, CMEs need specific industrial relations institutions to overcome poaching and holding up (Hall & Soskice, 2001). As a means to counter poaching, CMEs traditionally trusts trade unions and employer associations with bargaining on wages at the industry level. Thus, coming up with industry-wide standard wages, it is secured that the same skill level, that is, the same work, is remunerated equally across companies. As a consequence, first, companies cannot entice away workers by offering higher wages and, second, employees find no need to artificially secure demands since they are guaranteed to receive the best wages in the long term. From a macro perspective collective bargaining protects employment, reduces wage inequality, and controls inflationary effects (Hall & Soskice, 2001; Jackson & Deeg, 2006). In an archetypal LME, following the libertarian idea, individual freedom is not limited by standard wages and binding working conditions. Equipped with the freedom to bargain over one's own means, the relation between employer and employee is subject to market forces (Schröder, 2014). Unions and associations exist but are much less encompassing and have less adhesive strength. Hence, bargaining at a higher level is beyond scope and most often takes place at the individual level. Highly fluid labor markets allow firms to act on short-term hiring and releasing employees according to market conditions and situational opportunities and threats. Accordingly, to be able to move across firms and sectors, workers invest in general skills. Within companies, unilateral control is granted to the top management (Hall & Soskice, 2001). In general, industrial relations in LMEs leave it mostly to market dynamics to decide on, for example, the level of employment and inflationary effects.

Inter-firm Relations (IFR)

In general terms, Hall and Soskice (2001, p. 7) define inter-firm relations as "...the relationships a company forms with other enterprises, and notably its suppliers or clients, with a view to securing a stable demand for its products, appropriate supplies of inputs, and access to technology." Consequently, in order to exploit synergies and to jointly add more value than each company alone could, cooperation can be a reasonable strategy to increase its own competitiveness and, thus, to secure survival. Most importantly, each company contributes proprietary information that can be exploited by the counterpart. Thus, referring to a one-time collaboration, each company can profit maximally by breaching agreements, using (stealing) information exclusively for its own benefits (Schröder, 2014). Accordingly, firms' relations with other firms imply a pretty high risk of deception. To avoid a deadlock situation in which no company cooperates due to the inherent risks and threats, coordination among the participating companies is required.

Referring to, for example, the diffusion of new technology, CMEs cannot refer to the circulation of labor (see above in industrial relations) as a source of knowledge. To compensate, CME firms rely extensively on collaboration. Hence, in CMEs inter-firm relations play a more important role than they do in LMEs; cooperation is more frequent and may be designed for the long term (repetitive cooperation). CMEs manage to overcome a deadlock situation by using various institutional devices. Of utmost importance, joint efforts are made possible through associations that serve as a lasting overarching structure uniting, observing, and—in case of defection—sanctioning firms (Hall & Soskice, 2001). Associations set various common standards valid for all firms within the structure. Among others, technical standards are included that facilitate cooperation in, for example, research and development. Furthermore, associations set standards that allow for relational contracting. Relational contracting includes open-ended clauses and, thus, leaves room for and copes with contingencies that may appear throughout joint efforts. Relational contracting falls back on the prevailing standards set within the given association. In a case of disagreement, the association serves as referee and has various sanction mechanisms at its disposal (Schröder, 2014). In LMEs, cooperation plays a less important role and—if at all—then it is based on standard market relationships and formal contracting. Regarding technology transfer, LME has two predominant ways to diffuse technology. First, circulating workers among firms act as Trojan horses that carry knowledge inside and offer it to the new company. Second, companies buy external knowledge either in the form of acquiring innovations and entire companies by gaining majority share or by licensing innovations. Incomplete contracting is not supported by the LME's legal system[7] and can be conducted—if at all due to the absence of adequate associations—relying on costly reputation building. In the same vein, absent or weak associations impede effective standard setting and leave it to a market race in which the winner decides on which standards to use.

Employee Relations (ER)

The institutional domain of employee relations is unique inasmuch as it is the only internal one. Nonetheless and despite being internalized into a corporate hierarchy, coordination problems arise. Employee relations are decisive for the performance of a company for two reasons. First, it is of utmost importance that employees are equipped with the right competencies, since together they aggregate to the firm's competencies. Second, employees need to work and cooperate with others according to the interests of the corporate management, or the company's owner. The overarching objective of the entire workforce should be to jointly advance the objectives of the company to the best of one's knowledge and belief (Hall & Soskice, 2001). Typical problems within this domain are the one of adverse selection, principal-agent problems, moral hazard, and, thus, the conscious holding up of information and efforts. Emphasizing the micro perspective of VoC, Hall and Soskice state that the entirety of employer–employee relations also condition "...the character of an economy's production regimes" (Hall & Soskice, 2001, p. 7).

[7] As Hall and Soskice (2001) indicate, until the National Cooperative Research Act of 1984 it was prohibited to conduct close inter-firm collaboration.

Unlike in LMEs, CMEs do not grant unilateral control to the top management. For corporate decision-making, consensus among the major stakeholders needs to be reached. Co-determination, through a works council and by generally including the supervisory board in decision-making, employee representatives (and major shareholder plus, for example, major suppliers and customers) have a voice and can significantly shape major corporate decisions and distributional issues of profits made. Contributing to the design of the corporate future and being equipped with long-term employment contracts, holding up information and efforts to artificially secure demand is a rather unnecessary endeavor. The same applies to top management. Benefitting from long-term contracts and a specifically designed remuneration system aligns management incentives with those of the firm (respectively its owners). Management's premium is calculated based on the ability to secure consensus among the stakeholders and less on current earnings. Logically, management's and firms' incentives are not contradictory and aforementioned problems do rarely occur, if at all. In LMEs, current earnings play the major role when talking about managerial performance (see also corporate governance) and, thus, about managers' premium. On that account, the workforce, first, is paid for performance (incentive contracts), which is rather volatile and workers are hired and fired following frequently conducted make (internalize) or buy (market) considerations (Schröder, 2014). Along the same lines, employees have no institutional device through which to participate in decision-making and therefore have no means of making their voice heard. If an employee is left unsatisfied, its exclusive option is to exit the company and to find a new job. As complementarities in the next section indicate, finding a new job is not too difficult in a volatile labor market as a worker with a general skill set. As one can see, both employers and employees in LMEs rely heavily on the market to coordinate employee relations.

Corporate Governance (CG)

Corporate governance is often used as a showpiece domain to demonstrate differences between LMEs and CMEs. Corporate governance is described by Hall and Soskice as the issues of coordination "…to which firms turn for access to finance and in which investors seek assurances of returns in their investments" (Hall & Soskice, 2001, p. 7). This allegedly simple issue is sweeping and of major relevance since it informs a firm's organizational and incentive structure and general management style. Due to the heated debate around financialization in the aftermath of the latest financial crisis in 2008, this domain has gained major prominence (Christophers, 2015; Davis & Kim, 2015; Palley, 2013).

The principle coordination problem depicts a classical principal-agent problem between shareholders (principals) and firm's management (agents). In general, the firm offers the means of generating value. Translated into capitalist language that means to use money (i.e., resources that have a monetary value) to make more money. Investors offer money—basically—expecting to receive more money after a certain period of time. Even clearer, the investor expects the highest return on investment possible. Apparently, the relation between investor and firm seems like a good match. However, certain confidence problems arise that hamper cooperation.

Within this relation there is an inherent one-sided tendency to cheat. Maximizing firm's profits or one's own salary, corporate management is inclined to, for example, either repay less than possible or nothing at all or to cheat on key performance indicators (Schröder, 2014). Thus, without coordination, an investor would certainly hesitate to give his money randomly to any firm. Investment could only take place if either the investor invests a lot in monitoring or the investor would require tremendous interest rates that cope with the very high default risk. Both would make finance too expensive (transaction costs too high) so that the firm could not operate at all. Bringing together the firm in need of money and the investor in need of more money is a main task in capitalism. The underlying task is to make managers act the way the owners want, even though this may go against the manager's own interests (maximization interest). CMEs and LMEs approach this coordination problem quite differently which brings major differences in corporate structure and management style.

General basic differences between financial systems in CMEs and LMEs are the firm's ownership structure and corporate control. Archetypally, company shares in CMEs are concentrated to one or a very few investors (shareholders/owners/creditors). Major investors (most often banks as creditors, families as owners, and other firms as cross-shareholders) are directly present within the respective firm's board of supervisors, directly controlling management and shaping corporate decisions (Jackson & Deeg, 2006). Beyond that, as a so-called insider, an investor has unlimited and genuine access to information and key performance indicators (Schröder, 2014). Networks of cross-shareholding further strengthen tight inter-firm relations and a detected deception could cause severe reputational damage within the cross-shareholding networks and within CME-typical associations. In LMEs, company shares are dispersed and traded on the stock market. Having a countless number of unknown investors, it is not feasible to include all of them into decision-making or control. As control becomes obsolete in situations of aligned interests, top managers in typical LME countries are usually made partners that hold equity. Being remunerated by an increasing company value (market capitalization), managers and shareholders both strive for the same goals. Thus, a control body is not needed, supervisory boards are not existent, and unilateral power is granted to the Chief Executive Officer (CEO) of the company, whose objective is to make the hugest profit possible in the short term. If shareholders are not satisfied with the returns they get, they will withdraw their investments, leading to a decreasing share price because of which the firm runs the risk of being taken over and the CEO of being fired. Due to the dispersed nature of investors, LMEs are called outsider systems in which investors lack a voice inside, and information from within, the company. Thus, deciding whether to initially invest, to expand commitment, or to withdraw money, investors must rely on publicly accessible information: above all on the current share price.

Literature on capitalism distinguishes between flexible "short-term" and patient "long-term" capital. Relying heavily on retained earnings and—if a firm opens the door to investors—offering close long-term cooperation, comprehensive information and active contribution on future corporate strategy make those who invested money in CMEs more patient (Deeg & Hardie, 2016). Investors as insiders are able to recognize potential long-term profits and, thus, are willing to forego current earnings expecting higher and more stable returns in the long run. Further, banks are primarily interested in the debtor's repayment capacity and will use their power in the supervisory board to evoke a certain financial prudence (Schröder, 2014). Even for quoted companies, networks of cross-shareholding protect each firm from potential hostile takeovers when share prices are low. All in all, firms in CMEs are less sensitive to current company valuation (mostly affected by current earnings) and, thus, are able to conduct long-term strategies. In LMEs, the institutional surroundings induce managers to align their type of management in order to raise financial performance indicators. In general, money's flexibility can be advantageous and disadvantageous. On the one hand, firms are subject to the volatility and potential short-termism of the financial markets and associated performance indicators. On the other hand, raising venture capital especially for new companies that have not yet had any opportunity to improve reputation through networks and cooperation but promise high return rates, the financial market offers the right source.

Education and Vocational Training (EV)

The institutional domain of EV holds the coordination problem between firms demanding labor and workers offering labor. Firms need to secure a workforce with suitable skills and (potential) workers need to decide how much to invest in what kind of skills to secure employability and decent career prospects. In a nutshell, EV is the domain in which human capital—understood as the "the accumulated knowledge and skills that make a workforce productive (FARLEX, 2019)"—is generated. Beyond individual gains of workers and firms, in a VoC fashion, individual skill levels accumulate and determine the productivity level and competitiveness of the entire economy.

Both firms and workers are generally interested in reaching a high-skill level, which generates high productivity. However, also for both parties, this domain is situated in a "mist of uncertainty" about future values of current investments and bears the risk of sunk costs.[8] Without coordination that severely hampers the generation of human capital. Workers' investments in education that will not pay off in the future are sunk. Hence, if a worker is left in a state of total uncertainty about suitable job prospects (regarding salary and content), he or she will most likely hesitate to invest in the required education. Companies, on the other side, require skills but prefer to free-ride, relying on skilled workers educated by others. Conversely, company's investments in skills that will move to another firm are sunk (Schröder, 2014). As such, if a company is left in a state of uncertainty about future values of its investments, it will most likely hesitate to invest. Consequently, to

[8] Usually sunk costs refer to decision-making and are understood as costs that are not refundable. Rationally deciding actors should not include——different than future costs—these costs when deciding over future prospects. Here, sunk investments are understood as investments already made, which cannot be recovered and that will not generate any return in the future.

overcome such a market failure, which may be the worst case for the firms, workers, and the entire level of human capital, coordination is needed twofold to assure that efforts will pay off (Thelen & Busemeyer, 2008; Schröder, 2014). First, to assure the worker that education will lead to a suitable job and, second, to assure the firm that skilled workers will add value within the company that paid for his or her education and will not be poached by other companies.

Adding analytical depth, the degree of certainty required before investing is heavily related to the specificity of jobs and skills and, thus, with the probability of generating sunk costs. Hall and Soskice already opened the door to the concept of asset specificity, using it to understand economic structures in CMEs and LMEs.

> ... firms and other actors in coordinated market economies should be more willing to invest in specific and co-specific assets (i.e. assets that cannot readily be turned to another purpose and assets whose returns depend heavily on the active cooperation of others), while those in liberal market economies should invest more extensively in switchable assets (i.e. assets whose value can be realized if diverted to other purposes) (Hall & Soskice, 2001, p. 17)

Williamson (1995) already mentioned the centrality of asset specificity to transactions, since specific assets that endure over time but cannot be redeployed to other usages and users—except at either additional costs or significant losses of productive value—are transaction specific. The extension of specificity to skills and the interdependent relation between specificity of skills and specificity of assets has come into view in the aftermath of Hall and Soskice's seminal work (Busemeyer, 2009; Cusack et al., 2006). Following Iversen and Soskice's Asset Theory (2001), skills vary relating to their specificity. Most importantly, specificity of skills is related negatively with its transferability. Thus, the higher the job specificity, the higher the skill specificity, the fewer outside options a worker has (Iversen & Soskice, 2001). In the most general terms, Iversen and Soskice's taxonomy of the skill system is dichotomous and follows VoC inasmuch as a general skill system describes that of LMEs and a specific one describes CMEs. In general, Iversen and Soskice (2001) put it as follows: "...Specific skills are valuable only to a single firm or a group of firms (whether an industry or a sector), whereas general skills are portable across all firms" (2001, p. 876).

Specificity under uncertainty makes investors (workers and firms likewise) subject generally to two risks, one caused by market conditions and one caused by opportunism. First, since it is as difficult for the worker to replace the job as it is for firms to replace workers, adverse market conditions depict a major risk for both. In case of dismissal, workers in CMEs often face long periods of unemployment or a major decline in income (Busemeyer, 2009). In case of an economic downswing, firm's future strength partly depends on the ability to hold the specifically skilled workforce. In a generally weak economic phase resulting in forced dismissals, firms' prior investments would be futile. Second, in line with Williamson, specificity can also be understood as "...a measure of bilateral dependency" (1995, p. 225). Along with the low transferability of specific skills, in CMEs, workers' dependence on the employer is very high (Iversen & Soskice, 2001). Less in focus but the same also holds vice versa. A firm that invested a lot in a specifically skilled worker can hardly replace the worker. The firm's dependence on individual workers increases, putting workers in a powerful position (Moe, 1995; Schröder, 2014). Depending on the direction of dependence, one party is at the other's mercy and, without coordination, can easily be exploited. In LMEs, such dependencies rarely occur. Generally skilled workers can easily switch jobs and firms find replacement rapidly. All in all, strategic coordination is needed to clarify the mist of uncertainty and, thus, to overcome a failing market. Uncertainty about future values of investments is the result of specificity combined with opportunism and market forces. In order to assure tomorrow's value of today's investments in education, CMEs and LMEs developed different approaches.

CMEs are characterized by both a high-skill pattern and a high degree of asset specificity. Attempting to provide both, the market—as discussed above—is very likely to fail. CMEs manage to overcome market failure by applying nonmarket governance. As Schröder (2014) indicates, in CMEs, it is the restriction of market that is the sine qua non for strategic coordination. Complementarity regarding, among others, coordination of industrial relations is crucial. Imperfect markets caused by, for example, collective wage bargaining protects the firm against potential poaching. Furthermore, already introduced co-determination within firms enables workers to participate in decision- and strategy-making. Hence, corporate strategies are very unlikely to counter the workers' interests. Workers therefore come up with channels to incorporate their interests in long-termism and to counter potential labor cost-cutting strategies in times of economic downswing (Dias et al., 2012). Nonmarket approaches allow genuine long-term commitment, restrain opportunism, and reduce uncertainty about future value of investments. CMEs stand out for their system of collective skill formation. Generally, industry-wide business associations and trade unions supervise CMEs' publicly subsidized dual vocational system (Hall & Soskice, 2001). Associations encourage firms to participate as training organizations in the system. Equipped with monitoring and sanction mechanisms (such as exclusion), associations have the capability to limit free-riding. Furthermore, industry-wide associations aggregate firms' demand for skill categories and prepare suitable training protocols. In CMEs' corporatist structure, associations contribute firms' insider knowledge to deliberation about and design of the training system. Such information provided by associations secures, first, training that fits firms' demand and, second, demand for graduates (Hall & Soskice, 2001). Deliberation and corporatist efforts further allow for cost coordination. Within the system of dual vocational training, the firm pays for practical training internally, the state pays for theoretical parts in associated schools, and the apprentice contributes inasmuch as accepting a relatively low salary (Schröder, 2014). All in all, relying heavily on the dual vocational system, a CME manages to generate a highly and industry-specific skilled workforce.

Archetypally, LMEs' skill production regime is coordinated by market mechanisms. As discussed above, the market works only at a very general skill level (switchable assets) that again complies well with (and to a certain degree also contributes to) LME-typical highly fluid labor markets and subsequent generally short job tenures. Companies refrain from investing in workers' skills since poaching by free-riding firms is quite likely. Workers need to comply with short-termism and invest in the most general skills that are applicable throughout various companies across sectors and industries. The two actors' strategies are applied in order to secure that investments today will not be sunk tomorrow. Nonetheless, LMEs developed mechanisms that make the market work well, especially in sectors that are characterized by low asset specificity, such as the entire service sector (Hall & Soskice, 2001). Throughout the entire range of educational programs from secondary school to university, certification of general skills is emphasized. Experiencing a generally good university education, people entering the labor market are highly and generally skilled. Top universities are financed partly by the state, but for the most part by private individuals. High tuition fees pay off in working life since firms are not bound to standard wages and, thus, may pay a high premium for good graduates (Schröder, 2014). Easy hiring and firing of employees make firms in LMEs capable of responding flexibly and rapidly to new opportunities by shifting highly skilled workers across industries and sectors in which demand is highest. However, there is no pool of readily available specifically tailored skills. In order to equip generally educated employees with the right, more specific, skills, firms in LMEs carry out in-house training. Since LME firms demand significantly less specificity, in-house training is less extensive than CME apprenticeship schemes. High levels of general skills depict the foundation on which more specific skills can easily be built in-house at relatively low costs of additional training. As Thelen and Busemeyer (2008) emphasize, LME equivalents to CMEs' apprentices partly fall out of the costly university system. Hence, a large part of the society remains untrained and composes a large low-wage sector. Dividing society into well-educated university graduates and untrained low-paid workers makes LMEs a less equal society.

Table 3.2 below summarizes the various institutional domains regarding content, actors, and consequences of the relationship's quality for the firm and the entire economy. Empirical flesh will be put on the theoretical bones in Chaps. 5, 6, and 7.

The section on institutional domains above improved the understanding of both action situations and actors, both embedded in two different institutional ideal types. Domains, interactions, actors, behavioral choices (either to rely on the market or on strategic interaction), and performance outcomes (at stake) were first examined theoretically and then applied within ideal institutional settings of either CMEs or LMEs. The next section briefly discusses the interconnectedness of domains that make up for coherent and stable systems.

Systemic Coherence

The section above discussed the five institutional domains in which various actors build relations by interaction, determining a nation's overall economic success. Up to now, the domains above have been explained in a rather isolated manner. Nonetheless, systemic stability and strength depend heavily on the complementarity of the domains. Based on VoC, each interaction can be conducted either in a market-oriented or in a coordinated fashion. Following Aoki's (2001) notion of complementarity combined with VoC indicates that institutional settings across the five

Table 3.2 Institutional domains: content, actors, and consequences

Domains	Content	Actors	At stake
Industrial relations	Coordinate bargaining over wages and working conditions	Firms, labor force, employee, and labor force organizations	• Firm: wage and productivity level • Economy: rates of unemployment and inflation
Vocational training and education	• Firm: securing a suitable workforce (skills) • Workers: decision of workers on how much to invest in skills	Firms, workers	• Firm (worker): fortunes of individual workers and companies • Economy: skill levels, productivity, and competitiveness
Corporate governance	• Access to finance • Consequences for management	Firms, investors	• Firm: availability and terms of external finance • Shareholder or stakeholder focus • Time horizon of economic planning
Inter-firm relations	• Stable demand for its products, appropriate supplies of inputs, access to technology → Standard setting, technology transfer, collaborative R&D	Firms, other firms	• Firm: competitiveness • Economy: technological process
Employees	• Availability of requisite competencies, cooperation in the sense to advance objectives of the firm →Adverse selection, moral hazards, information sharing	Firms, employees	• Firm: cooperation, right competencies • Economy: which production regime

Source: From the author, based on Hall & Soskice (2001), Schröder (2014), and Jackson and Deeg (2006)

domains are aligned creating a “grand coordination principle” inasmuch as supporting systemically either market-based or coordinated action. As has already been hinted at, for example, the functioning of a coordinated EV system depends quite a lot on the institutional support from industrial and employee relations. Beyond, path-dependently grown LMEs and CMEs have developed widespread complementarities that generate a coherent national system of institutions and, consequently, a coherent pattern of how to solve coordination problems. Figures 3.5 and 3.6 depict some of the interdependent and complementary relations between the institutional domains. The two systems indicated follow this chapter’s logic and show ideal types of complete complementarity. In both systems, each of the five domains coherently follows the same coordination principle. As the arrows indicate, each of the domains connects with the other four and significantly supports and is supported by each of them. Furthermore, as the notion of equifinality indicated, both systems seem to be capable of generating decent economic growth. Nonetheless,

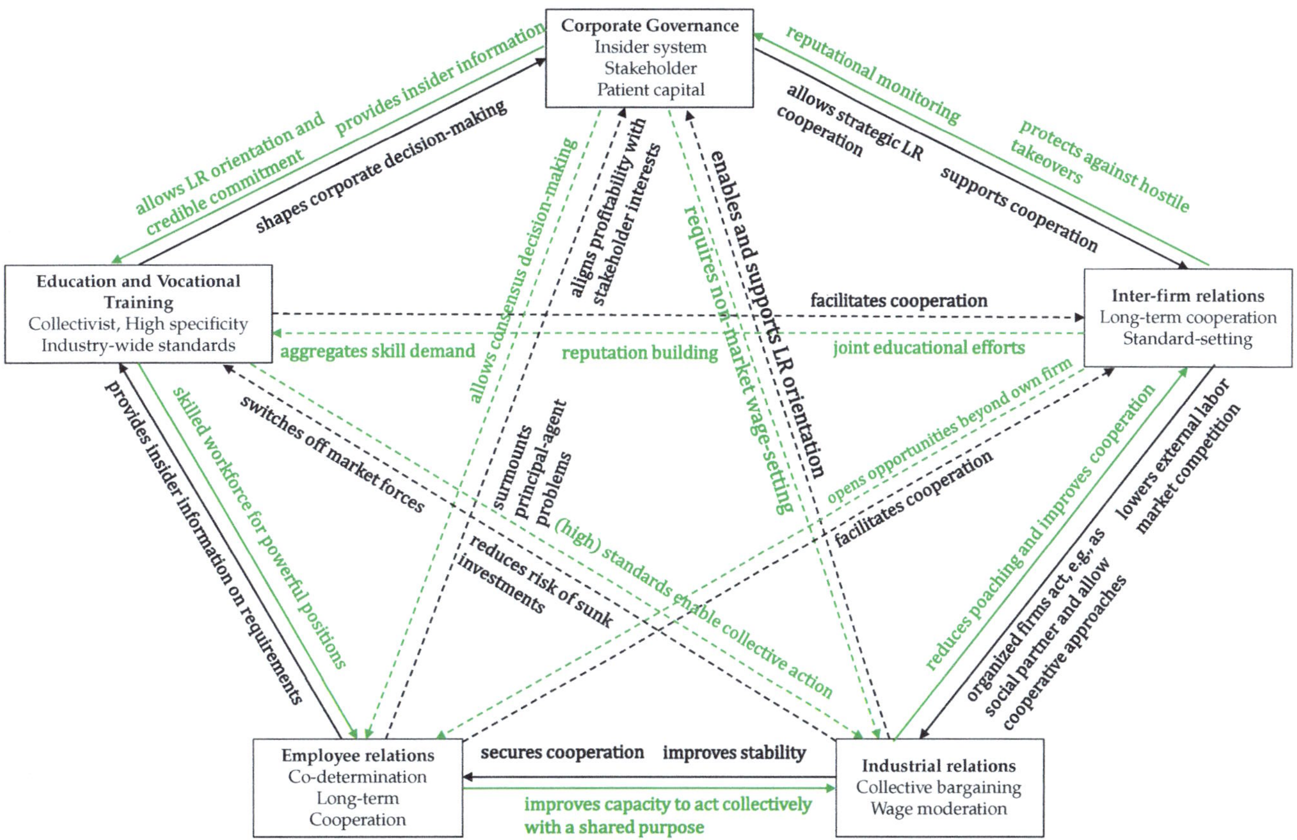

Fig. 3.5 CME as a system of institutional complementarities. Source: From the author, based on Hall and Soskice (2001)

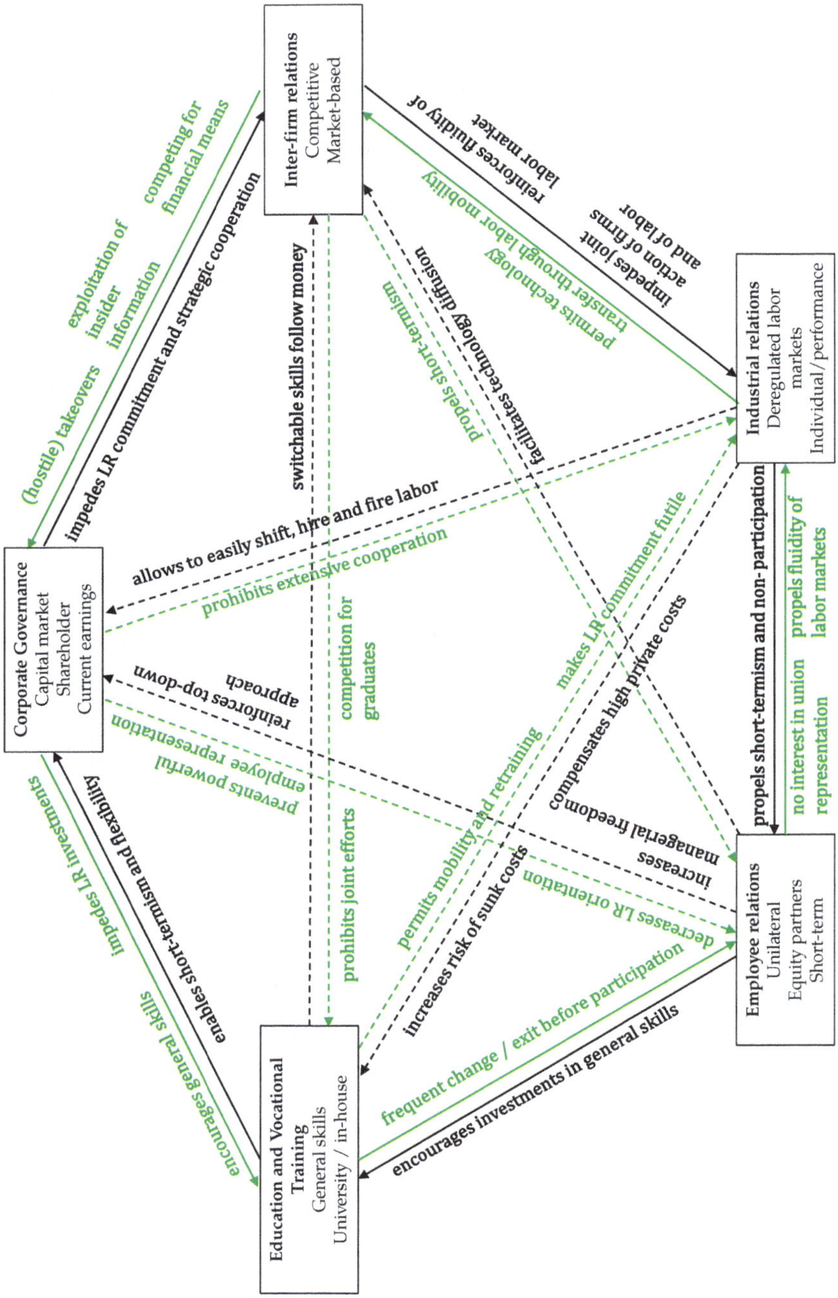

Fig. 3.6 LME as a system of institutional complementarities. Source: From the author, based on Hall and Soskice (2001)

institutional differences, complementarity, and subsequent predominant coordination principles lead to idiosyncrasies regarding the economy's structure, its composition, different specializations, and varying socioeconomic outcomes.

The text in Figs. 3.5 and 3.6 builds upon Hall and Soskice (2001), Schröder (2014), and the general discussion above.

Figure 3.5 exemplarily shows the interplay between the institutional domains in CMEs. All domains within an ideal CME make use of nonmarket arrangements that induce strategic interaction. Strong complementarities generally characterize CMEs as cooperative, participative, corporatist, deliberative, specific, and long-term oriented. Within such an ideal system, divergence from strategic coordination in one domain would cause efficiency losses since synergetic effects no longer operate.

In various ways, the tight CME setting may be understood in a Northian way as restraints for individual freedom. As such, an owner of a company that cannot unilaterally decide on major decisions certainly evokes a feeling of a "collectivist compulsion." Bearing risks but not fully determining strategy and not fully skimming profits may seem counterintuitive from a capitalist's point of view. Nonetheless, it is this "restricted" capitalism that open doors to specific comparative institutional advantages. Hall and Soskice, however, introduce tightly connected institutional settings as the base for comparative institutional advantage. Understanding institutions as Streeckian "beneficial constraints," CME firms use institutional support for long-term and specific activities and specialize in, for example, engineering, in which assets are highly specific and innovations are of incremental nature. As such, the availability of patient capital allows, for example, research and development without caring too much about current earnings. High-cost years can be more than compensated by future gains. The insider system gives investors enough information to estimate future trajectories and further protects firms from hostile takeovers due to, for example, potential decreasing stock prices. To further develop already well-advanced products, specific skills provided by CME's EV are of utmost importance. The EV system provides precisely the industry-specific skills required. Workers are willing to invest heavily in specific skills, since both employment and unemployment protection is very high. Furthermore, extensive R&D is further facilitated by joint efforts with other companies that contribute specific expert knowledge and financial means. Along the same lines, co-determination aggregates company-internal expert knowledge and allows corporate decisions on operations, education, and corporate management to be firmly consolidated. In addition, collectively bargained wages allow firms to build a workforce of highly skilled people at manageable costs. The workforce tends to be highly committed due to long-term employment and cooperative corporate culture. As one can see, all efforts are supposed to be sustainable over time. The institutional domains—of which each can only survive because of the other's existence—support incremental innovation, which means making a product that is already quite good even better. Hence, CMEs offer substantial institutional advantages, for example, for engineering, when compared to LMEs. Regarding the entire economy, CMEs are generally known for providing a high degree of productivity, stable economic growth, and a high degree of equality. A general sentiment for co-determination and the joint decision over distributional matters (providing a secured and equitable sharing of profits) further contribute to CMEs "inner peace."

In line with VoC's bipolar design of coordination principles, the liberal unregulated system is taking a rather opposite stance than the coordinated one does. As Fig. 3.6 shows, within an ideal LME, all institutional domains are characterized by market coordination. Complementarities make it a stable market-oriented system that is characterized by unilateral distribution of power, competition, shareholder orientation, short-termism, general assets, high volatility, and flexibility.

An LME may come closest to the market as understood by orthodox economists and comes almost without institutions as alleged constraints.[9] LMEs may be understood as the purest form of capitalism inasmuch as the owner of resources uses them in a productive manner to make more of it. To reach their goals, the capitalist owner comes up with power of decision and freedom to use their means the way they want. As CMEs do, the institutional design of LMEs offers idiosyncratic comparative institutional advantages. Using market's strength and coping with some of its failures, LMEs stand out for its fast reactivity and flexibility especially in, for example, the IT and service sectors. These sectors are constituted by firms that are capable of radically innovating and rapidly switching assets to seize erratic market opportunities.

Both "restless" capital and the danger of hostile takeovers propel orientation on current earnings. Relying on publicly available information, investors focus on short-term financial indicators (above all the stock price) and if unsatisfied shift capital to another more promising investment opportunity. Consequently, firms that need to satisfy shareholders are inclined to plan on the short run attempting to maintain flexibility when facing the chance to seize new opportunities.[10] Along the same lines, LMEs turn their weakness in providing specific skills to a strength in providing the general skills required by shifting markets. Switchable skills help firms to change focus and allow workers to cope with a fluid labor market (hire and fire). Skipping consensus building, unilateral CEO decisions make firms quick to act according to the market, and equity participation of the top management aligns interest in favor of the shareholders. Deregulated labor relations allow bargaining at the individual level that allows payment of high wages and, thus, hiring (poaching) of very good workers. Frequently moving workers across firms ensure technology and knowledge diffusion throughout the entire economy. Furthermore, responding to erratic market opportunities, the ease of hiring and firing workers is of utmost

[9] It certainly is constrained, among others, in generating specific skills or long-term cooperation (see discussion above).

[10] If the opportunity is very promising, investors are willing to run extremely high risks. Hence, LMEs—contrary to CMEs—are known to extensively provide venture capital for startups. The discussion about venture capital especially in Europe has gained major currency within the last decade. However, since startups are not in the focus of this work, the topic of venture capital will not further be elaborated on. For more information see, among others, Schneider et al. (2010) and Casper (2009).

importance, since an "adhesive" workforce may turn out being a millstone around the firm's neck.

Regarding the entire economy, LMEs are generally known for providing a high degree of productivity and stable economic growth. Absence of employment and unemployment protection, however, leaves some workers behind. Furthermore, the dividing education system in either highly skilled university graduates or untrained workers contributes to a relatively high degree of inequality within LMEs.

As the section above showed, institutional domains complement each other and form stable and successful capitalist systems. The coherence of coordination across domains builds general comparative advantages that put firms in a good position to specialize in certain markets. CMEs and LMEs production regimes seem to not get in each other's way and to be mutually beneficial. Each of the market economies is unrivaled in its segment. Whereas in LMEs all domains are aligned to flexible market arrangements, CMEs show coherence in supporting long-term cooperation. Market orientation strongly supports radical innovation in young industries characterized by high returns and high risks. Strategic interaction, in a bipolar fashion, propels stability and continual improvements in well-established markets (Schröder, 2014).

3.2.3 Merits Contributed and the Inclusion of Developing Countries

As the elaboration above shows, VoC overcomes some of the major shortcomings detected in the section on the theoretical puzzle and fits with requirements set in Sect. 3.2.2. VoC uses the firm's eye to deal with the inherent vector position firms take in market economies and, of course, to follow the approach of this paper and to emphasize the social embeddedness of interaction in both liberal and coordinated capitalist systems. Liberal and coordinated systems induce different rationalities of economic interaction. Whereas the former supports market mechanisms, the latter makes use of strategic coordination (nonmarket arrangements) to solve coordination problems. Accordingly, generally, firms can decide to rely either on markets or on strategic cooperation to interact with others. According to the specific institutional environment, VoC suggests clear idiosyncratic behavioral patterns in LMEs and CMEs. Hence, firms in LMEs and firms in CMEs behave (act) differently. Along these lines, VoC contributes heavily to this work since it:

- First, considers the variety of games being played
- Second, the non-identical nature of actors (behavior differences; overcoming the perception of firms as homogeneous bulk).

The ongoing variety of games being played combined with the notion of equifinality overcomes the exclusive reliance on markets and hierarchies and the inherent concept of a single best practice. It thereby raises doubts on one-size-fits-all approaches to different political economies and recognizes the need for tailored "remedies." Firms need a suitable, stable, and comprehensive system to conduct idiosyncratic interaction. In the same vein, VoC allows one to relate micro-agent interactions with (socio)economic outcome at the national level. Hence, success or failure of entire political economies can be examined at the microlevel.

To make these interactions investigable and to build this work's conceptual framework of Conflating Capitalisms, this chapter contributed manifold. On that count, VoC highly benefits the endeavor of this work since it provides information on action constellations by indicating actors, institutional domains, and specific interactions. Furthermore, VoC helps to understand both the variety of games being played and the subsequent non-identical nature of actors. It is exactly these multifaceted concepts that are most beneficial but are also the ones that make VoC rather weak when applying to interchanging systems at the international level, especially to the "Global South."[11]

Following this line of argumentation is certainly a good but not perfect match and comes up with some major shortcomings, in particular when developing political economies come to the fore. The following chapter analyzes in what sense more current VoC literature may be able to overcome certain limitations. In order to improve VoC's applicability to this work's endeavor, certain properties need to be adjusted and further developed. First, VoC as understood by Hall and Soskice is exclusively applied to highly developed countries. Since it is of prime interest to understand capitalism in less developed countries where economies are less successful, institutional settings and their interplay especially in Latin America need to be included. Along the same lines, second, above all, VoC emphasizes institutional stability of capitalist systems. Building on the aforementioned points of critique, this view most likely overestimates complementarity in—at least—other economies than "Western" ones, and underestimates complex MNCs as actors. Despite the theoretical supplement of Hall and Thelen (2009) allowing for divergent behavior and potential institutional change, the deterministic institutional approach will most likely not cope with developing countries where institution may be significantly weaker. The upcoming chapters attempt to further develop the aforementioned necessary points of adjustment in order to cope with this work's analytical requirements.

[11] Here, the term "Global South" is understood as an approximation for the entirety of developing countries in Latin America, Asia, and Africa. Lopez (2007) coins it as largely equivalent but not identical with Third World. For a more detailed comment, see Pagel et al. (2014).

3.3 Capitalism in Developing Countries and Latin America's HME

Along with its prominence, VoC has faced various points of critique. One of the main points of critique within the VoC debate, its non-application to the "Global South," is vital for this work. Hall and Soskice (2001) focus exclusively on the well-developed countries, including mostly North America and Western Europe. Following this orientation, the vast majority of successive scholars remained within the high GDP per capita delimited geographic areas. Along with the economic strength of the scrutinized political economies, the majority of countries under scrutiny have a rather stable institutional environment. As it has been argued, some of VoC's analytical constituents may reach their limits when being applied to developing countries. On that account, various scholars further applied VoC approaches to the Global South and, thus, contributed heavily to the wealth of this literature body. For Asian capitalism see, for example, Witt and Redding (2013a), Carney et al. (2009), Storz et al. (2013), Zhang and Whitley (2013), and Amable (2003). Within Asia, China's economic system mostly labeled as state capitalism takes a specific stance and is investigated by, for example, Fligstein und Zhang (2011), Peck and Zhang (2013), Otero-Iglesias and Vermeiren (2015), and Witt and Redding (2013a, b). Mostly "crony" capitalism in some major African countries is elaborated on by, among others, Leon (2010), Bond (2008), and Padayachee (2013). Eastern Europe most famously is investigated in the context of "dependent market economies" by, for example, Nölke (2018), Nölke and Vliegenhart (2009), Drahokoupil and Myant (2010), and Adam et al. (2009). Since the prime focus of this work lies on MNCs in Latin America, the remainder of this chapter remains within the corresponding literature body.

The Latin American political economy has been among the areas most contested within the social sciences for decades. Latin American history of (socio)economic development may be described as a cyclical trial and error in which relatively brief developmental heydays are succeeded by enduring states of instability, political turmoil, and stagnation (e.g., "La Década Perdida"[12]).[13] In line with this dramaturgy of development history, associated theories gain and lose validity correspondingly. As a heritage, Latin America offers an enormous wealth of development theory ranging from Latin American structuralist import substitution industrialization (ISI) (Furtado, 1965; Kay, 2005), over opposing Marxist dependency theory (Cardoso &

[12]La Década Perdida (The Lost Decade) describes the process of development of Latin American countries in the 1980s. Prior to this crisis, various countries developed well in the 1970s. However, in a nutshell, most of the wealth generated was built upon a tremendous amount of foreign debts. Hence, Latin American countries have slid into a situation of unaffordable foreign debts, fiscal deficits, and high inflation leading to recession and stagnation. For more detailed information, see, among others, Ocampo (2004) and Boris (2009).

[13]For an historical overview on Latin American countries and developmental efforts, see Boris (2009), Bodemer (2008), and Cypher (2018).

Faletto, 1979; Frank, 2009) and neoliberalism (Biglaiser, 2002; Bockmann, 2019), to the desire for a new "capitalismo del siglo XXI" (Ferrari, 2016).

Since one theory most often replaces another that failed shortly before, there is little ground for commonalities in between. However, the adjustment of VoC on Latin America copes with certain issues that seem insurmountable for all of them. Above all, VoC literature—as the others likewise are—is preoccupied with the origin of an ongoing (socio)economic underdevelopment. Regarding foreign capital, theories seem to be irreconcilable. Whereas ISI and dependency theory clearly reject foreign capital since it is supposed to conduct predatory exploitation, neoliberalism clearly aims at attracting foreign capital and propels integration into the global economy, since foreign capital brings more capital and knowledge. It is VoC that may be able to take a middle position. In line with Ferrari (2016), who generally acknowledges the potential strength of capitalism, including for Latin America, VoC may allow one to gain a more nuanced view on systematic distortions of local capitalist systems. Hence, rather than the binary yes/no attitude toward foreign capital (especially MNCs) supported by the aforementioned theory, one may overcome certain problems by improving the existing capitalist system, particularly its institutional setup.

In the context of Latin America, there are various strands of CC that partly disagree significantly with one another. Raising doubts on orthodox economics' "best way" in Latin America, CC has been applied to Latin America in multifaceted ways. As discussed above, being also the case in Latin America, various scholars decided differently between "parsimony and complexity." The following section discusses various CC approaches on Latin America and examines which one fits best with Hall and Soskice's VoC approach.

Struggling with North's reliance on the legal framework as an explanatory variable and the inherent one-size-fits-all indication, Bizberg and Théret (2015) stress the idea of equifinality and emphasize specific local requirements. Bizberg (2014) states that trajectories of the Latin American countries have bifurcated since the 1970s—within, according to Bizberg (2014, p. 45), "...época de divergencia"—and may no longer be seen as one system. According to him, the last time that Latin America was depicted by one system was in the times of ISI. Relying heavily on "thick descriptions" of social conflicts and the state as an active actor, Bizberg and Théret introduce as many different types of capitalism—that are not yet consolidated—as cases investigated. For Brazil, they develop a state capitalism aiming at the domestic market, for Chile a state capitalism aiming at foreign markets, a deregulated capitalism subordinated to foreign markets for Mexico, and an instable hybrid switching between the already mentioned ones in Argentina.[14] Categorizing capitalist systems according to the degree of integration into the global economy, the

[14] For original wording, see Bizberg and Théret (2015, p. 14): Brazil—capitalismo orientado por el estado y dirigido hacia el mercado interno; Chile: Capitalismo regulado por el estado dirigido hacia el mercado externo; Mexico—capitalismo desregulado subordinado al mercado externo (capitalism de subcontratación); Argentina—híbrido inestable.

relation between state and economy, and wage bargaining, Bizberg and Théret (2015) come close to what above is described as being complementary to VoC. However, there is very small common ground with VoC and it may rather be seen as belonging to SSP literature.

Along the same lines, Bresser-Pereira (2012) focuses on the role of the state and introduces the "liberal-dependent"[15] variety of capitalism for middle-income countries that most often fail at promoting equal and stable development. Focusing on Latin America, Bresser-Pereira recognizes a long and extensive phase of economic policy making according to the Washington Consensus since ISI. Favoring market-oriented solutions, a liberal-dependent market economy is characterized by the absence of a national development strategy as would be the case in mostly Asian developmental capitalist states. Further, emphasizing dependency on elitist groups in a Marxist fashion, similar to Evans' theory of dependent development (1979), Bresser-Pereira recognizes a tripartite, rather exclusive, structure consisting of the industrial bourgeoisie, the public, and the private bureaucracy, aligning the system in their own favor at the expense of wider society. Approaching development by focusing on the elites, Bresser-Pereira's approach may be fruitful inasmuch as an interventionist state may be able to "externally" impose structures that, as Sheahan (2002, p. 49) puts it, may be able to protect the society "...against destructive forms of profit-seeking."

Investigating the BRIC states (Brazil, Russia, India, and China) with a special focus on Brazil, Nölke (2010) follows a similar approach, but puts emphasis on the dominance of dense networks in which public authorities[16] collaborate in a clan-like manner with mostly huge domestic companies. Nölke describes the dense relationships between public actors and national capital as clans, that just like market, hierarchy, and coordination serve as a mode for social coordination (Nölke, 2018). Similar to Evans' triple alliance[17] (Evans, 1979), Nölke recognizes public authorities, national capital, and MNCs as major players. Nölke, however, rearranges power positions in a so-called state-permeated market economy (SME)—in contrast to smaller and less powerful DME—inasmuch as the national elites are capable of imposing conditions onto foreign capital. MNCs and FDI in general are only left in selectively as a modernizing factor. Recently, Nölke (2018) partly withdrew Brazil from the BRIC group of SMEs. Certainly, Brazil's huge domestic market brings the state itself into a relatively powerful position *vis-à-vis* companies that aim at generating sales in the said country. However, in comparison to China, Russia, and India, Nölke perceives Brazil as less capable of exercising state control over (foreign) capital. OECD data confirm that view, since the level of state control in

[15] Besides Argentina and Brazil, Bresser-Pereira assigns Turkey, Mexico, and South Africa to the liberal-dependent model.

[16] Further, Nölke stresses that state permeation in the sense of public authority's omnipresence is not to be equaled with a strong and centralized state. He rather suggests that public authorities are actors that may act according to their very vested interests.

[17] According to Evans (1979), the triple alliance consists of MNCs, the state, and local capital.

Brazil, for example, over FDI (FDI regulatory restrictiveness index) can rather be found in the group of LMEs than in the proposed interventionist SME one (OECD, 2019). An illustrative example of an SME may be China and it is high local content requirements that require foreign companies willing to sell in the Chinese market to set up 50/50 joint ventures with local companies.[18] Latin American countries, including Brazil, have no such instruments applied.[19] Nölke's attempt to generalize the BRIC countries may also fall short of expectations, since the importance of FDI especially in Brazil can hardly be compared with that of China or India. Thus, Brazil's dependence on foreign capital (FDI stock roughly 38 percent of GDP in 2017) is much higher than in the latter ones (China and India both below 15 percent) (UNCTAD STAT, 2019). Brazil's categorization with the other BRIC countries and the notion of the interventionist state may also be cast into doubt regarding the other empirical observations in Chap. 2 that suggest a clear orientation to market-oriented policies.

The three aforementioned approaches doubtless all provide distinct and valuable knowledge, but seem to move outside of the VoC ontology. Bizberg, Presser-Pereira, and Nölke mostly focus on the state activity within the distinct forms of capitalism and, thus, most likely provide the complementary knowledge mentioned above. By focusing on the state as a potential *leviathan* their—excepting partly Nölke—inherent focus lies on the macro rules of the game and therefore faces certain limitations considering the institutions in work in relation to the actors. Furthermore, as has been mentioned above, the past few decades—since the 1970s—have been characterized by strong economic liberalization. Hence, *vis-à-vis* corporations (especially multinational ones), the three approaches tend to overestimate the role of the state to a certain degree.

Most famously, gaining a canonical status for Latin American CC, Schneider introduces the hierarchical market economy (HME) overcoming major analytical obstacles that come along with local development (Schneider, 2009, 2013; Schneider & Soskice, 2009). To anticipate, HME's main characteristic also depicts its main difference *vis-à-vis* Hall and Soskice's (2001) original VoC taxonomy. In comparison to ideal-typical LMEs and CMEs, HMEs do not provide decent economic development. On the contrary, HMEs continuously reinforce systemic dysfunctions and find themselves in a so-called low-skill trap that hampers economic dynamics and culminates in stagnation, high inequality, low education, and low productivity. Even in times of, for example, the commodity-led period of economic upturn, according to HME literature, created if—at all—"growthless jobs"[20]

[18]This means that ownersip of JV is split into 50% foreign company and 50% Chinese company. For example, a German car manufacturer is allowed to sell cars in China only when conducting a 50/50 joint venture with a local company. Consequently, local production and technology transfer is propelled.

[19]One exception is the Brazilian oil and gas sector (Presidência da República, 2016).

[20]Growthless jobs are characterized by their inability to contribute to sustainable development. They most often are characterized by low productivity and low skill requirements.

(Schneider, 2013, p. 90). Hence the systemic weakness materializes in the inability to generate quality jobs on a larger scale.

In comparison to standard VoC literature in which institutional complementarity provides positive outcomes on a systemic level, expanding such analyses to the developing world, where complementarities stabilize failing systems, can be highly beneficial. The application of VoC to developing countries follows this work's understanding of development and allows one to approach ongoing developmental distortions as a matter of idiosyncratic institutional setups.

Schneider's work on the HME contributes positively to the work at hand, since it:

- Generally follows a VoC fashion as it indicates capitalist actor constellations in Latin America, including the players, the game being played, and potential outcomes
- Follows Hall and Soskice and perceives the entire political economy's performance as explainable by interaction at the micro-level
- Uses similar structures such as LMEs and CMEs and, thus, allows us to reasonably merge the different strands within the investigation of Conflating Capitalisms
- Uses VoC's strengths and offers systemic explanations for socioeconomic performance

In comparison to the approaches discussed above, following a rather clear VoC fashion, HME acknowledges the firm as a crucial actor within Latin America's political economy and uses the "firm's eye" for (socio)economic analyses. Highlighting the importance of (corporate) hierarchies, he states:

> In an oversimplified sense, economic activity in Latin America is still largely subject to planning rather than to the spontaneous free play of market forces, but the planning shifted after the 1990s from ministry offices to corporate boardrooms. (Schneider, 2013, p. 11)

Introducing the concept of business-led development, Schneider (2009) relies on the firm's interaction as an explanatory variable for the performance of the entire economy. He copes with both the aforementioned vector position of firms in capitalist societies and idiosyncrasies of Latin American development. Such firm-related developmental idiosyncrasies are, first, the retreat of the state since the 1990s, second, the corresponding Coasian onslaught in the wake of extensive privatization, and third, the relatively neglected and sometimes even nonexistent active role of corporations in Latin American political economy literature.

In comparison to Hall and Soskice, Schneider assigns firms an even more important role. Perceiving institutions as constraints, in comparison to CMEs and LMEs, HMEs certainly exert the fewest limitations. As a consequence, "...MNCs are freer from these constraints, and thus, their internally generated strategies and behaviors are more consequential for development outcomes..." (Schneider, 2013, p. 8). Sufficing for now and dealt with in more in detail in Chap. 4, a lack of enabling institutions in a Streeckian sense certainly limits firms in HMEs in other ways.

Noteworthily, within the specific Latin American surrounding, strong economic liberalization (discussed in Chap. 2) did not lead to the establishment of a (functioning) LME but—according to Schneider—culminated, to a large degree, in large hierarchical structures. As with LMEs and CMEs, HMEs are also deeply penetrated by market relations (and some coordinated as well). Nonetheless, Schneider perceives Latin America's core relations of capitalism (general principle of solving coordination problems) to be more pervaded by hierarchy than other countries. Generally in HME literature, hierarchy implies more than a mere decision to either buy or make. Going beyond the Williamson (1973) question of vertical integration and inherent efficiency considerations, Schneider understands hierarchy as a device to order social relations and to coordinate action. Hence, interactions conducted by relying on either strategic coordination in CMEs or the market in LMEs are mostly coordinated through hierarchy in HMEs (Schneider, 2013, p. 29). In a VoC fashion, within HMEs hierarchy determines, for example, the relation between owners and managers, between workers and managers, between firms and unions, and between employees and education.

Beyond the ongoing tremendous degree of socioeconomic inequality that generally propels hierarchical social relations one may, following Sheahan (2002), explain the phenomenon of internalization as follows. An HME, roughly speaking, is characterized by rather weak institutions. This absence of impartial and strong institutions—that are typical for LMEs—to rely on when playing the market severely hampers trust building among the social actors and prohibits further development toward LMEs (Sheahan, 2002). Hence, following a Coasian understanding, the (external transaction) costs of using the market's price mechanism are high (Coase, 1937). Keeping transaction costs at an affordable level, rather than through market organization, coordination is conducted based on nonmarket allocation through stable hierarchies, which *vis-à-vis* the local market produce lower (internal) transaction costs.

In conjunction with the stability postulates of historical institutionalism that emerge from path-dependent development, copying and pasting liberal market policies into an unfitting environment characterized by idiosyncratic contextual factors, not considering the entire system and complementary institutions, potentially ends up in either inefficient markets or hierarchies. One could certainly argue, according to Williamson's institutional hierarchy (Williamson, 2000), that the development of a level institutional playing field at all four hierarchy levels is beyond the scope of general scholarship and everyday politics since the time frame necessary may exceed the explorable.[21] Further, the distinct historical roots and contextual factors are not considerable in their entirety. However, the lesson that can certainly be drawn is that if institutions are changed, approaching it selectively (single domains, or even subunits within the domains), neglecting complementary institutions may not lead to the desired outcome. VoC in general and especially the

[21] According to Williamson's institutional hierarchy, first-level institutions (informal institutions, customs, traditions, norms, and religion) may need a thousand years to genuinely change. Second-level institutions such as formal rules, bureaucracies, etc., may need up to 100 years to change (Williamson, 2000).

work of Schneider et al., considering the various institutional domains and its interplay, certainly improves the systemic understanding that seems to be beneficial in Latin America.

3.3.1 HME's Analytical Adjustments and Limitations

Schneider's approach on Latin American capitalism indeed mostly moves within the frame set by Hall and Soskice (2001). Nevertheless, HME conducts various analytical adjustments that turn out to be crucial in order to cope with local realities in Latin American political economies. The following section discusses analytical adjustments, their general added value, their fit to the purpose of this work, potential shortcomings, and necessary further developments that will be conducted in the subsequent chapters. In general, most importantly for this work, changes take place at five fronts. First, Schneider reinterprets the Northian split between actors and institutions. Second, along the same lines, rather than relying on the institutional domains proposed by Hall and Soskice, Schneider emphasizes actors' behavioral responses to surrounding institutions. Third, the general concept of the firm is split into local business groups and MNCs. Fourth, institutional complementarity may also have negative effects on the socioeconomic development. Fifth, above all, the institutional system is approached by its capability to generate quality jobs.

Northian Split

Schneider clearly rejects the Northian (1992) divide between institutions as the rules of the game and organizations such as firms as the mere players. Hence, of utmost importance for this work, Schneider conducts an analytical shift away from scrutinizing mostly formal institutions toward behavior as a better proxy to understanding reality in Latin America. Schneider (2013, p. 7) states that the "... approach is less concerned with standard formal institutions—and how and why they lack force—and focuses instead on the organizational and behavioral responses to weak or absent institutions...." This analytical shift has already been partly conducted by Hall and Soskice inasmuch as organizations also have rules "...that contribute to the institutions of the political economy" (2001, p. 9). Furthermore, Hall and Soskice's division between rules and actors is at best vague as they indicate that "...from time to time, we refer loosely to the institutions or organizations of the political economy to refer to both the organizations and institutions found within it" (2001, p. 9). Schneider emphasizes the notion of organizations as independently affecting the political economy, since the very same formal institutions may work on various organizations (Schneider distinguishes between business groups and MNCs) entirely differently. As such, perceiving organizations as pure reflections of the surrounding institutions may fall short. On the contrary, Schneider indirectly states that across different institutional rule systems, behavior can be equal and, thus, builds de facto rules. In line with Ostrom's (1990) introduction of the institutional task to reduce uncertainty—by increasing predictability of other actors' future behavior—the definitional extension and inclusion of institutions "...as sets of regularized practices with a rule-like quality, structure the behavior of political and economic actors" (Hall, 2010, p. 204) seems to be fruitful especially in a region with rather weak formal institutions. Schneider's approach is reasonable, above all, in Latin America, which is characterized by a gap between *de jure* and de facto rules. For example, labor market regulation in Latin America is *de jure* even higher than in CMEs but clearly lacks extensive implementation, monitoring, and sanctioning (Schneider & Karcher, 2010). It—if at all—exclusively covers a small segment of labor elite and neglects the vast majority of low-skilled workers (Schneider, 2013, p. 12). De facto, the Latin American labor market is highly segmented, which does not allow organized labor either in corporatist bargaining or in employees' plant-level representation.

This definitory expansion of institutions also holds up with Aoki's (2001, 2010) concept of complementarity since within HMEs it is the institutionalized patterns of behavior in one institutional domain that impacts the incentives of workers and employers in the other domains. As such, a specific institutionalized behavior in one domain urges a similar kind of behavior in the others. As this chapter will show, this institutional complementarity is causing a relatively strong behavioral coherence across the entire system. Furthermore, regarding the work at hand, shifting the analytical focus from institutions to behavior is of utmost importance for the feasibility of this work. Even though it was not Schneider's goal to incorporate a multifaceted and dynamic investigation of MNCs, relying on behavioral responses allows for a nuanced investigation of MNCs and the research design applied throughout the empirical study later on.

Ontological Adjustments

In line with the aforementioned incorporation of organizational behavior into the institutional analysis, Schneider changes the ontological grounding inasmuch as he replaces Hall and Soskice's five institutional domains with—as he names it—four core features of HMEs. According to Schneider, HME's core features are diversified local business groups, MNCs, segmented labor markets, and low levels of education. In a Schneiderian meaning, these features are to be understood as (ongoing and habitualized) responses to the surrounding weak or absent institutions (2013, p. 7). Also emphasizing institutional complementarity, Schneider scrutinizes systemic adhesives as occurring between the mentioned response categories rather than between the institutional domains proposed by VoC. Such an approach certainly makes sense when introducing an apparently new variety of capitalism aimed at disclosing systemic coherence across Latin American countries. Whereas, for example, legislation within the institutional domains proposed by Hall and Soskice varies significantly between the political economies, it is these four key features that show a general Latin American pattern. Thus, one may say that though institutions vary *de jure*, patterns of real action and socioeconomic organization seem to be de facto similar. On that account, Schneider counters some major points of critique that criticize the applied parsimony regarding capitalism in Latin America. However, to anticipate, in order to make HME fit with LME and CME and to build one firm base for the three types of capitalism under scrutiny, this chapter translates these four core features into the five institutional domains already used to understand CMEs and LMEs. To consider Latin American realities, patterns of behavior will be included within a Schneiderian meaning.

Two Kinds of Firms

Schneider distinguishes two forms of firms: the huge mostly family-owned local business groups and MNCs that can both be seen as constituting the Latin American political economy. As mentioned above, this distinction seems to be fruitful, since the two forms of organization show different behavioral patterns though working under the same umbrella of institutions. Among others, different effects on the two firms may also be explained by the degree of formal institutions' de facto enforcement. According to Schneider, MNCs tend to be more regulated and, consequently, more likely to comply with regulations than domestic firms (2013, p. 109). Since it is the MNC that is of prime interest for this work, national business conglomerates will only be discussed inasmuch as they affect or are affected by MNCs.[22] Recognizing and including MNCs as a major player into the institutional analysis of national capitalisms is very beneficial for this work and complies with local conditions since "...a purely domestic focus would miss major players; in most countries, MNCs constitute a third to a half of the largest firms" (2013, p. 73). However, Schneider—owing to the nature of VoC—remains in the rather static field, explaining a status quo within national boundaries a posteriori rather than open doors for dynamics that occur between multinational actors and local institutions. Schneider discusses potential impacts of MNCs on Latin American political economies and, from time to time, finds himself confronted with the same pitfalls as those of orthodox economics. He follows the generalist assumption of homogeneous flows of MNCs. Consequently, though discussing behavior, the firm's impact on socioeconomic indicators is most often examined within the frames of FDI flows (2013) as an explanatory variable for capital accumulated, the number of created jobs, money spent in R&D (2013, p. 86), etc. This approach seems to be inconsistent also within HME. The HME approach emphasizes both the unilateral power of MNCs and its close ties with corporate headquarters (in terms of corporate governance) in the country of origin (Schneider, 2013, p. 7). Consequently, neglecting a potential variety of MNCs—according to their home country—is certainly a shortcoming of the HME approach. Assuming that MNCs behave in conformity makes sense—if at all—only within the traditional institutional analysis where structure determines action, perceiving MNCs to be entirely embedded (more on that in Chap. 4) within the local (national) institutional setting. That combined with the perception of FDI mainly originating in the USA, the inclusion of MNCs in socioeconomic analysis is certainly beneficial, but relatively rapidly reaches some of the same limits as orthodox economics.

[22]For more information and summaries on Latin American business groups and multilatinas, see Andonova and Losada-Otálora (2018), Schneider (2009, 2013).

Complementarity with Negative Consequences

Whereas systemic coherence across the institutional domains in CMEs and LMEs positively contributes to the performance of the entire political economy (Hall & Soskice, 2001), institutional complementarity in HMEs continuously hampers socio-economic development. Complementarity in HMEs neither leads to LME-like comparative institutional (dis)advantages in radical innovation nor to CME-like ones in incremental improvements. HMEs complementarities reinforce, among other things, low skills, short-term employment, and an absence of labor representation. Hence, it lacks both LME and CME capacities and offer an advantageous area rather for commodity production, natural resources, and low-complexity manufacturing (Schneider, 2013, p. 33). Schneider therefore extends the concept of complementarities, deviating from Hall and Soskice's beneficial relation between complementarity and socioeconomic performance. Institutional complementarity is, thus, neutral with respect to the outcomes. From an analytical point of view, a positive complementarity—as one institution improves the efficiency of another one and vice versa—can equally have a negative socioeconomic effect. Extending the concept of institutional complementarities to political economies that constantly underperform contributes to the understanding of not only why well-functioning economies work well—as Hall and Soskice did—but also why major developing economies continue to fail.

It Is All About Jobs

As the major analytical focus connecting major issues such as the skill regime, labor relations, productivity, and inequality, Schneider (2013) puts special emphasis on the system's ability to generate quality jobs.

> Experience shows that economic growth, on its own, is not sufficient. We must do more to empower individuals through decent work, support people through social protection, and ensure the voices of the poor and marginalized are heard (UN Secretary-General Ban Ki-moon, 2014).

Decent work (ILO),[23] good jobs (IDB),[24] *Gute Arbeit* (DGB),[25] and *buen trabajo* (PET),[26] in line with former UN Secretary-General Ban Ki-moon, various organizations across the north and the south recognize the quality of jobs as key to sustainable socioeconomic development. As such, within Latin American political economies, it is exactly the absence of quality jobs on a large scale that stalls development. It is Schneider who joins the aforementioned line of consensus and offers a systemic institutional explanation for a self-enforcing low-skill trap that prohibits quality jobs resulting in stagnation, inequality, and low productivity. Following a Schneiderian argumentation, socioeconomic development at the national level can only be achieved by high-quality jobs on a comprehensive scale.

---

[23] ECLAC/ILO (2013).

[24] IDB (2003).

[25] DGB (2019).

[26] Socioeco (2019).

This line of reasoning holds up with VoC's general approach in which the entire political economy may be approached as a product of infinite elements and interactions that each contribute to the aggregated result. Broadly put, following Schneider's (2013) general argument, a decent job may be a matter of the required skill level, personal security, and the corresponding remuneration.

Limitations

Approaching MNCs and Latin American development via the road of CC and adjusting it for this work's endeavor comes with certain limitations regarding the explanatory power for the whole political economy. However, it complies with the objectives set above, which is to scrutinize MNCs' role in Latin America.

First, the informal economy that accounts for 40 percent of GDP in Latin America and the Caribbean (OECD, 2018) is included only as far as providing a large pool of unskilled labor. That approach makes sense because it ensures a high degree of analytical clearness and generally seems to be sufficient since MNCs are not known for engaging too much with the informal economy. Nonetheless, entirely neglecting the informal economy certainly offers a limited view. On that account, the informal economy should be taken into account as an amplifier for hierarchical relations. Understanding the informal economy as an alternative to the formal one implies that every time firms are not satisfied with the *modus operandi* of the formal one, they have the opportunity, for example, to evade extensive regulation by switching business operations to the informal side of the economy.[27] Furthermore, in terms of power relations, the huge "reserve army" of labor in the informal economy lining up for formal jobs clearly strengthens the already skewed power relations between top management and labor to the detriment of the latter. One could also argue that the entire system characterized by short-termism, high risk, and low commitment may only be viable due to the informal economy's capacity to absorb low skilled workers that stand to lose their jobs within the informal one. As a consequence, the entire status quo of the Latin American game may only work due to the workers' safety net—the informal economy—constituting the "employer of last resort." According to Schneider (2013) and IDB (2003), confirming this argumentation, eight out of ten laid-off workers in Argentina will find their next job in the informal economy. However, as indicated above, the more negative the impact of the informal economy may be, the more important the development of the formal one should be. A focus on structure and potential change of the formal economy is crucial since a successfully inclusive formal economy logically leads to a decreasing informal economy, which should be an inherent objective of every political economy.[28]

Second, local business groups are included in the analysis exclusively as part of the system and insofar as they affect MNCs but not as active actors themselves. As indicated above, MNCs and local business groups act differently and follow

[27] World Bank's World Development Report 2005 on Latin America shows a strikingly positive correlation between levels of labor market regulation and noncompliance (evasion).

[28] The informal economy is characterized by nonexistent employment protection, bad working conditions, an absence of social security, healthcare, pensions, etc.

sometimes opposing incentive structures. In order to secure analytical clearness, the focus—corresponding with the general concern—therefore lies on MNCs and their interaction within Latin American HMEs.

3.3.2 HME's Institutional Dimensions

As indicated above, HMEs in Latin America are dysfunctional inasmuch as they are not providing a conducive environment for socioeconomic development. According to Schneider (2009, 2013), it is the local institutional setup that reinforces systemic weaknesses leading to low productivity, low levels of education, and high measures of inequality. The bottom line is the system's inability to generate quality jobs that hampers development. The next section develops the five institutional domains in a fashion following Hall and Soskice (2001) in which the institutional roots of a lack of development may be found. On that account—to match VoC's traditional categories of LME and CME with Schneider's HME—HME's four behavioral response categories are translated into the traditional institutional domains. The basic coordination problems that occur within the domains remain unchanged to those introduced in Sect. 3.2. However, using Schneider's extension of institutions—including behavioral patterns—the institutional domains are adjusted in order to cope with Latin American realities. Certainly, HME's institutional dimensions are introduced in a Weberian sense of ideal types. In reality, just like with the VoC in general, significant deviations can occur within an HME.

Industrial Relations

Bringing together those that own the means of production (employers) and those that own manpower (employees), in Latin America, takes place within an—to put it in the words of Schneider (2013)—atomized, segmented, and anomic field. This field may best be described using the following indicators. First, organization among both labor and employers is extremely weak. Unions are either nonexistent or a rather politicized[29] entity that lacks shop-floor presence (Schneider, 2009, 2013). According to the equal weakness of business associations (see also IFR below)—beyond their own disorganization and poor equipment of resources—both parties lack the corresponding counterpart to negotiate working conditions and wages, which again reinforces their limited role (Schneider, 2004, 2013). Accordingly, collective bargaining coverage is low and is substituted by negotiation on lower, more individualistic levels in a hierarchical manner, most often unilaterally decided by top management. Unilateral management control includes the capacities of the very few to decide about work organization, wage setting, and hiring and firing of the masses (Schneider & Soskice, 2009, p. 42).

[29] Unions willing to exert influence are politically bargaining with governments directly rather than with associations.

Formal sector employment[30] indeed provides certain benefits and protection due to an extensive regulation of labor markets. To protect employees against the high local risks of income loss, national governments commonly implemented extensive regulations (higher than in developed countries) that according to the IDB (2003, p. 9) "...constitute a primitive method of insurance and can be costly." As major means of employment protection, regulation relies heavily on the instrument of severance pay[31] that proportionally increases with the time of corporate affiliation. In a comparative perspective, severance costs for firms are among the highest in the world (Schneider, 2013, p. 116). In the same vein, World Bank data imply that a high degree of labor market regulation is perceived as a major constraint on firms in Latin America (World Bank, 2004).[32] However, regarding the entire political economy, lax enforcement, and subsequent employers' noncompliance and evasion make labor market regulation a vague matter and may be well approached by the already introduced *de jure*—de facto gap. Nonetheless, as indicated above, this picture may change when referring to MNCs that are supposed to comply more firmly with labor market regulations (2013, p. 109) than local firms do.

Education and Vocational Training

The "mist of uncertainty" postulated above is more or less what suitably describes the situation in HMEs' system of education and vocational training. This domain that is responsible for the accumulation of social capital succumbs to the inherent market failure and indeed generates general skills but at a (very) low overall quality (Schneider, 2013, p. 127). Like LMEs, HMEs have no nonmarket governance mechanism that helps to overcome high levels of uncertainty and the subsequent high risk of sunk investments. In comparison with LMEs, that manage to cope with market forces and opportunism, HMEs show "severe inefficiencies in the process of investment in human capital" (Schneider, 2013, p. 114) culminating in the worst-case scenario for all participants, which is stagnation of educational levels and low productivity. This negative outcome seems paradoxical, since on both sides employers and employees are supposed to have a vested interest in the generation of high skills on a large scale. While individuals' interest in attaining a decent job is not in question, World Bank investment climate survey data indicate that a large number of firms in Latin America also rate low levels of skills and education "...as a major or severe obstacle to their operations" (World Bank, 2004, p. 136).

---

[30] According to Schneider (2013), the formal sector accounts for approximately 60 percent of the entire employment in Latin America. He further distinguishes the formal sector as two-thirds regular workers (low skills, short tenure) and one-third as labor elite (long tenure, high skills, union representation).

[31] Apart from that, Latin American countries have no system (exceptions may be found to some degree in Brazil and Chile) of extensive unemployment or social insurance systems (Schneider, 2013, p. 95).

[32] Notably, Brazil takes the first rank in this ranking with almost 60 percent reporting that regulation depicts a problem for business operations.

Consequently, one can reasonably assume that firms are interested in overcoming obstacles by hiring more higher skilled workers.

Similar to LMEs, HMEs react to issues of specificity, opportunism, and market forces—being situated in an "ungoverned" environment—by producing a skill regime characterized by its generality, as opposed to specificity (or vocational) (Schneider & Soskice, 2009; Schneider, 2013). In the light of atomized labor relations, short-termism, and the absence of compensation mechanisms for workers who lose their job, a general skill set allows workers to switch between firms and sometimes even sectors and promises the highest cumulated returns over the span of a working life. Firms, as the direct counterpart, require generally skilled workers since any kind of specificity would require investments in education that again may be sunk tomorrow due to extensive poaching in Latin American political economies.

Facing potential sunk costs from investments in education, beyond the degree of specificity that certainly resembles LMEs, HMEs are not able to produce quality education and a highly skilled workforce as LMEs do. Uncertainty about future values of current investments is present for both workers and employers. Consequently, in order to avoid sunk costs, employers hardly invest in the skill creation of workers and employees hardly invest in their own skills. The immense pool of unskilled workers makes, for example, activities in commodities and low-technology production cheap, which in turn makes it costlier to engage with high-skilled workers. Furthermore, atomized labor relations and a consequently highly volatile workforce make it an urgent requirement to be able to easily replace employees in a short period of time. Since employees' substitutability most often negatively correlates with their skill level, firms' reliance on low-skilled workers is further strengthened. Along the same lines, workers putting efforts into intensive education may produce skills that are not in demand by the private sector and, thus, run the risk of sunk investments. If the skills gained are not to be applied in future employment, education becomes (from an economic perspective) a futile matter. Confirming this argument, the latest studies (Schneider, 2013, p. 124) show that Latin American political economies promise the world's lowest and further decreasing—even in times of economic growth—returns on individual investments in education. One may therefore argue that expecting marginal returns, if any at all, on additional education, potential employees' waiver of education follows the maxim of rationality insofar as to stop education when opportunity costs exceed the expected gains from additional (marginal) investments (2013, p. 125).

The disentanglement of the educational system from business reinforces the aforementioned dynamics. As such, even if firms had specific requirements, the demand would most likely not be matched and would not be translated into suitable training programs, due to a lack of exchange of expertise. Such a systemic error continuously generates and reinforces the misfit between skills acquired and skills demanded and logically propels decreasing returns on education.

As in the case of LMEs, a certain necessary degree of specificity is attained through firms' in-house training. However, the low quality of overall education deprives firms in HMEs of this opportunity. In-house training such as that of LMEs is only possible by building upon a generally strong educational background and highly developed general skills. Hence, in-house training is used much less in HMEs than in LMEs and firms remain in low-skill activities.

Notable in developing countries but following a certain LME logic is the very low availability of vocational training that according to Schneider depicts a remarkable indication of the mismatch between education and labor market demands (Schneider, 2013, p. 126). As trajectories of former development countries indicate, vocational training has often served well to upgrade the general skill level relating to both quantity and quality (Schneider, 2013, p. 101).

The situation described above culminates in a Latin American low-skill trap in which low demand for and a lack of supply of skills reinforce one another. Without any doubt, negative educational outcomes produced by the HME inherent system depict a major problem when discussing the entire system.

Corporate Governance

Within HMEs the realm of corporate governance is characterized by apparent simplicity but raises some questions. In general, MNCs and business groups are perceived as the major conduit for organizing access to capital and, thus, both kinds of firms' internal channels substitute both financial markets and banks (Schneider, 2013, p. 10). Top management in subsidiaries is therefore not preoccupied with keeping up relations either with shareholders or with bank managers that makes classical principal-agent problems less relevant. Instead, firms' top management is concerned with intra-firm hierarchical relations to the corporate headquarters (for MNCs) or to the owner family (business groups) (Schneider, 2013, p. 47). The principal, thus, is the company and other large external investors have—if any at all—little leverage over the subsidiaries' top management (agent). Consequently, corporate governance in HMEs resembles CMEs in various stances (Schneider, 2013, p. 25).

Ownership concentration is even higher than in CMEs. Generally, both business groups and subsidiaries—at least in wholly owned ones—are owned entirely by one proprietor and the owner is not supposed to change as long as the entity remains under the business group's or MNC's umbrella. In comparison with LME- and to a certain degree also CME-like obligations toward third parties, Schneider perceives subsidiaries as being freer from constraints exerted by external financial pressures. Following that line of thought, without the need to justify decisions and to find consensus between external investor and managers, decisions made internally seem to be more crucial than in LMEs and CMEs. Furthermore, since information is the principal's key to understanding and monitoring the agent, an MNC with centralized and comprehensive controlling systems and a frequent exchange of personnel can be seen—similarly to CMEs—as insider-oriented, overcoming information asymmetries (Deeg & Hardie, 2016) favoring the more proximate agent. Unlimited access to subsidiary information plus the ability to steer subsidiary business allows the headquarters to genuinely evaluate performance and to estimate future profits and risks. All these elements together seem to confirm Schneider's HME–CME resemblance postulate. However, in general, there may also be a tendency toward short-termism in multinationals' subsidiaries in HMEs, as it is simply easier to enter and exit in relation to business opportunities.

From a traditional VoC perspective, the aforementioned matters of ownership concentration and insider/outsider orientation should ultimately culminate in a certain degree of "patience" of capital (Hall & Soskice, 2001). The "level of patience" then again informs the time horizon of investments and the reliance on current earnings as a performance indicator. Relating to MNCs, considering the headquarters' hierarchical influence on corporate decisions, high ownership concentration and the corresponding privileged insider information should make headquarters able to recognize potential long-term profits and—as is the case in CMEs—thus, to overcome adverse short-term conditions without using the exit strategy. In line with that, patient capital is capable of relying less on short-term profits, expecting the crystallization of potential profits in the longer term. On that account, Schneider is certainly right comparing HMEs with CMEs. However, there may be differences according to the headquarters' country of origin. Schneider dispenses with such differences assuming that foreign firms are mainly US-owned MNCs (Schneider, 2013; Schneider & Soskice, 2009). As Chap. 2 indicates, MNCs originate equally from Europe as they do from the USA. Hence, Schneider's statement is somewhat misleading. Considering the diversity of subsidiaries' home systems and the assumption that headquarters are ultimately responsible for satisfying their investors in the country of origin, it would seem reasonable to assume that the degree of "patience" present in the home country certainly filters through to the performance requirement on the subsidiary to a certain degree set by the headquarters. According to this reasoning, one could assume that subsidiaries of MNCs originating in CMEs may be funded by capital that is more patient than the one of LME counterparts.

Furthermore, Schneider's perception of MNCs' headquarters as internal investors may be beyond debate in terms of access to information but may raise certain doubts when talking about desires, requirements, incentives, and expectations. Certainly, capital stems from within the corporate family, but headquarters may approach certain issues of interest differently to subsidiaries. In a hierarchical fashion, the desires of the main funder are decisive and local management needs to adhere to the decisions taken abroad. As a consequence, one may argue that economic planning has not only shifted "...from ministry offices to corporate boardrooms" (Schneider, 2013, p. 9) but to corporate boardrooms abroad in the MNCs' headquarters. Hence, the headquarters may better be considered as a quasi-external investor. Interestingly, corporate governance with such a quasi-external investor (principal) shifts requirements and desires from sheer monetary returns—as it is with traditional external investors—to a variety of demands and expectations that need to be met by the agent. In addition to the expected financial returns, agents within subsidiaries need to incorporate HQ's strategic directives, organizational structures, etc. Hence, when referring to MNC subsidiaries, the domain of corporate governance should be considered from a more comprehensive and more complex account beyond the provision of capital.

Employee Relations

Employee relations in HMEs resemble the dispersed and unorganized appearance of industrial relations. One difference certainly is the (power) position in HMEs. Workers' conscious withholding of information and efforts as described in Sect. 3.2 may not be that crucial for HMEs as it is for LMEs and CMEs. Due to the high staff turnover, workers in HMEs rarely come into the position of having unique knowledge or capabilities that may be used as a source of power *vis-à-vis* the management. The average job tenure in HMEs is significantly shorter even than the one in LMEs. Hence, strong rotation makes the workers' own future within the company uncertain and increases the certainty of leaving the firm soon. Such a high degree of workforce volatility makes a genuine incorporation of workers into corporate decision-making a futile endeavor. Furthermore, organization of workers via any kind of business labor forums is not feasible and labor representation within the corporate board is nonexistent. Consequently, employees lack a voice, representation, and any kind of formal grievance procedure (2013). Co-determination is neither desired nor possible to conduct. General atomized (disorganized) labor on shop-floor levels make joint management—workforce negotiation meaningless and costly *vis-à-vis* returns of hierarchical decision-making (2013, p. 35). An alignment of workers' and management's incentives and participation in decision-making on distributional issues is beyond scope. It is beyond the scope of a worker to ensure that good performance culminates in good wages. Decisions on the competences required and the renumeration among the workers, managers, and owners are decided by a combination of markets and hierarchy, with an emphasis on unilateral decisions by the top management.

Inter-firm Relations

IFR in HMEs resemble the ones in LMEs inasmuch as both have no shared coordination mechanisms for cooperation between firms (Schneider, 2013, p. 27) and rely on a combination of markets and hierarchies. The difference between LME and HME lies within the more frequent usage of hierarchies in the latter. As already mentioned above, firms are rarely organized into business associations, which generally hampers inter-firm cooperation.[33] This general weakness of associated business within HME is especially valid when referring to subsidiaries of MNCs. They are supposed to take powerful and dominant positions within whole sectors that make any further effort in collaborating with other firms rather unnecessary. On the contrary, subsidiaries are tightly controlled by intra-firm hierarchies that again reduces returns on cooperation and negotiation in the host countries and makes it more difficult to conduct. Further, accelerating isolation of MNCs' subsidiaries, Schneider recognizes a frequent cultural and linguistic misfit of, for example, expatriates in the host country and a strong tendency to short-termism that make cooperation of subsidiaries with local companies less likely (2013, p. 35). Along the

---

[33] Schneider undertook a reasonable effort to examine the potential impact of association, or the impact of their very absence, on development in Latin America; see Schneider (2004), Doner and Schneider (2000).

same lines, relations with, for example, suppliers are hierarchical either through a high degree of dependence of suppliers on large MNCs or through internalization processes (vertical integration).

Most often throughout Latin America, roughly speaking, subsidiaries of MNCs find themselves on a low-value stage of the global value chain. Hence, the prime objective of subsidiaries is most likely not to benefit from local technology diffusion when cooperating with other firms. Similarly, it is rather unlikely that the environment of HME will contribute significantly to the development of new technology. Hence, inter-firm cooperation aiming at attaining a technology edge is very unlikely and technology diffusion takes place along MNCs' hierarchy. However, if knowledge or technology spillover takes place, then the fluid labor market is certainly the main driver, just like the one in LMEs.

3.3.3 HME's Institutional Complementarities

Just like with CMEs and LMEs, HME's institutional domains developed above form a relatively stable economic system through the working of institutional complementarities. Complementarities and their adhesive character follow Aoki's (2001) understanding in which institutions' interplay raises one another's efficiency. However, as mentioned above, Schneider analytically adjusted complementarities insofar as they may produce negative outcomes and, thus, are able to stabilize a dysfunctional (in terms of outcomes) system, as is the case in Latin American political economies. HMEs' coherent pattern of how to solve coordination problems leads to a deadlock in which—even if desired—Latin American political economies are incapable of generating quality jobs. Whereas most domains show some tendency toward either LME- or CME-like coordination, within HMEs the unilateral hierarchical control plays a major role. Figure 3.7 indicates the institutional domains and some of the complementarities between them.

Complementarities Between EV and CG

High ownership concentration within HMEs has certain characteristics that CMEs do not. The expanded requirements of HQs and their capability to impact on local decisions need to be taken into account. It is the HQ that generally decides the subsidiary's position in the global value chain and therefore decides which activity is to be conducted in Latin America. Most often, high value adding departments such as research and development remain within the country of origin. On that account, decisions taken in corporate boardrooms abroad highly impact the constant very low demand for higher skilled labor. Depending on the strategy selected of the firm, for example, efficiency-seeking, capital may not be as patient as one could expect following Schneider's CME-similarity postulate. Since efficiency-seeking companies are mostly looking for low-skilled cheap labor, the corporate focus most often lies on realizing short-term gains. Enforcing this situation, local business groups generally remain (moved due to MNCs presence) in low-skill activities which again

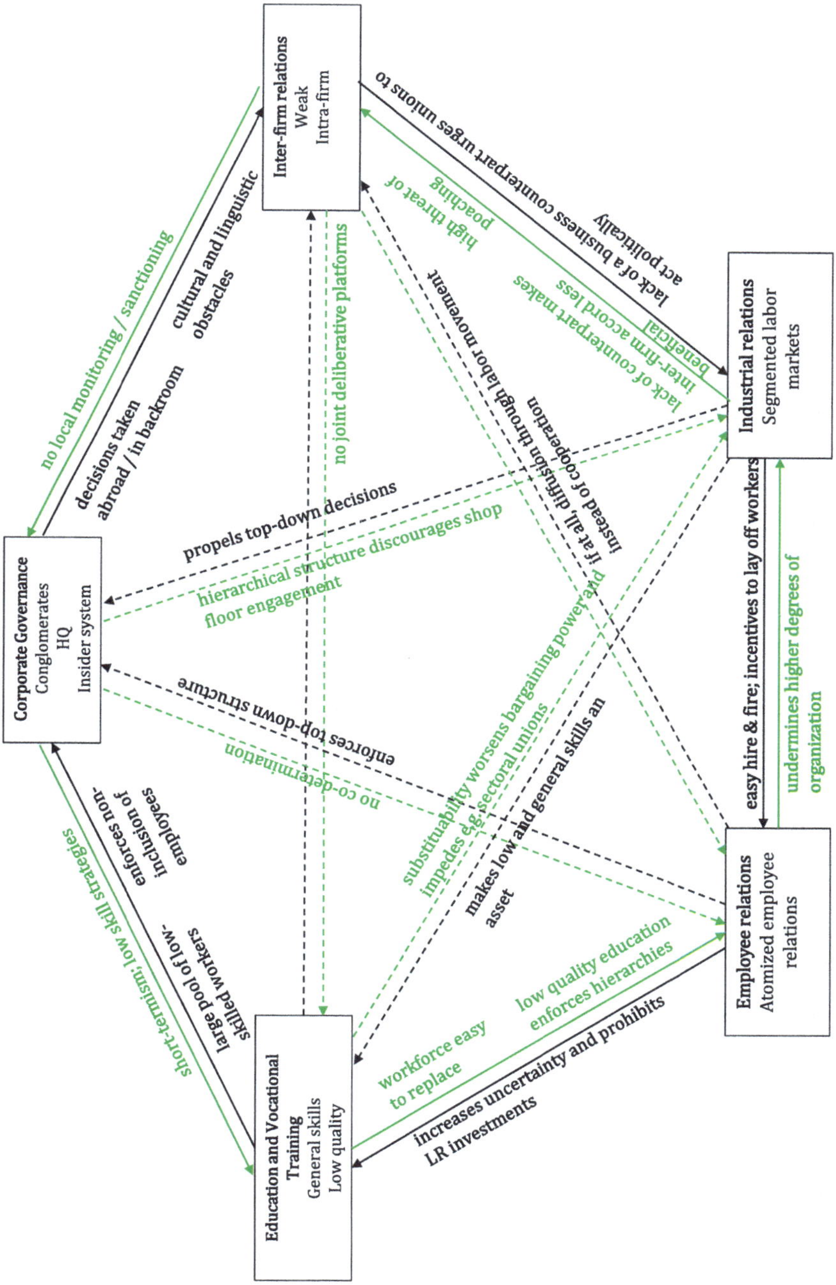

Fig. 3.7 HME as a system of institutional complementarities. Source: From the author

propels demand for low-skill workers. The enormous abundance of low-skilled workers—having the informal economy's unskilled reserve army in mind—makes it cheap for firms to conduct activities that rely on cheap and low-skilled workers.

Complementarities Between CG and IFR, CG and ER, CG and IR
The hierarchical structure of MNCs' and business groups' decision-making also highly affects other institutional domains. First, IFR is affected inasmuch as decisions taken in HQs are mostly final and not subject to local cooperative adjustments. Hierarchical order and a relatively powerful position—for both MNCs and mostly oligopolistic business groups—make joint efforts of various independent companies relatively futile. In the same vein, MNCs are supposed to bear relatively high costs when cooperating with local companies, since cultural and linguistic differences require additional efforts to overcome. Reversing the perspective, the general disorganization of employers and the lack of encompassing associations make hierarchically taken decisions in HQs or within families weigh more heavily. Second, families' and HQ's powerful position *vis-à-vis* local ER make employees' local voices less likely to be incorporated into decisions partly taken abroad. Implementing costly forums of employee participation and co-determination seems to be unnecessary when potential voices will not be heard anyway. Furthermore, the decision of the HQ regarding which part of the value chain to locate in Latin America directly informs the firm's specific skill set. Since most often higher value adding activities are left in the home country, MNCs' workforce do not need to be highly skilled. Low-skilled workforce and the high turnover raise skepticism in HQs and in families on the ability of the firm's workforce to make important decisions. That again makes both forms of companies rely on top managements' decisions. The absence of shop-floor employee representation amplifies the impact of hierarchical decisions since quasi-external authority has unfiltered impact on local operations. Third, between labor and workers, Schneider perceives a general level of distrust (Schneider, 2013, p. 103). Labor unions perceive management as hostile which, certainly, lowers unions' efforts to cooperate. Similarly, the gains from local negotiation are not of major importance neither for business groups nor for MNCs. Even more clearly, thoroughly organized labor may even counter firms' interest in maintaining a relatively voiceless workforce. Since the status quo of firms' activity may at best be described as low skilled, the very stability of the resource of relatively cheap labor may be a priority and would be countered by extensive and strong unions. However, since firms' interest in negotiation with unions is very low, unions generally lack shop-floor representation and rather become politicized actors. Since negotiation with firms is beyond scope in Latin American political economies, unions have high incentives to interact directly with governments and local officials.

Complementarities Between EV and ER, EV and IR, EV and IFR
EV in Latin America that at large produces a general and low-quality skilled workforce shows significant complementarities that are among the major adhesives stabilizing the Latin American low-skill trap.

The large pool of unskilled labor in HMEs propels hierarchical ER twice. It makes relatively low-skilled labor cheap, and it provides enough equally skilled labor that allows the very high turnover rates that are common across all HME countries. Reversing the point of view, very short average employment tenure increases employees' uncertainty about future income and makes investments in education in general—and especially in specific skills—a high-risk endeavor (Schneider, 2013, p. 104). Reinforcing this tendency, the lack of participation of employees in corporate decision-making deprives the workforce from co-determined distributional issues. Hence, workers have no means to make sure that they will receive a fair share of the monetary pie. That again decreases certainty about future gains and makes workers invest in very general skills on a superficial level or not at all. Additionally, the very high demand on low-skilled workers (and conversely the low demand on high-skilled ones) set incentives to align the EV domain accordingly. In comparison to CMEs, the absence of plant-level presentation makes certain expertise from workers within the company unlikely. However, it is this knowledge that is urgently needed to aggregate skill demand that informs a demand-oriented education. This lack of insider knowledge contributes to the relatively high degree of imbalance between the skills available and the ones required by the firms.

Segmented labor markets and the de facto absence of unions on the shop floor significantly hamper the EV from upgrading. First of all, the absence of a lobby and a strong representative when it comes to disputes about wages and working conditions clearly puts the individual employee in a less powerful position *vis-à-vis* the firm. On that account, the employee as an individual may be subject to the "whim" of the employer. Conversely, beyond dispute, strong unions and, for example, wages that are set on a high sector spanning level increase certainty regarding future income flows. Vice versa, weak organized labor makes the employees' investment a risky endeavor. Along the same lines, very low levels of unemployment protection make workers apply everywhere where they can secure a certain level of income. That most often takes place alongside the worker's movement across sectors and industries. In order to ensure an ability to accept every job that may be offered and to secure stable income, workers rationally invest in very general skills that can be applied across various parts of the economy (Schneider, 2013). Weak organization generally makes joint efforts for strategical alignment difficult; that applies equally to a weak organization of employers. The lack of encompassing associations—that provide monitoring and sanctioning capabilities for vocational training in CMEs—does not allow for joint education programs or for cooperatively formulating a demand on specifically required skills. Furthermore, the weak organization of both employers and associations may be a severe drawback when improving quality and quantity of training (Schneider, 2013, p. 101; Sehnbruch, 2006). Schneider (2013, p. 95) emphasizes the importance of strategic coordination of EV efforts since "the absence of plant-level representation, and certainly anything formal like German-style works councils, is crucial in foreclosing possibilities for negotiations over skills and work organization. . . ."

Atomized labor relations and segmented labor market reinforce each other on various stances. The high level of regulation most famously relies on measures that aim at securing employment such as severance pay, which increases dismissal costs.[34] Such measures that increase the costs of firing a worker according to their time of affiliation further supports short-termism on the ER level. Since the costs of firing a worker increase over time—in order to avoid the highest severance costs all over the world—firms in HMEs frequently fire workers after a short period of time without reimbursing severance pay. Hence, high levels of labor regulation lead to intensive evasion and, thus, to a lower de facto regulation at the expense of workers' security. Additionally, regarding another potential measure of employment protection, legislation leaves space for the wide application of temporary contracts that makes it less costly to separate from a worker that again propels turnover rates (Schneider, 2013). Worsening the situation for workers, while the reliance on severance pay is strong and contributes to high turnover rates, the already sacked worker finds almost no means of unemployment protection[35] or social insurances and is dependent on finding a new job within a very short period of time regardless of the job's suitability (Schneider, 2013, p. 95). As such, the specific design of regulation contributes to high turnover rates and puts workers that are searching for jobs in an uncomfortable and insecure situation.

Similarly, low unionization and union absence at the shop-floor make organization at the firm level very unlikely to occur. Further contributing to atomized labor relations, an impeded aggregation of the workers' voice makes employees less powerful. Internal hierarchical decision-making prefers to negotiate with the small fraction of labor elite, if at all (Schneider, 2013, p. 103). In order to keep decisions on organizational structure and bureaucratic processes within the top management, Schneider perceives an inherent vested interest of the top management to actively favor atomized labor relations and low unionization (Schneider, 2013, p. 104). Furthermore, short average job tenures negatively correlate with labor organization in general. Hence, there is hardly any horizontal link between workers in one firm. The absence of union or union-like plant-level representation certainly impedes higher level voice aggregation. Furthermore, being member of a specific union may be less beneficial in Latin America since, for example, a standard wage or certain working conditions attained by unions in one sector most likely will not be applied in any other sector in which workers are working the next day. The uncertainty that benefits in one sector achieved by one union will still count in the sector where the same employee works the next day generally weakens the workers' interest in union representation. In Latin American political economies one can, thus,

[34] According to the Muravyev (2014), employment protection encompasses regulations on hiring and firing thereby determining the costs connected with both dismissal and hiring.

[35] As defined by the ILO Employment Promotion and Protection Against Unemployment Convention in 1988 "unemployment protection is a combination of income security measures (under the form of contributory or social assistance schemes) aimed at guaranteeing a certain standard of living for workers until they can return to work and policies to help unemployed workers increase their employability and search for new jobs" (ILO, 2017a, b, p. 1).

reasonably argue that organized labor in general is very weak (Schneider, 2013) and the lack of representation at firm level and, for example, industry level reinforces each other to the workers' detriment.

The absence of organized business reflects itself in the domains of IR and ER insofar as it impedes cooperative efforts at both the firm and the higher sector or industry levels. Since technology diffusion does not materialize through cooperation, workers moving across firms may be the only opportunity available. Hence, volatile labor markets and rapidly shifting workforces from one firm to another may diffuse technology, though one should be aware of the very limited degree of the general level of technology diffusion in Latin America. Along the same lines, absent associations hamper the aggregation of employers' voices that again severely undermines any kind of organized bipartite or tripartite coordination. Making organization in associations even less interesting, the very lack of unions as a counterpart further decreases gains from employer organization since the value of potential union-association bargaining is quasi nonexistent; the same counts vice versa. As a response, unions generally bargain—if at all—with public authorities and are politicized to a high degree (Schneider, 2013, p. 95).

As one can see, the single interactions may be found on a scale between liberal and coordinated and, thus, may be seen as a hybrid as supposed by Hall and Soskice (2001). However, since the systemic adhesives complementarities are in force and continuously reproduce this different and unique sytem, HME may be a stand-alone capitalist system. Additionally, as described by Schneider, different to CME and LMEs, the stable system of HMEs is reproducing negative outcomes. The complementarities stabilize each other leading to negative outcomes of inequality, low education, low productivity, etc.

3.4 Summary and Reflection

This chapter contributed strongly to the understanding of both the actors of interest and the systemic differences that make the capitalist universe composed of a variety of different games. Along these lines, the complex and multifaceted nature of MNCs was introduced alongside the different market entry strategies that significantly change the local *Gestalt* in the developing country and intra-organizational dynamics that occur within the parent company and the foreign subsidiary. The specifics of different forms of ownership, various degrees of commitment and the corresponding differences in risk, knowledge, and corporate control improve the understanding of the actor of interest and clearly delimit MNCs from conventional firms that are located within one country. Furthermore, the discussion on MNCs elaborated on the subject of analysis as being the wholly owned subsidiary that is established through a greenfield investment. The WOS as the entry strategy with the highest commitment, densest ownership, and the highest risk promises the purest relationship between the foreign subsidiary and the parent company in the country of origin and makes it most intensive as being a local player.

Table 3.3 Behavioral Responses VoC

		Liberal	Coordinated	Hierarchical
Corporate governance	Stock ownership	Dispersed	Blockholding	Family blockholding
	Predominant type of large firms	Specialized managerial corporations, MNCs	Bank-controlled firms, business groups	Hierarchical business groups, MNCs
Inter-firm relations	Firm relations within sectors	Competitive	Sectoral associations	Oligopolistic, nonexistent
	Firm relations across sectors	Few	Encompassing associations	Few (save acquisitions)
	Supplier relations	Competitive bidding	Long term, negotiated	Vertical integration
Labor relations	Employment relations	Short term, market	Long term, negotiated	Short term, market
	Industrial relations	Fewer unions	Encompassing unions	Few unions
	Labor-management committees	No	Yes	No
Skills		General	Sector specific	Low
Comparative institutional advantages		Radical innovation, services	Incremental innovation, manufacturing	Commodities, simple manufacturing
Cases		USA, UK	Germany, Scandinavia, France	Latin America
Socioeconomic development		Mostly	Yes	No

Source: From the author, based on Schneider (2013)

Regarding the different institutional systems discussed, Table 3.3 summarizes the three types of market economies introduced. Table 3.3 indicates information and differences relating to the major institutional domains and socioeconomic outcomes. In general, HMEs seem to share various characteristics with LMEs, especially in the institutional dimensions of EV, IF, IR, and ER. One of the very few characteristics that are common to both HMEs and CMEs is the degree of ownership dispersion.

However, even the one structural similarity between CMEs and HMEs in the dimension of corporate governance (ownership dispersion) may be questionable since it may lead to entirely different consequences. Major funders (the HQs) are located in different systems that again most likely lead to different degrees of capital's "patience." The different degrees of patience materialize in different efficiency requirement and can therefore be consequential for the subsidiaries' strategies selected. Accordingly, considering the entire picture, one can reasonably see HMEs as significantly closer to LMEs than to CMEs.

The analysis of VoC, the incorporation of Schneider's HME, and the alignment of the latter with the former strongly benefit the endeavor at hand. It provides information on actor constellations and action situations by indicating actors, institutional domains, and specific interactions for all country and systems of interest. In general, this chapter develops major cornerstones of this work and allowed one to grasp the non-identical *Gestalt* of both the actor and the political economy. Such consideration is the necessary condition for the genuine development of an analytical framework that attempts to overcome the drawbacks of blueprints. However, so far, the picture of systemic differences is rigid inasmuch as it, indeed, recognizes differences, but does not offer instruments to capture the dynamics that occur when actors move across and are a constitutive part of more than one system. In order to cope with an MNC that transcends systemic borders, in particular in the context of a developing country, a deeper institutional understanding that allows for contradiction and dynamics of change is required. On that account, the next chapter further develops institutional understanding to fit the requirements of the endeavor at hand.

References

Adam, F., Kristan, P., & Tomsic, M. (2009). Varieties of capitalism in Eastern Europe (with special emphasis on Estonia and Slovenia). *Communist and Post-Communist Studies, 42*, 65–81.

Amable, B. (2003). *The diversity of modern capitalism*. Oxford University Press.

Amable, B., Demmou, L., & Gatti, D. (2011). The effect of employment protection and product market regulation on labour market performance: Substitution or complementarity? *Applied Economics, 43*, 449–464.

Amblard, F., Ferrand, N., & Hill, D. R. (2001). How a conceptual framework can help to design models following decreasing abstraction. In *13th SCS-European Simulation Symposium* (pp. 843–847).

Andonova, V., & Losada-Otálora, M. (2018). *Multilatinas: Strategies for internationalisation*. Cambridge University Press.

Aoki, M. (2001). *Toward a comparative insitutional analysis*. The MIT Press.

Aoki, M. (2010). *Corporations in evolving dinversity*. Oxford Universtiy Press.

Biglaiser, G. (2002). The internationalization of Chicago's economics in Latin America. *Economic Development and Cultural Change, 50*(2), 269–286.

Bizberg, I. (2014). *Variedades de Capitalismo en América Latina: los Casos de México, Brasil, Argentina y Chile*. El Colegio de México.

Bizberg, I., & Théret, B. (2015). *Variedades del capitalismo en América Latina: los casos de México, Brasil, Argentina y Chile*. El Colegio de México.

Blomström, M., Kokko, A., & Zejan, M. (2000). *Foreign direct investment: Firm and host country strategies*. Macmillan Press.

Blomström, M., & Lipsey, R. E. (1989). The export performance of US and Swedish multinationals. *Review of Income and Wealth, 35*(3), 245–264.

Blomström, M., & Lipsey, R. R. (1991). Firm size and foreign operations of multinationals. *Scandinavian Journal of Economics, 93*(1), 101–107.

Bockmann, J. (2019). Democratic socialism in Chile and Peru: Revisiting the "Chicago Boys" as the origin of neoliberalism. *Comparative Studies in Society and History, 61*(3), 654–679.

Bodemer, K. (2008). *Del "viejo" Cepalismo a la crítica de la globalización Cambio y continuidad en el debate sobre las estrategias de desarrollo en América Latina*. Retrieved from http://www.redalyc.org/home.oa, http://www.redalyc.org/pdf/774/77411616001.pdf

Bond, P. (2008). South Africa's "developmental state" distraction. *Mediations, 24*(1), 8–27.

Boris, D. (2009). *Lateinamerikas Politische Ökonomie: Aufbruch aus historischen Abhängigkeiten im 21. Jahrhundert*. VSA Verlag.

Bresser-Pereira, L. C. (2012). Five models of capitalism. *Brazilian Journal of Political Economy, 32*(1), 21–32.

Buckley, P. J., & Casson, M. C. (1976). *The future of the multinational enterprise*. Macmillan.

Buckley, P. J., & Casson, M. C. (2009). The internalisation theory of the multinational enterprise: A review of the progress of a research agenda after 30 years. *Journal of International Business Studies, 2009*, 1–18.

Buckley, P. J., & Casson, M. (2010). *The multinational enterprise revisited: The essential Buckley and Casson*. Palgrave Macmillan.

Buckley, P. J., & Pearce, R. D. (1979). Overseas production and exporting by the world's leading enterprises. *Journal of International Business Studies, 10*(1), 9–20.

Busemeyer, M. R. (2009). Asset specificity, institutional complementarities and the variety of skill regimes in coordinated market economies. *Socio-Economic Review, 7*, 375–406.

Cardoso, F. H., & Faletto, E. (1979). *Dependency and development in Latin America*. University of California Press.

Carney, M., Gedajlovic, E., & Yang, X. (2009). Varieties of Asian capitalism: Toward an institutional theory of Asian enterprise. *Asia Pacific Journal of Management, 2009*, 361–380.

Casper, S. (2009). Can new technology firms succeed incoordinated market economies? A response to Herrmann and Lange. *Socio-Economic Review, 2009*, 209–215.

Chang, S.-J., Chung, J., & Moon, J. J. (2013, March). When do wholly owned subsidiaries perform better than joint ventures? *Strategic Management Journal, 34*(3), 317–337.

Chao, J., Rinaudo, E. K., & Uhlaner, R. (2014, January). mckinsey.com. Retrieved from Avoiding blind spots in your next joint venture https://www.mckinsey.com/~/media/McKinsey/Business%20Functions/Strategy%20and%20Corporate%20Finance/Our%20Insights/Avoiding%20blind%20spots%20in%20your%20next%20joint%20venture/Avoiding%20blind%20spots%20in%20your%20next%20joint%20venture.ashx

Christophers, B. (2015). The limits to financialization. *Dialogues in Human Geography, 5*(2), 183–200.

Coase, R. (1937). The nature of the firm. *Economica, 4*, 386–405.

Crouch, C., & Streeck, W. (1997). *Political economy of modern capitalism: Mapping convergence and diversity*. Sage.

Crouch, C., Schröder, M., & Voelzkow, H. (2009). Regional and sectoral varieties of capitalism. *Economy and Society, 2009*, 654–678.

Crouch, C., Streeck, W., Boyer, R., Amable, B., Hall, P. A., & Jackson, G. (2005). Dialogue on 'Institutional complementarity and political economy'. *Socio-Economic Review, 3*, 359–382.

Cusack, T. R., Iversen, T., & Rehm, P. (2006). Risks at work: The demand and supply sides of government redistribution. *Oxford Review of Economic Policy, 22*, 365–389.

Cypher, J. M. (2018). From structuralism to neoliberal depredation and beyond: Economic transformations and labor policies in Latin America, 1950–2016. *Latin American Perspectives, 45*(1), 24–46.

Davis, G. F., & Kim, S. (2015). Financialization of the economy. *Annual Review of Sociology, 41*, 203–221.

Deeg, R., & Hardie, I. (2016). What is patient capital and who supplies it? *Socio-Economic Review, 14*(4), 627–645.

Deeg, R., & Jackson, G. (2007). Towards a more dynamic theory of capitalist variety. *Socio-Economic Review, 5*, 149–179.

DGB. (2019, April 5). *DGB.Index Gute Arbeit*. Retrieved from https://index-gute-arbeit.dgb.de/

Dias, D. A., Marques, C. R., & Martins, F. (2012). Labour cost-cutting strategies: Microeconomic evidence from survey data. *Economic Bulleting, 2012*, 37–55.

Powell, W. W., & DiMaggio, P. J. (1991). The iron cage revisited: Institutional isomorphism and collective rationality in organizational fields. *American Sociological Association, 48*(2), 147–160.

Doner, R. F., & Schneider, B. R. (2000). Business associations and economic development: Why some associations contribute more than others. *Business and Politics, 2*(3), 261–288.

Drahokoupil, J., & Myant, M. (2010). Varieties of capitalism, varieties of vulnerabilities: Financial crisis and its impact on welfare states in Eastern Europe and the Commonwealth of Independent States. *Historical Social Research/Historische Sozialforschung, 35*(2), 266–295.

Dunning, J. (1979). Toward an eclectic theory of international production: Some empirical tests. *Journal of International Business Studies, 11*, 9–31.

Dunning, J. H. (1993). Internationalizing Porter's diamond. *Management International Review, 33*, 7–15.

Dunning, J. H. (2009). Location and the multinational enterprise: A neglected factor? *Journal of International Business Studies, 40*(1), 5–19.

Dunning, J. H., Suhk Pak, Y., & Beldona, S. (2007). Foreign ownership strategies of UK and US international franchisors: An exploratory application of Dunning's envelope paradigm. *International Business Review, 16*(5), 531–548.

ECLAC/ILO. (2013, May). *CEPAL.* Retrieved from The employment situation in Latin America and the Caribbean https://repositorio.cepal.org/bitstream/handle/11362/37580/1/ECLAC-ILO-Bulletin8_en.pdf

Erramilli, M. K., Agarwal, S., & Dev, C. S. (2002). Choice between non-equity entry modes: An organizational capability perspective. *Journal of International Business Studies, 33*(2), 223–242.

Evans, P. B. (1979). *Dependent development: The alliance of multinational, state, and local capital in Brazil.* Princeton University Press.

FAO. (2019, February 5). fao.org. Retrieved from http://www.fao.org/3/w5973e/w5973e0b.htm

FARLEX. (2019, May 4). *The Free Dictionary.* Retrieved from https://www.thefreedictionary.com/human+capital

Ferrari, C. A. (2016). *Capitalismo: Crisis, cambios, y evolución en el siglo XXI.* Retrieved from Pontificia Universidad Javeriana https://www.javeriana.edu.co/documents/16113/9477233/N+1+Capitalismo+crisis+cambios+y+evoluci%C3%B3n+en+el+sXXI+%28WEB%29.pdf/939499f0-2d3f-4e87-ac23-6215fbc2fccc

Fligstein, N., & Zhang, J. (2011). A new agenda for research on the trajectory of Chinese capitalism. *Management and Organization Review, 7*, 39–62.

Forsgren, M., & Johanson, J. (2010). A dialogue about the Uppsala model of internationalization. In U. Andersson & U. Holm (Eds.), *Managing the contemporary multinational: The role of headquarters* (pp. 283–304). Edward Elgar Publishing Limited.

Frank, A. G. (2009). *Capitalism and underdevelopment in Latin America: Historical studies of Chile and Brazil.* Monthly Review Press.

Fukuyama, F. (1992). *The end of history and the last man.* Penguin Group.

Furtado, C. (1965). *Development and stagnation in Latin America: A structuralist approach.* Social Science Institute.

Ghoshal, S., & Bartlett, C. A. (1990). The multinational corporation as an interorganizational network. *The Academy of Management Review, 15*, 603–625.

Ghoshal, S., & Westney, D. E. (1993). *Organization theory and the multinational corporation.* St. Martin's Press.

Granovetter, M. (1985, November). Economic action and social structure: The problem of embeddedness. *American Journal of Sociology, 91*(3), 481–510.

Gulati, C., Lin, Y.-X., Mishra, S., & Rayner, J. (2002). *From Adam Smith to Michael Porter: Evolution of competitiveness theory.* Mainland Press.

Hall, P. A. (2010). Historical institutionalism in rationalist and sociological perspective. In J. Mahoney & K. Thelen (Eds.), *Explaining institutional change* (pp. 204–223). Cambridge University Press.

Hall, P. A., & Gingerich, D. W. (2004). Varieties of capitalism and institutional complementarities in the macroeconomy: An empirical analysis. *MPIfG Discussion Paper 04/5.*

Hall, P. A., & Gingerich, D. W. (2009). Varieties of capitalism and institutional complementarities in the political economy. *British Journal of Political Science, 39*(3), 449–482.

Hall, P. A., & Soskice, D. (2001). *Varieties of capitalism: The institutional foundations of comparative advantage.* Oxford University Press.

Hall, P. A., & Thelen, K. (2009). Institutional change in varieties of capitalism. *Socio-Economic Review, 7*, 7–34.

Herrigel, G. (1996). Crisis in German decentralized production. *European Urban and Regional Studies, 3*, 33–52.

Hollingsworth, J. R., Schmitter, P. C., & Streeck, W. (1994). *Governing capitalist economies: Performance and control of economic sectors*. Oxford University Press.

Hollingsworth, J. R., & Boyer, R. (1997). *Contemporary capitalism: The embeddedness of institutions*. Cambridge University Press.

Höpner, M. (2009). "Spielarten des Kapitalismus" als Schule der vergleichenden Staatstätigkeitsforschung. *Zeitschrift für Vergleichende Politikwissenschaft, 3*(2), 303–327.

Hymer, S. H. (1976). *The international operations of national firms: A study of direct foreign investment. Unpublished 1960 PhD thesis*. MIT Press.

IDB. (2003). Good Jobs Wanted: Labor Markets in Latin America. Washington D.C.: The Johns Hopkins University Press.

ILO. (2017a). *Unemployment protection: A good practices guideand training package*. International Labour Organization.

ILO. (2017b). *Labour relations and collective bargaining*. Retrieved from https://www.ilo.org/wcmsp5/groups/public/%2D%2D-ed_protect/%2D%2D-protrav/%2D%2D-travail/documents/publication/wcms_409422.pdf

Iversen, T., & Soskice, D. (2001). An asset theory of social policy preferences. *American Political Science Review, 95*, 875–893.

Jackson, G. (2010). Actors and institutions. In G. Morgan, J. L. Campbell, C. Crouch, O. K. Pedersen, & R. Whitley (Eds.), *The Oxford handbook of comparative institutional analysis* (pp. 63–87). Oxford University Press.

Jackson, G., & Deeg, R. (2006). *How many varieties of capitalism? Comparing the comparative institutional analyses of capitalsit diversity*. MPIfG Discussion Paper.

Jackson, G., & Deeg, R. (2008). Comparing capitalisms: Understanding institutional diversity and its implications for international business. *Journal of International Business Studies, 39*, 540–561.

Johanson, J., & Vahlne, J.-E. (1977). The internationalization process of the firm: A model of knowledge development and increasing foreign market commitments. *Journal of International Business Studies, 8*(1), 23–32.

Johanson, J., & Vahlne, J.-E. (2009). The Uppsala internationalization process model revisited: From liability of foreignness to liability of outsidership. *Journal of International Business Studies, 40*(9), 1411–1431.

Kay, C. (2005). Celso Furtado: Pioneer of structuralist development theory. *Development and Change, 36*(6), 1201–1207.

Kogut, B. (2001). Multinational corporations. In I. N. J. Smelser & P. B. Baltes (Eds.), *International Encyclopedia of social & behavioral sciences* (pp. 10197–10204). Pergamon Press.

Leon, P. (2010). *Address to 'miners from the frontiers' conference Macquarie Connections–Macquarie Capital (Europe) Ltd, London.* Retrieved from https://www.moneyweb.co.za/mw/action/media/downloadFile

Lindenberg, S. (1992). The method of decreasing abstraction. In T. Fararo (Ed.), *Rational choice theory: Advocacy and critique* (pp. 3–20). Sage.

Lopez, A. J. (2007). *Introduction: The (post) global south*. Indiana University Press.

Luo, Y. (2007). Are joint venture partners more opportunistic in a more volatile environment? *Strategic Management Journal, 28*, 39–60.

Martinelli, A. (1998). Contemporary capitalism: The embeddedness of institutions. *American Journal of Sociology, 104*(1), 233–235.

Mayntz, R., & Scharpf, F. W. (1995). Der Ansatz des akteurzentrierten Institutionalismus. In R. Mayntz & F. W. Scharpf (Eds.), *Gesellschaftliche Selbstregelung und politische Steuerung* (pp. 39–73). Campus Verlag.

Moe, T. M. (1995). The politics of structural choice: Toward a theory of public bureaucracy. In O. E. Williamson (Ed.), *Organization theory: From Chester Barnard to the present and beyond* (pp. 116–153). Oxford University Press.

Muravyev, A. (2014). *Employment protection legislation in transition and emerging markets.* IZA World of Labor.

Nitsch, D. (1999). *The determinants of foreign entry mode.* National Library of Canada. https://www.nlc-bnc.ca/obj/s4/f2/dsk1/tape7/PQDD_0013/NQ40282.pdf?is_thesis=1&oclc_number=1006907534

Nölke, A. (2013, August 15). linksnet.de. Retrieved from https://www.linksnet.de/sites/default/files/pdf/130-131_14_noelke_0.pdf

Nölke, A. (2018). Dependent versus state-permeated capitalism: Two basic options for emerging markets. *International Journal of Management and Economics, 54*(4), 269–282.

Nölke, A., & Perry, J. (2007). The power of transnational private governance: Financialization and the IASB. *Business and Politics, 9*(3), 1–25.

Nölke, A., & Vliegenhart, A. (2009, October). Enlarging the varieties of capitalism: The emergence of dependent market economies in East Central Europe. *World Politics, 61*(4), 670–702.

North, D. C. (1992). Institutions and economic theory. *The American Economist, 36*(1), 3–6.

Ocampo, J. A. (2004). La América Latina y La Economía Mundial en El Largo Siglo XX. *El Trimestre Económico, LXXI*(284), 725–786.

OECD. (2018, September 18–19). *OECD.* Retrieved from Latin American and Caribbean Competition Forum-Session I: Informal Economy in Latin America and the Caribbean: Implications for Competition Policy: https://one.oecd.org/document/DAF/COMP/LACF(2018)4/en/pdf

OECD. (2019). *FDI Regulatory Restrictiveness Index.* Retrieved from https://www.oecd.org/investment/fdiindex.htm

Osland, G. E., Taylor, C. R., & Zou, S. (2001). Selecting international modes of entry and expansion. *Marketing Intelligence & Planning, 19*(3), 153–161.

Ostrom, E. (1990). *Governing the commons: The evolution of institutions for collective action.* Cambridge University Press.

Ostrom, E. (2005). *Understanding institutional diversity.* Princeton University Press.

Ostrom, E. (2010a). Analyzing collective action. *International Association of Agricultural Economist, 41*, 155–166.

Ostrom, E. (2010b). Institutional analysis and development: Elements of the framework in historical perspective. In C. Crothers (Ed.), *Historical developments and theoretical approaches in sociology* (Vol. II, pp. 261–288). Eolss Publishers.

Ostrom, E. (2011). Background on the institutional analysis and development framework. *The Policy Studies Journal, 39*, 7–27.

Otero-Iglesias, M., & Vermeiren, M. (2015). China's state-permeated market economy and its constraints to the internationalization of the renminbi. *International Politics, 52*(6), 684–703.

Padayachee, V. (2013). Introducing varieties of capitalism into the South African debate: Uses and limits. *Transformation: Critical Perspectives on Southern Africa, Number, 81*(82), 5–32.

Pagel, H., Ranke, K., Hempel, F., & Köhler, J. (2014). *The use of the concept "global south" in social science & humanities.* Globaler Süden/Global South: Kritische Perspektiven. Institut für Asien- & Afrikawissenschaften, Humboldt-Universität zu Berlin.

Palley, T. I. (2013). *Financialization: The economics of finance capital domination.* Palgrave Macmillan.

Paunescu, M., & Schneider, M. (2004). Wettbewerbsfähigkeit und Dynamik institutioneller Standortbedingungen: Ein empirischer Test des "Varieties-of-Capitalism"-Ansatzes. *Schmollers Jahrbuch, 124*, 31–59.

Paunescu, M., & Schneider, M. R. (2012). Changing varieties of capitalism and revealed comparative advantages from 1990 to 2005: A test of the Hall and Soskice claims. *Socio-Economic Review, 1*, 731–753.

Peck, J., & Zhang, J. (2013). A variety of capitalism ... with Chinese characteristics? *Journal of Economic Geography, 13*, 357–396.

Pope, R. A. (2002). Why small firms export: Another look. *Journal of Small Business Management, 40*(1), 17–26.
Porter, M. E. (1990). *The competitive advantage of nations*. Free Press.
Presidência da República. (2016). *DECRETO N° 8.637, DE 15 DE JANEIRO DE 2016*. Retrieved from http://www.planalto.gov.br/ccivil_03/_ato2015-2018/2016/decreto/D8637.htm
Pries, L. (2000). Globalisierung und Wandelinternationaler Unternehmen. *Kölner Zeitschrift für Soziologie und Sozialpsychologie, 52*, 670–695.
Redding, G. (2005). The thick description and comparison of societal systems of capitalism. *Journal of International Business Studies, 36*, 123–155.
Root, F. R. (1994). *Entry strategies for international markets*. Lexington Books.
Roy, A., Shah, M., & Sharma, R. (2017, April). Need for foreign investment. *Journal of Accounting, Finance & Marketing Technology, 1*(1), 18–21.
Rugman, A., & Verbeke, A. (2008). Internalization theory and its impact on the field of international business. In J. Boddewyn (Ed.), *International business scholarship: AIB fellows on the first 50 years and beyond. Research in global strategic management* (Vol. 14, pp. 155–174). Emerald.
Sayer, A. (2000). Contemporary capitalism: The embeddedness of institutions by J. Rogers Hollingsworth and Robert Boyer. *Work, Employment & Society, 14*(3), 600–602.
Scharpf, F. W. (1997). *Games real actors play: Actor-centered institutionalism in policy research*. Westview Press.
Schneider, B. R. (2004). *Business politics and the state in 20th-century Latin America*. Cambridge University Press.
Schneider, B. R. (2009, August). Hierarchical market economies and varieties of capitalism in Latin America. *Journal of Latin American Studies, 41*(3), 553–575.
Schneider, B. R. (2013). *Hierarchical capitalism in Latin America: Business, labor, and the challenges of equitable development*. Cambridge University Press.
Schneider, B. R., & Karcher, S. (2010). Complementarities and continuities in the political economy of labour markets in Latin America. *Socio-Economic Review, 8*(4), 623–651.
Schneider, M. R., Schulze-Bentrop, C., & Paunescu, M. (2010). Mapping the institutional capital of high-techfirms: A fuzzy-set analysis of capitalist variety and export performance. *Journal of International Business Studies, 41*, 246–266.
Schneider, B. R., & Soskice, D. (2009). Inequality in developed countries and Latin America: Coordinated, liberal and hierarchical systems. *Economy and Society, 38*(1), 17–52.
Schröder, M. (2014). *Varianten des Kapitalismus: Die Unterschiede liberaler und koordinierter Marktwirtschaften*. Springer VS.
Sehnbruch, K. (2006). *The Chilean Labor Market: A key to understanding Latin American labor markets*. Palgrave Macmillan.
Sheahan, J. (2002). Alternative models of capitalism in Latin America. In E. Huber (Ed.), *Models of capitalism: Lessons for Latin America* (pp. 25–52). The Pennsylvania State University Press.
Sherman, A. J. (2011). *Franchising & licensing: Two powerful ways to grow your business in any economy*. AMA.
Smith, A. (1776). *An inquiry into the nature and causes of the wealth of nations*. Oxford University Press.
socioeco. (2019, May 15). *Sitio de recursos de la economía social y solidaria*. Retrieved from Programa de Economia del Trabajo (PET) http://www.socioeco.org/bdf_organisme-302_es.html#type_PUB_plusieurs
Storz, C., Amable, B., Casper, S., & Lechevalier, S. (2013). Bringing Asia into the comparative capitalism perspective. *Socio-Economic Review, 11*, 217–232.
Streeck, W. (2009). *Reforming capitalism: Institutional change in the German political economy*. Oxford University Press.
The Law Dictionary. (2019, February 5). *The Law dictionary: Featuring Black's law dictionary free online legal dictionary* (2nd ed). Retrieved from https://thelawdictionary.org/multinational-corporation-mnc/

The World Bank. (2004). *World Developmen Report 2005: A better investment climate for everyone*. Oxford University Press.

Thelen, K. (2001). Varieties of labor politics in the developed democracies. In P. A. Hall & D. Soskice (Eds.), *Varieties of capitalism: The institutional foundations of comparative advantage* (pp. 71–103). Oxford University Press.

Thelen, K., & Busemeyer, M. R. (2008). *From collectivism towards segmentalism: Institutional change in German vocational training*. MPIfG Discussion Paper.

UN Secretary-General Ban Ki-moon. (2014, February 20). *United Nations Secretary-General*. Retrieved from Secretary-General's message for the World Day of Social Justice https://www.un.org/sg/en/content/sg/statement/2014-02-20/secretary-generals-message-world-day-social-justice-scroll-down

UNCTAD. (2017). *United Nations conference on trade and development: Properity for all*. Retrieved May 25, 2017, from http://unctad.org/en/Pages/DIAE/Foreign-Direct-Investment-(FDI).aspx

UNCTAD STAT. (2019). *United Nations Conference on Trade and Development*. Retrieved from https://unctadstat.unctad.org/wds/TableViewer/tableView.aspx

Wach, K. (2014). Market entry modes for international businesses. In E. Horská (Ed.), *International marketing: Within and beyond Visegrad Borders, Edition 1, Chapter 7* (pp. 135–147). Wydawnictwo Episeteme.

Walker, K., Schlosser, F., & Deephouse, D. L. (2014, March 5). Organizational ingenuity and the paradox of embedded agency: The Case of the Embryonic Ontario Solar Energy Industry. *Organization Studies, 2014*, 613–634.

Welch, L. S., & Luostarinen, R. (1988). Internationalization: Evolution of a concept. *Journal of General Management, 14*(2), 34–55.

Whitley, R. (1998). Internationalization and varieties of capitalism: The limited effects of cross-national coordination of economic activities on the nature of business systems. *Review of Inernational Political Economy, 5*, 445–481.

Williamson, O. E. (1973). Markets and hierarchies: Some elementary considerations. *The American Economic Review, 63*, 316–325.

Williamson, O. E. (1995). Transaction costs economics and organization theory. In I. O. E. Williamson (Ed.), *Organization theory: From Chester Barnard to the present and beyond* (pp. 207–256). Oxford University Press.

Williamson, O. E. (2000). The new institutional economics: Taking stock, looking ahead. *Journal of Economic Literature, 3*, 595–613.

Witt, M. A., & Redding, G. (2013a). Asian business systems: Institutional comparison, clusters and implications for varieties of capitalism and business systems theory. *Socio-Economic Review, 11*(2), 265–300.

Witt, M., & Redding, G. (2013b). Asian business systems: Institutional comparison, clusters and implications for varieties of capitalism and business systems theory. *Socio-Economic Review, 11*(2), 217–232.

Yan, A., & Luo, Y. (2015). *International joint ventures: Theory and practice*. CRC Press.

Zhang, X., & Whitley, R. (2013). Changing macro-structural varieties of East Asian capitalism. *Socio-Economic Review, 11*(2), 301–336.

Chapter 4
Transcending Borders and Institutional Dynamics

Up to now, this work elaborated on who plays the game and what game is being played. However, as indicated at the discussion on the building blocks in Sect. 2.2, MNCs as actors who transcend borders require particular attention. This chapter builds upon the previous theoretical development and attempts to equip institutional analysis with a more sensitive understanding of structure and agency. It aims at incorporating systemic institutional differences and the non-identical *Gestalt* of MNCs and attempts to breathe life into their potentially mutually constitutive relationship. On that account, of special interest in this chapter are:

- The relation between MNCs and institutions.
- Specifics of behavior of foreign subsidiaries.
- The potential impact that divergent behavior may have on the game.

This chapter, first, reconsiders traditional institutional analyses that mostly assumes actors and clearly assignable institutions. Valuable insights are extracted and major requirements for analytical adjustments are set out. Whereas the former elaborations focused on the isolated games being played in form of different varieties of capitalism, this chapter develops theory in order to grasp dynamics that occur when various games (forms of capitalism) conflate with one another. On that account, this chapter broadly follows a two-step structure. First, analysis is brought up to the meso-level,[1] scrutinizing the overlap of different games and the impact on behavior of affected actors. Second, specifics of behavioral patterns are brought back to the local national level on which behavior affects the institutional setting. At the end of this chapter, all required building blocks are developed and the analytical framework Conflating Capitalisms is constructed.

[1] Here, the macro-level describes the entire universe of existing institutions. The meso-level grasps the different institutional settings that are demarcated, for example, by national borders, and the micro-level describes the institutional setting of one isolated field.

M. Kappler, *Western Multinational Corporations in Latin America*, Contributions to Economics, https://doi.org/10.1007/978-3-030-93805-5_4

4.1 Reconsidering Institutional Analysis

Institutional analysis here is analyzed in three ways, regarding the degree of fit with the requirements of this work. First, definitions of institutions and the inherent spectrum and direction of causation vary heavily. In order to cope with the requirements, set out above, a concept of institutions is required that copes with the interaction as a unit of analysis and the potential mutual relation between institutions and actors. Second, the assumed conception of man behind various approaches is analyzed. This conception should be able to capture certain varieties of change. Third, the question of institutional embeddedness may be the most crucial in the context of MNCs. As the section on rather technical peculiarities of MNCs has indicated, specific control and ownership constellations make embeddedness vague and needs further elaboration.

Adjusted Definition of Institutions

The bandwidth of institutions varies according to their definitions and set limitations. In the course of the previous chapters, various ideas and definitions of what institutions actually are have been introduced. Different approaches seem to be reasonable, since, in line with Cole (2013, p. 397), the definitions of institutions and their mechanisms vary and follow the specific analysis a scholar carries out. Since this work conducts an MNC-specific analysis, it requires a definition of institutions that cope with the requirements set out above.

North's (1991) "rules of the game," including formal and informal institutions, have gained a predominant role in institutional economics and seem to be a valid base for further elaboration. Equally, Hall and Soskice (2001) follow the Northian divide, though, the border between organizations and institutions becomes partly blurred and certain behavioral patterns are equipped with an institution-like quality. Following Schneider (2013), however, the Northian clear-cut divide between organizations and institutions hampers the inclusion of behavior into the institutional analysis, which is especially important in rather weak institutional surroundings. As Sect. 2.2 indicated, there are certain models that overcome the limitations set by North. For example, as discussed above, ACI by Mayntz and Scharpf (1997) allows the entry of actor behavior into institutional analysis by narrowing down the concept of institutions to mostly regulatory issues. However, this limitation inevitably leads to a clearly set focus on policy issues that perfectly copes with ACI inherent interest but may deprive this investigation of capturing more subtle dynamics caused by (divergent) behavior. Ostrom's (2005) IDA seems to be without formal restriction by definition, since institutions are generally seen as prescriptions that humans use to organize interactions. In order to be able to capture the role of MNCs, however, the concept of institutions should also include the potentially impactful role played by, for example, corporations. Hall (2010) extends the idea of institutions while also moving within an equally unlimited concept of institutions as Ostrom does. Emphasizing the constitutive role of action, Hall (2010, p. 204) introduces institutions as "...regularized practices with a rule-like quality...". Similar to Hall, Huntington highlights the importance of specifically conducted action by introducing institutions as "...stable, valued, recurring patterns of behavior" (Huntington, 1968, p. 12).

Hence, in order to, first, avoid limitations relating to both the bandwidth of institutions and the divide between organizations and institutions that may conceal the potentially mutual constitutive nature of institutions and action, the following definition of institutions may best fit with the requirements introduced above.

Institutions have a rule-like quality, facilitate joint understanding of actors and increase predictability of actors' future behavior. Institutions include both formal and informal ones and may come about as a product of regulatory processes and regularized behavioral patterns.

Traditional Analysis, Postulates of Local Embeddedness, and the Question of Conformity

A game being played by actors that are not (entirely) subject to the institutions that structure the specific game and, thus, actors that do not adhere to the rules may best be described as chaos and lands ideas of traditional institutional analysis in difficulty. As the elaboration on CC indicated, across countries there are various different games being played and, consequently, players within the specific institutional areas are supposed to play differently. In conjunction with the discussion on MNCs' specific border crossing structure and the inherent peculiarities of control and ownership above, MNCs may best be recognized as playing various games at a time: the one at home and the one abroad. Hence, the assignment of one player (MNC) to one game (institutional environment) seems to be questionable.

The following section analyzes traditional institutional analysis relating to its capabilities to reasonably include players who play various games at a time. Traditional analysis mostly sees actors under the umbrella of clearly assignable institutions and succumbs to the "temptation" of determinism within one set of institutions, or as put by Powell and Colyvas (2008, p. 277), traditional analysis tends to assume "...over-socialized individuals who seemed slavishly devoted to habit and fashion." Hence, they most likely have problems capturing institutional tensions and potentially deviant behavior. To keep things manageable, the following section recaps and briefly discusses institutional economics, historical institutionalism, and a broader sociological view on institutions. Despite having different assumptions on, for example, the adhesive that links actors and institutions and institutional development, they come up with some crucial intercepts. The schools of thought—in their traditional analysis—cannot capture dodgy embeddedness and, thus, mostly neglect the divergent behavior of systemic actors.

Institutional economics' rationality postulate and the ultimate objective of minimizing transaction costs make actors conform, since each divergent behavior deviates from the counterpart's expectations and, thus, raises costs for monitoring and sanctioning (Dequech, 2006). Behavior that increases transaction costs is not within the scope of NIE. According to North (1992), a player is confronted by the institutional surrounding and given pay-off matrices that induce them to recontract with existing institutions rather than investing resources in order to change institutions.

Historical institutionalists rely on the path-dependent cumulative causation perspective, and see institutions as historically grown and, thus, as very stable in the short and medium term. According to Tilly (1989), historical institutionalism does not investigate the operative[2] micro-level of a society as source of change. According to Tilly, historical institutionalism is the right instrument for understanding "big structures, large processes, and huge comparisons" (1989). In line with the inherent postulate of path dependency and the belief in "history matters" (Immergut 2006, p. 242)—that are equally followed by Hall and Soskice (2001)—historical institutionalists mostly dispense with divergent behavior of endogenous actors within a certain institutional setting.

The same shortcomings account for most of the neo-institutionalist perspectives, in which it is—most basically—explained how institutional pressures make organizations respond in similar ways through the process of isomorphism (DiMaggio & Powell, 1983, p. 147; Meyer & Rowan, 1977). Striving for legitimacy and survival, organizations (here, firms) are supposed to conform to institutional pressures and make it very unlikely for divergent behavior to arise. Along the same lines, DiMaggio and Powell (1983, p. 148) expect an "inexorable push towards homogenization" within an established field. Going one step further, important for MNCs, DiMaggio and Powell (1983, p. 148) further expect a "...homogenization of (...) new entrants..." that enter an established field. Considering MNCs' subsidiaries as new elements of the HME, that may be assumed to be a well-established field, conformity to the local environment may be expected. However, as this chapter will show, it is the broader understanding of sociological institutionalism that offers concepts that help this work.

Having a closer look at VoC, in general, emphasizes "...rational strategic behavior within a set of fixed institutions (Jackson & Deeg, 2008, p. 688). Implicating both, the nature of clearly assignable institutions and rational behavior that follows the given structure, exhibits the same shortcomings as the approaches above. VoC further strengthens the notion of determinism and institutional stability, since it combines the (boundedly) rational actor with historical institutionalism's path dependence and extends it with institutional complementarities and CIA that make it even less likely for behavior to deviate from the predominant one, respectively, to change historically developed systems. The incorporation into VoC of institutions as Streeckian "beneficial constraints," as opposed to Northian "humanly devised constraints" (North, 1991, p. 97), make an action that counters the institutional *status quo* even less likely since deviators would undermine the pillars on which their own capabilities are grounded. As examined in Chap. 3, in VoC, firms use the opportunities that existing institutions provide and, thus, actors' strategies are expected to conform, by gravitating toward a certain manner that uses and reinforces existing

[2]Operative here is meant to indicate analyses that focus on the short term.

institutions. Accordingly, companies face coordinating institutions that are not (entirely) under their control (Hall & Soskice, 2001, p. 15).

In line with VoC's theoretical foundation, Hall and Soskice (2001, p. 57) do not say much about the internationalization of companies. Following VoC's line of argumentation, according to Hall and Soskice (2001), a foreign subsidiary of an MNC is expected to entirely adjust to the institutional environment of the host country. Companies are supposed to go international and build subsidiaries in other countries because of institutional arbitrage (Hall & Soskice, 2001). Companies are supposed to only shift certain activities along their value chain into other countries to use the advantageous institutional environment that allows conducting certain activities to be better (at lower transaction costs) than at home. As empirical examples, they showcase General Motors moving its engine plant to Germany and various German pharmaceutical companies opening up research labs in the United States. In both cases, the MNCs use the institutionally advantageous environment of the other country to conduct specific operations. Logically, in order to benefit from foreign institutions, relying on home country institutions seems to be an unfertile endeavor and, thus, adjustment on the host country's institutions can be expected.

Schneider (2013), attempting to soften the aforementioned approaches' straightforward direction of causation, indeed, perceives MNCs in Latin America as different from local companies, but dispenses with subsidiaries' behavioral idiosyncrasies owing to systemic differences. Work on HME continuously describes MNCs as "... more than simple institution takers..." (Schneider, 2013, p. 40) and emphasizes that MNCs are not be seen as "institution takers that come to countries and blend into the corporate landscape" (2013, p. 73). However, as already indicated, Schneider's perception of subsidiaries as a homogeneous group, just like the approaches above, hampers grasping dynamics of institutional contradiction. Investigations in the context remain under the umbrella of local institutions. Further depriving MNCs of the potential to induce change, due to "political mousiness" (2013), Schneider does not allow MNCs to take on a position as a Northian "powerful player" (North, 1991) that may be capable of impacting its institutional surrounding.

Traditional institutional analysis generally follows a relatively straightforward causation in which action is—at least in the short and medium term—determined by surrounding institutions offered by the country in which the firm is located. The proposed conformity to local institutions logically banishes potential behavioral contradictions from most of the literature. Neglecting agency and deviant interaction have far-reaching consequences for investigations on institutional change. As Burns and Nielsen (2006, p. 451) put it: "institutional change is initiated by the existence of contradictions." However, dispensing with divergent behavior makes actor-induced institutional change not feasible. Thus, institutional change originating endogenously is largely out of scope and change is caused, if at all, by exogeneous forces. The change caused by endogenous actors would require divergent behavior that is considered—if at all—as a paradox of embedded agency (DellaPosta et al., 2017; Walker et al., 2014).

The present chapter has so far introduced certain aspects of MNCs and institutional analysis that cast traditional institutional analysis into doubt when applying it to this work. First of all, in conjunction with the in Sect. 3.1 introduced peculiarities of MNCs with full control over subsidiaries as the mechanism that transfers and replicates organizational practices from one country to another one (Kogut, 2001). Among all possible forms of internalization, the WOS depicts the only form in which a company has effective control of operations in a foreign country (Buckley & Casson, 2010; Buckley & Pearce, 1979; UNCTAD, 2017). Furthermore, overcoming Hymer's notion of foreign liability (combined with Kogut's theory of competitive advantage), MNCs can reasonably be assumed to replicate abroad what has worked well at home. If this assumption is right, combined with the knowledge of systemic differences in the distinct varieties of capitalism, contradiction and, consequently, locally divergent behavior seem to be entirely feasible when actors from one institutional setting move to another one. The assumption of a HQ's influence on subsidiaries is supported by HME's CG dimension discussed above. Apart from general tendencies to replicate practices in host countries, the system of HME implies the subsidiary's obligation to report to the HQ rather than to, for example, local banks or shareholders.

Review on Potential HQ Influence

This theoretically derived doubt on traditional analyses' capacity to capture MNCs' complexity is further backed by several empirical studies investigating the relationship between HQ and subsidiary. Javorcik and Spatareanu (2011) investigate MNCs' COOs in terms of distance from the host country. While the former relates to the physical distance, the latter scrutinizes cultural or institutional distance. Both investigations lead to quite similar results in so-far-as distance is negatively correlated with the degree of resemblance between HQ and subsidiaries. Even though distance is not part of prime interest here, it nonetheless indicates that the CoO may play a role. However, in the context of this work, in which distance seems to be quite high, both studies may limit the expectations of the relatedness of company behavior at home and abroad. Along the same lines, Xu and Shenkar (2002) approaching distance through institutions, suggest that the intensity of HQ practice transfer to its subsidiaries also depends on the "institutional distance" between home and host country; the less distant the institutional setting, the more likely practice transfer from HQ to international subsidiary.

Approaching MNCs as a matter of FDI, Fortanier (2007) shows that the CoO plays a vital role in estimating causalities between FDI and varying impacts on, for example, development or GDP growth. Fortanier (2007) investigates the differing impacts of FDI on GDP growth, depending on the home country of the parent company. According to Fortanier's research, one unit of, for example, German FDI has a reasonably different impact on GDP growth than a unit from the USA. As such, despite sticking to monetary indicators, Fortanier indicates that the same amount of currency may differ regarding CoO. Certainly, that observed difference does not indicate a specific form of behavior, but it clearly points to differences that can be traced back to the specific CoO. Translated into the language of this chapter, one may assume that a company from the USA acts differently than one from Germany. Adding Fortanier's research into analysis, the institutional background of the CoO and, thus, the HQ's behavior may be important for action conducted abroad.

Along the same lines, de Jong and Van Vo (2010) investigate headquarter—subsidiary relations in the context of granted autonomy. De Jong and Van Vo rely on the CoO only in as much as it seems to be decisive for the applied corporate structure abroad and internationalization strategy. It is argued that MNCs originating in liberal Anglo-Saxon countries impose rather centralized, global strategies on their subsidiaries and MNCs from coordinated countries prefer a rather local, decentralized organizational structure. As a consequence, MNCs from, for example, Germany generally grant their subsidiaries more autonomy with regard to resources and responsibilities, aiming at cooperation through networks similar to the proceeding in the CoO. On the other hand, for example, US companies using a standardized global strategy impose a high level of control and clear standards and requirements on their subsidiaries. Following this logic, the CoO of origin is decisive for international subsidiaries. International subsidiaries are supposed to follow—to a higher (LME) or lesser (CME) degree—guidelines of the parent company which are at least partly determined by the home country institutions. To put it in the language of this paper, subsidiaries are supposed to follow the HQ to a certain degree; however, a subsidiary with a HQ in a liberal economy is supposed to clearly reflect its origins.

The literature up to now mostly scrutinizes the CoO as a dummy variable and, thus, as proxies for physical and psychic distance, organizational structure, and corporate strategy. This chapter's logic—to directly scrutinize the behavior and actions of HQs and subsidiaries—has not yet reached mainstream literature. To date, there is—to the best of the author's knowledge—one exception with Kuznetsov and Jacobs (2015) that applies the VoC perspective on behavior of MNCs from the UK and Germany with subsidiaries in Germany and the UK. Their investigation tests the "power" of either the home or the host country. They recognize certain patterns of institutional adjustment. MNCs from both countries seem to prefer liberal approaches abroad. That points to (1) a significantly differing behavior of German subsidiaries in comparison to their HQs and (2) a tendency of UK companies to follow home country institutions. These observations, combined with de Jong and Van Vo (2010), may also be traced back to certain differences in the general internationalization strategy and the subsequent corporate structure. However, this research design is limited in explanatory power. In very general terms, it is stated that a shift toward market-based interaction is easier than building up networks and reputational systems based on strategic joint cooperation. Hence, as it is the inherent higher complexity of "coordinated" institutions, shifting to liberalism means abandoning complexity and shifting to "simplicity." Consequently, one can reasonably argue that it is easier to give up coordination and shift to market-based interactions than vice versa.

More fine-grained and of equal importance for this work, Kuznetsov and Jacobs (2015, p. 16) detect patterns relating to VoC's institutional domains. They assert that within the domain of industrial and employee relations, companies in foreign settings are most likely to blend both home and host country institutions. Such strategies may be best described as hybrid forms. HR management is supposed to be deeply embedded in national legal and cultural contexts. On that account, HR strategies are most likely to be adaptive to foreign institutions. Strategies relating to technology, finance, and marketing will most likely follow a trajectory determined by home country institutions.

In comparison to the research of Kuznetsov & Jacobs, this work investigates both behavioral patterns and the potential impact of differing behavior. Furthermore, moving beyond well-functioning systems in OECD countries such as Germany and the UK, this work focuses on subsidiaries in Latin American countries. As this chapter will show, the here applied analysis of behavior is more detailed and, therefore, allows conclusions relating to the entire institutional environment. Furthermore, behavior will be put under scrutiny as a source for change. As described above, Latin America is generally held to be a rather weak institutional environment. One could assume that—as Marinova (2015) put it—the power of the host's institutional system may be weaker than in the UK or in Germany and, consequently, the impact of the CoO institutions should be higher. In the context of German companies in Latin America, this view of a stronger influence of host country institutions is supported theoretically by Martinsons' theory of institutional deficiencies. In very general terms, Martinsons argues that companies from coordinated countries that build up subsidiaries in an environment characterized by either deficient or poorly enforced "rules" keep strongly to their relationship-based behavior to fill "...in institutional structural holes" (Marinova, 2015, p. 4).

This brief literature review indicates—sufficient for now—a general agreement that MNCs' home country institutions may matter to a certain degree. Since this is the first time that such an investigation is being conducted in the context of subsidiaries in Latin America, estimating the impact of CoO institutions on the actions of, for example, Western subsidiaries is a rather difficult task. In summary and sufficing for now: on the one hand, the general issues of distance, both physical and psychic, between the home and host countries under scrutiny, as discussed by Kuznetsov and Jacobs (2015), demonstrated a tendency of subsidiaries to embrace a rather market-based behavior. Furthermore, the presumed corporate strategy—at least by CME companies—of relying on local responsiveness may lower expectations of a high impact of home country institutions on the behavior of MNCs' subsidiaries. In line with the majority of literature on strategy and institutions, CME companies are known for a more local and LME ones for a more global focus. Translated into the language of this study, CME companies are generally expected to exercise less control over their subsidiaries than LME ones. Thus, one should expect subsidiary behavior of LME companies to be much more as a mirror of home country behavior. On the other hand, the rather weak institutional environment in Latin America combined with Martinsons' theory of institutional deficiencies; the distinct pattern of motivation to move to Latin America; and the specific business activities conducted strengthen the argument of CoO impact.

Reflection

The previous sections briefly discussed traditional institutional analysis as mostly succumbing to the "temptation" of determinism. In line with this rather deterministic approach, Wooten and Hoffman (2016) generally interpret "institutional theory" as looking to the "...source of action as existing exogenous to the actor" (2016, p. 130). Consistently with the rationale of conformity, DellaPosta et al. (2017) ask "...how initially illegitimate organizational and institutional innovations arise..." (2017, p. 6).

This determinism undermines agency and deviant behavior and, thus, cumulates in institutional rigidity and—if at all—a very shallow notion of endogenously induced institutional change. Traditional analysis' determinism, lack of agency, and neglection of change are generally contested and part of an ongoing and heated debate on institution. However, one may argue that approaching institutions and action in such a determinist fashion may make sense within a model-like, isolated and very firm institutional environment in which actors are entirely embedded. This rather theoretical assumption, though, certainly does not cope with MNCs that are physically present in more than one institutional setting, among which may also be weak ones.

The theoretically derived doubts above on traditional analysis capacity that mostly build upon the theory of MNCs and CC are further supported by various empirical studies on HQ—subsidiary relations that show HQ, that is to say CoO, impact on foreign subsidiaries. In the context of MNCs, following traditional institutional analysis and the assumption of embeddedness within and conformity to the local context may limit the understanding in various ways.

- It limits the understanding of the subsidiary as institutional tension field pressurized by both host and home institutional environments.
- Consequently, neglecting deviant behavior limits the understanding of the host country as an institutional tension field pressurized by alien-to-the-system behavior.
- It deprives analyses from incorporating dynamics (of change) that may be caused by subsidiaries in strange environments.

To capture institutional tension and triggered dynamics, institutional analysis in this work needs further elaboration at two ends. First, the subsidiary needs to be understood as being pressurized by various institutions. Considering a limited local embeddedness allows the inclusion of divergent behavior into the analysis that may solve the paradox of embedded agency within the context of MNCs. Second, being able to grasp divergent behavior from that induced by local institutions changes the understanding of rigidity built upon the conform actor. Considering the host country's environment as being subject to alien-to-the-system behavior leads to a continuous state of contradiction and, thus, it may find itself in a state of contestation and potential change. Hence, if acknowledging divergent behavior, institutional change endogenously induced by MNCs' subsidiaries needs to be taken into account and requires further theoretical development.

4.2 Broadening the Conception of Man

In the following sections, concepts of institutional plurality and actor-induced change will be introduced. Both concepts improve the capability of capturing tensions within both the subsidiary and the host country. They generally rely on a broader sociological institutionalist grounding, which makes it necessary to leave behind the temptation of determinism and—at least partly—VoC's idea of rational institutional arbitrage discussed above. On that account, sociological institutionalism's underlying conception of man is introduced within the frame necessary for this investigation.

Within the wide field of sociological institutionalism, actors' behavior does not necessarily reflect the optimal response to increase means—ends efficiency. The assumed relation between actors and institutions is more complex and less rigid than the assumption of a prescribed way to the optimal (most efficient) outcome would indicate. Hall and Taylor (1996, p. 949) emphasize that the addressed relation "... is built on a kind of 'practical reasoning' whereby the individual works with and reworks the available institutional templates to devise a course of action." Following this line of reasoning, rather than a response to rationality, behavior is based on the valuation (shared belief) of what is considered natural, expected, rightful, and legitimate within the broader social environment. Consequently, actors most likely conduct certain practices, and others not, in order to obtain legitimacy within their social environment (DiMaggio & Powell, 1983; Hall & Taylor, 1996; Meyer & Rowan, 1977; Popal, 2019). Whereas legitimacy is gained through appropriate and desirable action, it is lost by action that counters the shared belief mentioned above. Most generally, when "weighing" between alternative actions, Goodin, March and Olsen (2004, p. 478) perceive specific behavior as following the "...rules of appropriate or exemplary behavior..."[3] and the "logic of social appropriateness." Following Scott (2010, p. 6), translated to this work, firms approach appropriateness as: what is required of a firm like me in a situation like this?

Hall and Taylor (1996) further distinguish sociological institutionalism from rationality postulates insofar as granting the opportunity that a specific behavior—based on the evaluation of the society—may hamper or even counter the same actor's formal goals. Along the same lines, DiMaggio and Powell (1983) see that behavioral patterns of legitimation, indeed, make organizations and practices more similar but not necessarily more efficient (DiMaggio & Powell, 1983).

This broadened conception of man does not get in the way of MNCs as the actors under scrutiny. On the one hand, certainly, one can assume MNCs are relatively rational, since, first, MNCs move within the costs and benefits demarcated area and their formal goal is to maximize efficiency. As such, strategic considerations, behavior and interactions should be aligned with that goal. Second, according to the Uppsala internalization model, one may assume a company with subsidiaries abroad is relatively familiar with local conditions (see Sect. 3.1). Third, as a

[3] In contrast to the ‚logic of instrumentality' proposed by rational institutionalism.

composite actor, in line with Mayntz and Scharpf (1995), MNCs (i.e., their subsidiaries) are assumed to be more rational than individuals and not rely too heavily on things "taken-for-granted." Hence, a WOS in a foreign country may be assumed to be as rational as a foreign-owned entity may be. On the other hand, conducting the optimal interaction and showing the best possible behavior in the complex situation a WOS finds itself may at best be described as ambitious; more likely as beyond scope. Applying a broader conception of man does not rule out actors being rational. What indeed changes is the perception of what rationality is. In that regard, Hall and Taylor (1996, p. 949) state that what is perceived "...as 'rational action' is itself socially constituted...". In conclusion, an actor who may be assumed to be rational works and reworks institutional templates to devise the course most appropriate within the social environment, which in the case of WOS is complex and appropriate action may become a difficult matter.

This broadened conception of man, as has been indicated above, most often serves to conduct investigations within the traditional realm of "institutional" analysis. Nonetheless, it offers more space for behavioral contradiction and conflict beyond rationality and, thus, serves as a base for the following chapters that introduce institutional plurality and actor-induced change.

4.3 Institutions Matter, but Which Ones?

Of course, just like any other economic action, also the one of an MNC can be seen as a special case of social action. The institutional arrangement in force makes subsidiaries coordinate themselves with other actors following a specific logic of interaction. However, as the chapter above indicated, the institutional arrangement in force may not be equalled with exclusively the local one in isolation.

Figure 4.1 indicates that in comparison to traditional institutional analyses, in which action is determined by a clearly demarcated set of institutions, the subject matter changes when replacing a "normal" firm with an MNC, specifically its foreign subsidiary. The MNC and its WOS are crossing systemic borders. Consequently, the WOS that is physically situated in the host country, from a sociological view, is situated in an institutional tension field facing two institutional settings. In order to cope with the plurality of institutions, this chapter further develops institutional understanding by incorporating the idea of institutional duality that is: a subsidiary being pressured "...by two distinct sets of isomorphic pressures and a need to maintain legitimacy within both the host country and the MNC" (Kostova & Roth, 2002, p. 216). Multiplicity of governance principles that act upon the same actor simultaneously enables one to capture institutional tension, conflict and divergent behavior and, thus, is a possible way to overcome the paradox of WOS' embedded

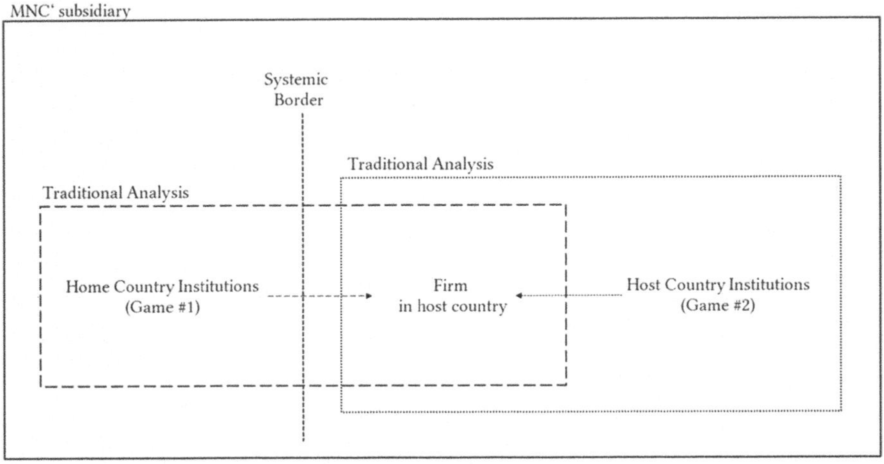

Fig. 4.1 Which Institutions Matter? Source: From the author

agency.[4] The idea of duality allows different sets of institutions to enter that may be in force at the same time. Hence, it allows one to grasp actors as being pressurized by various governance structures. If Game#1 and Game#2 are of different nature, one can reasonably argue that the subsidiary may find itself within an institutional tension area, as subject to two conflicting institutional settings.

In a VoC logic, the question of which institutional setting an MNCs relies on can be translated to "Which behavior does a company show?" On that account, the underlying logic of VoC certainly changes. The investigation is no longer restricted to the boundaries of single national political economies. The firm is replaced by the MNC and that change in view requires some theoretical reflections. WOS' interaction as social action, certainly, follow appropriate rules and, thus, also for WOS "institutions matter." However, this assertion has to be somehow adapted. The question now is "Which institutions matter?"

To better understand the concept of "dodgy embeddedness" in a state of institutional duality, the following section introduces the notions of organizational fields and isomorphism in more detail.

[4] Certainly, there also exist other solutions to the theoretical paradox of embedded agency, which are mostly grounded in notions of political dynamics, power, and interests (DiMaggio, 1991; Seo & Creed, 2002), or, for example, in a narrowed definition of institutions such as the one of Mayntz and Scharpf (1995).

4.3.1 The Organizational Field and Isomorphism

Attempting to understand patterns of rule-based action, homogeneity of practices and organizational forms, a central construct of institutionalist theory is one of organizational fields (DiMaggio & Powell, 1983; Powell & DiMaggio, 1991; Scott, 2010). DiMaggio and Powell (1983, p. 148) depict the organizational field as "those organizations which, in the aggregate, constitute a recognized area of institutional life: key suppliers, resources and product consumers, regulatory agencies, and other organizations that produce similar service or products." Subsequently, DiMaggio and Powell broaden the understanding and define an organizational field as the aggregate of "the totality of relevant actors" (1983, p. 148). Emphasizing the relational aspect of fields, DiMaggio and Powell indicate that the area of institutional life is made up of social or economic activity that establish relationships among themselves, setting up social structure and action models (Machado-da-Silva et al., 2006). Along the same lines, emphasizing inherent social dynamics, Scott (2010) defines an organizational field as a community of organizations that participate in the same meaning system and whose actors interact more frequently with each other than with someone from outside the field.[5]

The establishment of a field takes place through a mutually constitutive process with action and structure (DiMaggio & Powell, 1983). Building upon Giddens theory of structuration (Giddens, 1984; Machado-da-Silva et al., 2006), DiMaggio and Powell (1983) indicate that the structuration process of an organizational field results from increased interaction among organizations within the field, the building of an interorganizational structure, an increase in shared information, and development of mutual awareness that organizations are part of the same undertaking. Scott (2010) describes the process of structuration as "...over time, actions and relations within fields work together with beliefs and norms" to become more coherent.

Accordingly, also in this original conception of organizational fields the mutually constitutive relation between agency and structure within the process of structuration is incorporated, however, from a certain point on, a field can be labeled as established and individual behavior, that may deviate, has a negligible impact on the entire field. Hence, once actors are structured in a field, an "...inexorable push towards homogenization" (DiMaggio & Powell, 1983, p. 148) is supposed to take effect. Organizational forms and practices that become institutionalized, according to Powell and DiMaggio (1991), force organizations to be assimilated with other organizations that face similar situations. Hence, within an established organizational field, in line with the conception of man discussed above, behavior reflects collective patterns of legitimate forms and practices (Maurer, 2012) and shows homogeneity of practices. Organizations attempt to conduct practices that correspond to the rule-like perceptions of what is socially correct (Scott, 1991) achieving legitimacy in their surroundings and increasing the change of survival; and success

[5] For a review of alternative definitions of organizational fields, putting emphasis on, among others, functionality aspects and power and conflict, see Machado-da-Silva et al. (2006).

(DiMaggio & Powell, 1983). A shared belief system, that is to say, a common sense for what is a desirable and appropriate practice—or what is supposed to be good, rightful, and generally legitimate—is diffused within (or to put it in the words of Zajac and Kraatz (1993, p. 85) is "dictated by") the organizational field. This process of diffusion and stabilizing patterns of institutional reproduction leading to homogeneous and coherent forms and practices across the field is called isomorphism and describes organizations' similar responses to coercive, mimetic, and normative pressures (DiMaggio & Powell, 1983; Meyer & Rowan, 1977; Scott, 2010); of which all proceed "... in the absence of evidence that they increase internal organizational efficiency" (DiMaggio & Powell 1983, p. 153). Most general, Gardiner et al. (2013, p. 143) define isomorphism as "...being of identical or similar form or shape or structure to that prevailing in the environment."

Anticipatory, the forces of institutional isomorphism that are discussed below have the capacity to "overlap and intermingle" even though they are based on different conditions and may affect organizational practices and behavior in different ways (Frumkin & Galaskiewicz, 2004, p. 285). Along the same line, DiMaggio and Powell (1983) already indicate that the different types of isomorphism are of a rather analytical nature and may become blurred when approached empirically.

Sociological institutionalists refer to coercive isomorphism when pressure on organizations is exerted by external forces through direct authority relationships; power relations (DiMaggio, 1991). Organizations may be subject to formal or informal, direct or indirect pressure that can be exerted by a variety of entities, such as other organizations, the state, standards, legislation, or by general expectations that are firmly rooted within society, of which the organization is a part and dependent on (DiMaggio & Powell, 1983). Oliver (1991, p. 152) from the point of the individual organization, defines such compliance to coercive pressures as a "conscious obedience to or incorporation of values, norms, or institutional requirements." Showcasing political influence and organizational legitimacy, Sampaio de Freitas & de Aquino Guimarães (2007) demonstrate governments' impact through, for example, regulations, laws, and accreditation processes. Indicating another hierarchical relationship beyond the state,—and of a good fit with this work's overarching argument—DiMaggio and Powell (1983) recognize huge corporations as to impose standardized reporting mechanisms and performance evaluations across the subunits to assure compatibility with the parent company. However, coercive isomorphism can be seen not only in such clear top-down relationships. Showing a very basic and subtle example, Swidler (1979) describes the necessity of having the formally defined role of a "principal" in a school that serves as a proper negotiator when struggling with the district superintendent regarding resources and support. Without such a role at eye level with the district superintendent, the school had serious disadvantages. Consequently, without explicit enforcement of such hierarchical structure within the school, the structure of the municipality implicitly forces the school to do so likewise and depicts coercive pressure as well. Following this relatively wide range, DiMaggio and Powell indicate that coercive pressures "...may be felt as force, as persuasion, or as invitations to join in collusion" (1983, p. 150).

Normative isomorphism works through forces that are internal to the field (in contrast to coercive isomorphism) and explains the spread and reinforcement of occupational norms and values through the process of professionalization (DiMaggio & Powell, 1983; Frumkin & Galaskiewicz, 2004). The basic cornerstone of individuals that belong to a specific profession inhibiting norms and showing behavior that is associated with the profession they are part of. To attain legitimacy within a specific profession, members of such show characteristic (homogeneous) practices and behavior to appear legitimate. Norus (1997) extends the concept of professionalization beyond the determination of practices and behaviors deemed to be appropriate by including the creation of an appropriate cognitive framework in which decisions on organizational routines and behavior are made. On that account, thinking that takes place within a specific cognitive frame, again, leads to decisions that—if made by various individuals within the same profession but part of different organizations—are relatively homogeneous.

On that account, generally, professionalization is associated with the collective efforts of an occupation, i.e., sum of organizations and their members, to control the conditions and the conduct of their work; i.e., to define characteristics, and appropriate ways in which to act.[6] Along the same line, professionalization includes the efforts to establish and retain a cognitive grounding for occupational autonomy (DiMaggio & Powell, 1983). Most roughly, according to Kostova and Roth (2002, p. 216), normative isomorphism occurs when "organizations adopt patterns considered appropriate in the environment."

As major sources of normative isomorphism, DiMaggio and Powell (1983) introduce first, formal education and legitimation in a by university and professional training institutions led process. In such process, organizational norms are developed among professional managers and their employees and serve as common cognitive base. Second, professional cross-organizational networks such as associations serve as sources of normative pressure inasmuch as they may best be seen as a mechanism for definition, promulgation, and diffusion "...of normative rules about organizational and professional behavior" (DiMaggio & Powell, 1983, p. 152). Furthermore, occupational socialization serves as a force of normative isomorphism in the role of a communicator of appropriate behavior to its members through, on-the-job socialization and certification processes with accreditation by professional bodies (Sampaio de Freitas & de Aquino Guimarães, 2007). Picking various examples, Galaskiewicz and Wasserman (1989) indicate several venues for normative pressure, for example, professional networks, seminars, workshops, professional development, workshops, formal education, and professional magazines. Accordingly, pressure on behavior may be exercised by behavioral patterns shown by professionals and professional communities in general whose action is legitimated by virtue of a cognitive founding (Hall & Taylor, 1996).

To understand the difference between professions and organizations, two aspects of a profession's nature are to be considered. First, within an organization most

[6] As Larson (1977, p. 17) named it to control the "production of producers."

likely various professions exist and, second a profession goes beyond the borders of an organization. Following, DiMaggio and Powell (1983) recognize that different professionals within the same organization may differ significantly, though professionals within a certain organization may show a relatively high degree of conformity with members of their profession in other organizations. Concluding, professionalization/normative isomorphism generates a mass of individuals that are very similar regarding orientation and disposition and contribute strongly to homogeneous professions.

Mimetic isomorphism—also one whose forces are internal to the field—is grounded in organizations' uncertainty (DiMaggio & Powell, 1983). Being in a state of uncertainty with the compulsion to establish organizational legitimacy—for example, due to shocks, ambiguity, inexperience—organizations seek and fall back on behavioral patterns observed within the institutional area of interest. Following Hanson (2001) an organization consciously models itself after another similar organization that is perceived "to do better"; i.e., to be more successful and more legitimate. Such an allegedly better organization represents success and achievement in the eye of the public. In comparison to the oppressive counterpart coercing behavior and practices, the modeled organization unintentionally serves as an easily available and apparently viable source of practice. Along the same line, the diffusion of models can also happen unintentionally and indirectly through, for example, the circulation of labor and industry associations. Further relating to the viability of practice assumed, if success and legitimacy of one organization—that serves as model—within the same area (respectively facing a similar situation) can be somehow connected to a specifically conducted pattern of action, other organizations are pressurized to mimic (copy) this pattern of action that proved to be successful. Following this line of reasoning, a certain degree of uniformity in parts of the business world is partly to be explained by organizations' pursuit of proven best practices (Sampaio de Freitas & de Aquino Guimarães, 2007).

Not intended as a specific kind of isomorphism, though, one could extend the above-mentioned mechanisms by "complementarity" isomorphism; though this may be understood rather as a system effect than a societal one. Nonetheless, relying on the concept of institutional complementarity, as Hall and Soskice (2001) indicate, if a firm that experiences benefits when relying on a specific set of institutions (relying on a specific pattern of practices)—in terms of VoC either the ones of LMEs or of CMEs—within one realm of the institutional life, it "...encourage[s] stakeholders to adopt the full package of complementary institutions..." (Schneider, 2013, p. 38). Kuznetsov and Jacobs (2015, p. 8) bring in the notion of a "bandwagon effect" insofar as a change in one institution can prompt changes in interdependent institutions. Along the lines of complementarity and normative issues, as indicated by VoC, when changing one institution, institutional instability may arise due to a lack of specific behavior supporting institutions, that again, theoretically, may lead to pressure for a potential systemic wholesale change (Allen, 2004; Deeg & Jackson, 2007; Hollingsworth & Boyer, 1997). However, limiting the expectations on the field effect of "complementarity" isomorphism on HMEs, Schneider further emphasizes the nature of hierarchically internalized interaction inasmuch as both decisions and actions mostly take place within one firm. Accordingly, HMEs are supposed to lack the inter-organizational efforts and joint gains that are otherwise realized through trust or bargaining. Such a lack of the relational aspect—as introduced above—certainly limits the effect of complementarity isomorphism in HMEs *vis-à-vis*, for example, CMEs.

Setting Boundaries of the Organizational Field

The organizational field understood as an area of institutional life and the aggregate of all relevant actors can lead to challenges to clearly define the field's boundaries. In line with Machado-da-Silva et al. (2006), demarcating a theoretically optimal field may be beyond scope, since it seems at best ambitious to capture the totality of relevant actors and an exhaustive account of the shared belief system. Most generally, a field can take almost every form of social life, though it certainly makes sense to fulfill certain preset limitations. As Chap. 3 on "the game" indicate, this work generally relies on the market economy as an organizational field. It thereby defines the boundaries from two sides. First, as discussed above, the fields of a CME, LME, and HME are demarcated geographically by the borders of a nation-state and, thus, follows, among others, Morgan (2001) who perceives the national border as most important, since it is the state that is decisive for crucial issues such as social security, political regime, specifics of training and education, labor law, public administration, taxation, and so on. Along the same lines, Rosenzweig and Singh (1991) argue that most reasonably one can delimit areas of institutional life to national borders, since major elements such as the legal system and culture vary corresponding to the country.

Second, in line with Scott (1991, p. 117) who emphasizes the notion of functionality, fields may also be defined as a "collection of organizations operating in the same domain, as identified by the similarity of their services, products or functions, together with those organizations that critically influence the performance of focal organizations." VoC clearly defines actors that operate in the "domain" called market economy and, thus, demarcate the specific organizational field functionally. In sum, the VoC set market economies seem to serve well as organizational fields, since they provide the major aspects of an organizational field. The VoC approach and the associated varieties of market economies are well defined and indicate actors, the relevant relationships (of which actors are aware), the multidimensional and interdependent system of institutions, and within this work the further developed mutually constitutive dynamics between actors and institutions.

The discussed concept of organizational fields and isomorphism are valuable for understanding dynamics specific to MNCs' subsidiaries and host countries. Whereas this chapter hitherto discusses organizational fields within the concept of "traditional" analysis described above, understanding fields and potential dynamics within turns out to be crucial to better understanding what happens when organizational fields may overlap or come into conflict. The context of MNCs, in particular, may be a valid case since their subsidiaries seem to be simultaneously pressurized by different sets of institutions that may be contradictory.

4.3.2 *Various Institutional Fields and the Situation of Institutional Duality*

Investigating MNCs, crossing borders of nations and institutional areas, the investigation is no longer restricted to the boundaries of single national political economies. The firm is replaced by the MNC subsidiary that is physically existent in the host country while being subject to direct control and ownership of HQs located in the CoO.

Responding to institutional ambiguity, Kostova et al. (2008) raise doubt on the general applicability of coherent organizational fields to the MNC. Certainly, traditional analyses of organizational fields reach their limits, though in line with, among others, Philips and Tracey (2009), Geppert et al. (2006), Mattes (2013), Jackson and Rathert (2017), Kostova et al. (2018) and Clark and Geppert (2010) that the lack of clearly assignable organizational fields makes institutional analyses even more interesting and a source for conflict, tension, agency, change, and development. As Fig. 4.1 indicates, MNCs, most likely, are subject to more than one institutional setting and, consequently, face various, may be contradictory, and isomorphic pressures. Being subject to various—maybe contradictory—isomorphic pressures at a time, maintaining legitimacy in "all" its environments may become a difficult task. Contradictory isomorphic pressures may cause the subsidiary to act differently than it would if only pressured by the local one, as is the case with national firms. This behavior may be characterized as an alien-to-the-system practice.

The concept of the organizational field allows for a more complex understanding of MNCs facing various institutional settings simultaneously. Even though it was not part of earlier institutional thinking, the notion of the organizational field allows one to embed MNCs in multiple fields simultaneously. Thus, MNCs—as suggested by both theoretical and empirical considerations above—can be captured as entities that may face institutional plurality and find themselves in a tension field created by a multitude of institutional settings.

The debate on MNCs' embeddedness in host countries and general HQ—subsidiary relations is vivid, especially in the international business and international management literature (Heidenreich, 2012; Kostova et al., 2008; Mattes, 2013). In comparison to the approach of this work, however, these investigations aim at dismantling and understanding indicators that are crucial for corporate success. Recognizing behavioral tensions and the distinctness of environments, variables that are common to be maximized aim at improving organizational efficiency, employee motivation, and innovation (Heidenreich, 2012; Kostova et al., 2016). A major issue on IB's agenda, for example, is, as Doz and Prahalad (1991) put it, the dilemma of local responsiveness and global integration. Similarly, other scholars with Ghoshal and Bartlett (1990) at the forefront investigate the organizational structure ranging from local strategies to transnational one-size-fits-all aimed at grasping the one that promises highest profits operating in different environments simultaneously. Within IB literature, there are various recurring themes. Among others, various scholars emphasize the relevance of a subsidiary's autonomy, whereas others focus on the central role expatriates may take within the management of a foreign subsidiary (Vora et al., 2007). Further issues are, for example, the transfer of people, processes, technology and competences and, as a more concrete example, corporate social responsibility patterns from HQ to subsidiaries, or how to design a corporate control system; for example, financial or performance controls (Bartlett & Ghoshal, 1989; Cantwell et al., 2010; Jackson & Rathert, 2017; Kim & Park, 2008; Morgan & Kristensen, 2006). Indeed, all of these themes indicate that IB literature recognizes potential problems and systemic differences when relating to subsidiaries. However, generally, investigation takes place within the MNCs and the variables of interest are mirroring corporate success; the surrounding systems are mostly treated as black boxes. The home and host county environment, as systems of different institutions, rarely found access to IB literature. Nonetheless, it is the work of Kostova and colleagues that depicts an exception that theorizes HQ—subsidiary relations shedding light on the MNC as an organizational field itself (Hoenen & Kostova, 2015; Kostova, 2016; Kostova et al., 2008, 2018; Kostova & Roth, 2002; Kostova & Zaheer, 1999; Roth & Kostova, 2003; Vora et al., 2007).

Just like the theoretical introduction into organizational fields above indicated, similarly, an intra-organizational field is characterized by an aggregation of actors that interact socially and economically with each other more frequently than with others outside of the MNC. On that account, they build up social relationships and over time beliefs, norms, and formal rules become more coherent. Additionally, the awareness of the single actors that they are involved in a common enterprise may be higher and more self-evident than in countries. Certainly, an MNC is knit together mostly by hierarchies and the purpose of reaching common goals rather than by "officially" set jurisdictions and law. Thus, certainly, an intra-organizational MNC field is more diffuse geographically; it fully copes, however, with a Scottian understanding of functionally based organizational fields. Further strengthening the idea of the intra-organizational fields, Heidenreich (2012) coins the concept of "organizational embeddedness" perceiving the MNC as is integrated not only by financial and technical means but also by social networks and relations. Along the same lines, Morgan (2001) perceives the MNC as a "transnational social space" in which social relationships are structured internally in complex ways (Kellogg, 2009). Further, indicating potential tensions, Morgan (2001, p. 12) recognizes the "precarious and conflictual nature of the social order that develops within them."

Within the MNCs that are situated in a state of institutional ambiguity and potential conflict, an intra-organizational field undertakes an important task by providing a—to a certain degree—shared cognition and belief system and, thus, aligns subunits and reduces uncertainty over what is perceived to be appropriate. Kostova et al. (2008) expect intra-organizational fields to be stronger than the country delimited ones. Subunits of MNCs are supposed to be more dependent on the parent company than they are on their external environment. Beyond resource dependence, subsidiary managers are directly dependent on its parent company regarding their future career prospects (Kostova & Zaheer, 1999). Hence, one may expect subsidiary managers to act in a way perceived as appropriate by HQ managers that decide, for example, their next promotion.

As theoretically derived above, practices and forms are supposed to diffuse throughout the intra-organizational field according to their appropriateness, just like in any other clearly set area of institutional life. Diffusion of what is perceived appropriate takes place through the above discussed three isomorphic mechanisms. However, further carving out the coercive aspect of such hierarchies through a formal authority, Kostova and Roth (2002, p. 216) assume "... if a practice is mandated by the parent, the subsidiary is obligated to comply." Making the case for direct coercive pressure, Kostova et al. (2008) and Morgan and Kristensen (2006) notice a general trend in global management (especially regarding social responsibility) to establish globally valid codes of conduct, management guidelines, and general expectation for the entire MNC. Further strengthening the account of a powerful HQ, Ferner et al. (2011) recognize that, despite network- and flat hierarchical experiments, the norm still remains the authoritative central HQ. Similarly, working at the interface of coercive and mimetic pressures within MNCs, Kim and Park (2008), Heidenreich (2012) and Cantwell et al. (2010) see a general tendency of HQs, which find themselves in a relatively high state of uncertainty about foreign economies, to strongly replicate the practices of the parent company that have proven their validity at least once in the CoO context in the different host countries. In general, Kim & Park perceive the pressure for mimicry higher within the intra-organizational field than in the local one.

For the sake of analytical clarity, it is important to state that this work builds upon the work of, among others, Kostova et al. (2008) and Marinova (2015) and interprets the intra-organizational field as a quasi-carrier of the CoO institutions. Hence, the impact of home country institutions on MNCs abroad is an indirect one, since "...practices that an MNC attempts to diffuse are formulated in the MNC's home institutional context" (Kostova & Roth, 2002, p. 218). The line of causality goes as follows: home country institutions cause the HQ to act in a certain way. Then, an MNC itself functions as an organizational field "...where distinct patterns of organizational action emerge and become institutionalized, institutional pressures are exercised..." (Kostova et al., 2008, p. 997).

Figure 4.2 depicts the organizational fields in effect relating to MNCs and their subsidiaries. As one can see, the subsidiaries find themselves in a state of overlapping fields. Figure 4.2 depicts home and host country as having different institutional systems. For the sake of simplicity, different institutional principles between the institutional systems of the home and host country are represented by either left-turning or clockwise arrows. Postulated by institutional duality in combination with the specific characteristics of MNCs, one can reasonably assume the arrows within the intra-organizational field to be more or less aligned with the ones of the CoO. Certainly, equating the institutional system within the MNCs with the one of the CoO reaches its limits.

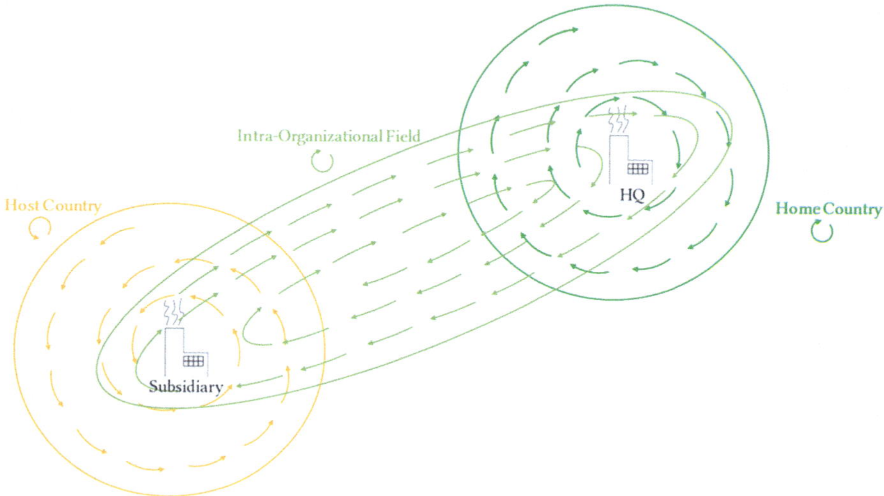

Fig. 4.2 MNCs' Organizational Fields. Source: From the author

Nota bene:

There also exists a literature body on the subsidiary impact on HQ and the entire MNC, well known as the concept of "reverse diffusion" (Edwards & Ferner, 2004; Ferner et al., 2005). Reverse diffusion is defined as "…the transfer of practices from foreign subsidiaries to the domestic operations" (Edwards & Ferner, 2004, p. 49). Despite not examining this issue further within this work, the idea of reverse diffusion certainly holds up to a certain degree and various scholars endorse the idea that MNCs contribute to an overall increase in diversity within the CoO as well (Sako, 2005). However, to put it in extremes, since the large MNCs are intertwined all over the world, granting each subsidiary a genuine impact on the entire MNC would make—ultimately—most of the MNCs homogeneous. As will be discussed below, though, MNCs within their CoO show a relatively high degree of resilience and mostly resemble local domestically oriented firms. Furthermore, literature on reverse diffusion inevitably implies a shared understanding of some globalization narratives that imply that MNCs are homogeneous, disembedded, and—if at all—belonging to a "detached" global class of actors (Dacin et al., 1999). This perspective of a global detached class of actors, however, in addition to the mentioned considerations above, is raised into question by a large body of literature on MNC resilience and, thus, is beyond the scope of this work. Along the same lines, Kostova et al. (2008) and Whitley (1998) and others, depict the institutional meta-level analysis—that is talking about one global system—within the scope of MNCs as relatively fruitless since the

(continued)

international business environment is still relatively weak. Certainly, there are scholars endorsing a more global stance on institution building (Ferner et al., 2011; Geppert et al., 2006). Nonetheless, since the main interest of this work lies within the differences between MNCs according to the CoO, the transnational institution building is beyond the scope of this work. One could certainly argue that MNCs from different CoOs may interact differently at the interface between a triad of different institutional settings including the host, the home, and the transnational global setting.

The intra-level analysis rather depicts a form of the "traditional" kind of analysis and the one proposed by, for example, Kostova et al. (2008), is the analysis of the meso-level, where different fields come into play, producing institutional ambiguity. *Vis-á-vis* the weak international/global business environment, institutional analysts are in line with this approach and assume that "...MNCs are likely to pursue more idiosyncratic ways of organizing at the interface with host and home environments" (Kostova et al., 2008, p. 1004).

In conclusion, this work's approach seems to be reasonable for reasons of the solid grounding in MNCs resilience to home country institutions and the theoretical considerations throughout the previous chapters.

In tradition with Meyer and Rowan (1977) who perceive the totality of institutional environments as potentially pluralistic and pointedly inconsistent, assuming cross-national institutional dissimilarities one may reasonably see MNCs' subsidiaries situated in a state of polycentricity, facing institutional duality "...confronted with two distinct sets of isomorphic pressures and a need to maintain legitimacy within both the host country and the MNC" (Kostova & Roth, 2002, p. 215). Most famously (Brewster et al., 2008; Kostova & Roth, 2002; Vora et al., 2007), institutional duality has been theorized as the situation when an entity is facing more than one institutional setting: the ones of the home and the host country. In a similar vein, Morgan & Kristensen describe institutional duality as the situation in which "...actors are pressured to conform to the expectations of their home context whilst also being subject to the transfer of practices from the home context of the MNC itself" (2006, p. 1467). Similarly, Geppert et al. (2006, p. 1455) see MNCs' subsidiaries as "...locally embedded in home and host countries...", and Geppert et al. (2003) interpret the situation of foreign subsidiaries as one in which different contextual rationalities from both home and host country come into play, putting the subsidiary in a dilemma situation inasmuch as they need both internal (intra-organizational) and external (host country) legitimacy (Geppert & Williams, 2006). Similarly, Mattes (2013) and Kwok and Tadesse (2006) recognize subsidiaries as embedded in the host country while being strongly aligned with contradictory demands of companywide control and coordination mechanisms that are shaped by the MNCs' home country context. In general, following Seo and Creed (2002) one can reasonably state that MNCs work at the crossroads of multiple interpenetrating institutional settings that are akin but often incompatible. That again, according to Seo and Creed (2002, p. 225), leads to the inevitable by-product of institutional "...contradictions, continually generating tensions and conflicts within and across social systems... ."

Discussing the degree of compliance with either home or host country institutions, literature provides a rather heterogenous account. As an example, Morgan and Kristensen (2006) further state, due to transfer practices, resources, dependency, and general control mechanisms, most often MNCs produce "subsidiary clones" of the HQ with little leverage to use/adapt to the opportunities/restrictions offered by the host country. Others, such as Cantwell et al. (2010) find increasing autonomy of MNC subsidiaries that makes them more likely to—to a certain degree—coevolve with local host country institutions. The various factors that may impact specific patterns of compliance are further discussed throughout the following sections. Among others, Ferner et al. (2005) scrutinizing US firms and their subsidiaries in the UK, tend to relativize the rather extreme poles and bring in a middle ground by stating:

> the "isomorphic pulls" exerted by corporate headquarters were not sufficient to ensure. .. subsidiary "acquiescence"—that is, full compliance in form and spirit with institutional pressures . . . managers were able to derive bargaining resources from their rootedness within the specific institutional configuration of the host country (2005, p. 316).

Recognizing subsidiaries as complex organizations facing various pressures simultaneously is key to this investigation insofar as it open doors to understanding behavior of subsidiaries that deviates from the one expected and induced by the subsidiary's local environment. The subsequent section gives some indicators that may be informative when discussing the impact of the two organizational fields on the actor.

Which Institutions Matter?

Situated in the state of polycentricity, behavioral responses of subsidiaries can be different, and conformity to a specific field becomes a matter of degree. In general, foreign subsidiaries of MNCs can either attempt to overcome local institutions, or defy HQ's transfer efforts (Ferner et al., 2011). Hence, theoretically, subsidiaries' practice can range from either conformity with the local environment to conformity with the intra-organizational one, including any kind of hybrid form within these extremes (Brookes et al., 2017). The notion of hybrid remains valid for two different observations. Observing multiple practices as elements of one total, a hybrid may indicate that some practices show conformity to field A, whereas others show conformity to field B. However, observing one specific practice, this single practice may be hybridized inasmuch as, for example, a practice from field A is either combined or adapted to characteristics of field B. For example, Edwards et al. (2007) make the case for the latter and expect MNCs to disseminate broad framework policies that locally adapt rather than concrete practices. Correspondingly, foreign subsidiaries are subject to either the host country environment, the internal field, or to both at the same time. However, by practical means, subsidiaries are social actors within both fields, in need of resources offered by both fields and heavily dependent on interaction with other social actors in both fields. Hence, foreign subsidiaries may neither be expected as being part of "hierarchical monoliths" (Birkinshaw & Hood, 1998, p. 778) nor as being rootless and entirely embedded locally. Summing up the discussion, Heidenreich (2012, p. 562) puts it as follows: "Thus, MNCs do not operate in a homogeneous organizational field characterized by a clear pattern of legitimacy and strong isomorphic pressures, but have to face heterogeneous and, in general, even conflicting demands for national or regional legitimacy." In a similar vein, relying on Seo and Creed (2002), assuming dissimilar institutional settings in which the subsidiary finds itself, it is the subsidiaries' "intrainstitutional conformity that creates interinstitutional incompatibilities" resulting in institutional contradiction. Further, already Meyer and Rowan (1977) recognized actors as being potentially embedded in pluralistic institutional settings that trigger pointedly inconsistent patterns of practices.

Following this argumentation, it is a major challenge for the subsidiary to deal with the misfit between local work practices and the one induced by the intra-organizational field. The state of dual embeddedness makes exclusive reliance on one of the fields at the same time taking the risk of conducting entirely inappropriate practices in the other one rather unlikely. Consequently, a foreign subsidiary can neither be expected to mirror home-based practices of the MNC nor be expected to entirely blend in with other actors in the host country context. Considering the dual pressure, in line with the theoretical and empirical considerations throughout Chap. 2, Morgan and Kristensen (2006), Kostova and Roth (2002), Smets et al. (2012), and Kuznetsov and Jacob (2015) expect an institutional hybrid form showing behavior originating in both institutional settings. Hence, one may assume subsidiaries' practice patterns are characterized by a certain adaptation to the local conditions while preserving certain imported elements of the home country. However, the degree to which behavior is reflecting either the local or the intra-organizational field is—at best—difficult to estimate. Whereas, partly in line with traditional analyses, among others, Whitley (1998) emphasizes the shaping power of the "direct" local environment, others such as Lane (2008) perceive local "shallow embeddedness" and, thus, strongly champion the diffusion of practices through the intra-organizational field.

Nonetheless, various studies, among others by Kuznetsov and Jacobs (2015), Kostova and Roth (2002), Morgan and Kristensen (2006), Kostova et al. (2008), Ferner et al. (2005), Zander and Sölvell (2004), indeed indicate that behavioral adaptation of a foreign subsidiary to a local host environment does not follow a preset recipe and depends on the specific case under scrutiny. Beyond the rather binary "either local or intra-organizational" conceptualization, Heidenreich (2012, p. 572) depicts the handling of subsidiaries' polycentricity as a "precarious task because it requires balancing the conflicting demands of local and corporate embeddedness." An institutional hybrid form may find itself at all steps on the spectrum between either the local or the intra-organizational field. The strength of a field, i.e., the degree by which an actor's behavior gravitates to the corresponding logic depends on both the field (of host and intra-organizational field) and on actor characteristics. Since the penetrative power of a field shares major indicators with the stability of a field, a discussion on field strengths will follow in Sect. 4.5 when potential institutional change will be derived theoretically.

Having introduced the institutional duality in which firms find themselves in a tension field facing dissimilar and, thus, conflictual isomorphic pressures, this work sheds light on the complex environment of a foreign subsidiary. Aligning practices in order to gain legitimacy within two different organizational fields simultaneously is strongly suspect to not entirely conform to either of the two fields in effect. On that account, MNCs are likely "...to pursue idiosyncratic ways of organizing at the interface with host and home environments." (Kostova et al., 2008, p. 1004) and, thus, show behavioral patterns that deviate from the one induced by local institutions. Incorporating deviant behavior into institutional analyses unties the strait-jacket of traditional analyses, allows behavioral contradiction and opens doors for a new source of agency within the host country. The process of adaptation and the dynamics within the host country caused by "alien-to-the-system" practices introduced by the subsidiary will be under closer scrutiny in the following chapter.

4.4 Alien-to-the-System, Agency and Institutional Change

The previous chapters indicated that deviant behavior is within scope. Foreign subsidiaries of MNCs as embedded actors are prone to act differently from other local actors. This, as a form of embedded—and transformative—agency, seems to be paradoxical since the question arises as to how organizations whose actions are supposed to be determined by their surroundings institutions can tackle these same institutions. The paradox of embedded agency raises certain barriers in institutional analysis (Walker et al., 2014; Leca et al., 2009; Seo & Creed, 2002; Friedland & Alford, 1991) and, thus, has long caused the role of agency and conflictual behavior to be out of scope, even though being a potential cause for institutional change (Jackson & Deeg, 2008; Garud et al., 2007). Levi, already (1990) recognized that an actor's noncompliance with an institution may be a source of institutional change. Nonetheless, in line with the traditional analyses' temptation of rigidity, Oliver (1991, p. 151) confirms that institutional theorists "...have tended to limit their attention to the effects of the institutional environment on structural conformity and isomorphism and have overlooked the role of active agency and resistance in organization-environment relation." Ever since Oliver (1991), very few scholars have engaged in the debate around divergent behavior of embedded actors and potential institutional change (Oliver, 1991; Seo & Creed, 2002, Burns & Nielsen, 2006; Powell & Colyvas, 2008; Smets et al., 2012). However, further investigating the specific behavior of MNCs and the subsequent potential impact is important as the diffusion of practices within the firm impacts outside its borders as well and may affect the society around in general (Meyer et al., 2011).

The previous chapter indicated that foreign subsidiaries of MNCs have a specific characteristic—a source of behavioral conflict—that makes them of utmost interest for institutional analysis. These subsidiaries act on "on behalf" of two not congruent—indeed rather conflictual—institutional environments, while being physically present in only one. Hence, economic interaction as a special case of social relationships remains rule-based, though rules become blurred and may even be conflictual. As indicated, relying on institutions that are not the local ones in the host country makes subsidiaries, to a certain degree, an alien-to-the-system importing new practices. As discussed above, it is the subsidiaries' intra-institutional conformity—reaching for legitimacy within both the MNC and the host country—that creates interinstitutional incompatibilities and, thus, institutional contradictions in the host country (Seo & Creed, 2002). Allowing for and integrating deviant behavior into analyses is key for a microfoundationalist attempt to scrutinize potential institutional change within the host country driven by subsidiaries that are both locally embedded and locally constitutive. This mutually constitutive account of structure and agency is in line with the above elaborated broader sociological conception of man and Gidden's theory of structuration and the concept of organizational fields of DiMaggio & Powell, respectively. Along these lines, translated to the context of this work, Forsgren, Holm, & Johanson argue against the neglection of MNCs as active actors in major parts of the literature and state that "(t)he environment adapts to the MNC as much as the MNC adapts to the environment" (2005, p. 186).

Simplified, large parts of the debate on dynamics within environments consider organizations to have a behavioral arsenal of either compliance, avoidance, or defiance with existing institutions (Fenton-O'Creevy et al., 2007; Hall & Thelen, 2009; Oliver, 1991). Whereas compliance is likely to confirm existing institutions, avoidance, and defiance indicate an inherent (institutional) contradiction. As (partly) alien-to-the-system, subsidiaries' avoidance, and defiance of existing institutions depicts deviant behavior from that which is appropriate at the local level. Hence, subsidiaries' polycentricity and the subsequent contradictions with host country institutions are of utmost importance, since, to put it in the words of Burns and Nielsen (2006, p. 451), "institutional change is initiated by the existence of contradictions." Applying a meso multilevel approach on endogenous field level contradictions on actors and change, among others, Boxenbaum (2006), Friedland and Alford (1991), and Seo and Creed (2002) see contradictory practice at the interface of dissimilar (incompatible) institutional settings as a necessary driving force of institutional change. Following Seo and Creed (2002, p. 223), it is contradiction that "transform embedded social actors into the change agents of the very institutional arrangement..." they are embedded in. Emphasizing MNCs as a source of conflict, Kwok and Tadesse (2006), Mitchell (2010), and March and Olsen (2009) state that alien-to-the-system practices can challenge the legitimacy of existing institutional patterns in various ways and, simultaneously, prompt debates and contestation on potentially better practices in the host country.

Broadly put, translated to this work, to deviate in behavior means to employ "strange" institutions as Streeckian enablers to solve coordination problems in a way that is not normal to the local environment but suits the achievement of the underlying objectives. Figure 4.3 roughly depicts the subsidiary within the organizational field of the host country importing and conducting practices that originate

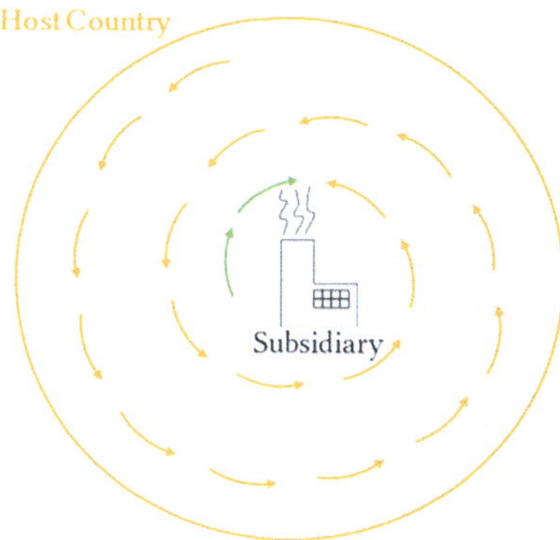

Fig. 4.3 An Alien-to-the-System. Source: From the author

from outside; following institutional duality, it stems from within the home country. As the previous chapter elaborated, the specific situation of foreign subsidiaries makes them subject to various isomorphic pressures, though having an effect endogenously within the host country. Simplified, the red arrows depict practices that are contradictory to the local ones imported from the home country. This is the initial situation on which the remainder of this chapter further builds.

This work perceives the conduct of practices that are not congruent with the locally appropriate ones as a materialization of agency. Accordingly, the concept of agency is widely defined as the "capacity to make a difference" (DiMaggio, 1988). Equally broadly defined by Giddens (1984, p. 9), agency is referred to as "...not to the intentions people have in doing things but to their capability of doing things in the first place...". In general terms, all that has happened due to a specific action (s) that otherwise would not have happened implies agency (Giddens, 1984). Furthermore, more specifically in line with theory on institutional entrepreneurship below, it is the actor's capacity to act reflectively and to create its own frame and structures in a situation described by institutional duality that explicitly shows agency (Kostova et al., 2008). Emphasizing agency's effect, particularly the behavioral impact on institutions, Powell and Colyvas (2008) categorize actions as ones that either reinforce existing institutions and others that change and reframe them. Hence, in conjunction with the potential response categories "comply, avoid, and defy," it is the latter two responses that contradict the local practice pattern, that show agency—according to this work's definition—and, consequently, that feed back to the field level and therefore most likely are the ones that cause institutional change.

Forms of Actor-Induced Institutional Change

Within the scope of this work, subsidiaries' agencies can be incorporated reasonably based on the knowledge of systemic differences and the importation of foreign practices into the host country's institutional settings. Hence, this idea follows, among others, Seo and Creed (2002) and Kostova et al. (2008, p. 1103) who recognize internationalization as bringing "...forth the power of firms as institutional change agents."

Above all, the point of origin for and key to actor-induced institutional change is behavioral contradiction. Based on such institutional conflict, actors can have an effect on the surrounding organizational field in various ways. Since "[c]hange is not likely to be governed by a single coherent and dominant process" (March & Olsen, 2004, p. 17), the following sections elaborate on two forms of subsidiary-induced change. First, actors can change institutions through the subtler and sometimes unconscious exertion of isomorphic pressure on the organizational field. Second, actors can act on purpose pursuing a specific institutional change. Regarding the second type of institutional change, the subsidiary itself acts as an institutional entrepreneur. Importantly, day-to-day mechanisms of actor-induced change can also be coercive and, thus, may counter the intuition one may have on unconscious day-to-day action. However, in comparison to the institutional entrepreneurship, it is understood as evoking institutional change rather passively as a by-product of business action and not as one as an objective of purposeful action (Ferner et al., 2011).

As discussed above, either the response of avoidance or the one of defiance is necessary to cause potential change of existing institutions. Relating to the two types of actor-induced change, "avoidance" may be understood as the more subtle response to local isomorphic pressure, whereas "defiance" requires a more active attitude including a notion of strategically approached resistance. Nonetheless, both mechanisms can have equal outcomes inasmuch as they can change both formal and informal rules, shift entire field-level logics, or may change nothing at all.

4.4.1 Institutionalization

Since host country environments can hardly be seen as *tabula rasa*, one best approaches the local context by assuming a (relatively) structured setting at the initial point in time of the investigation. Certainly, assuming host countries as a clean slate would make the investigation of the inter-institutional incompatibilities and subsequent institutional contradiction induced to change a futile endeavor, since no contradiction could occur. However, scrutinizing firms that move from one market economy to another one changing institutions, one rarely talks about a *genesis* of a certain institution but rather about a change, complementation, or supersession. In line with challenging the legitimacy of the existing and the recognition of the new and potentially better, an institutional change comprises both an institutionalization of, for example, a new practice and, simultaneously, a de-institutionalization of the corresponding existing one. Whereas the former describes a process in which legitimacy of a practice gradually increases, the latter one—vice versa—describes a process in which "...legitimacy of an institutionalized practice gradually erodes" (Seo & Creed, 2002, p. 233).

However, as is the case within this work, it is relatively well known how things were yesterday, but what happens today and how things will be tomorrow are of specific importance when talking about change. On that account, focusing on the process of change induced by actors that carry "inappropriate" practices with them, it is of utmost interest for this work to scrutinize change as a positive concept of something new, rather than as the negative one relating to the erosion of the past. Nonetheless, moving in a relative environment, the increased validity/legitimacy of something new always indicates the decreased validity/legitimacy of the (corresponding) old. All the positive in engaging with a new alternative, comes inevitably at the costs of disengagement from the existing. In that respect, each investigation of institutionalization also indicates the degree of de-institutionalization of the preceding institution.

Building upon the basic categories of institutionalization by Tolbert and Zucker (1996), a deviant practice needs to pass chronologically three stages until it finally becomes an appropriate part of institutional life. Over time, according to the increasing degree of institutionalization, the percentage of adoption of an institution among the institutional inhabitants increases constantly.

The first stage of institutionalization, as introduced by Tolbert and Zucker (1996) is called "pre-institutional." In this stage, new practices are introduced as innovations when responding to organizational problems. In this stage, knowledge about the practice is very limited and only a few adopters conduct the newly introduced practice. New practices are not yet permanent. Lawrence et al. (2002) refer to such new practices that are both weakly embedded and narrowly diffused as proto-institutions. Accordingly, proto-institutions "are institutions in the making: they have the potential to become full-fledged institutions if social processes develop that entrench them and they are diffused throughout an institutional field (Lawrence et al., 2002, p. 283). In the second stage that is called "semi-institutional," a new practice has a brief history, but is fairly diffused, added value is understood, and the practice gained a certain degree of normative acceptance among decision makers (Kostova & Roth, 2002). According to Tolbert and Zucker (1996, p. 179), the practice's "dissemination in other organizations of the same field" is important and mostly depends on the "leaders (defenders of change)" that aim at the establishment of cognitive and normative legitimacy. In the final stage of institutionalization, a practice is fully institutionalized and has "become taken for granted by members of a social group as efficacious and necessary" (Tolbert & Zucker, 1996). Institutions are equipped with self-activating mechanisms that can be understood as a firm set of rewards and sanctions that accompany usage and contestation of fully institutionalized practices (Lawrence et al., 2002).

It is this process along the stages of institutionalization—the trajectory of the new alternative in comparison to the old one—that depicts change. In the following chapters, it is the actors (MNCs) that may impact directly on these trajectories and, hence, change institutions.

4.4.2 Day-to-Day Operations: Reversing Isomorphism

Relating to practice-driven institutional change, based on institutional contradictions, the specific enactment of day-to-day operations indicates that it may be defective[7] and re-interpretive actions that may undermine some institutions and strengthen others gradually over time (Hall & Thelen, 2009; Mahoney & Thelen, 2010; Powell & Colyvas, 2008). Hall and Thelen emphasize the importance of a more subtle type of bottom-up change from within as a result of "defection" and "re-interpretation" (2009, p. 18). According to Hall and Thelen (2009, p. 18), defection and reinterpretation are the main mechanisms that may lead to shifts of existing processes and practices in a "...piecemeal fashion from below." One may perceive such incremental changes as a kind of "layering" that—translated to MNCs—signifies that deviant behavior of subsidiaries may indicate new, alternative practices *vis-à-vis* the existing one and, thus, also shows local actors different ways to pursue their strategies (Streeck & Thelen, 2005). In the same vein, Smets et al. (2012) observe institutional contradiction causing a chain of everyday mechanics without "dramatic" events that lead to both formal and informal institutional change one while "getting the jobs done." However, most importantly for now, due to the situation of institutional duality, it may be the foreign subsidiary of a MNC that deviates from the local ones and, thus, defects and re-interprets host country institutions.

Incorporating the conduct of alien-to-the-system practices and its impact on the local environment, Kwok and Tadesse (2006) and Mitchell (2010) propose that actors themselves are capable of exerting pressure on the organizational field; in this work's case: subsidiaries on the host country environment. Kwok and Tadesse more or less rely on institutionalization, which DiMaggio and Powell (1983, p. 148) labeled "...the process of institutional definition...". Carving the reciprocal duality of structure and agency, the concept of a mutually constitutive relation has been introduced in detail throughout the previous chapters. Here, even though Kwok and Tadesse remain on a macro level—using aggregate indices during their empirical study—they theorize on the potential impact of behavior on institutions, using a Giddensian structurationist view, by reversing causality of "traditional analyses." Including various actors and structures into analysis, they investigate corruption by scrutinizing how far "... the presence of MNCs could shape the institutional environment of corruption" (2006, p. 768). Kwok and Tadesse, building upon DiMaggio and Powell's isomorphic pressures elaborate on three mechanisms through which subsidiaries can exert force on and may shape their corresponding surrounding.

These are, first, regulatory pressure effects corresponding to coercive isomorphism. Second, demonstration effect, corresponding to mimetic isomorphism and, third, professionalization effect corresponding to normative isomorphism. Among

[7]Defection stems from game theory and describes strategies that deviate from a certain mode of cooperation. Defection may be followed by institutional displacement and institutional conversion.

others, Kim and Park (2008) emphasize the privileged position of foreign subsidiaries of a MNC as an agent of change referring to their strong presence and high visibility to domestic firms, government, and the public in general; after all, the necessary requirements is the actor's "...active participation in a practice itself" (Smets et al., 2012, p. 895).

Regarding regulatory pressure effects, Kwok and Tadesse (2006), using corruption as example, describe the situation in which corruption is part of the "...business as usual" between managers and government officials in the host country (2006, p. 769) and, thus, depicts an appropriate practice. However, within the HQ's home country, corrupt practices are not appropriate. Since subsidiaries also reach out for legitimacy within this intra-organizational field, subsidiaries will not conduct corruptive action abroad. Furthermore, subsidiary behavior may be directly informed by regulatory pressure from the home government. Remaining in the corruption example, the US Foreign Corrupt Practices Act does not allow US firms to give anything expecting a business advantage. Hence, for government officials and regulatory bodies in general, doing business with foreign subsidiaries of MNCs, is not business as usual and affects (puts pressure on) their behavior. Government officials interacting with MNCs have to either think creatively about bribing and not being caught, or just stop it. Either practice is certainly restrained *vis-à-vis* and, therefore different from the usual practice.

Beyond Kwok and Tadesse' concept of a subsidiary's impact on the host country's regulatory bodies, the subsidiary itself may act like a quasi-regulator exerting coercive pressure on dependent firms within the host country. As a prominent example, a firm promises a certain standard of the final product to its end customers. As a matter of fact, there is hardly any firm out there that has vertically integrated all stages of the value chain. On average, firms buy a high two-digit percentage of components from other companies rather than make it themselves. To guarantee the final product's fulfillment of the promised standards (no matter if that standard is one of quality, safety, technology, environmental impact, or one of human rights), the responsible firms need to ensure that the entire value chain complies. Hence, if the foreign subsidiary is responsible for local suppliers' compliance, practices that are crucial for the attainment of a standard are coerced upon all the firms that want to participate in the specific product's value chain. In short, in such a case, local firms that interact with the subsidiary either adopt the required practices or do not participate at all.

In general, the basic idea of the demonstration effect is that local firms model themselves after the foreign subsidiaries by altering their practices incrementally. Elaborating the demonstration effect, Kwok and Tadesse (2006) build upon mimetic pressure under conditions of uncertainty and extent it with literature on productivity and technological spillover effects and therewith apply it to practices. This effect heavily builds on the relational aspect of organizational fields, inasmuch as it is the joint action that serves as a medium to show local actors new practices that may deviate from the one they find appropriate. There are several venues that serve to exert pressure: first, increased competition may urge local firms to adopt certain practices that are perceived/deemed to be more efficient. Second, local firms may observe new practices and learn how things can be done differently. More than other forms of actor-induced pressure, the demonstration effect's strength heavily depends on the characteristics of actors, fields, and the action in play (see Sect. 4.5).

Regarding professionalization, Kwok and Tadesse (2006) mostly remain in the by DiMaggio and Powell (1983) suggested areas of university experts' influence and of the growth of networks of organizations across which new practices and behavior may diffuse. Assuming young people aiming at a career at a foreign subsidiary of an MNC in combination with expected partly scientific skill requirements, Kwok and Tadesse recognize a simultaneous movement that is the spread of "Western" business schools, that is "...sophisticated management practices" (2006, p. 771) within host countries. As an example, according to Kwok and Tadesse, students learn from globally accepted textbooks that generally ban corrupt practices from business, making corruptive behavior within the corresponding profession inappropriate. Reinforcing the strength of credentialing and education, ambitious young people ate inclined to internalize the new alleged more efficient models also to increase their chances to be recruited by an MNC. The MNC—not only by means of attracting certain skills and behaviors, but understood as an educational institution itself—may train employees and socialize young people within an environment of "...professional business values" (2006, p. 771). Returning to the example of corruptive behavior, such educated people are supposed to be more critical toward the (corrupt) status quo of practice patterns and, later, move to other firms implementing new anti-corruption practices and again teach other employees and, thus, spreading the new practices learned from the subsidiary.

Furthermore, of great importance to this study but mostly neglected by Kwok and Tadesse (2006), the company may act as a driving force of professionalization (though mostly unintentionally) itself, through a constitutive role in the various venues of normative pressure. Such an active role within the definition of occupational characteristics and appropriate ways in which to act is strongly supported by the notion of an MNC as a potential role model. MNCs are mostly perceived as being generally superior inasmuch as they are seen as advanced, experienced, and highly rationalized—and serve as corporate role models and, of equal importance, as representatives of the successful home countries (Kim & Park, 2008).

Regarding the concept of "complementarity" isomorphism introduced above in, first, holds up and, second is of specific interest within the context of foreign subsidiaries of MNCs in strange settings. Building upon the basic idea of complementarity and the application to the different capitalist systems, a newly implemented practice from another system most likely will have difficulties to proper functioning without the existence of institutions that support it. Translated for the study at hand, when a specific strange practice or behavior shown by an MNC may be perceived as more legitimate than the one existent in the home system, any form of institutionalization of such strange practice may have rigid limitations when implemented without the necessary complementary institutions. On that account, any form of institutionalized practice may be amplified by the "bandwagon in effect" introduced above. Consequently, a properly newly institutionalized practice in an originally strange system makes the entire system more homogeneous with the practice's system of origin insofar as complementary institutions are required.

In the longer term, based on the new practices, the *modus operandi* within a field (field logic), including the new practices brought in by aliens to the system, may develop a momentum of its own when institutional inhabitants develop a shared cognitive frame and a sense of what is appropriate, which again are more widely applied (Hall & Taylor, 1996). Accordingly, newly implemented practices can find further acceptance, by becoming legitimate and appropriate, even without the MNC as an exclusive driver of change. On that account, institutionalization of new models can be self-enforcing and may happen through either the realization of more favorable results when relying on the new practices in comparison to the old ones, or through an increase in trust that the counterpart will also comply with the new practices. The former can be understood, in line with March and Olsen (2009), as new experiences that over time either become institutionalized or eliminated through a competition of practices. In general, practice competition as introduced by March and Olsen (2009) can be understood as "Rule-driven behavior associated with successes or survival is likely to be repeated. Rules associated with failures are not." The latter, simultaneously, comes along with the diminishing trust in others' compliance with the old practices; that is de-institutionalization (Praça, 2009; Levi, 1990).

Similar to DiMaggio and Powell's (1983) notion of blurred lines between the categories of isomorphic pressures, the same counts for the reverse approach applied by Mitchell (2010) and Kwok and Tadesse (2006). Whereas there are "relatively" clear lines analytically, things become vaguer empirically. In that respect, Mitchell (2010, p. 386) argues that the three mechanisms may be difficult to distinguish since they are highly interdependent "...reinforce each other and manifest themselves in an ongoing and evolving dynamic system." Nonetheless, reversing traditional analyses insofar as the actor is granted agency to exert influence on other actors, allows the grasping of the "subtle" venues for institutional change. Despite not acting on behalf of a specific "political purpose," everyday action of firms that includes "conflictual" practices may cause change; theoretically ranging from minor adjustments up to entire shifts of organizational fields. Furthermore, a certain degree of vagueness comes into play, when discussing the difference between the "subtler" coercive type of actor-induced change and the one of institutional entrepreneurship. Certainly, theoretically relatively clearly distinguishable by means of consciousness and target orientation, empirically things seem to overlap every now and then.

4.4.3 Institutional Entrepreneurship[8]

Already DiMaggio (1988, p. 14) recognized that it may be actors that, first, see in new institutions that do not correspond to the *status quo* "...an opportunity to realize interests that they value highly" and, second, come up with sufficient resources to

[8] A similar account of the purposeful actor is offered by the concept of "institutional work" by Lawrence et al. (2011).

create new and/or change existing institutions. In an Oliverian tradition (Oliver, 1991) who premiered the concept of actors' "strategic responses" to the institutions in force, scholars of institutional entrepreneurship (Leca et al., 2009; Kostova et al., 2008; Ferner et al., 2005, 2011; Crouch et al., 2009; Smets & Reihlen, 2012), bringing in a further venue of actor-induced institutional change see, indeed, institutional contradiction as the necessary, though not sufficient, condition for institutional change. Within this institutional strand, conflict may be better understood as a source of diversity that broadens behavioral options (practice portfolio) for actors; however, one still needs to put them into practice. Similarly, Morgan and Kristensen (2006, p. 1472) express the increased portfolio in combination with a notion of Streeckian institutional enablers that in "contexts of 'dual institutional' pressures, the range of manoeuvre for actors is increased as they can draw on various institutional resources from the home and host context." Crouch et al. (2009) emphasize a Schumpeterian form of innovation labeled "creative incoherence," since actors as institutional entrepreneurs at the interface of different institutional settings (Crouch et al. remain within a nation, through elaborating on local differences within that nation) can combine existing—maybe even incompatible—practices in an unprecedented way and, thus, provide institutional innovation.

Practice Portfolio:

Certainly, one could argue that a purposeful and powerful actor may come up with the capability to also take other institutional logics into consideration that do not originate within the organizational fields in which it moves, maybe even inventing new ones. Following this line of thought, institutional duality would turn into a general notion of institutional (indefinite) plurality, which would turn the entire idea of institutional analysis into a questionable endeavor. However, there is relatively large consensus that potential institutional change agents find alternatives within their own portfolio of "proven" practices; at least these practices have shown to work well in a specific constellation of space and time (Seo & Creed, 2002; Morgan & Kristensen, 2006; Heidenreich, 2012). Along the same lines, an entirely new alternative would also evoke severe problems when approaching mobilization and collective action, since introducing, convincing, and reaching a consensus with other actors who are entirely unfamiliar with the alternative would be both extremely difficult and costly. On that account, Seo and Creed (2002, p. 236) reaffirm actors' reliance on the practice portfolio emerging from within the organizational fields in force by stating that:

> ...agents are likely to adopt a frame[9] or set of frames available in the broader, heterogeneous institutional context-a frame that is sufficiently incompatible with

(continued)

[9] A frame, according to, for example, Boxenbaum (2006), is an interpretative lens that people use to understand the world and events that happen within this world. They are built based on experience and guide actors' action.

the existing institutional arrangements to generate a fundamental departure from the past while also sufficiently resonant with some existing societal systems of belief to mobilize substantial support and resources from other participants.

Facing the situation of institutional duality, a practice portfolio may best be seen as compound of both home and host country practices. On that account, regarding the difference between home and host country environment, a practice portfolio can be characterized as either heterogeneous or homogeneous. Actors that find themselves in a state of institutional duality characterized by extreme differences between home and host countries have a wider more heterogeneous portfolio including very different and contradictive practices.

A basic understanding of institutional entrepreneurship may be best put in words by Philips and Tracey (2009, p. 170) and shows "...how actors can attain their goals by intentionally constructing and/or altering the institutional structures in which they are embedded." On that account, Garud et al. (2007, p. 962) describe the entrepreneurs' task as to "...break with existing rules and practices associated with the dominant institutional logic(s) and institutionalize the alternative rules, practices or logics they are championing." Similarly, Lawernce (1999, p. 168) describes institutional entrepreneurship as "...patterns of organizational action concerned with the formation and transformation of institutions, fields, and the rules and standards that control those structure." Digging deeper into the conditions of institutional entrepreneurship, following Seo and Creed (2002), institutional change is further mediated by a purposeful account of social action depicted by the concept of "human praxis." Human praxis, understood as a type of agency, is depicted as "...political action embedded in a historical system of interconnected yet incompatible institutional arrangements" (2002, p. 223). It mediates between institutional contradictions and change and is shaped by reflection and active target-oriented action and generally follows three steps (Geppert & Dörrenbacher, 2011; Seo & Creed, 2002).

First, the actor needs to understand the situation. That includes both the cognition of which institutions do not work according to their own interests and the search for adequate alternatives[10]; in general this "reflective" step is termed "actor's self-awareness." This reflective notion of praxis requires a shift away from the actor understood as a rather passive "playball" between the institutional pressures toward the "partially autonomous actor situated in a contradictory social world" (2002, p. 230). This actor is capable of reflecting about situative drawbacks and to consciously, skillfully and artfully exploit institutional contradictions in order to "...infuse new beliefs, norms, and values into social structures" (Rao et al., 2000, p. 240) that are in line with own expectations and interests. To cope with this active

[10]Noteworthy, Jackson and Deeg (2008) state that within this step, actors do not always know a priori about what fits best. Hence, according to Jackson and Deeg, actors continuously experiment with new combinations of institutions.

notion of actors, building upon Meyer and Rowan's (1977) notion of pluralist institutions within the wider society, Whittington (1992) grants actors transformative agency that includes the capacity to purposefully exploit institutional contradictions that originate from divergent structural principles. Similar to the concept of the "partially autonomous actor" (Seo & Creed, 2002), Kostova et al. (2008) introduce the MNC as a reflective and pro-active actor with an important agency role. Their position in between different and incompatible institutional pressures make them to—building upon the available portfolio of practices—"...manipulate, negotiate, and partially construct their institutional environments" (Kostova et al., 2008, p. 1001). Hence, MNCs are granted a purposeful role in building their own architecture of institutions in force and, consequentially, decide—to a certain degree—themselves the degree of compliance to the distinct institutional pressures. Kostova et al. (2008), as an example, recognize the situation in which subsidiary managers use the inherent institutional complexity to play, in this case, the parent company and the host country, to attain for themselves the most beneficial institutional situation. In conjunction with the idea of institutional entrepreneurship, within the range of the two institutional settings, MNCs may reflectively choose the practices—to a certain degree—that fit best with their interests, that may compensate for systemic weaknesses (Crouch et al., 2005), that may seem to produce legitimacy, that makes interaction more efficient, or that puts the actor into a position to develop specific capacities. However, certainly, practices that are entirely inappropriate in one institutional setting—which are accompanied by an enormous loss of legitimacy—are not within the potential portfolio of practices, especially not when the subsidiary aims above all at gaining legitimacy.

Second, a phase of "mobilization" is required to "spread the word" to other institutional inhabitants that may face the same situation. This intermediate step aims at producing a joint understanding of the situation and, then, mobilizing both resources and commitment of other actors in order to jointly reconstruct the negatively perceived social arrangement finally aiming at challenging the given structures and endorsing and enacting the proposed alternative social arrangements. The institutional entrepreneur, therefore, applies "framing strategically" that involves clearly expressing its idea of desired change, defining drawbacks, diagnosing causes, assigning the blame, and providing alternative solutions; all that is needed to give other actors and groups reason to cooperate (Garud et al., 2007). Furthermore, in line with the note on practice portfolio above, it is one of the crucial challenges for change agents to embed their idea of change within frames that are already available within the wider society and that are most likely to successfully mobilize collective action (Seo & Creed, 2002). Through such framing, the entrepreneur's own idea can be justified and may become appropriate which again is helpful to mobilize a wider range of coalition that is necessary to generate the collective action to back the institutional change (Garud et al., 2007).

As indicated, the efforts at mobilization are crucial with regard to success and failure of the third step, that is "collective action." Only if frames, interests, and logics of action of a "significant number" of institutional inhabitants have been realigned successfully, a group of institutional entrepreneurs act collectively to change specificities of the institutional setting. Collective action aiming at the replacement of a certain rule or behavior certainly is not a straight-forward process and may again be mediated by, among others, the resistance of an opposition, varying degrees of institutional stability, and the process of intense negotiation and contestation over the proposed alternatives to the existing practices. White (1992) labeled the political struggle over the primacy of specific practices as "institutional war" in which existing frames and perceptions are aligned, misaligned, and realigned. Broadly put, such a struggle may find its end in either a failure to change the institutional status quo or in the successful reconstruction of (parts of) the social arrangements.

Similar to the three steps indicated by Seo and Creed, Rao et al. (2000) refer to institutional entrepreneurs as primarily identifying opportunities, reframing issues, and mobilizing constitutive actors. Certainly, neither Seo and Creed's nor Rao et al.'s steps above can be understood as comprehensive. A theoretical account of institutional entrepreneurship cannot grasp all potential situations in real life. Processes in each of the steps vary significantly with the specific composition of the indefinite number of different situations, which are made up of different actors, a variety of organizational fields, and a specific practice of interest. Following the indefinite number of different situations, a universal theory explaining how reflection generally turns into collective action does not exist. Nonetheless, Seo and Creed (2002) and Rao et al. (2000) aim at roughly introducing the theoretical idea of institutional entrepreneurship and provide—taken in conjunction with both scholars of institutional duality/multiplicity and, in general, literature from within the more active agency perspectives—a valuable venue for institutional change caused by alien-to-the-system practice.

4.4.4 Summary and Reflection

From day-to-day change to the purposeful entrepreneur, there can be seen a shift from a (rather) passive and unreflective to a reflective and (pro-)active actor. For both, the institutional contradiction is the starting point, though the actual mechanism of change varies significantly. In both cases, the practice portfolio of the actors facing institutional duality is larger than the one of the local ones. However, whereas the day-to-day change may be induced by the very existence of institutional conflict, entrepreneurship is characterized by institutional choice. Hence, rather than a "play ball" within the tension field of home and host country that exerts isomorphic pressure on the organizational field, the subsidiary understood as a purposeful and partially autonomous actor, first, uses the multiple embeddedness as a source of alternative institutional logics and, second, aims at making the individually most suitable practice also appropriate on the field level. However, whether rather passive or active, new practices are rarely transmitted intact and without problems. Both forms of actor-induced change are not straightforward and the outcome, understood as the degree of institutionalization, of both isomorphic pressure and political action

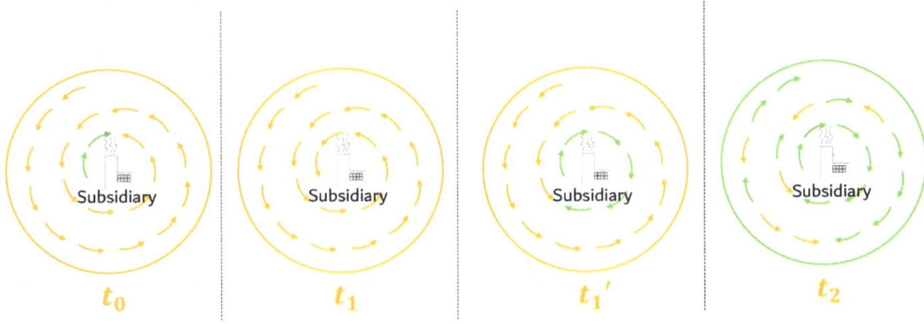

Fig. 4.4 Institutional dynamics over time. Source: From the author

is contingent on several conditions. Whether institutional contradiction, embodied by deviant corporate practices, indeed depicts alternative institutional logics and becomes appropriate within a field, certainly depends on the actor itself, the quality and appropriateness of the practice, and the strengths and stability of the fields in play. On that account, the next section further elaborates on the ‘condition triangle that indicates certain factors that may impact the process of institutional change.

Figure 4.4 indicates the field of the host country at four analytical points in time t0, t1, respectively, t1’, and t2. T0 indicates the initial point in time at the pre-institutional stage in which the subsidiary first imports alien-to-the-system practices; these are depicted by the red counterclockwise arrows, which are a misfit to the local field. As discussed throughout the present chapter, these subsidiaries act as institutional change agents, either as a subtler type, as an institutional entrepreneur, or as both at once. Both t1 and t1’ indicate alternative situations at the same point in time that take place after t0. Within this time period, subsidiaries worked on the institutions either through isomorphic pressure or political action. Nonetheless, institutional contradiction and induced change can develop differently and either dissolve or impact the field on a larger level. T1 indicates that subsidiaries’ imported practices do not impact the host country field at a noteworthy level. Hence, despite institutional contradiction and contestation, the new practice does not impact the field. T1’, however, shows a different situation in which institutional contradiction induced by the subsidiaries works on the field and institutions change. The new practice is now more appropriate and used by an increasing number of institutional inhabitants. T1’ depicts the situation of semi-institutionalization. T2 indicates a field-level change and depicts the stage of full institutionalization. In this case, the new practices have gained the status of full appropriateness within the once strange institutional setting.

Hence, one can see that the same efforts of change may lead to different outcomes in both degree of impact and speed—as a matter change per time between t0, t1’, and t2. Both institutional impact of new practices and speed of change—at ceteris paribus efforts of the subsidiaries as change agents—depend, just like the strength of the different organizational fields, on a triad of variables consisting of the actor properties, the field characteristics, and the quality of the practice itself. The subsequent elaborates on these sets of indicators.

4.5 Institutional Condition Triangle

Throughout the previous part, the concept of institutional duality and that of actor-induced institutional change have been introduced and further elaborated on to fit with this work's field of application. It is, thus, theoretically derived that, first, institutional contradiction can exist and, second, that subsequent deviant behavior may result in institutional change. Field strength and institutional change have been introduced as the corresponding indicators. Both concepts are of relative nature and inevitably become a matter of degree. Relating to field strength, an actor facing two different institutional pressures simultaneously will most likely not conform entirely to one of them and will most likely behave in a hybrid-like manner. The degree of compliance, though, to either the one field or the other may vary and can be found somewhere within the range between total compliance with either one of the fields. The same applies to deviant action as a driver of institutional change. Institutional change may take different degrees—at assumed ceteris paribus behavioral patterns—that can be found on a range between no change at all and field-level change.

Field strength and the potential impact on the field expressed as change (actor or practice strength) indicate the mutually constitutive process of structuration. Change is always also a (inverse) matter of stability and institutional stability is most often also a sign of field strength; the factors that condition both strength and change are very similar and are relative to each other. Oversimplified, what benefits a field's strength most often comes at the costs of actors' ability to change the field and vice versa. Hence, in order to estimate both specifics of behavior and impact of deviant behavior on the field, one needs to take the condition triangle, which includes actor properties, the (organizational) field characteristics, and the practice (action) itself into account and weigh it relatively. The single factors of the condition triangle are interdependent, meaning that, for example, a specific action (newly introduced practice) most likely impacts idiosyncratically on different fields or may impact differently on the same field when conducted by different actors.

4.5.1 The Strength of Organizational Fields

An actor facing institutional duality attempts to conduct appropriate behavior—thereby attaining legitimacy—within both surrounding fields: the local institutional setting and the intra-organizational one. As indicated above by, among others, DiMaggio and Powell (1983), institutional inhabitants within a specific organizational field are pressured to act appropriately by mimetic, coercive, and normative pressures. The degree of conformity with one of the two fields—and, thus, the strengths of each pressure, though, depends on specific characteristics of the fields in play and the action itself.

Literature up to now provides a rather heterogenous picture on how actors—in this case, foreign subsidiaries of MNCs—behave according to either the home or the host country's environment. Rather than finding a middle ground, some scholars emphasize almost exclusively the MNC as determining subsidiaries' action (Cooke, 2008; Birkinshaw & Hood 1998) and others based in "traditional analyses" do not distinguish between local actors and foreign subsidiaries, thus, assuming complete embeddedness within the host country. Morgan and Kristensen (2006, p. 1467) introduce the two corresponding appearances of subsidiaries labeled as either "boy scout" subsidiaries that do what the upper hierarchy tells them and "subversive subsidiaries" that aim at deepening local connections. Whereas the former mostly refers exclusively to the home country effect, the latter does so with the host country effect. On this ground, the former pole is criticized for undermining the notion of economic interaction as a specific social relationship, detaching subsidiaries from their local surroundings, and overemphasizing globalization narratives. The latter, subject to an equal amount of critique, is criticized for its rootless conception of MNCs' subsidiaries and the neglect of the complex structure of multinational organizations. Even if variation in conformity is accepted, investigations mostly remain exclusively either within the home or host country effects (Brookes et al., 2017; Ferner et al., 2005, 2011; Ferraz, 2018; Fortanier, 2007; Geppert et al., 2006; Morgan & Kristensen, 2006).

However, since the strength of dissimilar fields is relative in nature—the more conformity an actor shows with field A implicitly indicates less conformity with field B—to estimate behavior, one needs to take both fields into account simultaneously. Following this line of reasoning, this work understands foreign subsidiaries neither as part of MNCs as "hierarchical monoliths" (Birkinshaw & Hood, 1998, p. 778) nor as "pipelines of HQ" (Fortanier, 2007), nor as entirely autonomous from its parent company. Even though theory up to now mostly shows an either-or attitude, there are various conceptualizations of field characteristics that serve to improve understanding of strength. On that account, the following sections will shed light on specifics of the organizational fields that indicate their distinct assertiveness on the actor's behavior, mostly in the context of embeddedness, stability, dependence, and resistance.

Local Organizational Field

The impact of the local organizational field on the actor varies with, first, the degree of structuration, second, the degree of actor's embeddedness, and, third, the economic performance of a field in a given area. First, structuration is decisive for accompanying issues of coherence, resilience/stability and a potential gap between *de jure* and de facto institutions. As Scott (2010) describes, the more structured a field, the more coherent the actions and relations within that field. Along with DiMaggio and Powell (1983), within a structured field, new entrants face an inexorable push to adjust behavior to local appropriateness, that is, to show coherence. Hence, new entrants may have a hard time—struggling for survival—in a structured field when relying on alien-to-the-system practices and, consequently, adopt the local appropriate ones. Following this line of thought, resilience of the original characteristics is more likely in a well-structured field; meaning that despite institutional contestation by challengers (such as new entrants), the field and its major characteristics remain relatively stable. Furthermore, if a field is structured well, a shared belief system should be widely accepted and diffused among the majority of institutional inhabitants. If that is not the case—when a field is fragmented and different expectations of what is right and what is wrong exist—there may be a certain kind of decoupling; a gap between expected and de facto institutions (Boxenbaum & Jonsson, 2017). Ostrom (2005) working on differences between local models of lawful behavior and illegal actions due to a lack of monitoring and genuine sanctioning, lays the foundation for a wider understanding of a potential gap between expectation and reality. Whereas Ostrom remains within the area of laws and, thus, regulatory pressures (gap between *de jure* and de facto), one can reasonably expand the idea of gaps to normative rules and prescriptions for behavior. Just like an actor that cheats when not facing potential legal penalties, it is easier for an entrant to show new (inappropriate) practices when a field is relatively unstructured and fragmented, and therefore when society does not punish inappropriate behavior. Even though the level of structuration informs the matters of coherence, stability, and potential gap between expectation and reality, measuring structuration directly is at best a vague endeavor. As such, reversing causality, one may best approach the level of structuration by investigating coherence, resilience, and the gap directly and then deducing to overall structuration.

Translating structuration into the language of VoC, according to Hall and Soskice (2001) a field may be labeled as structured only when having achieved the status of being either coordinated or liberal. However, relating to the work of others on, for example, HMEs, DMEs, or NMEs, they argue that the concept of CME and LME is not comprehensive and that other types of market economies can depict final states of institutional development, too. Consequently, in order to estimate the degree of structuration of single market economies, one may best approach it by scrutinizing the matters of coherence stability, and assertiveness of expectations. Beyond structuration, within the conceptualization of VoC, one needs to expand the understanding of stability, especially, by the concept of institutional complementarities. Even though complementarity depicts a systemic rather than a societal phenomenon, it certainly impacts the stability and, thus, the strength of the local organizational field.

Furthermore, at the interface between local institutional conditions and the actor itself, embeddedness plays a major role when referring to a field's normative assertiveness on the actors in reach (Kostova & Roth, 2002; Mattes, 2013). Embeddedness can be seen from two perspectives, one based on relational aspects with others, and one as a matter of penetration of local beliefs of the actor (for example, a firm) itself. According to both perspectives, a higher degree of embeddedness comes with a stronger impact of the respective field. However, also in both perspectives, within the context of foreign subsidiaries, the strength of the local field has a certain threshold and, most likely, will never attain a status of entirely determining the subsidiaries' actions. First, relating to relational aspects, reasoning by extremes, assuming an actor that is physically present but not at all coupled with the local institutions (not embedded) is, indeed, a rather theoretical consideration but an interesting one. An actor that has no relation with others is not dependent on the opinion of others and is more likely to show deviant behavior (Mitchell, 2010; Oliver, 1991). Without local interaction, isomorphic pressures hardly work on the actor as, from a societal perspective, one can hardly behave inappropriately and if it happens anyway, societal penalties have no impact on the alien actor, since its success and survival does not depend on others. Even more drastic, penalties would most likely not occur at all, since no one would notice inappropriate behavior in the first place. In reality, within the context of foreign subsidiaries, the actors that most resemble the theoretical consideration on the decoupled actor above, maybe so-called *maquiladoras*. *Maquiladoras* are foreign-owned, low-value adding assembly facilities in Latin America that, generally speaking, import components, assemble them by exploiting abundant low-cost labor, and export them as intermediate goods or finished products mostly back to the firms' HQ. Hence, apart from hiring low-cost workers locally, the *maquiladora* hardly interacts with any other local actors such as suppliers, customers, competitors, financial firms, and educational institutes. In such isolated islands, not only are societal effects of the host country led *ad absurdum*, but also the effect of complementary institutions is neither needed nor does its absence affect such a decoupled actor. In general terms, a *maquiladora* is independent of its direct societal surrounding. In summary, the logic behind the rather extreme case of the more or less decoupled actor holds up vice versa as well and the degree of embeddedness, in general, is positively related to the strength of the respective field. Nonetheless, as long as ownership and control remain MNC-like centered at the parent company, one may reasonably assume that complete local embeddedness is not possible.

Second, an actor—in this case a firm—may itself be infiltrated by its surroundings and, thus, by its local belief system. Most obvious and previously used by various scholars (Kostova & Roth, 2002; Mattes, 2013), recognizing the importance of people within firms as potential institutional carriers, "…institutional elements enter organizations through the people working in them" (Kostova & Roth, 2002, p. 218). In particular, local employees that take decisive positions along the corporate decision-making process inevitably bring in their local belief system when deciding about organizational forms and practices. On that account, organizational practices and forms also mirror the institutional setting in which the employees' belief systems have been built. One step further, the more employees that are hired locally—or more detailed, the higher the ratio of local employees to entire workforce—the more people participate in decision-making that take a stand relying on the local belief system. In conclusion, the more infiltrated a subsidiary by local employees, the higher the impact of the local organizational field. However, within the organizational structure of an MNC, even with an infusion of local beliefs—and even with a local employee to entire workforce ratio of 100 percent—a subsidiary cannot be assumed to be independent of the parent company when deciding about organizational forms and practices.

Third, relating to performance, first of all, poor performance perceived as systemic weakness, opens windows for MNCs to rely on alien-to-the-system firm-level practices of MNCs as an attempt to compensate for local dysfunctions (Crouch et al., 2005). Furthermore, among others, Ferner et al. (2011) emphasize the relationship between the international institutional spaces insofar as the business systems that are extraordinarily successful (in a specific area or in general) may be dominant. Dominance effects are exerted by organizational fields that are perceived as the area of "best practice" for a specific activity through representative actors such as firms. Such effects facilitate both the stability within a field of best practice *vis-à-vis* entrants from "inferior" fields and the import of best practice from a dominant business system to an inferior one. In general, best practices have a greater influence by virtue of their success and the inherent presumption of superior efficacy and general supremacy. Furthermore, best practices (practices stemming from well-functioning dominant countries) are generally recognized as such and, thus, increase the host country's actors' receptiveness to transfer (Ferner et al., 2011). The status of "dominance," though, is dynamic and changes over space and time. Looking deeper into the economic history of the past 50 years, one can generally see changing national business systems as being dominant over others. Observing the past decades, one can see a primacy of the highly productive *Wirtschaftswunder* Germany throughout the 1960s, superseded by the highly efficient Japanese economy in the 1980s ending in Japan's "Lost Decade," followed by a more or less unquestioned hegemonic position of the USA in the aftermath of the fall of the Iron Curtain, a victory march of free markets policies and financial capitalism climaxing in the financial crisis of 2007–2008.

Besides the level of the nation-state as the base for dominance, one may also approach the issue on a more fine-grained level. Building upon a general understanding of "comparative advantage" (in this case understood in Smithonian absolute terms) one can reasonably argue that some countries conduct some practices better than others.

Hence, following this line of thought, to best recognize dominance one may break national economies down functionally by, for example, sectors (Crouch et al., 2009). As such, just as put forth by, for example, Hall and Soskice (2001), a nation offers fertile ground for specific sectors that again rely on specific action. Thus, one may state that, for example, the IT and financial service sectors in the USA, which is to say the actors from the USA in that sector, can be seen as dominant. Similarly, remaining within the spectrum of VoC, Germany and the firms originating from within may be perceived as being dominant in, for example, engineering and the automotive sector in general. In conclusion, if a host country (or specific sector within) itself is dominant, an import of an "inferior" practice is rather unlikely. In such a case, the organizational field of the host country is deemed to be relatively strong. The same holds up vice versa: the host country's field may be rather weak when the underlying economic system is perceived as inferior.

In conclusion, Morgan and Kristensen (2006) further state that practice transfer may be more feasible when international subsidiaries are in weak—referring to a lower degree of structuration, lower level of embeddedness, and lower performativity—institutional contexts, "...allowing the MNC to reproduce its home model" (2006, p. 1471).

Intra-organizational Field (Actor)
Generally, all organizational fields work similarly. Just like the local field, that of the MNC is a terrain of relationships and certain beliefs. A foreign subsidiary is confronted with pressures from within the MNC to conform to organization based practices and structures (Kostova & Roth, 2002). Just like above, field strength is understood as the degree of an agent's determination. Following the logic of the section above, the penetrative power of the home institutions is higher if the parent company commands "dominance" either by virtue of its home country or the specific sector. Since dominance most likely includes measures of institutional coherence, one may suggest that the more structured the CoO, the more likely there is to be a degree of dominance relating to the home country. Furthermore, analogue to the rationale of ratio of local workers in the workforce, people that most likely carry their institutional baggage from the home country to the foreign subsidiary are expatriates sent from the HQ working within the subsidiary. On that account, the number of expatriates within the local workforce likewise informs the degree of institutional penetration through CoO workers. Nonetheless, the intra-organizational field technically deviates from the local one, since there is a clearly recognizable principal called HQ within the MNC that entirely owns and controls the foreign agents (subsidiaries). In that regard, the specific relationship between the HQ and the foreign subsidiary is of utmost importance and matters of structuration, performance, and embeddedness need to be approached slightly differently. This relationship and the pressures within this intra-organizational field are shaped by, first, the MNC's overall organization and strategy and, second, the relation between the HQ and the subsidiary.

Along these lines, some scholars, such as Ferner et al. (2011) make the case for a general authoritative HQ as a centralized regulative body. For a more fine-tuned understanding, some decisions relating to corporate organization and international strategy may impact the subsidiary's degree of autonomy and, thus, clearly inform the strength of the intra-organizational field. Most importantly and widely discussed in Sect. 3.1, an MNC has various ways of entering foreign markets. The specific market entry mode chosen strongly informs both control and ownership (Fortanier, 2007). As derived through the application of the Uppsala model, WOS built through greenfield investments is the only mode in which full ownership and, thus, control remains with the parent company. Hence, talking about entry strategies, the one chosen is deemed to be the one where the HQ has the purest and highest regulative impact. From that viewpoint, the intra-organizational field may be strongest for WOS established through greenfield investments *vis-à-vis* other entry modes. Further following the concept of Hymer's liability of foreignness (Hymer, 1976; Johanson & Vahlne, 2009; Kogut, 2001), one can reasonably expect a relatively strong account of firm-specific advantages originating within the parent company that is applied abroad to offset the costs of foreignness. On that account, to put it in Kogut's words (2001, p. 10197), the intra-organizational field may be expected to be relatively strong, since the MNC as an international organization can be seen as "…the mechanism by which organizational practices are transferred and replicated...". In addition, reversing the concept of institutional distance between home and host country as a losing game for an intra-organizational field's power, the liability of foreignness can be used to make the opposite case. The more distant the host country, the higher the costs of foreignness. Logically, in order to offset these increasing costs, an MNC needs to use more of the firm-specific advantages stemming from the home country to continue to be competitive. Consequently, the more distant the host country may be, the stronger the penetration of home practices on which the original corporate success was built.

On the contrary, further interpreting the Uppsala model in the context of this work, considering the high degree of market knowledge that is needed for reasonably establishing a WOS abroad, one may suspect that MNCs should be aware of at least major local institutional peculiarities and therefore should not commit too many major errors that may end up in severe institutional clashes. On that account, one may argue that the intra-organizational field is somehow limited in order to not generate too many and too costly conflicts. However, making the case for a strong intra-organizational field, one could also argue that within the developing country context, MNCs may know about drawbacks and how to apply firm-specific advantages to compensate for certain local dysfunctions.

In summary, the nature of an MNC and WOS—in terms of control exerted, knowledge required, risk committed, and costs of foreignness caused—suggests a rather strong intra-organizational field and is, thus, in line with, for example, Levy (2008) who perceives HQ's position as a "field dominant" (Levy, 2008). Along the same lines, one may suggest a limited degree of a subsidiary's uncertainty and, consequently, a relatively low effect of the local organizational field's mimetic pressure exerted on the subsidiary. The strength of the intra-organizational field is built upon the pillars discussed above. It is suggested that a labelling of HQ as either authoritative or as rather laissez-faire is most likely limited when understanding the fine-grained characteristics of the intra-organizational field. Rather than putting emphasis on the political confrontation between the HQ and the subsidiary itself, the section on strength of the intra-organizational field indicated the conditions deemed to be crucial when approaching the transfer of business practices from the CoO to the local environment. The different indicators categorized around the organization and the specific subsidiary characteristics shed light on the permeability of practices and, thus, indicate the likelihood of HQ resemblance abroad and the potential overall strength of the intra-organizational field.

Action

Within the state of institutional duality, subsidiary resemblance of either the home or the host country institutional setting is further mediated by the action/practice itself. As indicated above, even though strengths of fields vary and certain situations favor one or the other, a state in which isomorphic pressures from one of the governance modes are entirely switched off is not realistic. Consequently, in order not to entirely lose legitimacy in one of the institutional settings, there may be lines of inappropriateness for each field that should not be crossed when introducing alien-to-the-system practices. A practice that is, indeed, appropriate in one of the fields and is, according to the corresponding field's strength, transferred to the other field, but entirely breaches the minimum requirements of compliance with the corresponding local normative or/and regulatory frames is beyond scope. An illustrative example may be corruption that is part of the appropriate practice portfolio within the home country but not at all in the host country. A HQ as a driving force for subsidiaries' practice adoption will most likely either be unsuccessful because of the subsidiary's resistance or will bear the costs of subsidiary failure. Hence, in such a case of extremes in which a practice strongly breaches legal and/or normative frames is most likely not a matter of degree but of absoluteness. Certainly, a mature field characterized by conformity and clearly shared belief systems and, thus, a high level of structuration makes the occurrence of a clear "line of appropriateness" more likely to occur and makes large-scale resistance to entirely inappropriate practices more probable. From extremes to degrees, one may state that the more inappropriate a specific behavior as may be perceived in the host country, the less likely is the transfer. On that account, similarly to Kostova and Zaheer's (1999) concept of institutional distance, emphasizing societal effects, one may argue that the higher the difference between the different institutional settings, the higher the probability of legitimacy struggles and the occurrence of "lines of appropriateness" and therefore the transfer of practices is less likely.

A further characteristic of practice is the degree to which it is dependent on either home or host country institutional peculiarities. Following a system-oriented VoC fashion, a certain kind of action is conducted specifically because of the surrounding institutions that either enable or restrict the actor in a distinct way. If a company sets up foreign subsidiaries abroad to use such specific advantages of a given host country institutional setting—that is, institutional arbitrage (Hall & Soskice, 2001)—a large-scale transfer of home practices would be a rather futile endeavor. Importing practices from home to a host country, despite the attempt of institutional arbitrage, would undermine the institutional advantages of the host county and would simultaneously lead the corporate strategic decision to move abroad *ad absurdum*. The other way around, also in line with the firm-specific advantages discussed above, if a company that developed its specific structure and, above all, practices according to the conducive CoO context aims at conducting the same action abroad, it may tend to also copy practices and structures that have been proved to be successful in the CoO. Following this line of thought and of special importance for this work, Hall and Soskice (2001, p. 57) in one of the very few notes on other than OECD countries, indicate that apart from LMEs it is also institutionally relatively weak developing countries that are supposed to not provide the institutional infrastructure needed to conduct CME practices but mostly provide market structures sufficiently equipped to implement liberal policies. Hence, following Hall & Soskice one may suppose that specific action from a CoO that builds upon liberal coordination may find easier access to the host country.

One may approach this topic through the concept of "asset specificity" as already discussed in the chapter on VoC. To recall briefly, the most basic idea of specificity is that specific assets cannot easily (or not at all) be used for another purpose. The more specific an asset may be the less transferable it is. Accordingly, someone who invests in specific assets runs the risk of losses when the planned purpose fails to materialize; either due to market conditions or by opportunism of others. On that account, from VoC's interaction perspective, an actor that contributes relatively specific assets is highly dependent on the successful completion of the interaction and therefore also on the cooperation of others (Busemeyer, 2009). As a response to potential losses resulting from investments in specific assets, the actor in danger needs to assure future returns on the investment and needs to protect themselves against possible future loss of income (Iversen & Soskice, 2001). As Chap. 3 indicated, CME's institutional setting manages to secure investments in specific assets and allows long-term cooperation and enables investment in specific assets. LMEs, on the other hand, support investments in more universal and switchable assets that fit well with interaction based on arm's-length exchange. If, for example, a firm from a CME—that uses the CoO inherent institutional advantages; assume a firm that innovates incrementally, based on long-term relationships—moves to an LME while still carrying out the action that is induced by their CoO environment may be struggling, as LMEs do not offer the necessary insurance needed for the CME-like action. On that account, if a practice is enabled by the home country but not (or to a significantly lesser degree) by the host one, a relatively strong reliance on home country practices seems to be expected. Regarding matters of specificity and the action conducted abroad, most roughly, Kuznetsov and Jacobs (2015) distinguish between foreign subsidiaries that produce and others that do not. Whereas the former is supposed to rely on firm-specific advantages (developed under the umbrella of CoO institutions), the latter aims at ensuring access to the local market and needs no specific local advantage to survive. In comparison to sales subsidiaries, accordingly, production subsidiaries abroad are supposed to exploit firm-specific advantages in foreign environments and, thus, tend to reproduce the wining practice known from operations within the CoO and, simultaneously, to be less receptive to host country institutions. Hence, one may conclude that a production subsidiary opens doors for a stronger intra-organizational field.

Contradiction Cube

Figure 4.5 presents the Contradiction Cube that, first, summarizes the discussion above and, second, indicates the expected behavior of a foreign subsidiary. Depending on characteristics of the actor (MNC), the local institutional field, and the specific action of interest, the Contradiction Cube suggests the strength of the intra-organizational field. This strength is translated into the likelihood that a home country practice finds its way to the foreign subsidiary. If such transmission occurs, the subsidiary is likely to conduct practices in the host country that are alien-to-the-system.

In this approach, the three factors are balanced inasmuch each one loads equally on the likelihood of a foreign practice appearing in the host country. Indicated by the array from rose to dark red, one can derive the strength of the intra-organizational field and, accordingly, the likelihood of transferring a practice into a strange system.

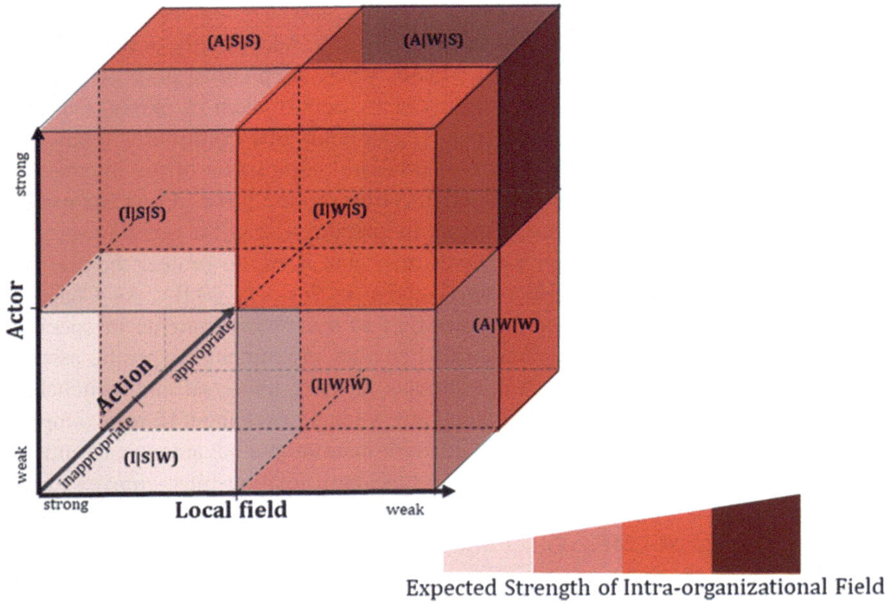

Fig. 4.5 Contradiction Cube. Source: From the author

The array ranges from very unlikely (rose) when the action is inappropriate, the local field strong, and the actor weak (i.e., inappropriate/strong/weak is ISW). At the other end of the array, dark red indicates an AWS that means that the action is perceived as appropriate, the local field is rather weak, and the actor strong.

4.5.2 Potential Impact of Actor-Induced Change

As indicated throughout this chapter, deviant behavior is the initial condition that precedes both day-to-day and the entrepreneurial mechanisms of change. Certainly, the degree of deviance also informs the form and strength of potential change; however, local receptiveness toward new practices further depends on various characteristics of the condition triad. Whereas the previous section discussed potential behavior as being prescribed either by home or host institutions, this section aims at dismantling the potential impact of deviant action on the local institutional setting. Whether a new practice may cause a change in the host country also depends on the degree of local changeability and receptiveness, which again is strongly connected to some characteristics of the condition triangle. Most characteristics that are decisive for the degree of impact on the local environment also have somehow to do with the characteristics that factor into strengths of the fields. In the following part of this work, ceteris paribus institutional contestation—in the form of deviant behavior—is assumed. Despite consistent pressure exerted by the alien-to-the-system actors, impact on local institutions may vary significantly in relation to characteristics of the local field, the intra-organizational field, and of the actor itself.

Whether a new practice is perceived well or not depends on various factors. The following factors inform both the possibility that institutional contradiction leads to an initial adoption of a new practice and the practice's further development and persistence over time. Broadly, though, the perceived success of the initial adoption (and each experience that follows) decides if the new practice is equipped with "action-generating" properties or not (Kostova & Roth, 2002). Only by gaining such properties are further stages of institutionalization in reach.

Local Organizational Field

First, above all, since change is the inverse of stability, the level of structuration strongly informs the receptiveness of the local field toward new practices. On that account, matters of institutional coherence and resilience are negatively correlated with the impact a new practice may have on the local field. Despite institutional contestation by challengers (such as new entrants), a well-structured field and its major characteristics are supposed to remain relatively stable. Furthermore, a profound penetration of a shared belief system makes alien-to-the-system practices very unlikely to become institutionalized themselves. If this is not the case, though, if a field is rather fragmented, new practices may enter the institutional stage more easily, since competing institutions can be maintained simultaneously over a relatively long time period (March & Olsen, 2009). In addition, if the gap between expected and de facto institutions is very small (or theoretically non-existent), a genuine sanctioning of deviant behavior in the form of losing legitimacy can be expected. In conclusion, following Seo and Creed's (2002) notion of "degree of misaligned interests," the degree of structuration is generally positively correlated with the scope for deviant behavior, praxis, and, thus, institutional change. Summarizing, in line with Ferner et al. (2011), the institutional context of the host country provides an MNC with specific capabilities that facilitate, block, or adjust potential practice transfers.

Second, embeddedness as a matter of both relational aspects and the penetration of local actors is decisive for potential impact on the field, as it is crucial for the impact of the field. As Scott (2010) and DiMaggio and Powell (1983) indicate, it is frequent interaction between actors within a field that defines the organizational field through the building of a shared belief system and development of mutual awareness as being part of the same game. Consequently, interaction is necessary to make beliefs, norms, and, thus, action more coherent. Applied to institutional change, a new practice may only come into force over time through ongoing interaction and the exertion of corresponding isomorphic pressures. However, different systems may vary according to the degree of interaction they encourage and may on that account provide grounds with distinct fertility for new practices. An extreme case for a low degree of interaction among the institutional inhabitants may be the *maquiladora* system expanded in the late 1960s within the area at the Mexican–US border by the Mexican government's maquiladora program. As discussed above, a *maquiladora* is largely independent from its direct societal environment based on the non-existence of local relationships. In such a system constituted by *maquila* firms, practices hardly diffuse and remain firmly within the borders of the single companies.

However, as Morgan and Kristensen (2006) argue, interactions may be different in nature relating to their degree of social cohesion. Resting on VoC's categorization, they distinguish between either cooperative, enduring partnerships on eye level in CMEs or rather weak inter-actor links in LMEs. Within the former, the majority of actors can make their voices heard. Hence, a practice needs to be perceived as appropriate by various actors. On that account, it is more likely that some actors within CMEs perceive the practice as inappropriate and respond to new practices with resistance. Within the latter, hierarchies are pretty common, meaning that a few have power over many. The rather voiceless mass, therefore, lacks both the institutional venue for communicating dissatisfaction and consequently has little capacity for joint resistance. Certainly, since resistance is negatively correlated with the likelihood of a new practice of becoming institutionalized, the more cooperative interaction patterns may be, the more difficult it will be for new practices to enter the game.

Furthermore, embeddedness does not only work through interaction with others, but also through the penetration of the local field with elements representing the alien-to-the system practice. Hence, just as the infiltration of local elements within the subsidiary increases the strength of the local organizational field, the infiltration of the local field with (similar) alien-to-the-system actors increases the strength of the new practices on the organizational field. In order to have such an effect, the alien-to-the-system needs to be aligned regarding their practices and specific belief system. On that account, one may reasonably argue that the quantity of actors within the host country that have a similar practice portfolio tend to work similarly as agents of change favoring a similar set of practices. Certainly, a higher number of similar agents of change exerts a stronger influence on the local field favoring the new practice. Stronger influence may be expected for both types of influence. First, a higher number of similar aliens-to-the-system multiplies the specific isomorphic pressures that are exerted through day-to-day operations and, second, due to familiarity with the practice, facilitates the stage of actor mobilization when strategically approaching institutional change as purposeful entrepreneurs.

Third, the performance of the local organizational field is crucial when referring to potential change. Generally speaking, the better the institutional *status quo* performs, the less likely is to change. Whether performance is either good or bad depends on the perception of the institutional inhabitants and mirrors their satisfaction with the current state of the field. For instance, a new practice entering into a well-performing field with satisfied inhabitants may struggle to find legitimacy. A well-performing field is most likely characterized by a widely shared belief system, coherence, stability, and the support of actors resulting in delegitimization of, and resistance against, new practices. However, a field in crisis and institutional instability can work in reverse as a breeding ground for new practices. Similar to the strength of "dominant" nations, an institutional area in crisis has certainly lost—if it once had—the perception as being an area of "best practice." Hence, the local environment is perceived as being "inferior" *vis-à-vis* institutional challengers, especially if they themselves come from an acknowledged "dominant area of best practice." Each crisis leads to a transformative period in which the institutions that paved the way to the crisis in the first place experience decreasing legitimacy and increased contestation, potentially resulting in disengagement from past behavioral patterns. Then, to put it in the words of Goodin et al. (2011, p. 489) ". . .institutions and their constitutive rules are discredited as unworkable and intolerable and change initiatives are presented as emancipation from an order that is a dysfunctional, unfair, or tyrannical relic of an unacceptable past." In the aftermath of a crisis, actors attain a critical perspective regarding the disadvantageous social arrangement and rethink who they and others are, to whom they belong and what is appropriate and what not (Seo & Creed, 2002). In search of a better way of organization, new legitimate institutional models are searched and inevitably include either institutional adjustment or substitution by "better" ones. Crisis and subsequent disorientation, therefore, propel a normative restructuring and an atmosphere of uncertainty about what and how best to do things. On that account, highly receptive for especially normative and mimetic pressures, crises can open windows for new practices to enter the game.

Furthermore, reinforcing the relative power of new entrants *vis-à-vis* the local field, acting as a catalyst for the transfer of practices, in a state of disorientation and uncertainty—or in general to improve economic performance-, it may be a part of national economic policy programs to attract MNCs. MNCs, understood as potential remedies against chronic diseases of economic dysfunctionality, are very likely to be well heard by policy makers. That certainly facilitates their potential endeavors as institutional entrepreneurs.

MNC's Peculiarities

Whereas MNCs are certainly part of various heated debates, their perception as a "role model" within the economic area of institutional life is mostly beyond dispute. As already indicated several times, MNCs embody economic success and efficiency, are perceived as well advanced in both technology and organizational issues, and are highly equipped with resources and, above all, with capital (Koene & Ansari, 2011). These characteristics and the matter of fact that the vast majority of national economic policies target the attraction of MNCs as a major pillar of economic development, makes MNCs a considerably important agent of change through both the venue of day-to-day operations and purposeful institutional entrepreneurship. However, their potential impact as agent of institutional change depends, apart from the practices' quality and the characteristics of the host country environment, on various factors such as national origins (or even more specifically, sectors within nations), involvement in local interaction, and the number of similar MNCs.

MNCs' origins can improve their social position and, thus, may strengthen their potential impact with the dominance effects as introduced above (Leca et al., 2009). If a company originates in a certain field that is acknowledged to show best practice, the firm itself acts as representative of a "superior" system *vis-à-vis* the host country system. Both venues of change benefit from an improved (social) position either through the ability to exert higher pressure or political clout and the resources available to successfully participate in political action. Vice versa, change induced by representatives of "inferior" systems may be limited.

Involvement of the MNC within the local organizational field regarding both day-to-day interactions and political participation is decisive for potential change. As indicated above, a system constituted by *maquiladoras* is very limited regarding societal effects. Along the same lines, an MNC that establishes a *maquiladora* abroad is not supposed to exert strong isomorphic pressure on the field. The lack of interaction makes it isolated and rather disembedded from the local field. Of course, the maquiladora embodies the extreme of noninvolvement and, certainly, a more locally involved subsidiary is the usual case. In general, each interaction with other actors increases a subsidiary's influence on the field, whether through increased visibility and ability to demonstrate alien-to-the-system practices or through shaping normative and cognitive frames. In particular, a subsidiary that educates people that will move to other firms and the participation in professional communities are interactions with others that can contribute significantly to institutional change. Hence, each subsidiary's effect is closely connected to the degree of local involvement.

Along similar lines, also catalyzing MNCs' capacity as "rule makers," the quantity of aligned actors multiplies isomorphic pressures exerted through day-to-day operations and facilitates actor mobilization when strategically approaching institutional change as purposeful entrepreneurs. On that account, the number of similar agents of change positively correlates with potential for institutional change. Each actor that is equipped with the same practice portfolio and faces the same situation in a host country tends to apply the same familiar non-systemic alternatives. In a state of institutional duality between home and host country environments, the practice portfolio of actors from the same CoO is supposed to be similar. Following this line of reasoning, one may reasonably expect firms originating in the same home country to rely on similar alien-to-the-system practices. Even if foreign subsidiaries do not show home country practices, their receptiveness toward familiar home country practices is supposed to be relatively high due to an already existing appropriate normative expertise (Ferner et al., 2011). Such familiarity makes foreign subsidiaries susceptible to being mobilized more easily by like-minded others that attempt to change institutions and, thus, significantly improves the process of institutional entrepreneurship.

Action Characteristics

As introduced in the section above, a specific action that takes place frequently and that is conducted by a large number of actors is more likely to result in institutional change. Each additional actor pressurizing for a similar change contributes to potential institutional adaptions. Furthermore, in order to mobilize support and resources from others, a new practice that is already resonant with some of the institutional inhabitants' belief systems is more promising than others (Seo & Creed, 2002). Hence, through both venues of change, the more actors coming up with a similar practice portfolio increases the likelihood of striving for aligned change that builds upon overlapping belief systems.

Apart from being present among some of the actors' practice portfolios, the practice has some characteristics that—interdependent with peculiarities of the local field and the actor—partly determine its validity within the local area of institutional life. Particularly within the context of an institutional setting that inheres dysfunctional properties, new practices—being the likelihood of their successful institutionalization—may also be determined by their distinctiveness in comparison to the existing institutional arrangement. In order to depict a contrast to the past institutions that proved to be dysfunctional and to fundamentally depart from crisis, new practices need to be perceived as sufficiently incompatible with the ones that led to the crisis in the first place (Seo & Creed, 2002). This idea of a practice being "different" to the existing ones, can be further developed with the notions of inappropriateness and solution orientation. Crisis in a specific area of institutional life certainly contests the practice of interest (and those connected) but rarely leads to a general collapse of the entire societal system, including the entirety of the shared belief system. If a situation of crisis leaves certain parts of the institutional inhabitants' belief system intact, new practices that entirely counter the existing normative and cognitive frames may result in local resistance. Following this reasoning, new practices, indeed, should be perceived as sufficiently incompatible with the existing social arrangement, but should not cross the systemic "line of appropriateness." Logically, the same holds true in well-functioning institutional arrangements as well. Generally, if a new practice is brought into play either through isomorphic pressures or political participation, a positive reception of the practice is more likely when the existing arrangement is favorable for the specific action conducted (Kostova & Roth, 2002) and is favorable inasmuch as its inhabitants are cognitively better equipped to understand the practice and its value. Furthermore, referring to institutional differences, it may be less likely to transfer a different practice from one institutional environment to the other. Nonetheless, and of utmost importance for this paper, it may be exactly the quite (sufficiently incompatible) different practices that survive the journey from the home to the host country that provide sources of institutional change, especially in situations of crisis. In line with the heterogeneity of the practice portfolio introduced above, Seo and Creed (2002, p. 238) support this view by stating that "The degree and number of interinstitutional incompatibilities increase the likelihood of praxis for institutional change by increasing the number of frames and logics available for the construction of alternative models of institutional arrangements...".

Furthermore, if systemic dysfunctions are recognized, understood, and labeled, a new practice that is assumed to be supportive of overcoming this specific situation of crisis may have the best future prospects. On that account, if the new practice is different and somehow solution oriented to the specific problem, it may be granted with a relatively high value. One step further, relatively new practices that have proven their ability to counter distinct problems and that have already led to "feasible" and visible improvements may gain additional value over time (Garud et al., 2007). In general, an increase of a practice's perceived value further strengthens pressures on the field and makes a potentially successful institutionalization more likely.

Beyond societal properties, actions also vary according to systemic characteristics. It is said that market-oriented practices are more prominent and easier to implement than more coordinated ones. Within the context of VoC, beyond the perceived hegemony of the liberal idea of life and the tendency of international actors to adopt rather liberal practices (Pudelko & Harzing, 2007; Streeck, 2009), one may argue that liberal practices are easier to put in place in comparison to coordinated ones. As Chap. 3 discussed, whereas LMEs rely on market relationships, CMEs tend to coordinate interaction through nonmarket modes, including extensive relational contracting, network monitoring, consensus orientation, and general cooperation (Hall & Soskice, 2001, p. 8). Hence, rather than relying on demand and supply, the functioning of CME practices requires deliberative platforms and suitable mind-sets of institutional inhabitants that allow for wide participation, joint consultation, and cooperative and strategic interaction.[11] Considering CMEs' deeply entangled system of complementarities and the required extensive demands on companies to enter into tight relationships, Hall and Soskice (2001, p. 48) argue that "Coordination-oriented policies will be more difficult to implement in liberal market economies..." than vice versa. Applied to potential actor-induced change, following a strict VoC approach, application and spillover on the field of liberal practices may be in scope, whereas, due to the systemic complexity of CMEs that allow for strategic coordination, an actor-induced change toward more long-term cooperation within a generally unfavorable environment is very unlikely.

In very general terms, one may state that a shift toward market-based interaction is easier than building up networks and reputational systems based on strategic joint cooperation. Hence, as it is the inherent higher complexity of "coordinated" institutions that makes it is easier to abandon complexity and to shift to "simplicity" than vice versa, it is easier to give up coordination and shift to market-based interactions.

The Change Cube

Figure 4.6 presents the Change Cube that, first, summarizes the discussion above and, second, indicates the expected impact of strange behavior on the local organizational field. Just like the Contradiction Cube above, depending on characteristics of the actor (MNC), the local institutional field, and the specific action of interest, the Change Cube suggests the potential impact of a subsidiary's demonstrated alien-to-the-system practice on the local institutional setting.

In this approach, the three factors are balanced inasmuch each one loads equally on the expected impact of a foreign practice on the host country's institutional setting. Indicated by the array from rose to dark red, one can derive the expected impact of a new practice and, accordingly. The array ranges from very—if at all—very small impact (rose) when the action is passive, the local field strong, and the

[11] Granovetter (1985) also implies a certain degree of trust and familiarity within market-based coordination. Here, Hall and Soskice (2001), though, do not deny this but emphasize the higher degree of trust and familiarity in CMEs.

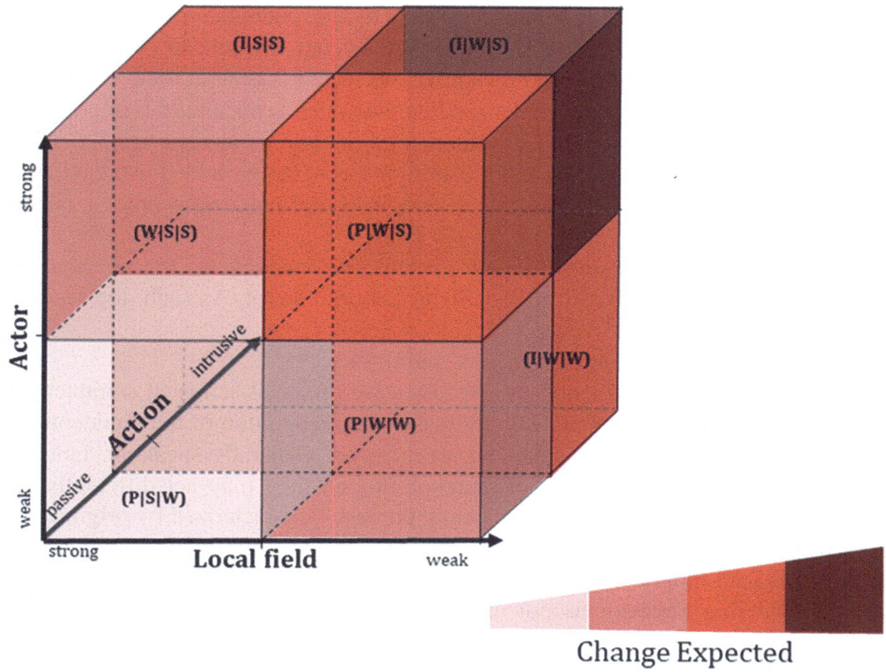

Fig. 4.6 Change Cube. Source: From the author

actor weak (i.e., inappropriate/strong/weak is PSW). At the other end of the array, dark red indicates an IWS that means that the action is intrusive, the local field is rather weak, and the actor strong.

4.6 Summary and Assembly of Conflating Capitalisms

In general, this work attempts to deal with the ubiquitous position of MNCs in developing countries and the idea that social phenomena are explainable as an outcome of interactions. This work suggests that underdevelopment is rooted in a dysfunctional systemic configuration that hampers successful interaction. On that account, developmental issues are understood as a matter of the institutional setting rather than one of a sheer lack of a quantifiable resource (such as money). Logically, MNCs' impact on development needs to be translated as being caused by potential institutional change. In order to recognize MNCs' impact on the development of countries, major propositions of this work set at the outset are:

1. To overcome the assumption of economic systems' uniformity.

   The consideration of the distinctness of political economies makes orthodox assumptions of developmental blueprints—at best—a vague endeavor. The distinctness of political economies inheres to the potential for idiosyncratic distortions that hamper development. On that account, the concepts of "growing the pie" and an assumed trickle-down effect on society's general socio-economic well-being reach their limits. Understanding the systemic peculiarities of political economies allow one to grasp developmental distortions at their idiosyncratic roots. Understanding developmental distortions as being grounded in a dysfunctional institutional setting means that development as a process becomes a matter of institutional change.

Along with the consideration of systemic distinctiveness, the concept of MNCs as a homogeneous flow of USD is cast into doubt. As such, the second major proposition is:

2. To overcome the assumption of actors' uniformity.

   Assuming economic action as a special case of social action in conjunction with the idea of institutional diversity makes the recognition of the nonidentical *Gestalt* of MNCs across systems an urgent need. Generally speaking, indeed, actors interact with others in all systems, though they may act differently in different ones. MNCs that cross systemic borders—characterized by originating in one system and being physically present in another one—may show distinct behavior accordingly.

   Considering behavior as potentially varying, requires an understanding of action, institutions, and potential change that goes beyond the rather determinist concepts of "traditional" analyses. Consequently, the third major proposition is:

3. To leave behind the "deterministic temptation of institutionalism."

   Applying IAD's and AIC's understanding of action situations as being adjacent—meaning that one action is connected to the previous one, as its output partially shapes the institutional setup under which the following actions take place—to MNCs in developing countries creates a more dynamic understanding of the interplay between both the idiosyncratic systems and the specific behavior. Further developing the relation between behavior and potential institutional change allows one to grasp dynamics of inter-systemic exchange of different actors within unique institutional environments.

   Considering these major propositions, the objective of this work's theory development throughout the previous chapters was to develop the major building blocks—derived in Chap. 2, which are:

- Actor
- Actor constellation
- Action situation
- Specific relationship of institutions and actors

Conflating Capitalisms aims at providing an analytical framework guiding and allowing for institutional analyses of dynamics that may occur through inter-systemic exchange of MNCs within the host country. According to this work's basic understanding of development, a potential contribution to development needs to be understood as induced potential institutional change. Furthermore, the concept of adjacency suggests that a specific conduct of action may affect the

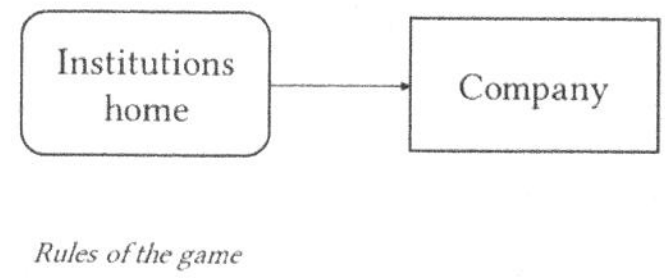

Fig. 4.7 Traditional institutional analysis. Source: From the author

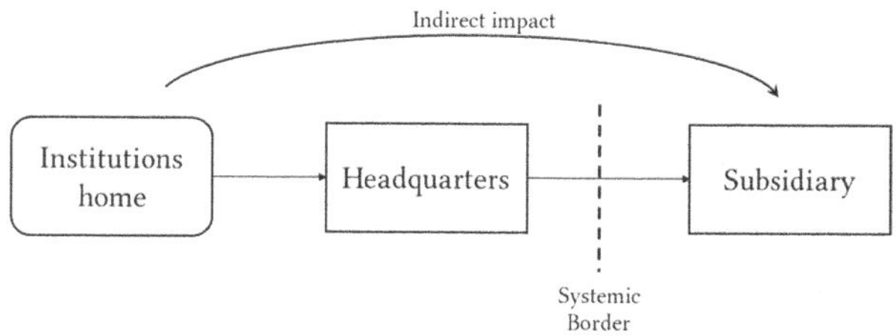

Fig. 4.8 Institutional analysis and crossing borders. Source: From the author

subsequent action situations, though indirectly, through institutional change. Following this short version of this work's logic, Conflating Capitalisms should be able to respond to two major questions.

– How do subsidiaries from parent companies in A and B behave in C?
– How does behavior from subsidiaries with parent companies in A and B impact on the distinct system of C?

As the initial point, there is the Actor constellation, which is the distinct game being played. Here, as Fig. 4.7 indicates, there is a straightforward causal relationship between the institutional surrounding and the company within the borders of a single country. The VoC approach and the various extensions on the Global South, follow this relatively deterministic line of traditional institutional analyses. Translated into the concept of organizational fields, the company is clearly assignable to one institutional setting and, thus, to one set of rules.

What Conflating Capitalisms extracts out of these traditional studies is, among other things, the variety of games (actor constellations), major actors (most importantly, firms), and the institutional domains and interactions of interest. Furthermore, studies that take place within an isolated nation-state allow for the understanding of developmental distortions as a matter of interaction and enable one to detect dysfunctional institutions and the assigning of the interactions of interest.

According to this work's requirements, the actor changes inasmuch the company is replaced by a multinational corporation with a special focus on the foreign subsidiary, see Fig. 4.8. Chapter 3 introduced the MNC, indeed, just like a nationally limited company, as generally motivated by the pursuit of (the largest possible) profit, though, showing major organizational differences that cry for far-reaching analytical changes. The MNC crosses the dashed systemic border and builds foreign subsidiaries in other, different, systems. The MNC, hence, is a unique actor within the universe of institutions since it is—at the same time—present in different institutional settings, and therefore, playing different games simultaneously.

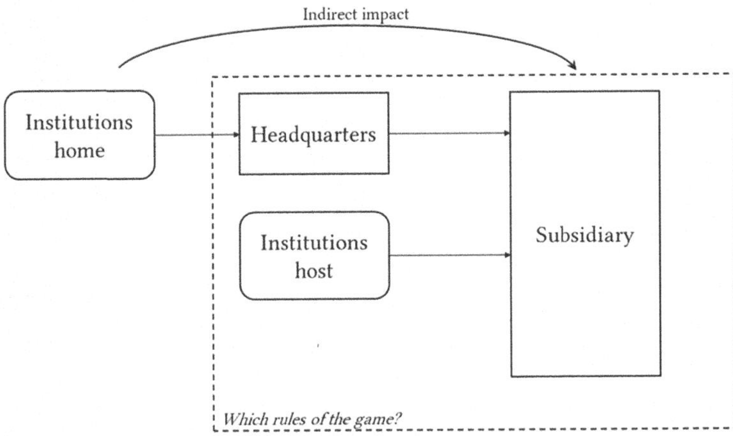

Fig. 4.9 Institutional analysis and various pressures. Source: From the author

Understood in terms of organizational field, the subsidiary is still subject to the institutional setting of the home country, though indirectly, through the Scottian functionally coined intra-organizational field.

HQs having a dominant position within the intra-organizational field are firmly situated in their respective home countries. Built on, among others, the pillars of control, dependence, ownership, and in general frequent interaction, the HQ transmits institutional pressures of the home country onto its foreign subsidiary. Hence, even though being physically located in another system, an MNCs' foreign subsidiary continues to be subject to the parent company's home country institutional setting. Responding to pressures, the subsidiary is expected to strive for legitimacy and following the logic of appropriateness within the intra-organizational field can be expected to show conformity with the HQ and, thus, also with the home country institutional setup.

Being physically present in a foreign and different institutional setting, though, being continued to be pressurized by the home country setting, brings the foreign subsidiary in a state of institutional duality. The subsidiary is facing more than one set of institutional pressures simultaneously, that of the home and the host country. Hence, the subsidiary, primarily, plays the "local game" though being subject to two sets of different and sometimes contradictory rules (Fig. 4.9).

Just like within the intra-organizational field, the subsidiary needs to show conformity with the local host country organizational field to gain legitimacy and toto not put its survival at stake. It is exactly the intra-institutional conformity that may create inter-institutional incompatibilities. As a result of the attempt to gain legitimacy in both fields, a certain degree of conformity with each of the fields can be expected. Hence, assuming systemic differences, conformity to both fields logically implies a certain degree of unconformity (incompatibility) to each of the fields. A subsidiary can therefore neither be expected to mirror home-based practices of the MNC nor to entirely blend in with other actors in the host country context.

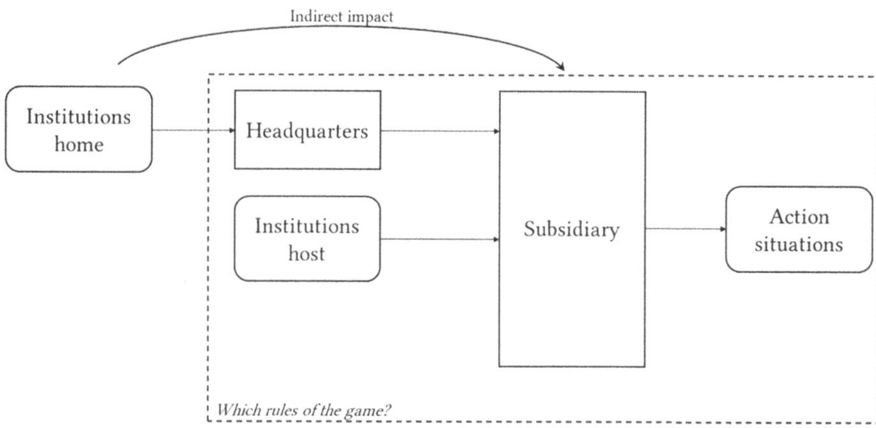

Fig. 4.10 Institutional analysis and the action situation. Source: From the author

The specific conduct of interaction materializes within the action situation. The action situation of a foreign subsidiary is unique since its institutional input is diverse and sometimes contradictory. The action situation, as indicated in Fig. 4.10) is the most important step within Conflating Capitalisms, as it is the crucial stage where different rules work, actors meet and interact, make decisions, generate certain outcomes and contradiction materializes.

The action situation induces action by confronting the subsidiary, generally, with (coordination) problems. Furthermore, it offers various options on how to behave, i.e., which practice to choose, when confronted with a given problem. The alternative approaches on how to solve the problem can broadly be found within the range offered by actors' practice portfolios—including home and host country practices. At a broad level, behavior describes the specific practice chosen when approaching a coordination problem. In the context of VoC, for example, a subsidiary originating from an LME located in a CME may "solve" the problem to raise funds by either liberal practices such as listing stocks or by coordinated practices such as raising credit from the house bank; or a combination of both. Since both CMEs and LMEs are market economies in a general sense, both practices are conductible though being pushed to a certain degree by the corresponding institutional environments.

If a foreign subsidiary chooses a move according to strange rules of the game—i.e., showing practices that resemble the home country—alien-to-the-system practices can challenge the legitimacy of existing institutional patterns in various ways and, thus, simultaneously, prompt debates and contestation on potentially better practices in the host country. According to the basic understanding developed above, institutional change is initiated by contradiction that transforms embedded social actors into change agents of the institutional arrangement. Therefore, the integration of deviant behavior into analyses is key for a microfoundationalist attempt to scrutinize potential institutional change within the host country driven by subsidiaries. A subsidiary's deviant behavior is the behavioral manifestation of institutional contradiction, inherently shows patterns of avoidance or defiance and serves as the initial point for potential MNC-induced institutional change within the host country.

Within Conflating Capitalisms, action is feeding back to the field level and, thus, may cause institutional change through two major channels. Deviant behavior as the condition for institutional change may induce institutional change through:

- Day-to-day Operations
- Institutional Entrepreneurship

Building upon a more dynamic interplay between action and institutions, the specific conduct of action can feedback on the field level. Day-to-day operations that show either avoidance or defiance may undermine some institutions and strengthen others gradually over time. Such a notion of bottom-up change from within happens without "dramatic" events. Actors, in this case subsidiaries, can exert force on the institutional surrounding through the concept of "reverse" isomorphic pressures. Analogue to coercive, mimetic, and normative pressures exerted by the field affecting the subsidiary, a subsidiary itself may be capable of exerting isomorphic pressure on the host country field through regulatory pressure effect, demonstration effects, or professionalization. Relating to day-to-day operations and subsequent impact on the institutional setting, the relational aspect of actors is of utmost importance.

Also initiated by contradiction though a more strategic approach on actor-induced institutional change, institutional entrepreneurship depicts the conscious and purposeful actor that strategically proceeds to change the surrounding institutional structure for its own advantage. The concept of "praxis" and subsidiaries describes the process of institutional entrepreneurship in three steps. First, the subsidiary needs to be aware of the perceived institutional dysfunctions and come up with an allegedly better alternative. Second, a phase of mobilization is required to mobile both resources and commitment of other actors in order to jointly reconstruct the negatively perceived social arrangement. The ultimate aim is to challenge the given structures and to endorse and to enact the proposed alternative social arrangements. Third, change itself is attained through collective action, meaning that a "significant number" of institutional inhabitants has been realigned successfully, a group of institutional entrepreneurs act collectively to change specificities of the institutional setting.

For both channels of institutional change, foreign subsidiaries of MNCs may turn into agents of change. Due to reasons of institutional duality, their practice portfolio is larger than the one of the local actors. Hence, foreign subsidiaries as carriers of new and alien-to-the-system practices can reasonably lead to contradiction and may cause institutional change. Nonetheless, both crucial stages of "Conflating Capitalisms," the specific behavior (action situation) and the strength of impact on the field (feedback channels) are matters of degree. Both may reasonably be approached and hypothesized relying on the Condition Triangle. The relative measures of the field, the actor, and the introduced action determine—to a certain degree—the relative strengths of the fields that inform the specific action situation and the potential degree of field change.

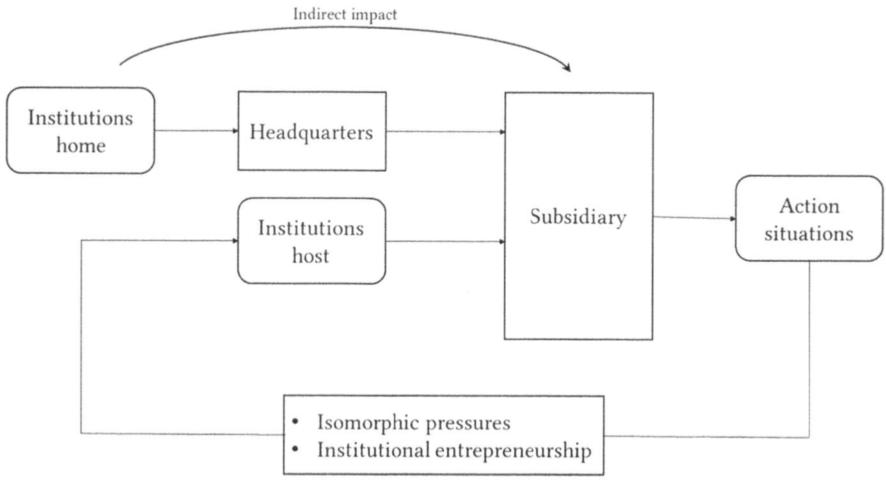

Fig. 4.11 Institutional analysis and the MNC as change agent. Source: From the author

Conflating Capitalisms, as finally assembled in Fig. 4.11, offers a sound analytical framework for the institutional analysis of MNCs in developing countries. Its single building blocks that have been developed throughout the chapters in theory development have been assembled above. Conflating Capitalisms overcomes major pitfalls of mostly orthodox theory and allows for a tailor-made approach considering systemic distortions as a major obstacle for development. It copes with the MNC as a social actor, embedded in various different institutional environments simultaneously. Allowing for institutional contradiction and actor-induced institutional change, political economies—especially the ones of developing countries—that are coined by institutional tensions, may become an area of institutional contestation. In the following chapters, Conflating Capitalisms is applied empirically to the case of MNCs from CMEs and LMEs that are present HMEs through foreign subsidiaries.

References

Allen, M. (2004). The varieties of capitalism paradigm: Not enough variety? *Socio-Economic Review, 2*, 87–108.

Bartlett, C. A., & Ghoshal, S. (1989). *Managing across borders. The transnational solution*. Harvard Business School Press.

Birkinshaw, J., & Hood, N. (1998). Multinational subsidiary evolution: Capability and charter change in foreign-owned subsidiary companies. *The Academy of Management Review, 23*, 773–795.

Boxenbaum, E. (2006). Corporate social responsibility as institutional hybrids. *Journal of Business Strategies, 23*, 45–63.

Boxenbaum, E., & Jonsson, S. (2017). Isomorphism, diffusion and decoupling: Concept evolution and theoretical challenges. In R. Greenwood, C. Oliver, T. B. Lawrence, & R. E. Meyer (Eds.), *The SAGE handbook of organizational institutionalism* (pp. 77–101). Sage.
Brewster, C., Wood, G., & Brookes, M. (2008). Similarity, isomorphism or duality? Recent survey evidence on the human resource management policies of multinational corporations. *British Journal of Management, 19*, 320–342.
Brookes, M., Brewster, C., & Wood, G. (2017). Are MNCs norm entrepreneurs or followers? The changing relationship between host country institutions and MNC HRM practices. *The International Journal of Human Resource Management, 2017*, 1690–1711.
Buckley, P. J., & Casson, M. (2010). *The multinational enterprise revisited: The essential Buckley and Casson*. Palgrave Macmillan.
Buckley, P. J., & Pearce, R. D. (1979). Overseas production and exporting by the world's leading enterprises. *Journal of International Business Studies, 10*(1), 9–20.
Burns, J., & Nielsen, K. (2006). How do embedded agents engage in institutional change? *Journal of Economic Issues, 40*(2), 449–456.
Busemeyer, M. R. (2009). Asset specificity, institutional complementarities and the variety of skill regimes in coordinated market economies. *Socio-Economic Review, 7*, 375–406.
Cantwell, J., Dunning, J. H., & Lundan, S. M. (2010). An evolutionary approach to understanding international business activity: The co-evolution of MNCs and the institutional environment. *Journal of International Business Studies, 41*, 567–586.
Clark, E., & Geppert, M. (2010). Subsidiary integration as identity constructionand institution building: A political sensemaking approach. *Journal of Management Studies, 48*(2), 395–416.
Cole, D. H. (2013). The varieties of comparative institutional analysis. *Articles by Maurer Faculty, Paper 834*.
Cooke, W. N. (2008). Multinational companies and global human resource strategy. In P. Boxall, J. Purcell, & P. Wright (Eds.), *The Oxford handbook of human resource management*. Oxford University Press.
Crouch, C., Schröder, M., & Voelzkow, H. (2009). Regional and sectoral varieties of capitalism. *Economy and Society, 2009*, 654–678.
Crouch, C., Streeck, W., Boyer, R., Amable, B., Hall, P. A., & Jackson, G. (2005). Dialogue on 'Institutional complementarity and political economy'. *Socio-Economic Review, 3*, 359–382.
Dacin, M. T., Ventresca, M. J., & Beal, B. D. (1999). The embeddedness of organizations: Dialogue & directions. *Journal of Management, 25*, 317–356.
de Jong, G., & Van Vo, D. (2010). The impact of the institutional environment on the autonomy of MNCs' subsidiaries. *Problems and Perspectives in Management, 8*(2), 53–63.
Deeg, R., & Jackson, G. (2007). Towards a more dynamic theory of capitalist variety. *Socio-Economic Review, 5*, 149–179.
DellaPosta, D., Nee, V., & Opper, S. (2017). Endogenous dynamics of institutional change. *Rationality and Society, 29*(I), 5–48.
Dequech, D. (2006). The new institutional economics and the theory of behaviour under uncertainty. *Journal of Economic Behavior & Organization, 59*, 109–131.
DiMaggio, P. (1988). Interest and agency in institutional theory. In L. Zucker (Ed.), *Institutional patterns and organizations: Culture and environment* (pp. 3–21). Ballinger Publishing.
DiMaggio, P. (1991). Social structure, institutions, and cultural goods: The case of the U.S. In I. P. Bourdieu & J. Coleman (Eds.), *Social theory for a changing society*. Westview Press.
DiMaggio, P. J., & Powell, W. W. (1983). The iron cage revisited: Institutional isomorphism and collective rationality in organizational fields. *American Sociological Association, 48*(2), 147–160.
Doz, Y. L., & Prahalad, C. K. (1991). Managing DMNCs: A search for a new paradigm. *Strategic Management Journal, 12*, 145–164.
Edwards, P., Edwards, T., Ferner, A., Marginson, P., & Tregaskis, O. (2007). *Employment practices of MNCs in organisational context: A large-scale survey*. Retrieved from University of

Warwick http://www2.warwick.ac.uk/fac/soc/wbs/projects/mncemployment/conference_papers/full_report_july.pdf

Edwards, T., & Ferner, A. (2004). Multinationals, reverse diffusion and national business systems. *Management International Review, 44*(1), 49–79.

Fenton-O'Creevy, M., Gooderham, P., & Nordhaug, O. (2007). Human resource management in US subsidiaries in Europe and Australia: Centralisation or autonomy? *Journal of International Business Studies, 17*, 151–166.

Ferner, A., Almond, P., & Colling, T. (2005). Institutional theory and the cross-national transfer of employment policy: The case of 'workforce diversity' in US multinationals. *Journal of International Business Studies, 36*(3), 304–321.

Ferner, A., Edwards, T., & Tempel, A. (2011). Power, institutions and the cross-national tranfer of employment practices in multinationals. *Human Relations, 65*, 163–187.

Ferraz, R. L. (2018). bibliotecadigital.fgv.br. Retrieved from Operations decisions and the influence of host-country institutions: An exploratory study under the Paraguayan 'Maquila regime'. Retrieved from https://bibliotecadigital.fgv.br/dspace/bitstream/handle/10438/27235/20190322.%20Disserta%c3%a7%c3%a3o%20Renan%20Lucas%20Ferraz_FINAL%20BIBLIOTECA.pdf?sequence=4&isAllowed=y

Forsgren, M., Holm, U., & Johanson, J. (2005). *Managing the embedded multinational: A business network view*. Edward Elgar.

Fortanier, F. (2007, August). Foreign direct investment and host country economic growth: Does the investor's country of origin play a role? *Transnational Corporations, 16*(2), 41–76.

Friedland, R., & Alford, R. R. (1991). Bringing society back. In I. W. W. Powell & P. J. DiMaggio (Eds.), *Symbols, practices, and institutional contradictions. The new institutionalism in organizational analysis* (pp. 232–263). University of Chicago Press.

Frumkin, P., & Galaskiewicz, J. (2004). Institutional isomorphism and public sector organizations. *Journal of Public Administration Research and Theory, 14*(3), 283–307.

Galaskiewicz, J., & Wasserman, S. (1989). Mimetic processes within an interorganizational field: An empirical test. *Administrative Science Quarterly, 34*(3), 454–479.

Gardiner, L., Summers, E., & Raftl, G. (2013). By invitation only? In S. R. Whittle & R. C. Stevens (Eds.), *Changing organizations from within*. Routledge.

Garud, R., Hardy, C., & Maguire, S. (2007). Institutional entrepreneurship as embedded agency: An introduction to the special issue. *Organization Studies, 2007*, 957–969.

Geppert, M., & Dörrenbacher, C. (2011). *Politics and power in the multinational corporation: The role of institutions, interests and identities*. Cambridge University Press.

Geppert, M., Matten, D., & Walgenbach, P. (2006). Transnational institution building and the multinational corporation: An emerging field of research. *Human Relations, 59*, 1451–1465.

Geppert, M., & Williams, K. (2006). Global, national and local practices in multinational corporations: Towards a sociopolitical framework. *The International Journal of Human Resource Management, 17*, 49–69.

Geppert, M., Williams, K., & Matten, D. (2003). The social construction of contextual rationalities in MNCs: An Anglo-German comparison of subsidiary choice. *Journal of Management Studies, 40*(3), 617–641.

Ghoshal, S., & Bartlett, C. A. (1990). The multinational corporation as an interorganizational network. *The Academy of Management Review, 15*, 603–625.

Giddens, A. (1984). Elements of the theory of structuration. In A. Giddens (Ed.), *The constitution of society: Outline of the theory of structuration* (pp. 1–28). University of California Press.

Goodin, R., March, J., & Olsen, J. (2011). The logic of appropriateness. In *The Oxford handbook of political science*. Oxford University Press. Retrieved from https://www.oxfordhandbooks.com/view/10.1093/oxfordhb/9780199604456.001.0001/oxfordhb-9780199604456-e-024

Granovetter, M. (1985, November). Economic action and social structure: The problem of embeddedness. *American Journal of Sociology, 91*(3), 481–510.

Hall, P. A. (2010). Historical institutionalism in rationalist and sociological perspective. In J. Mahoney & K. Thelen (Eds.), *Explaining institutional change* (pp. 204–223). Cambridge University Press.
Hall, P. A., & Soskice, D. (2001). *Varieties of capitalism: The institutional foundations of comparative advantage*. Oxford University Press.
Hall, P. A., & Taylor, R. C. (1996). Political science and the three new institutionalisms. *Political Studies, XLIV*, 936–957.
Hall, P. A., & Thelen, K. (2009). Institutional change in varieties of capitalism. *Socio-Economic Review, 7*, 7–34.
Hanson, M. (2001). Institutional theory and educational change. *Educational Administration Quarterly, 37*(5), 637–661.
Heidenreich, M. (2012). The social embeddedness of multinational companies: A literature review. *Socio-Economic Review, 10*(3), 549–579.
Hoenen, A. K., & Kostova, T. (2015). Utilizing the broader agency perspective for studying headquarters–subsidiary relations in multinational companies. *Journal of International Business Studies, 46*, 104–113.
Hollingsworth, J. R., & Boyer, R. (1997). *Contemporary capitalism: The embeddedness of institutions*. Cambridge University Press.
Huntington, S. P. (1968). *Political order in changing societies*. Yale University Press.
Hymer, S. H. (1976). *The international operations of national firms: A study of direct foreign investment. Unpublished 1960 PhD thesis*. MIT Press.
Immergut, E. M. (2006). Historical-institutionalism in political science and the problem of change. In A. Wimmer & R. Kössler (Eds.), *Understanding change* (pp. 237–259). Palgrave Macmillan.
Iversen, T., & Soskice, D. (2001). An asset theory of social policy preferences. *American Political Science Review, 95*, 875–893.
Jackson, G., & Deeg, R. (2008). Comparing capitalisms: Understanding institutional diversity and its implications for international business. *Journal of International Business Studies, 39*, 540–561.
Jackson, G., & Rathert, N. (2017). Private governance as regulatory substitute or complement? A comparative institutional approach to csr adoption by multinational corporations. *Research in the Sociology of Organizations, 49*, 445–478.
Javorcik, B. S., & Spatareanu, M. (2011). Does it matter where you come from? Vertical spillovers from foreign direct investment and the origin of investors. *Journal of Development Economics, 96*, 126–138.
Johanson, J., & Vahlne, J.-E. (2009). The Uppsala internationalization process model revisited: From liability of foreignness to liability of outsidership. *Journal of International Business Studies, 40(9)*, 1411–1431.
Kellogg, K. C. (2009). Operating room: Relational spaces and microinstitutional change in surgery. *American Journal of Sociology, 115*, 657–711.
Kim, S., & Park, C. (2008). The influence of multinational corporations on institutional diffusion in emerging markets: Evidence from hiring the disabled in Korea. *Seoul Journal of Business, 14*, 4–30.
Koene, B., & Ansari, S. (2011). Institutional change and the multinational change agent: A study of the temporary staffing industry in Spain. *Journal of Organizational Change Management, 24*, 511–531.
Kogut, B. (2001). Multinational corporations. In I. N. J. Smelser & P. B. Baltes (Eds.), *International Encyclopedia of social & behavioral sciences* (pp. 10197–10204). Pergamon Press.
Kostova, T., Marano, V., & Tallman, S. (2016). Headquarters–subsidiary relationships in MNCs: Fifty years of evoling research. *Journal of World Business*, 176–184.
Kostova, T., Nell, P. C., & Hoenen, A. K. (2018). Understanding agency problems in headquarters-subsidiary relationships in multinational corporations: A contextualized model. *Journal of Management, 44*, 2611–2637.

Kostova, T., & Roth, K. (2002). Adoption of an organizational practice by subsidiaries of multinational corporations: Institutional and relational effects. *Academy of Management Journal, 45*, 215–233.

Kostova, T., Roth, K., & Dacin, M. T. (2008, October). Institutional theory in the study of multinational corporations: A critique and new directions. *The Academy of Management Review, 33*(4), 994–1006.

Kostova, T., & Zaheer, S. (1999). Organizational legitimacy under conditions of complexity: The case of the multinational enterprise. *Academy of Management Review, 24*(1), 64–81.

Kuznetsov, A., & Jacob, M. (2015). Convergence versus divergence: Testing varieties of capitalism on the globalization of buiness practices. In I. S. Marinova (Ed.), *Institutional impacts on firm internationalization* (pp. 12–39). Palgrave Macmillan.

Kwok, C. C., & Tadesse, S. (2006). The MNC as an agent of change for host-country institutions: FDI and corruption. *Journal of International Business Studies, 7*, 767–785.

Lane, C. (2008). National capitalisms and global production networks: An analysis of their interaction in two global industries. *Socio-Economic Review, 6*, 227–260.

Larson, M. S. (1977). *The rise of professionalism: A sociological analysis*. University of California Press.

Lawernce, T. B. (1999). Institutional strategy. *Journal of Management, 25*, 161–187.

Lawrence, T. B., Hardy, C., & Phillips, N. (2002). Institutional effects of interorganizational collaboration: The emergence of proto-institutions. *The Academy of Management Journal, 45*, 281–290.

Lawrence, T., Suddaby, R., & Leca, B. (2011). Institutional work: Refocusing institutional studies of organization. *Journal of Management Inquiry, 20*, 52–58.

Leca, B., Battilana, J., & Boxenbaum, E. (2009). Agency and institutions: A review on institutional entrepreneurship. *The Academy of Management Annals, 2009*, 2–51.

Levi, M. (1990). A logic of institutional change. In K. Schweers, K. Cook, & M. Levi (Eds.), *The limits of rationality* (pp. 402–418). Universtiy of Chicago Press.

Levy, D. L. (2008). Political contestation in global production networks. *Academy of Management Review., 33*(4), 943–962.

Machado-da-Silva, C. L., Guarido Filho, E. R., & Rossoni, L. (2006). Organizational fields and the structuration perspective: Analytical possibilities. *Brazilian Administration Review, 3*, 32–56.

Mahoney, J., & Thelen, K. (2010). A theory of gradual institutional change. In J. Mahoney & K. Thelen (Eds.), *Explaining institutional change* (pp. 1–37). Cambridge University Press.

March, J. G., & Olsen, J. P. (2004). *The logic of appropriateness*. Retrieved from Centre for European Studies https://www.researchgate.net/publication/5014575_The_Logic_of_Appropriateness/link/55d2f0c808aec1b0429f03e4/download

March, J. G., & Olsen, J. P. (2009). The logic of appropriateness. In R. E. Gooding (Ed.), *The Oxford handbook of political science* (pp. 478–497). Oxford University Press.

Marinova, S. (2015). Institutions and international business. In I. S. Marinova (Ed.), *Institutional impacts on firm internalization* (pp. 1–11). Palgrave Macmillan.

Mattes, J. (2013). The regional embeddness of multinational companies: A critical perspective. *European Planning Studies, 21*(4), 433–451.

Maurer, A. (2012). "Social embeddedness" viewed from an institutional perspective, revision of a core principle of new economic sociology with special regard to Max Weber. *Polish Sociological Review, 180*, 475–496.

Mayntz, R., & Scharpf, F. W. (1995). Der Ansatz des akteurzentrierten Institutionalismus. In R. Mayntz & F. W. Scharpf (Eds.), *Gesellschaftliche Selbstregelung und politische Steuerung* (pp. 39–73). Campus Verlag.

Meyer, K. E., Mudambi, R., & Narula, R. (2011). Multinational enterprises and local contexts: The opportunities and challenges of multiple embeddedness. *Journal of Management Studies, 48*(2), 235–252.

Meyer, W. J., & Rowan, B. (1977). Institutionalized organizations: Formal structure as myth and ceremony. *American Journal of Sociology, 83*(2), 340–363.

Mitchell, M. C. (2010). An institutional perspective of the MNC as a social change agent: The case of environmentalism. *Journal of Global Responsibility, 1*(2), 382–398.

Morgan, G. (2001). The multinational firm: Organizing across institutional and national divides. In G. Morgan, P. H. Kristensen, & R. Whitley (Eds.), *The multinational firm* (pp. 1–24). Oxford University Press.

Morgan, G., & Kristensen, P. H. (2006). The contested space of multinationals: Varieties of institutionalism, varieties of capitalism. *Human Relations, 59*, 1467–1490.

North, D. C. (1991). Institutions. *Journal of Economic Perspectives, 5*(1), 97–112.

North, D. C. (1992). Institutions and economic theory. *The American Economist, 36*(1), 3–6.

Norus, J. (1997). The role of personal and professional networks in the process of technological transformation. *American Behavioral Scientist, 40*(4), 514–522.

Oliver, C. (1991). Strategic respones to institutional processes. *Academy of Management Review, 16*(1), 145–179.

Ostrom, E. (2005). *Understanding institutional diversity*. Princeton University Press.

Philips, N. W., & Tracey, P. (2009). Institutional theory and the MNC. *The Academy of Management Review, 34*(1), 169–173.

Popal, P. (2019). *Small to medium sized enterprises and corporate social responsibility: The role of international networks*. Routledge.

Powell, W. W., & DiMaggio, P. J. (1991). *The new institutionalism in organizational analysis*. University of Chicago Press.

Powell, W. W., & Colyvas, J. A. (2008). Microfoundations of institutional theory. In R. Greenwood, C. Oliver, K. Sahlin, & R. Suddaby (Eds.), *The SAGE handbook of organizational institutionalism* (pp. 276–298). Sage.

Praça, S. (2009). *Preference formation and institutional change*. Retrieved from brazilian political science review http://socialsciences.scielo.org/pdf/s_bpsr/v4nse/a04.pdf

Pudelko, M., & Harzing, A.-W. (2007). Country-of-origin, localization, or dominance effect? An empirical investigation of HRM practices in foreign subsidiaries. *Human Resource Management, 46*, 535–559.

Rao, H., Morrill, C., & Zald, M. N. (2000). Power plays: How socialmovements and collectiveaction create neworganizational forms. *Research in Organizational Behaviour, 2000*, 239–282.

Rosenzweig, P. M., & Singh, J. V. (1991). Organizational environments and the multinational enterprise. *The Academy of Management Review, 27*, 340–361.

Roth, K., & Kostova, T. (2003). Organizational coping with institutional upheaval in transition economies. *Journal of World Business, 38*, 314–330.

Sako, M. (2005). Does embeddedness imply limits to within country diversity? *British Journal of Industrial Relations, 43*(4), 585–592.

Sampaio de Freitas, C. A., & de Aquino Guimarães, T. (2007). Isomorphism, institutionalization and legitimacy: Operational auditing at the court of auditors. *Brazilian Administration Review, 4*, 35–50.

Scharpf, F. W. (1997). *Games real actors play: Actor-centered institutionalism in policy research*. Westview Press.

Schneider, B. R. (2013). *Hierarchical capitalism in Latin America: Business, labor, and the challenges of equitable development*. Cambridge University Press.

Scott, W. R. (1991). Unpacking institutional arguments. In W. W. Powell & P. J. DiMaggio (Eds.), *The new institutionalism in organizational analysis*. University of Chicago Press.

Scott, R. W. (2010). Reflections: The past and future of research on institutions and institutional change. *Journal of Change Management, 10*(1), 5–21.

Seo, M.-G., & Creed, D. W. (2002). Institutional contradictions, praxis, and institutional change: A Dialectical perspective. *The Academy of Management Review, 27*(2), 222–247.

Smets, M., Morris, T., & Greenwood, R. (2012). From practice to field: A multilevel model of practice-driven institutional change. *The Academy of Management Journal, 55*(4), 877–904.

Smets, M., & Reihlen, M. (2012). Institutional entrepreneurship: A literature review and analysis of the maturing consulting field: Discussion Paper #6. *Leuphana Discussion Paper Series*, pp. 1–37.

Streeck, W. (2009). *Reforming capitalism: Institutional change in the German political economy*. Oxford University Press.

Streeck, W., & Thelen, K. (2005). *Beyond continutiy: Institutional change in advanced political economies*. Oxford University Press.

Swidler, A. (1979). *Organization Without Authority: Dilemmas of Social Control of Free Schools*. Harvard University Press.

Tilly, C. (1989). *Big structures, large processes, huge comparisons*. Russell Sage Foundation.

Tolbert, P. S., & Zucker, L. G. (1996). The institutionalization of institutional theory. In S. Clegg, C. Hardy, & W. Nord (Eds.), *Handbook of organization studies* (pp. 175–190). Sage.

UNCTAD. (2017). *United Nations conference on trade and development: Properity for all*. Retrieved May 25, 2017, from http://unctad.org/en/Pages/DIAE/Foreign-Direct-Investment-(FDI).aspx

Vora, D., Kostova, T., & Roth, K. (2007). Roles of subsidiary managers in multinational corporations: The effect of dual organizational identification. *Management International Review, 47*, 595–620.

Walker, K., Schlosser, F., & Deephouse, D. L. (2014, March 5). Organizational ingenuity and the paradox of embedded agency: The Case of the Embryonic Ontario Solar Energy Industry. *Organization Studies, 2014*, 613–634.

White, H. (1992). *Identity and control: A structural theory of social integration*. Princeton University Press.

Whitley, R. (1998). Internationalization and varieties of capitalism: The limited effects of cross-national coordination of economic activities on the nature of business systems. *Review of Inernational Political Economy, 5*, 445–481.

Whittington, R. (1992). Putting giddens into action: Social systems and managerial agency. *Journal of Management Studies, 29*(6), 693–712.

Wooten, M., & Hoffman, A. J. (2016). Organizational Fields: Past, Present and Future. In R. Greenwood, C. Oliver, K. Sahlin, & R. Suddaby (Eds.), *The SAGE handbook of organizational institutionalism* (pp. 130–148). Sage.

Xu, D., & Shenkar, O. (2002). Institutional distance and the multinational enterprise. *The Academy of Management Review, 27*(4), 608–618.

Zajac, E. J., & Kraatz, M. S. (1993). A diametric forces model of strategic change: Assessing the antecedents and consequences of restructuring the higher education industry. *Strategic Management Journal, 14*, 83–102.

Zander, I., & Sölvell, Ö. (2004). Cross-border innovation in the modern multinational: Three dilemmas. In M. G. Serapio & T. Hayashi (Eds.), *Research in international business* (Vol. 8, pp. 13–40). Elsevier.

Chapter 5
Conflating Capitalisms: Western MNCs in Latin America

The empirical part of this work puts flesh on the bones of the framework Conflating Capitalisms that was developed throughout the previous chapters. As Fig. 5.1 indicates, it does so by investigating MNCs originating in France, Germany—as representatives of CMEs—the USA, and the UK—as representatives of LMEs—that established WOS through greenfield investments in Argentina, Brazil, Chile, and Colombia—as representatives of HMEs.

Following the investigative logic proposed by Conflating Capitalisms, investigation can reasonably be split into two pivotal stages, answering the research questions that were raised at the outset of Sect. 2.2:

1. How do WOS from parent companies in CMEs and LMEs behave in HMEs?

   Putting the action situation of alien-to-the-system WOS in Latin America under empirical scrutiny attempts to shed light on the specific behavior of actors that originate in a different system to the one in which they are actually working. At this stage of investigation, it may be cautiously hypothesized that WOS potentially act partly as still being embedded in the home country of its parent company. Putting the action situation in the focus of interest and investigating the behavior shown allows us to detect potential contradiction and is pivotal regarding potential dynamics that may emerge within HMEs. The action situation is put under empirical scrutiny in Chap. 6. Depending on the specifics of WOS behavior, the second major question raised is:
2. How does behavior from WOS with parent companies in CMEs and LMEs impact on the distinct system of HMEs?

   Analyzing idiosyncrasies of WOS' behavior allows one to understand their role as potential agents of institutional change. Investigating behavior as feeding back on the institutional level in Chap. 7 attempts to improve understanding of how behavior may impact the local institutional setting of the host country.

This chapter discusses further in detail the so far briefly introduced case of Western MNCs in Latin America. First, the MNC–Latin America nexus is highlighted by emphasizing the general importance of MNCs for Latin American

M. Kappler, *Western Multinational Corporations in Latin America*, Contributions to Economics, https://doi.org/10.1007/978-3-030-93805-5_5

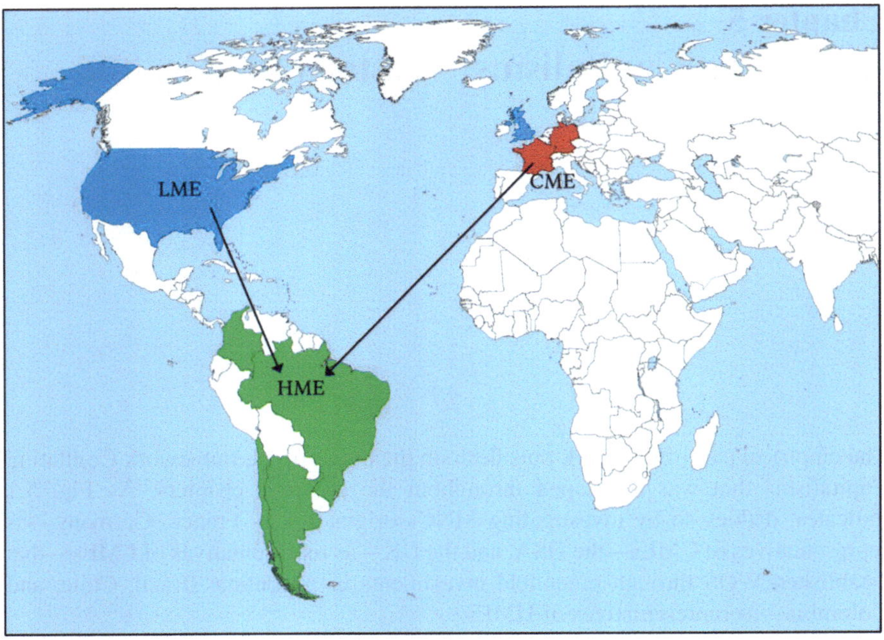

Fig. 5.1 Schematic investigation. Source: From the author

economies, the dispersion of FDI relating to its (systemic) origins, and the general attitude of Latin American politics *vis-à-vis* MNCs. Second, developmental distortions already introduced on a theoretical basis are introduced and empirically complemented. On that account, the "developmental" situation of the HMEs under scrutiny is depicted within the context of productivity and equality. Building upon the theoretical grounding of HMEs, the focus lies on an institutional diagnosis of developmental distortions and a brief discussion about potential ways out. Third, the political economies chosen are investigated on the degree of fit—as representatives—with the systems proposed by Chap. 3. Fourth, the case study under scrutiny is translated to the framework Conflating Capitalisms. Fifth, the framework of Conflating Capitalisms offers guidance on how both the action situation and the feedback channel can potentially be investigated using a variety of methods. As such, methodological considerations that will inform empirical investigations are made.

5.1 Latin America: MNCs

Ever since the early 1990s, after critical phases of ISI and the consequential "Década Perdida", Latin American political economies have opened doors to external finance and companies. Ongoing deregulation, economic liberalization, and extensive privatization paved the way for MNCs to engage in Latin America. As Chap. 2 discussed, FDI is a major constituent of each of the four countries under closer scrutiny. Overall, FDI stocks as a percentage of GDP increased between 1990 and 2015 by a two-digit factor and can be found among the highest in the world. On average, MNCs and their WOS contribute over a third of the largest companies in the HME region. Within the time frame from 2003 until 2017, 14.401 FDI projects with a volume of approximately 1.2 trillion USD were conducted in total within the wider Latin America and the Caribbean (The Financial Times, 2017). FDI flows are relatively concentrated with the five largest destination countries within the region (Brazil, Mexico, Argentina, Colombia, and Chile) accounting for approximately 80 percent of the total FDI inflows within the time frame set.

The four countries under closer scrutiny can all be found among the five largest FDI destination countries within the region and receive roughly half of the entire FDI inflows generated. FDI projects conducted between 2003 and 2017 within Argentina, Brazil, Chile, and Colombia created more than 1.3 million new direct jobs, all situated within the formal economy. Considering these numbers, the constitutive role of MNCs within the Latin American economies is beyond dispute. MNCs' dominant position is not expected to be severely contested in the near future; on the contrary witnessing further deregulation and increasing efforts in international trade and investment agreements, there is a clear tendency toward continuing investment liberalization and FDI promotion.

Besides general openness of national investment policies, the four countries under scrutiny improve investment climate by both promoting FDI flows and reducing risk for foreign investors through pro-market regulation as discussed in Chap. 2 and, particularly, various forms of trade treaties and international investment agreements. Reinforcing the relevance of MNCs for Latin America and propelling integration into the global economy, various investment and free-trade treaties with other countries and regions of the world facilitate access to the corresponding markets and improve protection of foreign investors against potential—in Latin America generally—high[1] risk of default (UNCTAD, 2018a, b, 2019).

Indeed, Latin American efforts to attract FDI seem to work well. Comparing FDI inflows 2016–2017, in a phase generally defined by major global trade disputes and protectionist tendencies of especially the USA, Latin America and the Caribbean is the only region worldwide that increased FDI inflows by roughly ten percent (UNCTAD, 2018a, b).

Apart from the magnitude of FDI inflows, the dispersion of FDI relating to its country of origin is of importance for two reasons. First, as Table 5.1 indicates, the four source countries of interest—France, Germany, the UK, and the USA—are among the seven major source countries investing in the entirety of Latin America

[1]Country risk—describing the default risk a foreign investor faces—is generally high in Latin America. Approaching it by Moody's country rating, only Chile is ranked A, with Argentina at B2, Brazil Ba2, and Colombia Baa2. These relatively low rankings indicate a generally high risk for foreign investors (NYU, 2019).

Table 5.1 FDI trend by source country

Source country	No of projects	No of companies	Jobs created		Capital investment	
			Total	Average	Total (USD m)	Average (USD m)
USA	4188	2350	883,416	210	268,305.40	64.10
Spain	1545	698	323,192	209	139,423.00	90.20
Germany	954	477	216,327	226	70,533.80	73.90
Japan	847	493	214,418	253	58,369.40	68.90
UK	793	464	129,104	162	64,200.50	81.00
Canada	686	402	247,592	360	118,860.50	173.30
France	666	340	129,223	194	47,243.90	70.90
Switzerland	367	152	51,120	139	21,974.10	59.90
Italy	328	181	101,634	309	51,159.30	162.10
Brazil	307	154	71,614	233	31,996.60	104.20
Other source countries	3720	2131	910,860	244	366,032.50	98.40
Total	**14,401**	**7793**	**3,278,500**	**227**	**1,240,099.20**	**86.10**

Source: From the author, based on The Financial Times (2017)

and the Caribbean. Around roughly half of all FDI inflows therefore originate in the countries under scrutiny. This picture remains constant when examining the four receiving countries individually. If deviant at all, the four source countries are even more important for the relevant destination than for the Latin American average. This holds up especially in Brazil, where the four source countries are among the five major investors, completed by Spain. Second, taken from a systemic perspective, Table 5.1 shows a heterogeneous picture. On a country level, the USA is the largest source country within the region. However, in total the USA contributes less than a third of total FDI inflows. Taking the LME-labeled source countries (USA, UK, and Canada) together, they account for less than 40 percent. Logically, more than 60 percent of the companies invested in Latin America originate from a political economy whose institutional setting does not conform with that of an LME. Three of the four major source countries (Spain, Germany, and Japan) are not LMEs.

Considering the institutional setting of the home country as important for behavior abroad, the inclusion of the four source countries of interest considers the largest part of FDI in total and the corresponding systemic heterogeneity.

5.2 Developmental Status Quo, Institutional Diagnosis, and Potential Ways Out

As discussed in detail in Chap. 3, the HME depicts a dysfunctional institutional setting that reproduces developmental stagnation created by, above all, high socio-economic inequality and very low measures of productivity. Schneider (2013) sums

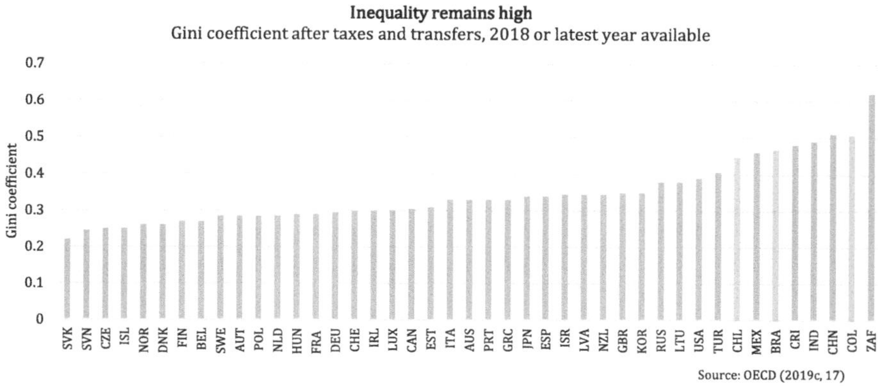

Fig. 5.2 Inequality. Source: From the author, based on OECD (2019b, p. 17)

it up as Latin American countries being caught in a "low-skill trap" that makes them incapable of generating quality jobs. Beyond the lack of socioeconomic development, in line with Boris (2009), such a polarized society is prone to social and political upheavals, as is shown at the time of writing in the majority of Latin American countries, to a greater or lesser extent.

As Chap. 2 already indicated, Latin America in general and the destination countries chosen in particular are united in terms of the indicators mentioned and clearly show similar patterns of productivity and inequality that suggest ongoing systemic distortions generated by HMEs. There is a wide consensus on unequal distribution of wealth hampering sustainable development in the long term. Confirming, the ILO (2014, p. xvii) states that "...high levels of inequality can adversely affect well-being and social cohesion as well as reducing medium- and long-term economic growth." The four countries of interest come up with very high GINI values that imply very unequal societies. As Fig. 5.2 indicates, ranked globally, Brazil, Chile, and Colombia take—in a negative sense—leading positions and can be found among the 20 most unequal countries. Excluding Sub-Saharan Africa, Colombia and Brazil are among the three most unequal countries in the world in terms of wealth distribution.

In general, levels of income equality are strongly determined by the labor market through either the number of people in paid employment (employment effects) or the level of wages (wage effect). Even though the quantity of paid employment increases, the expected flattening effect fails to materialize. What actually happens is that inequality either remains very high or—most often—the gap between the poor and the rich keeps growing. The distribution of wages is therefore key. As Fig. 5.3 demonstrates for Argentina and Brazil, the countries of interest show tremendously unequal relative wage distributions to the detriment of the majority.

That situation is even worse when comparing intra-nationally inequality by age. As Fig. 5.4 shows, the destination countries of interest largely fail at incorporating

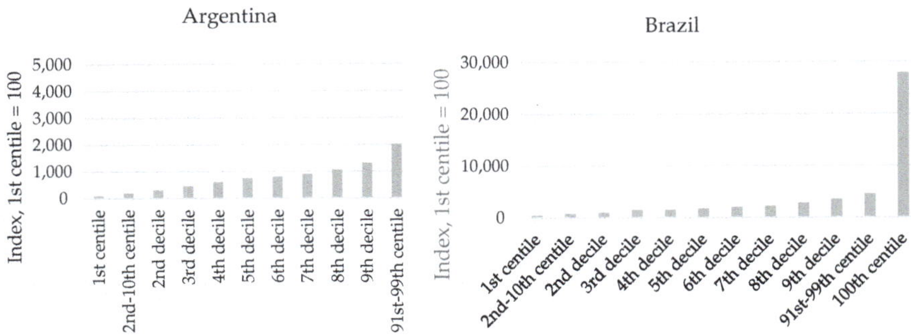

Fig. 5.3 Relative wage distribution. Source: From the author, based on ILO (2016, p. 38)

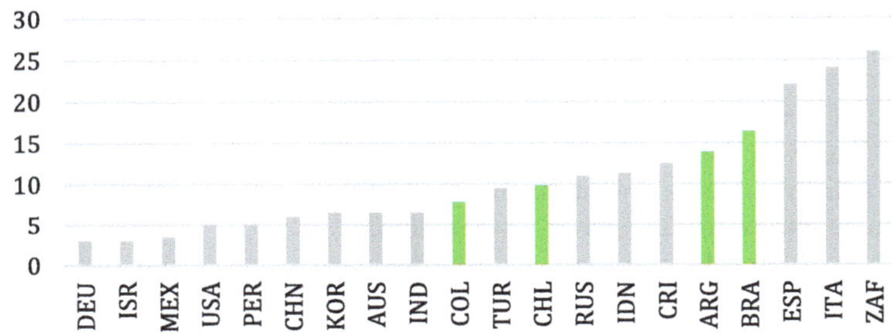

Fig. 5.4 Youth unemployment rate. Source: From the author, based on OECD (2019a, p. 26)

their youth into the labor market. Here, the effects from lack of employment intensify the situation for the younger people.

Productivity patterns are similar to those of inequality. Again, the countries of interest are leading, though, in a negative sense. Across the four countries, according to the recent Conference Board and Eurostat data (2019), labor productivity measured in absolute terms as GDP (PPP[2]) per person employed and hour worked is tremendously low. As a comparison, Chile is ranked highest as 43rd out of 62 countries. Argentina (52.), Colombia (55.), and Brazil (57.), on average, show roughly one-sixth of labor productivity compared to the levels in the source countries. Comparing productivity on a cross-national level, OECD data in Fig. 5.5 affirms the low levels of productivity.

Looking at productivity levels over time, the trajectory of Latin America is shaped by the worst development globally. That especially holds up for Brazil and Colombia where productivity levels either remained stagnant or even recorded a net loss within the time period 1990 and 2005. This picture remains stable in the phase

[2]GDP is measured in purchasing power parity, based on the value of the 2013 USD.

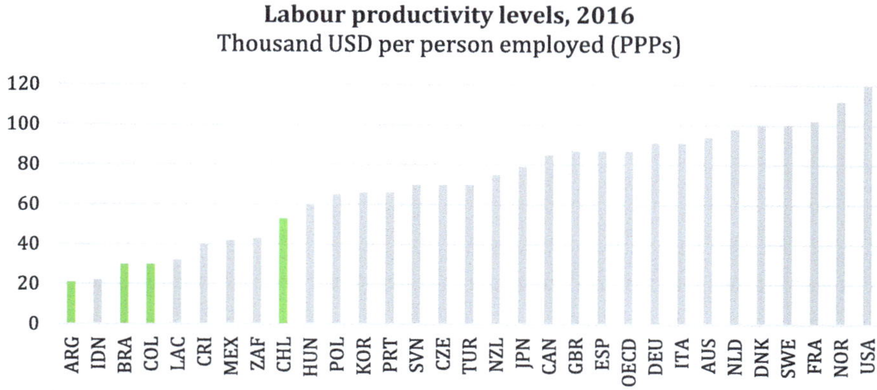

Fig. 5.5 Labor productivity levels. Source: From the author, based on the OECD (2018, p. 35)

between 2008 and 2018. Latest Knoema (2019) data affirm the notion of stagnant productivity levels and even indicate a net loss also for Argentina. Depending on the specific source of data, slight variations may be possible. According to data from the Banco do Brasil, for example, labor productivity is assessed even worse and reports a net loss of Brazilian productivity of more than 15 percent. Likewise, World Bank and OECD (2019a) data imply a slight net loss for Argentina from 2010, but an equally slight gain of productivity in Chile and Colombia (Trading Economics, 2019).

Even though the relation between measures of productivity and wages—especially in Latin America—may not be described linearly[3] (Pessoa & Van Reenen, 2013), Fig. 5.6 indicates consequences of, among other things, stagnant productivity levels on the trajectory of real wages; that again severely hampers positive wage effects. On average, according to ILO data Latin America shows the slowest growth of real wages across the developing regions between 2006 and 2013.

Reaffirming the notion of "growthless jobs," dismantling GDP growth, Fig. 5.6 indicates that the Latin American economy grew very slowly. The composition of GDP growth is even more remarkable. Paid employment coverage, indeed, has increased over time. Nonetheless, specifically for Latin America, where growth in general is very slow, the numbers need to be taken cautiously. Hence, increased coverage may not be on such a high scale as indicated by Fig. 5.7. However, it contributes almost four-fifth to moderate economic gains. Affirming the observations above, productivity gains that contribute to GDP growth in Latin America are dwindling. In comparison to the other regions of the world, Fig. 5.7 shows that,

[3]Generally, economic theory expects the worker's hourly compensation to mirror GDP in the long term. If trajectories of productivity and wages bifurcate, mainstream economics refer to "gross decoupling" (Pessoa & Van Reenen, 2013). Certainly, due to failure to "trickle down" in Latin American countries, one can find "gross decoupling," and orthodox economics understanding only serves as first approximation.

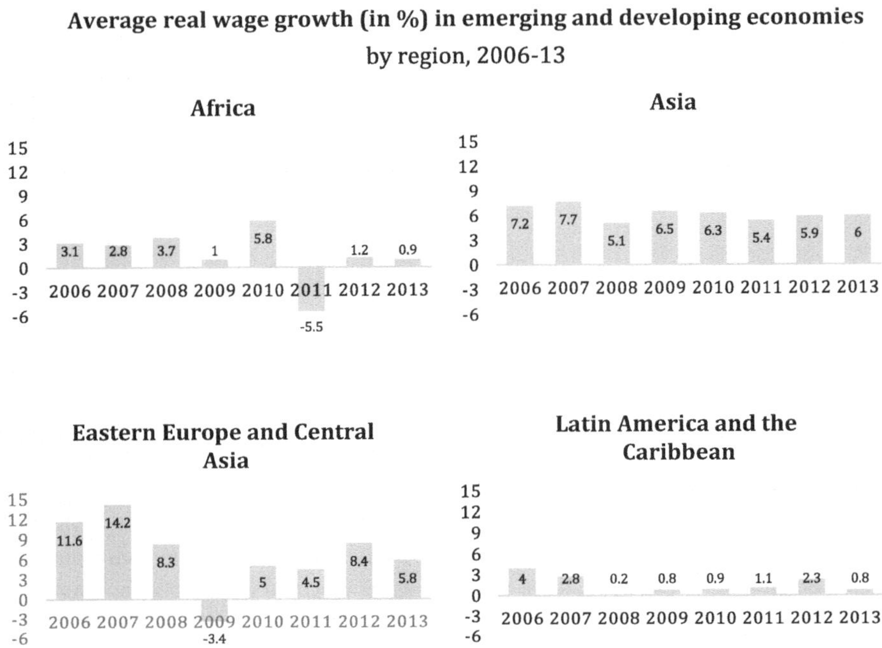

Fig. 5.6 Real wage growth. Source: From the author, based on ILO (2015, p. 13)

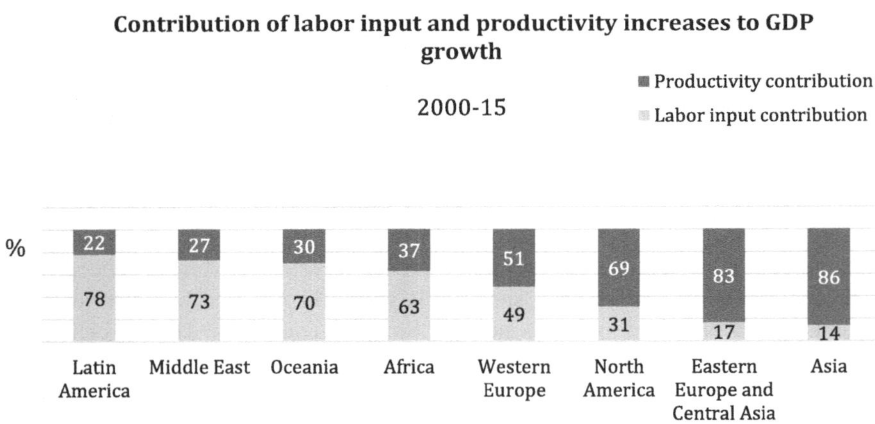

Fig. 5.7 Growthless jobs. Source: From the author, based on Cadena et al. (2017, p. 5)

indeed, Latin American countries have increased the actual number of jobs. Nonetheless, since Latin American countries can hardly show any productivity gains, only a few of those jobs created are those described by Schneider as quality jobs.

While a stable job is not to be equated with a quality job, a precarious job is definitely not of high quality. In that respect, one may cautiously approach the

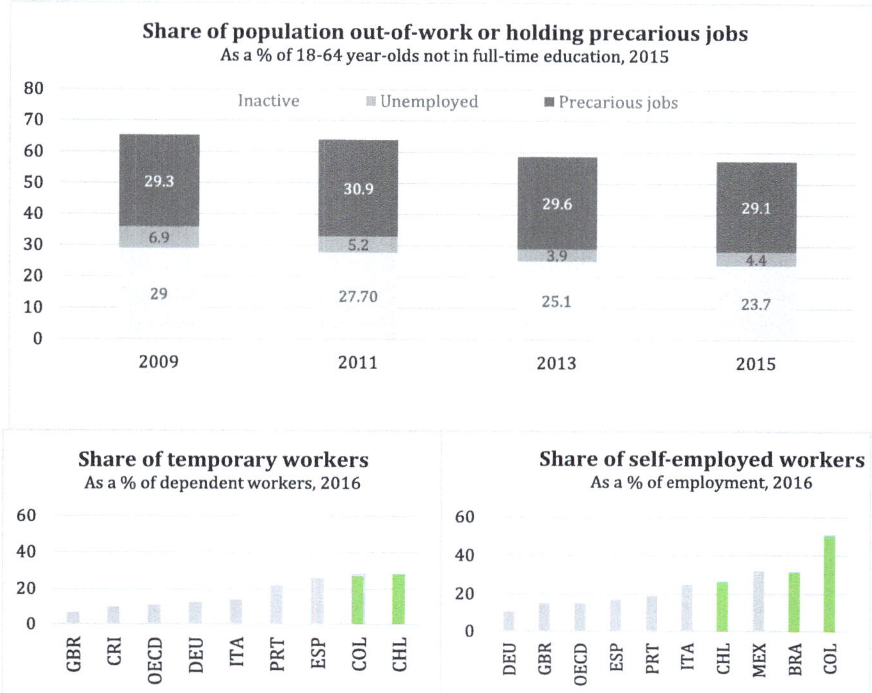

Fig. 5.8 Precarious jobs. Source: From the author, based on OECD (2018, p. 43)

magnitude of quality jobs through the reciprocal value of the number of precarious jobs that are the more quality ones. Figure 5.8 indicates both the continuance of precarious jobs over time and the unmatched importance of precarious jobs to the economy in comparison to other political economies.

Strengthening Schneider's notion of growthless jobs, HMEs were incapable of producing quality jobs created by either better education levels or more capital intensity that could contribute sustainably to socioeconomic development. Possible shocks that could introduce turbulence into the economies are abundant, and the occurrence of such is only a matter of time.

Institutional Diagnosis and Potential Ways Out

In order to overcome the developmental distortions discussed above and in the previous chapters, a general consensus among major development players (see Sect. 3.3) and Latin American economists in particular was reached to put "good jobs" (IDB) and "decent work" (ILO) at the core of developmental efforts. It is exactly here where a micro-institutional approach departs. HMEs are not capable of generating "...skilled, productive, and well-paid jobs" (Schneider, 2013, p. 16). The situation described above is triggered by the ubiquitous low-skill trap in which low demand and a lack of supply of skills reinforce one another.

Section 3.3 introduced in detail the dysfunctional institutional setting of HMEs. Indeed, it seems to be relatively constant over time but still not in a final state of a CME or LME. Hence, the work on HME and the further development discussed above breaks down the institutional setting and delivers an institutional diagnosis of what goes wrong in Latin America. It, therefore, contributes to the explanation of low productivity, high inequality, low education, etc. as a matter of dysfunctional institutions. In line with the actor-centered approaches of IAD and ACI in Chap. 2, and Conflating Capitalisms, institutional diagnosis (institutional status quo ante) is the cornerstone of institutional investigations. Diagnosis delivers an operationalization of grievances and serves as reference when investigating institutional change regarding both its direction and its quality. As introduced above, one may label movements as desirable according to their perceived ability to counter a problem. In line with the understanding of development as being mostly a systemic matter, in the first place, the question occurs of how to possibly change the malfunctioning game's rules in order to improve its outcomes.

Regarding potential ways out, according to VoC, one may argue that either direction toward an LME or CME may be beneficial. Emphasizing the notion of equifinality, empirically strengthened by archetypes of the USA and Germany, both CMEs and LMEs can provide a decent life for its inhabitants and, thus, development toward either one of them may be perceived as generally desirable. As a matter of numbers, as Chap. 3 indicates, four of five institutional dimensions seem to rather resemble an LME; hence, one may reasonably argue that further development toward a real LME may be more reasonable since Latin America may already be halfway there. Furthermore, institutional change toward LME certainly seems to be carried by the momentum of liberal policies indicated by, among other, tendencies to deregulate markets and the expected "general advantage" of market-based practices in comparison to coordinated ones that allegedly require more complex institutional support. However, it is this general tendency toward liberal policies that has taken place since the early 1990s and the nonetheless stagnant development ever since that raises doubts on the potential functioning of Latin American political economies designed as LMEs. As Schneider (2009, p. 574) puts it: "One of the neglected ironies of liberalization in the 1990s is that market-oriented reforms in trade, privatization and deregulation often resulted, in the end, in more hierarchy than market." Along the same lines, various scholars such as Franz (2017) and Ferrari (2016) reaffirm Schneider and raise strong doubts on the desirability of further liberalization and forced development toward impersonal markets as the choice for coordinating economic activity.

Ferrari (2016, p. 45) confirms Bizberg and recognizes a Latin American "...economía de mercado mal copiada...."[4] He pronounces a general cry for a new "capitalismo del siglo XXI" (Ferrari, 2016, p. 7) and emphasizes negative consequences of the ongoing neoliberally created trust in markets' self-regulatory capabilities. Arguing from various perspectives, Ferrari deplores the abolishment of

[4] Translated: "a badly copied market economy."

social security systems based on solidarity, their respective replacement through intense privatization, and the exclusive nature of the local economy. As outcomes of the "old capitalism," he refers to social conflicts, political instability, and a "reprimarización" of the economy meaning a de facto de-industrialization at the costs of the productive sectors. Amplifying already existing grievances, self-regulating markets led to a growing dependence on natural resources (Argentina and Brazil mostly on agricultural products, Colombia extensively on petroleum, and Chile mostly mining and metals (mostly copper)). The heavy reliance on raw materials can be seen as a major hurdle toward more sustainable, inclusive, and productive development. Dependence on natural resources can be dangerous since local well-being depends on commodity prices obtained and volume demanded on the world market (Ahumada, 2019). Hence, each crisis of a major trading partner—with a certain inertia—translates into a severe Latin American crisis. As recent history has shown, demand breakdown within the past decade led Latin American countries into serious problems and further strengthened existing problems in the region. Additionally, potential high returns within the primary sector led to a general decrease of education efforts and—due to their capital intense nature of upstream activities—further propelled inequality to the advantage of a few capital owners.

The "new capitalism of the 21st century" in Latin America, according to Ferrari (2016), is built upon, among other things, increased social security (such as universal employment protection) and actors' comprehensive and inclusive participation as active and vital parts of the political economy. The urgent need to increase productivity, to raise equality, and to support inclusiveness is amplified by the need to leave behind dependence on natural resources, i.e., a de facto dependence on the well-being of others. Although not giving systemically based propositions on how to improve the situation, Ferrari, sufficiently for the context of this work, may be summarized as follows. First, Ferrari further strengthens the importance of increased productivity and improved quality. Second, he doubts the functionality of a political economy entrusted to the governance of the market. Notions of social security and an improved inclusiveness of the economy seem to resemble rather a more strategically approached form of capitalism.

Royo (2009), similar to Ferrari, makes the case for a capitalist development of Latin American countries toward a German-like system in which, according to Royo, economic and social objectives are not trade-offs but go hand in hand. As major distortions, Royo emphasizes Latin American general low wages, shallow—if at all—social protection, and job instability that led to low levels of productivity. Among others, decentralization of wage bargaining, according to Royo, undermined social actors' position and impedes solidaristic European approaches. Likewise, without digging deeper into institutional analysis, he observes capitalism in continental Europe as being capable of reconciling high wages, high skills, high levels of education and specifically vocational training, social protection, and general high employment quality. Accordingly, Royo implicitly makes the case for an orientation toward a coordinated system that has shown:

Table 5.2 Systemic belonging

CME	LME	HME
France, Germany	UK, USA	Argentina, Brazil, Chile, Colombia

Source: From the author

> . . .that it is possible to maintain a competitive position in world markets in countries that maintain an extensive system of social protection to cushion to adjustment problems, invest in human capital, increase labor participation (particularly among women), and promote cooperation among the economic actors (Royo, 2009, p. 7).

One may strengthen these arguments game-theoretically, as information and deliberation—that clearly exceeds the information provided by the price mechanism—may be able to solve certain problems (in more detail, see Van Lieshout, 2008) and—in line with Ostrom—make "tragedies" disappear to increase general welfare, as is done in CMEs.

Furthermore, slightly disagreeing with the notion of equifinality of the VoC systems, given the overwhelming inequality in Latin America, one certainly needs to counter that with a prime interest. As indicated throughout the discussion on VoC, LMEs, despite generally providing a decent life, are characterized by a relatively high degree of inequality *vis-à-vis* a CME.

Theoretically, regarding the feasibility of change either toward LME or CME, under assumptions of equifinality, they are crucial: from a VoC perspective, the hitherto adopted strategy of following the liberal path toward development should continue to be followed. Off-track change may be beyond scope due to complementarity and historically chosen paths. From a broader sociological perspective, arguments may be reversed and off-track change may become feasible, if not even easier, to implement. Since it is mostly liberal ideas that led Latin America to the situation in which it is in now, a potential development toward a CME may be even easier to conduct. It is the existing social arrangement that led to a situation of crisis, and in line with, for example, Seo and Creed (2002), change may best be achieved through sufficiently incompatible concepts. Hence, applying CME ideas to "LME-torn" systems may precisely be perceived as sufficiently incompatible.

5.3 Country Selection

This section briefly analyzes both source countries and destination countries of interest regarding its fit as representing the different archetypal systems discussed in Chap. 3. Within CC literature, each of the countries is considered as representing the purest form observable of the corresponding capitalist system (Table 5.2).

5.3.1 Source Countries: CMEs and LMEs

This section briefly verifies the degree of compatibility relating to both output and systemic variables. Anticipating, the selected home countries serve well as archetypal representatives of their systems.

Relating to economic strength, the four source countries of interest can be found among the six largest economies globally (IMF, 2019). Similarly, in comparison with an OECD average, the source countries chosen relatively clearly outperform their major peer group in terms of GDP per capita (current USD), too. Figure 5.9 indicates similar patterns for labor productivity for the time frame 1995–2018. Despite having started at an already high level of productivity in 1995, all four countries—although slightly less true for the UK since 2008–09—could have continued to increase output per hour worked due to significant improvements in, among others, education and technology (OECD, 2019c). All source countries outperform the OECD average indicated (black line) in Fig. 5.9.

Comparison at an international level indicates a similar pattern for level of education. Using a composite indicator including various factors from primary school to university, latest World Population Review data (2019) rank the four source countries among the five best countries for education; complemented only by Canada, ranked third.

Showing similar patterns relating to the general economic strength and productivity levels, though, the source countries show differences regarding the income distribution across their corresponding population. Reaffirming the theoretically derived propositions in Chap. 3, both CMEs show significantly lower GINI levels than their LMEs counterparts do. World Bank (2019) data implies Germany (31.7 in

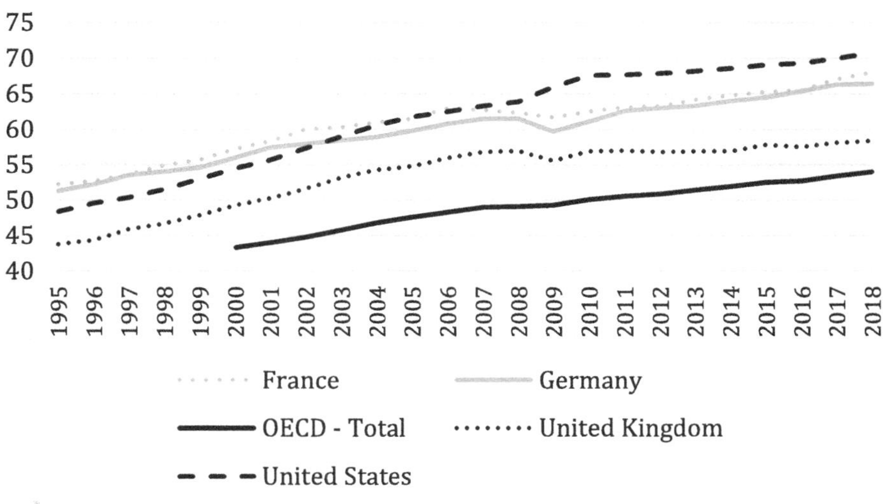

Fig. 5.9 Labor productivity as GDP per hour worked (1995–2018). Source: From the author, based on OECD (2019c)

Table 5.3 Host country information

	Argentina	Brazil	Chile	Colombia
Population[a]	44,969,597	211,684,941	19,041,930	50,613,389
GDP (PPP in mil.)[b]	912,816	3,216,031	455,941	720,151

Source: From the author, based on United Nations (2019)[a]; IMF (2017)[b]

2015) as being the most equal country, followed by France (32.7 in 2015), the UK (33.2 in 2015), and the US clearly ahead—in a rather negative sense—with a value of 41.5 in 2016. Hence, as assumed theoretically, LMEs' economic success seems to be built, at least partially, on the shoulders of a more unequal society. The notion of equifinality may therefore only be applied to the achievement of more economic goals and—if at all—rather cautiously to socioeconomic indicators.

Relating to the systemic fit, several studies investigated the categorization of countries as either CMEs or LMEs. The two investigations testing the VoC approach's validity that examined all institutional domains are Hall and Gingerich (2009) and Paunescu and Schneider (2004, 2011). Both Hall and Gingerich (2009) and Paunescu and Schneider (2011) investigate the institutional domains by relying on major aggregate indices (mostly retrieved from OECD databanks) and come to similar findings. Paunescu and Schneider's longitudinal analyses in the years 1990, 1995, 1999, 2003, and 2005 give remarkable insights. First, over time there has been a tendency toward liberalization among various countries that have been originally labeled CMEs (Denmark, Finland, the Netherlands, and Sweden). Second, certain countries remained unchanged regarding their institutional design throughout that time and, thus, show a high degree of institutional persistence. Even though being exposed to, among others, strong EU liberalization tendencies, Germany and France (also Belgium and Austria) remain strong representatives of CMEs throughout all points in time observed.[5] Showing an equal amount of stability, the UK and the USA (and Canada) remain equally strong representatives of LMEs. This institutional stability, despite major changes in the political economy, very likely supports stability theses of Hall and Soskice and the inherent design of institutions that keep shaping and enabling economic activity in a certain way.

5.3.2 Destination Countries: HMEs

The LatFour are four of Latin America's largest countries measured by both population and economic strength. As Table 5.3 indicates, regarding people living on the entire continent, roughly four-fifth of South Americans live in the LatFour.

[5] Interestingly and of utmost importance for this work, the political economy of France—which, within the original work of Hall and Soskice (2001), was labeled a Mediterranean market economy with a strong statist notion—is one of four countries that throughout the named investigations on the "recent history" constantly embodied an archetypal CME.

Regarding the LatFour economies, they contribute more than 55 percent of GDP generated in the entire region of Latin America and the Caribbean. Referring to the continent of South America, they present almost—mirroring the size pattern observed with the population—80 percent of the entire continental economic force. Hence, if one wants to approach Latin American socioeconomic development, the countries chosen seem to be a reasonable point of departure.

This work—for now—consciously dispenses with Mexico for the quantitative analysis as a destination country, even though it is the second largest Latin American economy after Brazil. The proximity to the USA and its membership in the NAFTA make Mexico slightly different. Mexico is, indeed, also categorized as an HME and fits pretty well with theory, though, the perceived homogeneity within the LatFour is even higher than the one within any other constellation including Mexico.

More important than the economy's sheer size, this section attempts to verify the degree of systemic compatibility of the LatFour with the theoretical concept of an HME; the degree of fit with the output variables has already been verified in Sect. 5.2. On that account, the subsequent part follows the theoretically derived institutional domains and reviews the match between theory and Latin American reality using various representative key indicators. Being aware that some of the subsequent issues raised are part of an ongoing and sometimes heated debate, this section follows the VoC's inherent relatively high degree of abstraction and makes do generally with tendencies rather than exact and possibly spurious accuracy.[6]

The employer–labor nexus is—according to HME—described as an atomized, segmented, and anomic field. Mostly, that holds up well for the LatFour where coordination is hardly observable. Within the past two decades, LatFour witnessed a strong weakening of industry-wide collective bargaining toward firm-level bargaining especially in Brazil and Argentina. Within LatFour, however, there are relatively clear differences, ranging from highly decentralized systems in Brazil, Colombia, and Chile with a collective bargaining coverage of less than 15 percent (LaMarche, 2015) to fairly centralized systems in Argentina with coverage of almost 30 percent (ILO, 2017). Furthermore, as indicated by the IDB (2003) and Schneider (2013), employment protection, indeed, is very high and constitutes a "...primitive method of insurance and can be costly" (IDB, 2003, p. 9). Theoretical notions of HME are affirmed inasmuch as the instrument of severance pay is used extensively and, in all LatFour, is among the highest in the world and strongly exceeds the OECD average (OECD, 2019a). As the outcome of an unorganized labor market and high volatility, average job tenure in Latin America is very short. Clearly showing the highest fluctuation, average job tenure is less than 3 years and, thus, is by far the shortest when comparing with CMEs (7.4 years) and LMEs (5 years).

As HME theory suggests, education and vocational training in general produce a skill set that is on average both general and of very low quality. All the LatFour seem to fit well with the general HME characteristics and show major inefficiencies in the

[6]Since most of OECD data is not available for Argentina, Brazil, and Colombia, indicators are chosen and vary from the ones used by, for example, by Paunescu and Schneider (2011).

creation of human capital. Even though education coverage has improved significantly, the quality of education remains a major challenge in Latin America. The Programme for International Student Assessment (PISA) evaluates Chile as the best Latin American performer, performing ten percent lower than the world average. Brazil, Argentina, and Colombia can be found locked among the worst performing ten percent among all countries (OECD, 2013). This trend is confirmed across all levels of education and can equally be verified regarding the quality of university education. Such low levels of educational attainments—with a certain inertia—translate into the skill level of the adult workforce. Low quality of education is clearly reflected by the provision of generally low-quality jobs and the tremendous share of the adult population with low skills. Among the LatFour, Chile is performing best with roughly 60 percent of adult population with low skills compared to an OECD average of below 20 percent (OECD, 2018).

The notion of inefficiencies is further strengthened when considering the public expenditure that is channeled into the educational sector. Approaching education expenditure as percentage of GDP, Colombia and Chile can be found pretty close to the OECD average; Argentina and Brazil take outstanding positions by investing almost six percent of GDP on education. Compared with, for example, Germany which is characterized as a high-skilled country investing roughly four percent of its GDP, all LatFour clearly invest more of their economic wealth on education (OECD, 2019a). This clear deviation between real outcome and what could be expected regarding the monetary input raises questions on the functioning of the educational system.

Furthermore, relating to the issue of specificity, HME theory urges the corresponding countries to show patterns of general skill sets that allow individuals to switch between firms and sectors and, thus, serves to prevent sunk costs. This is clearly affirmed across all LatFour countries. Dismantling tertiary and further education, the share of university graduates compared to VET ones is very high and equals LME levels (OECD, 2019b).

HME postulates regarding the dimension of corporate governance emphasize the importance of intra-firm (business groups and MNCs) finance that compensates for weak financial markets and banks. Affirmative, Fig. 5.10 indicates that the financial sector within the LatFour countries is less developed than, for example, the average country of the OECD. Whereas LMEs and CMEs are either well developed in terms of banks or stock markets, in HMEs both bank deposits and stock market capitalization as percentage of GDP—apart from Chile's stock market capitalization—show values that clearly fall short of the OECD average (OECD, 2019a). Hence, in order to finance corporate endeavors companies seem to rely neither on finance through banks nor through the stock market and, thus, suggest an ubiquitous alternative of finance through business groups' and MNCs' company-internal channels as proposed by HME theory.

The dimension of inter-firm relations in HMEs is theoretically coined by companies that coexist rather than cooperate. Hence, HMEs show no shared coordination mechanisms or deliberative platform for cooperation such as a joint organization in

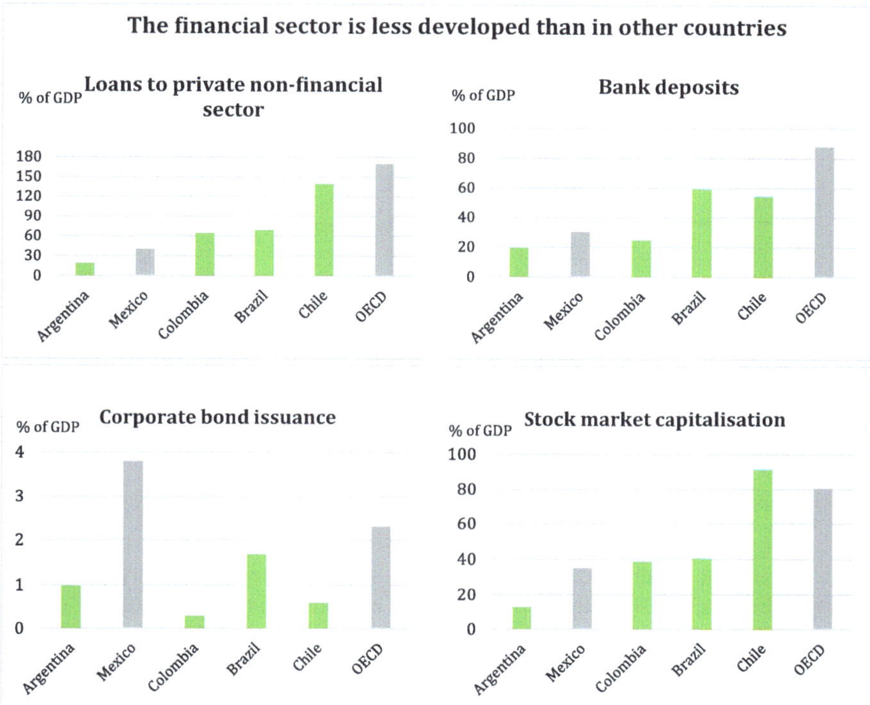

Fig. 5.10 The financial sector. Source: From the author, based on OECD (2019a, p. 51)

business associations. Indeed, affirming the fit of the LatFour as HMEs, belonging to a business association in Argentina, Brazil, Chile, and Colombia is very rare.

5.4 Conflating Capitalisms: Western MNCs in Latin America

In general, the following empirical study attempts to shed light on the dynamics that occur through the establishment of WOS of MNCs originating in France, Germany, the USA, and the UK in Argentina, Brazil, Chile, and Colombia. Applying Conflating Capitalisms, translated into a more systemic language, the following empirical investigations contribute to responding to the two leading research questions raised in Chap. 2.

- How do WOS from parent companies in CMEs (France and Germany) and LMEs (UK and USA) behave in HMEs (Argentina, Brazil, Chile, and Colombia)?
- How does behavior from WOS with parent companies in CMEs and LMEs impact on the distinct system of HMEs?

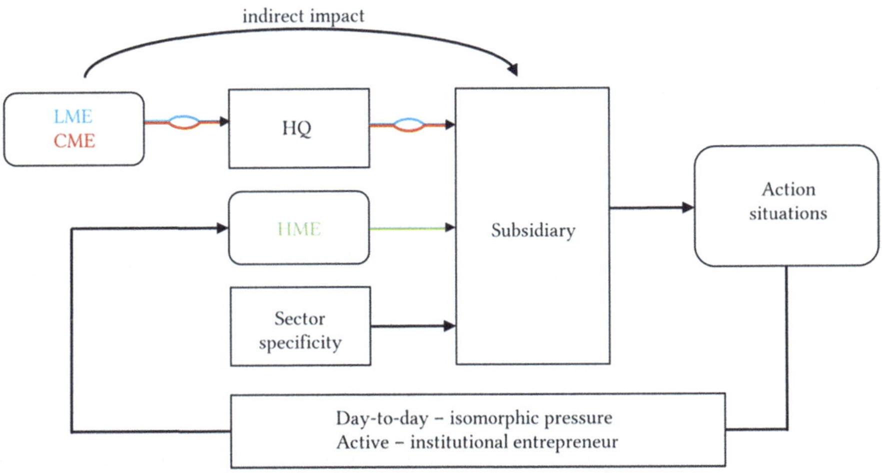

Fig. 5.11 Applied Conflating Capitalisms. Source: From the author

As this chapter introduced, the countries selected present archetypes of the corresponding capitalist systems discussed and elaborated in previous theory development. The actor of interest is the MNC that crosses (systemic) borders through the establishment of WOS through greenfield investments. The WOS as the entry strategy of interest is chosen due to its organizational peculiarities including the parent company's full ownership and the inherent high degree of control. Despite a high degree of market knowledge required (according to the Uppsala school), these close ties across borders promise the purest influence possible of one entity on another one, although situated in different institutional systems in the universe of international business.

Approaching institutional analysis through interaction, replacing the national company within an HME with a WOS in an HME though owned by a parent company from a CME or LME is consequential. The framework of Conflating Capitalisms, as indicated in Fig. 5.11, enables investigations on both WOS' behavior in and subsequent impact on the host country's institutional setting. Corresponding to the theoretical grounding developed, the following section applies the framework Conflating Capitalism to the present case study.

The MNCs under scrutiny cross their respective national institutional border and build up WOS in an HME. Hence, termed in a Northian fashion, each of the MNCs plays two different games—HME and CME, or HME and LME—shaped by distinct rules, simultaneously. The WOS, being physically present in the host country, finds itself in a situation of institutional duality in which it is pressured by two different fields, the intra-organizational (blue and red dyed arrow) and the host country one (green dyed arrow). The intra-organizational field, with the HQ in a dominant position, transmits rather indirectly institutional pressure originating in the corresponding LME or CME. Hence, being subject to two different institutional pressures, the WOS needs to show conformity to both the HME and the LME/CME.

It is this intra-institutional conformity to both HME and LME/CME at the same time that may create inter-institutional incompatibility. Each conformity of a WOS that reflects LME/CME pressure is likely to lead to behavior that may deviate from what is expected following exclusively HME pressures. Different pressures materialize in the action situation in which WOS build relations and interact with other actors within the HME. Within each Action Situation, the WOS needs to solve coordination problems relating to matters of, for example, education, finance, and human resources. The different institutional pressures exerted demand for and, thus, induce different ways of solving coordination problems. Striving for legitimacy in both organizational fields and being equipped with the relatively broad practice portfolio constituted by both home and host country institutional arrangements may lead WOS in HMEs to approach similar problems differently from companies from HMEs. Most roughly, a WOS may show behavior created by a stronger reliance on market forces if the parent originates in an LME, or by rather strategic and collaborative coordination when the parent company originates in a CME.

WOS' conformity to pressures that originate in the home country—whereas the degree of incompatibility between CME and HME may be higher than the one between LME and HME—leads to the conduct of alien-to-the-system practices, which again depicts a contradiction with the local field. It is this contradictive behavior of WOS that may be capable of contesting the institutional setting of the HME. The WOS as potential agent of institutional change has two major channels of impacting the local HME, the one of reversing isomorphic pressures on the field, and the one of purposefully and strategically attempting to change HME institutions. Due to reasons of legitimacy and the specific practice portfolio, both potential channels of change are assumed—if at all—to lead to institutional change in direction to the home system of the respective MNC.

Regarding socioeconomic indicators, the HME shows a dysfunctional institutional setting. As introduced above, among major socioeconomic indicators the HME can be perceived as the negative picture of both the CME and the LME. Following this logic and the quality of impact discussed in Chap. 2, a consolidation of a dysfunctional system does not depict the outcome of WOS' presence mostly desired. Of special interest, as already mentioned, is the contradiction that may lead to change. Considering the alleged superiority of the LME and the CME in comparison with the HME, each institutional change that leads an HME to be either more CME or more LME may be desired. Above all, change may generally be desirable inasmuch as it improves the system's capacity to support the creation of quality jobs—as they are abundant in both CMEs and LMEs—and, thus, to generally counter problems of low productivity and high inequality. Certainly, behavior that either consolidates or even worsens the dysfunctional *status quo* may be perceived as not desired.

5.5 Methodological Considerations: A Deductive Sequential Mixed Design

In line with the concept of development understood as a matter of (dys)functioning institutional setup, Conflating Capitalisms allows investigation of MNCs' behavior and its subsequent impact on the institutional roots of developmental distortions. Conflating Capitalisms offers guidance for empirical investigation inasmuch as it indicates the analytical logic of the investigation and the stages of analysis, as well as establishing the necessary links between actors, capitalist systems, behavior, and change.

Indeed, the overarching objective of this research is to better understand MNCs' impact on developing countries. Analytically, though, Conflating Capitalisms suggests a logical split into two observable social phenomena which are, first, the Action Situation and, second, the Feedback Channel. These two stages require distinct approaches of empirical investigation. The following empirical study takes a pragmatic stance inasmuch as it follows the rationale of the method following the requirements of the research problem (Glogowska, 2011; Maudsley, 2011; McEvoy & Richards, 2006; Simons & Lathlean, 2010). It puts the twofold research problem at the core of interest and makes—roughly speaking—"...use of whatever philosophical and/or methodological approach (that) works for the particular research problem under study" (Tashakkori & Teddlie, 2008, p. 9).

To provide a more comprehensive account of the research problem, the empirical study moves within both a positivist and a rather interpretative paradigm. The investigation makes use of the different lenses, frames, and processes offered and benefits from both "quantitative breadth" (external validity) and "qualitative depth" (internal validity). It therefore uses quantitative and qualitative data collection and analyses at different stages of the research process and, thus, is best characterized as a mixed-method approach (Halcomb & Hickman, 2015; Terrell, 2012).

The investigation of the Action Situation attempts to observe behavioral patterns and to test whether a general link between MNCs' behavior at home and behavior abroad exists. This quantitative study follows a deductive design inasmuch as the theoretically set general relation of MNCs' subsidiaries in foreign systems is applied to the specific case of French, German, US, and British companies in Argentina, Brazil, Chile, and Colombia. Hence, through operationalization of behavior, the carrying out of a larger scale survey and the statistical analyses, the Action Situation enables one to observe the behavior of representative agents.

The Feedback Channel is certainly of equal complexity as the Action Situation. Generally, it scrutinizes how distinct behavior may feed back on the institutional environment and attempts to understand institutional processes of contestation and change. Furthermore, since the process of MNC-induced institutional change is less understood and offers less work upon which to build, the investigation on the Feedback Channel is less clearly a priori and thereby it is more difficult to formulate clear assumption about how things work. In addition, depicted by the interplay of the Condition Triangle, situations of interaction and their specific conduct and impact depend on a variety of factors and, thus, may be even more case specific. Due to the high degree of case specificity and relatively low state of knowledge, investigation on subsidiary-induced institutional change is rather exploratory in nature (Diekmann, 1995). Above all, it aims at understanding local processes and providing information that may improve understanding of actor-induced changes in general. Furthermore, since the feedback channel views the political economy as the dependent variable, an institutional delta caused by MNCs may, indeed, be there, though it may be too small to be detected using quantitative studies using variables that reflect the entirety of the political economy. The risk of slurring institutional movements that may be within the initial stages may best be countered by applying a rather qualitative stance. Additionally, qualitative analyses may be able to offer complementary information that was missed by numerical analyses.

In general, moving within different methodological paradigms, using specific strength of each, and, thus, compensating partly for each other's weaknesses, the application of a mixed-method approach in the context of Conflating Capitalisms may be able to provide a more comprehensive picture on MNCs in developing countries than may be achieved by relying exclusively on either qualitative or quantitative analysis.

Triangulation, indeed, takes place, though is not in the center of interest. Since two different stages are investigated, mixed-method analyses are rather complementary than corroborative. Nonetheless, Chap. 7 certainly attempts to put findings from the quantitative study under strong contestation.

Since Conflating Capitalisms depicts a logical flow in which both behavior and institutional feedback require idiosyncratic approaches, the research design is arranged accordingly. The empirical study follows, most roughly, a sequential mixed design (Schoonenboom & Johnson, 2017) since quantitative and qualitative strands take place in chronological phases and the latter's procedure and question is informed by the former. On that account, this work sheds light on different facets of the empirical reality under investigation, even if each has its own particular leading methodology.

From a more detailed perspective, one may label it as both a sequential-dependent and a nested design (Halcomb & Hickman, 2015; Klassen et al., 2012; Schoonenboom & Johnson, 2017) that comprises two rather separate but dependent and complementary data collections and subsequent analyses. The quantitative analysis of the Action Situation, as discussed above, indicates behavioral patterns upon which the subsequent qualitative study on the Feedback Channels builds. Here, standardized data and statistical methods to observe behavioral patterns of the action situation are applied. The conduct of the qualitative study therefore directly depends on the outcomes of the quantitative analysis (Schoonenboom & Johnson, 2017). It is used to understand the multilayered process of potential institutional change induced by contradictory behavior. Since this research attempts to quantitatively scrutinize all major institutional domains indicated by VoC, the qualitative study exclusively uses a case of specific interest from the entirety of quantitative findings. Within the context of the behavioral pattern selected, the embedded qualitative dataset is used to

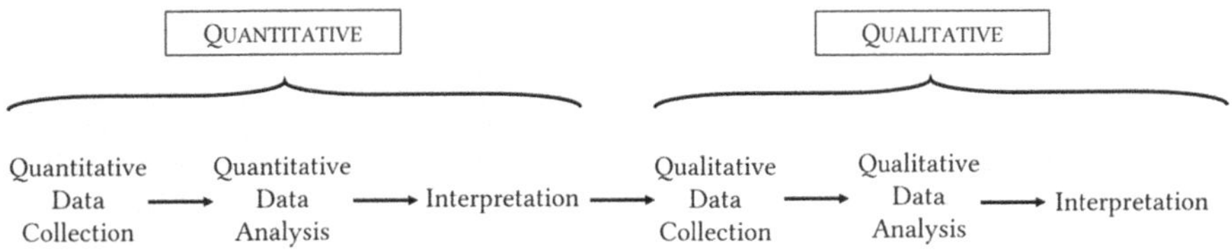

Fig. 5.12 Logic of the applied mixed-methods research design. Source: From the author

answer the complementary question regarding institutional feedback to validate plausibility of quantitative findings and, if partly overlapping, to corroborate them.

Since the sine qua non for every actor-induced institutional change is behavioral contradiction, the Action Situation, *vis-à-vis* the Feedback Channel, is treated more prominently. In terms of relative priority, the smaller qualitative part is therefore nested within the quantitative study.

The empirical study follows, in line with Fig. 5.12, a segregated model (O'Cathain, 2009) inasmuch as quantitative and qualitative investigations are presented separately, even though the former informs the latter. The specific methods in use from within the corresponding methodological universes and the distinct conduct of investigation are introduced in detail in the respective subsequent chapters.

References

Ahumada, J. M. (2019). Latin America since the 1990s: Deindustrialization, reprimarization and policy space restrictions. *The Political Economy of Peripheral Growth, 2019*, 49–72.

Boris, D. (2009). *Lateinamerikas Politische Ökonomie: Aufbruch aus historischen Abhängigkeiten im 21. Jahrhundert.* VSA Verlag.

Cadena, A., Remes, J., Grosman, N., & de Oliveira, A. (2017). *McKinsey Global Institute: Where will Latin America's growth come from?* McKinsey & Company.

Diekmann, A. (1995). *Empirische Sozialforschung. Grundlagen, Methoden, Anwendungen.* Reinbek.

Ferrari, C. A. (2016). *Capitalismo: Crisis, cambios, y evolución en el siglo XXI.* Retrieved from Pontificia Universidad Javeriana https://www.javeriana.edu.co/documents/16113/9477233/N+1+Capitalismo+crisis+cambios+y+evoluci%C3%B3n+en+el+sXXI+%28WEB%29.pdf/939499f0-2d3f-4e87-ac23-6215fbc2fccc

Franz, T. (2017, May 4). lse.ac.uk. Retrieved from Latin America's productivity problems can only be overcome by incentivising, underwriting, and enforcing technological investment https://blogs.lse.ac.uk/latamcaribbean/2017/05/04/latin-americas-productivity-problems-can-only-be-overcome-by-incentivising-underwriting-and-enforcing-technological-investment/

Glogowska, M. (2011). Paradigms, pragmatism and possibilities: Mixed-methods research in speech and language therapy. *International Journal of Language & Communication Disorders, 46*, 251–260.

Halcomb, E. J., & Hickman, L. (2015). Mixed methods research. *Nursing Standards: Promoting Excellence in Nursing Care, 29*(32), 41–47.

Hall, P. A., & Gingerich, D. W. (2009). Varieties of capitalism and institutional complementarities in the political economy. *British Journal of Political Science, 39*(3), 449–482.

Hall, P. A., & Soskice, D. (2001). *Varieties of capitalism: The institutional foundations of comparative advantage*. Oxford University Press.

IDB. (2003). *Good jobs wanted: Labor markets in Latin America*. The Johns Hopkins University Press.

ILO. (2014). *Poverty, inequality and employment in Chile*. International Labour Office.

ILO. (2015). *Global wage report 2014/15: Wages and income inequality*. International Labour Office.

ILO. (2016). *Global wage report 2016/17: Wage inequality in the workplace*. International Labour Office.

ILO. (2017). *Labour relations and collective bargaining*. Retrieved from https://www.ilo.org/wcmsp5/groups/public/%2D%2D-ed_protect/%2D%2D-protrav/%2D%2D-travail/documents/publication/wcms_409422.pdf

IMF. (2017, April). *World Economic Outlook database*. Retrieved from https://www.imf.org/external/pubs/ft/weo/2017/01/weodata/weorept.aspx?pr.x=43&pr.y=10&sy=2017&ey=2022&scsm=1&ssd=1&sort=country&ds=.&br=1&c=336%2C213%2C218%2C223%2C228%2C288%2C233%2C293%2C248%2C366%2C298%2C299&s=NGDPD%2CPPPGDP%2CPPPPC&grp=0&a=

IMF. (2019). *IMF DataMapper*. Retrieved from https://www.imf.org/external/datamapper/NGDPD@WEO/OEMDC/ADVEC/WEOWORLD

Klassen, A. C., Creswell, J., Plano Clark, V. L., Clegg Smith, C., & Meissner, H. I. (2012). Best practices in mixed methods for quality of life research. *Quality of Life Research, 21*, 377–380.

Knoema. (2019). *Total economy database: Output, labor, and labor productivity, 1950-2018*. Retrieved from https://knoema.de/TEDOLLPCD2018Nov/total-economy-database-output-labor-and-labor-productivity-1950-2018?country=1000750-argentina

LaMarche, C. (2015). *I Z A World of labor*. Retrieved from https://wol.iza.org/uploads/articles/183/pdfs/collective-bargaining-in-developing-countries.pdf

Maudsley, G. (2011). Mixing it but not mixed-up: Mixed methods research in medical education (a critical narrative review). *Medical Teacher, 33*(2), 92–104.

McEvoy, P., & Richards, D. (2006). A critical realist rationale for using a combination of quantitative and qualitative methods. *Journal of Research in Nursing*, 66–78.

NYU. (2019). *Country default spreads and risk premiums*. Retrieved from http://pages.stern.nyu.edu/~adamodar/New_Home_Page/datafile/ctryprem.html

O'Cathain, A. (2009). Reporting results. In S. Andres & E. Halcomb (Eds.), *Mixed methods research for nursing and the health sciences*. Blackwell Publishing.

OECD. (2013). *PISA 2012 Ergebnisse im Fokus: Was 15-Jährige wissen und wie sie dieses Wissen einsetzen können*. .

OECD. (2018). *OECD economic surveys Chile*. OECD.

OECD. (2019a). *OECD economic surveys Argentina*. OECD.

OECD. (2019b). *OECD economic surveys Colombia*. OECD.

OECD. (2019c). *OECD productivity statistics*. Retrieved from GDP per capita and productivity growth https://data.oecd.org/lprdty/gdp-per-hour-worked.htm

Paunescu, M., & Schneider, M. (2004). Wettbewerbsfähigkeit und Dynamik institutioneller Standortbedingungen: Ein empirischer Test des "Varieties-of-Capitalism"-Ansatzes. *Schmollers Jahrbuch, 124*, 31–59.

Paunescu, M., & Schneider, M. R. (2011). Changing varieties of capitalism and revealed comparative advantages from1990 to 2005: A test of the Hall and Soskice claims. *Socio-Economic Review, 10*, 1–23.

Pessoa, J. P., & Van Reenen, J. (2013). *Wage growth and productivity growth: The myth and reality of 'decoupling'*. Retrieved from CentrePiece Autumn 2013 http://cep.lse.ac.uk/pubs/download/cp401.pdf

Royo, S. (2009). Varieties of capitalism for Latin America? *Jean Monnet/Robert Schuman Paper Series, 9*(12), 2–23.

Schneider, B. R. (2009, August). Hierarchical market economies and varieties of capitalism in Latin America. *Journal of Latin American Studies, 41*(3), 553–575.

Schneider, B. R. (2013). *Hierarchical capitalism in Latin America: Business, labor, and the challenges of equitable development*. Cambridge University Press.

Schoonenboom, J., & Johnson, R. B. (2017). How to construct a mixed methods research design. *Kolner Zeitschrift für Soziologie und Sozialpsychologie, 2017*, 107–131.

Seo, M.-G., & Creed, D. W. (2002). Institutional contradictions, praxis, and institutional change: A Dialectical perspective. *The Academy of Management Review, 27*(2), 222–247.

Simons, L., & Lathlean, J. (2010). Mixed methods. In K. Gerrish & A. Lacey (Eds.), *The Research Process in Nursing* (6th ed.). Wiley-Blackwell.

Tashakkori, A., & Teddlie, C. (2008). Introduction to mixed method and mixed model studies in the social and behavioral science. In V. L. Plano-Clar & J. W. Creswell (Eds.), *The mixed methods reader* (pp. 7–26). Springer.

Terrell, S. R. (2012). Mixed-methods research methodologies. *The Qualitative Report, 17*(1), 254–280.

The Financial Times. (2017, May). *fDi Intelligence from the Financial Times Ltd.* Retrieved from https://www.fdimarkets.com/

Trading Economics. (2019). *Brazil productivity*. Retrieved from https://tradingeconomics.com/brazil/productivity

UNCTAD. (2018a, November). *United Nations Confrence on Trade and Development*. Retrieved from https://unctad.org/en/Pages/DIAE/World%20Investment%20Report/Country-Fact-Sheets.aspx

UNCTAD. (2018b). *World investment report 2018*. United Nations.

UNCTAD. (2019). *Investment policy hub*. Retrieved from https://investmentpolicy.unctad.org/international-investment-agreements/countries/8/argentina

United Nations. (2019). *DESA/Population Division*. Retrieved from https://population.un.org/wpp/, https://population.un.org/wpp/

van Lieshout, H. A. (2008). *Different hands. Markets for intermediate skills in Germany, the U.S. and the Netherlands*.

Chapter 6
The Action Situation and Behavioral Patterns: A Quantitative Approach

Applying Conflating Capitalisms to empirical testing, this chapter quantitatively scrutinizes the pivotal point of the action situation. Investigating a situation that is understood to be inducing action (to solve a coordination problem) and offering different behavioral options within the context of foreign subsidiaries' institutional duality, the interest is to scrutinize whether, and to what extent, company behavior abroad (through MNCs' subsidiaries) can be explained by the specific behavior of the parent company, which is transferred through the intra-organizational field. Applying the case study introduced in Chap. 5, the overarching question is to what extent typical LME or CME behavior may be observed in Latin American HMEs. Since any form of subsidiary's conduct of alien-to-the-system practices depicts a potential contradiction with the local institutional setting, the Action Situation is the primary and pivotal point for investigating actor-induced institutional change, which follows in Chap. 7.

This chapter puts major efforts into conducting the investigation in order to allow a reasonable and controlled examination of what is derived theoretically with what is observed empirically, approximating reality to a fair degree. In general, this chapter quantitatively investigates the subject matter at the interaction level and attempts to keep conditions of the study as constant[1] as possible and to provide the highest degree of standardization feasible in order to secure objectivity and to allow for intersubjective verification (Kromrey et al., 2016, p. 32). Certainly, aiming for the detection of general behavioral patterns, this study attempts to be as representative as possible within the context given and, thus, to make the study's validity ascend the borders set by the sample.

In brief, this chapter investigates behavioral patterns and the relationship of two corporate actors that are, first, MNCs' headquarters in France, Germany, the UK, and

[1] Constancy is required to keep control, so that differences in respondents' replies can be traced back to the respondents' characteristics themselves and not to the variations in the way data are gathered (e.g., through differently raised questions) (Flick, 2011).

M. Kappler, *Western Multinational Corporations in Latin America*, Contributions to Economics, https://doi.org/10.1007/978-3-030-93805-5_6

the USA and, second, their foreign subsidiaries in Argentina, Brazil, Columbia, and Chile. It is attempted to detect general patterns of MNCs' practice transfer from the home to the host country. This investigation relies on firm-level data and, prior to this work, no suitable secondary data exist. To reasonably approach and to improve understanding of the Action Situation, the study develops and carries out a survey among MNCs—including both the HQ and foreign subsidiary level—and puts newly gained data under scrutiny through statistical analyses.

This chapter structurally follows the logical chronology of a quantitative investigation (Flick, 2011; Kromrey et al., 2016; O'Leary, 2010). It, first, applies the "Condition Triangle" to the case of interest. The objective here is to reasonably derive hypotheses that both serve as orientation for the entire quantitative study and propose relationships between dependent and independent variables in a way that can be tested. Second, building upon the relationship hypothetically indicated and the general design proposed by the VoC approach, a research design is set out and appropriate methods are selected. Third, operationalization of hypotheses into entities that can be observed or questions that can be answered is conducted and is followed by the development of a new questionnaire inquiring into corporate behavior. Furthermore, to improve validity of the newly developed questionnaire, a cognitive pretest is conducted. This step is of importance especially in the context of a cross-cultural research setting such as the one in this case. The fourth section involves sampling, the gathering of survey-based data, and data processing for subsequent analyses. Fifth, analyzing the tailor-made and newly gathered data, statistical methods are applied, results are presented, and findings are discussed and interpreted. Finally, a discussion on both the results and the applied methods in the context of their reliability and validity concludes the quantitative study.

6.1 Condition Triangle and Hypotheses

Due to the subsidiaries' situation of institutional duality, they are affected by both the local and the home country institutional setting. The degree to which each environment affects the subsidiaries is decisive for the behavior shown. On that account, aiming for the derivation of a leading hypothesis, the condition triangle scrutinizes field strengths of both the intra-organizational field and the local institutional setting in the context of a specific practice shown. The brief application of the condition triangle below follows the cornerstones set throughout the theoretical consideration made in Chaps. 3 and 4.

6.1.1 Condition Triangle

The degree of structuration of an HME is part of an ongoing debate. Polar positions are represented by, for example, Schneider (2009, 2013) assuming a Latin American

HME to be a stand-alone form of capitalism and, at the other end of the spectrum, Ferrari (2016), Bizberg (2014), and Royo (2009) that perceive regional HMEs as still developing and the status quo rather as a dysfunctional version of an LME. If approaching an HME from the perspective of institutional complementarities, one can certainly assume self-enforcing and, thus, reproducing forces to be relatively strong. Friel (2011, p. 11), along the same lines, recognizes HME's complementarities to be "strong enough to prevent HMEs from converging toward another ideal type." However, regarding other characteristics of the local organizational field, one may conclude differently. As the discussion in Chap. 3 shows, local institutions are rather weak—if not, as Schneider (2013) puts it "absent"—and allow major decisions to take place within hierarchical structures rather than being predetermined by the local perception of appropriateness. Along the same lines, the limited magnitude of interaction with other actors and the focus on in-house solutions may limit isomorphic pressures on actors to show conformity. All in all, one can reasonably expect a relatively low degree of local embeddedness. Furthermore, as Chap. 5 discussed in detail, regarding major socioeconomic indicators, the HMEs under scrutiny find themselves in a situation of constant crisis. That again does not allow local practices to gain a dominant status and, at the same time, may allow alien-to-the-system practices to enter. Following these lines, the local institutional field is described as rather "weak."

The actor and the corresponding intra-organizational field are of further interest. As a matter of fact, as the archetypes of their capitalist systems, the subsidiaries' countries of origin can be reasonably assumed to be highly structured and—in terms of performance—come along with a certain notion of dominance *vis-à-vis* the HME host countries. Since this investigation exclusively focuses on WOS that are established through greenfield investments, the related concepts of control, risk, and knowledge certainly argue for a relatively dense and strong intra-organizational field. Furthermore, high institutional distance increases the liability of foreignness that points to close connection with the parent company as a source of advantage compensating for the burden of being alien-to-the-system. Further increasing dependence and, thus, impact of the parent company, as Schneider (2013) clearly depicts, corporate finance of the foreign subsidiaries is mostly highly dependent on the home country HQ rather than on local stakeholders (banks or stock markets), which again lowers local, and increases intra-organizational, embeddedness. Following this argument, the intra-organizational field is termed "strong."

Since action in all institutional dimensions is put under scrutiny, there is no general degree of appropriateness with the local field. However, in terms of institutional distance, asset specificity, and generally the reliance on home country institutions, the conduct of liberal practices seems to be more feasible than that of coordinated practices. Since the quantitative study throughout this chapter is especially sensitive to differences shown by CME and LME subsidiaries, it may be the CME action and its alleged worse fit with the local field that prohibit large behavioral differences. On that account, based on CME practices, one may assume home country prescriptions for action as rather "inappropriate."

Bringing together the characteristics of the Contradiction Cube's indicators, one can assume a moderate to strong impact of the intra-organizational field. On that account, due to the inherent force to act according to parent company's perception of appropriateness, one can reasonably assume foreign subsidiaries of the source countries under scrutiny to show behavior that is appropriate in their home, rather than in the host, country.

6.1.2 Hypothesis

In general, a hypothesis is a logical presumption about relationships of variables that are expressed in the form of a testable statement (O'Leary, 2010, p. 55). Accordingly, the hypothesis offers a tentative proposition that guides one through investigation and is subject to empirical verification through the same. Hypothesis development in this section builds upon theoretical considerations made throughout the chapters on theory and the investigation in Chap. 5, and the previously applied condition triangle. On that account, the fundamental analytical orientation, the object area, and aspects of reality to consider (Kromrey et al., 2016, p. 52) are firmly set.

Briefly recapitulating, the hypothesis needs to formulate the action situation in which the subsidiary finds itself in the state of institutional duality, situated in two fields with different perceptions of what is appropriate and what is not. In order to scrutinize the effect of the intra-organizational field, the hypothesis needs to grasp the relationship between behavior of the parent company and the subsidiary in Latin America.

Here, hypothesis development uses the Hempel–Oppenheim (H-O) scheme that builds upon a theoretically derived hypothesis and accordingly derived statement pairs that allow it to be observed in reality. In general, the H-O scheme involves an issue that requires explanation (*explanandum*) and an explaining argument involving a cause and the connecting cause-effect principle (*explanans*) (Kromrey et al., 2016, p. 2016). Generally applying the H-O scheme to the specifics of the study at hand, using the characteristic of behavior moving on the bipolar axis between liberal and coordinated, the hypothesis can look as follows:

Explanans:	(1) If an MNC behaves more coordinated in the home country, then the corresponding subsidiary in Latin America behaves more coordinated as well. (2) Behavior of the MNC in the home country is coordinated.
Explanandum:	(3) Behavior of the MNC's subsidiary in Latin America is coordinated.

That, of course, holds up as well vice versa:

Explanans:	(1) If an MNC behaves more liberal in the home country, then the corresponding subsidiary in Latin America behaves more liberal as well. (2) Behavior of the MNC in the home country is liberal.
Explanandum:	(3) Behavior of the MNC's subsidiary in Latin America is liberal.

Accordingly, the subsequent quantitative analysis aims at, first, observing (2) and (3) in order to, second, test the assumed relationship in (1). Up to now, behavior is a rather abstract term. This chapter operationalizes behavior and allows one to grasp behavior at various levels of abstraction. Hence, developed explanans and explanandum in the overarching H-O scheme are valid for all measurements of behavior at the various levels of abstraction throughout this chapter.

6.2 Research Design

The previously developed H-O scheme that guides the subsequent investigation needs to be translated into a basic research model that indicates investigative logic, structure, and procedure. First of all, since a research project cannot grasp the complexity of reality, it is of utmost importance to decide about the specific section of reality that can be put under empirical scrutiny (Kromrey et al., 2016, p. 49). In line with Zetterberg (1973), a descriptive scheme of the conceptual arrangement is needed that leads to the phenomena and to the aspects of interest. Translated to the investigation on the Conflating Capitalisms' Action Situation, the section of reality that is targeted follows the logic of Hall and Soskice's (2001) VoC approach and the theoretical advancements made in Chap. 3 and is depicted in Fig. 6.1. Each market economy is characterized by interactions that take place in five dimensions, which are IR, IF, CG, EV, and ER.

Each of the five dimensions can again be split into different aspects (subdimensions). For example, the dimension of IR can be split into, among others, issues of "wage bargaining" and "employment protection." It is the dismantling and translation of these sub-dimensions into one-dimensional aspects of reality (action situations) that are both measurable and testable and which will follow in Sect. 6.3.1 "Operationalization." For now, the rather abstract basic model as proposed in Fig. 6.1 is sufficient to discuss the general design and proceeding of this study.

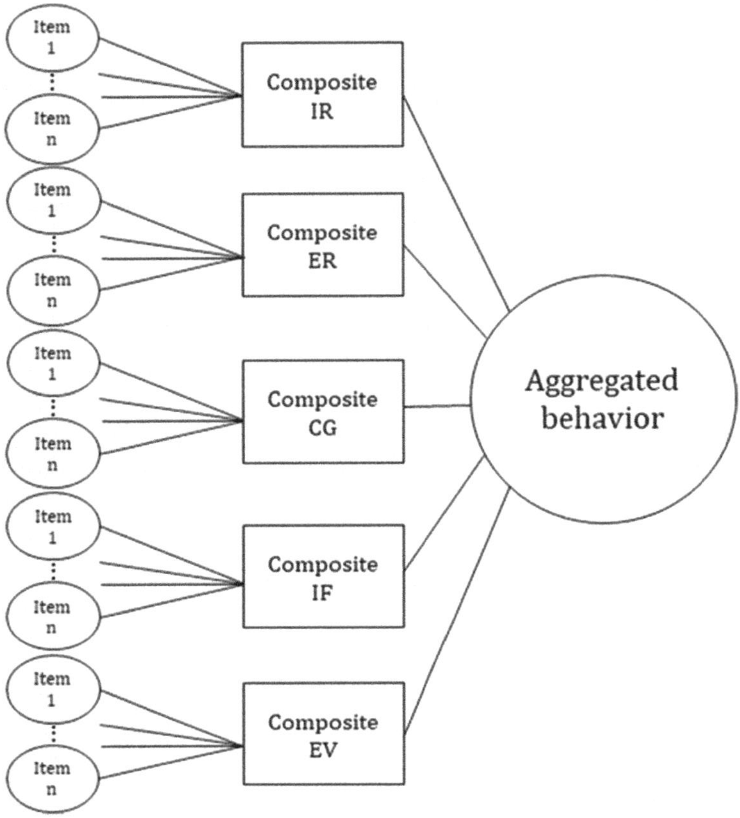

Fig. 6.1 Basic model of behavior. Source: From the Author

Discussing the targeted section of reality, Fig. 6.1 indicates a basic model for behavior within an isolated nation. Since, however, the main interest of the study lies in the relationship between behavior of MNCs at home and the behavior of WOS abroad, this section of reality needs to be captured twice: once in the reality of the parent company in the home country and once in the reality of the WOS in the host country.

On that account, the subsequent section indicates the study's design depicting a cross-country intra-organizational investigation which allows one to analyze dependencies and dynamics between HQ and subsidiaries—and, thus, the intra-organizational field—on different levels of abstraction. Figure 6.2 depicts the (first) research design of this study.

The research design indicated allows one both to grasp the relationship of interest and to make statements regarding how far behavior abroad as the dependent variable (DV) can be explained by behavior at home as the independent variable (IV). Relating to the hypotheses in the form of the H-O scheme, this design serves the interest of better understanding the relationship between behavior at home and

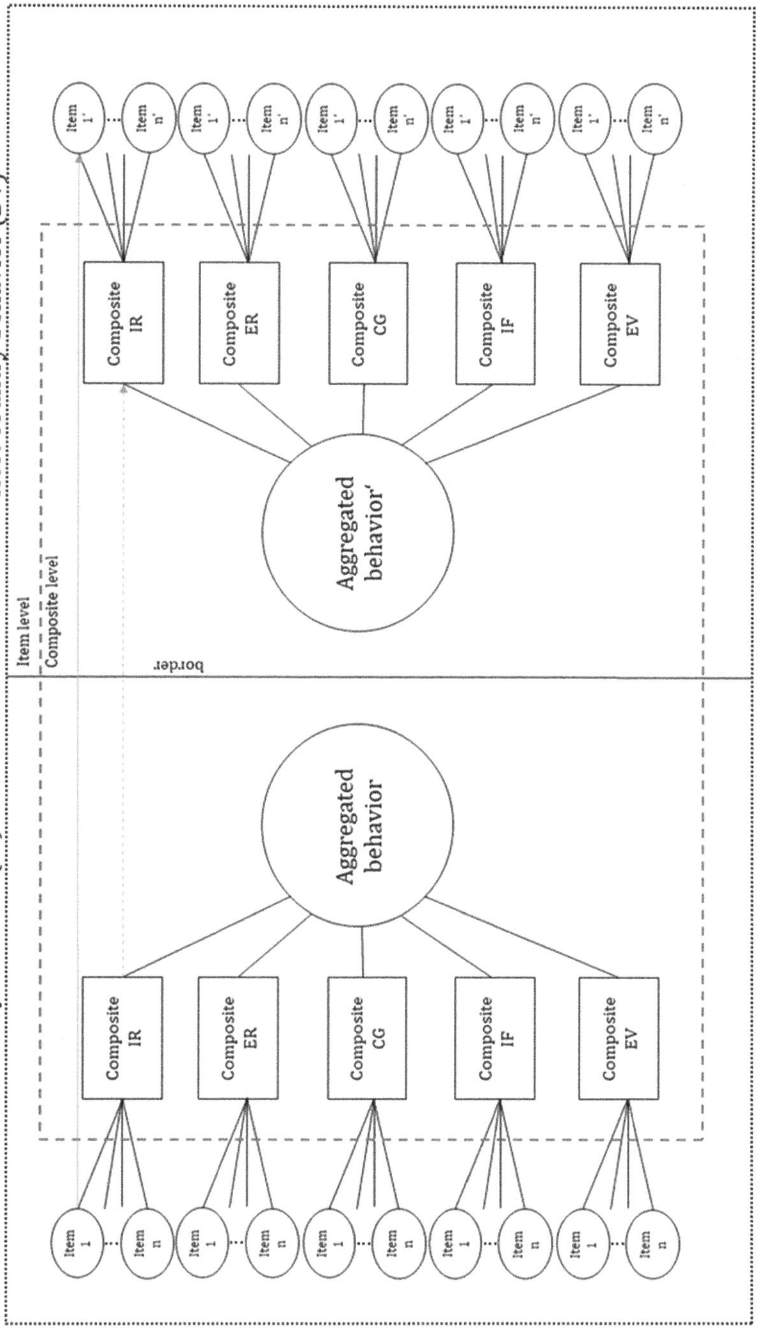

Fig. 6.2 Study design—two-step approach. Source: From the Author

behavior abroad as indicated by the effect-cause principle (1), indicating whether and to what degree a change of the condition statement (2) leads to an effect in the explanandum (3).

The relationships between behavior abroad and behavior at home can be scrutinized using the measurements at the different levels of abstraction. Measurements of behavior are largely possible at two different levels, which each show different degrees of abstraction. At the item level, one-dimensional aspects of reality are directly observable. At this least abstract level, it is possible to directly estimate the relationship between the items, as indicated by the dotted arrow exemplarily between "Item 1" and "Item 1." The composite level depicts the five institutional dimensions of VoC. Each dimension at the composite level is multidimensional and is characterized by various one-dimensional, directly observable aspects (items). At the composite level, again, estimations of relationships at this more abstract level are conductible and allow one to recognize general patterns, as indicated by the dashed arrow exemplarily between "composite IR" and "composite IR." The most abstract level possible is depicted by aggregated behavior level that subsumes the five institutional dimensions of the composite level. However, there is a large risk of blurring valuable information and important details. Hence, the added value by such abstract indicator and the statistical analyses that it builds upon is low and, thus, the creation of such is dispensed with here.

In anticipation, the research design depicted in Fig. 6.2 requires a complex data gathering process that reaches limits when generating a huge number of observations. In order to raise the number of observations and thereby putting the statistical investigation on a firmer and more solid foundation, the research design has been adapted toward a conventional cross-sectional analysis. Figure 6.3 depicts the adjusted research design. The change of the design of the general study, indeed, comes with different analytical opportunities, though the dimensions and aspects of reality of interest remained unchanged and, thus, are allowed to continue with the use of the hitherto applied data gathering instrument and to reasonably merge data (more details in the subsequent section of this chapter).

As Fig. 6.3 indicates, relating to the adjusted design, observation takes place exclusively within the host country. This leaner data collection process, indeed, comes with certain limitations regarding potential inferences but attains a higher number of respondents, which again puts the analysis on a more solid base. Whereas the DV remains unchanged, the IV no longer measures degrees of behavior but distinguishes groups according to either the system or country of origin. Accordingly, differences at the composite and item level are analytically dependent on national and systemic belonging, as indicated by the dotted and dashed arrows. Moving within the Hempel–Oppenheim scheme, the condition statement (2) is no longer a matter of degrees but one of group belonging. Consequently, this approach allows one to analyze the relationship between belonging to a specific country (system) and the behavior abroad.

This approach, indeed, does not provide the same analytical precision and width as that shown in Fig. 6.2 but still provides valuable information on behavior abroad as being affected by systemic belonging of the parent company. In line with Chap. 3,

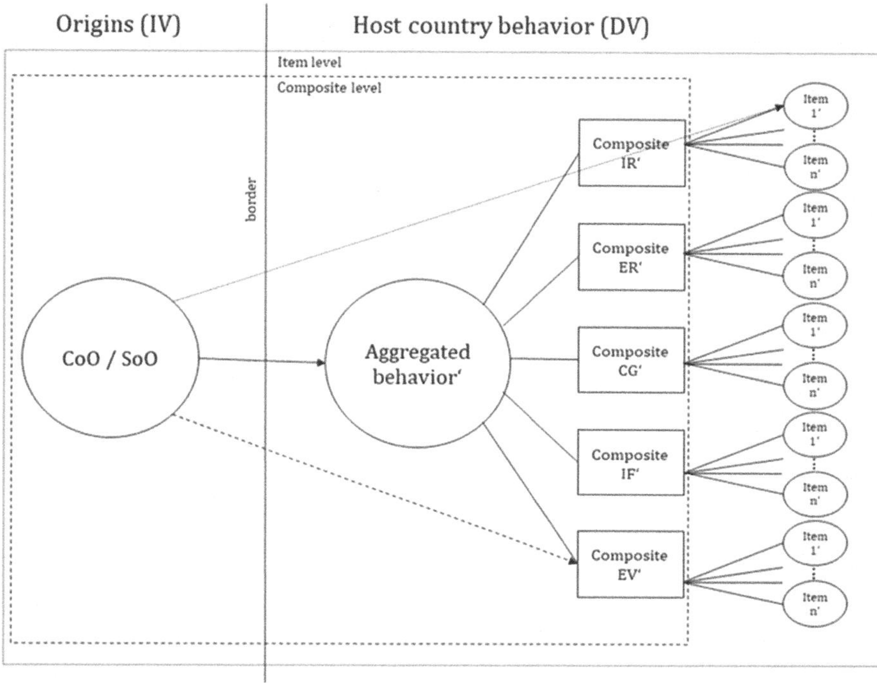

Fig. 6.3 Study design—one-shot approach. Source: From the Author

which introduced theory on systemic functioning of the different market economies in detail, and Chap. 5, which contributed to the understanding of the home countries of interest as the archetypes of coordinated and liberal market economies, assuming a certain systemically appropriate behavior of the parent companies in their home countries and the subsequent grouping of MNCs according to their home country seems to be reasonably justified. Most importantly, though not measuring HQ behavior directly, the potential impact of the parent company's systemic belonging on the WOS' behavior is exerted in an unchanged manner through the intra-organizational field.

The design indicated in Fig. 6.3 allows one to estimate the impact of the parent company's systemic belonging on the WOS' behavior along the two aforementioned degrees of abstraction. The dashed arrow connects the IV directly with the one-dimensional aspects of reality in the host country and depicts the least abstract variant possible within this approach. The relationships between IV and the first- and second-degree level follow the same rule of abstraction as the one explained above. The composite indicators of the first- and second-degree level of the DV are constructed just like those above.

Of further interest, an isolated view on the host country behavior side allows one to investigate institutional (behavioral) complementarities between the actions conducted in the different institutional domains. This additional investigation on complementarities is conducted for various reasons. First, it contributes to the general aim at understanding dynamics and adjustment of MNCs' subsidiaries in a strange system. Second, it can improve understanding of how alien-to-the-system practices can be applied in an unfavorable environment in which complementary institutions are lacking. Third, such data and accordingly such investigation cannot be found in the literature and therefore contributes to general knowledge.

6.3 Instrument Development

In order to conduct the research as proposed by the previous chapter, data on behavior at the interaction level is needed. However, data that sheds light on how companies decide to interact when being situated in the specific action situations of interest are not available. On that account, to reasonably generate knowledge that can contribute to responding to the research questions raised, primary data need to be gathered that meets certain requirements.

Moving within the data gathering universe, one most frequently finds three general methods of data collection, which are (i) content analysis, (ii) observation, and (iii) surveying (Kromrey et al., 2016, p. 301; O'Leary, 2010). The objective of this study's data collection is manifold and requires some further discussion. Without any doubt, the data collected should be able to capture the aspect of reality of interest and thereby to provide a reasonable base for analyses. Beyond the quality of information, the quantity of participants is of utmost importance since only information from a relatively large number of participants allows statistical analysis, improves external validity, and, finally, enables to draw conclusions from the sample to the population. Consequently, the method of choice needs to be capable of reaching a relatively large number of potential participants. Additionally, as is the case in this research, participants are located in eight different countries on three different continents and are, consequently, relatively difficult to reach in person. Similarly, this geographical remoteness and the inherent relatively poor accessibility of potential participants make personal introduction into the research difficult. On that account, the method of choice needs to be easy to understand for the participants and relatively clear to conduct. In conclusion, in order to comply with the specific setting of this research and the need for comparable data for statistical analysis, the method of choice needs to be as standardized, as easy to understand, and as easy to spread around the world as possible.

The data collection of choice is a written standardized online-based survey, since it is the one that complies best with the aforementioned requirements. Most generally, surveying is the "...process of collecting data by asking a range of individuals the same questions related to their characteristics, attributes, how they live, or their opinions through a questionnaire" (O'Leary, 2010, p. 181). This indicates the unique character of an expert (elite) survey as an indirect measuring method, in which it is the respondent himself or herself that measures characteristics of objects and situations and not the interviewer (or observant). On that account, the questions raised and the carrying out of the survey need to be especially well prepared to secure a proper understanding both of the concepts and of the measuring.

The design of the study's survey is structured into two sections and meets the requirements of the two approaches discussed above. First, the comparative two-tier design includes two measurements per respondent: one in the MNC's HQ and one in the corresponding foreign subsidiary. The two-tier approach requires asking the same sample of respondents twice. In contrast to a panel study, though, the survey is not conducted at two different points in time but at two different locations (institutional environments). In order to include a company as a participant in the study, it therefore needs to respond to the same questionnaire twice at the logical same point in time within two different institutional settings. Accordingly, the objective is not to see if behavior changes over time but over institutional differences to see if behavior abroad is influenced by the one at home. Second, the one-sided investigation, as depicted above, is a one-shot process and thereby is a traditional cross-sectional survey. Such surveys use a sample (for sampling in detail, see Sect. 6.4) of respondents and asks them one time. In order to extrapolate findings back to the larger population, the sample should be as representative as possible (O'Leary, 2010, p. 2010). In this study's case, the sample is drawn from foreign subsidiaries and the investigation attempts to deduce behavioral patterns back to the entire corresponding population. Hence, behavioral analyses in the context of the one-shot approach is less concerned with dynamics between HQ and subsidiaries but with the particular behavior shown in the host country.

In both investigations, the same standardized questionnaire is used to translate the action situations of interest into answerable questions in order to ask about their specific conduct as either coordinate or liberal, or somewhere between. Generally, a survey's relative ease of conduct for a rather large number of participants comes at the cost of a rather high vulnerability for inaccuracies due to (perceptual) differences of participants and the fact that generated data rely on statements about natural situations rather than on the natural situation itself (Kromrey et al., 2016, p. 337).[2] To counter such potential distortions and thereby to provide adequate data, the conduct of the actual survey is preceded by an operationalization process, instrument (questionnaire) development, piloting, modifying, and participant selection. These cornerstones of survey-based empirical investigation are discussed in the subsequent chapters.

6.3.1 Operationalization

Most generally, statements (2) and (3) of the Hempel–Oppenheim scheme require visibility to test hypotheses raised. To test the assumed relationship between variables, expressed through both the if and the then components need to be empirically captured in order to observe potential "deflection" of the then component depending

---

[2] Empirical social sciences always inhere certain inaccuracies due to two major asymmetries, i.e., first, between operationalized measurement and empirical statement. Second, between empirical Basissatz and theoretical Basissatz.

on changes of the if component (Kromrey et al., 2016, p. 80). Since the hypothesized relationships describe behavior with the broad concepts of coordinated and liberal, this chapter translates abstract ideas into measurable questions (O'Leary, 2010). The final objective is to derive manifest variables that indicate latent dimensions.

In this study on the Conflating Capitalisms' action situation, it is of utmost importance to detect behavior as coordinated or liberal. On that account, using surveying as the method of choice, above all, questions need to be developed whose answers allow one to measure companies' specific conduct/behavior shown when interacting with others. The translation of the behavioral concepts of liberal and coordinated within the dimensions and sub-dimensions (discussed in detail throughout Chap. 3) into measurable variables and the bringing together of the former and the latter by adequate correspondence rules, above all, follow an approach that involves the basic scheme of the VoC approach including the five institutional dimensions: corporate governance, industrial relations, employee relations, education and vocational training, and inter-firm relations. Similarly, there is a relatively wide consensus on the matter of the sub-dimensions and their corresponding indicators. Besides the in-depth discussion in Chap. 3, various studies that empirically investigate VoC's sub-dimensions measure institutions through proxy variables such as the well-known OECD and World Bank composite indicators (Glennerster & Lieberman, 2011; Hall & Gingerich, 2009; Paunescu & Schneider, 2004, 2011; Schneider, 2013). Nonetheless, the studies mentioned provide a frame that indicates the most important sub-dimensions. Due to this study's analytical change from measuring institutions to the measurement of behavior as discussed in Chap. 4, the pivotal objective is therefore the operationalization of the sub-dimensions into one-dimensional, measurable questions that indicate the specific conduct of companies as either more liberal or more coordinated.

Figure 6.4 indicates the five institutional dimensions and their inherent behavioral ranges using exemplary characteristics. In general, industrial relations' important factor of wage bargaining can be either assigned onto the individual level in LMEs or to the collective one in CMEs. Regarding finance, LMEs tend to rely on the capital market, whereas CMEs mostly include banks as both creditors and long-term partners. Education in LMEs largely produces generalists and CME experts in more specific areas. Relations between the firms are either based on market transactions or a matter of strategic cooperation. Finally, employee relations are characterized either by inclusion of employees in CMEs into decision-making or exclusion of such in LMEs.

In the context of indicator formation and operationalization, certain steps are conducted and objectives pursued. First, in order to both make responding to questions as valid as possible and decrease the number of dropouts, the questions need to be both semantically clear and relatively easy to respond to. Formulating questions, Porst (2014) is considered insofar special emphasis is put on semantic clarity, meaning the clarity of concepts and the avoidance of ambiguity and long and complex interrogation. The ease of response was attempted to be reached though the reliance on the respondent's (directly retrievable) memory rather than relying on exact numbers that may need some research. Memory, in this case, means

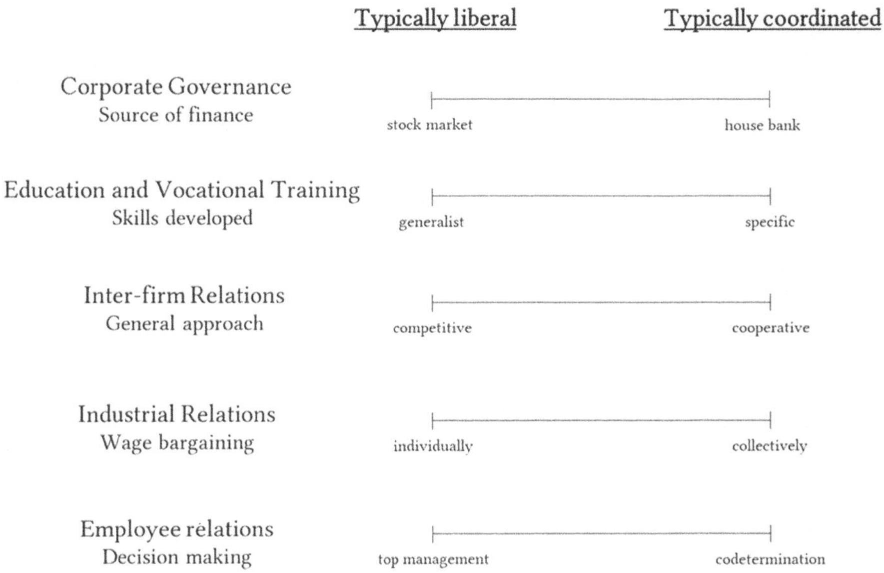

Fig. 6.4 Liberal–coordinated range. Source: From the Author

remembered information and reconstructions of former behavior. Hence, the reliance on perception rather than on factual data decreases the dropout rate, especially in the context of a survey among MNCs' top management, where time-consuming questionnaires run a very high risk of not being completed. Table 6.1 shows the questions raised through the survey.

Similarly, a major objective of instrument development and data gathering (see the upcoming chapters) is to secure a decent level of semantic and empirical validity. Semantic validity, in brief, is the translation of the concept definition into a reasonable, operationalized rule. The question whether one properly approaches and measures what was theoretically supposed is of utmost importance (Kromrey et al., 2016, p. 188). On that account, this study applies correspondence rules (below) and conducts a cognitive pretest in the upcoming chapter. Furthermore, empirical validity, as the avoidance of systematic distortions[3] stemming from either the measuring instrument or the survey situation itself, ensures that measurements reflect as best as possible what is going on in reality. A decent level of empirical validity is attempted to be gained through the (comprehensible) wording (see above), a careful design of the questionnaire, a standardized surveying procedure, and the carrying out of a cognitive pretest in the upcoming chapter. Validating questioning through such a pilot was especially important within the study's cross-cultural and multilingual context. This pretest is part of this chapter below.

[3] Systematic errors affect the entirety of respondents and thereby cannot be compensated with a larger number of respondents.

Table 6.1 Operationalization

Dimension/sub-dimension	Survey item	Shorthand	Source of Survey Item	Response scale	Correspondence rule
CG—Source of money: Banks	According to your experience in your company's country of origin in the recent past (approximately 2–3 years), please indicate the importance of the following sources of finance for your company: Banks	CGb	Own item, relying on Kuznetsov and Jacob (2015).	1 not at all important 2 not so important 3 somewhat important 4 very important 5 extremely important	The more bank-oriented, the more coordinated The less bank-oriented, the more liberal
CG—Source of money: Capital market	According to your experience in your company's country of origin in the recent past (approximately 2–3 years), please indicate the importance of the following sources of finance for your company: Capital market	CGc	Own item	1 not at all important 2 not so important 3 somewhat important 4 very important 5 extremely important	The more capital market-oriented, the more liberal The less capital market-oriented, the more coordinated
CG—Ownership	Regarding your subsidiary, please indicate which statements are correct and which ones are wrong: Our subsidiary has cross-shareholdings with other companies (not parent company)	CGo	Own item, relying on Kuznetsov and Jacob (2015)	1 correct 2 wrong	If correct, then typically coordinated
CG—Leadership stability	Relating to your subsidiary, please indicate which statements are correct and which ones are wrong: Within the past 1–2 years we had major changes within our top management	CGl	Own item	1 correct 2 wrong	If correct, then typically liberal
IR—Associations	Regarding your subsidiary, please indicate which statements are correct	IRa		1 correct 2 wrong	If correct, then typically coordinated

	and which ones are wrong: Our subsidiary is part of a local business association		Own item, relying on Kuznetsov and Jacob (2015)		
IR—Wage setting	Regarding the employees in your subsidiary, who predominantly determines the wages? For the largest part of our employees, we pay wages based on:	IRw	Own item, relying on CRANET (2015)	1 economy/cross-industry-wide wage agreements 2 industry-/sector-wide wage agreements 3 company/plant-level wage agreements 4 other kinds of wage agreement	The higher the coverage of wage agreements, the more coordinated
IR—Payment	Considering your subsidiary, please indicate if the following statements are correct or wrong: Most common, out employees are paid according to their performance	IRp	Own item.	1 correct 2 wrong	If correct, then typically liberal
IR—Contract	Considering your subsidiary, please indicate if the statements are correct or wrong: "For our employees permanent work contracts prevail over fixed-term and temporary contracts"	IRpc	Own item, relying on Kuznetsov and Jacob (2015)	1 correct 2 wrong	If correct, then typically coordinated
IR—Notice period	Considering your subsidiary, please indicate if the statements are correct or wrong: "For our employees employment contracts generally contain notice periods no shorter than 90 days"	IRn	Own item, relying on Kuznetsov and Jacob (2015)	1 correct 2 wrong	If correct, then typically coordinated
IR—Severance pay	Considering your subsidiary, please indicate if the following statements are	IRs	Own item	1 correct 2 wrong	If correct, then typically coordinated

(continued)

Table 6.1 (continued)

Dimension/sub-dimension	Survey item	Shorthand	Source of Survey Item	Response scale	Correspondence rule
	correct or wrong: If released, employees generally receive severance pay/compensation				
IR—Unions1	According to your experience in your subsidiary, please indicate to what degree you agree with the following statements: Unions are an important partner in setting wages and working conditions	IRu1	Own item, relying, on CRANET (2015):	1 strongly disagree 2 disagree 3 neutral 4 agree 5 strongly agree	The more important unions are, the more coordinated
IR—Unions2	Approximately, what proportion of the total number of employees in your subsidiary is member of a union?	IRu2	Own item, relying, on CRANET (2015):	1.0% 2.1%–10% 3.11%–25% 4.26%–50% 5.51%–75% 6.76%–100%	The more unionized, the more coordinated
IFR—Industrial relations1	Please indicate the following frequency: "Our subsidiary works together with other companies and/or organizations (not parent company) to: cooperatively avoid problems such as poaching (poaching means: stealing a skilled worker from another company without investing in skill formation oneself)"	IFip	Own item	1 never 2 rarely 3 occasionally 4 a moderate amount 5 a great deal	The more cooperation, the more coordinated
IFR—Industrial relations2	Please indicate the following frequency: "Our subsidiary works together with other companies and/or organizations (not parent company) to: bargain	IFic	Own item	1 never 2 rarely 3 occasionally 4 a moderate	The more cooperation, the more coordinated

	over industrial relations (wage and working conditions) with unions or other groups of employees"			amount 5 a great deal	
IFR—Standard setting	Please indicate the following frequency: "Our subsidiary works together with other companies and/or organizations (not parent company) to: set industry standards"	IFs	Own item, relying on Kuznetsov and Jacob (2015)	1 never 2 rarely 3 occasionally 4 a moderate amount 5 a great deal	The more cooperation, the more coordinated
IFR—Education	Please indicate the following frequency: "Our subsidiary works together with other companies and/or organizations (not parent company) to: secure the right education for our future workforce"	IFe	Own item.	1 never 2 rarely 3 occasionally 4 a moderate amount 5 a great deal	The more cooperation, the more coordinated
IFR—Suppliers and buyers1	According to your experience in your subsidiary, please indicate the following information: In our strategic planning, we include major suppliers and buyers	IFsb	Own item.	1 strongly disagree 2 disagree 3 neutral 4 agree 5 strongly agree	The more cooperation, the more coordinated
IFR—Suppliers and buyers2	According to your experience in your subsidiary, please indicate the following information: Links with local suppliers and buyers are very important for the success of our subsidiary	IFsb	Own item.	1 strongly disagree 2 disagree 3 neutral 4 agree 5 strongly agree	The more cooperation, the more coordinated
IFR—Research and development	Please indicate if the following statements are correct: "Regarding our R&D efforts in the country of our subsidiary, we cooperate with suppliers	IFr	Own item, relying on Kuznetsov and Jacob (2015).	0 not quoted 1 quoted	The more cooperation, the more coordinated
	Please indicate if the following statements are correct: "Regarding our R&D	IFr		0 not quoted 1 quoted	The more cooperation, the more coordinated

(continued)

Table 6.1 (continued)

Dimension/sub-dimension	Survey item	Shorthand	Source of Survey Item	Response scale	Correspondence rule
IFR—Research and development	efforts in the country of our subsidiary, we cooperate with clients		Own item, relying on Kuznetsov and Jacob (2015)		
IFR—Research and development	Please indicate if the following statements are correct: "Regarding our R&D efforts in the country of our subsidiary, we cooperate with competitors or other enterprises	IFr	Own item, relying on Kuznetsov and Jacob (2015).	0 not quoted 1 quoted	The more cooperation, the more coordinated
IFR—Research and development	Please indicate if the following statements are correct: "Regarding our R&D efforts in the country of our subsidiary, we cooperate with higher education institutions	IFr	Own item, relying on Kuznetsov and Jacob (2015)	0 not quoted 1 quoted	The more cooperation, the more coordinated
IFR—Research and development	Please indicate if the following statements are correct: "Regarding our R&D efforts in the country of our subsidiary, we cooperate with government, public, or private research institutions	IFr	Own item, relying on Kuznetsov and Jacob (2015)	0 not quoted 1 quoted	The more cooperation, the more coordinated
ER—Co-determination1	Regarding your subsidiary, please indicate which statements are correct and which ones are wrong: Our subsidiary has an active works council or a comparable employee representation	ERc	Own item, relying on CRANET (2015)	1 correct 2 wrong	If correct, then typically coordinated
ER—Co-determination2	According to your experience in your subsidiary, please indicate to what degree you agree with the following statements: In our subsidiary, including	ERc	Own item, relying on Kuznetsov and Jacob (2015).	1 strongly disagree 2 disagree 3 neutral	The more inclusion of stakeholders, the more coordinated.

	employees and/or employee representatives in decision-making is very important			4 agree 5 strongly agree	
ER—Staff turnover	Approximately, please indicate the annual staff turnover for the past year in your subsidiary	ERa	Own item, relying on CRANET (2015):	%	The higher the annual staff turnover, the more liberal
ER—Crisis strategy—Labor costs	According to your experience in your subsidiary, please indicate to what degree you agree with the following statements: In our subsidiary, in times of serious crises, reducing labor costs is a reasonable strategy to ensure the well-being of the company	ERl	Own item	1 strongly disagree 2 disagree 3 neutral 4 agree 5 strongly agree	The more volatile the workforce, the more liberal
EV—Firm/industry specificity	According to your experience in your subsidiary, please indicate to what degree you agree with the following statements: We train employees in firm-specific skills rather than in industry-specific skills	EVf	Own item	1 strongly disagree 2 disagree 3 neutral 4 agree 5 strongly agree	The more specific, the more coordinated
EV—Communication	According to your experience in your subsidiary, please indicate the following frequency: We actively inform educational institutions about our demand on specific skills	EVc	Own item	1 never 2 rarely 3 occasionally 4 a moderate amount 5 a great deal	The more communication between firms and educational institutions, the more coordinated
EV—Vocational training	According to your experience in your subsidiary, please indicate the following frequency: Our subsidiary educates our young workers in the context of a vocational training scheme. (Most often that means parallel training in both your	EVv	Own item	1 never 2 rarely 3 occasionally 4 a moderate amount 5 a great deal	The more vocational training, the more coordinated

(continued)

Table 6.1 (continued)

Dimension/sub-dimension	Survey item	Shorthand	Source of Survey Item	Response scale	Correspondence rule
	company and in a vocational institution such as vocational school, technical college, professional school, etc.)				
EV—Investment in apprentices	Generally, most of the money spent in education, our subsidiary invested in. . .: . . .the education of apprentices (most often recent school graduates)	EVia	Own item	1 strongly disagree 2 disagree 3 neutral 4 agree 5 strongly agree	The more money spent in apprentices, the more coordinated
EV—In-house training	Generally, most of the money spent in education, our subsidiary invested in. . .: . . . further in-house training for employees (excluding apprentices)	EVii	Own item	1 strongly disagree 2 disagree 3 neutral 4 agree 5 strongly agree	The more money spent in in-house training, the more liberal
Country of origin	In which country is your parent company located in?	CoO	Own item	1 France 2 Germany 3 UK 4 USA	
Country of subsidiary	In which country is your subsidiary located in?	CoS	Own item	1 Argentina 2 Brazil 3 Chile 4 Colombia	

Source: From the Author

Second, since indicators have the inherent function to draw conclusion about the corresponding superordinate concept, they are equipped with a "*Überschussbedeutung*" (Kromrey et al., 2016, p. 163). This means that empirically measurable indicators used cannot be seen as grasping the theoretical entirety of the abstract but as proxies that depict only a facet of the theoretical concept. In order to bridge the information value gap between the measured and the indicated, to reasonably deduce from the observable to the non-observable (measurable to the non-measurable)—to equip a variable with the nature of an indicator for the corresponding concept—Table 6.1 indicates explicit correspondence rules that indicate how one can deduce back on the entire concept using the variable of interest. Correspondence rules may best be defined as hypotheses about the relationship between indicator and the corresponding concept. In the case of this study, correspondence rules are built upon the entire body of theoretical and empirical literature of the VoC approach discussed in detail throughout the previous chapters.

Third, existing studies have been reviewed in order to extract potential surveys that have already addressed suitable variables that proved to be both valid and reliable. In so doing, if possible, efforts for question development and pretesting were economized by relying on existent findings. If a suitable variable is used from another study, Table 6.1 indicates the source of the item. Specific indicators that have not yet been established are newly developed and cognitively tested.

Fourth, questions are supposed to be raised in order to benefit from VoC's one-dimensional bipolarity (liberal–coordinated) as discussed in Chap. 3. On that account, each question is supposed to be answerable within a spectrum ranging from liberal to coordinated. As such, in each Action Situation, a respondent can show behavior within the range from liberal to coordinated. Indeed, there is no final line that makes a company act in a liberal or coordinated manner. Using the range indicated, one can exclusively state that someone acts, for example, more or less coordinated or liberal than a subject of comparison. Table 6.1 indicates the corresponding logic of the question. All of the questions raised are closed in nature and vary in the level of differentiation. All questions have a limited and predefined number of potential response categories in which respondents need to format their responses.

Fifth, measuring is the numerical (symbolic) assignment of an object's characteristic categories. The result of measuring is the symbolic depiction of the empirical characteristic (Kromrey et al., 2016, p. 203). The information value of measuring can vary in its level of differentiation ranging from binary information (existing/nonexisting) to the exact registration as the precise "degree of existence." Accordingly, variables can be measured in various scales, such as the nominal, the ordinal, the interval, and the ratio scale,[4] chronologically showing an increase in information value and levels of differentiation and thereby also in statistical opportunities. As Table 6.1 indicates, mostly nominal, ordinal, and ratio scales are used. According to the decision taken before targeting the respondents' ability to use memory to answer,

[4] For a more detailed introduction into scale levels, see, for example, Kromrey (2016, p. 205).

the decision regarding the level of differentiation needed is targeting as much information as possible to allow nuanced statistical analysis and as few as needed to secure the relative ease of conducting and to avoid spurious accuracy. In addition to, for example, dichotomous variables or the precise indication of percentages, the scale most often used is the Likert scale. It has proven valuable in social sciences, among others, due to its potentially high level of differentiation and the relative ease of responding.

Item construction is informed—to a relatively large degree by a broad literature review in VoC-related work. However, in particular, various items follow the work of Liebmann (2009), Kuznetsov and Jacob (2015), Albert (1992), and CRANET (2015). As Table 6.1 indicates, IFr and IFs are exceptions inasmuch as being composed by more than one item. They are calculated as additive indicators as indicated in Sect. 6.4 on data processing. All items developed are summarized in the subsequent table.

6.3.2 Questionnaire Development

The questionnaire represents this quantitative study's major data gathering instrument. Whereas questions were developed in the previous section, this section, first, introduces various considerations on the questionnaire configuration and, second, briefly discusses the cognitive-pretest aiming at designing a transparent, interesting, valid, reliable, and easy-to-handle questionnaire.[5]

Relating to the general considerations on questionnaire building, following Porst (2014) and Kromrey et al. (2016, p. 350), to secure a high level of transparency, it is of utmost importance to explain the major content, interest, and purpose of the investigation, the role of the respondent as a valued expert, to indicate information about the investigators, and to reassure respondents regarding anonymity and the exclusively scientific use of information. Of further importance, the first couple of "introductory" questions are supposed to provide an unproblematic, easy, yet interesting entry to the questionnaire. Since most respondents feel rather uncomfortable with questions that may be answered with a relatively negative response category, such as "no," they are avoided in the beginning (Kromrey et al., 2016, p. 356). Furthermore, the middle passage of the questionnaire plays a vital role since it is the stage in the questionnaire where potential symptoms of fatigue take place (Kromrey et al., 2016, p. 357). In order to motivate the respondent to finish the questionnaire, the middle passage indicating that the respondent is already "half way there" is amended to the questionnaire.

Filter questions are applied when reasonable; in this case regarding questions on research and development, since not all subsidiaries have such a department. It helps

[5]Due to restrictions of time and matters of a limited population, this study does not conduct a standard pretest of the questionnaire as a whole.

to reduce the workload and to focus on what matters. It furthermore helps to avoid contradictory responses. In the same vein, throughout the entire questionnaire, a progress bar is applied. It informs the respondent in percent about how much of the questionnaire has already been answered and how much still needs to be answered. Beyond transparency, information about progress is generally considered to contribute positively to matters of transparency and motivation. Following this line of argument, individual pages of the questionnaire are designed to not be too long. Progress seems to be more dynamic and motivates the respondent. Questions are clearly legible and questions are made clearly separable through the alternating use of gray and white as background dye. In general, the structure of the questionnaire is built according to the related topic in dimensional blocks. On that account, as far as possible, successive questions mostly logically belong to the same topic.

The line between mandatory and non-mandatory questions is, indeed, easy to draw but has wide-reaching consequences. On the one hand, non-mandatory fields make missing values more likely and risk a "jumping" respondent cherry-picking the questions he or she feels most comfortable with. On the other hand, mandatory fields increase the risk of dropouts. A respondent who does not want to answer a particular mandatory question is forced to not participate in the survey at all. Hence, a dropout means a loss of the entire information just because of the unwillingness to respond to one question. That seems inappropriate. On that account, this questionnaire finds a middle way. No question is mandatory, though each question not answered leads to an information text popping up reminding that responses are missing. On that account, easy skipping through the questionnaire is not possible, thereby increasing the probability of indicating values, and if not at all willing to answer a certain question, a respondent can just skip the question by consciously expressing the desire to leave this question blank. Finally, the closing question provides a platform in which the respondent can comment, give feedback, and indicate additional information that is deemed important.

Cognitive Pretesting

In general, the method of cognitive pretesting approaches the issue of questions' validity—both semantic and empirical. Cognitive pretests belong to the active techniques inasmuch as the interviewer actively questions the respondent regarding the general interpretation and understanding of questions and concepts, the cognitive process toward decision-making, and the assignment of the internal evaluation of a situation to a formal response category (Lenzner et al., 2015; Porst, 2014; Prüfer & Rexroth, 2005).

Evaluating and testing a questionnaire (respectively the questions formulated) before the actual field phase is an essential part of questionnaire development. It helps to secure a decent level of validity and reliability,[6] to reduce the number of dropouts, and to increase the quality of data gathered (Lenzner et al., 2015; Porst,

[6]Reliability is understood as the absence of systematic errors. Consequently, reliability describes the intertemporal, intersubjective, and inter-instrumental stability of the measured values (Kromrey et al., 2016, p. 243).

2014; Prüfer & Rexroth, 2000). The imperative nature of a pretest is further reinforced by the diverse cultural and linguistic backgrounds of this investigation's participants. Without ensuring that interpretations of concepts and words align across countries and individuals, the validity of the entire research project is put at stake. Table 6.2 summarizes the in-depth pretesting.

Table 6.2 Pretesting summary table

Number of Cognitive Interviewers	1
Number of interviews conducted (audio-recorded)	6
Selection of target population	Quota sample
Quotas	The selection of the pretest participants was primarily based on the mother tongue and cultural backgrounds. Accordingly, the sample was selected to represent each mother tongue and type of market economy with participants from Brazil (Portuguese), Germany (German), Colombia (Spanish), the USA (English), and France (French). Furthermore, the participants of the pretest resembled the target population with regard to major characteristics such as an economic work field, corporate experience, staff and budget responsibility, gender, and age (Lenzner et al., 2015).
Procedure	In person interviews. Interviewee receives a printed version of the questionnaire. Conversation is led and additional questions are raised by the questionnaire. Conversation is led and additional questions are raised by the interviewer in a quasi-standardized fashion. This pretest is conducted in an iterative manner by carrying out three consecutive rounds with each two participants (Prüfer & Rexroth, 2005; Lenzner et al., 2015). After each round, changes and adaptations are edited. This leads to improvement over time and includes the different cultural and linguistic backgrounds. Rounds two and three are conducted in the same way but through Skype Video calling. Instead of a printed version, the interviewee receives the questions as a Word document. Each interview should take no longer than 60–90 min and should not exceed the number of 20 to 25 questions (Lenzner et al., 2015). Questions that are put under cognitive scrutiny are selected relating to complexity and their prior state of validity. The more complex a question is the more necessary it is to pretest it. If a question is not new and already tested, further pretests are mostly avoided. Following the recommendation of, e.g., Porst (2014) and Lenzner et al. (2015), the pretest is limited to around 20 questions
Cognitive techniques applied	Concurrent thinking aloud, comprehension probing, information retrieval probing, elaborative probing, paraphrasing, confidence rating
Analysis technique	Informal analysis. After the interview, the conversation is selectively transcribed (Lenzner et al., 2015) and eclectically and subjectively evaluated. Phases of evaluation and analyses take place after each round of interviews

The only alteration between home and host country questionnaire is the replacement of the word "company" with "subsidiary."

6.4 Data Gathering

Fielding the survey and collecting and processing data are part of the subsequent chapter. As indicated above, mainly due to the wide geographic dispersion and the corresponding poor accessibility of respondents, the survey is carried out online. As tool, the survey provider Unipark[7] is used. The subsequent chapter discusses the survey-related aspects of population and sampling, the actual carrying out of the survey itself and the processing of data for subsequent statistical analyses.

6.4.1 Population and Sampling

Sampling is the process of "...making a selection from a group for which propositions will be advanced at the end" (Flick, 2011, p. 70). Expected characteristics of and relationships within the mentioned group (population) are supposed to be mirrored by a smaller representative selection (Kromrey et al., 2016).

As a particularity of this study, the subject of interest is the MNC. On that account, first of all, the population of the corporate actors is defined. Later on, though, considerations about who within the MNC may best be suitable to respond on behalf of it are made. Following, regarding the corporate actors of interest, the mentioned group (target population) is empirically well-defined and unambiguously determined by theoretical considerations in Sect. 3.1. MNCs of interest need to share the following characteristics:

- Being a company/for-profit corporation
- Having its HQ in France, Germany, the UK, or the USA
- Having foreign subsidiaries in Argentina, Brazil, Chile, or Colombia
- Being the sole owner of the subsidiaries (i.e., WOS)
- Having built the subsidiaries through greenfield investments

Information about the presence of companies in general and especially in conjunction with the specific form of foreign market entry is very scarce and could be retrieved from fdimarket.com, which offers a comprehensive database on FDI-related processes worldwide. This database provides information about all greenfield investments within the time frame from 2001 until today (2017 at the date of sampling) and allows one to observe every single FDI made connected to, among others, the company of interest, project date, name of the investing company,

[7] © Copyright 2021 UNIPARK & QuestBack.

the parent company, destination country, industry sector, capital investment, the industry activity, and the number of jobs created (directly).

In total, according to the dataset of fdimarkets.com, within the time frame of 2003 to 2017, relating to the home and host countries of interest, 3280 FDI[8] projects have been conducted by MNCs. Correcting for multiple investments of one company in more than one country, in total 1650 companies from France, Germany, the UK, and the USA invested in the Latin American countries of interest and thereby represent the target population.

However, information of fdimarkets.com does not include whether the subsidiary as indicated still exists or not. Assuming $B(t)$ as the quantity of companies that exist today after t years regarding the time period 2001–2017, a as the annual hazard rate of foreign subsidiaries, and c the number of annually newly invested companies. $B(t)$ can be calculated as follows:

$$B(t) = c \cdot \sum_{n=0}^{t} a^t$$

Assuming a conservatively calculated hazard rate of 5%[9] over 16 years, and a number of newly investing companies p.a. on average of 103,[10] the total existing target population nowadays is:

$$B(17) = 103 \cdot \sum_{n=0}^{16} 0,95^{17} = 1241.74$$

Certainly, the actual population is larger than the one assumed here. Also, before 2001, Western MNCs did make FDI in the host countries of interest. However, those that entered the Latin American market before 2001 are not accessible. Since it was neither possible (time and access restrictions) nor practicable to conduct a "census," which is a survey of each of the 1242 companies, the following section describes the process of selecting elements of the 1242 companies that can be included into this study. In order to reasonably generalize findings, the sample is supposed to be representative, appropriate, and unbiased (O'Leary, 2010).

As a general rule, the more sophisticated statistical analysis may be, the more respondents are required to reasonably generalize findings back to the wider population. Using a "sample size calculator"[11] that suggests the size of the sample based on the target population size (1242), the confidence interval accepted, and the

---

[8] Thereof 2003 projects were conducted in Brazil, 497 in Argentina, 425 in Colombia, and 355 in Chile (The Financial Times, 2017).

[9] In emerging markets, usually a higher hazard rate is applied.

[10] On average: 1650 companies over 16 years makes on average 103 companies per year.

[11] See https://www.calculator.net/sample-size-calculator.html?type=1&cl=90&ci=8&pp=50&ps=1200&x=0&y=0

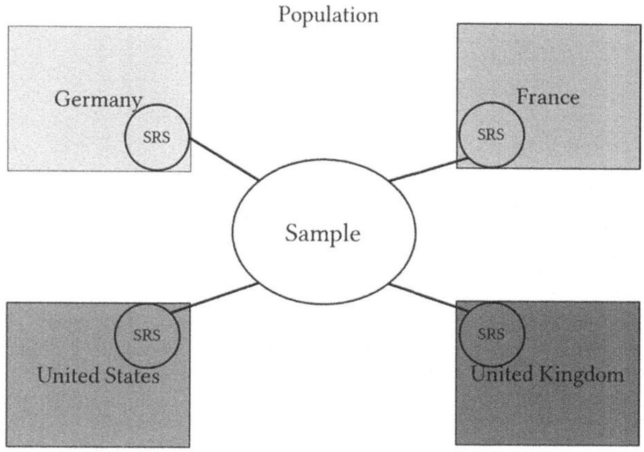

Fig. 6.5 Stratified random sampling. Source: From the Author

confidence level applied, a minimum size of 99 is recommended. This number is based on accepting a relatively low confidence level of 90 percent and a confidence interval (margin of error) of about 7 percent. Both values, indeed, are relatively laxly chosen and consequently cause a relatively high risk of reliability issues. Nonetheless, since the survey targets experts (to be distinguished from citizen surveys), the quality of information is high and the response rate is expected to be rather low within the specific setting of this study. On that account, these measures are accepted and can be found as such in comparable studies. Translated to the study at hand, this means that there is a nine in ten chance that results of this sample fall between a score + − 7 percent of the result gained, if all 1242 companies were surveyed. Accordingly, safeguarding the sample to approximate the characteristics and inherent heterogeneity of the wider population (Flick, 2011), representativeness is addressed in detail below.

As Fig. 6.5 demonstrates, the applied sampling strategy is a systematic stratified sampling, since the population is first divided into non-overlapping subgroups. Since the MNCs' home country as potential driver of specific behavior is of utmost importance, the division into subgroups is conducted according to companies' country of origin. Then, within each subgroup a random sample is taken in order to secure adequate representation of companies from each home country.[12]

As Table 6.3 indicates, in order to reasonably compare MNCs according to their home country, representation of the subgroups within the sample is disproportionate and attempts to attain equal sizes of subdivisions rather than mirroring the population regarding its actual distribution. For the complete list of sampling units, see Appendix 1.

Consequently, the sample of MNCs is deemed to be representative for the target population, covering more than 400 MNCs, thus depicting almost a third of the

[12] The selection in alphabetical order is, indeed, systematic, though still to be evaluated as randomized, since there are no known relationships between the first letter of a company name and potential biases regarding characteristics and behavior shown of a company or a distinct hazard rate.

Table 6.3 Population and sample proportions

	Target population		Disproportionate stratified sample	
	N	Share of the target population[a]	*n*	Share of frame population
Germany	200	16%	100	25%
France	200	16%	100	25%
UK	200	16%	100	25%
US	650	52%	100	25%

Source: From the Author
[a]Since the hazard rate is assumed to be equal for all country groups, the relative figures are informed by the corresponding shares of the original 1.650 MNCs

entire target population (Kromrey et al., 2016). Nonetheless, the assumption of a low response rate due to the complex survey process in conjunction with the decision against a census sampling intuitively evokes skepticism. However, the sampling method applied is led by reasonable pragmatism in the context of non-identity between MNCs as the sampling units (*Auswahleinheiten*) and managers within the MNCs as the survey units (*Erhebungseinheiten*) giving actual information (Kromey et al., 2017, p. 261). Anticipating the subsequent section, one MNC can be approached through various individual representatives (experts/informants) making "vertical" contacting (contacting various individuals per company) advantageous in comparison to horizontal diffusion (one individual per company) among a larger number of MNCs.

The subsequent chapter elucidates the selection of informants as the final survey units and the carrying out of the survey. The selection of survey units, indeed, is part of the sampling process. Nonetheless, since it motivates the specific conduct of the survey, embedding the selection of the survey units within the survey procedure seems to be reasonable and is therefore part of the next chapter.

6.4.2 *Survey*

In the case of the study, the actual test subject, the MNC and its Latin American subsidiary, cannot serve as a respondent itself. Accordingly, respondents in this study are company-internal experts that do not evaluate on its characteristics or behavior, but the ones of an object of interest that belongs to the rather narrow living context[13] of the expert (Kromrey et al., 2016, p. 241). The informed expert as informant decides himself or herself about specific situations, corresponding response categories and the measurement, not the interviewer. Hence, in comparison to "direct measuring" where the scientist measures directly, here, the measurement

[13] *Engerer Lebenskontext* in the original German version of Kromrey et al. (2016).

and assignment of conditions and situations to specific response categories is done by the interviewee himself or herself. On that account, the respondent of choice needs to be a real expert that is capable of giving representative responses for the hierarchical structure he or she belongs to. That need for comprehensive expertise is intensified by the coverage of all five institutional domains of the VoC approach that transcends the functional borders of single corporate departments (Bardasi et al., 2010; Battaglia et al., 2008). On that account, to give valuable and valid information, this study focuses on the top management as key informants. Accordingly, a manager is considered when having budget and staff responsibility and being in a position that allows a certain macro knowledge about various departments and the relationships between them.

The survey is conducted using the online platform Unipark.[14] In line with the two study designs applied, data gathering applies two different approaches. First, the "horizontal approach" (generating data for the "two-step approach" design) investigates both relevant sides of the MNC, the HQs, and the Latin American subsidiary. As such, one valid observation involves two completed questionnaires per MNC. This approach, indeed, opens analytical opportunities but falls short of expectations due to a relatively low number of complete observations of 51, with a relatively strong German bias among the participating HQs (number of respondents per country: 1 France, 42 Germany, 4 UK, 5 USA) due to reasons of awareness level of the research institution. Referring to the approximately 800 potential subsidiaries (on average, each MNC has two relevant subsidiaries), which equals a response rate of roughly 6.38 percent. However, the more "honest" response rate differs significantly. Considering the various potential respondents per MNC, a total of more than 2000 contacts, the number of roughly 1.5 percent indicates the approach's limitations.

Second, to increase the number of respondents, complexity was reduced and data gathering changed toward the "one-shot approach" that requires only one completed questionnaire at the subsidiary level in order to be valid. An additional number of 83 respondents was generated, making it a total of 134 observations at the subsidiary level that—especially in the context of an expert survey—copes well with quantitative requirements. Along these lines, this approach increased the response rate up to sound 12.9 percent making it well in line with comparable online survey studies.

Discussing the representativeness of the sample, Table 6.4 shows various size measures of the subsidiaries' workforces. In total, the subsidiaries that are part of the study employ slightly more than 80,000 employees. Furthermore, they show a proper variation of workforce size that copes well with reality.

Frequency distribution of the home country indicates that the German bias of the "horizontal approach" disappeared with relatively similar response rates across the different home countries. Different subsamples according to the respective home countries attain a very similar size, as is expected with stratified randomized sampling. Furthermore, the host country structure of the N134 resembles well the

[14] © Copyright 2020 UNIPARK & QuestBack.

Table 6.4 Number of employees in subsidiaries under scrutiny

Total	80,086
Average size of subsidiary	602
Smallest subsidiary	2
Largest subsidiary	15,000

Source: From the Author

Table 6.5 Number of observations per CoO and per host country

France	31	Argentina	22
Germany	43	Brazil	71
UK	30	Chile	19
USA	30	Colombia	22

Source: From the Author

structure of the frame population. Argentina and Colombia make up around 16 percent of the cases, matching the percentages of the population very well. Brazil, clearly making up the largest section, accounts for up to 53 percent of the cases, though, remaining a bit below population's share. Consequently, regarding the composition there is a slight shift toward Chile being slightly overrepresented with around 14 percent. However, in total, deviations are marginal and the sample represents population fairly well (Table 6.5).

Examining the main motives and motivations behind the establishment of a subsidiary in the host countries of interest confirms representativeness. The sample and the frame population is very similar with the major seven reasons being identical only varying slightly in order (Table 6.6).

Further affirming the good fit of the sample, analyzing the business activities, foreign subsidiaries are engaged in (for an overview and corresponding definitions of all 15 business activities, see Appendix 2) of the N134 supports representativeness.[15] Indicating the four most important business activities are "sales, marketing, & support," "manufacturing," "business services," and "logistics, distribution, & transportation," the sample shows a very similar pattern to that of the frame population.

Bridging from data to analyses, it is the two-step approach that conducts two complete surveys at two different levels within the same MNC. On that account, through independently completed questionnaires on behavior, the survey allows one to grasp different degrees of behavior in both home and host country and enables one to establish links and to recognize patterns between them. Accordingly, with N51 data one can contribute to the understanding of how variation in behavior in the home country may explain variation in behavior abroad. Interpreting data with the appropriate caution due to German overrepresentation, the data gathered allows one

[15] Apart from the German bias, other indicators such as size, motivation, business activities conducted, and relative dispersion relating to the host countries do not significantly differ between the datasets N51 and N134.

Table 6.6 Comparing motivations for FDI (N134)

Rank	N134	Frame population[a]
1.	Domestic market growth potential	Domestic market growth potential
2.	Proximity to markets or customers	Proximity to markets or customers
3.	Skilled workforce availability	Regulations or business climate
4.	Infrastructure and logistics	Skilled workforce availability
5.	Regulations or business climate	Infrastructure and logistics
6.	Lower costs	Lower costs
7.	Natural resources	Natural resources

Source: From the Author
[a]The Financial Times (2017)

to conduct unprecedented fine-tuned analyses on how behavioral patterns are and develop over different fields within the same MNC. However, especially in conjunction with the follow-up investigation in the context of the N134, some findings of the N51 can further be contested, verified, and falsified and, thus, be put on a firm base.

Changing the fielding approach, the one-shot approach managed to increase the quantity of observations to a sufficient number. Even though the survey process changed slightly, the questionnaire remained the same. Accordingly, data could be merged reasonably. The inclusion of 134 respondents that are all to be evaluated as real experts in their field copes well with the requirements on the sample size and, thus, allows for robust quantitative analysis. It allows for analyses on behavior abroad as being dependent on the specific systemic origin and enables to coherently investigate on behavioral differences between the groups of subsidiaries.

6.4.3 Data Processing

Raw data gained through the survey is processed by certain measures in order to allow proper statistical analyses. In terms of missing values, the survey produced a generally very low number of missing data. In total, missing values account for less than five percent of all values. Such marginal amount of missing values is very good and allows us to draw accurate inference about the data. Accordingly, missing values are not computed or substituted by any estimated value (Statistics Solutions, 2020b). All missing values are replaced with the number "−77." This number is used since there is no real response that may be "−77," and as such, this number can be consciously left out of calculations. On that account, missing values are left out of subsequent analyses.

For some variables scoring was reversed. Since questions are purposefully raised differently, meaning that sometimes agreement expresses liberal and sometimes coordinated behavior, all scales need to be aligned for comparison and for proper formation of composite indicators. Hence, reverse coding is conducted in order to have all variables aligned; for all indicators a higher value indicates "more coordination" and a lower value always indicates a more liberal behavior. Certainly, a higher value does not correspond to a potential desirability and is meant to be normatively neutral.

For reasons of better comparison, all variables are re-scaled using min-max normalization that re-scales a value with distribution value between 0 and 1 (Sirra, 2020). Min-max normalization follows the formula:

$$x_{\text{new}} = \frac{x_i - \min(x)}{\max(x) - \min(x)}$$

After processing the data, all variables are comparable and summable with values between 0 (typically liberal) and 1 (typically coordinated).

Furthermore, in order to scrutinize behavior at a more abstract level than the item one, five composite indicators—that capture the five institutional domains—are constructed. All composite indicators are constructed through an additive method of indicator formation. On that account, items are grouped according to theoretically derived superordinate latent dimensions (Kromrey et al., 2016). All items are considered equally important, and, therefore, the additive index is a simple arithmetic mean of all constituent items.

6.5 Statistical Analysis

In order to better understand the Action Situation in the case of MNCs' subsidiaries that are hypothesized to being situated in a state of institutional duality, the following chapter is putting primary data gathered under statistical scrutiny. In general, the statistical research allows deductions (theoretical *Basissätze*) to be compared with statements about real situations (through empirical observation conducted) (Kromrey et al., 2016, p. 81). If the theoretical *basissätze* correspond to the empirical statements (empirical *basissätze*), the corresponding hypothesis developed above is empirically confirmed. If not, the hypothesis is empirically refuted, or as Kromrey et al. (2016, p. 81) state it, shocked in terms of its claim of validity.

In line with the research design developed above, benefitting from both the N51 paired observation and the N134 larger dataset, statistical analysis is applied, first, to understand how behavioral patterns at home may explain behavioral patterns abroad. Translated to the concept of differing institutional belongings of MNCs' subsidiaries and HQs, relationships between the two behaviors provide insights into the nature of an intra-organizational field. Furthermore, if such field is existent—building upon the independently completed questionnaires—the strength of the relationship between behavior at home and abroad directly corresponds to the field strength of the intra-organizational field. On that account, statistical analyses that make use of the N51 data mostly apply bivariate regression. Depending on the scale of the variables under scrutiny, different forms of regressions are applied to both the first-level indicators and the item level. Second, the larger dataset of N134 is applied mostly to test for group differences in behavior shown. Following this logic of investigation, it is attempted to investigate inasmuch differences in systemic origin—CME or LME—may affect behavior in a "third" system. If differences in behavior can be found in the first place, one can reasonably assume variation based on systemic origins. Along these lines, strength and direction of differences then may indicate if subsidiaries act according to what is appropriate in their home country, which again would strengthen the concept of the intra-organizational field. To scrutinize differences relating to systemic origins, various forms of variance analyses are applied to the data of N134. Third, to contribute to the concept of institutional complementarity, this is the first study that scrutinizes subsidiaries' behavior along all the VoC dimensions relating to institutional complementarity shown. Institutional complementarity is approached through the relationships between the behavioral patterns shown in the single dimension in the host country. Especially in connection with the previously conducted analyses, the investigation of complementary behavior can significantly improve understanding of behavioral dynamics that occur when potentially transferring practices across systemic borders leaving the supportive ground upon which the practice has originally been legitimated and gained the status of appropriateness.

Generally, due to the absence of reference studies, it is not (yet) possible to draw a clear line at the behavioral spectrum between what is liberal and coordinated. In this first study of this kind, nonetheless, the focus does not rest on the assignment of behavioral categories but on dynamics of behavior that allow one to better understand the functioning of the organizational fields in play. On that account, rather than being either liberal or coordinated, behavioral variation, changes, and differences are of interest.

6.5.1 N51

First, inferential statistics are conducted for data stemming from N51 in order to test the following hypothesis:

Explanans:	(1) If an MNC behaves more coordinated in the home country, then the corresponding subsidiary in Latin America behaves more coordinated as well. (2) Behavior of the MNC in the home country is coordinated.
Explanandum:	(3) Behavior of the MNC's subsidiary in Latin America is coordinated.

Pairing data from both subjects of interest—the HQ and the foreign subsidiary—allows one to scrutinize the relationship between behavior at home and behavior abroad. With the N51 data, both (2) and (3) are observable for each participating company and makes it reasonable to dig further into the testing of (1). In this case, the underlying interest is to test if and to what degree behavior abroad (dependent variable) can be explained by behavior at home (independent variable). As variables' scales vary, so do statistical regressions. However, differences within data are considered when choosing the right statistical method.

6.5.1.1 Composite Indicators

As a first approach, the relatively abstract dimensional aggregate indicators are put under scrutiny using bivariate linear regressions. This form of regression is applied to evaluate the linear relationship between (2) and (3) of the hypothesis raised above. In this study, the linear regression for the entire population models as such (exemplary for composite ER dimension):

$$\text{Beh\_ER}_{\text{home}} = \beta_0 + \beta_1 * \text{Beh\_ER}_{\text{host}} + \varepsilon.$$

where β_0 is the intercept, β_1 the slope coefficient, and ε the errors. Regarding the specific sample drawn, the model is:

$$\text{Beh\_ER}_{\text{host}} = b_0 + b_1 * \text{Beh\_ER}_{\text{home}} + e.$$

where b_0 is the sample intercept and serves as an estimate for β_0, b_1 as the sample slope coefficient estimates β_1, and e as the sample errors estimating ε.

Translating the leading hypothesis into one for a bivariate linear regression, the null hypothesis is:

$$H_0 : b_1 = 0, \text{the slope coefficient equals zero.}$$

And the alternative hypothesis:

$$H_A : b_1 \neq 0, \text{the slope coefficient does not equal zero.}$$

The bivariate linear regression serves well to test the hypothesis of interest since it allows one, first, to determine if the linear regression is statistically significant, second, to assess the major characteristics of the relationship direction and magnitude (interpreting the slope coefficient and the corresponding sign), and, third, to predict behavior abroad based on different behavior at home (Laerd Statistics, 2015a; Urban & Mayerl, 2006).

Exemplary ER Dimension

Reporting in brief, a linear regression is run to understand the effect of average behavior of MNCs in the exemplary dimension of ER at home on the one abroad (Carifio & Perla, 2007; Cohen, 1988; Laerd Statistics, 2015a, 2018; Statistics Solutions, 2020a, b; Sullivan & Artino, 2013; Weisberg, 2014). To assess linearity, a scatterplot of behavior at home against behavior abroad with superimposed regression line is plotted. Visual inspection of the normal P–P Plot indicates a linear relationship between the variables. There is homoscedasticity and normality of the residuals. There are no outliers detected. The prediction equation is:

$$\text{Beh\_ER}_{\text{host}} = 0.503 + 0.144 * \text{Beh\_ER}_{\text{home}}$$

Average behavior at home does not predict statistically significant behavior abroad, $F(1, 49) = 1.50$, $p > 0.05$, accounting for 3% of the variation on behavior abroad with adjusted $R^2 = 1\%$, a low size effect according to Cohen (1988). An extra unit of coordination leads to a 0.144 increase in behavior abroad. Predictions are made to determine mean behavior abroad for MNCs who behave 0.7. The mean behavior abroad is predicted as 0.604 (95% CI, 0.564 to 0.643).

The results are graphically presented in the scatterplot below in which the behavior abroad is plotted against behavior at home including the line of best fit. The curved lines indicate the corresponding confidence intervals that demonstrate the confidence to which one can predict the mean values of the DV for each value of the IV (Fig. 6.6).

Correlation Matrix: Composite Dimensional Indicators

Summarizing bivariate regression for the other composite indicators of IR, CG, IFR, and EV, the correlation matrix below indicates two major findings: first, generally,

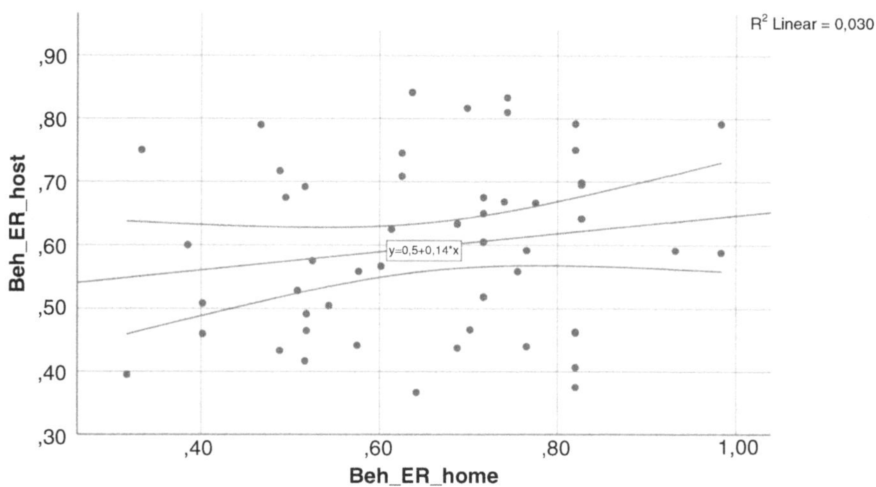

Fig. 6.6 Scatterplot ER. Source: From the Author

there are relatively weak relationships between the composite behavioral indicators in the home and the host country. Even though, one may not reject the null hypotheses finally, it may be noteworthy that all the five-dimensional pairs indicate—as shown by the Pearson correlation coefficient—a positive relationship (Table 6.7).

That can cautiously be interpreted as a hint that the intra-organizational field can be caught analytically even though the abstract first-level indicators are applied. Furthermore, the total number of relationships between home and host dimensions is—just like the direct pairs indicated—not significant. However, in eight of ten cases the figures have a positive sign suggesting a positive correlation. Such potential inter-dimensional cross-systemic complementarity within the intra-organizational field cannot be sufficiently approached here and is beyond the scope of this research, though it may provide an interesting point for further research. However, lacking significance makes the interpretation of the direction and effect sizes above at best a vague endeavor and needs to be done cautiously. It nevertheless does certainly not negate the existence of intra-organizational fields as a whole. What it does though is provide evidence to raise doubts on the strong wholesale adoption of practices by foreign subsidiaries that can be detected when applying abstract composite indicators.

Not of major interest in this study, though noteworthy and confirming the concept of institutional complementarities within the home countries, there is a rather strong relationship between the aggregate dimensional indicators in the home country. Despite measuring on such an abstract level, all bivariate regressions relating to the relationships of the dimensions within the home country, eight out of ten relationships demonstrate significantly positive correlations with relatively strong effect sizes. This is remarkable and provides evidence for suggesting strong complementarities in the home country, here mostly in Germany.

In conclusion, the results for the inter-systemic bivariate regressions conducted, one can state that in general, at least at this level of abstraction, effect size is very low. One could argue that this raises doubts on the wholesale adoption of a parent company's practice in the corresponding Latin American subsidiaries. The general positive correlation between the variables of interest, though, may give a hint that some information is to be found within the dimensions. If there is an intra-organizational effect at all, it may exist in certain activities and not in others. Aggregation of variables in composite indicators certainly does not allow a more fine-grained analysis. Indeed, the composite indicators include various different activities that can certainly be attributed to the same category but are of very distinct nature and can be conducted in an entirely dissociated manner. Such blurred information may hide relationships on a less abstract level, for some practices. This, however, can neither be proposed nor negated by hitherto analyses. On that account, dismantling the composite indicator seems to be a reasonable next step in analyses. Along this line of thought, the subsequent section conducts a less abstract and more fine-grained analysis that focuses on the item level.

Table 6.7 Correlation matrix composite home-host dimensions ($N = 51$)

		EVhome	EVhost	IFhome	IFhost	CGhome	CGhost	IRhome	IRhost	ERhome	ERhost
EVhome	Pearson correlation	1	0.121	0.539**	0.200	0.370**	0.187	0.348*	0.219	0.363**	0.024
	Sig. (2-tailed)		0.397	0.000	0.159	0.007	0.188	0.012	0.122	0.009	0.868
IFhome	Pearson correlation	0.539**	0.168	1	0.211	0.324*	0.203	0.301*	0.076	0.240	−0.051
	Sig. (2-tailed)	0.000	0.239		0.137	0.020	0.153	0.032	0.594	0.089	0.723
CGhome	Pearson correlation	0.370**	0.095	0.324*	−0.093	1	0.127	−0.070	0.089	0.346*	−0.240
	Sig. (2-tailed)	0.007	0.507	0.020	0.517		0.375	0.624	0.534	0.013	0.090
IRhome	Pearson correlation	0.348*	0.055	0.301*	0.100	−0.070	0.189	1	0.081	0.419**	0.138
	Sig. (2-tailed)	0.012	0.700	0.032	0.484	0.624	0.183		0.572	0.002	0.336
ERhome	Pearson correlation	0.363**	−0.071	0.240	0.090	0.346*	0.011	0.419**	−0.070	1	0.173
	Sig. (2-tailed)	0.009	0.622	0.089	0.528	0.013	0.940	0.002	0.627		0.226

Source: From the Author
*Correlation is significant at the 0.1 level (2-tailed)
**Correlation is significant at the 0.05 level (2-tailed)
***Correlation is significant at the 0.01 level (2-tailed)

6.5.1.2 Item Level

Following Lindenberg's rule of diminishing abstraction (Lindenberg, 1992) and the limited explanatory value of the analyses at the aggregated dimensional level, the subsequent analyses reduce abstraction. In the following, the single variables are tested item by item.

Likert and Metric Items

This section scrutinizes various items, of which some are interval and others Likert scaled. Along these lines, this section applies simple linear regression and ordinal logistic regression. Since the method of statistical analyses depends, among others, on the measurement of the variable, it is of utmost importance to briefly examine the debate surrounding Likert and interval scaled measurements. Whether a Likert scaled variable, ordinal in nature, can be treated as a metric one and, therefore, be analyzed by a broader variety of statistical methods is part of a vivid debate. From a conservative point of view, one certainly does not approve of some missing characteristics such as clear equidistance. Nonetheless, especially in the social sciences some compromises are made and, hence, have found their way into the scientific community. Among the more progressive part of the community, especially Likert scales that aggregate various Likert items are well accepted for metric analyses (Statistics Solutions, 2020a, b; Sullivan & Artino, 2013). Whether single Likert items can be used for metric analyses is part of the debate too. The application of 7 and 5-point scales to metric analyses somehow found its way into general practice (Norman, 2010; Sullivan & Artino, 2013), and such variable is referred to as an "ordinal approximation of a continuous variable" (Statistics Solutions, 2020a, b). In line with the more progressive camp, the subsequent section applies various methods assuming continuity. However, if such analyses are conducted, results will be double-checked for validity using further nonparametric tests. For each of the ordinal variables, additional nonparametric correlations (using Kendall's tau) and cumulative odds ordinal logistic regressions with proportional odds are conducted (Laerd Statistics, 2015b).

As a first step, all interval and ordinal scaled relationships between home and host behavior are approached through bivariate linear regression. Regarding all regressions conducted, all observations are included; no outliers are removed. Certainly, in such a small sample, potential outliers can have a large impact on the entire relationship. As a means to avoiding general rejection, the significance level required is lowered to 90%.

Table 6.8 summarizes the statistically significant results of the linear regressions conducted at the item level (for all others, see Appendix 3). Regressions are conducted to understand the effect of average behavior of MNCs at home on the one abroad. Regarding the data pairs indicated in Table 6.8, average behavior at home statistically significantly predicts behavior abroad at a medium effect size, on average, according to Cohen (1988). On that account, it is possible to predict the value of the DV by implying the value of the corresponding IV.

As a preliminary summary, there, indeed, seems to be a statistically significant positive relationship between behavior at home and abroad, though not on a

Table 6.8 Correlation matrix item level (Pearson correlations)

	CGt_host	IRw_host	IFe_host	IFg_host	ERc_host	ERl_host	EVv_host
CGt_home	0.248*						
IRw_home		0.263*					
IFe_home			0.283**				
IFg_home				0.270*			
ERc_home					0.290**		
ERl_home						0.289**	
EVv_home							0.235*

Source: From the Author
*Correlation is significant at the 0.1 level (2-tailed)
**Correlation is significant at the 0.05 level (2-tailed)
***Correlation is significant at the 0.01 level (2-tailed)

wholesale level including all practices. As hypothesized by H_A, the slope coefficient of the bivariate linear regressions above with behavior at home in the parent company as IV and behavior abroad in the corresponding foreign subsidiary does not equal zero. Hence, H_0 can be reasonably rejected. Furthermore, due the small sample, one may also look behind the notions of statistical significance, though interpreting it very cautiously.

Without digging too much into details, the entirety of 21 relationships investigated shows a relatively clear pattern. The total of relationships investigated in this section that are described by a positive sign (positive relationship) amount to 16, which outnumbers the relationships described by neutral or negative signs of five (three negative and two neutral) by far. Moreover, the absence of a single negative relationship that is statistically negative further hints at the existence of an intra-organizational field characterized by positive relationships, as behavioral variation in one explains behavioral variation in the other. This finding further validates the plausibility of the existence of an intra-organizational field. At least, though it does not thwart the findings discussed above.

As indicated above, all Likert scale variables are also put under nonparametric scrutiny. On that account, ordinal logistic regressions cumulative odds ordinal logistic regressions with proportional odds are applied to double-check findings derived from testing Likert-type data with bivariate linear regressions. Securing validity of the findings gained, nonparametric testing generally reaffirms the findings introduced above.

6.5.2 N134

Along with the methodical change in data collection discussed in Sect. 6.4, this chapter scrutinizes the one-sided, though significantly larger, sample of the N134. In comparison to the sample of N51 that is scrutinized with a suitable analytical toolkit for the relationships between exact measures of behavior abroad and at home, the

N134 serves to better understand whether that relationship holds up across the different systems of the home countries. Accordingly, rather than working with regressions and correlations between behaviors, here the focus lies on the investigation of mostly group differences in behavior between the foreign subsidiaries in Latin America according to their system and country of origin. In addition to behavioral group differences, though, as will be shown in this chapter, the sample of N134 allows one to gain valuable insights into the concept of institutional complementarity in the behavior of MNCs' subsidiaries in Latin America.

6.5.2.1 Group Differences

This part of the study is cross-sectional in nature and, accordingly, built as a "between-subjects design." Generally, as Table 6.9 indicates the cases are assigned to independent groups either to the corresponding country or to the system of origin.

Where the System-Group#1 involves France and Germany, the System-Group#2 involves the UK and USA. In general, for both country and system groups independence of observations is secured. Regarding country groups, for example, a German company cannot also be a French company. It is either the one or the other. No company can be found in more than one group. The same applies to the systemic perspective. An MNC cannot have origins in both CME and LME.

Regarding the behavioral differences relating to the MNCs' origins, this chapter follows the guiding puzzle of whether there is a difference in behavior between MNCs according to their origins. Since the IV changes between system and country groups, appropriate tests are conducted for each.

Composite Indicators and Systems of Origin (SoO)

First of all, the composite indicators are put under scrutiny to test whether or not behavioral differences can be detected at the abstract dimensional level. The investigation at the abstract level is conducted according to the system of origins exclusively. Differences on country level are reemphasized in the following chapter on differences at the item level.

In order to test group differences in one continuous DV relating to one IV that consists of two independent dichotomous groups (CME and LME), the subsequent

Table 6.9 SoO and CoO grouping

Differences regarding...	Grouping
...the system of origin	System-Group#1: CME
	System-Group#2: LME
...the country of origin	Country-Group#1: France
	Country-Group#2: Germany
	Country-Group#3: UK
	Country-Group#4: USA

Source: From the Author

section conducts a variety of independent-samples t-tests. Such test determines, first, if a difference exists, and if so, second, if such difference may be statistically significant; that means that such difference can also be assumed to exist in the corresponding population (Laerd Statistics, 2015c). The basic idea behind it is to determine whether (mean) behavior in foreign subsidiaries differs (significantly) between subsidiaries with either origins in CMEs or LMEs. As discussed above, the composite dimensional indicators are treated as continuous in nature. In line with the previous investigations, testing on the existence of an intra-organizational field, one hypothesizes that, first, differences exist and, second, that subsidiaries with origins in CME act more coordinated than their LME counterparts.[16]

In the subsequent section, applying independent-samples t-test, the corresponding null hypothesis is:

$$H_0 : \mu_{\text{CME}} = \mu_{\text{LME}}$$

In which μ is the population mean and the different independent groups are "LME" and "CME." Verbally expressed, the null hypothesis states that mean behavior of foreign subsidiaries independent of their systemic origins is equal.

Alternatively, one can hypothesize:

$$H_A : \mu_{\text{CME}} \neq \mu_{\text{LME}}.$$

With CME and LME mean behavior not being equal in the population, indicating that differences in systemic origins of the parent company affect subsidiaries inasmuch their behavior differs. The applied test provides evidence to either reject or accept the H_A, and reject, or to fail to reject the H_0. Whereas the hypotheses introduced focus exclusively on the question whether differences can also be found in the population, there are other effect size measures that can be used to determine the explanatory power of the IV. As such, in the following, the size measure "d" will be used to indicate corresponding effect sizes.

As Table 6.10 indicates, descriptive group statistics indicate the means for subsidiaries grouped by the system of origin. Data is mean ± standard deviation, unless otherwise stated. There are 74 subsidiaries originating in CMEs and 60 originating in LMEs.[17] As a rough first view, mean scores of the different aggregated dimensions show—apart from ER—a relatively clear tendency inasmuch as subsidiaries that originate from CMEs do also behave more coordinated abroad, LME subsidiaries behave more liberally than their coordinated counterparts. Especially in the

[16]The same holds up vice versa, meaning that it can equally be hypothesized that subsidiaries with origins in LME act more liberally than their CME counterparts.

[17]With regard to the composition of the sample, despite having more subsidiaries with origins in CME (74) than one with LME origins (60), the difference in numbers is small enough to assume a relatively balanced design that avoids heavy negative effects of potential violations of assumptions on the test's validity. Furthermore, the number of cases clearly outreaches the recommended number by Laerd Statistics, (2015c) of at least six participants per group.

Table 6.10 Group statistics composite dimensional indicators

Group statistics				
	SoO	*N*	Mean	Std. deviation
IF	CME	74	0.48474	0.16371
	LME	59	0.45862	0.18490
EV	CME	74	0.48202	0.12105
	LME	60	0.44833	0.12365
ER	CME	74	0.57854	0.13504
	LME	60	0.58701	0.13947
IR	CME	74	0.52808	0.15150
	LME	60	0.50093	0.15450
CG	CME	74	0.48761	0.16780
	LME	60	0.44166	0.14549

Source: From the Author

dimension of "EV," behavior of CME subsidiaries is indeed more coordinated showing a higher mean behavioral score (0.482 ± 0.121) than LME subsidiaries do (0.445 ± 0.124). Similarly, subsidiaries from Germany and France act more coordinated in terms of "CG" attaining a mean score of (0.488 ± 0.168) compared to those from the USA and the UK (0.441 ± 0.145).

Independent-samples *t*-test are run to determine whether there are differences in behavior within the dimensions between subsidiaries originating in liberal and coordinated systems. Behavioral scores for each level of systemic origin are normally distributed, as assessed by Shapiro–Wilk's test ($p > 0.05$), and there is homogeneity of variances, as assessed by Levene's test for equality of variances. Behavioral scores from subsidiaries originating in CMEs are for CG 0.046 (95% CI, −0.008 to 0.110), for IR 0.027 (95% CI, −0.025 to 0.100), for EV 0.034 (95% CI, −0.008 to 0.076), and for IF 0.026 (95% CI, −0.034 to 0.086) higher than the behavioral scores from subsidiaries originating in LMEs. ER scores are relatively equal with a mean difference of 0.008 (95% CI, −0.056 to 0.039). There was a statistically significant difference in behavioral scores between CME and LME subsidiaries in Latin America only within the CG dimension at a 90% confidence level, with a *p*-value <0.1 and one for the EV dimension, which is only slightly above. As such, there is a statistically significant difference in mean behavioral CG score between CME and LME subsidiaries, $t(132) = 1.672, p = 0.097$.[18] The effect size Cohen's d (Cohen, 1988) remains across all dimensional indicators small to moderate (for CG: $d = 0.30$; for IF: $d = 0.15$; for EV: $d = 0.12$; for ER: $d = 0.06$; for IR: $d = 0.18$).

Figure 6.7 demonstrates behavioral scores across the institutional domains according to systemic differences in a bar chart.

[18] t means that here comparison to a *t*-distribution (*t*-test) is conducted, df here is 132 indicating the degrees of freedom; *t* here is 1.672 indicating the obtained *t*-value, and *p* here is 0.097 indicating a 9.7% chance of obtaining the observed *t*-value if the null hypothesis is true.

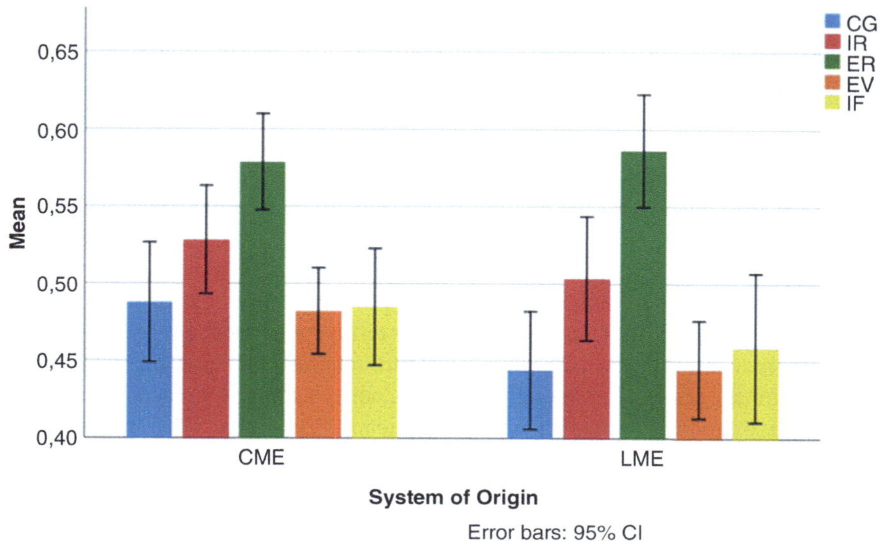

Fig. 6.7 Bar chart group differences composite dimensional indicators. Source: From the Author

The general tendency of the mean behavioral scores across the aggregated dimensional scores certainly solidifies the assumption of an existing intra-organizational field within the MNC. Generally, subsidiaries originating in coordinated countries, indeed, behave more coordinated abroad in Latin American countries. Expressed the other way round, moving between the bipolar axis of behavior, subsidiaries from liberal countries stick to the behavior most common in their home countries. Hence, both groups behave abroad in Latin America—a different system to their home one—as is deemed to be appropriate in their "home system."

Nonetheless, here, at such an abstract level of measurement, it is only the CG dimension that has a statistically significant difference between means ($p < 0.1$), and therefore, the corresponding null hypothesis ($H_0 : \mu_{\text{CME}} = \mu_{\text{LME}}$) can be rejected and the alternative hypothesis ($H_A : \mu_{\text{CME}} \neq \mu_{\text{LME}}$) can be accepted.

Item Level and Country of Origin

In order to dismantle the composite indicators and to avoid the risk of missing dynamics within the dimensions, the following chapter scrutinizes group differences in subsidiaries' behavior at the item level according to their country of origin. To consider each CoO as a distinct group, certain one-way analyses of variance (ANOVA) plus post hoc Tukey HSD and Games-Howell tests are conducted. The mentioned post hoc tests differ inasmuch as the latter does not assume homogeneity of variances. The ANOVA as an omnibus test statistic indicates whether there are at least two groups that are different from one another (Laerd Statistics, 2017a). Where such a difference lies exactly, further testing on which country groups differ exactly can be approached using post hoc tests.

Continuous and Ordinal DVs

Just like above, the DVs of interest—both continuous and ordinal one (here 5-point Likert items)—are as a first step approached as measures at the continuous level. Later on, all ordinal variables will further be double-checked by nonparametric Kruskal–Wallis H tests. The IV consists of four different groups, which are France, Germany, the UK, and the USA.

Testing differences for four groups—i.e., six pairwise comparisons[19]—leads to an accumulation of the Type I error, increasing the chance of falsely rejecting a null hypothesis if all null hypotheses are true and, therefore, demands multiple testing correction. Therefore, running a one-way ANOVA including—if statistically significant—a follow-up with a Tukey HSD post hoc test is recommended. In comparison with running manifold pairwise comparisons through independent-samples t-tests—it corrects for the accumulation of Type I errors when testing differences for various groups and, therefore, depicts "honestly significant differences" (HSD) (Keppel & Wickens, 2004; Laerd Statistics, 2017a; Wuensch, 2012). Such adjustment for multiple comparisons makes requirements relating to an alpha level, at which one accepts statistical significance, much more conservative. For example, if generally a 10% (5%) alpha level is used to indicate statistical significance, a Bonferroni adjustment in the context of four groups and six pairwise comparisons decreases the alpha level at which one accepts statistical significance to 1.66% (0.83%).[20] Furthermore, besides the question of (statistically significant) differences between groups, in the following effect sizes eta squared (η^2) and omega squared (ω^2) will be calculated to estimate the importance of the results, notably the strength of the CoOs' impact on subsidiary behavior (Ferguson, 2009).

In this part of the study, investigating group differences according to the country origin of the subsidiaries, the null hypothesis states that there are no differences in population means between the subsidiaries with different home countries.

$$H_0 : \mu_{\text{France}} = \mu_{\text{Germany}} = \mu_{\text{UK}} = \mu_{\text{USA}}.$$

Since the intra-organizational field is assumed to impact the behavior abroad, evidence against the null hypothesis is of utmost interest here. Accordingly, the alternative hypothesis states that there is a difference between at least two group population means.

$$H_A : \text{at least one group population mean is different.}$$

[19] One could have also tested only the inter-systemic group differences, i.e., Germany-UK, Germany-USA, France-UK, France-USA, using predefined custom contrasts. However, to keep the exploratory nature of this quantitative study and continue the relatively wide approach that also allows for counterintuitive findings, here also the differences France-Germany and UK-USA are also part of the investigation.

[20] Bonferroni adjustment divides the alpha level by the number of pairwise comparisons conducted. Here a Bonferroni adjustment follows the formula: alpha/6 = alpha adjusted.

Analyzing the various boxplots of the variables of interest indicates the absence of extreme outliers. Generally, no data point has a distance of three or more box-lengths from the corresponding box. Accordingly, all data is kept within subsequent analyses and calculations are based on the full datasets available. As a next step, approaching normality of data distribution, the Shapiro–Wilk test of normality is conducted for each group of the IV for each of the DVs. As a general finding, the different behavioral scores are not normally distributed, as assessed by Shapiro–Wilk's test ($p < 0.05$). Since the assumption of normality is violated, this study conducts various data transformation methods that can correct non-normality to secure the highest validity possible (Laerd Statistics, 2017a). Accordingly, various square root or logarithmic transformations are applied, though do not correct non-normality. Consequently, despite transformation, data still violates the assumption of normality. Since the one-way ANOVA is fairly robust to deviations from the normality assumption, for now, this study proceeds regardless of non-normality. In this study, sample size is sufficiently large and the single group sizes are generally balanced. Under these circumstances, non-normality does not affect Type I error heavily (Laerd Statistics, 2017a; Maxwell et al., 2017). As a second step, to double-check results gained from the one-way ANOVA, the nonparametric Kruskal–Wallis H test is applied, which does not require normality and can therefore be a suitable alternative to the one-way ANOVA (Laerd Statistics, 2015d).

Regarding the assumption of homogeneity of variances, as assessed by Levene's test for equality of variances, except for the variables CGc, IFe, ERa, EVf, and EVii that violate the assumption of equality of variances (with $p < 0.05$), all other data shows homogeneity having Levene's test statistics $p > 0.05$. Differences in the level of homogeneity require different forms of testing. The cases in which the assumption of homogeneity of variances is met are analyzed differently from those indicated. Whereas the former is put under scrutiny of the Tukey HSD, the four mentioned are further investigated using Games-Howell tests that do not require equality of variances.

If the assumption of homogeneity of variances is met, one can proceed with the standard procedure of the one-way ANOVA with Tukey post hoc tests. Several behavioral scores were statistically significantly different for different CoO categories.

- The behavioral score of CGb is statistically significantly different for different CoO categories, $F(3, 128) = 3.540$, $p = 0.017$.[21]
- The behavioral score of IFic is statistically significantly different for different CoO categories, $F(3, 127) = 2.378$, $p = 0.073$.

[21] Reporting of a one-way ANOVA follows the schema: $F(df1, df2) = F$-statistic, $p = p$-value. F stands for F-test, i.e., comparing to an F-distribution, $df1$ indicates "between groups degrees of freedom" and $df2$ the "within groups [error] degrees of freedom, F is the value of the F-statistics (F-value), and the p-value indicates the likelihood of attaining the observed F-value if the null hypothesis is true (Laerd Statistics, 2017a).

- The behavioral score of IFs is statistically significantly different for different CoO categories, $F(3, 129) = 2.279$, $p = 0.083$.
- The behavioral score of EVia is statistically significantly different for different CoO categories, $F(3, 126) = 2.875$, $p = 0.039$.

Conducting, the Tukey post hoc test begins where the one-way ANOVA indicated that at least two group mean differences do statistically significantly differ. The Tukey post hoc test conducts all possible pairwise comparisons (four groups allow for six different comparisons) and, therefore, allows one to explore further where these differences (between which categories) exactly lie (Laerd Statistics, 2017a). Here, the differences between Germany and France and the UK and the USA are scrutinized too, meaning that the Tukey post hoc test corrects the aforementioned accumulation of Type I error in the context of six pairwise comparisons. This is noteworthy since the major interest of this study lies within inter-systemic behavioral differences (between CME and LME countries). Testing all six potential differences in mean behavior leads to more conservative calculations of statistical significance than when comparing exclusively inter-systemically (four pairwise comparisons).

In the subsequent section, exclusively statistically significant inter-systemic differences are further discussed.[22] The Tukey post hoc statistics in detail shows mean inter-systemic differences as follows:

- There is an increase in the behavioral CGb score from 0.308 ± 0.333 in the UK group to 0.534 ± 0.339 in the France group, an increase of 0.226 (95% CI, 0.029 to 0.423), which is statistically significant ($p = 0.044$).
- There is an increase in the behavioral IFs score from 0.466 ± 0.358 in the UK group to 0.653 ± 0.239 in the France group, an increase of 0.188 (95% CI, 0.016 to 0.358), which is statistically significant ($p = 0.059$).
- There is an increase in the behavioral EVia score from 0.371 ± 0.300 in the UK group to 0.558 ± 0.252 in the France group, an increase of 0.188 (95% CI, 0.035 to 0.340), which is statistically significant ($p = 0.026$).

Despite the one-way ANOVA indicating a difference between groups in the behavioral score of IFic, pairwise comparison using a Tukey post hoc test does not confirm statistical significance. This may be due to the more conservative characteristic of a specific test (here the Tukey post hoc test), or due to different distributions used in the two tests (Coolidge, 2012; Laerd Statistics, 2017a). On the other hand, though not "detected" by the one-way ANOVA, according to the Tukey post hoc test, there is a statistically significant difference in the behavioral score of EVv between the group Germany and the group UK.

[22]The only intra-systemic statistically significant difference is to be found within the behavioral score CGb from 0.308 ± 0.333 in the UK group to 0.558 ± 0.306 in the USA group, an increase of 0.250 (95% CI, 0.054 to 0.446), $p = 0.019$.

Table 6.11 Effect size item-level

Behavioral score	η^2	ω^2
CGb	0.077	0.055
IFs	0.050	0.028
EVv	0.044	0.022
EVia	0.064	0.042

Source: From the Author

- There is an increase in the behavioral EVv score from 0.383 ± 0.269 in the UK group to 0.552 ± 0.320 in the Germany group, an increase of 0.169 (95% CI, 0.008 to 0.330), which is statistically significant ($p = 0.077$).

Regarding an effect size of the IVs, one most often either relies on the measures called omega squared (ω^2) or eta squared (η^2). The latter indicates the effect size for the sample; the former one estimates the effect size in the population (Laerd Statistics, 2017a). Table 6.11 reports both measures for the statistically significant differences. Both $\eta^2$and ω^2 effect sizes, according to Cohen's rule of thumb (Cohen et al., 2001; Field, 2013), are categorized as follows: a small effect at a value of 0.01, a medium one at 0.06, and a large one at 0.14.

Generally, the effect that differing CoOs have on subsidiaries' behavior is medium, with equal amplitude toward large and small effect sizes.

If the assumption of homogeneity of variances is violated—as is the case with data of CGc, IFe, ERa, EVii, and EVf—the process of a modified ANOVA is recommended, in this case the Welch ANOVA (Laerd Statistics, 2017a). Different to the standard one-way ANOVA above, the Welch one—if statistically significant—is followed by the Games-Howell post hoc test to see between which groups differences lie. The Games-Howell post hoc test does not assume equality of variances.

There are two statistically significant results. Significance levels for CGc and ERa indicate that within these variables not all country groups are equal in the population. Hence, it can be concluded that there is a statistically significant difference in the mean behavioral scores CGc and ERa regarding the different CoO groups. Briefly verbalizing the results for the statistically significant group differences:

- The behavioral score CGc of the foreign subsidiaries is statistically significantly different for the different country groups, Welch's F (3, 66.277) = 7.060, $p < 0.0005$.
- The behavioral score ERa of the foreign subsidiaries is statistically significantly different for the different country groups, Welch's F (3, 63.294) = 2.604, $p = 0.060$.

Henceforward, only statistically significant findings are reported. Just like the Tukey post hoc test, the Games-Howell test tests all six possible combinations of group differences. Consequently, and along the same lines, correcting for multiple comparisons, results are based on rather conservative alpha levels at which one accepts statistical significance. Games-Howell post hoc test indicates inter-systemic significant differences for both CGc and ERa between the groups of Germany and the USA.

- There is an increase in the CGc behavioral score from 0.558 ± 0.364 in the group USA to 0.855 ± 0.269 in the group Germany, an increase of 0.296 (95% CI, 0.113 to 0.480), which is statistically significant ($p = 0.002$).
- There is an increase in the ERa behavioral score from 0.748 ± 0.230 in the group USA to 0.873 ± 0.111 in the group Germany, an increase of 0.125 (95% CI, 0.016 to 0.234), which is statistically significant ($p = 0.047$).

Having heterogeneity of variances, using Welch's F test, to report the effect size, an adjusted omega squared formula is used.

$$\omega^2_{\mathrm{CGc}} = 0.1410 = 0.141.$$

$$\omega^2_{\mathrm{ERa}} = 0.1410 = 0.035.$$

Therefore, one can state, for example, that approximately 14.1% of the DV's total variance (CGc behavioral score) can be explained by the IV (CoO). In line with the effect sizes introduced above, this depicts large effect. Regarding the behavioral score of ERa, the CoO has a small to medium effect on subsidiaries' behavior in Latin America.

Summing up all effect sizes for the detected statistically significant differences in behavior in relation to the CoO, Cohen's d is calculated and results in relatively large effect sizes as indicated in Table 6.12.

All findings retrieved during the process of the one-way ANOVA when treating 5-point Likert scaled variables as continuous ones are double-checked by applying nonparametric Kruskal–Wallis H test and follow-up Dunn's (1964) procedure with Bonferroni adjustment. Sufficing for here and summarizing, significance levels retrieved through the one-way ANOVA are generally confirmed across all variables under scrutiny. Kruskal–Wallis H tests show even lower alpha levels *vis-à-vis* the ones generated by the one-way ANOVA and, therefore, indicate a lower chance of committing a Type I error. Generally, Dunn's procedure generates the same findings

Table 6.12 Cohen's *d*—group differences item level

Variable	Comparison	Cohen's *d*	Interpretation[a]
CGb	France—UK	0.68	Middle to large effect
CGc	Germany—USA	0.93	Large effect
ERa	Germany—USA	0.71	Middle to large effect
IFs	France—UK	0.61	Middle to large effect
EVia	France—UK	0.68	Middle to large effect
EVv	Germany—UK	0.57	Middle to large effect

Source: From the Author
[a]Interpretation according to Cohen (1988)

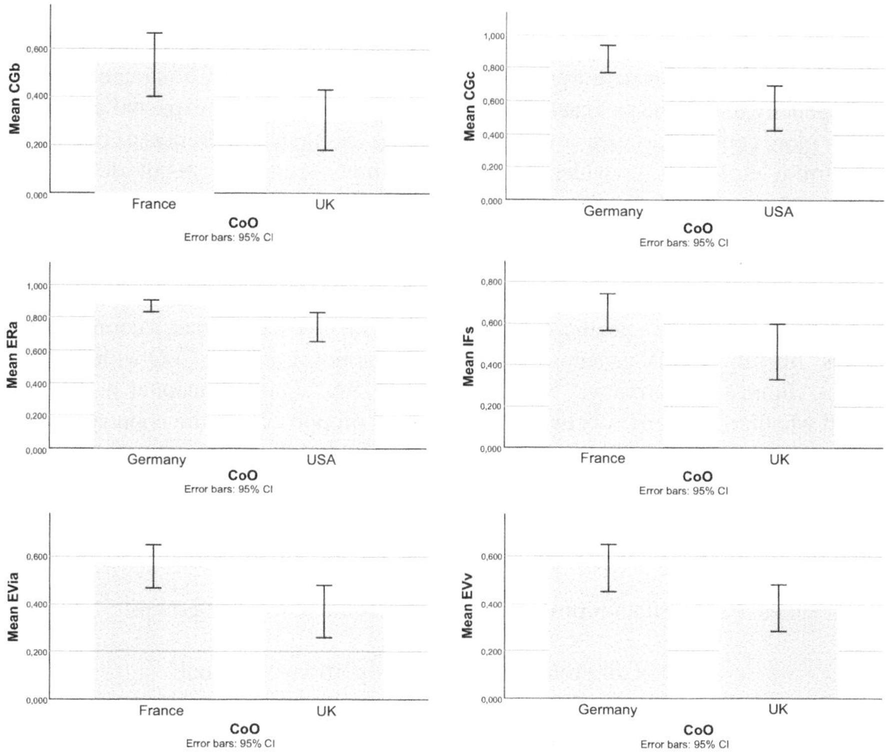

Fig. 6.8 Bar charts group differences item level. Source: From the Author

and, therefore, validates results from Tukey HSD and Games-Howell post hoc tests conducted above.[23]

As a preliminary conclusion, regarding the DVs that are scrutinized in detail above, one can reject H_0, which states that there are no differences in population means between the subsidiaries with different home countries. As the investigation indicates, relating to the DVs of interest, at least one group population is different. All statistically significant group differences indicate that, indeed, subsidiaries that originate in either France or Germany do also act more coordinated in Latin America when compared with their counterparts originating in the UK or the USA. Figure 6.8 summarizes the statistically significantly different behaviors.

[23] Furthermore, Dunn's procedure also indicates significance levels as if each pairwise comparison was considered in isolation. It applies alpha levels without Bonferroni corrections and indicates further statistically significant differences in mean behavioral scores of CGb (Germany and UK) and IFic (Germany and USA). However, they are not reported here, since the chance of committing a Type I error is too high.

Dichotomous Behavior Variables

Dichotomous DVs and potential differences according to the origins of the subsidiaries are put under scrutiny using the two omnibus tests: Chi-square tests of homogeneity and Fisher's exact test (2 × *c*). The latter is run if expected count for one or more cells of the corresponding cross tab is less than five. Both tests conduct a Bonferroni correction considering multiple comparisons. The major differences between the tests is that rather than approximating to the chi-squared distribution, it calculates an exact sampling distribution (Laerd Statistics, 2017b).

The two tests are used to determine if the proportions of subsidiaries with different CoOs that behave rather coordinated versus rather liberal are equal. Hence, each DV is a specific type of action with two categories, "coordinated" versus "liberal." The IV remains unchanged and demonstrates the CoO with the four groups "France," "Germany," "UK," and the "USA." On that account it is determined whether differences between the binomial proportions of the country groups exist regarding the specific behavior of subsidiaries in Latin America.

H_0 stating that population proportions are the same for all groups:

$$H_0 : P_{\text{France}} = P_{\text{Germany}} = P_{\text{UK}} = P_{\text{USA}}$$

H_A states that population proportions are not equal across the groups.

$$H_A : \text{not all group population proportions are equal.}$$

Following the same logic as the calculations above, if statistically significant difference in proportions exists, post hoc tests can be applied to scrutinize between which country groups significant differences exactly lie (Laerd Statistics, 2017b). Whereas a statistically significant Chi-square test of homogeneity is followed by multiple z-tests, a significant Fisher's exact test (2 × *c*) is followed by multiple Fisher's exact tests (2 × 2).[24]

Briefly reporting significant differences, regarding the DV CGl, a total of 134 foreign subsidiaries are randomly assigned to CoO groups France, Germany, the UK, and the USA. Observing behavior in Latin America between coordinated and liberal market economies, 13 French (41.9% of all French subsidiaries), 30 German (69.8%), 20 UK (66.7), and 13 US (43.3%) subsidiaries show coordinated behavior, a statistically significant difference in proportions, $p = 0.027$. Post hoc analysis involved pairwise comparisons using the *z*-test and indicates a statistical difference in proportions between two specific groups only if neglecting Bonferroni correction. Running a relatively high risk of underestimating potential chance of committing a Type I error, the proportion of subsidiaries acting in a coordinated manner is

[24] The Fisher's exact test (2 × c) tests for statistically significant differences between all groups; the Fisher's exact test (2 × 2) compares two proportions. Here, for example, group Germany versus group USA.

statistically significantly higher for German subsidiaries than for US subsidiaries, $p < 0.05$ (with Bonferroni adjustment $p > 0.05$).[25]

Regarding the DV IRpc, a total of 134 foreign subsidiaries are randomly assigned to CoO groups France, Germany, the UK, and the USA. The assumption of sample size (expected count for each cell of the $2 \times c$ cross table equal or greater than five) is not met. Observing behavior in Latin America between coordinated and liberal market economies, 31 French (100.00% of all French subsidiaries), 37 German (86.0%), 23 UK (76.7), and 28 US (93.3%) subsidiaries show coordinated behavior, a statistically significant difference in proportions, as assessed by Fisher's exact test ($2 \times c$), $p = 0.016$. Post hoc analysis involves pairwise comparisons using multiple Fisher's exact tests (2×2) with a Bonferroni correction. Statistical significance is accepted at $p < 0.0083$. The proportion of subsidiaries acting in a coordinated manner is statistically significantly higher for French subsidiaries than for UK subsidiaries, $p < 0.0083$.

Concluding the dichotomous behavior variables: there is a statistically significant difference between the four independent binomial proportions ($p < 0.05$) in CGl and IRpc. Therefore, in the context of these variables the null hypothesis can be rejected and the alternative hypothesis can be accepted.

The next section uses the large dataset N134 to test for complementarities across the behavioral dimensions investigated. This investigation further improves understanding of behavioral dynamics that occur when—as the previous analyses indicates—the foreign subsidiary relies on certain home country practices.

6.5.2.2 Complementarities

According to a systemic understanding, in which a coherent way of conducting specific practices requires the embedment in a general supportive environment, complementarity is understood—in line with the detailed discussion in Chap. 3—as the presence of one institution increases the returns of the other. Accordingly, if a single alien-to-the-system practice is applied in a strange environment, neglecting the support from other institutional dimensions, the practice is likely to perform poorly. However, as the previous quantitative analyses indicate, one can reasonably assume that certain practices find their way from the home country into the Latin American host country in which the specific practice is rather inappropriate. If that practice is deemed to be successful, it needs to be embedded in a supportive (coherent) environment. Hence, regarding the action situation under scrutiny, for example, if subsidiaries act rather coordinated in one action situation, one may expect a rather coordinated behavior in other action situations too. Making use of the dataset N134, the subsequent section allows one to grasp whether complementarity exists for the subsidiaries that are situated in a state of institutional duality.

[25] Here, the 0.05 level is used since SPSS Statistics does not allow for alpha level adjustments when conducting multiple z-tests.

Here in the quantitative analysis, complementarity in behavior is suggested if there is a positive relationship between the behavioral variables.

Relating to the abstract dimensional indicators, EV, IF, CG, IF, and EV, inter-dimensional correlations are scrutinized using Pearson's product-moment correlation. It provides the Pearson correlation coefficient that allows strength and direction of the relationship to be grasped. On that account, a positive correlation between behavioral variables may indicate that if one is "active" (that is being more coordinated or more liberal) the other one is "active" in a supportive role, indicating complementarity (Laerd Statistics 2018). Being located in the spectrum between the poles of typically coordinated and typically liberal in the various action situations, a positive relationship between the variables of interest indicates that if a subsidiary tends to approach a specific action situation in, for example, a coordinated manner, it also tends to approach another specific action in a coordinated manner, indicating complementarity.

The Pearson correlation coefficient r indicates strength and direction for relationships exclusively for the sample. Regarding the Pearson correlation coefficient p that exists in the population, the following null hypothesis is raised, indicating that there is no relationship between the behavioral dimensional variables.

$$H_0 : p = 0, \text{the population correlation coefficient is equal to zero.}$$

The alternative hypothesis stating that there is a relationship between two variables is:

$$H_A : p \neq 0, \text{the population corelation coefficient is not equal to zero.}$$

First of all, data needs to be checked to see if it fits the requirements of the Pearson correlation well. On that account, linearity of the relationships, existence of outliers, and the assumption of bivariate normality is put under scrutiny. Visual inspection of scatterplots indicates both linearity of the relationships and the absence of extreme outliers. Behavioral scores are normally distributed, as assessed by visual inspection of normal Q-Q plots. In general, in conjunction with the relatively large sample size, the Pearson's correlation test is fairly robust to deviations from normality (Laerd Statistics, 2018).

Table 6.13 indicates the major results of the Pearson's correlations. It indicates the Pearson's correlation coefficient value r (or p), which indicates direction and strength of the relationship tested. In general, nine out of ten relationships investigated show a positive relationship. The only negative one is the one between EV and ER and is the one closest to zero. Following Cohen (1988), there are four small ($0.1 < |r| < 0.3$) and two moderate ($0.3 < |r| < 0.5$) correlations observable.

Summarizing the statistically significant correlations: Pearson's correlations are run to assess the relationship between the composite dimensional indicators. A total of 134 subsidiaries participate in the investigation.

Table 6.13 Complementarity composite

Correlations						
		EV	IF	ER	CG	IR
EV	Pearson Correlation	1	.438***	−0.019	.268***	0.167*
IF	Pearson Correlation		1	0.142	0.046	.353***
ER	Pearson Correlation			1	0.132	0.052
CG	Pearson Correlation				1	0.052
IR	Pearson Correlation					1

Source: From the Author
*Correlation is significant at the 0.1 level (2-tailed)
**Correlation is significant at the 0.05 level (2-tailed)
***Correlation is significant at the 0.01 level (2-tailed)
$N = 134$

- There is a statistically significant, moderate positive correlation between behavior in the dimension of EV and the one of IF, $r(134) = 0.438, p < 0.01$, with behavior in EV explaining more than 19% of the variation in IF. Therefore, the null hypothesis can be rejected and the corresponding alternative hypothesis can be accepted.
- There is a statistically significant, small positive correlation between behavior in the dimension of EV and the one of CG, $r(134) = 0.268, p < 0.01$, with behavior in EV explaining more than 7% of the variation in CG. Therefore, the null hypothesis can be rejected and the corresponding alternative hypothesis can be accepted.
- There is a statistically significant, small positive correlation between behavior in the dimension of EV and the one of IR, $r(134) = 0.167, p < 0.1$, with behavior in EV explaining more than 3% of the variation in IR. Therefore, the null hypothesis can be rejected and the corresponding alternative hypothesis can be accepted.
- There is a statistically significant, small positive correlation between behavior in the dimension of IF and the one of IR, $r(134) = 0.353, p < 0.01$, with behavior in IF explaining roughly 12% of the variation in IR. Therefore, the null hypothesis can be rejected and the corresponding alternative hypothesis can be accepted.

The relatively strong correlations imply that variation in one variable can be reasonably explained to a certain degree by another variable. This aligned movement across the behavioral variables along the spectrum with liberal and coordinated poles suggests that the specific behavior within an action situation is closely connected with similar behavior in other action situations, suggesting a recognizable degree of institutional (behavioral) complementarity for MNCs' subsidiaries within the Latin American system. Recognizing a specific pattern, coherence across the dimensions seems to be strong for EV in particular. As the tests above indicate, action conducted, especially within the dimension of EV, seems to be strongly supported by complementary action in the other institutional dimensions. Furthermore, the occurrence of complementarity indicates that, indeed, if a subsidiary introduces foreign practices, other practices are potentially adjusted accordingly. That again confirms the rather weak institutional setting in the Latin American countries, since such an orchestrated alignment with foreign practices may be beyond scope in firmer systems such as those found in the home countries of interest.

In addition, correlations are conducted at the item level (see Appendix 4). Pearson's correlations and nonparametric tests relying on the Kendall rank correlation coefficient (Kendall's tau) are applied to consider the different scales. Briefly summarizing findings, correlations at the item level further strengthen the notion of complementarities. Expressed in numbers, a total of 90 relations between the single variables is statistically significant out of which the vast majority of 75 is positive. Some clusters characterized by a relatively high density of strong relationship can be found especially between the dimensions of IR, EV, and IF. These findings confirm the analyses on the composite indicators above.

Concluding, given the context of the study, these findings that suggest complementarity are remarkable. MNCs' subsidiaries that are located in a strange system, nevertheless, show coherence across the different actions. On that account, this evidence strongly suggests complementarity in action regarding coordinated and liberal action. Hence, the specific conduct of an alien-to-the-system practices most likely does not come "alone" but is accompanied by various supportive practices that may allow its proper conduct in the first place. Such a finding cannot be found in the existing literature and depicts a new insight into the behavior of MNCs in strange systems. Even though being located in a strange and rather fragmented organizational field such as the Latin American HME, MNCs show a relatively strong systemic coherence regarding their actions.

6.5.3 Behavioral Patterns

Following the findings of complementarity, the subsequent chapter investigates whether there are more adequate factors describing certain behavioral patterns than the theoretically predetermined institutional dimensions and their corresponding composite indicators. On that account, this chapter conducts an exploratory factor analysis (EFA). Furthermore, potential composite indicators are applied to the methodological variety indicated up to now. First, regression analysis sheds light on the variations of behavior and their relationship. Second, group differences allow behavioral differences relating to the specific groups' distinct CoO to be detected.

6.5.3.1 Exploratory Factor Analysis

In comparison to the theoretically predetermined composite indicators of EV, IR, ER, CG, and IF, notions of complementarity require further investigation as to whether there may be other composite indicators that may better describe certain behavioral patterns.

An EFA is conducted using the sample N134 since it is the one most suitable in terms of sample size. Even using this dataset, due to the number of variables, the Kaiser–Meyer–Olkin measure of sampling adequacy of 0.465 is slightly lower than 0.5, which is normally taken as the lower limit (Ludwig-Mayerhofer, 2016). However, as a rule of thumb, some scholars indicate at least five to ten participants per question. That sets a lower limit to 130 respondents, which the study at hand can cope with. However, being aware of the rather low sample size, the application of an EFA is a reasonable endeavor.

As a first step, Bartlett's test of sphericity indicates a reliable correlation with a significance level $p < 0.005$. This basically means that there is at least one significant correlation between two of the items. Furthermore, the communalities table in the column "extraction" indicates how much of the variance of each factor can be explained by the specific item. It contains no item with less than 0.3, which means that all items can be kept in further analysis. Further, "total of variance explained" and the "scree plot" suggest ten new factors with an *eigenvalue* greater than one. In order to double-check the number of factors, Horn's parallel analysis (Horn, 1965) is used to determine the number of factors (Patil et al., 2017). In brief, an item is kept in the analysis if Horn's parallel analysis shows *eigenvalues* that are less than the calculated *eigenvalue*. Using the generated web-based parallel analysis engine by Patil et al. (2008), it is the ninth item in which, here, the calculated *eigenvalue* is lower than the minimum one indicated by Horn's analysis. Accordingly, eight factors are kept in analysis.

The component correlation matrix indicates values all smaller than 0.5 making it an orthogonal matrix (as compared to oblique). Such matrix indicates an orthogonal relationship between the new factors, meaning that there is no considerable correlation between the new factors. One step further, the rotated component matrix indicates the composition of the new factors. All variables under a factor may be contributed as being part of the same latent variable. Strong correlation between the variables indicates that no matter what they are measuring exactly, it is most likely the same thing. As a next step, data from the rotated component matrix is used to run a reliability test for each of the factors. The guiding indicator is Cronbach's Alpha indicating the internal consistency reliability. In general, Cronbach's alpha for a factor should be 0.7 or higher to be interpreted as "respectable" or "very good" regarding a sufficient level of reliability (DeVellis, 2012).

Testing the first new factor with the variables EVv, EVc, IFe, EVia, IRpc, and EVii indicates a Cronbach's Alpha of 0.557, which means that the factor is not reliable and requires further adjustment. The item-total statistics in the right column shows the Cronbach's Alpha if a specific item was deleted. If the variable "EVii" was deleted the Cronbach's Alpha for the first new factor increases up to 0.731, indicating a strong reliability. Reiterating without the variable "EVii," a reliable new factor is indicated.

A Cronbach's alpha of 0.491 of the second factor with the variables "IRu1," "IFic," IRu2," and "EVf" indicates low reliability. Deleting "EVf" leads to a Cronbach's alpha of 0.628 that still lacks reliability. Further deleting IRu2 leads to

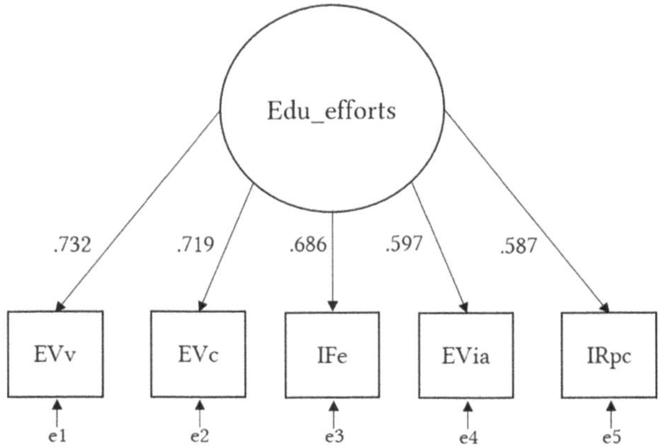

Fig. 6.9 Exploratory factor analysis. Source: From the Author

a value of 0.658. Since only two variables are left within the factor, there is no further adjustment possible. On that account, this factor is left out of further analysis.

A Cronbach's alpha of 0.606 of the third factor with the variables "IFip," "IFr," and IFs" and "IFsb" indicates low reliability. There is no possible adjustment that would lead to a higher degree of reliability. On that account, this factor is left out of further analysis.

A Cronbach's alpha of 0.533 of the fourth factor with the variables "IFs," "IRs," "IRp," and "CGo" indicates low reliability. Deleting "IFr" leads to a Cronbach's alpha of 0.594 that still lacks reliability. Since only two variables are left within the factor, there is no further adjustment possible. On that account, this factor is left out of further analysis.

All the other factors do not reach a sufficient level of reliability. In conclusion, the EFA conducted leads to a one-factor model as shown in Fig. 6.9.

Reduction of dimensions through an EFA crystalizes a latent variable that may best be described by the common underlying characteristic that is the specific manner of education. To consider this, the latent variable is called "Edu_efforts." All variables, apart from the "IRpc" one, are directly connected with educational efforts.

Three of the variables stem directly from the dimension of EV. That of the IF dimension (IFe) is the one that operationalizes inter-firm cooperation in the field of education, which is a key pillar of especially coordinated market economies. Finally, the variable "IRpc" may best be understood as strongly complementary—positively impacting (maybe even allowing) specifics of education—since the mutual will and security of both the company and the employee to cooperate in the long term are vital for future planning, especially whether or not to conduct a vocational training and, thus, to acquire firm-specific skills. Such notion of complementarity between the design of working contracts and the specific conduct of educational practices is already indicated by significant correlations between "IRpc" and the EV variables as can be seen in Appendix 4.

In the upcoming chapters this factor, "Edu_efforts" is used to dig deeper into the dynamics of inter-systemic exchange of economic entities within the field of education that in Latin America is coined by the generally low level of education, the ongoing mismatch between supply and demand of skills, and system inherent distortions that allow inequality and a very low level of productivity to reproduce and to coexist in the long term. Following the hitherto applied methods, the factor will be depicted by an arithmetic mean index of its constituting variables. Furthermore, such index is applied to both regression analysis for the sample N51 and the testing for group differences for the sample N134.

6.5.3.2 Education and Behavioral Relations: N51

The EFA above indicates the factor "Edu_efforts." Whether educational efforts of the foreign subsidiary can be predicted by educational efforts in the parent company is part of the subsequent analysis using paired data (N51). On that account, the composite indicators "Edu_efforts_home" and "Edu_efforts_host" are constructed as arithmetic means of the item of interest.

Investigation is based on bivariate linear regression, as follows:

$$\text{Beh\_Edu\_efforts}_{\text{host}} = \beta_0 + \beta_1 * \text{Beh\_Edu\_efforts}_{\text{\_home}} + \varepsilon,$$

where β_0 is the intercept, β_1 the slope coefficient, and ε the error.

Regarding the specific sample drawn, the model is:

$$\text{Beh\_Edu\_efforts}_{\text{host}} = b_0 + b_1 * \text{Beh\_Edu\_efforts}_{\text{\_home}} + e,$$

where b_0 is the sample intercept and serves as an estimate for β_0, b_1 as the sample slope coefficient that estimates β_1, and e as the sample error estimating ε.

First, data is scrutinized according to its fit with the method's requirements. First, a scatterplot of "$\text{Beh \_ Edu \_ efforts}_{\text{host}}$" against "$\text{Beh \_ Edu \_ efforts}_{\text{\_home}}$" is plotted. Visual inspection of the scatterplot indicates a linear relationship between the variables. Second, as assessed by a Durbin–Watson statistics of 2.060, there is independence of residuals. Third, regarding the existence of (extreme) outliers, case number 8 with a standardized residual $> \pm 3$ is removed from further analyses. The indicated value is, first, logically impossible and, second, characterized by too many missing values. Alternative results with the outlier kept in analysis show very small differences that do not change general characteristics of strength and direction. Fourth, there is homoscedasticity, as assessed by a visual inspection of a plot of standardized residuals versus standardized predicted values. Fifth, residuals are normally distributed as assessed by visual inspection of a normal P-P plot.

R^2, which is the proportion of variation explained by the regression model in the sample, is as a percentage 22%. Therefore, 22% of the variability can be explained by the corresponding IV. In order to derive results valid for the entire population, adjusted R^2 corrects R^2's positively biased estimates and leads to more conservative values. Consequently, *adjusted* R^2 is the proportion of variation explained by the model in the population. Here, 20.4% of the population's variability can be explained by the model.

As such, behavior in educational efforts of the parent company in the home country accounts for 22.0% of the variation in behavior in educational efforts of the corresponding foreign subsidiary with adjusted $R^2 = 20.4\%$, a very strong "substantial" effect according to Cohen (1988, 1992) and Gignac and Szodorai (2016). Further analysis indicates that the relationships under scrutiny are highly statistically significant. "Beh_Edu_efforts_home" statistically significantly predicts "Beh_Edu_efforts_host," $F(1, 48) = 13.55, p = 0.001$.

Substituting the values into the regression model, there is:

$$\text{Beh\_Edu\_efforts}_{\text{host}} = 0.272 + 0.455 * B\text{eh\_Edu\_efforts}_{\text{\_home}}.$$

The slope coefficient is statistically significant, meaning that it is different to zero. Taking a look at the 95% CI, the true value of the slope coefficient lies between 0.207 and 0.704. Given the regression equation retrieved throughout the chapter, one can reasonably calculate predicted values of behavior in education abroad for values of behavior in education at home. Such predicted value is the mean behavior abroad, which can be interpreted as if one measures behavior abroad for all the companies in the population that behave specifically at home (with a given value). Referring to contrast results, predictions are made to determine mean behavior in educational efforts of the subsidiaries for those companies that behave 0.2, 0.5, and 0.8 in educational efforts at home. For 0.2 behavior at home, mean behavior abroad is predicted as 0.363 (95% CI, 0.241to 0.485); for 0.5 it is predicted as 0.500 (95% CI, 0.440 to 0.559); and for 0.8 it is predicted as 0.636 (95% CI, 0.578 to 0.694).

Summarizing, Fig. 6.10 visualizes the bivariate linear regression on educational efforts. It depicts a statically significant very strong linear relationships between Edu_efforts at home and Edu_efforts at the host country.

6.5.3.3 Education and Group Differences (SoO, CoO)

Having found solid evidence suggesting a strong relationship between educational behavior in the home and the host country, further analyses are conducted to use the large dataset (N134) exclusively with the subsidiaries in Latin America scrutinizing behavior in the field of education relating to the system and country of origin.

System of Origin: N134

In line with the previous investigations, testing on the existence of an intra-organizational field, one hypothesizes that, first, differences relating to the behavior

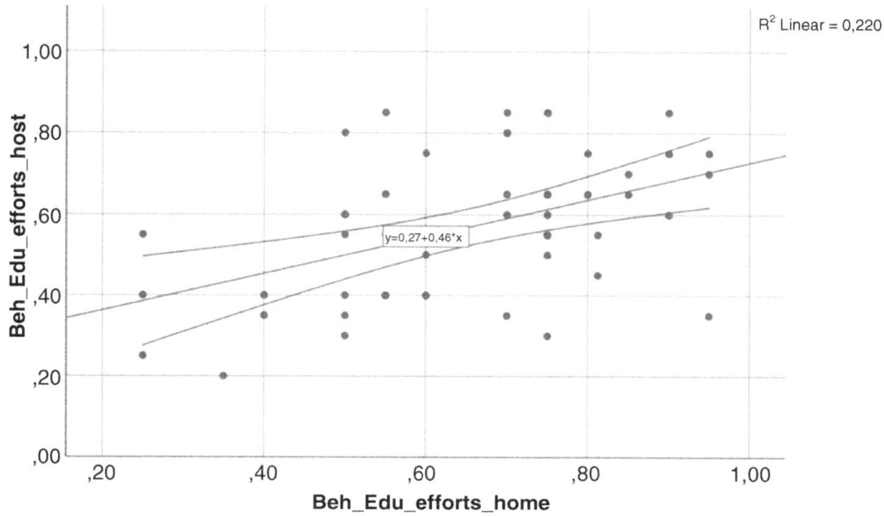

Fig. 6.10 Scatterplot Edu_efforts. Source: From the Author

in Edu_efforts exist and, second, that subsidiaries with origins in CME act more coordinated than their LME counterparts.[26]

In the subsequent section, applying independent-samples t-test, the corresponding null hypothesis is:

$$H_0 : \mu_{\text{CME}} = \mu_{\text{LME}}$$

in which μ is the population mean and the different independent groups are "LME" and "CME." Verbally expressed, the null hypothesis states that mean behavior of foreign subsidiaries independent of their systemic origins is equal.

Alternatively, one can hypothesize:

$$H_A : \mu_{\text{CME}} \neq \mu_{\text{LME}}.$$

CME and LME mean behavior being unequal in the population indicates that differences in systemic origins of the parent company affect subsidiaries inasmuch as their behavior differs.

In total, there were 73 CME and 60 LME subsidiaries. An independent-samples *t*-test was run to determine whether there are differences in educational behavior between CME and LME companies. There are no outliers in the data, as assessed

[26]The same holds up vice versa, meaning that it can equally be hypothesized that subsidiaries with origins in LME act more liberally than their CME counterparts.

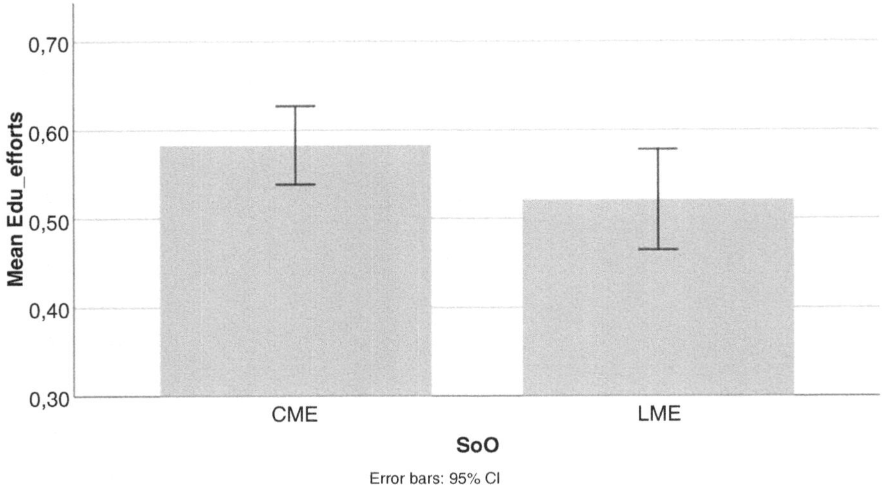

Fig. 6.11 Bar Chart Edu_efforts SoO. Source: From the Author

by inspection of a boxplot.[27] Behavioral scores for each category of CoO are non-normally distributed, as assessed by Shapiro–Wilk's test ($p < 0.05$),[28] and there is homogeneity of variances, as assessed by Levene's test for equality of variances ($p = 0.452$). Educational behavior of subsidiaries that originate from a CME is more coordinated (higher) (0.583 ± 0.190) than the one of subsidiaries that originate in an LME (0.521 ± 0.220), a statistically significant difference of 0.062 (95% CI, −0.009 to 0.132), $t(132) = 1.736$, $p = 0.085$, $d = 0.714$. This value of d indicates a large effect (Cohen, 1988), meaning that, indeed, there is a great difference in educational behavior relating to the different systemic origins.

Accordingly, found evidence strongly suggests that—in the context of Edu_efforts—mean behavior is not equal in the population and that differences can be found relating to the systemic origins of the parent company. Consequently, H_0 can reasonably be rejected and H_A accepted.

The bar chart below visually summarizes group differences in behavior according to the capitalist system of origin (Fig. 6.11).

[27] Nonetheless, one value is extracted due to multiple missing values. Four of the five variables of the additive index are missing. Using the indicator anyway would highly overweight the single response given and, thus, may distort representativeness of the sample.

[28] Due to the violation of the assumption of normality, to cross-check findings with a nonparametric test, a Kruskal–Wallis H test was run to determine if there were differences in educational behavioral score between two groups of SoO either from a CME or an LME: the "CME" and "LME" groups. Distributions of educational behavioral scores were similar for the two groups, as assessed by visual inspection of a boxplot. The distributions of educational behavioral scores though were statistically slightly insignificantly different between groups, $\chi^2(1) = 2.602$, $p = 0.107$.

Country of Origin: Brazil

Digging deeper into differences between the specific CoO representatives (countries of origin), in order to keep analysis of educational efforts clean relating to potentially differing host country effects, the upcoming analysis focuses on group differences exclusively within the host country best represented in the entire sample, which is Brazil with a total of 70 participating subsidiaries.

In this part of the study, investigating group differences in Edu_efforts according to the country origin of the subsidiaries, the null hypothesis states that there are no differences in population means between the subsidiaries with different home countries.

$$H_0 : \mu_{\text{France}} = \mu_{\text{Germany}} = \mu_{\text{UK}} = \mu_{\text{USA}}.$$

Since the intra-organizational field is assumed to impact the behavior abroad, here evidence against the null hypothesis is of utmost interest. Accordingly, the alternative hypothesis states that there is a difference between at least two group population means.

$$H_A : \text{at least one group population mean is different.}$$

A one-way ANOVA is conducted to determine if the educational behavior of foreign subsidiaries (educational behavioral score) is different according to their CoO. Participating companies were classified into four groups: France ($n = 17$), Germany (24), the UK ($n = 11$), and the USA ($n = 18$). There are no outliers, as assessed by boxplot; data is normally distributed for each group, as assessed by Shapiro–Wilk's test ($p > 0.05$); and there is homogeneity of variances, as assessed by Levene's test of homogeneity of variances ($p = 0.267$). Data is presented as mean ± standard deviation. Educational behavioral score is statistically significantly different between different CoOs, $F(3, 66) = 3.699, p = 0.016, \omega^2 = 0.14$, indicating a large effect. Educational behavioral scores increase from the LME groups the UK (0.511 ± 0.240) and the USA (0.509 ± 0.133) to the CME groups Germany (0.625 ± 0.169) and France (0.671 ± 0.160). Tukey post hoc analysis revealed that the increases of both from the UK to the France group (0.160, 95% CI, (0.005 to 0.315)) are statistically significant ($p = 0.085$), as well as the increase from the USA to the France group (0.161, 95% CI, (0.026 to 0.297)). The increase from the UK to the Germany group (0.114, CI (−0.032 to 0.260)) is insignificant ($p = 0.268$). The increase from the USA to the Germany group (0.116, CI (−0.009 to 0.241)) is slightly insignificant ($p = 0.144$). Since group means are statistically significantly different ($p < 0.05$), H_0 can be rejected and H_A can be accepted.

The bar chart below visually demonstrates mean behavioral scores within the field of education. French and German subsidiaries within Brazil act significantly more coordinated than their counterparts from the UK and the USA (Fig. 6.12).

The evidence found strongly suggests the existence of an intra-organizational field. Subsidiaries that originate in both CME countries act much more coordinated

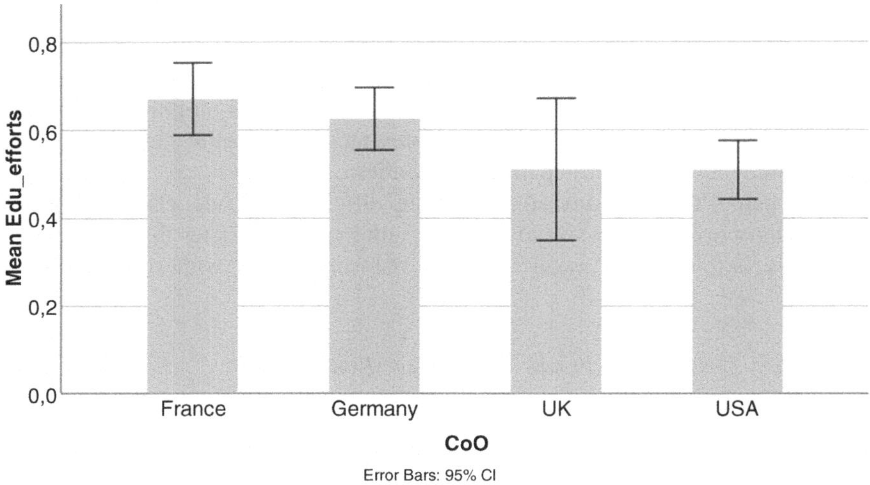

Fig. 6.12 Bar chart Edu_efforts CoO. Source: From the Author

than their counterparts from LMEs. The same holds up vice versa: subsidiaries that originate in liberal market economies tend to act more liberal than their counterparts from CMEs do.

6.6 Summary and Discussion: Quantitative Analysis

This quantitative study scrutinizes Conflating Capitalisms' decisive point of the action situation in the context of the case study of Western MNCs in Latin America introduced in Chap. 5. For the first time, evidence has been obtained at the micro-level regarding the inter-actor exchange between LMEs and CMEs on the one hand and Latin American HMEs on the other hand. As such, this investigation goes beyond the OECD countries, for the first time, and peculiarities of developing countries are considered in particular. Along these lines, it is the first time that investigation in this setting is based on quantitative analysis instead of case studies, aiming at detecting general patterns of behavior.

On that account, to grasp behavioral patterns and to better understand if and to what extent subsidiaries act in line with their system or country of origin, corporate behavior was operationalized along all institutional domains, a questionnaire was developed, a survey was carried out among corporate decision-makers, and in-depth statistical analyses were applied. The analysis throughout the chapter allows one to grasp and evaluate behavioral patterns as a source of institutional contradiction. Hence, the quantitative analysis contributes to a better understanding of the theoretically derived situation of institutional duality and the corresponding explanation of MNCs' subsidiaries' embedded agency (DellaPosta et al., 2017). In general, the previous statistical analyses find relatively strong evidence for the existence of institutional duality and, therefore, of an intra-organizational field. The investigation on behavior of the subsidiary in Latin America and the behavior of the parent company, indeed, suggests a firm and generally positive relationship. It therefore supports the hypothesis raised that "If an MNC behaves more coordinated in the home country, then the corresponding subsidiary in Latin America behaves rather coordinated as well" and, furthermore, confirms by the condition triangle moderate to strong effect of the intra-organizational field.

As such, various regression analyses that use the N51 dataset suggest that—to varying degrees at the item level—behavior abroad follows and, therefore, can be explained by behavior at home. Certainly, regression analyses by no means report wholesale transfers of practices. However, general direction and strength of the relationships suggest that, indeed, foreign subsidiaries are situated in a state of institutional duality and, partly, act in conformity with what is appropriate in their home country. Confirming this, the relation between corporate behavior abroad and at home is worth considering especially in the case of educational efforts. Analyses of the composite indicator of educational efforts indicate a very strong and statistically significant relationship, in which behavior of the subsidiary in Latin America can be largely explained by the specific behavior of the parent company in the country of origin.

Considering the strong representation of German companies, interpreting the results based on the N51 dataset requires certain caution. First, in general, findings need to be interpreted cautiously with respect to the general sample size. The complex data collection method in use for the two-step approach, unfortunately, did not allow to generate a larger and more balanced sample within the given setting of this work. Furthermore, such high weighting of German MNCs can call generalizability of the findings on the wider population into question. In fact, as introduced in Sect. 4.5, various studies exist that investigate differences between, for example, German and US companies relating to the degree of autonomy granted to the foreign subsidiary. To recall, subsidiaries are labeled as either "boy scout" subsidiaries that do what the upper intra-firm hierarchy tells them and "subversive subsidiaries" that aim at deepening local connections. Interestingly and supporting the validity of this research for the wider population, across all suitable studies, there is a consensus that it is always the German company that grants a high degree of autonomy and, therefore, is clearly assigned to the subversive category (De Jong & Van Vo, 2010; Javorcik & Spatareanu, 2011; Kuznetsov & Jacob, 2015; Xu & Shenkar, 2002). In general terms, it is stated that a shift toward market-based interaction is easier than building up networks and reputational systems based on strategic joint cooperation. This means that—even if intra-organizationally desired—a company from a coordinated home country may be less likely to transfer practices due to the high complexity and the non-supportive environment in the host country. Along the same lines, Kuznetsov and Jacob (2015) discuss the general subversive strategies used by German subsidiaries and the corresponding adjustment to local conditions as a deliberate "flight from the German model." Following this argumentation, German MNCs often perceive the home country institutions as too restrictive and, therefore, aim at using the institutional advantages of the liberal market economies that are allegedly freer from constraints. However, the "flight" is detected mainly when German companies move to LMEs as host countries. Certainly, the alleged freedoms of a well-functioning free market are not to be expected in Latin American countries. Nonetheless, following this line of thought, assuming German subsidiaries tend to adjust locally, the quantitative analyses using the dataset N51 with mostly German MNCs depict a least likely case in which the occurrence of such intra-organizational transfer of behavioral patterns is less likely than in subsidiaries from other countries. Therefore, the quantitative study based on the N51 dataset may strengthen the expectation of companies from countries other than Germany to have even closer relationships with their foreign subsidiaries and, thus, to generate higher levels of conformity with the home country's institutional logic. Consequently, the overrepresentation of German companies certainly affects the validity of the specific strength of the relationship but most likely does not affect (on the contrary, it rather strengthens) the findings that support the general existence of behavioral dynamics due to institutional duality and the intra-organizational field.

Confirming the general relationship detected before and further exploring behavioral patterns depending on the system and country of origin, analyses of the dataset N134 contribute to better understanding the behavioral dynamics in play. In-depth analyses demonstrate that foreign subsidiaries of MNCs that originate in coordinated countries also tend to act more coordinated when situated in a hierarchical environment. Along the same lines of argumentation, the same holds up vice versa inasmuch as subsidiaries from a liberal country act significantly more liberal than their counterparts from CMEs. Regarding the abstract institutional dimensions, such behavioral pattern is recognizable in CG, IR, EV, and IF in particular. The dimension of ER indicates no behavioral differences between the subsidiaries originating in different systems.

Similar behavior in ER in Latin America of both liberal and coordinated subsidiaries can indicate the existence of a third "global" organizational field that is composed of multinational organizations that affects all MNCs equally. However, if it exists at all, such strength of a global field exclusively in the dimension of ER, in conjunction with prior studies that emphasize national systemic resilience of, for example, Pauly and Reich (1997), Paunescu and Schneider (2011), and Hall and Gingerich (2009), the detachment of corporate actor of nation states is rather unlikely. On that account, discussing at the abstract level of composite indicators, one can reasonably assume that the local HME exerts sufficient pressure on the various companies to show conformity within the local organizational field.

Decreasing abstraction, moving at the item level, and testing for group differences according to the CoO, the actions regarding CGc, ERa, CGb, IFic, IFs, EVia, and EVv in particular, indicate significant differences in behavior. Regarding all these specific actions, the corresponding home country has a middle to large effect on the behavior shown by the subsidiaries. Across all differences identified, subsidiaries with parent companies from CMEs act more coordinated than the ones with liberal origins. Logically, all subsidiaries with liberal roots act more liberal. Considering this apparently strong impact, the assumption of an intra-organizational field that pressurizes conformity to the home country institutional setting is strongly supported.

Further analyses on educational efforts find strong evidence that behavioral patterns of the foreign subsidiaries can be reasonably explained by the systemic belonging of the parent company and thereby also confirm the findings gained through regression analyses of the N51. The composite indicator Edu_efforts that includes EVv, EVc, IFe, EVia, and IRpc finds a statistically significant difference in behavior relating to having origins in either LMEs or CMEs. Statistical analyses further find that this effect of origins is large, meaning that educational behavior is highly impacted by systemic belonging of the parent company.

In order to attain the highest degree of analytical clarity, further analyses approach one host country exclusively and estimate effects of origins regarding the country of origin. In so doing, all values can clearly be assigned to one country. Focusing the investigation on Brazil as the host country of interest, findings support the hypothesis raised even more clearly. Within Brazil, educational efforts of French and German MNCs show behavior that is firmly aligned with that induced by home country institutions. In comparison, both MNCs from the UK and the USA in Brazil show a statistically significantly more liberal behavior.

According to the general findings that support an intra-organizational field, this work in the given empirical setting, indeed, raises major doubts on a variety of theories and approaches. First, the comprehensively criticized treatment of MNCs as a featureless flow of FDI at the beginning of this work in Chap. 2, indeed, seems to come with major shortcomings and oversimplified generalizations. Differences in behavior on such a large scale, as indicated by the analysis of the action situation, strengthen the postulated need to understand economic interaction as a case of social relations rather than one characterized by automatisms and optimal corporate responses. By treating MNCs in such a misunderstood manner, in conjunction with the overwhelming importance of MNCs in Latin America, orthodox economics runs the risk of missing pivotal attributes that directly tackle the assumptions upon which orthodox economic theory is constructed. These findings that strongly suggest a systemically reproduced pattern of behavioral variety call for a severe ontological extension of economic orthodoxy, including the non-identical *Gestalt* of MNCs.

Second, identified conformity to home country institutions of foreign subsidiaries that are located in a strange system raises strong doubts on Hall and Soskice's (2001) postulate of institutional arbitrage. Intrinsically, an HME with complementarities between, among others, low skills, short-term employment, and absence of labor representation offers—if at all—a comparative institutional advantage for commodity production, natural resources, and low-complexity manufacturing (Schneider, 2013). However, reliance on home country practice, combined with the motives for moving to Latin America in the first place (The Financial Times, 2017), indicates that local institutions do not function as a major pull factor for MNCs. Along these lines, if the institutional setting is not decisive in the first place, then the idea of MNCs conforming to them as a source of benefits is questionable.

Third, the strongly supported concept of institutional duality and, hence, subsidiaries as subject to various different sorts of isomorphic pressures call large parts of institutional literature on MNCs that scrutinize actors within a nationally isolated field into question. The assumption of an "oversocialized" actor that responds to one clearly assignable set of institutions lacks the capability to approach actors that move across the borders of organizational field (Powell & Colyvas, 2008; Schneider, 2013). Following this line of thought, difficulties in understanding embedded agency requires—especially in the case of MNCs—one to incorporate the institutional meso-level into analysis in which different sets of rules overlap and intermingle. This need to approach MNCs as potentially showing hybrid forms of behavior may be further strengthened when applying institutional analysis to inter-systemic exchange between very stable and well-functioning and rather weak and poorly performing institutional settings, such as is the case in this study at hand.

In fact, this study confirms the rather small fraction of literature that considers MNCs as institutional tension fields that struggle for legitimacy in more than one institutional setting (Geppert et al., 2006; Heidenreich, 2012; Kostova et al., 2008; Kwok & Tadesse, 2006; Seo & Creed, 2002). However, this quantitative study's findings regarding behavioral dynamics that occur in the particular empirical context given are unique and, thus, comparison with other studies is rather difficult. The only study that investigates behavior across the five institutional dimensions is the one of Kuznetsov and Jacob (2015). They scrutinize MNCs that move from Germany to the UK and vice versa regarding the transfer of practices from the home to the host country. In comparison to the study at hand, the empirical setting is constituted by different systems but of which both are stable and well-performing archetypes. Approaching behavior and potential adjustment processes from a rather comprehensive perspective—as is done here through the condition triangle—including peculiarities of the organizational fields, actors, and actions in play, such change in the host country's characteristics most likely leads to different processes and makes comparison futile. A basis for comparison is not given, especially when the host country changes from an outstandingly successful to a rather institutionally weak one. Nonetheless, both Kuznetsov and Jacob (2015) and the study at hand support the concept of MNCs as hybrid forms that show neither full conformity with the local environment nor with the intra-organizational one. Furthermore, similar findings are made regarding the adoption of home country practices and the adaptation to the national setup inasmuch as it is not uniform across the institutional dimensions scrutinized. As the quantitative study above shows, uniformity is not even to be observed within the single dimensions. Therefore, a subsidiary most likely responds to the plurality of isomorphic pressures in one dimension differently than it does in another one.

The different adjustment processes across the five institutional domains may, at first, call postulates of complementarity into question. Indeed, complementarity across the dimensions is not found between all dimensions as may be the case in the liberal and coordinated home countries (that as a by-product has been strongly supported in Sect. 6.5.1). Considering MNCs as showing hybrid forms of behavior, such comprehensive systemic coherence is certainly beyond expectation. However, this study and the corresponding quantitative analysis is the first one that is able to find complementarity regarding the practices of alien-to-the-system actors in a strange variety of capitalism. It is the dimension of EV in particular that demonstrates strong complementarities with the dimensions of IF, CG, and IR. This remarkable finding may be explained by the high degree of EV's local embeddedness. In general, a high degree of local embeddedness indicates that the proper conduct of the EV generally depends highly on supportive institutions in the other domains that can be understood as Streeckian enablers. Along these lines, the complexity of EV and the high degree of EV's embeddedness into the local setting are usually used to explain the inability of MNCs' subsidiaries to transfer home country EV practices to the host country. However, one can reasonably argue that if EV practices are transferred in the first place, then such practice is required to be accompanied by complementary practices. On that account, deep local embeddedness of EV in this study does not explain the alignment with the host country but the comprehensive and intense transfer of home country practices that allow one to work in home country EV. Such comprehensive complementarity and corresponding extensive transfer of supporting practices have not been found before and depict a major contradiction with the local institutional setting.

Concluding, this quantitative analysis scrutinizes the action situation and finds that subsidiaries from LMEs and CMEs act differently from one another and also differently from the local actors. On that account, the previous investigation finds strong evidence suggesting institutional contradiction within the HMEs of interest that is caused by MNCs' subsidiaries. In comparison to other case studies, this quantitative study finds general contradictory behavioral patterns, meaning that this behavior can be assumed to be (partly) representative for the population of subsidiaries in Latin America with origins in France, Germany, the USA, and the UK. Following this line of thought, institutional contradiction caused by alien-to-the-system practices is not an isolated case but indicates a systemically produced behavioral pattern of MNCs' subsidiaries. Since institutional contradiction is the necessary condition for institutional contestation and, therefore, turns embedded social actors into agents of institutional change, this finding is applied to further investigation on institutional change (Boxenbaum, 2006; Burns & Nielsen, 2006; March & Olsen, 2009; Mitchell, 2010). How contradiction feeds back in the local institutional field depicts the second major step in the framework of Conflating Capitalisms. In particular, the finding of extensive institutional contradictions within the dimension of educational efforts is used to scrutinize potential institutional change caused by MNCs' subsidiaries. Beyond the remarkable findings of behavioral dynamics within the dimension of EV in the empirical study above, different approaches on education and vocational training and potential for institutional changes reach the core of the low-skill trap and the systemic incapability of generating quality jobs in the Latin American HMEs as theoretically introduced in Chap. 3 and empirically diagnosed in Chap. 5. Whether institutional contradiction is translated into actor-induced institutional change is scrutinized qualitatively in the subsequent chapter on German educational practices in Brazil.

References

Albert, M. (1992). *Kapitalismus contra Kapitalismus*. Campus.

Bardasi, E., Beegle, K., Dillon, A., & Serneels, P. (2010, January). Do labor statistics depend on how and to whom the questions are asked. *Policy Research Working Paper 5192*, pp. 1–56.

Battaglia, M. P., Link, M. W., Frankel, M. R., Osborn, L., & Mokdad, A. H. (2008). An evaluation of respondent selection methods for household mail surveys. *Public Opinion Quarterly, 72(3)*, 459–469.

Bizberg, I. (2014). *Variedades de Capitalismo en América Latina: los Casos de México, Brasil, Argentina y Chile*. El Colegio de México.

Boxenbaum, E. (2006). Corporate social responsibility as institutional hybrids. *Journal of Business Strategies, 23*, 45–63.

Burns, J., & Nielsen, K. (2006). How do embedded agents engage in institutional change? *Journal of Economic Issues, 40*(2), 449–456.

Carifio, J., & Perla, R. J. (2007). Ten common misunderstandings, misconceptions, persistent myths and urban legends about likert scales and likert response formats and their antidotes. *Journal of Social Sciences, 3*, 106–116.

Cohen, J. (1988). *Statistical power analysis for the behavioral sciences* (2nd ed.). Lawrence Erlbaum Associates.

Cohen, J. (1992). A power primer. *Psychological Bulletin, 112*(1), 155–159.

Cohen, L., Manion, L., & Morrison, K. (2001). *Research methods in education* (5th ed.). Routledge.

Coolidge, F. L. (2012). *Statistics: A gentle introduction*. Sage.

CRANET. (2015). *Strategic human resource management*. Retrieved October 05, 2017, from https://hrpepper.de/cranet/studie/

de Jong, G., & Van Vo, D. (2010). The impact of the institutional environment on the autonomy of MNCs' subsidiaries. *Problems and Perspectives in Management, 8*(2), 53–63.

DellaPosta, D., Nee, V., & Opper, S. (2017). Endogenous dynamics of institutional change. *Rationality and Society, 29*(I), 5–48.

DeVellis, R. F. (2012). *Scale development: Theory and applications*. SAGE.

Dunn, O. J. (1964). Multiple comparisons using rank sums. *Technometrics, 6*, 241–252.

Ferguson, C. J. (2009). An effect size primer: A guide for clinicians and researchers. *Professional Psychology: Research and Practice, 40*(5), 532–538.

Ferrari, C. A. (2016). *Capitalismo: Crisis, cambios, y evolución en el siglo XXI*. Retrieved from Pontificia Universidad Javeriana https://www.javeriana.edu.co/documents/16113/9477233/N+1+Capitalismo+crisis+cambios+y+evoluci%C3%B3n+en+el+sXXI+%28WEB%29.pdf/939499f0-2d3f-4e87-ac23-6215fbc2fccc

Field, A. (2013). *Discovering statistics using IBM SPSS Statistics* (4th ed.). Sage.

Flick, U. (2011). *Introducing research methodology*. Rowohlt Verlag.

Friel, D. (2011). Forging a comparative institutional advantage in Argentina: Implications for theory and praxis. *Human Relations., 64*(4), 553–572.

Geppert, M., Matten, D., & Walgenbach, P. (2006). Transnational institution building and the multinational corporation: An emerging field of research. *Human Relations, 59*, 1451–1465.

Gignac, G. E., & Szodorai, E. T. (2016). Effect size guidelines for individual differences researchers. *Personality and Individual Differences, 102*, 74–78.

Glennerster, H., & Lieberman, R. C. (2011). Hidden convergence: Toward a historical comparison of U.S. and U.K. health policy. *Journal of Health Politics, Policy and Law, 36*, 5–31.

Hall, P. A., & Gingerich, D. W. (2009). Varieties of capitalism and institutional complementarities in the political economy. *British Journal of Political Science, 39*(3), 449–482.

Hall, P. A., & Soskice, D. (2001). *Varieties of capitalism: The institutional foundations of comparative advantage*. Oxford University Press.

Heidenreich, M. (2012). The social embeddedness of multinational companies: A literature review. *Socio-Economic Review, 10*(3), 549–579.

Horn, J. L. (1965). A rationale and test for the number of factors in factor analysis. *Psychometrika, 30*(2), 179–185.
Javorcik, B. S., & Spatareanu, M. (2011). Does it matter where you come from? Vertical spillovers from foreign direct investment and the origin of investors. *Journal of Development Economics, 96*, 126–138.
Keppel, G., & Wickens, T. D. (2004). *Design and analysis: A researchers handbook* (4rd ed.). Pearson.
Kostova, T., Roth, K., & Dacin, M. T. (2008, October). Institutional theory in the study of multinational corporations: A critique and new directions. *The Academy of Management Review, 33*(4), 994–1006.
Kromrey, H., Roose, J., & Strübing, J. (2016). *Empirische Sozialforschung*. UVK Verlagsgesellschaft mbh.
Kuznetsov, A., & Jacob, M. (2015). Convergence versus divergence: Testing varieties of capitalism on the globalization of buiness practices. In I. S. Marinova (Ed.), *Institutional impacts on firm internationalization* (pp. 12–39). Palgrave Macmillan.
Kwok, C. C., & Tadesse, S. (2006). The MNC as an agent of change for host-country institutions: FDI and corruption. *Journal of International Business Studies, 7*, 767–785.
Laerd Statistics. (2015a). *Simple linear regression using SPSS Statistics*. Retrieved from Statistical tutorials and software guides https://statistics.laerd.com/
Laerd Statistics. (2015b). *Ordinal logistic regression using SPSS statistics. Statistical tutorials and software guides*. Retrieved from https://statistics.laerd.com/
Laerd Statistics. (2015c). *Independent-samples t-test using SPSS statistics. Statistical tutorials and software guides*. Retrieved from https://statistics.laerd.com/premium/spss/istt/independent-t-test-in-spss-24.php
Laerd Statistics. (2015d). *Kruskal-Wallis H test using SPSS statistics. Statistical tutorials and software guides*. Retrieved from https://statistics.laerd.com/premium/spss/kwht/kruskal-wallis-test-in-spss-19.php
Laerd Statistics. (2017a). *One-way ANOVA using SPSS statistics. Statistical tutorials and software guides*. Retrieved from https://statistics.laerd.com/premium/spss/owa/one-way-anova-in-spss-28.php
Laerd Statistics. (2017b). *Chi-square test of homogeneity (2 x C) using SPSS statistics. Statistical tutorials and software guides*. Retrieved from https://statistics.laerd.com/premium/spss/cstoh2xc/chi-square-test-of-homogeneity-2xc-in-spss-22.php
Laerd Statistics. (2018). Pearson's product-moment correlation using SPSS Statistics. *Statistical tutorials and software guides*. https://statistics.laerd.com/
Lenzner, T., Neuert, C., & Wanda, O. (2015). *GESIS survey guidelines - Kognitives pretesting*. GESIS – Leibniz-Institut für Sozialwissenschaften.
Liebmann, D. (2009). *Insitutional change in a varieties of capitalism context*. Rainer Hampp Verlag.
Lindenberg, S. (1992). The method of decreasing abstraction. In T. Fararo (Ed.), *Rational choice theory: Advocacy and critique* (pp. 3–20). Sage.
Ludwig-Mayerhofer, W. (2016). *Faktorenanalyse. Internet-Lexikon der Methoden der empirischen Sozialforschung(ILMES)*. http://wlm.userweb.mwn.de/Ilmes/ilm_f3.htm
March, J. G., & Olsen, J. P. (2009). The logic of appropriateness. In R. E. Gooding (Ed.), *The Oxford handbook of political science* (pp. 478–497). Oxford University Press.
Maxwell, S. E., Delaney, H. D., & Kelley, K. (2017). *Designing experiments and analyzing data: A model comparison perspective* (3rd ed.). CRC Press.
Mitchell, M. C. (2010). An institutional perspective of the MNC as a social change agent: The case of environmentalism. *Journal of Global Responsibility, 1*(2), 382–398.
Norman, G. (2010). Likert scales, levels of measurement and the "laws" of statistics. *Advances in Health Sciences Education, 15*(5), 625–632.
O'Leary, Z. (2010). *The essential guide to doing your research project*. Sage.

Patil, V. H., Singh, S. N., Mishra, S., & Donavan, D. T. (2008). *Parallel analysis engine to aid determining number of factors to retain [Computer software]*. Retrieved from http://smishra.faculty.ku.edu/parallelengine.htm

Patil, V. H., Singh, S. N., Mishra, S., & Donavan, D. T. (2017). *Parallel analysis engine to aid in determining number of factors to retain using R [Computer software]*. Retrieved from https://analytics.gonzaga.edu/parallelengine/

Pauly, L. W., & Reich, S. (1997). National structures and multinational corporate behavior: Enduring differences in the age of globalization. *International Organization, 51*, 1–30.

Paunescu, M., & Schneider, M. (2004). Wettbewerbsfähigkeit und Dynamik institutioneller Standortbedingungen: Ein empirischer Test des "Varieties-of-Capitalism"-Ansatzes. *Schmollers Jahrbuch, 124*, 31–59.

Paunescu, M., & Schneider, M. R. (2011). Changing varieties of capitalism and revealed comparative advantages from1990 to 2005: A test of the Hall and Soskice claims. *Socio-Economic Review, 10*, 1–23.

Porst, R. (2014). *Fragebogen*. VS Verlag für Sozialwissenschaften.

Powell, W. W., & Colyvas, J. A. (2008). Microfoundations of institutional theory. In R. Greenwood, C. Oliver, K. Sahlin, & R. Suddaby (Eds.), *The SAGE handbook of organizational institutionalism* (pp. 276–298). Sage.

Prüfer, P., & Rexroth, M. (2000). www.gesis.org. Retrieved from Zwei-Phasen-Pretesting: https://www.gesis.org/fileadmin/upload/forschung/publikationen/gesis_reihen/zuma_arbeitsberichte/00_08.pdf

Prüfer, P., & Rexroth, M. (2005). *Kognitive interviews*. ZUMA How-to-Reihe, 15.

Royo, S. (2009). Varieties of capitalism for Latin America? *Jean Monnet/Robert Schuman Paper Series, 9*(12), 2–23.

Schneider, B. R. (2009, August). Hierarchical market economies and varieties of capitalism in Latin America. *Journal of Latin American Studies, 41*(3), 553–575.

Schneider, B. R. (2013). *Hierarchical capitalism in Latin America: Business, labor, and the challenges of equitable development*. Cambridge University Press.

Seo, M.-G., & Creed, D. W. (2002). Institutional contradictions, praxis, and institutional change: A Dialectical perspective. *The Academy of Management Review, 27*(2), 222–247.

Sirra, V. (2020). *GeeksforGeeks*. Retrieved from https://www.geeksforgeeks.org/ml-feature-scaling-part-2/

Statistics Solutions. (2020a). *Can an ordinal Likert Scale be a continuous variable?* Retrieved from https://www.statisticssolutions.com/can-an-ordinal-likert-scale-be-a-continuous-variable/

Statistics Solutions. (2020b). *Missing values in data*. Retrieved from https://www.statisticssolutions.com/missing-values-in-data/

Sullivan, G., & Artino, A. R. (2013). Analyzing and interpreting data from Likert-Type Scales. *Journal of Graduate Medical Education, 5*, 541–542.

The Financial Times. (2017, May). *fDi Intelligence from the Financial Times Ltd.* Retrieved from https://www.fdimarkets.com/

Urban, D., & Mayerl, J. (2006). *Regressionsanalyse: Theorie, technik und anwendung*. VS Verlag.

Weisberg, S. (2014). *Applied linear regression* (4th ed.). Wiley.

Wuensch, L. (2012). *East Carolina University*. Retrieved from Pairwise comparisons http://core.ecu.edu/psyc/wuenschk/stathelp/Pairwise.htm.

Xu, D., & Shenkar, O. (2002). Institutional distance and the multinational enterprise. *The Academy of Management Review, 27*(4), 608–618.

Zetterberg, H. L. (1973). Theorie, Forschung und Praxis in der Soziologie. In R. König (Ed.), *Handbuch der empirischen Sozialforschung* (pp. 103–160). Stuttgart.

Chapter 7
Institutional Contradiction and Actor-Induced Institutional Change: German Dual Vocational Training in Brazil (and Mexico): A Qualitative Approach

The quantitative study across all five institutional dimensions in Chap. 6 finds that foreign subsidiaries of MNCs show behavioral patterns that stem from their host country institutional setting. Hence, the choice within an action situation can systemically deviate from the "usual" local one. Therefore, facing certain coordination problems, foreign subsidiaries rely on their wider practice portfolio and solve a problem by relying on either liberal or coordinated strategies that are in each case alien-to-the-system, hence, not complying with and therefore avoiding or defying existing institutions. It is exactly such "play" following alien-to-the-system rules that demonstrates endogenous field level contradiction that is, as Chap. 4 discussed, a (necessary) condition for institutional change. Following the situation of contradiction, above all, this chapter scrutinizes the role of foreign subsidiaries as agents of change through the venues of institutional isomorphism and institutional entrepreneurship. It thereby completes Conflating Capitalisms' cycle back from the action situation to the local institutions and digs into the question of institutionalization and developmental impacts.

As quantitative analyses above have shown, institutional contradiction is most salient in the area of educational efforts. Accordingly, this chapter qualitatively scrutinizes the role of foreign subsidiaries relating to potential changes of the educational system using qualitative content analysis firmly built upon in-depth expert interviews with the most relevant actors in the educational area. In general, this investigation is comparative in nature and focuses on foreign subsidiaries of German MNCs and their role in reshaping the local institutional setting of an archetypal HME in Brazil, using the case of Mexico as reference where German education practices have reached a fairly prominent status. The decision for German MNCs rather than French ones is based on pragmatism, since availability and access to German MNCs were more extensive. Accordingly, the research question is:

> How does coordinated behavior in the context of vocational education and training (VET) from subsidiaries with parent companies in Germany impact on the distinct educational system of Brazil?

M. Kappler, *Western Multinational Corporations in Latin America*, Contributions to Economics, https://doi.org/10.1007/978-3-030-93805-5_7

This case is of special interest for three reasons. First, the analysis of institutional dynamics when CME practices enter an HME is characterized by a very large institutional distance (compared to the distance between LME and HME), inherently lacking supporting institutions, and, consequently, high potential for contradiction and contestation. Second, the issue of quality education hits the core of the HME, best described as a "low-skill trap" (Schneider, 2013) and depicts a major challenge of today's Brazilian realities. Any change toward a higher quality education that meets the demands of the economy is the *conditio* sine qua non for the creation of quality jobs, which contribute, among other things, to a more equal society, more stable development, lower youth unemployment, decreasing informal sector,[1] and higher labor productivity. Third, it may be the German dual vocational training (DVT) that is deemed to counter, in particular, problems of short-termism, low productivity, and skill mismatches, that may offer an alternative for most salient local developmental issues.

Generally, there is almost no empirical work on foreign subsidiaries importing DVT to HMEs. This is especially the case for Brazil where educational research is limited to higher education institutions and academic work on DVT is largely absent. This lack of empirical scrutiny is also the case for Mexico. A very few exceptions—that are all not to be found in the area of a broader VoC approach—have recently begun to explore the development of DVT in Mexico (Fuchs et al., 2016; Wiemann, 2018; Wiemann & Pilz, 2017). As such, subsequent empirical research may contribute positively by enhancing a VoC-based systemic perspective, thus bridging the scholarly gap of DVT in particular in Brazil and also in Mexico.

This chapter is set out as follows: first, a picture of education in both Germany and in Brazil is given. As a point of departure, the Brazilian *status quo* is introduced and, using the VoC logic, the educational system's (dys)functioning in Brazil and in Germany is shown and inter-systemic suitability is analyzed. Second, methodical considerations shed light on the qualitative approach used. Most importantly, data collection and the general design of the study are introduced. Third, applying the Change Cube developed in Chap. 4, potential for change is discussed along the indicators of organizational field, actor, and action and an overarching hypothesis is derived. Fourth, qualitative analysis is conducted along the corresponding analytical categories that are to be subsumed as general functioning and matters of complementarity, isomorphism and institutional entrepreneurship, and institutionalization and developmental impact. On that account, first, the reference case of Mexico is developed and, second, the Brazilian case is put under scrutiny. In a final section, major findings are discussed and summarized.

---

[1] Informality is a major problem within most of the HMEs. It leaves people behind with low levels of protection and provisions. Furthermore, workers in informal jobs do not pay taxes, which again strongly impacts the state since public finance is under pressure. As an approximation, according to OECD data (2019a, b, c, d), Argentina, Brazil, Chile, and Colombia are among the seven worst performing countries relating to the payment of income tax.

7.1 Education: Status Quo and the Systemic Perspective

Education is key to the creation of quality jobs that again are the necessary condition for both an equal society and a competitive economy (Ferrari, 2016; Gereffi et al., 2016; Schneider, 2013). However, as discussed in detail in the previous chapters, Brazil as an archetypal HME finds itself in a "low-skill trap" in which the institutional interplay strongly hampers educational efforts, leading to stagnant and negative development of skill levels that mostly do not fit the demands of the labor market.

To counter such deficiencies, i.e., to raise labor productivity, to make labor relations less volatile, more calculable, and more a matter of joint commitment, Sect. 5.2. on the institutional diagnosis concludes with Ferrari (2016) and Royo (2009) who plead for a reconstitution of capitalism to increase economic functioning alongside matters of solidarity, equality, and social stability, putting CMEs as the role model. However, as discussed in detail in Chap. 3, generally, HME's educational institutions show strong parallels to the liberal approach, though with HMEs "perishing in the mist of uncertainty" not overcoming the inherent market failure. Affirming this, Ferrari (2016) recognizes a dysfunctional, badly copied form of liberal market economy. The strong reliance on (relatively badly educated) university-educated generalists does not cope with the demand of the HME economy. The educational system that provides extremes, either "lawyers or unskilled workers" but no technicians, raises Ferrari's concerns (2016) who decries—in a quite informal but urgent manner—the majority of highly educated academics making their living from driving taxis and pleads an urgent synchronization of economic development and the higher education level, that is, to match labor supply with demand (Schneider, 2013).

As a matter of fact, there is recognition of technical and vocational training as a potential key to development that may fit better to realities in developing economies such as Brazil, leading to a more inclusive and equal economy and to increasing competitivity and productivity (Almeida et al., 2015; European Commission, 2012; ILO, 2008; OECD, 2019b, c; Portelo Souza et al., 2015; Schneider & Soskice, 2009). Unfortunately, if VET has found its way on the political agenda at all, the policy recommendations on VET given mostly target the scale and scope of VET programs exclusively. As such they attempt to improve the educational system by channeling resources into it (OECD, 2017) and, thus, make a malfunctioning system larger rather than grasping the systemic roots. In so doing, focusing exclusively on supply-led development, educational efforts are likely to end up in a misunderstood "Say's law" where supply does not generate its own demand. In such cases, the strongly subsidized skills are not demanded by companies, resulting in exorbitant public expenses without economic payoff and, from an individual's perspective, negative returns from investments in such education, culminating in such initiative's failure (Sehnbruch, 2016; Schneider, 2013).

7.1.1 VET in Brazil Today

After a long period of relative neglection, Brazil has recognized that for further socioeconomic development, a stronger reliance on VET (*vis-à-vis* university education) can be a reasonable strategy (Dornbach, 2016; OECD, 2014).[2] Accordingly, Brazilian authorities emphasized the development of a better and more comprehensive VET program quite prominently on their National Plan for Education (PNE), aiming at creating courses that secure higher employability prospects and that generally facilitate labor market access for young people (Câmara dos Deputados, 2020).

VET in Brazil is heterogeneous and programs differ according to educational level, complexity, and accreditation (for a general overview see Portelo Souza et al., 2015; Kauer, 2015). The one that is both by far the most important and similar to the German DVT is the VET in a subsequent modality[3] (INEP, 2019).[4] It is to be found at the upper secondary level in the Brazilian educational system and begins after completing high school. Just like its German counterpart, it is, first, a stand-alone vocational training that prepares students for their working life and, second, can provide its students with a general higher education entrance qualification (Câmara dos Deputados, 2020). Also, within the VET in a subsequent modality, there are differences mostly relating to the conduct of the program. This may be the municipality, the state, churches, or private (or parastatal) vocational schools.

Hereof, the latter takes a predominant position. It is organized as the "Sistema S" consisting of ten (delimited by sectors) private nonprofit educational institutions that are all financed by public funds through mandatory taxes on firm's payrolls and a minor share of fees charged for services (Portelo Souza et al., 2015).[5] The two most important organizations are the SENAI (Serviço Nacional de Aprendizagem Industrial or National Service of Industrial Apprenticeship) and the SENAC (Serviço Nacional de Aprendizagem do Comércio or National Service of Trade Apprenticeship) accounting for roughly 40 percent of all secondary level VET enrollments in Brazil (Confederação Nacional da Indústria, 2014). SENAI and SENAC are both obligated to allocate two-thirds of the tax income generated toward free VET. Consequently, a relatively large part of the students enrolled have access to free education (Portelo Souza et al., 2015). Both the SENAC and the SENAI are for secondary school graduates. They offer two-year programs that are based entirely at

[2] Indeed, VET opportunities have existed ever since. However, they were neglected heavily and enrollment rates have only increased relatively recently. Compared to university enrollments, VET still makes only a minor fraction in Brazil (Kauer, 2015; Dornbach, 2016; INEP, 2019).

[3] In comparison to ones that are either integrated or concomitant with high school education (Kauer, 2015).

[4] The PNE includes various forms of VET, such as continuing training for employees or as an integral part in high school. Here, only the one at the tertiary level is of interest (for further discussion on the various forms of VET in Brazil, see Kauer (2015).

[5] Contribution to the SENAI and SENAC is about 1 percent of total employees renumeration paid by the companies in their field of action.

school. The corresponding curricula involve *vis-à-vis* university education a larger part of more practical issues. On completing a VET program in the SENAI or SENAC, students receive a stand-alone federally accepted degree of the *tecnico* that qualifies them to work in a more manual occupation.

Generally, evaluations of the Brazil VET system are rather frustrating. As a matter of fact, governmental efforts toward VET increase the number of students and various studies find evidence for slight increases in both average earnings and the probability of being employed after doing a VET in the Sistema S (Oliva, 2014; Assunção & Gonzaga, 2010). However, VET (especially as supported by the PRONATEC[6]) in Brazil remains a measure to help the most vulnerable in society, rather than a measure to emphasize VET as an instrument for supplying the market with the demanded skills (CEPAL, 2015; UNESCO, 2016). Affirmatively, Portelo Souza et al. (2015) indicate a strong mismatch between skills supplied by VET and skills demanded by the market, with most of the VET graduates either unemployed, working in a different function than they were trained for, or in further university programs. Affirming this, CNI (2014) reports show that around two-thirds of VET graduates who are working today are not working in the same area of the completed VET. 58 percent of the workers aged 16 to 24 report that after graduation they never worked in an area related to their technical training. Portelo Souza et al. (2015, p. 24) refer to various experts of the Brazilian VET system that jointly state that:

> one of the fundamental flaws of the PRONATEC program is that its conception did not follow the common rationale for professional qualification—identifying the demands first and then designing technical courses tailor-made for the needs of the local labor market.

This view is backed by scholars and the Brazilian Federal Auditing institution likewise, whose major evaluative studies find a general lack of communication between the stakeholders, specifically a strong disconnect between the VET institutions and the employers (Mourshed et al., 2013; Portelo Souza et al., 2015; Silva et al., 2015). According to these studies, VET courses offered and the corresponding curricula are to a high degree subject to arbitrariness of the providers rather than led by the market.[7] It is this situation that urges a better understanding of educational initiatives that may be propelled by the ultimate demander: the firm. On that account, the German DVT system is introduced below, embedding it briefly in the German institutional setting.

[6]National Programme for Access to Technical Education and Employment—PRONATEC (Programa Nacional de Acesso ao Ensino Técnico e Emprego) was introduced under the presidency of Dilma Rousseff in 2011.

[7]Indeed, for example, SENAI has established the "Industry to Work Map" that is supposed to better consider market trends. However, again employers and other stakeholders are mostly left outside. Since its establishment, no significant improvement could be detected.

7.1.2 DVT in Germany

Germany is known as a textbook example for a CME having very low (youth) unemployment and generally highly qualified specialists that make the German economy strongly competitive. There is a consensus that a major contributor to this positive situation is the German DVT (Westervelt, 2012; Wiemann & Fuchs, 2018). DVT is Germany's major VET program and is embedded in the coordinated setting and—just like the coordinated practices in general—builds upon, inter alia, credible long-term commitment, strategic alliances, deliberation, cooperation, and social protection. Following this "grand principle," vocational and technical training in Germany's coordinated approach at the upper secondary level[8] is different to the one existing in other countries in terms of conduct and actors within. In comparison to the education that takes place entirely at school, the German coordinated approach of DVT is carried out in equal measures by companies and publicly funded technical schools that work closely together. The DVT is designed and organized mainly by the social partners (unions and associations) and orchestrated by strongly complementary regulations and curricula and the corresponding chamber,[9] which generally monitors and secures quality standards[10] to guarantee comparably educated workers (BiBB, 2017; BMBF, 2017). Following the principle of inter-actor coordination, the regulations upon which the DVT builds (*Ausbildungsordnung and Rahmenlehrplan*) are dynamic inasmuch as they are adjusted to changing realities and altering market relevancies, though keeping an equilibrium of interest by a council that includes employer representatives and trade unions (BiBB, 2017). Along the same lines, the chamber in charge serves as a platform for deliberation and allows a high degree of coordination. For further development of the DVT, they organize the "*Berufsbildungsausschuss*" (Dual Vocational Training Committee), which includes representatives of employers, employees, and teachers of the technical school, responsible for the further development the DVT system (BBiG § 77 Abs.1).

From the viewpoint of apprentices (from now on called "azubi" when referring to an apprentice in DVT following the German model; azubi is the abbreviation for "*Auszubildender*," which is the translation of "apprentice"), the course of the DVT is split into two major parts. Azubis frequently rotate between theoretical (generic) education in a technical school and practical education working in their training company. On that account, in their functions as both employee and student, they acquire both a rather general skill set (suitable especially to the sectoral/industry level) in school and a practical and firm-specific set of skills during their time working in the company. The degree that comes with completing the DVT is

---

[8] In Germany it is called Sekundarbereich II.

[9] For example, the Chamber of Crafts or in a non-manual occupation the Chamber of Industry and Commerce (BBiG § 71).

[10] Among others, the chamber carries out the final examination that is the same one for everybody from the same occupation.

officially recognized by law and demonstrates a full degree of upper secondary education.

Regarding the benefits of the DVT, azubis have a secure job after the DVT program in the training company, generally face a future as an expert in a specific area with their firm as a long-term partner (since workers have the skills the company needs), reasonably expecting stable employment relations, and, hence, secure flows of income (BMBF, 2018). Likewise, companies educating young talents over mostly three-and-a-half-years benefit from this system by having generally highly skilled employees with a strong firm-specific set of skills in the long run, allowing firms to focus on the production of very specific products and services. From a rather macro perspective, highly skilled education leads to quality jobs that, due to the match between market demand and labor supply, results in economic stability and in higher efficiency and productivity numbers. Through continuous contestation and direct involvement of employers, changing realities can be taken into account when designing, for example, the curricula.

Remarkably, the German DVT allows azubis to commit themselves to a high degree of specialization and, therefore, to align their education and career with the needs of a specific company (or sector) without the threat of being exposed to opportunistic behavior and potential income losses (Hölscher, 2012). Equally, the DVT system allows companies to invest heavily in the education of specifically educated employees without facing the threat of being poached by another firm or by asymmetric power relations *vis-à-vis* the employees. As such, the "mist of uncertainty" is dissolved by the coordinated institutional setting.

DVT is a textbook example of coordinated action and follows the logic of embeddedness in a coordinated and complementary institutional setting. Accordingly, here, having Chap. 3 in mind, a very brief introduction into DVT and the relevant institutional interplay suffices.

First of all, collective bargaining regarding wages and working conditions takes place mostly at industry level between employer associations and unions. Accordingly, due to a relatively dense unionization and wide coverage of collective bargaining (mostly negotiated at the industry level), the corresponding claim of a specialist worker to receive standard wages,[11] to work under standard working conditions, and to sign a permanent working contract means employers have—if at all—very little leeway either to pay less than such collective wage agreement allows or to easily hire and fire their employees (Fulton, 2020). Consequently, employees come up with a clearly calculable flow of income for the long term. The same holds up for the employer as well. Fixed wages increase planning security for the employer and make short-term strategies less likely and poaching a rather futile strategy. Since all companies pay the same wage for the same employee, poaching someone from another firm based on income differentials is no longer a

[11] Not to be confused with minimum wages. In Germany, standard wages (and standard conditions) are negotiated through collective bargaining between representative bodies of workers (associations) and employers (unions) and are valid for entire sectors and industries.

valid strategy. Noteworthy, in the German jurisdiction, collective wage agreements take precedence over firm-level or individual-level agreements. On that account, even if for specific employees' wage and working conditions are bargained individually, the collective wage agreements serve as minimum requirements and, therefore, are not to be dropped below (Ellguth & Kohaut, 2017).[12]

Next to the workers' representation through the venue of unions, German firms have relatively strong in-firm representative bodies. A works council (or a similar body)—which is also the executive body for collective wage agreements within each firm—is a legally recognized representative of the employees at the firm level. It is in constant communication with the higher-level union, serves as a point of contact for employees, aggregates their voices, and weighs the employees' voices into "regulation of working conditions as well as in economic planning and decision-making" (Page, 2018) through co-determination by, for example, board-level representation. On that account, matters of corporate governance, such as distributional issues of profits, cannot be decided without conceding the workers their fair share. Employees' opportunity to make their voices heard and their firm-specific skills puts them at eye level with the management and contributes to the dissolution of uncertainty.

The second social partner is the aggregated voice of employers through business associations. Beyond negotiating at eye level with strong trade unions and the representation of interests, encompassing sectoral associations are constituents of the DVT system inasmuch as they actively shape the DVT securing the entire system's market relevance, as indicated above. In general, though associations serve as deliberation platforms for employers, they allow voice aggregation, and serve as a monitoring instrument insofar as noncompliance of an employer is most likely to be punished in associations (Schneider, 2013).

Even though the government leaves the design and conduct of the DVT mostly to the social partners, it nevertheless serves as a solid base for action. This coordinated system of strategic alliances and long-term commitment is complemented by a supportive state as, inter alia, both funder of the public technical schools and additional social safeguard in the context of unemployment protection. The specific social security system and relatively generous unemployment protection allows an unemployed person to wait for the right vacancy that fits with his or her specific set of skills (for further discussion on the German welfare system, see Blank, 2016; Richmond, 2020; Fleckenstein & Lee, 2017). Hence, in the case of a job loss and a change of job and company, a worker can be "patiently" waiting for the right job for which they can be assured to make use of their specific assets.

One can see that all institutional dimensions are in play and allow the DVT system to be as it is. Consequently, the inherent question of suitability between the

[12] Collective bargaining coverage is about 62% in Germany (Fulton, 2020). However, the function of collective wage agreements as a guiding principle for other individually bargained agreements is important, since the majority of firms in Germany are not legally bound by collective wage agreements.

German DVT and the Brazilian reality is of interest. In the following work, the Brazilian political economy is briefly scrutinized through the institutional dimensions and their potential to support such coordinated DVT.

7.1.3 Brazil's Compatibility with German DVT

Brazil's educational system is embedded in an archetypal HME, which hampers progress in education and does not allow strengthening of technical and vocational training. The case of education in Brazil depicts a textbook example of HME's general shortcomings and the rather negative institutional complementarity as discussed theoretically in Sect. 3.3. Discussing education in an HME system considering Brazilian realities sheds light on the systemic burden of Brazil's VET efforts and provides a rather sobering picture of compatibility with German DVT.

First, the chronically high turnover rates of around 20 percent[13] (Pieczynski, 2016) increase employees' uncertainty regarding future incomes. Consequently, in order to diversify risk, skills—if at all—are required that are general and, thus, fit with a high number of companies across sectoral borders. Along the same lines, decisions are made most often in a hierarchical manner from the top-down. Such lack of representation in corporate decision-making processes excludes workers, first, from a joint decision about distributional efforts and, second, from participating in (increased) corporate gains. Such lack of co-determination also excludes knowledge from workers. Insider knowledge can be especially important in designing demand-led educational efforts.

Second, indeed, until the labor reform in 2017 union contribution was obligatory for all Brazilian employees (Neeser & Camargo, 2017). However, unions are rather politicized[14] and largely absent from the shop-floor, making employees less heard, joint action more difficult, and, on a higher level, less capable of negotiating with other collective actors (Murillo, 2001; Schneider, 2009, 2013; Schneider & Karcher, 2010). Consequences, such as a lack of standardized wages, contribute to employees' uncertainty around future gains and make "poaching" a valid corporate strategy. In addition, weak organized labor generally decreases employment protection that makes interruptions of income flows a matter of time. In the same vein, very low measures of unemployment protection make people out of work "impatient" to reenter working life, independent of the job's content and suitability.

[13] As da Silva Filho (2016) shows such turnover can be higher relating to the region. Evaluating the percentage of formal jobs that were less than 2 years in the industry concludes that around 54% of the employees had not finished their second year in the job. In total, 76 percent were less than 5 years in the job.

[14] Schneider describes the term "politicized" by the union's focus of "achieving blanket salary raises by government decree" (Schneider & Karcher, 2010, p. 9). Instead of negotiation with business, unions attempt to gain a leverage by lobbying governments.

Third, analogous to a lack of overarching employee agencies, companies do hardly interact with one another at an institutionalized level. Consequently, there is an equal lack of encompassing associations. Joint efforts of companies therefore seem to be out of scope due to the absence of platforms of deliberation and no meaningful way of monitoring and sanctioning behavior and compliance. Fourth, efficiency-related corporate policies make corporate boards deterred from costly education. That holds up especially in an environment characterized by a large pool of unskilled labor, correspondingly low labor costs, and the threat of being poached.

Being aware of these severe systemic differences in Brazilian and German VET systems improves understanding of the status quo and puts investigation on potential institutional change on a firm base. Certainly, the distinct EV programs in Brazil and Germany build upon highly contradictory institutional environments and, thus, add complexity to the processes of change.

7.2 Study Design, Data Collection, and Methodical Considerations

This study requires to capture certain complex multi-actor dynamics that may occur responding to German subsidiaries' behavior. Methods applied and the overarching research design need to deal with the three major issues that are, first, the functioning of alien-to-the-system educational practices in Brazil, second, potential isomorphic pressures exerted by German subsidiaries and perceived by Brazilian society, and third, the conscious application of institutional entrepreneurship.

Since existing knowledge on the implementation of coordinated educational practices into Brazil's HME environment is very limited, the following study is explorative in nature. Potential dynamics and interdependencies that characterize a process of institutionalization—if at all—hardly follow a prescribed pattern. In order to cope with the specifics of this study and the gap in literature, primary data needs to be collected and analyzed in a way that allows to grasp nuances of behavior and change.

7.2.1 Research Design

In general, literature on institutional processes in the context of coordinated practices in hierarchical environments is very scarce, in particular for Brazil. Accordingly, a lack of prior research comes along with a very low level of knowledge regarding which aspects of reality to focus. The absence of reference studies limits the exploratory power of a single case studied. On that account, to deal with the fairly complex research interest, the lack of comparable studies, and to put the study on

CME practices in Brazil on a solid basis, this chapter conducts a comparative study that applies a "Most Similar Systems Design" (Anckar, 2008). This design includes Brazil as the actually targeted country that, up to now, has flown underneath the radar and Mexico as the reference country as alleged "best case" where coordinated DVT practices gained a relatively prominent status. The set of instruments and the theoretical considerations made in Chap. 4 that attempt to recognize the impact of subsidiaries on the host country's institutional setup are applied to the case of DVT in Mexico first. Then, in the second step, building upon knowledge gained and analytical components and categories derived from the Mexican case, the case of Brazil is put under detailed scrutiny. Using the comparison with the alleged case of "best practice" in Mexico, differences in Brazil and potential behavioral and institutional deviations may allow one to understand the impact of German subsidiaries and to explain also differing trajectories of institutional development. Following this line of thought, one can reasonably rely on similar systems aiming at understanding different institutional trajectories: according to De Meur and Berg-Schlosser (1994) a design called "Most Similar With Different Outcome."

The Mexican case is conducted to derive major aspects and categories that serve for a proper analysis and to learn about dynamics, interdependencies, and mechanisms of institutional contestation from the case of perceived "best practice." Mexico serves well since, first, DVT according to the German model is installed in Mexico by a manifold of smaller "island solutions" in which companies organize their own educational centers and through the federally acknowledged Modelo Mexicano de Formación Dual (Mexican Model of Dual Vocational Training, MMFD) in place since 2015. It is officially recognized as a stand-alone education and is incorporated into Mexico's educational system and supported as such by Mexican authorities. Second, since the case of DVT in Mexico is by far the most prominent, it is also the case for which most supplementary literature, evaluative studies, and general information exist. Building upon a wider base of different sources helps especially for developing the right categories and aspects that are important for meaningful comparison. Third, Mexico being an HME shows strong similarities with the Brazilian institutional setting in which, among others, the threat of poaching prohibits long-term investments in people (Wiemann & Pilz, 2017). As such, the applied similar systems design is in accordance with Anckar (2008, p. 392) who states that "similar systems designs require an *a priori* assumption about the level of social systems at which the important factors operate." Following this argument, the case of Mexico—despite some differences owing to, for example, the proximity to the USA—allows us to apply a most similar systems design (Georg, 2005) with Brazil. Similar to an experimental design, a most similar design, here, allows us to explore behavioral and institutional processes in the context of vocational training, keeping other conditions as stable as empirical cross-systemic investigation at this rather low level of abstraction reasonably allows (Anckar, 2008). Shielding the actual issue of interest from disturbing influences allows us to analyze specifically differences, similarities, and peculiarities within the context of coordinated education in an HME and the aspects of systemic functioning, isomorphic pressures, and institutional entrepreneurship.

Table 7.1 Interviews

Name	Country	City/State	Entity	Specificities
MexMNC1	Mexico	Guadalajara/Jalisco	MNC	Large industrial MNC/part of the MMFD
MexMNC2	Mexico	Guadalajara/Jalisco	MNC	Large industrial MNC/part of the MMFD
MexOrg1	Mexico	Mexico City	Organization	Development agency
MexMNC3	Mexico	Puebla/Puebla	MNC	Medium sized supplier/having own DVT program
BraMNC1	Brazil	São Paulo/São Paulo	MNC	Consulting company
BraOrg1	Brazil	São Paulo/São Paulo	Organization	Supporting agency
BraMNC2	Brazil	São Paulo/São Paulo	MNC	Large industrial MNC
BraOrg2	Brazil	São Paulo/São Paulo	Organization	Technical school
BraMNC3	Brazil	São Paulo/São Paulo	MNC	Large industrial MNC

Source: From the author

7.2.2 Data Gathering and Processing

Since this study is novel relating to both theoretical grounding and empirical setup, no secondary data available suits with the approach of Conflating Capitalisms and the specific case of German educational practices in Latin American countries. On that account, data is gathered through the conduct of semi-structured interviews with experts from MNCs and educational agencies in Brazil and Mexico.

The corresponding interview guide (semi-structure questionnaire) is developed according to the objectives of this chapter following the theoretical discussion in Chaps. 3 and 4. It has three categories that operationalize the general functioning of DVT in the given institutional setting, institutional isomorphism, and institutional entrepreneurship. The questionnaire deals with the exploratory nature of the topic by allowing new ideas and perspectives to enter the analysis. On that account, each of the three main topics is approached by raising very broad questions. Only if a respondent is off track, or the interviewee requires more information, more closely guiding sub-questions serve as opportunities for re-adjustment.

Here, the conduct of semi-structured interviews is conversationally with one expert at a time. This procedure enables the dialogue between the interviewer and the interviewee to detach from a specific agenda set a priori and, thus, potentially unveil new and unforeseen issues and relationships (Adams, 2015). Especially in areas where reference studies are lacking—as the one at hand—the ability to grasp dynamics within a very wide pre-set frame can help to include otherwise potentially omitted explanatory factors. As Table 7.1 indicates, in total, nine interviews were conducted in the time frame between April 4, 2019 and October 21, 2019. Each of the interviews—on average—took 45 min. Four interviews (three subsidiaries and one supporting organization) are conducted in Mexico and five (three subsidiaries and two organizations) in Brazil. All interviewees have positions characterized by a high degree of responsibility and competence. These are country heads (CEO) and directors of the foreign subsidiaries and leading managers of educational programs within the corresponding organizations such as development agencies and the German Chamber of Commerce. Before each interview, anonymity was guaranteed and informed consent was attained and a nondisclosure agreement was attached to the invitation to the study. As indicated in Table 7.1, the interviews are conducted in a rather small part of the host countries. As such, the Mexican interviewees are located in either the city of Guadalajara in the state of Jalisco (capital city of Jalisco) or in the city of Puebla (capital city of the state of Puebla) in the wider surroundings of Mexico City. Brazilian interviewees were all situated in the city and in the surrounding of São Paulo. These mentioned locations are known as hotspots for MNCs. On that account, dynamics and mechanisms of potential institutional change are certainly different in other parts of the countries that are not characterized by a high MNC density.

Interviews were conducted in English, Spanish, and German by one interviewer, securing high inter-personal reliability. Since qualitative analysis is conducted by the same person—able to understand and analyze texts in English, Spanish, and German—a complete translation intro the English language was not necessary. Again, there is no indication that there is systemic difference in responses relating to the language used. All interviews were digitally recorded, transcribed (using the software MaxQDA[15]), and partly translated into English, as far as directly quoted in the subsequent analysis. Transcriptions of the interviews serve as a basis for the qualitative analysis throughout this chapter (Mayring et al., 2005) that is supposed to do both testing the theory developed above and exploring in-depth behavioral dynamics in a multi-actor setting and to understand the partly counterintuitive findings of Chap. 6.

7.2.3 *Qualitative Content Analysis*

The method of data analysis applied is a qualitative content analysis according to Mayring (2014). Since content analysis is not a standardized instrument, it follows the research design and the objects of interest set above. Transcribed semi-structured interviews and supplementary documents such as newspapers, organizational white papers, protocols, web pages, and related empirical studies are put under scrutiny and build the basis for an ongoing and critical discussion throughout the chapter. All input is considered exclusively inasmuch as it contributes to responding the overarching research question (Mayring, 2003).

---

[15] © VERBI GmbH.

Major assets of content analysis are, for example, that it allows us to interpret text beyond its manifest context as latent content. Furthermore, QCA suits well with the solidly founded theoretical frame but still exploratory nature of this study (Mayring, 2003). Accordingly, Wenzler-Cremer (2007) distinguishes QCA from the approach of grounded theory inasmuch as categories are primarily not developed from within the material but exogenously derived. However, categories derived from prior knowledge mostly serve as guiding heuristics with which material are worked through. Accordingly, QCA enables one to further develop analytical categories by, for example, exposing them to continuous contestation through feedback loops within the process of analysis (Mayring, 2000). Alongside the inclusion of various sources of information, it allows ongoing comparison with other empirical data as a means of triangulation.

In brief, the procedure of this study's analysis is as follows: the main areas of interest, the level of abstraction, and the overarching research question that are derived theoretically determine "...the aspects of the textual material taken into account" (Mayring, 2000, p. 12). In line with the widely set questions of the questionnaire, a "first" system of categories is deduced and applied to work through the material (Kruse, 2007). Text passages are systematically assigned to and subsumed in corresponding categories. Following, various feedback loops in the form of revising categories and corresponding sub-categories allow us to further sharpen and adjust the aspects of interest and to check for their reliability. In the final step, results are interpreted attempting to attain a coherent argument considering the variety of information structured along with the categories developed.

7.3 Applying the Change Cube

The quantitative study indicated that there is indeed deviating behavior of MNCs in Brazil. If at all, to what degree isomorphic pressures or institutional entrepreneurship leads to changes in the environment depends, however, mostly on the condition triad of factors including the action itself, the specific actor conducting the action, and the organizational field in which the action is being conducted.

The Local Organizational Field: The Organizational Field of Brazil's VET
To recall, the local organizational field and its stability provides actors with power capabilities with which to engage in institutional change. Regarding the educational system's degree of structuration, one may perceive it as a rather less structured field. Indeed, VET in Brazil has existed ever since, though for quite a long time only formally on paper. Within the past two decades, as prior discussions have shown, the field of VET has changed significantly regarding both reach and design. Furthermore, the ongoing governmental program that aims to support the VET system indicates that the system depends on governmental support and that in an isolated manner may hardly work by itself. In addition, facilitating the way in for new practices, in the case of an insertion of new (normal) educational ideas, there is no

threat of being sanctioned in the case of deviation. On a general basis, Brazilian jurisdiction may be seen as relatively open toward educational issues, best to be seen by the rather heterogenous picture of VET and the official legitimation of DVT already back in the 1990s.

The field of VET in Brazil depicts a lowly embedded subsystem. As shown above, the VET system in Brazil is rather detached from other institutional domains and other actors. In general, the Brazilian political economy—being an HME—can be described as mostly hierarchical. The same is the case for the Brazilian VET system, which is a product of top-down decisions rather than one by interaction between its stakeholders. Hence, the local VET system rests on the goodwill of individual actors ("defenders") and can be supposed to not be stably anchored in a shared inter-actor set of beliefs and norms.

Furthermore, from the ongoing mismatch between supply of skills and market demand combined with the generally low quality of Brazilian education, one may reasonably understand the Brazilian educational system as being in a constant state of crisis. Each crisis goes along with both the decrease of the current system's legitimacy and an increase of contestation. If other or new legitimate institutional models are examined, an adjustment or even substitution of the current one by perceived better ones may be in scope. Disorientation and uncertainty—which are major components of a crisis—may further increase receptiveness of local actors, particularly if the local system is felt as being "inferior" *vis-à-vis* that of the institutional challengers.

The Actor: The Foreign Subsidiary of Coordinated MNCs

Coordinated subsidiaries can reasonably be assumed to be a role model by virtue of both their belonging to a successful and efficient MNC and by their national origins which—in the case of vocational training—may provide additional weight. Since Germany is commonly known as having a very well-functioning VET system, subsidiaries' role as a representative of a better functioning "superior" system may equip a subsidiary with a notion of "dominance effect."

A subsidiary's impact certainly also depends on the degree to which it commits itself to interaction with other local actors. Generally, one may expect a rather low degree of local participation, as one of the major characteristics of HMEs is that companies—both local business groups and MNCs—mostly act within their own borders. Additionally, foreign subsidiaries of MNCs may act more within the intra-organizational field of the MNC than in the local field. It is difficult to estimate the extent of inward orientation, though being part of such a hierarchic structure of an MNC raises reasonable doubts on the active local involvement. Consequently, not being locally involved would severely decrease local visibility and, hence, also the ability to exert isomorphic pressures.

Furthermore, the relatively strong presence of foreign subsidiaries of coordinated MNCs may also call for a noticeable impact of coordinated action on the local setting. Chapter 5 shows the large flows and therefore stock of FDI in Brazil. Certainly, MNCs from CMEs do not depict any kind of majority and are, indeed, a minor fraction relating to the entire economy. Nevertheless, it is not one isolated case. If various actors with the same practice portfolio act in a more orchestrated manner, combined with the strongly pronounced coordinated behavior of German MNCs in Brazil (see Chap. 6), influence may be in reach. The quantity of aligned actors certainly positively correlates with both isomorphic pressures exerted and the potential of acting jointly, such as a strong alliance of institutional entrepreneurs.

The Action: Education Through DVT

Along with the quantity of aligned actors, the more frequently the same strange practice is conducted, the more likely it may result in change. As Chap. 6 indicates, a German subsidiary in Brazil is quite likely to show coordinated behavior in the context of education. On that account, pressures exerted can be multiplied by the number of companies that exert the same one, increasing the likelihood of having an impact on the local field.

Connecting the notions of crisis and perceived superiority of German DVT, one may expect the new practice to enter more easily due to the practice's perceived value. Since DVT in Germany has proven to counter precisely the educational problems that are very present in today's Brazil, locals may open doors to welcome such solution-oriented practice for their own best practice.

Regarding the conduct of DVT and the degree of compatibility with the local field, one may argue from two perspectives. However, as Sect. 7.1 discussed, what certainly remains the same is that DVT seems to be very different from Brazil's educational system. First, the difference between the German and the Brazilian practice can be interpreted as a plus factor for change. Assuming the Brazilian system to be in a severe crisis, the German practice is without any doubt "sufficiently incompatible" with the existing social arrangement that led to the situation of crisis in the first place. On that account, combined with the alleged superiority of the German DVT system, one may expect a high degree of receptiveness toward the DVT. However, the second perspective may be weighting in even more heavily. As Sect. 7.1 remarkably shows, the German DVT as a typical deeply entangled coordinated practice (*vis-à-vis* liberal ones) heavily depends on, among other things, long-term commitment, deliberation, cooperation, and strategic alliances. It works well in Germany since all coordinated institutional dimensions are in effect, supporting the specific conduct of DVT. All these complementary institutions are lacking in Brazil. On that account, incompatibility may also depict a hurdle that cannot be overcome. The very different practice of DVT runs the risk of encountering local actors that are not suitably cognitively equipped (not having this practice in their own practice portfolio) to understand the DVT and its value.

Reflection and Impact Expected

In order to estimate the potential of institutional change in Brazil induced by foreign subsidiaries from Germany, the three major factors discussed above need to be categorized within the framework of the Change Cube developed in Chap. 4.

First, to finally evaluate the practice of DVT as either "passive" or "intrusive" is not entirely possible. Indeed, it is highly conflictual with the existing setting and may demonstrate a solution for the existing local crisis. Nevertheless, one should further consider the possibility of incompatibility being insurmountable. As a working hypothesis, the high degree of incompatibility makes German DVT rather "passive." Second, the local educational system can certainly be classified as rather weak. Heterogeneity, substantial changes within the recent past, severe and constant problems of performance, and the found isolation of the system from other stakeholders make the system vulnerable to institutional contention. Third, despite assuming a rather hierarchical management, the foreign subsidiary as representative of the generally perceived successful class of MNC and of a country in which VET works very wells is assumed to be characterized as "strong."

Described by PWS (passive action, weak local setting, and strong actor) on the cube, subsidiaries of German MNCs that show coordinated behavior of DVT in Brazil may be supposed to have a moderate (to strong) impact on the local institutional setting. In line with the research design developed above, the subsequent study qualitatively investigates behavior and institutional dynamics when coordinated DVT enters an HME. In a first step, the issues of institutional functioning, isomorphic pressures, and the institutional entrepreneurialism are put under scrutiny in the context of German subsidiaries in Mexico. Knowledge gained from the alleged "best practice" case of Mexico will provide a solid reference to better understand behavioral and institutional dynamics in Brazil. In fact, described as an HME too, the discussion throughout this section on the impact cube is valid largely for Mexico as well.

7.4 DVT in Mexico

Being described as an HME, most of the discussion above on Brazil also applies to Mexico. Accordingly, the Mexican institutional setting needs no repeated in-depth systemic introduction. This chapter on the Mexican DVT experience has two objectives. First, to understand how DVT can work in an HME environment and, second, to understand what role subsidiaries of German MNCs may play. The Mexican educational system is consciously included in this work only inasmuch as is necessary to understand the DVT efforts. A more detailed analysis of the very complex Mexican VET system is not part of this chapter (for more details on Mexican VET, see Artega García et al. (2010)) and Wiemann (2018).

7.4.1 An Outline of DVT in Mexico[16]

German DVT arrived more than 50 years ago in Mexico. It was imported by major German MNCs such as Volkswagen and Bosch, though in the early stages as a pure

---

[16]For a more detailed chronology of efforts that led to the creation and implementation of DVT programs in Mexico, see Aragón (2019).

in-house form of education. For the first time, in the year 1993, a formalized collaborative version of dual training was implemented in—and regionally delimited to—the city of Santiago Tianguistenco as a collaboration exclusively between Mercedes-Benz (the company's plant was located in Santiago Tianguistenco) and *Colegio Nacional de Educación Profesional Técnica* (CONALEP). This initial version of DVT in accordance with the German model in Mexico soon ended. According to CONALEP of the State of México, the DVT program was stopped by virtue of Mercedes-Benz in 2000 due to a sufficient number of qualified workers (720 *técnicos*); some information indicates a general recruitment freeze as the major reason. According to ALTRATEC (2012), graduates from the first pilot programs significantly improved their employability, followed excellent career paths, and were highly appreciated by both the company and general society.

However, Mercedes-CONALEP cooperation from the 1990s was not an evolutionary end, but served as an initial point from which efforts on DVT were re-emphasized in 2008 (López-Fogués et al., 2018). Since this resumption, German-like DVT in Mexico gained momentum, inter alia, with the first agreement (Carta de Intención) in which the government of the State of México and the German Embassy in Mexico promised joint efforts for developing a pilot DVT program in the State of México. The CONALEP of the State of México and the German companies led ALTRATEC (German-Mexican Alliance for Technology Transfer) in cooperation with the Germany's Federal Institute for Vocational Training (Bundesinstitut für Berufsbildung, BiBB) and the Mexican-German Chamber of Commerce (Cámara Mexicano-Alemana de Comercion e Industria, CAMEXA).

The period between 2012 and 2014 depicts a phase of acceleration in DVT development in Mexico. Members of both the Secretary of Public Education (Secretaría de Educación Pública, SEP) and the participating business association (COPARMEX) learned in-depth and firsthand about the DVT in Germany. The SEP and the Subsecretary of Media and Superior Education (Subsecretaría de Educación Media Superior, SEMS) together with stakeholders of existing "pilot programs" such as the one in the State of México and the CAMEXA established the *Modelo Mexicano de Formación Dual* (MMFD; translated: Mexican Model of Dual Vocational Training) (SEP, 2014). This development culminated in 2015 with the announcement of the agreement 06/06/15 that established the DVT in Mexico as an officially legitimated, upper secondary component of the federal Mexican educational system.

Generally, the cooperation of mostly the SEP and the COPARMEX with Germany is close and mainly expressed by the involvement of the CAMEXA—which controls education and takes exams—and the GIZ (Cooperación Alemana para el Desarrollo Sustentable)—as the operative arm of the German Federal Ministry for Economic Cooperation and Development—which mainly supports both the private and public sector in their efforts to improve performance and coverage of the Mexican DVT program (funded by the German Federal Ministry of Economic Cooperation and Development). Today, 24 of 32 Mexican states are part of the MMFD (BiBB, 2018) offering courses in, among others, electro mechanics, mechatronics, IT, and administration.

Importantly, even though the MMFD is certainly the DVT initiative with the widest coverage, parallel to the higher-level formation of the MMFD, lots of individual German companies and also German company groups—in cooperation with the CAMEXA[17]—established their own DVT programs with their own educational centers within their corporate boundaries. Notably, there are around 1500 subsidiaries of German MNCs in Mexico including the companies Volkswagen and Schuler[18] (Wiemann, 2018). Volkswagen in Puebla established its *Instituto para Formación Dual y Desarollo Volkswagen* (own educational center for their DVT scheme) in 1996 in the automotive cluster of Puebla. In 3-year courses, they teach mechatronics, electronics, and toolmaking. Per year, more than a hundred students graduate from the Volkswagen institute. Accumulated, Volkswagen reports of roughly 6000 graduating from the institute (Weiss, 2016). Since 2016, Volkswagen has used the certification of the CAMEXA as well, for both the examination and some educators (BiBB, 2018). Another text book example of an "island solutions" is the company, Schuler, which established the *Centro de Especialización Dual (CEDUAL)* in Puebla as well (Schuler, 2020). Since 2012, the CEDUAL offers 3-year DVT programs in industrial mechanics and toolmaking and is closely aligned with the German DVT. Schuler follows a rather strict German-led system and describes its system emphasizing the German origins as "*Sistema alemán, instructores alemanes y máquinas alemanas*"[19] (Schuler, 2020). Educators are certified by the CAMEXA. Similarly, intermediate and final examinations are CAMEXA certified according to German standards. Hence, in addition to the Mexican degree, graduates receive the German equivalent (*Gesellenbrief*) (Wiemann & Pilz, 2017). There are other interesting examples of German subsidiaries in Mexico that educate through the DVT program such as the in 2001 established and by the CAMEXA-certified Centro de Capacitación Técnica (in total Bosch runs three Technical Training Center) of Bosch in San Luis Potosí, Toluca, and Juarez (Bosch, 2018b). Another one is the close cooperation of Audi with the Universidad Tecnológica de Puebla and the establishment of a DVT program in the Centro de Especialización (Wiemann, 2018).

Interestingly, some German-led initiatives that were originally pushed by companies have developed to stand-alone organizations. For example, ALTRATEC, strongly pushed by Mercedes-Benz in its beginnings, established a supra-company DVT center in the State of Mexico. Today, ALTRATEC is a private educational institution and serves as the educational counterpart for other companies. DVT takes place, just like those mentioned above, theoretically in the ALTRATEC and practically in the participating companies. Another example is the company, Festo, which offers a relatively wide variety of vocational training courses through its

[17]The CAMEXA, for example, certifies training companies, controls educational framework, teaches the educators, organization of the exams, and the certification of the azubis by means of both the AHK and DIHK; see CAMEXA (2020).

[18]Other examples would be Bosch, Schaeffler, and Audi.

[19]Translated: "German system, German instructors, and German machines."

own business unit, Festo Didactics, though for a rather short time period and not in the form of a German-like DVT (Wiemann, 2018).

7.4.2 Functioning of DVT in Mexico's HME

Before exploring the role of the foreign subsidiaries of German MNCs in spreading the practice of German DVT, this chapter outlines how such highly coordinated practice can work in an HME environment. Some of the developments and actions that are simultaneously happening to the establishment of DVT are also to be understood as complementary isomorphism as discussed in Chap. 4.

From a "mechanical" perspective, both the island solutions and the federally acknowledged MMFD work just like the German DVT as a coproduction of educational institutions[20] where the azubis learn theoretically (generically) and the training companies in which practical and firm-specific skills across different departments are developed.[21] Regarding the cost side, in both forms, the costs for their azubis are mainly borne by the training (and finally benefitting) companies. Such costs arise, for example, through training measures, training staff, workplace, clothing, IT, and examinations at the CAMEXA. Azubis usually do not receive a regular salary. Most of the azubis are under 18 and are still officially students. On that account, companies are not obliged to pay wages according to local labor law. The vast majority of companies, however, pay a minor contribution to compensate for expenses (nutrition and transport) of the azubis (Cáceres-Reebs & Schneider, 2020). In the context of the MMFD, to make it more attractive for the azubis and to reduce the burden on the company, the SEP introduced a scholarship system that equips the MMFD azubis with a scholarship that covers per year a one-month minimum wage. If a company conducts its own DVT program, the training company covers full costs plus potential compensation. In general, all DVT programs mostly take 3 years. Depending on the certification and the inclusion of various certificating actors, graduates receive a *Técnico Bachiller* and the *Técnico Dual* from the SEP, and in a reasonable number of cases also the German equivalent to the *técnico* (*Gesellenbrief*). Certification of the MMFD is based on local legislation and thereby graduates do not obtain the German *Gesellenbrief* (Wiemann & Fuchs, 2018). However, graduates from the MMFD receive, in addition to the standard Mexican VET certificate, an additional proof of competences that is relatively renowned in Mexico.

Whereas the "mechanics" of DVT in Mexico are relatively clear, the question as to how such coordinated practice can work in an HME is not yet clear. How can an

---

[20] For example, Instituciones Públicas de Educación Media Superior (IPEMS) and Colegio Nacional de Educación Profesional Tecnológica (CONALEP).

[21] The design of the program is different to the one in Germany. In Mexico, azubis start to work in the company after the second semester (SEP, 2014).

azubi invest in firm-specific skills facing an uncertain future? How can a company invest in the education of its employees when they may be poached each moment? In order to conduct the DVT according to the German model, the DVT systems introduced in Mexico somehow need to solve the "mist of uncertainty." Furthermore, the alignment of educational supply and corporate demand within an environment that hampers joint coordination is a further puzzle to solve. In the following, specific action of DVT-relevant actors in Mexico is under scrutiny against the background of weak (or missing) complementary institutions.

In Mexico, there is no statutory inclusion of employee or employer representatives in deciding about which competences or learning fields should be included into DVT's curricula. However, the specific requirements of the companies find their way into the curricula and the design of the DVT program via various avenues. According to MexMNC3 who conducts its own DVT program the leeway regarding content and design of an own program is quite limited. MexMNC3 aligns its DVT program entirely with the German "*Rahmenausbildungsplan*" according to German law. Accordingly, the demands of MexMNC3 mostly do not find their way directly into the DVT program. However, one may suggest that the requirements of the counterparts (within the same sector) in Germany are similar, so that demands are met properly in any case also for the Mexican subsidiary. In line with MexMNC3, one of the most important cases of German DVT that is Schuler and its CEDUAL is built just like the one of MexMNC3 (Schuler, 2020). As examples of CAMEXA-certified training companies (*Ausbildungsbetriebe*) according to German law, all graduates from Schuler and MexMNC3 have both a Mexican *tecnico* and the German *Gesellenbrief*. Of major importance, all DVT programs that culminate in a German degree are built in close cooperation with the CAMEXA. Along these lines, MexOrg1 and MexMNC3 report the importance of the CAMEXA as platform of inter-firm deliberation. Every company sends their training manager (*Ausbildungsleiter*) to workshops and reunions hosted by the CAMEXA. Here, potential minor adjustments can be discussed. Furthermore, the conduct of the examinations (where, when, and by whom) is coordinated between the companies.

Furthermore, since alignment with German framework treaties is voluntary, conformity of, for example, Schuler's and MexMNC3's planning with the official German one indicates a relatively high degree of congruence in corporate demands on skills. Affirming the opportunity to design the program oneself, MexMNC3 implies that other German companies in Mexico deviate significantly from the official German planning. One such example is Volkswagen that also conducts an "island solution," though locally adapted their DVT program relatively clearly.[22] Logically, companies that do their own planning are perfectly in a position to adapt it to their demands.

In the context of the MMFD, input of the stakeholders is relatively limited when it comes to the ongoing development of the DVT program. However, companies can

[22] As an example, Volkswagen's DVT program takes 3 years as well, though is ordered chronologically in 1 year purely at school and two purely within the company.

make their voice heard indirectly through interaction with the major MMFD partners such as the CONALEP, the ALTRATEC, or the CAMEXA (Cáceres-Reebs & Schneider, 2020; López-Fogués et al., 2018). MexMNC2 reaffirms this notion of, first, low means of inter-firm deliberation (if at all informal) and, hence, a limited voice aggregation of the companies, and accordingly, second, a rather low influence on the design of the MMFD. In line with Cáceres-Reebs and Schneider (2020) and the statements of MexMNC3 above, MexMNC2 emphasizes the role of the CAMEXA as an intermediary between the system (mostly the educational institutions) and the MexMNC2. Consequently, despite relatively little influence, as GIZ (2019) data shows, Mexican companies in general (in total around 150 entities that have some experience with MMFD) indicate that labor supply of the MMFD meets the demand of the company. 74.5 percent of the entities answered *"The professional competences of graduates correspond to the requirements of the companies"* with either "very good" or "good" (GIZ, 2019). Along the same lines, more than 80 percent indicate that the graduate from the MMFD clearly outperforms the one from a conventional VET program. In general, especially for the CAMEXA-certified DVT programs and the MMFD, impact of the MNCs on the curricula, etc. is limited. However, as first evaluation studies find, market relevance of the courses is clearly higher than the ones offered by conventional VET measures.

German subsidiaries that conduct DVT somehow have to convince people to, first, invest 3 years in sector- and firm-specific skills and, second, to stay within the firm in the long term. From the perspective of azubis, security in times of both employment and unemployment is of utmost importance. From the perspective of the employers, it is of major importance to keep the azubis after graduation within the company. Since, indeed, Mexico is—in line with Schneider (2013)—an archetypal HME that does not offer security either for the company or for the employee—with very shallow unemployment protection and absent higher level wage agreements (that control actors' inter-firm movement)—companies need to compensate this with a future perspective of secure employment, a fair distribution of profits, and, most general, a desirable future. Indeed, MexMNC3 reports a "gentlemen agreement" between the German companies to not poach from each other, though he further indicates that experience proves this agreement to be out of commission. Poaching seems to be intensified for companies that have a DVT program. MexMNC3 reports that its DVT-educated workforce is highly regarded across the companies and, thus, comes to the fore for poaching as well. He mourns various highly skilled employees poached by huge companies paying higher salaries in the recent past.

Relating intra-firm co-determination and especially to the participation in distributional issues, MexMNC1 reports that there are work councils in effect, though they do not have a comparable clout like the ones in Germany. Management in MexMNC1 makes decisions in a strongly hierarchical manner and also, in respect of wage issues. On that account, in line with Jürgens and Krzywdzinski (2016), concerns of employees and azubis are most often subject to bilateral bargaining between management and worker, or are not dealt with at all.

Accordingly, all three interview partners indicate that it is a major concern to increase employment security, and therefore to decrease personnel fluctuation and to keep employees in the long term. Most directly and most remarkably, MexMNC3 legally gives its azubis the highest guarantee possible by assuring them a transfer guarantee after the completion of the DVT. On that account, young people have guaranteed employment after their education. MexMNC3 though is not the only company offering job guarantees. Among others, Volkswagen does so too (Weiss, 2016). In a country such as Mexico with a very high youth unemployment, such offer is unique in the Mexican career universe. Not having a statutory guaranteed employment as part of its educational contract, MexMNC2 reports that up to now (only having two generations of DVT graduates so far), all azubis were further employed after graduation and were equipped with permanent working contracts. Affirming this, López-Fogués et al. (2018) in a pilot evaluation find evidence for a positive impact of the MMFD with more than 90 percent of the graduates actively employed.

Beyond the high retention rate, all subsidiaries of German MNCs interviewed in Mexico report a reputational advantage of the company through its renowned brand and through its position as one of the top employers in Mexico. According to MexMNC1, the characteristic of the company as a potential bridge to the German market is an asset in recruiting high-quality azubis and to plan with them for the long term. He states that the most eager azubis are mostly interested in gaining a corporate function in the HQ in Germany. In line with that, he adds that the best azubis are part of business delegations to Germany and other foreign markets. Such future prospects contribute heavily to the commitment azubis show for the company. MexMNC3 similarly mentions business travels to Germany and China with the azubis and further emphasizes the reputational advantage of a company in which one can obtain the German *Gesellenbrief*. Accordingly, this door opener to a job in Germany weighs heavily when choosing a company. Also indicated by MexMNC3, a very good reputation allows the company to select the best azubis in terms of both cognitive capacity and endurance (ability to commit in the long run). He refers to a number of applicants numbering more than 100 times the number of vacancies. Through a relatively complex recruitment process, the company gets to know the entire family and can, thus, comprehensively estimate with whom they can plan in the long term.

Interestingly, none of the companies interviewed report salaries for their employees that are much higher than the ones of their competitors. MexMNC2 emphasizes that it is especially the additional benefits offered that outperform competitors. Among others, she mentions a special transport system to the place of work, a free canteen, a corporate savings bank, and various purchase coupons.

Furthermore, since the design of the DVT curricula mostly follows the theory at school and practice at the firm rotation typical for DVT in Germany, skills gained are not entirely firm-specific. Following this line, skills acquired are transferable to other firms and, hence, dependence of the employee on one employer is not too high. That certainly secures the employee from potential income losses or the risk of working somewhere where his or her skills are not appreciated and, thus, not paid. This, next to the general desire for long-term commitment discussed above, strongly improves the situation of the worker and allows them to consecutively build upon and to benefit in the long run from the DVT.

Certainly, every form of employees' long-term commitment also improves calculability for the corresponding firm. Further increasing security and planning capability for the employer, most remarkable, and in line with the employment guarantee of MexMNC3, MexMNC3 has an obligatory article in educational contracts that binds the azubis to work at least 3 years within the company after graduation. In case of a breach of duty, the parents of the azubi (that are required to sign the contract as well) act as bailsman and are forced to refund the costs incurred to the training company.

Investment in education is not only a rather risky endeavor; it is also huge and may need years to pay off. How the companies interviewed manage such a long-term investment in an environment that is mostly characterized by means of efficiency and low labor costs sets a further puzzle. All companies interviewed establish the link between the HQ and their subsidiary. MexMNC1 and MexMNC2 are both from a company that entered the Mexican market decades ago and has somehow taught through a DVT program ever since. On that account, the imported practice from Germany has never been seriously questioned. Contrarily, MexMNC3 may give more insights into the corporate decision-making process relating to the DVT. The company established its own training center a few years ago. The interviewee representing MexMNC3 attaches importance to the fact that the training center was built upon his conviction (to recall, the interviewee is a German expatriate, as the responsible person for, among others, education) and following a strong request to the HQ and not upon a directive of the German mother company. He refers to the history of his parent company as a renowned DVT educator in Germany. However, he further indicates that it is the efficiency-thinking due to his parent company's stock market listing that made the HQ rather reluctant to invest in Mexico in the first place. However, after "a long way" he convinced them to approach the Mexico business with a long-term strategy. One may draw the lesson that the value added by a DVT program needs to be present to the people that decide about whether or not to engage in DVT. In this case, a strongly convinced expatriate can be made largely responsible for the setup of the training center in accordance with German law.

In a preliminary conclusion, demand seems to be met by the supply, even though complementary institutions are not entirely in effect. Employment and unemployment security are highly increased by the DVT itself, since it makes both partners (company and employee) more valuable for each other. Companies largely compensate for a lack of complementary CME institutions by offering credible long-term cooperation and a reasonable future prospect. Usually, money invested in Mexico is expected to pay off in the short run and to avoid any additional risk. However, the cases under scrutiny, however, show that all companies scrutinized make major investments in the long-term development of their workforce. Apparently, they do so because they know the value of DVT as a means to improve both their employees and the business operations in general.

7.4.3 Institutional Entrepreneurship

Within the blue-collar area, Mexican companies typically react to the ubiquitous low-quality education in their HME system with a strong reliance on in-house education that, unfortunately, is mostly nothing more than a mere form of technical familiarization, and does not include any in-depth technical education. That again does not allow one to escape from "precarious jobs" being a major share of the Mexican labor market (Schneider, 2013). Wiemann and Pilz (2017) affirm this point empirically by showing Mexican companies hiring people directly after school and equipping them with a shallow technical understanding. Accordingly, since day one, new employees are treated just like any other that may have been working there for 10 years.

The sections above on the various German-led initiatives and the compensation of lacking complementary institutions already indicate that some of the German subsidiaries indeed break with the existing Mexican rules and, falling back on known and proven practices from their home country, introduce alternative practices and rules. In fact, German practices have somehow found their way into the Mexican system of education. Whether that change—although not yet clear how profound that change may be—is also to be traced back to the conscious enactment of German subsidiaries is part of the upcoming section. Certainly, being located in a complex field of development over decades, clearly assigned contributions to the single actors are not possible. However, the idea is to get a basic understanding of the role of German subsidiaries as a factor within change.

In the context of vocational training in Mexico, German subsidiaries have a quite heterogeneous and contradictory practice portfolio including both CME and HME practices. However, having a larger practice portfolio than the local counterparts, it is this apparent incompatibility that can make them an agent of institutional change. In fact, as the various DVT programs in Mexico show, even some incompatible practices are being merged in an unprecedented manner providing institutional innovation. The German subsidiaries scrutinized are all to be labeled as institutional entrepreneurs to differing degrees. These issues was approached under the main category in the questionnaire as "action undertaken to establish DVT in Mexico that is not to be ascribed to normal business operations." The three steps through which institutional entrepreneurship can be described that are reflection, reframing and mobilization, and collective action are to be captured.

First of all, reflection and awareness of the situation is the initial point upon which any conscious action aiming at change builds. Without any exception, all interviewees in Mexico indicated a high degree of dissatisfaction with the existing local educational system and, accordingly, an awareness of the system's misfit with their own requirements and expectations. As an example, MexMNC3 expresses the reasons for engaging in DVT in Mexico relying on his awareness of systemic misfit as follows:

> …there was the necessity to find well-educated employees. Without any doubt, against this background we were searching for alternatives. Generally, in Mexico, a suitable school or

> training system does not exist. They do not know such technical professions in the form needed. On that account we face major difficulties to find well-educated technical personnel, for example, in the area of tool manufacturing. All the instrument mechanics we had employed, they learned it somehow from their uncle or father, and, of course, the according levels of education and of knowledge of these employees were very low. (interview MexMNC3; original German interview is translated by the author).

Similar explanations with the negative situation in the Mexican labor market as cause for own initiatives can be found beyond the sample of this study and equally for other German subsidiaries that actively engage with DVT such as Schuler, Mercedes-Benz, and Audi. (Wiemann, 2018).

Generally, Mexico takes a special position in the educational landscape since it, indeed, is a relatively well-developed country with quite a reasonable amount of industry but is equipped with a rather inappropriate education system. Consequently, Mexico is quite known as a "*Industrieland ohne Facharbeiter*" (industrialized country without technicians) (Janert, 2017). Affirming this, Wiemann and Fuchs (2018) bring the existing VET system into play and find that large parts of the subsidiary manager in Mexico are unsatisfied with the existing VET system, condemning the detachment of VET from practical experience and requirements. In their study, a German subsidiary manager comments:

> We are really not satisfied [with the vocational education in Mexico]; in reality the people learn once they enter the company. [...] They teach you a career that gives you a title but no experience or cleverness. [...] School and reality are a little separated in Mexico.

Similarly, MexMNC1 indicated that well-educated technicians are not available in Mexico and that the education of such is just not possible. He further intuitively connected the lack of highly skilled education with the "hire and fire mentality," short-cycle planning of both companies and people, and very high personnel fluctuation. Accordingly, one can expect that, in this case, MexMNC1 did not only recognize the incapacity of the local system to generate suitably educated employees, but also recognized the need for complementary institutions for a proper VET to function.

On that account, the efforts put in the establishment of a DVT in Mexico clearly follow from awareness regarding, first, the problems they face in the conduct of their business activities in the HME institutional setting of Mexico and, second (here starts the second step of institutional entrepreneurship), the solution that fit best with their interests, which may compensate for systemic weaknesses they carry in their practice portfolio. The awareness of the inappropriate situation in the Mexican labor market can therefore be seen as cause for the conscious enactment of institutional innovation in the HME.

Mobilization and collective action (second and third) are tightly interconnected and, therefore, are discussed together. Due to the negative situation found in Mexico, subsidiaries are searching for alternative solutions in their wide practice portfolio. MexMNC3 emphasizes the long and very successful tradition of the parent company's DVT in Germany to further strengthen his choice of German DVT. One can reasonably argue that such choice perfectly fits the requirements. Due to the similarity of business operations (see "nota bene" above) between the parent company and the subsidiary, the labor required is similar as well. Logically, if the home country practice provides suitable workers for the parent company, then it should also be able to provide suitable workers for their operations in Mexico. It is exactly here where German subsidiaries access their wider practice portfolio and fall back on well-proven DVT practices. Contesting and reinterpreting the same educational issue as other companies, German subsidiaries use their wider portfolio, which allows them to reframe the issue of VET and to embed the alternative in the frames that are already conversant with the actors with whom one wishes to jointly act. Since institutional change is difficult, complex, and costly, a single actor of change (in this case a single HR department or subsidiary) is limited in making a difference. As such, mobilization of resources and partners is key in successful institutional entrepreneurship to jointly reconstruct the negatively perceived educational arrangement. As Chap. 4 introduced theoretically, only a significant (sufficient) number of companions with sufficient resources in a collective action allow an institutional entrepreneur to reasonably "fight in the institutional war."

Mobilization can be conducted through various venues. For example, MexMNC3 reports of a long way from the idea of implementing DVT in Mexico toward its operation. He refers to high costs of building the school, buying machines, hiring training and teaching personnel, and receiving the CAMEXA certification, all necessary for the execution of DVT. For so doing, MexMNC3 emphasizes the importance of the parent company's support. In this case, the parent company was quite reluctant to invest such an amount of resources in a long-term project in Mexico. However, as MexMNC3 further reports, he could convince the people in charge in the HQ to fund the project by forcefully expressing the idea and providing a coherent and feasible solution. The bottom line is that mobilization efforts of MexMNC3 gave the HQ reason to cooperate and, thus, to jointly tackle educational issues of the subsidiary in Mexico. In this case of intra-company mobilization, the issue of framing and making the idea of change appropriate for the potential collaborator (here the HQ) is not too complex, since the HQ knows the value of DVT pretty well and the overall idea is perfectly appropriate for it.

However, aside from mobilization and "collective action" in terms of intra-company flow of resources, the conduct of a new practice can also take place between companies in Mexico. As an example, the establishment of the CEDUAL in 2012 was made possible due to the collective action of various actors of change. Due to the complexity of such a huge project, under the lead of Schuler, five more German (Allgaier, Gestamp, Schäffler, ThyssenKrupp, and PWO) subsidiaries joined Schuler and, thus, jointly implemented a large-scale DVT center. Illustrating the supra-firm claim of the CEDUAL, the CEDUAL is described by a representative of the German embassy right from the outset as "*factor clave para las empresas automovilísticas alemanas en México al igual que para sus proveedores*"[23] (Centro

[23]Translated by the author: "key factor for the German automotive companies in Mexico as well as for its suppliers."

Alemán de Información para Latinoamérica, 2015). Again, the necessary efforts invested in explaining the idea of DVT and to reframe the participating companies were—if at all existent—limited. All companies that collectively act are German companies with German managers in charge.

Another example of mobilization and collective action is Audi in San José Chiapa, in the State of Puebla. To meet the requirements of Audi's premium model factory, the car manufacturer mobilized the *Universidad de Tecnológica de Puebla* and has found itself in active and ongoing joint cooperation with the same since 2016. This large-scale joint venture (with a size of more than 20,000 sqm) called *Centro de Especialización* allows the burden to be shared among various shoulders. The State of Puebla pays for the building of the facilities and the wages of teachers and trainers. Audi equips the educational center with machines and a state-of-the-art apprentice workshop and assures quality of training through regular training courses in its HQ in Ingolstadt, Germany. Notably, by doing a DVT program in the *Centro de Especialización* azubis of the Universidad de Tecnológica de Puebla are able to deduct the time spent for the DVT program from potential further studying. On that account, by investing two more years in university after graduation from the DVT program, students can acquire a *Licenciatura* (the usual university degree) in engineering sciences (Otto, 2014; Wiemann, 2018). Without further information available on the specific development of Audi's joint efforts in Mexico, one could argue that, indeed, the counterpart being Mexican significantly changes the game of reframing and restructuring. The design of this DVT program with, among others, the potential for ongoing studies aiming at a *Licenciatura* deviates significantly from the more German-like DVT actions introduced above. Instead of copying the German practices, this DVT initiative includes parts that are appropriate to a Mexican university. Accordingly, one can reasonably state that the *Centro de Especialización* is rather a product of institutional negotiation and certainly more embedded within the frames that were already in existence with the Mexican counterpart, though still heavily influenced by institutional innovation brought in by the institutional entrepreneur Audi.

Finally, the MMFD is the DVT project with by far the widest coverage and highest impact at a federal level. However, by exploring the history of DVT in Mexico from the early 1990s, one can reasonably argue that the German subsidiaries were pioneers in the conduct of DVT according to their home country model and served as role model for the MMFD (Elbling, n.d.). Of special importance, the collaboration between Mercedes-Benz and the CONALEP marked the point of departure for the MMFD, even though with an inertia of approximately two decades. Affirmatively, MexMNC2 especially emphasizes the prime and major impulse given by the German subsidiaries. Similarly, the establishment of German certification of DVT in Mexico is seen as a very important precursor to the wider establishment of the MMFD, which is strongly supported by the CAMEXA (MexOrg1). Interestingly, the CAMEXA introduced the certification and, thus, a legal base for the German DVT in Mexico on demand by German subsidiaries. Aragón (2019) remarkably illustrates the succession of events that made the CAMEXA a major safeguard of German DVT in Mexico. According to Aragón (2019), German subsidiaries made their voice heard at their HQs in Germany, which again pressurized the German Confederation of Chambers and the BDA (Federal Employer Association) to convince the DIHK (Association of Chambers of Commerce and Industry in Germany; umbrella organization of the CAMEXA) to equip the CAMEXA with the mandate to organize German DVT in Mexico. Confirming this, VETNet[24] states that the CAMEXA is supported and mandated by German authorities by demand of German companies abroad. As the *raison d'être* for the active AHK involvement in, for example, Mexico, VETNet states:

> Die AHKs werden so in ihrer Rolle als Außenwirtschaftsförderer gestärkt, indem sie den Fachkräftebedarf der (deutschen) Wirtschaft vor Ort durch nachfrageorientierte und wirtschaftsnahe Angebote zur dualen Berufsausbildung sichern[25] (VETNet, 2020).

For a more detailed discussion on the chronology of CAMEXA becoming the major DVT certification agency in Mexico, including the efforts of the German government (and the GIZ), see Aragón (2019).

As the elaboration above has introduced, today's MMFD is a very complex, multi-actor endeavor in which the role of German subsidiaries has become blurred. Ever since the resumption of the MMFD in 2009, different actors have entered the field claiming major contribution to the development of the MMFD. Therefore, the trajectory of the MMFD, from a certain point in time, cannot be understood without the inclusion of political and developmental actors such as both the Mexican CONALEP, SEP, and COPARMEX and the German CAMEXA, BiBB, and the GIZ (MexOrg1). In fact, today, the MMFD is a top priority on the Mexican-German bilateral agenda (for an overview of bilateral Mexican-German interaction, see Negrín and Pérez (n.d.)).

Additional information: MexMNC2 has been participating in the MMFD right from the outset. Interestingly, MexMNC2 also had an internal "island solution" DVT program before participation in the MMFD ever since the establishment of the German subsidiary in Mexico. The former island solution was also connected to the CAMEXA and allowed to confer official German and Mexican degrees. However, according to MexMNC2, the company stopped its own education center and joined the MMFD due to a corporate crisis that made MexMNC2 unable to bear the costs for its own DVT program.

In line with that, MexMNC2 emphasizes the support received by the government, but also distinguishes the active role of MexMNC2 during the development of the

[24] VETNet is the German Chambers worldwide network (AHK) for cooperative, work-based vocational education and training.

[25] Translated: "The AHKs, thus, comply with their role as supporting international business by securing the rightly skilled workers for the (German) business locally through the offer of demand-led dual vocational training."

MMFD. She reports frequent interaction and a relatively close relationship between the Mexican government and MexMNC2 in the context of MMFD development.

> MexMNC2 was working hand in hand with the government, in order to implement the DVT. As a matter of fact, there were various conferences and assemblies in which MexMNC2 participated. (MexMNC2; original Spanish interview is translated by the author).

As an example, MexMNC2 reports in particular from a DVT conference in which representatives of the Mexican government, the CAMEXA, the German government, and German subsidiaries participated. At this conference, she puts clearly, the directors of MexMNC2 and, of special importance, the director of HRM participated actively. However, in a concluding argument, MexMNC2 reports that the strongest impact German companies had was through the influence on other companies to also participate in the DVT initiative and as somewhat of a counselor of the government.

Next, major focus on the sum of actors is required. Aragón (2019) describes the policy process that led to the creation and establishment of the MMFD. He affirms MexMNC2 as the private sector (in particular, German subsidiaries that had knowledge and experience with DVT in Mexico), indeed, had a relatively strong representation in the agenda setting "strategic core group" (Aragón, 2019) forming the MMFD along with other actors such as the government, educational institutions, and the CAMEXA. However, major attributes of institutional entrepreneurship can rather be assigned to governmental actors, first at state level with—most prominently—the State of Mexico and then on national level with the federal government as the driving force. Interestingly, the president in charge at the time of MMFD's beginnings at the federal level in 2009 was the same as the governor of the State of México when Mercedes-Benz was strongly supported by the respective state government in 1993: Enrique Peña Nieto. Nieto's presidency brought both a general interest in DVT and people with experience in DVT issues into the right position. Oversimplified and consciously dispensing with some information on the detailed policy process, both the State of Mexico and the Mexican government, each under the lead of Nieto, acted consciously, knowing about the situation in Mexico characterized by high youth unemployment and low productivity. Accordingly, he applied what both the German subsidiaries in Mexico and the German CME in general had already successfully proven to serve as a potential remedy against the drawbacks mentioned. Consequently, Nieto used the practice portfolio broadened by the German subsidiaries. Accordingly, one needs to contribute a major share of entrepreneurship to the government in charge that, nonetheless, was strongly influenced by what German subsidiaries had imported successfully.

Indeed, one finds all the steps to be conducted that are characteristic for institutional entrepreneurship, though with the Mexican government as major driver (MexOrg1). The Mexican government shows awareness of the situation in Mexico (youth unemployment, informality, low productivity, etc., and a rapid upsurge of the automobile sector in the 2010s with a strong increase in demand for technical skills[26]) and of the inclusion of the private sector as a necessary condition for the DVT to function. Furthermore, taking care of the gathering of major stakeholders and as major partner in collective action, the government under Nieto can be understood as an institutional entrepreneur.

Notably, as a product of major Mexican and German actors, the MMFD has paid its national appearance and legitimacy by the various actors with a strong degree of "tropicalization," which is a deviation from the original German model through adjustment to Mexican realities. Whereas Mexican governmental and supra-firm agencies (SEP, CONALEP, COPARMEX) were quite aware of the value the German DVT and the specific design, it required, however, thorough embedding of the DVT in the known frame of especially Mexican companies, resulting in certain adjustments. According to Aragón (2019), Mexican companies had a hard time (and are still in the process of) understanding VET efforts that take longer than 2 weeks and require a long-term commitment. Additionally, the advantage German subsidiaries have (reputation, bridge to the German market, etc.) that makes employees stay is not available to Mexican companies. They also, for example, face a significantly higher threat of poaching than German subsidiaries do. To counter such threats, the Mexican government developed the scholarship program to disburden Mexican companies. Furthermore, the MMFD is shorter and the practical part is, *vis-á-vis* the German DVT, weighed more heavily. Accordingly, the added value of the azubi is immediately higher than in a more German DVT and costs for companies are significantly lower. However, theoretical knowledge and in-depth technical competences are lower than those certified by the CAMEXA.

Concluding for the MMFD one may, indeed, assign German subsidiaries an active role in the creation and establishment of the nation-wide initiative. They certainly gave the first impetus, broadened the government's practice portfolio, strongly supported the design of the MMFD with their specific knowledge, and above all provided the MMFD with a certain degree of legitimacy and acted as role models. However, attaining this massive and unprecedented mobilization of business, political, and developmental actors and the following international, multi-level, and cross-occupational collective action is beyond the reach of solely German subsidiaries. The active and continuous support of various actors is needed. However, above all, regarding the actual institutional entrepreneur that shifted DVT on a national scale in Mexico, one needs to particularly emphasize the government in charge that recognized the value of DVT as a measure to counter ongoing developmental issues, further triggering creation and establishment of DVT. It negotiated with the German government and in an ongoing manner strongly supports the ongoing operations of the MMFD, for example, by means of the scholarship granted to MMFD's students.

Up to now, this chapter has discussed various avenues through which German subsidiaries have acted as institutional entrepreneurs. Among others, intra-firm efforts leading to island solutions of one company (+CAMEXA), inter-firm efforts

[26] For an overview of the increasing automobile sector, see Aragón (2019).

with joint action of various like-minded actors (CEDUAL + CAMEXA), inter-actor efforts with cooperation between a subsidiary and an educational institution, and the multi-level efforts culminating in the development of an unprecedented DVT initiative outside of Germany, the MMFD, indicated how German subsidiaries changed the Mexican status quo through consciously acting beyond their usual corporate duties. All in all, through the various avenues of establishing DVT in Mexico, German subsidiaries clearly show institutional entrepreneurship. Relying on the wide practice portfolio and adjusting it to a strange institutional setting is what makes institutional innovation a product of conscious (joint) action.

However, as the section—in particular on the MMFD—has anticipated, German MNCs as the pioneers of DVT and representatives of a CME also acted as role models giving DVT in Mexico momentum and, thus, may have allowed MMFD to occur in the first place. Such rather passive contribution and the potential avenues through which (reversed) institutional isomorphism can be exerted by German subsidiaries on the field are part of the next section.

7.4.4 Reversed Isomorphism: German Subsidiaries in Mexico

Analytical lines may become blurred every now and then between institutional entrepreneurship and institutional isomorphism and also between the categories of institutional isomorphism themselves. However, to secure the highest degree of analytical clarity possible, here, only the usual corporate duties are put under scrutiny. Nonetheless, sometimes exerted pressure can be interpreted as the one or the other, and from time to time, a specific action can exert various pressures at a time. On that account, the categories are not strictly discussed separately but are incorporated into a coherent flow of argumentation.

Since a political economy is inhabited by various actors and organizational structures at different levels, this study breaks new ground by putting societal dynamics originating with German subsidiaries under scrutiny relating to both vertical (on organizations and individuals at other levels such as ministries, political leaders, universities, and families) and horizontal (on organizations at the same level such as local companies, other international subsidiaries, and German subsidiaries) diffusion of practices. Affirmatively, emphasizing the scope of societal impacts, Elbing refers to German subsidiaries as affecting the entire Mexican with regard to DVT.

> Muchas empresas alemanas establecidas en México, conscientes de la ventaja del Sistema dual, son pioneras en la aplicación de la Formación Dual en México. Sus centros de capacitación tienen carácter ejemplar para todo el país (Elbling, n.d., p. 2).[27]

[27] Translated: "Lots of German companies that are established in Mexico, well aware of the advantages of the dual system, are pioneers in applying DVT in Mexico. Their training centers serve as role models for the entire country."

Subsidiaries such as those interviewed, in line with the general consensus among scholars and practitioners, served as role models representing a coordinated system that has proven to counter the most urgent problems in the Mexican economy (Elbling, n.d.; López-Fogués et al., 2018; Negrín & Pérez, n.d.; Wiemann & Fuchs, 2018). Following this line of thought, one may add and emphasize two circumstances in which the Mexican government found itself, when thinking about DVT initiatives. First, the country found itself (certainly still finds) in a crisis situation characterized by, among others, low productivity and high (youth) unemployment (MexOrg1; Negrín & Pérez, n.d.). Second, a major wave of investment of automobile companies stood in line in the time of the MMFD pilot phase. Car producers alone (not considering the entire supplying industry that will follow) promised new investment, exclusively in the years 2014–2018, of more than 18 billion USD, creating around 43,000[28] new jobs (Aragón, 2019; Chicago Tribune, 2015). Knowing about the mismatch between educational supply and corporate demand of especially high technology manufacturers, the government felt pressurized to align with the German model that was perceived to be more successful (more legitimate) in order to cope with the already existing and continuously increasing demand for well-skilled technicians. Being in a state of uncertainty, due to both developmental stagnation and increased future demand from a dysfunctional system, the government has been very receptive for DVT demonstrations by the German subsidiaries. Certainly, as already discussed above, the German subsidiaries acted as a best practice example in Mexico and as representatives of CME systems (that cope with exactly the requirements of the Mexican government back then). One can reasonably assume that the demonstration of the German practices, the education of future employees to match the demand of car producers, and the smooth inclusion of young people into working life exerts pressure on the Mexican field to model their VET system after the German system. Thus, one can assume the German subsidiaries to have exercised a strong demonstration effect on the government to draw attention to the DVT according to the German model.

Another form of vertical diffusion of DVT takes place between the German subsidiaries and potential future workers, i.e., the Mexican people. Referring to such diffusion, MexMNC3 and MexOrg1 state that the reputation of the DVT programs of German subsidiaries among the Mexican people is generally very high. This, indeed, is contradictory to what one could expect, due to the general unfamiliarity of people with the German DVT. However, MexMNC3 reports usual ratio for the industry of DVT vacancies to applicants of three to 400 and, therefore, clearly affirms the popularity of the DVT. Consequently, one can reasonably argue that due to the perception of German companies as "top employers" offering promising careers, at least in industrial hotspots such as Puebla (coined by a dense population of MNCs and a long history of such), the general orientation toward

[28] This number needs to be adjusted by the additional surround supplier industry that goes along with the movement of car producers in particular. On that account, one may expect significantly more vacancies than 43,000.

university education in Mexico is also legitimately enriched with DVT education as a valid alternative among the people, not only legally accepted but also socially. Further contributing to the perceived appropriateness among the people, MexMNC3 reports of the inclusion of the entire family into their recruitment process. Inviting the entire family to "open house days" that include, for example, general introductions to the company, DVT, workshops, and future career prospects and the exchange with former azubis, MexMNC3 familiarizes larger parts of the society with the DVT. All this happens in the conduct of recruiting that is a daily operation of MexMNC3. From a corporate side, the inclusion of the family into the recruitment process enables them to integrate more socioeconomic indictors into the selection procedure and enables them to find the most promising future azubis. In line with that, Wiemann and Fuchs (2018) affirm the relatively high acceptance of DVT among the people in Mexico. Accordingly, people that face the decision of what educational path to follow become aware of DVT's recognition by the industry and, along with that, also the fact that "today, they [graduates] earn more as if they would work as an [academic] engineer" (Wiemann & Fuchs, 2018, p. 8).

Relating to horizontally exerted pressure, since serving as a role model can be especially valid for similar organizations, isomorphic pressures exerted on the peer group (consisting of other companies) are very important. Digging deeper, all three corporate interviewees negated any form of formal and direct coercion mechanism that, for example, requires a supplier or any kind of partner company to conduct DVT. However, MexMNC2 and MexMNC3 in particular report of indirect, more subtle avenues of exercising coercive pressure on the cooperation partners. In fact, German companies that conduct DVT indirectly force others to incorporate DVT through high quality standards and certifications. MexMNC3 refers to audits in which, here, German companies check, for example, potential suppliers, in an initial inspection or frequently in an ongoing manner to secure their compliance. According to MexMNC3, typical questions that constitute an audit are, for example:

> How can you secure quality standards? How can you properly conduct machine maintenance? What kind of personnel do you have for these tasks? What educational background do they have? (MexMNC3, original German interview is translated by the author).

Following this argument, MexMNC3 emphasizes the heavy weight such (more or less) subtle questioning can have on suppliers, especially if the one who raises questions is a major company such as Volkswagen, Daimler, or BMW that knows the benefits of DVT and, thus, highly appreciates the *Gesellenbrief*. He further states that this weight of the demander is multiplied if it is a very important or sometimes even exclusive client. Accordingly, the receptiveness of coercive pressure directly correlates with the perceived dependence on a pressurizing entity. Further increasing the quality requirements, MexMNC3 notes that the Mexican, here, car production is becoming an industry of higher technology. As an example, he refers to the shift of car production only for the Latin American continent (which requires fewer quality standards than, for example, the European Union) to, for example, Audi's production of its premium model Q5 that is exclusively manufactured in Mexico for the global market. Accordingly, both quality standards and products' complexity have increased significantly, which again requires better educated employees to cope with. Going one step further, he gives insights into the business conduct and inter-firm relations that further propel the transmission of quality standards, indirectly evoking DVT. In fact, a relatively large amount of supplying companies has machines within their production halls that are partly (or even entirely) owned by their clients. These assets can easily have a value of hundreds of thousands EUR and require highly skilled maintenance. In such a scenario, a German owner of the machinery will certainly be reassured if the person responsible for maintaining the assets has undertaken recognized and trusted education. In this vein, MexMNC3 emphasized the very high value of employees that are certified with a German *Gesellenbrief*.

It is right here, where the lines between coercive pressures and cognitive ones become blurred. The *Gesellenbrief* over and above its usage as an instrument to deal with coercive pressures as described above is, of course, a major pillar of a wider CME credentialing system that contributes greatly to the clear demarcation and identification of belonging to a certain profession, which may be labeled as "high quality, high reliability, and long-term oriented company."[29] Hence, in line with MexMNC2, beyond a means of securing quality, German DVT certification describes an entire profession and, thereby, symbolizes occupational belonging. In an attempt to describe MexMNC3, he does so by setting it apart from the "others" that do not have a German certificate and that cannot award their graduates with a *Gesellenbrief*. Emphasizing the superiority of the German DVT and delineating the profession even more closely as "quality producers in Mexico with German origins," MexMNC3 affirmatively states:

> . . .the companies with German origins, they know the advantages of our educational system, of course. A German tool instrument mechanic who, as a matter of fact, has a good education, has a higher knowledge level as an [academic] engineer from here. I had to notice that a couple of times. The value, especially here in Puebla, or generally in Mexico, also San Luiz where lots of automobile producers are located, the valence of a Gesellenbrief has certainly a different value (MexMNC3, original German interview is translated by the author).

The strong concerns he expresses if other companies without DVT can conduct the complex tasks reasonably clearly affirm the idea of a desired identification with the profession of the reliable, long-term oriented company. Along these lines, he clearly shows professional affiliation to those that are certified German training companies. In so doing, he reveals the inner workings of the profession and makes German quality standards and the corresponding certification a constituent element of the profession. Similarly, MexMNC2 strongly emphasizes the company as having instructors and trainers that are all certified by the CAMEXA. A further strong

[29] Connecting German credentialing back to the audits discussed above, Volkswagen offers courses in its own Volkswagen Academy Mexico to understand and to better cope with requirements demanded by Volkswagen and Audi. As a matter of fact, the Volkswagen Academy in Mexico offers specific program that awards German certifications for auditors (licenciatario de VDA-QMC de Alemania) (see Volkswagen Group, 2020a, b).

example in which a company even incorporates professional belonging into its marketing strategy and uses and reinforces the discussed profession is Schuler, who describes its CEDUAL as "*Sistema alemán, instructores alemanes y máquinas alemanas*"[30] (Schuler, 2020). Along the same lines, although interpreting the concept of profession even more narrowly, Volkswagen and its Academy, which educates through DVT (both its own trainees and those of other firms), are rather interested in creating a profession of "high quality, German Volkswagen companies" and identification with the Volkswagen brand. Building upon the same foundations as the examples discussed above, Volkswagen offers, among others, DVT and other such German courses (e.g., German certifications for auditors) with the vision:

> Profesionalizamos a los colaboradores de la cadena de valor para fabricar los vehículos y componentes del Grupo Volkswagen (Volkswagen Group, 2020a).[31]

Hence, professionalization is propelled, indeed, according to the German model, though taken even more narrowly, it has directly connected with the company instead of the country of origin as a base for joint identification.

Furthermore, one can recognize a certain pattern of dispersion of company-owned DVT centers. Such an effect stems mostly from larger and resource-rich German subsidiaries that initially take up DVT programs in their own company and, from a specific point in time onwards, open doors to other companies, equipping them cognitively with all it takes to do DVT in Mexico. As such, various examples can be drawn upon. Most prominently, Volkswagen de México, established in 1964—and having a German CEO ever since—and today with more than 14,000 employees (Volkswagen Group, 2020b), built the Volkswagen Academy Mexico that also acts as a service provider offering DVT to other companies. As such companies that do not have their own educational centers can join the Volkswagen Academy and, thus, can also conduct proper DVT. Companies cooperating with the Academy pay in turn a (relatively high) fee to Volkswagen. Another prominent example is Schuler's CEDUAL that does it similarly—though officially CAMEXA certified—and opens doors to partner companies (Schuler, 2020). However, in a certain point of time, the cognitively well-equipped companies that use services by CEDUAL or the Volkswagen Academy face the high fees and consider their own solutions in the context of DVT. MexMNC3 sheds light on this process of dispersion and outlines the history of its own educational center along the lines drawn. He states that until a specific point in time, MexMNC3 had its trainees sent to external DVT providers to conduct the theoretical part of the DVT. Concluding in his company's own DVT center, considering external DVT providers as a large cost factor, he states:

> ...if they can do it [Volkswagen and DVT], then we can do it as well (MexMNC3, original German interview is translated by the author).

[30] Translated: "German system, German instructors, and German machines."

[31] Translated: "We professionalize partners along the value chain in order to produce cars and components for the Volkswagen Group."

As a matter of fact, MexMNC3 established its own DVT center as means to educate employees meeting its own demand. However, MexMNC3 also adds that they can imagine that once their demand is satisfied, they will open their center and offer DVT as service to other companies, hence, starting the cycle of dispersion a second time.

The idea of open doors for other companies and, thus, to induct the DVT in Mexico to others is also closely connected to the idea of demonstration effects German subsidiaries may have on their surroundings. No doubt, one can also reasonably understand the dispersion process described above as mimicry in which perceived best practices are learned and mimetically applied by other companies that face same problems of skill shortages and short-termism. In line with the very positive reputation of DVT and the position as role models referred to frequently in the previous chapters and sections, the desire of other companies that do not have DVT to join the promising endeavor of such is self-explanatory. All corporate interviewees affirm the role of their company as a role model for DVT in Mexico.

MexMNC2 describes the major contribution of her company to the MMFD as being that other firms perceive MexMNC2's action as best practice and, therefore, join the MMFD as well. Pressure on companies though seems to differ with regard to their home institutional setting. Indeed, from examining the companies participating in the MMFD, one recognizes various Mexican companies. That is different to other island solutions in which Mexican companies are up to now not engaged. Certainly, a major difference lies within the costs of a trainee out of the MMFD and one out of, for example, the CEDUAL. Whereas the MMFD is both highly adjusted to Mexican needs (as discussed above: shorter, more practical phases, etc.) and highly subsidized by the Mexican government, DVT through the CEDUAL is costlier and more complex. On that account, the MMFD, which is legitimized at the federal level, indeed, manages to incorporate Mexican companies as well. However, MexMNC1 does not trust this development too much and indicates her presumption that mostly Mexican companies follow the maxim of rent-seeking and, thus, benefitting from free workers who are paid by the government without sustainably implementing DVT in their companies. However, whether the MMFD is misused or not, comparing the MMFD with, for example, the CEDUAL, in relation to the number of Mexican companies participating, one can reasonably state that the governmental support and embedding in existing frames reduce the obstacles that a Mexican company faces when interested in DVT.

In the context of its island solutions that are based on German legislation, MexMNC3 sees very limited movement for Mexican companies and mostly refers to the "automobile universe" consisting of MNCs. Accordingly, indeed, there is awareness that quality standards need to be increased in the long run. However, mostly smaller Mexican companies—if included at all in the "automobile universe"—have neither the necessary knowledge nor the monetary resources to implement their own DVT program. Up to now, still a very small minority within the context of DVT, MexMNC3 reports from customers visits of international companies from, for example, Canada and the USA:

> ...also those other than German companies are very interested in DVT. If they are visiting us, they are highly enthusiastic about the training workshop, and the entire idea of the concept. As a matter of fact, in their country of origin, such DVT does not exist either. This is a eureka-moment and they ask how we do these things. In general, they are open-minded about DVT (MexMNC3, original German interview is translated by the author).

On that account, DVT may further be accelerated if MNCs not stemming from Germany recognize the value of DVT in Mexico.

7.4.5 Summary and Degree of Institutionalization

The Mexican case study leads to various findings and—as such, case of "best practice"—indicates the major categories and aspects of reality of interest for similar investigations in Brazil. This case demonstrates that behavioral contradiction can lead to institutional contestation and make MNCs agents of institutional change. Here, the reliance on home country patterns of DVT had and still has a significant impact on the Mexican institutional setting. This brief discussion on the Mexican case summarizes and discusses major findings and sheds light on the strength of impact as a matter of the degree of institutionalization.

The chapter on the functioning of alien-to-the-system DVT demonstrated how German subsidiaries manage to (partly) cope with this lack by compensating for absent or weak institutions in the four complementary institutional domains. In fact, building upon their positive reputation, strongly supported by the Mexican government (at least in the case of the MMFD), German subsidiaries are relatively successful in dissolving the "mist of uncertainty," allowing both the employer and the employee to credibly commit in the long term. Elaborations on the coherent CME alignment across all the five institutional domains strongly affirm the findings of complementarity in the context of educational efforts in Chap. 6.

In contrast to Schneider's (2013) notions of MNCs "mousiness" and exit as the preferred strategy if not satisfied with the environment, the case of Mexico shows that German subsidiaries, indeed, act as institutional entrepreneurs that consciously attempt to implement German DVT. On that account, these subsidiaries showed major efforts either alone, with help from the home country, in cooperation with the CAMEXA, as a joint project with other companies, as a joint effort with local educational institutions, or as part of a high-level initiative such as the MMFD. Nonetheless, the Mexican case indicated that entrepreneurship in this sense can only be successful as long as local receptiveness is greater than reluctance against institutional innovation. On that account, the sheer existence of willing partners, especially in the case of the MMFD, plays a major role when discussing the role of German subsidiaries in the establishment of DVT initiatives across Mexico. Furthermore, German subsidiaries exert reasonable isomorphic pressures on the Mexican field and its various levels and actors. The analysis of the various venues and forms of actor-induced isomorphism shows the impact German subsidiaries have on others to do it alike. Along these lines, the investigation above has shown how

German subsidiaries in the conduct of their usual duties can pressurize particularly the government and other companies to also educate in a manner similar to German DVT.

All in all, one can state that, indeed, German subsidiaries have a pivotal role in the introduction and establishment of DVT in Mexico. Nonetheless, today's Mexico is "the most successful DVT system" (GIZ, 2019) outside of Germany not exclusively because of the efforts of German subsidiaries. All areas investigated above—compensation of absent institutions, institutional entrepreneurship, and institutional isomorphism—have strongly benefitted from a relatively stable, supportive, and—above all—receptive surrounding in Mexico.

Approaching DVT in Mexico regarding the degree of institutionalization, without doubt, the practice of DVT according to the German model has gained reasonable legitimacy. Based on the prior analysis, one can reasonably assume that it has already left the status of a proto-institution (Wiemann & Fuchs, 2018; Lawrence et al., 2002) and, therefore, has also left the borders of German subsidiaries. As the textbook example, the MMFD today has more than 300 companies participating. Of these 300, the majority is Mexican and further includes numerous subsidiaries of MNCs from a variety of home countries such as—apart from Germany—the USA, France, Canada, Japan, South Korea etc. (DW, 2016; Wiemann & Fuchs, 2018). Following this line of thought, DVT and the corresponding added value are understood and, therefore, firmly present also in the cognitive frames of companies other than German. Furthermore, young people's acceptance of DVT as a solid educational choice and the relatively broad recognition of DVT's added value by other firms make DVT more than a mere institutional innovation. It has reasonably diffused throughout the corresponding institutional field and gained legitimacy in relation to the most important actors. Following this reasoning, one can reasonably assume DVT in Mexico has gained the status of a semi-institutional practice. In line with Kostova and Roth (2002), even though the history of DVT in Mexico is relatively brief (at least the one of DVT at a national level), it is already fairly diffused, the added value is understood, and therefore, it has gained a certain degree of legitimacy among the major decision-makers.

Approaching DVT from a more mechanical perspective may give further rise to DVT's future prospects. The various approaches of DVT in Mexico—in particular the MMFD—demonstrate that DVT can function in an environment in which originally supportive institutions are lacking. Through both compensation mechanisms of (German) companies and those of the government, the various DVT approaches demonstrate that coordinated DVT does not necessarily fail in an HME. In the situation given, the two major puzzles, which are the mist of uncertainty and the demand orientation of DVT, are dissolved to a reasonable degree.

Whether DVT in Mexico has attained the status of being fully institutionalized, though, is very questionable. In line with Wiemann and Fuchs's (2018) report of an as yet non-measurable impact of DVT on local labor markets or firms' competitiveness, today's scope of DVT seems to be limited. Following this line of thought, DVT is not yet taken for granted by members of Mexican society in general but rather by a minor share of it in various locations. DVT is still a local phenomenon rather than a

Mexico-wide one. DVT is present largely at the industrial hotspots that are characterized by a high density of higher technology and a strong presence of foreign—above all German—companies in the states of México, Puebla, Nuevo León, and Coahuila de Zaragoza (Wiemann & Fuchs, 2018). Therefore, one can reasonably argue that DVT is—at best—on the way to gaining general societal legitimacy. So far, it may best be described as legitimated in only some locations.

The limited geographic diffusion of DVT and the proximity to mostly international companies indicate an ongoing dependence on the leaders and "defenders of change" (Tolbert & Zucker, 1996). As the analysis of DVT in Mexico indicated, next to business actors, the government as defender of change needs particular attention. As the disruptive trajectory of DVT in Mexico has shown since the year 2013, governmental support was the *conditio* sine qua non to scale DVT up to the national level and, therefore, to semi-institutionalize it. On the other side of the coin, governmental withdrawal could result in a similarly disruptive, though negative trajectory (MexOrg1). The cooperative DVT initiative between Mercedes-Benz and the State of Mexico in the 1990s—considering its status as a proto-institution back then—and its sudden stop due to the withdrawal of one of the major drivers may serve as a warning example and are reminder of the potential fragility of such a promising initiative. Of course, the fact that the government is a pillar of a specific system is not negative per se. As Sect. 7.1.2 on the German DVT indicates, DVT in Germany is hardly imaginable without the support of the government. However, as the case study above discussed, the outstandingly positive and rapid development of DVT in Mexico took place under only one presidency of Nieto (Cáceres-Reebs & Schneider, 2020). Along these lines, various Mexican interviewees express their worries regarding the change of government in 2018 and the support of DVT. In particular, MexMNC2, who expresses his concerns as the "new government may have other initiatives" (translated by the author), shows that actors have a critical stance on governmental support. In fact, the government under Nieto was a major pillar compensating for lacking institutional support through, for example, the comprehensive scholarship system and governmental efforts allowed for a sufficient degree of tropicalization necessary to fit with the existing frames. Along these lines, a governmental withdrawal could put the entire development of DVT in Mexico—beyond German island solutions—at stake. As a first impression, though, the new presidency of Andrés Manuel López Obrador seems to further carry DVT in Mexico (MexOrg1). As such, indicating ongoing support, according to Mexican government information, the Mexican government under López Obrador renewed and strengthened cooperation with the German government and the AHKs to further push the MMFD in July 2019 (Gobierno del Estado de México, 2018). Supporting this, MexOrg1 reports the new government has already emphasized to shifting DVT in Mexico to systemic importance, scaling it up and reframing it from the rather piloting "Modelo" toward a "Sistema de Educación Dual." Along the same lines, the Mexican newspaper "Milenio" taking stock of the new president's first year in office, a major positive point is "continuidad y fomento al Modelo Mexicano de Formación Dual"[32] (De La Rosa, 2019).

The identified high degree heterogeneity of DVT in Mexico (according to MexOrg1, there are 19 different DVT initiatives in Mexico) and the ongoing dependence on both corporate actors and the Mexican government and the corresponding instability of the system indicate that DVT in Mexico lacks strong self-activating mechanisms that are required for a practice to reproduce itself, becoming stable over time and resisting contestations. On that account, DVT—at the time of writing—has not reached the status of being fully institutionalized. Considering the findings above, future prospects of German DVT in Mexico and the further process of institutionalization face various obstacles. In order to make the system more stable, less dependence on single actors is necessary. To attain a sufficient degree of independence and to equip DVT with self-enforcing dynamics and the capability of reproduction, institutional dimensions need to be complementary. Without reintroducing all aspects of institutional complementarity in CMEs that allow DVT, the investigation above suggests some points for potential improvement in HMEs more than others.

In fact, German subsidiaries in Mexico have managed to overcome the mist of uncertainty by relying on, for example, reputational advantages of the company and the characteristic as being perceived as a potential bridge to Germany and the European Union. Beyond doubt, this reputational advantage cannot be transmitted to and used by, for example, Mexican companies. Hence, on a broader level, the mist of uncertainty may only be dissolved by a coherent and more coordinated complementary institutional system that allows commitment to long-term cooperation and, here, to invest in firm- or sector-specific skills. Accordingly, it is necessary that azubis and future workers leave their rather weak position (Rutherford & Holmes, 2014) inasmuch as being safeguarded by, for example, a higher degree of co-determination that enables workers to secure their fair share of corporate profits. Along the same lines, a further example on potential institutional improvement, the low influence companies have on the content and design of DVT's curriculum may depict a large problem in the longer term. By now, the system relies largely on German guidelines indicated by, among others, the CAMEXA. In the longer term, to put Mexico's DVT on a solid basis, inter-firm deliberation and inclusion in decision-making need to be fostered. Consideration of local business information can be a major driver for the creation of a DVT program that fits well with the specific Mexican demand on skills.

The investigation and discussion on DVT in Mexico can, indeed, be regarded also as a stand-alone investigation. However, the categories and the variety of aspects of interest developed throughout the fields of interest serve as reference when scrutinizing the Brazilian case in the next chapter.

[32] Translated: "continuity and promotion of the Mexican Model of Dual Training."

7.5 DVT in Brazil

Following the logic of the Mexican study, this chapter scrutinizes DVT in Brazil relating to the general functioning of DVT practices in an HME and puts major focus on the subsidiary as an agent of institutional change through institutional entrepreneurism and reversed isomorphism. In order to benefit from the comparative analysis of DVT efforts in the two countries of interest, this chapter frequently compares with and discusses findings in Brazil alongside those from the Mexican study.

As a very first comparison, beyond the characteristics and the corresponding problems of an HME that characterized both Brazil and Mexico, important for potential institutional change, just like in Mexico, the number of German companies in Brazil is around 1500 of which a large part is located in the larger area of São Paulo (around 900), Santa Catarina, or Rio Grande do Sul (iMove., 2012). As such, the density of German subsidiaries—that can be key to actor-induced institutional change—is roughly comparable to that, for example, in Puebla or Jalisco, Mexico.

7.5.1 An Outline of DVT in Brazil

The beginning of VET that combines theory and practice in Brazil dates back to the year 1942 with the establishment of the SENAI, ever since oriented toward the German professional education system (DVT). In fact, as one of the very few VET systems outside Germany, it is mandatory that at least ten percent of VET's duration must take place in a company, conducting practical work in the course of an internship (Krzywdzinski & Jürgens, 2019; Weinstein, 1997). Securing firms' collaboration—relating to the short but mandatory practical phase of SENAI's VET—Brazil's Apprentice Law (*Lei do Aprendiz*) requires companies to cope with the *cota de aprendizagem*, which requires firms to have—regarding total work force—at least five to fifteen percent apprentices (nube, 2020; Presidência da República, 2000). Beyond that, the introduction of "real" German DVT in Brazil shows various parallels to the one in Mexico, though more regarding the role of the German subsidiaries and less in the proliferation across the country.

Also, in Brazil, among others, it was companies like Volkswagen and Bosch that as far back as the 1960s set up DVT programs for training azubis, for example, in mechatronics engineering according to the German model (Bosch, 2018a, b). In terms of acceptance, DVT according to the German model has been recognized by Brazilian legislation as an option in the upper secondary level in the subsequent modality since 1996 (Kauer, 2015). Despite—at first sight—quite similar conditions regarding business actors and legal status, the strong phase of acceleration and cross-level movement of DVT that characterizes the Mexican case cannot be found in Brazil. On the contrary, some figures may even suggest a declining proliferation of DVT since the "heydays" of German-like professional education in Brazil in the late

1990s and early 2000s (BraOrg2). Consequently, the shift of DVT up to the national level has not yet occurred and, according to various interview partners, is not expected to happen in the foreseeable future. On that account, in Brazil there is no comparable large-scale and nation-wide DVT program like the MMFD in Mexico. Nevertheless, various DVT initiatives exist in Brazil. For example, one of the oldest approaches with the widest coverage may be the one that was established in 1982 as *Formação Profissional Dual* as a joint effort between firms, the AHK, and the Colégio Humboldt[33] in the area of São Paulo (Colégio Humboldt, 2020). Regarding the partners, the AHK Brazil is equipped with a similar mandate to the CAMEXA, which is, among others, to provide the rightly skilled workforce for German companies abroad (VETNet, n.d.) by controlling and securing German education standards through coordination, training, and examination. The Colégio Humboldt is one of ten professional German schools abroad (worldwide) and depicts the educational counterpart to the firms that train azubis in practice. This initiative provides DVT courses in business administration such as industrial management and logistics. The Humboldt approach strictly follows the German model and is "100 percent comparable with the German professional school [in Germany]" (BraOrg2, translated by the author). On that account, through comprehensive AHK certification of the entire DVT program including curricula, teachers, training companies, and the professional school, more than 1750 graduates of the "Humboldt approach" up to now have been awarded with double degrees, including both the Brazilian *técnico* (from 1996) and the German *Gesellenbrief* (BraOrg1).

In line with the potential stagnation of Brazil's DVT, the trajectory of this approach is rather frustrating. In terms of numbers, within the entire span of operations, a total of more than 100 companies have participated (iMove, 2012; Kauer, 2015).[34] Of these 100, nine companies remain in the program today, of which all are German (BraOrg1). Affirming this, BraOrg2 recalls that for the Humboldt approach "the 1990s were fairly fat years, the beginning of the 90s and the early 2000s were the best years" (BraOrg2, translated by the author). In terms of numbers,

[33] Formerly IFPA (Instituto de Formação Profissional Administrativa), it is the largest German vocational school outside of German borders (iMove, 2012).

[34] IMove (2012, p. 32) lists more companies that participate in the Humboldt approach: "Allianz Seguros SA Copagaz Ltda, HDI Seguros SA, AHK São Paulo, Mercedes-Benz Corretora, Heidelberg do Brasil, Aliança Navegação Mercedes-Benz do Brasil, Hellmann Logistics, B. Grob do Brasil, DHL, Henkel Ltda, BASF, Elotrans, Hosp.Oswaldo Cruz, Bayer Epcos (Icotron), Horst Bremer, BodyCote Brasimet SA, Ferrostaal—IPP, Intergráfica, BSH Continental, Figwal, JAS Forwarding, Clariant, Fresenius, Jost Brasil, Coop.Agraria—Entre Rios, Giroflex S.A., Kuehne + Nagel Ltda, Coop.—Neuland, Hamburg-Süd/Aliança, Keiper do Brasil, KS Pistões Ltda, Real Seguros, Siemens VDO, Lanxess, Rehau, Stihl Moto Serras, Lear do Brasil Ltda, Rödl & Partner Ltda, Symrise, Lufthansa Cargo, Saargummi, ThyssenKrupp Metal, Logimasters-Dachser, Schaeffler Brasil Ltda, T-Systems do Brasil Ltda, Mahle—Metal Leve, Schenker do Brasil Ltda, Volkswagen do Brasil, Marítima Seguros, Schering do Brasil, Volkswagen Transports, Mitsui Brasileira, Schwing Equip. Ind. Ltda, Wabco Freios, Dr. Oetker, Senator International Ltda, ZF do Brasil, Panalpina, Siemens, ZF—Sachs and Zürich Seguros."

BraOrg2 indicates that today the entire approach produces around 30 graduates per year.

Before introducing the second larger scale DVT program, the Volkswagen case is depicted briefly. It serves as the foundation for further developments and proliferation. Volkswagen implemented the DVT program with the local SENAI (Krzywdzinski & Jürgens, 2019). In fact, Volkswagen's factory in Anchieta (São Bernardo do Campo) comes with its own SENAI professional school. Here, Volkswagen and the SENAI work together closely to align educational content and corporate requirements. This initiative combines a normal SENAI course as introduced in Sect. 7.1.1 and practical work in the Volkswagen company. Generally, due to the proximity of SENAI and Volkswagen, azubis go to school in the morning and to the company in the afternoon. Due to Brazilian legislation that prohibits minors from working in production areas, the first phase of practical courses takes place at either SENAI workshops or simulated workshops (e.g., Bosch has such simulation). After having turned 18, practical parts of the DVT are located within the company at the manufacturing areas (BraOrg1; Krzywdzinski & Jürgens, 2019).

Out of this DVT project, a larger scale inter-actor initiative to implement German DVT in Brazil has occurred. According to BraOrg1, the AHK together with the aforementioned collaborating actors, Volkswagen and SENAI, has developed a new project and broadened the DVT landscape in Brazil by introducing a 3-year AHK-certified DVT course in mechatronics, entirely conducted in Portuguese. Except for linguistic adjustment, according to the AHK São Paulo, the DVT is subject to the same requirement as it is in Germany (dos Santos Mayer, 2016) and graduates receive a German *Gesellenbrief*.

Since most azubis start this course aged 16, certain adjustments were made. In order to deal with Brazilian youth protection legislation introduced above, this technical DVT program is fairly "tropicalized" and separates theory and practice parts in two long-term phases. The first 2 years of the program are SENAI based with a few practical phases in SENAI workshops. During this first phase, azubis focus on theoretical foundation for future work and gain the degree of the Brazilian *tecnico*. It is the third year, having turned 18, in which the azubis move on to work in the training company. Being in the de facto third year of DVT, azubis are already employed as permanent "normal" employees remunerated with a normal salary. Nonetheless, in this third year, azubis rotate within the company and prepare themselves for the final AHK examination at the end of year three (BraMNC2). In terms of practice diffusion, the Volkswagen-SENAI cooperation opened doors and let in other companies to participate in the DVT program. Among others, companies such as Kostal, ZF, Grob, Mahle, and ThyssenKrupp have taken part within the past decade. Interestingly, similar to the pre-MMFD delegation that learned DVT in Germany firsthand, the Brazilian AHK sent a similar delegation with people from firms and the educational institutions to Germany to learn from locals, in particular at the largest worldwide fair for professional education, the "Didacta" in 2018 (VETNet, n.d.; Viehmann, 2017). Nonetheless, development of this program may best be characterized by relative stagnation. On the one hand, indeed, major companies such as Bosch[35] and Stihl joined the program (dos Santos Mayer, 2016). On the other hand, though, BarOrg1 indicates various companies that left the program due to relatively high costs, internal problems, and a general lack of acceptance. These reasons will be further elaborated on in the remainder of this chapter. Of specific interest, shedding light on the limited coverage of this initiative, the company ZF quit collaboration because of a relocation of its Brazilian subsidiary (BraOrg1). The new location was too distant from the SENAI of Volkswagen, which up to now remains one of the very few education providers for this DVT initiative.

In addition to the large-scale multi-actor DVT initiatives, just like in Mexico, various German subsidiaries have established their own DVT initiatives. In total, these clearly outnumber the initiatives introduced above, though each one is limited to its own corporate borders and is without AHK certification of German standards and, thus, without the *Gesellenbrief* after completing DVT. As an example, the company Voith works together with the Brazilian training institutions conducting training based on the German model "...intended to secure for the company a steady supply of skilled workers in industrial and commercial occupations" (Voith, 2019a). As a large representative of such DVT programs (though not all in a conventional DVT form), up to today, Voith has educated more than 2300 skilled workers locally in Brazil. Another example is Bosch who, as mentioned above, also participates in the Volkswagen-SENAI approach, though they also conduct a 2-year DVT program without the AHK and have their own SENAI school on company grounds with which they conduct DVT (BraOrg1). In a 2-year course, azubis go to the SENAI in the morning and to Bosch in the afternoon. Bosch also managed to align the idea of DVT for people under 18 with the Brazilian youth protection legislation. Bosch-SENAI DVT allows its azubis to gain practical experience even when they are still under 18, though fully complying with legal requirement through the establishment of a "simulated production" that only serves for the purposes and aim of learning and does not really produce for corporate purposes. Furthermore, similar to the Mexican case, German "educational companies" such as Festo Didactics are present and offer a similar range of courses as they do in Mexico (iMove, 2012).

As an interim conclusion, the German companies in Brazil show relatively similar efforts to those analyzed in the Mexican case. Strongly affirming quantitative findings of alien-to-the-system educational practices in Brazil, they commit themselves to German DVT through various venues either alone or in joint efforts with other companies and both German and Brazilian educational bodies. However, as indicated, the trajectory of DVT in Brazilian does not take the same course it took in Mexico. Strikingly, comparing the DVT initiatives in Brazil with the ones in Mexico according to the constitutive actors, it is apparent that the Brazilian government is not taking a comparable role in the development of DVT as its Mexican counterpart does. To better understand the role of German companies in Brazil, the impact their actions have vertically and horizontally on the surrounding institutional setting and,

[35] Bosch's DVT that has existed since the 1960s has been officially certified by the AHK since the mid-2010s.

thus, also the differences from the Mexican case are investigated in the upcoming sections.

7.5.2 Functioning of DVT in Brazil's HME

The underlying question is how—if at all—such an archetypal CME practice as the DVT can work in an HME. The Mexican reference case indicated—in line with the finding of complementarity of subsidiary action in Chap. 6—that it is often the companies themselves that activate CME-like practices also in the complementary institutional dimensions to compensate for local institutional weakness (for this specific action). This section investigates the categories and concepts developed throughout the Mexican case and compares the two cases. The final objectives are, first, to better understand and recognize behavioral patterns of German subsidiaries that conduct DVT in Brazil and, second, to detect major differences that may contribute to the explanation for the fairly different trajectories of DVT in Mexico and Brazil.

The vast majority of DVT initiatives in Brazil are constituted by the "usual" major pillars, which are the firm responsible for practical training and an educational institution responsible for teaching generic theoretical aspects, and sometimes the AHK as quality safeguard (some of the DVT initiatives also conduct the theoretical phase within the company). The rotation between the two first mentioned is subject to a Brazilian "tropicalization." As an example, azubis of the Volkswagen approach rotate once per day, having school in the morning and going to work in the afternoon (Krzywdzinski & Jürgens, 2019). At the other extreme, rotation takes place once in 3 months. BraOrg1 reports of the massive traffic problems they face in São Paulo and the corresponding impossibility for more frequent changes of working and learning spaces. Accordingly, azubis go to work for 2 months and then to school for 1 month. According to the experience of BraOrg1, this long-term alternation makes life difficult for managers since they frequently mourn that "as soon as they [azubis] understood a bit about the work, they go away to school" (BraOrg1, translated by the author). Furthermore, she emphasizes that this procedure can lead to internal conflicts with, for example, university students that are interning at the company full-time while studying full-time. They do not understand why the azubis have an entirely free month to learn and they do not.

Regarding the cost side of the DVT initiatives, both island solutions and joint efforts are relatively expensive for Brazilian realities. The two major joint efforts that are the Humboldt and the Volkswagen approach differ mostly in relation to the educational institution they are working with. The Colégio Humboldt is entirely private, slightly supported from the German government (posted teachers from Germany are paid), and not part of the Sistema S. According to BraOrg2, a company has to pay tuitions fees of about 72,000 BRL (Brazilian real) for the 2 years (around 600 EUR per month) if they send an azubi to conduct a DVT program with the Colégio Humboldt. In contrast with the minimum wage in Brazil of around 250 EUR per month, the tuition fee is very high. All interviewees state unanimously that such a high tuition fee is especially problematic when an alternative exists that provides employees who have already graduated from the Sistema S or universities to be recruited for free, independent of the quality of education and the fit with corporate demand. This is especially true as all companies do already pay an obligatory fee for the Sistema S (see above Sect. 7.1). In fact, a company that conducts DVT with the Colégio Humboldt pays twice the obligatory Sistema S and the Humboldt approach. In addition, all other expenses for the working space and the azubi itself are funded by the company.

If a firm conducts DVT within the context of the Volkswagen approach that works together with the SENAI, the first 2 years of schooling are paid through the national funds of the SENAI. Accordingly, the company is required only to pay the additional year, necessary corporate infrastructure, salaries, and examination fees of the AHK. Of specific interest, the issue of salaries is subject to Brazilian tropicalization, too. First, as a major difference to the Mexican case—in which the Mexican government introduced a large scholarship initiative for DVT azubis—in which azubis mostly receive—if at all—only a monetary compensation for food and transport from the training company, in Brazil azubis must be paid at least the national minimum wage (Chankseliani & Anuar, 2019). Additionally, the Volkswagen-SENAI approach needs further embedding within the existing educational system to cope with legal requirements. After graduating from and finishing the 2-year SENAI course, people in Brazil can no longer be considered as apprentices. On that account, in the third year of the Volkswagen DVT approach that takes place after the two-year SENAI, azubis need to be permanently employed and are paid just like any other full-time employee (BraOrg1). Consequently, tropicalization of DVT leads to lower costs through the inclusion of SENAI. Nonetheless, the higher costs through, among others, the fully paid third year seem to make the Volkswagen approach less convincing for firms, above all in an environment characterized by education for free. As an example, BraMNC2 reports of one of the major German subsidiaries in Brazil that participates in the Volkswagen approach but that, due to cost reasons, allows only one out of four apprentices (usually the one with the highest performance) to finalize the AHK-certified DVT program over the entire period of 3 years.

> We don't have every student in the course of the AHK, because there is a cost for doing this additional testing and so on, so we have a prioritization of the best students and we use them for the tests (BraMNC2).

All other apprentices stop DVT/VET after the second year, graduating from SENAI with a regular Brazilian degree *tecnico*. Companies that collaborate independently with the Sistema S face similar challenges. All other DVT initiatives that are conducted entirely within the corporate borders are paid entirely by the respective firm.

As the Mexican case shows, the value added by DVT should be clear to those who decide about whether or not to conduct DVT. The decision regarding investing lots of money in people that pays off—if at all—in the long-term requires experience, conviction, and, above all, "patient capital." Of course, there are the traditional DVT players such as Bosch, Volkswagen, and Voith that have conducted DVT ever since and that hardly question this practice. However, there is a consensus among all interviewees that the vast majority of companies in Brazil take a more critical stance. In particular the two organizations that are interviewed report the sheer impossibility of convincing Brazilian actors that do not have any affinity or experience with the German system. BraOrg1 refers to the situation of Brazilians that get in touch with DVT as a "culture shock" due to the higher costs, alternating practice-theory system,[36] and to the general sentiment of apprenticeships as being inferior *vis-à-vis* university education. Further widening the gap between Brazilians and the German DVT, the existing Sistema S is paid by all companies anyway. Hence, companies in Brazil are already obligated to pay for a VET program that is not the DVT with AHK certification. Accordingly, the existence of a well-known alternative one has already paid for certainly hampers enthusiasm when facing high costs for an unknown education if the known one is for free. Confirming this, BraOrg1 reports of experiences with potential participants of the DVT programs: "...why should I participate in this program, if get people from SENAI with a 2-year VET and I have to pay absolutely nothing additional" (BraOrg1, translated by the author). In addition, when referring to employing people who have already graduated, university graduates—that are generally perceived as "superior" by Brazilian society—*vis-à-vis* the known VET programs (more on this issue later on)—are abundantly available on the labor market at very low costs. BraOrg1 clearly makes the point as follows and states that even:

> the ones responsible also in German companies are Brazilians and they do not at all understand the [DVT] program and they see no sense to participating in the program. Even though the people are very well educated, awarded with three different degrees, fluent in three foreign languages that are German, English, and Spanish (BraOrg1, translated by the author).

Accordingly, one may argue that the decision in favor of DVT within the environment described above can only be made if the value added by DVT justifies additional efforts and costs. Following this line of argumentation, just like the Mexican case already indicated, this added value needs to be understood. Clearly emphasizing the importance of people that know the DVT system and recognize its value as the backbone of DVT in Brazil:

> ...if we didn't have such people, that know the system well, DVT [in Brazil] would collapse...you need either Germans or German companies. Otherwise, at many locations, it is really difficult to implement DVT (BraOrg2, translated by the author).

In line, BraOrg2 explains the strong impetus of the 1990s as a "gold-rush atmosphere in Brazil with lots of German expats that understood the system" (BraOrg2, translated by the author). Strengthening the argument of familiarity with

[36] According to BraOrg1, Brazilian employers cannot understand the idea of not having their own employees entirely within the company. Especially in the case of theory phases of 1 month, absence from the shop-floor is met with strong opposition.

DVT, BraOrg1 reports that all companies that participate within the joint DVT efforts are German companies. All in all, the unfamiliarity with DVT, the existence of (gratuitous) alternatives, and the high costs are all factors that weigh heavily in Brazil and heavier than in Mexico. In the course of the Brazilian interviews, some aspects turned out to strongly exacerbate the given situation that deters management from investing in DVT. Most prominently, these are the "exodus of expatriates" (Johanson, 2016) and the general and persisting crisis situation of the Brazilian economy, where certainly the former depends on the latter.

Expatriates as delegates from Germany are deeply embedded in the home country and firm with the corresponding DVT approach, carrying it within their practice portfolio and knowing about the added value. Analogous to the strong impetus in DVT in the 1990s that originated from German expatriates, the absence of such "experienced driver" has negative consequences. BraOrg1 reports changes in corporate decision-making positions as follows:

> In the course of the past five or eight years something happened. In earlier times lots of German people were responsible for the human resource management [in the German companies]. They knew about the system; how good the program is and that in any case it pays off to participate. But today, due to the crisis, in most German companies that are here in Brazil, the people that are responsible for it are Brazilians and do not understand the program at all and see no reason to be part of the program (BraOrg1, translated by the author).

The assumed declining number of expatriates is backed by official statistics and is labeled as a "mass expat exodus from Brazil" (Johanson, 2016). Foreign managers that entered Brazil with high hopes are today rather crisis-torn and leave the country due to a quite negative economic outlook or have to leave according to their parent company. Comparing the heydays of DVT with the year 2016, there has been a decrease of expatriates in large companies of more than 40 percent. Another supporting figure, the international headhunting firm, Boyden, in São Paulo reports that applications from global executives for jobs in Brazil have decreased to almost zero (Johanson, 2016). According to data from the Brazilian Ministry of Labor, in 2016 the demand for foreign worker permits has decreased by more than 60 percent.

As this trajectory of expatriates shows, the presence of expatriates highly depends on the well-being of the political economy. Brazil was a textbook example for a thriving (developing) economy and a prominent constituent of the BRIC countries, but spent years with political instabilities, a weak currency, high inflation rates, increased unemployment, and, generally, a significant economic recession. BraOrg2 set out the case of two car producers that are facing problems that were not to be expected a decade ago. As an example, he introduces the case of a German car producer that has established a new plant and, up to now, has not recorded figures in the black since. He further introduces the case of Ford that, indeed, partly left Brazil for good due to economic issues. In particular, the second case in which the plant closed, he describes as a "major shock for the Brazilian economy that someone leaves the Brazilian market. This actually is a declaration of bankruptcy" (BraOrg2, translated by the author). Accordingly, BraOrg1 and BraOrg2 unanimously state that many companies have entirely different and entirely existential problems to a potential introduction of DVT. As a consequence of the relatively constant economic downturn, in addition to the withdrawal of expensive (high-wage) expatriates, companies need to save money. In the direct context of DVT, this leads either to companies that do not join (alleged costly) DVT efforts or companies that already conduct DVT to decrease efforts or entirely quit DVT initiatives. BraOrg1 also knows of various German companies that hold back with investments and participation in DVT because of the ongoing crisis. Further, she reports of an example that hit the DVT efforts hard: one large founding company and a pillar of one of the major DVT programs introduced above has left the program for good due to economic problems.

As a preliminary summary, the dimension of finance and corporate decision-making in Brazil is strongly affected by both the large-scale withdrawal of expatriates that know the value of German DVT and the general economic downturns and need for cutting costs. Recognizing a decisive dynamic for DVT relating to this simultaneous (and dependent) process, one can reasonably argue that if the value of DVT is not clear to the managers in charge (not an expatriate), DVT may be one of the first corporate parts where one can cut costs. Following this logic, the withdrawal of expatriates and the general need for cutting costs mutually reinforce each other, culminating in rather "impatient capital" and DVT efforts coming under severe pressure.

Not to be misunderstood, the previous section on costs, expatriates, and crisis does by no means indicate that DVT in Brazil is dissolving or disappearing. It rather contributes to explanations of stagnation and the different trajectory to DVT in Mexico. However, in line with the quantitative findings of Chap. 6 and the DVT outline of initiatives introduced above, DVT does also exist in Brazil. As will be shown below, in contrast to the institutional dimension of finance and corporate decision-making, the other dimensions are more equal to those in Mexico. Here, also major issues circulate around the concepts of demand-led education and uncertainty of both employees and employers.

Just like the German subsidiaries in Mexico, those in Brazil have various but limited avenues for making their voice and specific skill demand heard. In general, BraMNC2 makes the case for DVT as a general means to making supply match demand. Emphasizing the alternating principle of DVT, he emphasizes:

> ... inside our house we can train them as we need, obviously following the course, following the topics that they must cover. But we can do this align to our strategy. (BraMNC2).

Digging deeper into content and design of the DVT, according to BraOrg1 and BraOrg2, both multi-actor DVT approaches introduced above follow the German "*Rahmenausbildungsplan*" (and also the SENAI curriculum partly in the first 2 years of the Volkswagen approach) according to German law. Accordingly, the impact of Brazilian subsidiaries on DVT content and design is mainly out of scope. Nonetheless, the congruence identified between companies in Germany and German subsidiaries in Brazil regarding the skills required ensures that supply of DVT meets the demand of companies. Underscoring the similarity of the subsidiaries to the major plants in Germany and, thus, distancing them from mere maquiladora companies,

BraOrg1 emphasizes the nature of most of the subsidiaries as fully-fledged companies with all value-adding steps, including research and development having thousands of employees. Confirming this, BraMNC2 states that the German benchmark fits their corporate realities well. Viehmann (2017) reports that the tight coupling with the German "*Rahmenausbildungsplan*" is much appreciated, since it comes with an increase in quality and an adjustment to the latest German content. Along the same lines, the head of Bosch's technical school in Brazil affirms that it is the state-of-the-art knowledge from Germany in particular that directly finds its way into Brazilian education. Nonetheless, to a smaller degree, for example, regarding the procedure of both the practical and theoretical phase, all interviewees report several feedback channels back to the educational institution and the AHK. BraOrg1 emphasizes the importance of informal feedback when the different actors come together, for example, in the examination board. In the same vein, BraMNC3 perceives informal feedback throughout meetings and discussions as the usual venue for exchanging best practices. Similarly, BraOrg2 reports of frequent company visits with extensive feedback and counseling conversations. An association-like aggregation of voices in the context of DVT exists but—in line with the situation described above—has virtually come to a complete halt. Regarding the SENAI-Volkswagen approach, there exists an association with its own committee on VET. BraMNC2 explains the functioning of the committee, which is composed of representatives from the participating company and is mostly occupied with the conduct of the examination and the evaluation of the azubis. Along the same lines, BraOrg1 states that one of the major goals of the committee is to incorporate the German subsidiaries because of their experience and knowledge. The same holds for the Humboldt approach that established a "Committee for DVT" in which the different actors can meet and discuss questions and potential problems (BraOrg2). However, both interviewees further report that due to a lack of demand, these channels came to a halt.

Companies such as Bosch and Volkswagen that have—beyond the AHK-certified course—a close partnership with the SENAI are subject to the SENAI planning, certainly. However, as the SENAI degree does not evaluate (include) the practical phases, the content and design of such is more or less left to the company. On that account, companies in cooperation with SENAI have more leeway in organizing the practical phase according to the firm's preferences. Using this leeway, for example, Bosch—as mentioned above—has established its own simulation of a real shop-floor in which specific Bosch-related tasks can be learned and conducted when under the age of 18 as well (BraOrg1). Indicating certain leeway, BraMNC2 reports of an ongoing process to improve DVT in the company. He reports of frequent meetings that include the top management in which they:

> define which are our main targets for the technical school; we define the main focus of the technical school at the beginning of the year. And then during the year I believe every three months he [vice president] comes and we have this overview about what is happening. (BraMNC2).

Retaining the people after graduation is a major objective of the BraMNC2. To do so, i.e., in order to match supply with corporate demands as best as possible, BraMNC2 further reports of the relatively wide leeway in cooperation with the SENAI that allows a detailed long-term planning to be conducted by connecting the different departments, azubis, and the educational instructors:

> So, for example, today, I already know where the students from the next year, so in which area each of the students of the next year will go. And I have already discussed it with the managers of the areas. So, we already have this vision for the next year. So what I am trying to do is that if I don't have a spot as a technician, some of these students can become for example... we try to put them now as an intern in another area, if they agree. So, we try to find opportunities and we try to diversify where to put them (BraMNC2).

Other island solutions that are detached from official educational systems and conducted mostly in-house, certainly, are freely designed and composed by the operating company.

Regarding the often cited "mist of uncertainty," just like in Mexico, Brazilian subsidiaries have somehow to convince people to, first, invest heavily in a relatively specific education and, second, to stay within the company in the long term. In the same vein, relating to the latter, companies that invest heavily in the education of their employees somehow need the security that their investments pay off and are not poached by other companies. According to BraOrg2, the largest problem in incorporating more companies in DVT is to convince the company that the graduates stay at the company after DVT. Along the same lines, BraOrg1 reports from Brazilian reality where lots of companies express their attitude toward DVT and poaching in Brazil as follows:

> If I invest such a huge amount of money and there is such a lot of competition in the branch, then someone will poach the azubis that I educated over three years, what can I do? (BraOrg1, translated by the author).

BraMNC1 reports of very high personnel fluctuation and emphasizes the typical ease for HME of quitting employment for both the employer and the employee, the conducive legislation for hiring and firing, and the attitude to follow maximum reimbursement.

> As soon as I find another job, where I earn a bit more, one changes jobs. Salary plays a significant role. Normal salaries are relatively low. Rapidly I change because of the salary (BraMNC1, translated by the author).

Being located in an HME that is characterized by low (or absent) employment and unemployment protection, fluid labor markets, and mostly individual wage agreements, companies can decrease their uncertainty and that of the employees by establishing the foundation for long-term cooperation. As the Mexican case shows, a sound combination of career prospects, fair reimbursement, and a desirable future generally can compensate the unfitting institutional surrounding.

Surprisingly, just like in the Mexican case, the firms conducting DVT do not counter the problem of poaching by paying ever higher wages. All of the interviewees indicate that German subsidiaries pay according to the market, which is higher than the minimum wage, though to be found within the "normal" range.

Hence, a young person may not decide in favor of DVT because of wage differentials. BraOrg2 emphasizes the responsibility of each firm to offer a sound perspective, also beyond monetary issues by stating that "the firms, if they want to keep them [DVT graduates], they really have to show them a perspective. According to my experience, they make surpassing careers" (BraOrg2, translated by the author). Affirmatively, BraOrg1 explains the position of the companies as follows:

> they [firms] need to be attractive. For most of the companies that is not a problem. Most of the companies that participate are really good. They offer various programs to its employees, so that employees do not want to change in the first place (translated by the author).

In so doing, strategies applied are similar to those of German subsidiaries in Mexico and mostly built on high retention rates, good reputation of the company, career prospects, and the bridge function to Germany and the entire European Union (in which the German degree is fully acknowledged).

Regarding the Humboldt approach, BraOrg2 reports of a retention rate of more than 75 percent and emphasizes the outstanding character of such numbers, especially in times of economic crisis. One step further, BraOrg1, shedding light on the Volkswagen approach adds that "they [graduates] do directly and immediately get full employment, because they are already employees in the third year" (translated by the author). Such a promise is relatively close to the contractually fixed job guarantee indicated by MexMNC3 in the Mexican case. BraMNC2 reports of a retention rate within his company for DVT graduates of 82 percent and adds that those who are not employed find a job somewhere else because of their very good educational background. These findings are further supported by the significantly lower staff turnover of subsidiaries with parent companies from Germany *vis-à-vis*, for example, staff turnover in subsidiaries with US-American origins, as found in the quantitative analysis. Of course, in today's Brazil even more than in Mexico, with an ongoing economic downturn and corresponding high rates of (youth) unemployment, such a "guaranteed "employment increases calculability, secures income flows, and offers "secure" career prospects that are unique in the Brazilian educational spectrum.

Reputation as a means of attraction, compensating for weak institutions, works in Brazil as well, though in a manner that is a bit more diffuse. In Brazil, reputation needs to be approached from two sides: that of the companies and that of DVT. Regarding the company side, just like in Mexico German subsidiaries have a very good reputation which, indeed, serves as a major factor of attraction. BraOrg1 states "almost everybody would like to work at a German company. It is very attractive" (BraOrg1, translated by the author). As an important element of reputation, companies in general and all interviewees emphasize the bridging function of German subsidiaries to Germany and the European Union. BraOrg2 highlights the DVT—where azubis graduate with both a German *Gesellenbrief* and a German advanced technical college certificate—as a way to work and study in Germany (Voith, 2019b). Along the same lines, BraOrg1 emphasizes the career opportunities azubis face and refers to various DVT alumni that now have leading positions in German companies in both the local subsidiaries and in the HQ in Germany. In the same vein, already within the course of the DVT, BraOrg1 refers to business trips to Germany of various Brazilian azubis. Approaching the issue of reputation from the DVT side, though, things are less positive in Brazil. Generally, BraMNC3 reports that "the people have lots of respect of what has been developed in Germany and these things are taken frequently as benchmark" (translated by the author) and thereby indicates a reputational advantage based on the country of origin. However, in terms of reputation, DVT itself faces a difficult situation and is, indeed, afflicted with some reputational disadvantages. In Brazil—just like most people in Mexico—people are not familiar with DVT according to the German model and, therefore, only distinguish between the categories of university education and VET. This, however, is more problematic in Brazil than in Mexico. Since DVT is to be found at the upper secondary level and is conducted within the Sistema S, people do not differentiate between VET and DVT. This low degree of distinction and the perception of DVT as a form of VET comes with severe problems (Dornbach, 2016). As Kauer puts it, in Brazil, "VET at secondary level in Brazil serves an underprivileged class of society who cannot afford private universities and are not intellectually prepared to pass an entrance examination at a public university" (Kauer, 2015, p. 250). This disadvantageous perception of DVT (actually VET in general) is unanimously backed by all interviewees. Summarizing the general problematic, BraOrg1 reports that:

> they just have to go to university. There is absolutely no culture of vocational training. This is important to say. Such culture does not exist here. Everybody wants to go to university. That's why we have a cultural problem (BraOrg1, translated by the author).

BraOrg2 affirms that DVT is largely perceived as inferior *vis-à-vis* university education. Nonetheless, he also emphasizes that over the years, especially in the area of São Paulo, good work and especially the high-quality graduates have slightly improved the reputation of DVT. Similarly, BraMNC3 states that ever since DVT graduates have received an internationally renowned German degree, the reputation is slightly improving. Certainly, this argument is closely connected to the bridge-functioning discussed above.

In this context, various scholars (Dornbach, 2016; Kauer, 2015) and also the interviewees discuss Brazilian governmental efforts counterintuitively as rather undermining DVT (VET) efforts. In contrast to Mexico, where the government integrated DVT (VET) in the educational system as a means to improve productivity and to decrease unemployment, Brazil has up to now promoted VET more or less exclusively as a means to "protect the orphans and the socioeconomically underprivileged" (Ministério da Educação, 2018). That has severely created a firm and disadvantageous picture of DVT, which makes all those who are neither orphans nor socioeconomically underprivileged (essentially those that do not want to be categorized as such) want to select university as their educational path of choice.

Briefly summarizing, in general, one may state that reputation in Brazil works in two directions and may, therefore, be less supportive for DVT in Brazil than in Mexico.

Finally, companies in Brazil that conduct DVT do mostly offer various additional benefits *vis-à-vis* the average Brazilian company. For example, BraMNC1 mentions some avenues through which attractiveness can be increased and introduces, among others, the opportunity of various provisions such as health insurance, pension schemes, and life assurances.

Regarding co-determination—the representation of workers in decision-making bodies that are internal to the company—and the corresponding possibility of representing interests in terms of monetary distribution, the picture in Brazil is very similar to the one in Mexico. Some of the companies indicate having a works council (or a similar body) in effect, though, according to BraMNC1, this is a "tropicalized" form of such. However, at the end of the day, there is a consensus that workers are not included into final decision-making and—if at all—are mostly involved in management boards insofar as information from the shop-floor is required (BraMNC2).

In summary, just like the companies investigated in Mexico, those in Brazil also conduct DVT. They cope with the disadvantageous institutional setting and compensate for major local weaknesses in all complementary dimensions, thereby affirming findings of complementarity in Chap. 6. In the status quo, companies and azubis manage to mutually promise a sufficient degree of certainty that allows both parties to engage in long-term cooperation. Nonetheless, as an interim conclusion, one can reasonably state that there are major differences within Brazil in comparison to Mexico. First, tropicalization to Brazilian realities severely complicates the conduct of DVT. Adjustments such as long-term alternations between theory and practice and the division of 2 years at school and 1 year at the company are met with resistance. Second, one may recognize that the practice portfolio, at the end of the day, is carried by people and less by organizational hierarchies themselves. Hence, the discussed "mass exodus of expats" as a response to the Brazilian economic crisis makes the German subsidiaries less German inasmuch as the decision-makers within are no longer German and, therefore, unfamiliar with DVT. That again, especially in combination with an ongoing crisis, makes money "less patient" when it comes to educational issues, especially if the value added by DVT is not recognized. Third, also reinforcing the issue of impatient money, costs of DVT are relatively high. Where large German subsidiaries may be able to afford such expensive programs, other companies may struggle with it. Contributing to the high costs, in comparison to Mexico, in Brazil there is much less governmental support. In Brazil such a comprehensive scholarship system does not exist, as it does in Mexico. On that account, costs are burdened entirely on the shoulders of companies. That again, in addition to the obligatory fees every company has to pay for the Sistema S, makes companies that participate in DVT (apart from the Volkswagen approach) pay twice for educational efforts. Fourth, the poor reputation of VET weighs heavily on DVT efforts (Dornbach, 2016; Kauer, 2015). Indeed, Mexico faced a similar perception of VET decades ago (and still does so in less industrial areas) combined with the university as a gold standard of education. Nonetheless, governmental actions in Brazil treat VET (and thus DVT) as a means of helping the poorest and not as a means of increasing productivity. Certainly not the intention, but efforts of the Brazilian government depict a strong disservice to the efforts of implementing DVT.

7.5.3 Institutional Entrepreneurship

Just like in the Mexican case, German subsidiaries in Brazil that conduct DVT break with local approaches that are known and perceived as appropriate. Falling back on practices that are appropriate within their home country, German subsidiaries introduce alternative practices. Combining practices from the two organizational fields (the Brazilian and the quasi-German intra-organizational one), German subsidiaries carry a wide and contradictory practice portfolio, whose full usage leads to institutional innovation in Brazil.

How far German subsidiaries are actively interested and engaged with the creation of German DVT in Brazil will be discussed throughout the subsequent section on institutional entrepreneurship. Following the steps of awareness, reframing and mobilization, and collective action, the role of German subsidiaries in the intentional creation of DVT in Brazil is put under scrutiny.

As Sect. 7.1.1 discussed in detail, the existing educational system does largely fail in providing the skills demanded by the companies. On that account, just like in Mexico, companies require technically qualified professionals that are not abundant locally. BraMNC1 confirms that by indicating quite drastically that "the Brazilian educational system is basically bad and not practically oriented" (BraMNC1, translated by the author). Along the same lines, he recognizes a strong shortage of specialists in Brazil. In the same vein, BraMNC2 mourns the low quality of technical skills that can be found in the labor market:

> ...we are a very technical company. When I say technical company, I mean we need at least a basic technical know-how for our new employees in the technical teams. So, it's not easy for us to go simply to the market and then hire someone, who is already prepared for what we have here, that fast and that suitable with our needs (BraMNC2).

As a solution to the problem, he refers to the installed DVT at his company in which they are "...preparing according to the COMPANYNAME's requirements and actually our needs for knowledge" (BraMNC2). Of major interest, beyond awareness of quality issues, BraMNC2 highlights DVT also as a means of complying with Brazilian law. The already introduced Brazilian Apprentice Law requires companies to have a certain percentage of the entire workforce as apprentices. According to BraMNC2, conducting DVT helps to attain a sufficient number of apprentices.

From the high degree of dissatisfaction with the local system—and the additional motivation to comply with the Brazilian Apprentices Law—one can reasonably state that potential actions conducted, related to the establishment of DVT, are based on a clear awareness relating to the dysfunctional system and the corresponding lack of suitable workers. Based on this knowledge, as the subsequent section analyzes, an institutional entrepreneur builds strategies and action plans, using practices in his or her wider practice portfolio to change the educational setting according to his or her preferences.

Relating to joint action, just like in Mexico, German subsidiaries in Brazil recognize its value when approaching the issue of DVT. Corporate actors use various venues that provide the means of pooling competences and power. The case of both Bosch's and Volkswagen's collaboration with the local Sistema S serves well to understanding corporate efforts that go beyond the borders of the company. To join forces with an educational counterpart, the companies mentioned actively cooperate with the SENAI that undertakes the theoretical part of the DVT program (BraOrg1; BraMNC2). This example demonstrates the actor-led combination and merging of different, partly contradicting, institutional setups well. The local Brazilian VET, which usually takes place entirely at school,[37] is enriched by the alien-to-the-system practical elements on the shop-floor rotating through different departments. The building of the shop-floor simulation at, for example, Bosch allows minor azubis to gain practical experience and clearly shows an innovational approach on how to adjust the setting according to the preference of conducting DVT. The collaboration with the SENAI, though, is a strongly tropicalized form of DVT inasmuch as it is adjusted to SENAI VET that takes only 2 years. In line with that, graduates from this two-year program attain the Brazilian *tecnico*, but not the German *Gesellenbrief*. Hence, instead of copying and pasting the German practice, this DVT initiative includes parts that are appropriate and well known in Brazil. Accordingly, one can reasonably argue that these initiatives are the product of institutional contestation and negotiation and that it is embedded within the Brazilian frames, though highly influenced by institutional innovation brought in by Volkswagen and Bosch. As indicated above, both Volkswagen and Bosch educate the majority of their azubis through this form of DVT. However, both companies are also part of the Volkswagen approach (discussed and introduced above) that further incorporates various other German subsidiaries and the AHK.

On that account, aiming at the introduction of a "real" German DVT, the Volkswagen approach is stemmed through joint efforts by various German subsidiaries. From the beginning, the firms Kostal Brasil, ZF do Brasil, Grob do Brasil, Mahle Brasil, and Volkswagen do Brasil participated in the program, actively engaged in constructing the complex program, and, in fact, enabled it to be implemented in the first place. For one isolated company, such a program that involves various actors would be certainly beyond scope. The active engagement of the mentioned companies in the context of the Volkswagen approach is depicted by BraMNC2 who reports of active participation at the AHK board.

> ...so there is a group of companies like Bosch, Volkswagen, Scania[38] and so on, so most obviously German companies. So, we have this committee and we have one representative from each company and then we define how the tests will happen and where. The team participates doing the evaluation of the students. So, we are part of this. So, after we finished this first batch, we can learn from it and continuously grow (BraMNC2).

In this case, though, BraMNC2 remains mostly in the topic of examination, and clearly indicates the intention to further consciously establish and increase DVT in

[37] Apart from the ten percent of practice, which is obligatory according to the Apprentices Law.

[38] Since 2008, Scania has been part of the Volkswagen group (Scania, 2020).

Brazil. Even though the Volkswagen approach today includes various actors, the leading role of, for example, Volkswagen is emphasized by BraOrg1 who states:

> …of course, Volkswagen would like to have the same program as they have in Germany across the different locations in different countries. Of course, that helped a lot. If someone from Germany says that they want it, then it works (BraOrg1, translated by the author).

Furthermore, as is the case with all DVT programs that are located outside of Germany that are capable of awarding the *Gesellenbrief*, the AHK takes on a pivotal position. Equipped with a similar mandate as the CAMEXA—that is to support, to consult, and in the case of education, to provide suitable employees to the German companies abroad—one can certainly argue that the AHK was initially attracted to Brazil by German subsidiaries as described by Aragón (2019) in the Mexican case. However, the AHK in Brazil developed a strong "life of its own." It cannot be seen as a mere service provider that acts according to the demand of German subsidiaries. The AHK developed into a major actor pushing DVT in Brazil. In fact, the AHK is a constituent actor that contributed significantly to both inter-actor approaches: the Volkswagen and the Humboldt ones. The AHK, just like in Mexico, also acts as a platform for inter-firm deliberation with its DVT committee and as a general coordinator of action between the firms, the educational institutes, and the German quality standards through monitoring, counseling, credentialing through German examination, and training of the DVT trainers (BraMNC2; BraMNC3; BraOrg1). Furthermore, the AHK is putting strong efforts into the further inclusion of more companies and the "proliferation of this good practice" (translation by the author), as BraMNC3 puts it. In the same vein, BraOrg1 reports that the AHK attempts to convince companies to join the DVT programs. As such, the AHK organizes information events and presents the DVT programs on-site at the plants. Additionally, the AHK is known among the interviewees to also cross the actor levels (companies, governmental bodies, people, etc.) in their attempt to broaden the field of actors, to improve the design of DVT in Brazil, and to generally move DVT on to the agenda at a political level. Along these lines, it is reported in the interviews that the AHK is involved in ongoing discussions with actors of both countries affected, for example, the local Brazilian Ministry of Labor and the German Ministry of Education and Research. As an example, for discussion, the AHK is attempting to convince the Brazilian government to expand the SENAI cooperation for the Volkswagen approach for the entire period of DVT of 3 years (BraOrg1). In so doing, DVT through the Volkswagen approach would be less costly for the firms, since the final third year would not need to be financed exclusively by them.

It is exactly here where one finds a major difference from the Mexican case, since, as BraOrg1 puts it, "things with the government are not that easy" (BraOrg1, translated by the author). The Brazilian government seems to be out of the game. Beyond the legal recognition of DVT and the adoption of the potentially supportive

Apprentices Law,[39] efforts to strengthen DVT are not recognizable. One can reasonably argue that, in line with the exclusive support of the Sistema S and the recognition of VET as a means to help socially and intellectually underprivileged (conform with Sect. 7.1), governmental efforts related to VET may even undermine efforts to establish DVT as a solid and valid educational path. BraMNC3 affirms the reluctant position of the Brazilian government in relation to DVT as follows: "That [discussion on DVT] is to be found at the AHKs. Up to now, I haven't seen the DVT at the level of the Ministry of Development and Industry. I think that takes place a level below. At least I haven't experienced it" (BraMNC3, translated by the author). Even though Brazilian government is not showing major efforts relating to the DVT, BraOrg1 reports:

> They [the government] told us already that they are interested. That is important. . .but I think, until some changes, it will take a very long time. But that is normal. Today we are in a political crisis and have financial problems. The new president has a lot to do. He has a lot of problems to find solutions for and, of course, education and professional education is an important topic, but he must set priorities (BraOrg1, translated by the author).

BraOrg2 reports similar experiences and expresses hope that the DVT will come on the Brazilian political agenda. Accordingly, the then mayor of the city of São Paulo (2017–2018) and today governor of the State of São Paulo (since 2019) João Doria Júnior (SP, 2020) put the DVT quite prominently at his election campaign's agenda and held the prospect of introducing DVT at the state and even national level. Further, emphasizing the promising position of João Doria Júnior's in relation to the next presidential election and simultaneously indicating the dependence of DVT development on single high-level supporters, BraOrg2 states that:

> . . .if Doria, that positions himself for the presidential election in two years; he is a great fan [of DVT]. He comes from the private sector, he is not a standard politician. If he came to power, then I could imagine that there may be new impetus (BraOrg2, translated by the author).

In addition, the absence of the Brazilian government severely hampers the mobilization of supporting German governmental actors. The German government, of course, is not able to interfere in local Brazilian issues. On that account, without a local governmental counterpart, the German government and its developmental agencies, such as the GIZ and the BiBB, are largely out of the game. As the chapter on the Mexican case indicates, these actors contribute positively to the development of DVT. Furthermore, other important players in the context of collective action around DVT, among others, the Colégio Humboldt, are to be mentioned. Even though its *raison d'étre* differs from, for example, the AHK inasmuch as its mission is to strengthen German culture rather than German companies, it is a major actor in joint action. In fact, it acts way beyond the actual mandate of an educational institute, which is lectureship. The Colégio Humboldt takes the role of a counselor for companies, a deliberative platform for companies though the installed corresponding

[39] The Brazilian Apprentices Law was not intentionally adopted to support DVT.

roundtable, and a "salesman" conducting field work and acquisition at both company and individual apprentice level (BraOrg2).

In conclusion, just like in Mexico, German subsidiaries in Brazil can be understood as proper institutional entrepreneurs that consciously act fully aware of problems and potential solutions, mobilize and pool both resources, and have power to adjust the given institutional setting according to their own preferences. They organize island solutions within the company, initialize and conduct joint action with other firms, and cooperate with other actors from different levels. Some of these actors, indeed, partly act beyond their initial mandate. All actors that act in concert, indeed, create something new and innovate in their institutional surroundings. However, in terms of expanding DVT, they seem to not be able to compensate for the lack of governmental support. Recalling the Mexican government, which, indeed, made DVT a matter of national relevance, reframed it to the Mexican realities, strongly mobilized actors and resources across the levels, and strongly supports the ongoing conduct of the MMFD, the absence of the Brazilian government makes it—at best—difficult to scale DVT up on a national level.

7.5.4 Reversed Isomorphism: German Subsidiaries in Brazil

Investigation follows the distinction between vertically and horizontally exerted pressures on the corresponding actors at the various levels to act alike. Translated to the study at hand, analysis covers mimetic, coercive, and normative pressures exerted on other firms, people, and the state to participate in and, thus, to support DVT. In order to understand the different trajectories of DVT, focus is put rather on differences from, than on similarities with the Mexican case.

German subsidiaries that conduct DVT exert pressure on their surroundings at various levels. Especially regarding the isomorphic pressures within the corporate peer group, certain mechanisms work just the way they do in Mexico. The German subsidiaries interviewed in Brazil do not demonstrate any formal coercion mechanism that forces, for example, supplying companies to adopt DVT. However, similar to the subtle pressures exerted through, for example, auditing activities in Mexico, the interviewees in Brazil indicated the informal urging of suppliers and the role of a quasi-regulator. As such, for example, suppliers are required to keep certain quality standards by conducting educational programs and, thus, to acquire certain skills in BraMNC2's own educational center (BraMNC2; BraMNC3). However, up to now, the courses offered to others by BraMNC2 are not yet full DVT courses. Since BraMNC3 joined the DVT program relatively recently, he states that before carrying DVT to the market, the company first wants to see how DVT works. Accordingly, BraMNC3 states:

> ...we thought about offering educational centers in the region of Campinhas. That means that they can use our infrastructure in order to train their people... but directly at the beginning of the DVT since the change two to three years ago. We thought that we better bring the first form to an end and then we talk about the diffusion. But the idea is existing, not

> yet reality, but the desire of COMPANYNAME to bring DVT is large (BraMNC3, translated by the author).

Emphasizing the importance of suppliers as potential multipliers within the market, BraMNC3 indicates that the large suppliers mostly serve as benchmarks for the larger supplying industry. Along the same lines, opening doors to other companies and introducing and showing DVT as a best practice, BraMNC2 gives the following insight:

> Well, I think that when some other companies come here, we receive a lot of visits from other companies to do any kind of benchmarks of manufacturing and so on, but they come and visit our technical school. What we can see from them is that they're really impressed about how we created this and how we're collecting these benefits. I would say, that this is a start of spreading some good ideas to other companies (BraMNC2)

Accordingly, showing DVT to a wider audience combined with the good reputation of German companies certainly has a demonstration effect on the (corporate) surroundings. Perception as best practice increases the desire of other companies to join in the DVT program. As an example, Volkswagen that has worked with SENAI for a long time is certainly the major building block when talking about the development of the Volkswagen approach with various other companies and the AHK. Accordingly, out of this single company DVT grew one of the largest joint DVT initiatives in Brazil. On that account, one can clearly recognize a DVT diffusion among German companies in Brazil. One can certainly assume that German companies that conduct DVT and open doors to others equip other German companies cognitively on how to train azubis in Brazil. As indicated, today various German companies participate in this initiative.

However, according to the interview sample, the German network seems to be less dense in Brazil than in Mexico. Accordingly, CME credentialing does not take a similar importance in Brazil as in Mexico. As an example, the German *Gesellenbrief* is mentioned frequently as a means to study and work abroad but rarely as a means to symbolize occupational belonging or to improve employability in Brazil. Along the same lines, a profession that is defined by, among others, DVT has not yet occurred to the same extent as in Mexico. Indeed, just like Volkswagen in Mexico, BraMNC3 in Brazil attempts to create a profession of high-quality manufacturing through the inclusion of suppliers into their DVT. BraOrg2 refers to the informal chat among managers of German companies in particular who exchange ideas and concepts of education that may contribute to the creation of a German profession. However, such efforts are relatively limited in size. Accordingly, Kauer (2015) finds that a DVT degree is recognized only by the small group of German companies. However, the Mexican case shows that—besides the MMFD—a relative dense network of German subsidiaries built a major pillar for both strong identification and a sufficient demand for DVT graduates. German subsidiaries in Brazil seem to be more loosely connected. Supporting this, in terms of DVT, BraOrg1 states that DVT is not equally supported by German subsidiaries. It was from the mid-2000s especially when German support for DVT decreased and when mostly Brazilians took decision-making positions in, for example, HR departments who "do not at all understand the program nor recognize any value of having such program in the company" (BraOrg1, translated by the author). Giving further insights, BraOrg1 tells about efforts to incorporate German subsidiaries into DVT and comes to quite a sobering result:

> these days, I visit lots of German companies, for example, COMPANYNAME. I have been there on Friday, to make them participate in the program. I talked to the president to convince him, but they are not one hundred percent convinced, as soon as they have to invest money. Even though these are German companies, it is unbelievable. (BraOrg1, translated by the author).

Thus, also contributing to the explanation of lacking professionalization, BraOrg1 highlights the limited receptiveness even of German subsidiaries regarding DVT. In line with Sect. 7.5.2 which discussed the "mass exodus of expatriates" in Brazil, the majority of interviewees report of the heavy decline of expatriates in German companies. Consequently, decision-makers on the corporate boards are mostly Brazilians who are not familiar with the concept and, thus, not interested in DVT. As a revealing anecdote, BraOrg1 gives insights into agencies that attempt to further push DVT locally who have become creative in order to attract new participants. Coping with the low receptiveness of German subsidiaries toward DVT in the past few years, agencies directly address the HQ in Germany and try to convince them that the Brazilian DVT makes sense. They hope for higher receptiveness from the HQ that knows the value of DVT and subsequent pressure on the affiliated Brazilian subsidiaries to increase efforts in DVT. BraOrg1 states that "if HQ tells them [the subsidiary] that we need it, then it will work in Brazil" (translated by the author). Compared to the anecdotal evidence of the subsidiary manager (MexMNC3) in Mexico that fought for the implementation of German DVT in his company, one recognizes the need in Brazil for exogeneous stimuli, whereas in Mexico the DVT system grew out of itself.

In times of absence of German expatriates, the interviewees find a consensus that the current development of DVT in Brazil may best be described as an organic process. In such, professionalization occurs through training azubis in a DVT environment that transmits corresponding professional business values. Being equipped with value, norms, and knowledge about DVT, today's azubis diffuse DVT tomorrow. As an example, BraMNC3 himself conducted a DVT program and today is a strong driver of DVT in his company. He knows content and the added value relating to the inclusion of practical phases and the alignment with corporate demands. Evaluating DVT in general, he states: "these people [DVT graduates] have a real strong background. This base still helps me today. It was a very good base" (BraMNC3, translated by the author). He further emphasizes the ongoing process of DVT development as:

> We already have a lot of German companies [conducting DVT]. But every great movement begins with the action by the one or the other... if we deliver good examples and the first apprentices show good results, others [other companies] will also participate. (BraMNC3, translated by the author).

BraOrg2 affirms BraMNC3 by stating that there are larger German subsidiaries that strongly pool DVT graduates. As an example, he states that roughly 25 percent of Hamburg Süd's workforce is constituted by DVT graduates from the Humboldt approach. With people in decision-making positions that know DVT, the corresponding company's participation in DVT is very likely. As such, BraOrg2 refers to various companies from, among others, Germany, Brazil, France, and the USA—all located in Brazil—that today actively participate in DVT due to the decision of an DVT alumnus who rose through the corporate hierarchy. In fact—still the exception—BraOrg2 gives the example of a huge German bank that today conducts DVT due to the decision of a Brazilian woman who did DVT herself and not, as one may assume, due to German roots. Accordingly, BraOrg2 indicates that the DVT alumni that are in management positions today strongly function as bridges that incorporate DVT into their own company. This strategy, indeed, seems to function though at a very low speed (BraOrg1).

As the previous discussion indicates, DVT in Brazil develops very slowly—if at all—and grows in an organic manner. As such, it is the absence of a scaling-up of DVT that clearly distinguishes Brazil from Mexico. On that account, in addition to reputational problems and the exodus of expatriates, the unreceptive government certainly depicts a major difference to the Mexican case.

DVT according to the German model has not yet been heard by the Brazilian (or state level) government. In line with the nonexistent role of the government as an institutional entrepreneur, Brazilian authorities do not seriously incorporate DVT into their educational system. In comparison to the Mexican case, there is a major lack of receptiveness in Brazil. This neglect is not clearly to be understood. In fact, the political economy of Brazil today shows various similar characteristics as the Mexican one did in the 2010s (respectively the State of Mexico in the 1990s) and is characterized by high (youth) unemployment and low productivity. Furthermore, besides systemic similarities, Brazil and Mexico show a relatively similar economic composition and are, for example, among the regional high technology manufacturers and major car producing countries globally. On that account, one may reasonably assume that the demand for qualified technical workers is similar across the countries, too. Nonetheless, DVT as a potential means to ameliorate the situation has not come to a state or national agenda, despite various leading politicians acknowledging DVT as a positive contribution to the Brazilian development. BraOrg2 described former mayor, current governor, and potential future president João Doria Júnior as a "fan" of DVT. Along the same lines, the company, Voith, which is a major pioneer in DVT in Brazil, was acknowledged by the former president, Cardoso, as a "firm that has contributed significantly to the positive development of Brazil" (Voith, 2019b). However, as a potential explanation for ongoing neglect, in Brazil—unlike in Mexico—there has not been (in recent years) and there is no line of car producers queuing with more than 18 billion USD. On the contrary, BraOrg2 reports various multinational car producers that are struggling heavily in Brazil. In fact, the car manufacturer Ford has closed down a major car plant and decided to exit the entire Latin American truck market (Bom Dia SP, 2019). According to BraOrg2, the process was unimaginable in the heydays of

Brazilian development in the 2000s but became reality from 2014 with Brazil in a severe economic crisis, with years of massive recession and the slowest ongoing economic recovery in Brazilian history (Gallas & Palumbo, 2019). However, one needs to add that the Brazilian government showed no genuine interest in DVT measures in the economic heydays either. As Sect. 7.1 introduced, VET has come to a more prominent position, though still rather as a means of including the poor and underprivileged. Along these lines, Brazilian government shows no receptiveness for DVT as demonstrated by German subsidiaries. Accordingly, DVT-related action of German subsidiaries does not reach the responsible bodies. Despite the recognition of valuable "German actions" the ongoing problems of the Brazilian political economy and—not least because of—the absence of an institutional entrepreneur at the political level such as Nieto prohibit up-scaling of DVT on a state or national level.

A lack of orchestrated political action further hampers the general effect DVT action by Germany subsidiaries may have on other actors at other levels, such as local companies and people (MexOrg1). As the Mexican case highlights, a "tropicalized" and subsidized form of DVT called the MMFD opened doors of DVT to local companies. Without the MMFD, the number of Mexican companies that conduct DVT would be very low, if not zero (MexMNC3). The MMFD has at least two major functions that culminate in generally lower barriers to DVT for locals. First, the embedding into local frames increases familiarity with such a new educational path. According to BraMNC2, such familiarity is very important, as changing the local mind-set is important to perceive DVT not as a "cost structure but an adding value structure" (BraMNC2). Second, strong financial subsidies allow Mexican companies to participate in the first place. Without any doubt, the latter is especially important in times of (economic) crises in which uncertainty is high and economic survival is at stake. Accordingly, BraMNC2 depicts financial hurdles for local by players by stating that "they'll [other companies] have some challenges regarding the costs, because unfortunately here in Brazil we're dealing with a hard cost battle, so we need to be more competitive" (BraMNC2). Since there is no MMFD equivalent in Brazil, neither function is performed. Unfortunately, both unfamiliarity and costs are mostly insurmountable obstacles for local companies. Hence, despite the generally high appreciation of what is developed in Germany and the action of German subsidiaries (BraMNC3), even if isomorphic pressures reach local companies—inasmuch as they recognize, understand DVT, and perceive it as desirable—DVT remains out of reach. Consequently, pressure exerted by German subsidiaries and felt by their local counterparts hardly leads to isomorphism.

Similarly, Brazilian people that are mostly strongly unfamiliar with DVT do not gain easy access to DVT as they do in Mexico through the tropicalized MMFD. The concept of DVT is alien-to-the-system and—as mentioned above—understood as a form of VET. As VET comes with a very negative reputation in Brazil (BraOrg1; BraOrg2), as mentioned before, it has a severely negative effect on the diffusion of DVT. Convincing Brazilian people to commit themselves to DVT is especially important, since as BraOrg2 reports, today's lack of expatriates entails a lack of children from German-speaking people that undertook German DVT in Brazil. On that account, despite the very good reputation of German companies in Brazil (BraOrg1), the attraction of DVT is—if at all—moderate. In addition, making the situation even more difficult for DVT, companies' and people's perceptions of DVT reinforce one another. People that recognize DVT's low degree of perceived appropriateness for the companies derive a disadvantage regarding employability. Affirmatively, Kauer (2015, p. 702) investigating DVT in Brazil indicates that "it [DVT] is only recognized by some companies, by German companies (,) but it does not replace a college degree." Along these lines, companies' general low acceptance of DVT downgrades opportunities for DVT graduates on the labor market. As a consequence, people will refrain from choosing DVT as an educational path.

As a preliminary conclusion, of course, it is by no means argued that there is no isomorphic pressure exerted by German subsidiaries either on the state or on local companies and people. However, the general environment of crisis, reluctant governments, unfamiliarity, and bad reputation seem to strongly undermine DVT in Brazil and prohibit isomorphic pressure from having a stronger effect. In general, across all levels, there is a limited receptiveness toward DVT.

7.6 Discussion and Degree of Institutionalization

Building upon both the theoretically derived and the empirically suggested categories and aspects of reality from the Mexican case, this chapter scrutinizes institutional dynamics that occur due to institutional contradiction caused by foreign subsidiaries of German MNCs in Brazil. As the most general findings, first, subsidiaries with origins in Germany exhibit a strong degree of behavioral contradiction inasmuch as they strongly rely on German DVT practices, despite being located in an archetypal HME. Second, the behavioral contradiction leads to institutional change. Today, the educational landscape in Brazil shows various DVT initiatives according to the German model that are largely carried by subsidiaries with German roots. Examples discussed in this chapter, such as Volkswagen approach, Humboldt approach, and various smaller island solutions within the corporate borders of a subsidiary, indicate the impact of subsidiaries as agents of institutional change.

Consequently, the in-depth investigation of DVT in Brazil throughout Sect. 7.5 firmly supports the findings of Chap. 6 that suggest a transfer of practices from Germany to Brazil. Along the same lines, foreign subsidiaries from German MNCs cope with the disadvantageous local institutional setting and compensate for major local weaknesses in all complementary dimensions. This finding confirms the observed patterns of complementarity in Chap. 6 and strongly supports the notion of institutions as Streeckian enablers.

Remarkably, reaching the core of the institutionally reproduced low-skill trap in Latin America, regarding the DVT initiatives discussed, German-owned training companies and local young people overcome the obstacles raised by HME's institutional setting and manage to mutually promise a sufficient degree of certainty, which allows both parties to engage in long-term cooperation. Along these lines, subsidiaries of German MNCs contest HMEs' status quo and act as agents of institutional change. In fact, major theories and approaches ranging from orthodox economics, over VoC, toward conventional sociological analyses are not capable of grasping institutional contradiction as an important source of change and, thereby, run a very high risk of omitting valuable explanatory factors. Here, understanding the institutional interplay as strongly determining the performance of a political economy, the approach of Conflating Capitalisms incorporates key aspects of institutional contradiction and its subsequent impact.

The empirical case in Brazil demonstrates that, in terms of institutional change induced by the subsidiaries, the impact on Brazil's institutional setting cannot keep up either with the moderate effect hypothesized by the "Change Cube" or the change observed in Mexico. Despite the most similar systems design chosen and the similar actions of subsidiaries, the trajectory of institutional development is different. Subsidiaries in Brazil equally demand higher technical skills and have the same potent partners with, among others, the AHK and the German school abroad as their counterparts in Mexico. However, qualitative analysis throughout this chapter indicates that, in comparison to the Mexican case, pressure exerted by the German subsidiaries has not resulted in comprehensive change due to local receptiveness in favor of DVT being lesser than the reluctance against such institutional innovation.

Along the same lines, the impact of everyday business operations on the surroundings (vertically and horizontally) is limited across the most important actors. Without any doubt, the subsidiaries of German subsidiaries act mostly like the ones in Mexico and, thus, potentially diffuse the practice in the roles of demonstrators, drivers of professionalization, and as quasi-regulators. However, the degree to which isomorphic pressures are received by the local surrounding is different to the one in Mexico.

The various existing DVT initiatives in Brazil, indeed, indicate that isomorphic pressure is exerted and also received by other companies. However, the strength of received isomorphic pressure is not as high as it is in Mexico. Regarding companies other than subsidiaries with German roots, pressure to conduct DVT is hardly received. In comparison to the Mexican case, in Brazil no comparable initiative to the MMFD exists. The MMFD has the function to tropicalize DVT sufficiently to suit the locally existing frames. The absence of such a perçeived sufficiently "appropriate" access to DVT increases the hurdles that need to be overcome for Brazilian companies to join an entirely "inappropriate" approach. Furthermore, the ongoing Brazilian economic crisis and the corresponding uncertainty make companies to refrain from costly endeavors such as DVT. The issue of costs depicts an unsurmountable obstacle for the vast majority of local and, in general, mostly smaller companies. Further contributing to the high costs, in comparison to Mexico, in Brazil there is much less governmental support. In Brazil, a comprehensive scholarship system—as exists in Mexico—does not exist. On that account, costs are burdened entirely on the shoulders of companies. That again, in addition to the obligatory fees every company has to pay for the Sistema S, makes companies that participate in DVT (apart from the Volkswagen approach that incorporates the existing SENAI) pay twice for educational efforts. Hence, the existence of a valid educational path that is already paid for further hampers the creation of an alternative form. Furthermore, increasing the obstacles of DVT to companies, DVT's adjustments to Brazilian realities are strong and severely complicate the conduct of DVT. Adjustments, such as long-term alternations between DVT's theoretical and practical phase and the division of 2 years at school and 1 year at the company—due to Brazilian youth protection law—are met with resistance. Furthermore, this Brazilian legislation that prohibits minors from working in production areas strongly undermines the idea of educating minors through DVT and downgrades azubis to exclusively cost units without "added value."

Regarding other German MNCs and their Brazilian subsidiaries, in line with the findings of the quantitative study, they show a strong tendency to conduct German-like DVT practices. However, also within the group of German subsidiaries, further development of DVT in Brazil has come to a halt since the heydays in the 1990 and early 2000s. Through the qualitative analysis in this chapter, in line with Kostova and Roth (2002) and Mattes (2013), one can recognize that the practice portfolio and the inherent will to use and defend it, at the end of the day, is carried by people and less by organizational hierarchies themselves. Hence, the discussed "mass exodus of expatriates" in Brazil makes the German subsidiaries less German inasmuch as the decision-makers within them are no longer German and, therefore, unfamiliar with DVT. This finding is supported by the newly gained quantitative primary survey data (question in this survey: Please give the proportion for: Local workers as percentage (%) of your management) that supports the strong representation of Brazilians in decision-making decisions. In Brazilian subsidiaries of German MNCs, on average more than 80 percent of the management is composed of Brazilian people that come with a Brazilian belief system. That again, especially in combination with an ongoing economic crisis, makes money less patient when it comes to educational issues, especially if the value added by DVT is not recognized. Further adding to the relatively low receptiveness relating to DVT, a German subsidiary without German people faces largely the same obstacles (see above) to DVT as the Brazilian companies do.

Finally, regarding both the Brazilian people and the companies led by Brazilians, the poor reputation of VET weighs heavily on DVT efforts. Indeed, Mexico faced a similar perception of VET decades ago (and still does so in less industrialized areas) combined with the university as a gold standard of education. Nonetheless, as Sect. 7.1 indicates, governmental actions in Brazil treat VET (and thus DVT) as a means of helping the poorest and not as a means of increasing productivity. Certainly not the intention, but efforts of the Brazilian government have done a strong disservice to the efforts of implementing DVT, since people that do not want to be categorized as the "poorest and needy" tend to refrain from educational paths that are promoted as being designed for such.

Regarding institutional entrepreneurship, just like in Mexico, German subsidiaries in Brazil can be understood as proper institutional entrepreneurs that consciously act fully aware of problems and potential solutions, mobilize and pool both resources, and have power to adjust the given institutional setting according to their own preferences. They organize island solutions within the company, initialize and conduct joint action with other firms, and cooperate with other actors from different levels. Some of these actors, indeed, put enormous efforts in the further diffusion of DVT and partly act beyond their initial mandate, such as the AHK and the Colégio Humboldt. All actors that act in concert, indeed, create something new and innovate in their institutional surrounding. However, in terms of expanding DVT, they seem to not be able to compensate for the lack of governmental support. Recalling the Mexican government, which, indeed, made DVT a matter of national relevance, reframed it to Mexican realities, strongly mobilized actors and resources across the levels, and strongly supported the ongoing conduct of the MMFD, the absence of the Brazilian government makes it—at best—difficult to scale DVT up on a national level. Interestingly, according to the analysis made, it was a similar (institutional) crisis in Mexico to that which Brazil now faces that made the Mexican government incorporate German DVT into the political agenda but that, in the case of Brazil, has contributed instead to the government further refraining from costly DVT practices.

Assuming ceteris paribus conditions of economic crisis and bad VET reputation that both severely undermine local receptiveness for DVT and, therefore, prohibit pressure exerted by German subsidiaries from having a stronger effect. One may therefore argue that without the government as either an entrepreneur itself or as an amplifier of corporate DVT efforts, the trajectory of DVT in Brazil will—at best—slightly increase through "organic professionalization" relating to alumni of DVT programs that consider it when in decision-making positions. However, the disruptive growth witnessed throughout the 2010s in Mexico is certainly beyond scope without a supportive government.

Approaching DVT in Brazil regarding the degree of institutionalization, without doubt, the practice of DVT according to the German model gained certain legitimacy and materialized through manifold different DVT initiatives. On that account, at the time of writing, DVT practices in Brazil have attained the pre-institutional stage. German subsidiaries make use of their wider practice portfolio and counter organizational problems that occur due to HME's dysfunctions. Such institutional innovation, though, is limited to the reach of German and Germany-related decision-makers at higher corporate hierarchical levels. In fact, DVT may not be newly introduced in Brazil, but finds only a limited number of adopters. The diffusion toward non-German actors depicts a hurdle that is not yet overcome and, accordingly, indicates the practice's relative low degree of local embeddedness. However, the Mexican case impressively shows that institutional development can be disruptive, despite relative stagnation over previous decades. The political engagement of the Mexican government under Nieto indicates that DVT in an HME is achievable, depicting a potential solid addition to the local educational landscape. As the analysis above introduced, with São Paulo's current governor, João Doria Júnior, there may be a Brazilian equivalent to Nieto in a promising position. In fact, taking the Mexican case prior to 2013, the institutional development of DVT looked fairly similar to the one today in Brazil. The Mexican government made use of the willing DVT actors and the already well-implemented DVT programs within the subsidiaries of German MNCs and brought DVT into a stage of semi-institutionalization within less than 10 years. On that account, if government actors find a genuine interest in DVT, Brazil is equipped with the same fertile conditions as Mexico in the early 2010s. In fact, German DVT already exists in Brazil and various initiatives are successfully implemented, proving that DVT can work well securing a decent fit with the Brazilian HME. Following these lines, various actors with German origins, in particular the subsidiaries of German MNCs, are present and could provide a solid basis to build upon.

Approaching the issue of institutional impact from a rather systemic side, as pre-set in Chaps. 3 and 4 and the institutional diagnosis in Chap. 5, the relationship between HME's institutionally constituted low-skill trap on the one hand and the highly coordinated DVT on the other hand is extraordinary and depicts a most different systems case. According to the vast majority of literature on Latin American development, both strategic action and credible inter-actor deliberation are deemed to be out of reach (Franz, 2017; Schneider, 2013). On that account, the ongoing long-term and generally well-functioning DVT initiatives in both Brazil and Mexico are institutional success stories in themselves. Accordingly, as discussed above, DVT as it is implemented today allows German-owned training companies and local young people to overcome the obstacles raised by HME's institutional setting and manage to mutually promise a sufficient degree of certainty that allows both parties to engage in long-term cooperation. Following this line of thought, in conjunction with the different qualities of behavior and change discussed, with the given caution relating to an ongoing process, German DVT introduced to Brazil by the subsidiaries of German MNCs can be normatively categorized as "good." It contests the institutional setting that is incapable of providing a "decent life" and has the potential to counter the distortions that hamper the creation of quality jobs.

Regarding the impact of DVT on development indicators, the Mexican government emphasizes the positive contribution DVT has on Mexican development and states that the DVT in Mexico:

> ha tenido un impacto positive en cuanto a: personal altamente calificado para mejorar la eficencia y productividad; en la reducción de la tasa de desempleo juvenile y el mejoramiento de la empleabilidad de los alumnus y la aceptación social de la formación dual; así como, en el aumento de competitividad industrial, identificación des los jóvenes con el trabajo y mejores perspectivas en el Mercado laboral (Ruiz-Velasco Sánchez & Bárcenas López, 2019, p. 754).[40]

Still, there is a lack of evaluative studies that test the impact of actor-induced institutional change in the context of DVT on performance indicators, such as labor productivity and (youth) employment. Most likely, from a macro perspective, in line with the pre-institutional stage of DVT in Brazil, developmental effects on, for example, increased productivity or lower (youth) unemployment in Brazil and

[40]Translated: "has had a positive impact in terms of: highly qualified personnel to improve efficiency and productivity; in reducing the youth unemployment rate and improving the employability of students and the social acceptance of dual training; as well as, in increasing industrial competitiveness, identification of young people with work and better prospects in the labor market."

Mexico are difficult to measure. Up to now, in line with Wiemann and Fuchs (2018), DVT is relevant for a rather small segment of skilled labor and therefore has not been able to reduce underemployment and unemployment significantly at the national level. Along the same lines, DVT is yet not more than a promising offer on productivity. However, the findings of this study strongly argue for the incorporation of such evaluative studies into the scholarly debate on development in Latin America.

The qualitative analysis further contributes to a better understanding of CME practices in strange systems. Major findings dissent from the literature proposing "flight from the German model" (Kuznetsov & Jacob, 2015). On the contrary, the findings made here indicate that German MNCs rely on practices of their home country and even remodel a coordinated environment by compensating for the local unsupportive institutional setting across all institutional domains. This work suggests that German MNCs, in particular in the DVT context, are defenders of institutional change and drive—either consciously or as by-product of their actual duty—local institutional development toward coordination. Along the same lines, this work finds evidence that raises severe doubts on the narrative of CME practices being too complex (too deeply embedded in the local institutional setup of CMEs) to apply in non-coordinated environments. Most often in both the scholarly debate and practitioner's reality, if inter-systemic consensus or a generally desirable development outcome needs to be formulated, all too often preference is given to the (ease of implementing the) liberal way.

The very few attempts to implement coordinated practices of, for example, DVT in developing countries, indeed, failed. However, the Chilean example in the late 1980s demonstrates clearly that, up to now, coordinated practices are introduced top-down without considering either complementary institutions or constitutive actors (Sehnbruch, 2016; Schneider, 2013). Focusing exclusively on the supply side of education without incorporating major actors, most importantly the final demander of skills—that are companies—most likely leads to failing initiatives. In brief, generating skills without generating demand for the skills leads to disastrous outcomes, such as negative returns of education followed by the collapse of DVT in Chile. However, in both cases put under scrutiny in this work, the Brazilian and Mexican one, DVT programs are implemented and driven by corporate demand. On that account, companies that understand the system compensated for institutional weaknesses and depict the immediate demander of the skills generated. Following these lines of thought, both cases strongly indicate that coordinated DVT can function well if complementarities and major actors are considered.

In line with Royo (2009), Ferrari (2016) Schneider (2009), Bizberg and Théret (2015), and Bresser-Pereira (2012) that investigate the long and mostly unsuccessful history of liberalization in Latin American, this work contributes to understanding economic organization according to CME standards as a valid alternative. Since it is mostly liberal ideas that led Latin America to the situation in which it is in now, from the perspective of incompatibility, a potential development toward a CME may be even easier to conduct. It is the existing social arrangement that led to a situation of crisis, and in line with, for example, Seo and Creed (2002), change may best be achieved through sufficiently incompatible concepts of CMEs.

Second, and of even greater importance, this work contributes to the developmental debate by showing inherent advantages of coordinated practices over liberal ones when implementing them in strange settings, in particular in hierarchical environments. In HMEs in which decisions are made top-down within corporate boardrooms rather than as a result of balancing stakeholder interests (as a response to societal pressures), new practices that may even contradict the local institutional setting (such as German DVT) can be established within the firm quite easily (Schneider, 2013). On that account, in line with Smets et al. (2012), alien-to-the-system practices require a solid consolidation within the corporate borders of a firm before radiating to the field. Along the same lines, Fortwengel and Jackson (2016) indicate that institutional change is triggered by small-scale "proto-institutions" that, through diffusion to other locations and actors, incrementally gain legitimacy and develop along the stages of institutionalization shown by Tolbert and Zucker (1996). Following this argumentation, the likelihood of a new practice of becoming successfully institutionalized reasonably depends on the practice's ability to be conducted within corporate borders.

Assuming the liberal idea of education—in a disruptively innovative system—that is characterized by short-term competitive relationships, the educational path of choice is the one of generalist education. Liberal generalists secure income flows through wide-ranging employability across sectors and industries. Briefly summarizing, the two major actors, being the people (that decide about what to learn) and the companies (that decide about what to demand), rely on, for the former, a large pool of highly skilled generalists, and, for the latter, a large pool of firms that require highly skilled generalists, neither of which are available in Latin American countries and—if at all—are partly compensated for by the informal sector. Following this line of thought, liberal educational practices require the final materialization of a market-oriented system to work well before even starting institutional development toward an LME setting. Accordingly, island solutions of individual actors—that may then radiate to the field—are hardly imaginable within the context of liberal practices.

It is exactly here where this work finds evidence suggesting that CME practices have an inherent advantage that is strongly worked out in the DVT cases discussed. Simply put, if a company can credibly guarantee lifelong employment and, thus, continuous income flows, a person can reasonably invest in a specific skill set demanded, even though the skills acquired are useless for other companies. Confirming this, the investigation above finds evidence of CME microcosms in Latin American HMEs. Both the Brazilian and the Mexican cases demonstrate DVT initiatives organized by individual German MNCs, compensating for all major complementary institutions. These initiatives remodel a coordinated system within such micro-environment and manage to enable both the company and the azubi to attain a sufficient degree of certainty to engage in CME-like long-term cooperation. As the investigation above shows, firms and workers manage to make credible long-term commitment and, therefore, neither of the two relies on the large pools of either supply or demand to secure themselves against income losses and sunk investments.

These findings argue that CME practices should by no means be left outside consideration of developmental thinking and, indeed, in comparison to liberal practices come with the advantage of being practicable in island solutions. The proper conduct and consolidation of alien-to-the-system practices within such a corporate island—as demonstrated by DVT in Brazil and Mexico—can lay the foundation for further institutionalization.

References

Adams, W. (2015). Conducting semi-structured interviews. In E. N. Newcomer, P. H. Hatry, & J. S. Wholey (Eds.), *Handbook of practical program evaluation* (pp. 492–505). Wiley.

Almeida, R., Anazawa, L., Menezes Filho, N., & Vasconcellos, L. (2015). *Policy research Working Paper 7246*. Retrieved from investing in technical & vocational education and training: Does it yield large economic returns in Brazil? Retrieved from http://documents.worldbank.org/curated/pt/465981468181787054/pdf/WPS7246.pdf

ALTRATEC. (2012). *Formación en el Sistema Dual*. Retrieved from http://www.altratec.mx/organizacion.html

Anckar, C. (2008). On the applicability of the most similar systems design and the most different systems design in comparative research. *International Journal of Social Research Methodology, 2008*, 389–401.

Aragón, E. (2019). nopoor: Working Paper n° 74. *Increasing employability of young people through policy changes in educational systems: The Mexican Model of Dual Formation*. Retrieved from Increasing employability of young people through Policy changes in Educational Systems: The Mexican Model of Dual Formation.

Artega García, A., Sierra Romero, S., & Flores Lima, R. (2010). The vocational training system in Mexico: Characteristics and actors, strenghts and weaknesses. In I. G. Bosch & J. Charest (Eds.), *Vocational training. International perspectives (Routledge studies in employment and work relations in context)* (Vol. 4, pp. 187–213). Routledge.

Assunção, J., & Gonzaga, G. (2010). *Educação Profissional no Brasil: Inserção e Retorno*. SENAI-DN.

BiBB. (2017). *Ausbildungsordnungen und wie sie entstehen*. Bundesinstitut für Berufsbildung.

BiBB. (2018). *Imove*. Retrieved from Mexiko und Deutschland vertiefen Zusammenarbeit in Berufsbildung https://www.imove-germany.de/de/alle_news.htm?content-url=/cps/rde/xchg/imove_projekt_de_2020/hs.xsl/Mexiko-und-Deutschland-vertiefen-Zusammenarbeit-in-Berufsbildung.htm

Bizberg, I., & Théret, B. (2015). *Variedades del capitalismo en América Latina: los casos de México, Brasil, Argentina y Chile*. El Colegio de México.

Blank, F. (2016). Unemployment and pensions protection in Europe: The changing role of social partners. In *OSE Paper Series, Research Paper No. 29*.

BMBF. (2017). *Bundesministerium für Bildung und Forschung (BMBF), Referat Grundsatzfragen der beruflichen Aus- und Weiterbildung*. Retrieved from Duale Berufsausbildung sichtbar gemacht https://www.freie-berufe.de/wordpress/wp-content/uploads/2017/09/BMBF_Duale_Berufsausbildung.pdf

BMBF. (2018). *Berufsbildungsbericht 2018*. Bundesministerium für Bildung und Forschung (BMBF) Referat Grundsatzfragen der beruflichen Aus und Weiterbildung.

Bom Dia, S. P. (2019). *g1 - Fechamento da fábrica da Ford*. https://g1.globo.com/sp/sao-paulo/edicao/2019/02/21/videos-bom-dia-sp-de-quinta-feira-21-de-fevereiro.ghtml

Bosch. (2018a). *Bosch in Brazil*. Retrieved from https://www.bosch-presse.de/pressportal/de/en/bosch-in-brazil-162240.html

Bosch. (2018b). *Factsheet: Bosch in Mexico*. Retrieved from https://www.bosch-presse.de/pressportal/de/en/press-release-146373.html

Bresser-Pereira, L. C. (2012). Five models of capitalism. *Brazilian Journal of Political Economy, 32*(1), 21–32.

Cáceres-Reebs, D., & Schneider, U. (2020). *Vocational education and training in Mexico - How the country has tropicalised the dual model*. Retrieved from https://www.bibb.de/en/22624.php

Câmara dos Deputados. (2020). *Biblioteca Digital*. Retrieved from LDB Lei de diretrizes e bases da educação nacional: Lei n° 9.394, de 20 de dezembro de 1996, que estabelece as diretrizes e bases da educação nacional http://bd.camara.leg.br/bd/handle/bdcamara/19339

CAMEXA. (2020). *Die deutsche duale Berufsausbildung in Mexiko*. Retrieved from https://mexiko.ahk.de/dual/deutsche-duale-berufsausbildung

Centro Alemán de Información para Latinoamérica. (2015). *El CEDUAL expande sus operaciones en Puebla, México*. Retrieved from https://alemaniaparati.diplo.de/mxdz-es/aktuelles/cedualexpansionpuebla/1087570

CEPAL. (2015). *National Programme for access to technical education and employment-PRONATEC (Programa Nacional de Acesso ao Ensino Técnico e Emprego) (2011-)*. Retrieved from https://dds.cepal.org/bpsnc/programme?id=80

Chankseliani, M., & Anuar, A. M. (2019). Cross-country comparison of engagement in apprenticeships: A conceptual analysis of incentives for individuals and firms. *International Journal for Research in Vocational Education and Training, 2019*, 261–283.

Chicago Tribune. (2015). *Key automotive investments in Mexico*. Retrieved from https://www.chicagotribune.com/business/ct-mexican-auto-plants-0711-biz-20150710-story.html

CNI. (2014). *Portrait of Brazilian population: Professional education*. CNI.

Colégio Humboldt. (2020). *Duale Berufsbildung*. Retrieved from Berufsbildung https://www.humboldt.com.br/de/berufsbildung/

Confederação Nacional da Indústria. (2014). *Pesquisa CNI-IBOPE: Retratos da Sociedade Brasileira: Saude publica*. CNI.

da Silva Filho, L. A. (2016). Labour market and turnover in the industrial employment in the Brazilian Northeast region. *Investigación Económica, LXXV*(295), 203–230.

De Meur, G., & Berg-Schlosser, D. (1994). Comparing political systems: Establishing similarities and dissimilarities. *European Journal of Political Research, 26*, 193–219.

De La Rosa, E. (2019). *Milenio*. Coparmex realiza balance negativo del primer año de AMLO. https://www.milenio.com/negocios/de-primer-ano-de-amlo-coparmex-hace-balance-negativo

Dornbach, S. (2016). *Berufsbildung in Brasilien*. Ribeiro do Espinho Fachmedien Berlin.

dos Santos Mayer, B. (2016). *Volkswagen führt mit der AHK São Paulo duale Ausbildung für Mechatroniker in Brasilien ein*. Retrieved from Kooperation international https://www.kooperation-international.de/aktuelles/nachrichten/detail/info/volkswagen-fuehrt-mit-der-ahk-sao-paulo-duale-ausbildung-fuer-mechatroniker-in-brasilien-ein/

DW. (2016). *Formación profesional dual: la experiencia mexicana*. Retrieved from https://alemaniaparati.diplo.de/mxdz-es/aktuelles/dwformaciondualbalance/1077542

Elbling, V. (n.d.). *La Iniciativa Alemana de Formación Dual en México*. Retrieved from https://mexiko.diplo.de/blob/875018/d3801d26df8bb017bb778b35b3abcc3a/flyer-formaci%25C3%25B3n-dual-data.pdf

Ellguth, P., & Kohaut, S. (2017). *wsi mitteilungen 4/2017: Tarifbindung und betriebliche Interessenvertretung: Ergebnisse aus dem IAB-Betriebspanel 2016*. Retrieved from https://www.boeckler.de/data/wsimit_2017_04_ellguth.pdf

European Commision. (2012). *Comunicación de la Comisión al Parlamento Europeo, alconsejo, al Comité Económico y Social Europeo y al Comité de las Regiones – Un nuevo concepto de educación: invertir en las competencias para lograd mejores resultados socioeconómicos*. Retrieved from https://eur-lex.europa.eu/legal-content/ES/TXT/PDF/?uri=CELEX:52012DC0669&from=EN

Ferrari, C. A. (2016). *Capitalismo: Crisis, cambios, y evolución en el siglo XXI*. Retrieved from Pontificia Universidad Javeriana https://www.javeriana.edu.co/documents/16113/9477233/N

+1+Capitalismo+crisis+cambios+y+evoluci%C3%B3n+en+el+sXXI+%28WEB%29.pdf/939499f0-2d3f-4e87-ac23-6215fbc2fccc

Fleckenstein, T., & Lee, S. C. (2017). The politics of labor market reform in coordinated welfare capitalism: Comparing Sweden, Germany, and South Korea. *World Politics, 69*(1), 144–183.

Fortwengel, J., & Jackson, G. (2016). Legitimizing the apprenticeship practice in a distant environment: Institutional entrepreneurship through inter-organizational networks. *Journal of World Business, 51*, 895–909.

Franz, T. (2017, May 4). lse.ac.uk. Retrieved from Latin America's productivity problems can only be overcome by incentivising, underwriting, and enforcing technological investment https://blogs.lse.ac.uk/latamcaribbean/2017/05/04/latin-americas-productivity-problems-can-only-be-overcome-by-incentivising-underwriting-and-enforcing-technological-investment/

Fuchs, M., Schamp, E. W., & Wiemann, J. (2016). Duale Aus-und Fortbildung goes global? Zur Internationalisierung von Wissen in der industriellen Fertigung durch global-lokale Qualifizierungsstrategien multinationaler Unternehmen. *Geographische Zeitschrift, 104*(3), 140–157.

Fulton, L. (2020). *National industrial relations, an update.* Labour Research Department and ETUI (online publication). Retrieved from http://www.worker-participation.eu/National-Industrial-Relations

Gallas, D. & Palumbo, D. (2019). *What's gone wrong with Brazil's economy?* BBC. https://www.bbc.com/news/business-48386415

Georg, W. (2005). Vergleichende Berufsbildungsforschung. In F. Rauner (Ed.), *Handbuch Berufsbildungsforschung* (pp. 186–192). Bertelsmann.

Gereffi, G., Bamber, P., & Fernandez-Stark, K. (2016). *Promoting decent work in global supply chains in Latin America and the Caribbean.* ILO.

GIZ. (2019). *GIZ program for strengthening the Mexican Model of Dual Vocational Education and Training (MMFD).*

Gobierno del Estado de México. (2018). *CONALEPMEX.* Retrieved from https://www.conalepmex.edu.mx/educacion-conalep/modelo-educacion-dual.html

Hölscher, M. (2012). Spielarten des Kapitalismus und Kompetenzen von Hochschulabsolventinnen und-absolventen: Eine komparative empirische Analyse. *Kölner Zeitschrift für Soziologie und Sozialpsychologie, 64*, 479–505.

ILO. (2008). *Vocational training and productivity. Montevideo: ILO/Cinterfor.* Retrieved from ILO https://www.oitcinterfor.org/sites/default/files/file_publicacion/trazos37_eng.pdf

iMove. (2012). *Developing skills for employability with German partners.* iMOVEat the Federal Institute for Vocational Education and Training (BIBB).

INEP. (2019). *Instituto Nacional de Estudos e Pesquisas Educacionais Anísio Teixeira.* Retrieved from Censo Escolar http://portal.inep.gov.br/censo-escolar

Janert, J. (2017). *Erfolgsmodell duale Ausbildung.* Retrieved from https://www.deutschland.de/de/topic/wissen/erfolgsmodell-duale-ausbildung

Johanson, M. (2016). *BBC.* Retrieved from There's a mass expat exodus from Brazil https://www.bbc.com/worklife/article/20160729-theres-a-mass-expat-exodus-from-brazil

Jürgens, U., & Krzywdzinski, M. (2016). *New worlds of work: Varieties of work in car factories in the BRIC countries.* Oxford University Press.

Kauer, M. (2015). *Unpublished Dissertation: The status (quo) of VET in Brazil: An empirical study about its function, meaning and impingements from the perspective of former dual system apprentices.* Retrieved from https://opendata.uni-halle.de/bitstream/1981185920/11937/1/Dissertation%20-%20Marcelo%20Kauer%20%28184027%29.pdf

Kostova, T., & Roth, K. (2002). Adoption of an organizational practice by subsidiaries of multinational corporations: Institutional and relational effects. *Academy of Management Journal, 45*, 215–233.

Kruse, O. (2007). *Keine Angst vor dem leeren Blatt. Ohne Schreibblockaden durchs Studium.* CampusConcept.

Krzywdzinski, J., & Jürgens, U. (2019). Transfer deutscher und japanischer Ansätze der Facharbeiter-ausbildung an die BRIC-Standorte: Volkswagen und Toyota im Vergleich. In M. Gessler, M. Fuchs, & M. Pilz (Eds.), *Konzepte und Wirkungen des Transfers Dualer Berufsausbildung* (pp. 281–320). Springer VS.

Kuznetsov, A., & Jacob, M. (2015). Convergence versus divergence: Testing varieties of capitalism on the globalization of buiness practices. In I. S. Marinova (Ed.), *Institutional impacts on firm internationalization* (pp. 12–39). Palgrave Macmillan.

Lawrence, T. B., Hardy, C., & Phillips, N. (2002). Institutional effects of interorganizational collaboration: The emergence of proto-institutions. *The Academy of Management Journal, 45*, 281–290.

López-Fogués, A., Rosado, R., Valiente, O., Fuentes, H., & Aragón, E. (2018). *Pilot evaluation of the Mexican model of dual TVET in the State of Mexico.* Retrieved from http://eprints.gla.ac.uk/159540/7/159540.pdf

Mattes, J. (2013). The regional embeddness of multinational companies: A critical perspective. *European Planning Studies, 21*(4), 433–451.

Mayring, P. (2000). Qualitative Content Analysis. *Forum: Qualitative Qualitative Social Research.* Vol. 1, no. 2, Art. 20.

Mayring, P. (2003). *Qualitative Inhaltsanalyse: Grundlagen und Techniken.* Beltz Verlag.

Mayring, P. (2014). *SSOAR.* Retrieved from Qualitative content analysis: theoretical foundation, basicprocedures and software solution http://nbn-resolving.de/urn:nbn:de:0168-ssoar-395173

Mayring, P., Gläser-Zikuda, M., & Ziegelbauer, S. (2005). Auswertung von Videoaufnahmen mit Hilfe der Qualitativen Inhaltsanalyse - ein Beispiel aus der Unterrichtsforschung. *MedienPädagogik, 9*, 1–17.

Ministério da Educação. (2018). *Secretaria de Educação Profissional e Tecnológica.* Retrieved from http://portal.mec.gov.br/setec/legisla_tecnico_parecer1699.pdf

Mourshed, M., Farrell, D., & Barton, D. (2013). *Educação para o Trabalho: Desenhando um Sistema que Funcione.* McKinsey Center for Government.

Murillo, M. V. (2001). *Labor unions, partisan coalitions, and market reforms in Latin America.* Cambridge University Press.

Neeser, R., & Camargo, L. (2017, May 17). *Brazil: Unions struggle after labor reform.* Retrieved from https://www.shrm.org/resourcesandtools/legal-and-compliance/employment-law/pages/global-brazil-unions-after-labor-reform.aspx

Negrín, A., & Pérez, A. V. (n.d.). México y Alemania: una agenda a futuro. *Revista Mexicana de Política Exterior, 105*, 135–154.

nube. (2020). *Núcleo Brasileiro de Estágios.* Retrieved from https://www.nube.com.br/cota-aprendiz

OECD. (2014). *All on board: Making inclusive growth happen.* .

OECD. (2017). *Education in Chile, Reviews of national policies for education.* OECD Publishing.

OECD. (2019a). *FDI Regulatory Restrictiveness Index.* Retrieved from https://www.oecd.org/investment/fdiindex.htm

OECD. (2019b). *OECD economic surveys Argentina.* OECD.

OECD. (2019c). *OECD economic surveys Colombia.* OECD.

OECD. (2019d). *OECD productivity statistics.* Retrieved from GDP per capita and productivity growth https://data.oecd.org/lprdty/gdp-per-hour-worked.htm

Oliva, B. T. (2014). *Três ensaios de economia da educação.* Fundação Getúlio Vargas.

Otto, F. (2014). audi.com. Retrieved from Audi México: Inaugurado nuevo Centro de Especialización https://www.audi.com.mx/dam/nemo/mx/compania/media-center/noticias/pdf/141021_centro-de-especializacion.pdf

Page, R. (2018). *ARBEITSPAPIER Nummer 313: Co-determination in Germany –A beginner's guide.* Hans Böckler Stiftung.

Pieczynski, D. (2016). *radford.* Retrieved from Employee Turnover Slows in Brazil, Even as the Tech Sector Remains an Economic Bright Spot https://radford.aon.com/insights/articles/2016/employee-turnover-slows-in-brazil

Portelo Souza, A., Lima, L., Arabage, A., Camargo, J., de Lucena, T., & Soares, S. (2015, June). *Inter-American Development Bank.* Retrieved from https://publications.iadb.org/publications/english/document/Vocational-Education-and-Training-in-Brazil-Knowledge-Sharing-Forum-on-Development-Experiences-Comparative-Experiences-of-Korea-and-Latin-America-and-the-Caribbean.pdf

Presidência da República. (2000). *LEI No 10.097, DE 19 DE DEZEMBRO DE 2000.* Retrieved from https://www.planalto.gov.br/ccivil_03/Leis/L10097.htm

Richmond, P. (2020). *European integration and labour market institutions: A varieties of capitalism perspective.* Retrieved from Birkbeck Politics Occasional Paper 3/2020 https://eprints.bbk.ac.uk/31241/1/31241.pdf

Royo, S. (2009). Varieties of capitalism for Latin America? *Jean Monnet/Robert Schuman Paper Series, 9*(12), 2–23.

Ruiz-Velasco Sánchez, E., & Bárcenas López, J. (2019). *Edutecnología y Aprendizaje 4.0.* Sociedad Mexicana de Computación en lad Educación A.C.

Rutherford, T. D., & Holmes, J. (2014). Manufacturing resiliency: Economic restructuring and automotive manufacturing in the Great Lakes region. *Cambridge Journal of Regions, Economy and Society, 7*, 359–378.

Scania. (2020). *Scania.* Retrieved from https://www.volkswagenag.com/de/brands-and-models/scania.html

Schneider, B. R. (2009, August). Hierarchical market economies and varieties of capitalism in Latin America. *Journal of Latin American Studies, 41*(3), 553–575.

Schneider, B. R. (2013). *Hierarchical capitalism in Latin America: Business, labor, and the challenges of equitable development.* Cambridge University Press.

Schneider, B. R., & Karcher, S. (2010). Complementarities and continuities in the political economy of labour markets in Latin America. *Socio-Economic Review, 8*(4), 623–651.

Schneider, B. R., & Soskice, D. (2009). Inequality in developed countries and Latin America: Coordinated, liberal and hierarchical systems. *Economy and Society, 38*(1), 17–52.

Schuler. (2020). *Centro de especialización cedual.* Retrieved from https://www.schulergroup.com/minor/mx/training_center/index.html

Sehnbruch, K. (2016). Unemployment insurance or individual savings accounts: Can Chile's new scheme serve as a model for other developing countries? *International Social Security Review, 59*(1), 27–48.

Seo, M.-G., & Creed, D. W. (2002). Institutional contradictions, praxis, and institutional change: A Dialectical perspective. *The Academy of Management Review, 27*(2), 222–247.

SEP. (2014). *Modelo Mexicano de Formación Dual.* Retrieved from https://www.gob.mx/sep/acciones-y-programas/modelo-mexicano-de-formacion-dual

Silva, J., Almeida, R., & Strokova, V. (2015). *Sustaining employment and wage gains in Brazil.* World Bank Group.

Smets, M., Morris, T., & Greenwood, R. (2012). From practice to field: A multilevel model of practice-driven institutional change. *The Academy of Management Journal, 55*(4), 877–904.

SP. (2020). saopauolo.sp.gov.br. Retrieved from https://www.saopaulo.sp.gov.br/orgaos-e-entidades/governador

Tolbert, P. S., & Zucker, L. G. (1996). The institutionalization of institutional theory. In S. Clegg, C. Hardy, & W. Nord (Eds.), *Handbook of organization studies* (pp. 175–190). Sage.

UNESCO. (2016). *Brazil.* Retrieved from http://www.unesco.org/new/en/gefi/partnerships/gefi-champion-countries/brazil/

vetnet. (2020). *German chambers worldwide network (AHK) for cooperative, work-based Vocational Education & Training.* Retrieved from Bundesministerium für Bildung und Forschung https://www.berufsbildung-international.de/de/projekte-und-kooperationslaender-strategieprojekte-vetnet.html

VETnet. (n.d.). *Elf Länder, ein Ziel: Erfolg durch berufliche Bildung.* Retrieved from https://mexiko.ahk.de/fileadmin/AHK_Mexiko/Dokumente/vetnet-deutsch.pdf

Viehmann, S. M. (2017). *Formação Dual e sua aplicação no Brasil*. Retrieved from http://www.brasilalemanhanews.com.br/formacao/formacao-dual-e-sua-aplicacao-no-brasil/?doing_wp_cron=1592298898.9241828918457031250000

Voith. (2019a). *A stepping stone for your dream career*. Retrieved from http://www.voith.com/corp-en/careers___students.html

Voith. (2019b). *Summer 1964 - summer 2014: 50 years of Voith in Brazil*. Retrieved from http://www.voith.com/corp-en/sala-de-imprensa__press-releases-77217_59346.html

Volkswagen Group. (2020a). *Volkswagen Group Academy Mexico*. Retrieved from http://www.vwi.com.mx/auditors.html

Volkswagen Group. (2020b). *Volkswagen de México*. Retrieved from https://www.vw.com.mx/es.html

Wenzler-Cremer, H. (2007). Grounded-Theory-Methodologie. *QUASUS. Qualitatives Methodenportal zur Qualitativen Sozial-, Unterrichts- und Schulforschung*.

Weinstein, B. (1997). *For social peace in Brazil: Industrialists and the remaking of the working class in São Paulo, 1920-1964*. University of North Carolina Press.

Weiss, S. (2016). *Vorreiter in Mexiko – die VW-Akademie*. Retrieved from https://www.deutschland.de/de/topic/wissen/bildung-lernen/vorreiter-in-mexiko-die-vw-akademie

Westervelt, E. (2012). *The secret to Germany's low youth unemployment*. Retrieved from https://www.npr.org/2012/04/04/149927290/the-secret-to-germanys-low-youth-unemployment

Wiemann, K. (2018). *Mexiko. Internationales Handbuch der Berufsbildung, Band 49*. Bundesinstitut für Berufsbildung.

Wiemann, J., & Fuchs, M. (2018). The export of Germany's "secret of success" dual technical VET: MNCs and multiscalar stakeholders changing the skill formation system in Mexico. *Cambridge Journal or Regions, Economy and Society, 11*(2), 373–386.

Wiemann, K., & Pilz, M. (2017). Berufliche Ausbildung durch mexikanische und deutsche Unternehmen in Mexiko - ein Home-International-Vergleich. *Journal für International und Interkulturell Vergleichende Erziehungswissenschaft 23, 2*, 217-245.

Chapter 8
Summary and Concluding Remarks

This work argues that striving for increasing GDP runs the risk of enlarging a dysfunctional game rather than attaining substantial socioeconomic development—particularly in the context of developing countries. Therefore, capturing MNCs' contribution to development as a matter of generated GDP is—at least in this study—questionable. On that account, rather than the size of the game, this work is primarily aimed at targeting its rules, which are made up of and reproduce dysfunctions and developmental stagnation.

In order to meet this objective, this work developed the analytical framework Conflating Capitalisms and shifted the role of MNCs from being a featureless flow of USD toward that of agents of institutional change. This approach allows systemic distortions to be addressed at their roots and to approach MNCs' contribution to development as a matter of positive institutional change caused rather than one of generated GDP. In order to construct an analytical framework that allows one to better grasp such a remodeled role of MNCs and their potential impact on institutional distortions in developing countries, this work succeeded in broadening analysis by incorporating the non-identical *Gestalt* of system-transcending MNCs and the different capitalist forms of socio-economic organization. That again allows for dynamics that occur when the former interacts with the latter to be captured. Such fine-tuned analysis required extensive theory development in order to prepare a solid grounding for the construction of Conflating Capitalisms.

Briefly summarizing, the general contestation of the related economic approaches with the detachment of GDP from socioeconomic development established the point of departure for theory development. It pointed out Drawbacks that need to be overcome and assets that serve to be built upon. Directed by the general logic of investigation and the building blocks derived from the analysis of ACI and IAD, the single cornerstones of, first, the actor and, second, the differently constituted

---

Supplementary Information The online version contains supplementary material available at [https://doi.org/10.1007/978-3-030-93805-5_8].

M. Kappler, *Western Multinational Corporations in Latin America*, Contributions to Economics, https://doi.org/10.1007/978-3-030-93805-5_8

institutional settings were discussed. Relating to the former, the MNC as a system-crossing entity was introduced alongside its different forms of appearance and the corresponding characteristics of ownership, dependence, and control. The MNCs' foreign wholly owned subsidiary that is characterized by the purest relationship with its parent company was selected as the actor of choice. Regarding the different organization of capitalist systems—building largely on the VoC approach and its advancements to developing countries—the institutional settings of coordinated, liberal, and hierarchical market economies were brought into line and incorporated into theory development. As such the diversity of socio-economic organization was widened beyond the concept of impersonal markets.

Of utmost importance, each distinct market economy contributed to this work by allowing micro-level interaction to relate with socioeconomic outcomes at the national level and by indicating distinct prevailing action constellations and corresponding unique behavioral interaction patterns. Firmly grounded in a comprehensive understanding of the MNC and the varying institutional settings, this work elaborated on a broader sociological understanding of structure and agency to improve the framework's capability of grasping contradiction caused by system-crossing MNCs. On that account, the general conception of institutional rigidity, the corresponding "temptation of determinism," and the postulated paradox of embedded agency were overcome by, first, broadening the narrow understanding of actor's rationality with the wider concepts of legitimacy and appropriateness and, second, considering MNCs' foreign subsidiaries as subject to more than one institutional setting at a time, being in a constant state of institutional duality. Along these lines, the concept of organizational fields was introduced and applied to foreign subsidiaries, locating them within the two contradictory intra-organizational and local host country organizational fields that both exert isomorphic pressures on the MNC's subsidiary to show conformity. Accordingly, understanding the foreign subsidiary as attempting to show conformity within both different organizational fields, in effect, necessarily generates inter-systemic contradiction leading to and, therefore, allowing for the occurrence of behavioral contradiction in the host country and alien-to-the-system practices to enter institutional analysis. As indicated in Fig. 8.1, behavioral contradiction materializes in the action situation.

Considering the impact of MNCs' action on the local institutional setting, foreign subsidiaries' contradictory behavior within the local field was put under scrutiny as behavioral patterns of avoidance and defiance that challenge the legitimacy of existing local institutional patterns and initiate potential institutional change. Following this general line of reasoning, this work further developed a feedback channel that connects contradictory behavior with potential generated institutional change. In order to capture the impact of deviating behavior in its surroundings and to genuinely include actor-induced institutional change into analysis, isomorphic pressures are applied in a reversed logic, allowing the MNC to exert isomorphic pressure on and to shape the corresponding institutional setting. In addition to the concept of reversed isomorphism, the feedback channel was further developed with the understanding of the MNC as an institutional entrepreneur that consciously exploits contradiction, mobilizes actors and resources, and collectively endorses and enacts

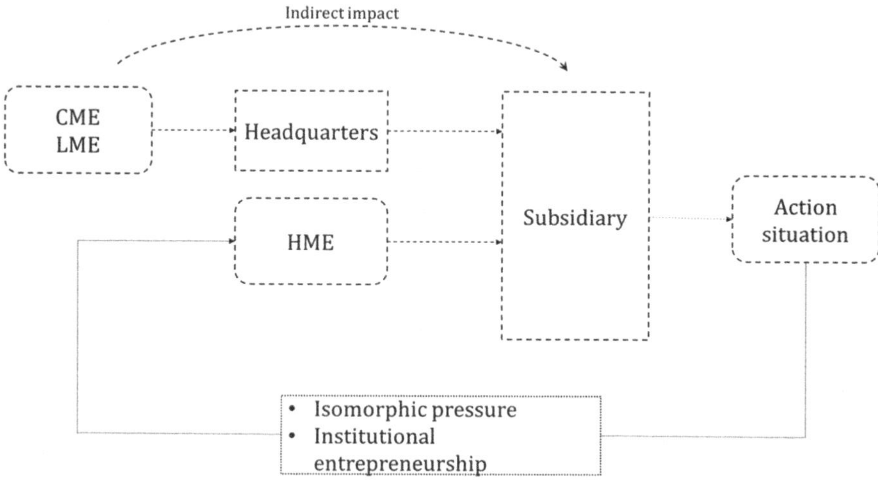

Fig. 8.1 Conflating capitalisms applied to the Latin American case. Source: From the author

the proposed alternative institutional arrangement. Accordingly, the feedback channel is capable of grasping actor-induced institutional change as both "by-product" of the subsidiary's actual duty and the more strategic and political action aiming at a specific institutional change.

Finally, in order to hypothesize about expected behavioral contradiction and institutional change caused within a specific case, the condition triangle was developed to consider characteristics and specificities of the actors in play, the specific action conducted, and the organizational fields involved. Considerations relating to the condition triangle culminate either in the "Contradiction Cube" estimating the strength of the intra-organizational field or in the "Change Cube" estimating the strength of impact on the local field.

Figure 8.1 indicates the analytical framework that Conflating Capitalisms applied to the empirical case of this study. Summarizing, the dashed lines depict the institutional dynamics that lead to the action situation which induces action and requires the actor to decide how to act. Hence, it is the action situation in which behavioral contradiction materializes. The dotted lines demonstrate the feedback channel and depict the venues for actor-induced institutional change in the local organizational field.

After establishing the analytical framework of Conflating Capitalisms, this work applied it in order to put a specific case study under empirical scrutiny. The application of the newly developed framework served, first, to contest theoretical considerations with empirical reality and, second, to improve understanding of MNCs' role in the particular setting of the case study. The case included MNCs from, first, France and Germany as archetypal representatives for CMEs and, second, from the USA and the UK, as archetypal representatives for LMEs. The Latin American countries of Argentina, Brazil, Chile, and Colombia were the host countries of choice, depicting archetypal representatives for HMEs. For each country, the high degree of representativeness for the corresponding capitalist system was verified by in-depth analysis of empirical indicators and existing studies. In line with the overarching rationale of this work, the empirical study aimed at understanding the role of MNCs in the Latin American countries and, above all, their contribution to development understood as a matter of institutional functioning. In so doing, a sequential mixed-method design was applied, first, quantitatively scrutinizing the action situation and detecting potentially contradictory behavior and, second, qualitatively investigating the impact of contradiction on the local field as potential actor-induced institutional change.

The quantitative study was the first of its kind and, therefore, was the first one that put interaction at the micro-level on a relatively large scale under scrutiny, generating a good degree of generalizability. In order to attain reasonable explanatory power, the quantitative analysis was conducted exhaustively by, first, translating and operationalizing the institutional dimensions and their major aspects into measurable behavioral indicators; second, cognitively pre-testing the questions developed; and third, conducting a relatively large-scale survey among senior managers within both the MNCs' foreign subsidiaries and the headquarters. In general, the analysis found fairly strong evidence suggesting a moderate to strong impact of the intra-organizational field on the behavior shown by foreign subsidiaries. On that account, it was found that behavior in the subsidiary can be explained to a reasonably high degree by behavior in the corresponding parent company. Furthermore, analyses of group differences between foreign subsidiaries from liberal countries and their counterparts from coordinated countries showed significantly different behavioral patterns, strongly reflecting the patterns deemed most appropriate in their corresponding home country. Whereas the intra-organizational was found to not be equally strong across all dimensions and aspects within them, it was educational efforts in particular that demonstrated a remarkably high degree of behavioral contradiction, meaning that the foreign subsidiaries in HMEs strongly applied educational practices originating from their home country. Of utmost interest and further contributing to understanding the dynamics of institutional contradiction, the quantitative study found institutional complementarity in particular between the institutional dimension of education and training and the other dimensions. Accordingly, one can reasonably assume that foreign subsidiaries that relied on home country educational practices compensated for a lack of local complementarity and embedded educational efforts in aligned and supportive behavior.

In line with the strongly contradictory behavioral patterns in the context of education, the qualitative study aimed at scrutinizing the impact of foreign subsidiaries from German MNCs in Brazil. Since no such investigation has taken place in this context before, categories and aspects of reality to consider needed to be developed. On that account, this work conducted a comparative study including both Brazil and (as reference case of alleged best practice) Mexico. To put the study on a solid grounding, in-depth semi-structured interviews were conducted with local corporate and other organizational decision-makers in the context of DVT in Brazil and Mexico. Transcribed versions of the interviews and supplementary documents, newspapers, etc. were put under the detailed scrutiny of a qualitative content analysis. Above all, the study indicated that, first, both venues for actor-induced institutional change were found to be active in the context of DVT following the German model in the HMEs and, second, that, indeed, the behavioral contradiction led to institutional change. Of further interest and supporting findings of complementarity in the quantitative analysis, subsidiaries of German MNCs compensated for the local institutional weakness by aligning behavior across the institutional domains, strongly supporting the concept of "enabling" institutions.

Today, the educational landscape in Brazil shows various DVT initiatives according to the German model that are largely carried by subsidiaries with German roots. Accordingly, the qualitative study found strong evidence that suggested an institutional impact in both Mexico and Brazil, though to differing degrees. Differences in local receptiveness were found to be decisive regarding the effect of both venues of change in respect of their subsequent institutional impact. Nonetheless, remarkably, reaching the core of the institutionally reproduced low-skill trap in Latin America, evidence was found that suggests DVT initiatives allow both the employers and local young people to overcome the obstacles raised by HMEs' institutional setting and to manage to mutually promise a sufficiently large degree of certainty that allows both parties to engage in long-term cooperation, to invest in each other, and, thus, to generate quality jobs. Along these lines, the quality of institutional change and the contribution to development can certainly be evaluated positively. While still on a relatively small scale, systemic distortions were overcome and allowed local companies to create quality jobs. However, DVT in Brazil in particular has not yet reached a sufficient degree of institutionalization to genuinely counter institutional distortions on a larger scale. However, given the capability of solving the mist of uncertainty and the positive trajectory of DVT demonstrated by the Mexican case, DVT according to the German model has the potential to significantly improve the situation in Brazil.

Relating to the overarching objective of this study, this work's extensive theoretical development culminating in the Conflating Capitalisms framework and the in-depth empirical scrutiny contributed to a better understanding of the nexus between developing countries and MNCs. It succeeded in overcoming the straitjacket of blueprints, considered the non-identical *Gestalt* of both MNCs and capitalist systems and made MNCs' contribution to development a matter of contradiction and actor-induced institutional change.

In a VoC fashion, through the expected aligned interest of both politics and business of conducting successful economic interaction, this work provided valuable insights for a wider, in particular, economic and political audience. For MNCs, being the very subject of institutional dynamics, a better understanding of such improves capabilities in a variety of managerial tasks. Most visibly, the study at hand indicated institutional matters to consider when introducing home country practices in a strange system. It provided a wide knowledge base that gives information on, among others, complementary institutions to consider, potential challenges occurring, potential design of initiatives and partners with whom to cooperate, and potential venues for local change. Beyond, this work improved general understanding of matters such as HQ–subsidiary relations, expatriate management, local institutional problems, and potential behavioral leeway in host countries.

For other stakeholders of the political economy at the macro-level, this work added a remodeled institutional perspective that allows the roots of developmental problems to be approached and to more comprehensively understand the MNC as a source of contradiction, a major constituent of the local institutional setting, and a source of potentially positive innovation. This newly developed perspective allows policy makers to move within the rather binary stances of either attracting or refusing FDI. As such this work generally benefits policy making inasmuch as it broadens the knowledge base and provides a fine-tuned institutional understanding that enables politicians to purposefully lead desired institutional development, considering complementarity and the inclusion of major actors. Furthermore, and of particular importance, this work equipped policy making with a larger arsenal of potential instruments by demonstrating potentially successful incorporation of coordinated practices in non-coordinated environments. Following these lines of reasoning, strongly informed by theoretical considerations made and empirical evidence found by this work, apart from the understanding of development as an institutional matter, this study endorses a more extensive and genuine incorporation of coordinated practices into the economic, business, and development debate. Regarding the general fit of coordination with business requirements, evidence was found that counters the narrative of a "flight from the German model" that mirrors the overarching rationale of a (too) highly restrictive institutional setting in CMEs. On the contrary, German MNCs remodel coordinated microcosms in non-coordinated host countries in order to conduct practices that would not be possible otherwise. Regarding the organization of economic activity, it is, for example, the coordinated practice of DVT in Brazil and Mexico that succeeded in overcoming the Latin American "low-skill trap" by enabling stakeholders to commit to the long term and, thus, to reasonably invest in each other. On that account, in conjunction with coordinated practices' inherent advantage of possible intra-firm consolidation, this work argues that a careful consideration of coordinated practices as a solid alternative of organization with a firm notion of complementarity and a wider inclusion of actors would benefit the general debate.

This work invites the scholarly debate to join investigations in the context of Conflating Capitalisms and to further improve the underlying theoretical grounding and further sharpen the instruments applied. As such, the link between, for example, the establishment of DVT in HMEs and the local improvement of equality and labor productivity is built on the concept of a market economy as the sum of interactions and on experience values from other countries, but it is not yet grounded in local empirical evidence. On that account, in order to reasonably reconnect specific interactions with the socioeconomic performance of a country, Conflating Capitalisms would strongly benefit from an analytical inclusion and connection of generated actor-induced institutional change with performance indicators at the macro-level. Furthermore, in line with the nature of institutional dynamics discussed throughout this work, findings from the empirical study of the Latin American countries are to be interpreted with the caution of an ongoing process. As was remarkably shown by the institutional development in Mexico, the process of institutionalization can proceed disruptively and the institutional setting investigated today may soon look different. On that account, rather than depicting a final state, findings of the empirical study in Latin America require ongoing contestation and would highly benefit from inclusion into a continuous research process.

Furthermore, Conflating Capitalisms is a universal analytical framework that serves for inter-systemic investigation for all market economies and is by no means limited to the Latin American case study applied here. On that account, this work encourages scholars from all regions of the world that can be described as having a specific type of a market economy to improve understanding of alien-to-the-system elements in their own political economy. Along the same lines, Conflating Capitalisms can also be equally applied to well-functioning host regions of the world. In comparison to developing countries such as Brazil or Mexico, market economies that are capable of providing a good life to the majority of inhabitants may be interested in maintaining the status quo rather than changing it. However, independent of what is "desired"—institutional change or consolidation—an in-depth understanding of institutional dynamics and the deduction of, for example, suitable and supportive policies are of unchanged importance.

This wide area of potential application can certainly contribute positively to further improving Conflating Capitalisms. Up to now, the newly developed analytical framework may best be described as a starting point for further investigation that adds a new perspective but which requires further application and development along both its quantitative and qualitative components.

Relating to the action situation, up to now, quantitative analysis—in particular for the Brazilian case—is based on a rather small sample size. On that account, general validity would gain from further empirical contestation of the findings made. Along the same lines, quantitative analysis has been limited to comparative studies and relative differences in behavior as being either more coordinated or more liberal. Along these lines, explanatory power and analytical accuracy would certainly benefit from a wider application generating more experience values that again allow giving absolute values to act either in a liberal or in a coordinated manner. Such improvements would allow one to conduct standalone studies focusing on, for example, MNCs from only one country of origin. Similarly, regarding the qualitative section of actor-induced institutional change, informative value would benefit from, for example, a wider inclusion of a larger variety of actors and, in general, more respondents across larger parts of the country. In both country studies conducted, dynamics observed occurred largely in the industrial hotspots of each country. In order to grasp the impact of change at the wider country level, the inclusion of a set of sectoral and geographically more diffuse actors would be beneficial. Furthermore, as found in the course of the Brazilian case, the Change Cube, indeed, considers various contextual factors and gives a certain direction but could gain by attaining a higher sensitivity to understanding different outcomes in very similar market systems. On that account, a more fine-tuned understanding of, in particular, the factor of local receptiveness would improve the quality of expected actor-induced institutional change. Accordingly, more local investigation and the incorporation of a wider spectrum of host country actors could further improve the analytical depth of Conflating Capitalisms.

References

Acemoglu, D., Johnson, S., & Robinson, J. A. (2005). Institutions as the fundamental cause of long-run growth. In I. P. Aghion & S. Durlauf (Eds.), *Handbook of economic growth* (pp. 385–472). Elsevier.

Adam, F., Kristan, P., & Tomsic, M. (2009). Varieties of capitalism in Eastern Europe (with special emphasis on Estonia and Slovenia). *Communist and Post-Communist Studies, 42*, 65–81.

Adams, W. (2015). Conducting semi-structured interviews. In E. N. Newcomer, P. H. Hatry, & J. S. Wholey (Eds.), *Handbook of practical program evaluation* (pp. 492–505). Wiley.

Agarwal, M., & Atri, P. (2015). Foreign direct investment and poverty reduction: India in regional context. In *Research and information system for developing countries discussion paper.*

Ahumada, J. M. (2019). Latin America since the 1990s: Deindustrialization, reprimarization and policy space restrictions. *The Political Economy of Peripheral Growth, 2019*, 49–72.

Albert, M. (1992). *Kapitalismus contra Kapitalismus*. Campus.

Alden, C., & Davies, M. (2006). A profile of the operations of Chinese multinationals in Africa. *South African Journal of International Affairs, 13*, 83–96.

Alexander, J. C. (1990, June). *Commentary: Structure, value, action* (pp. 339–345). American Sociological Association.

Allen, M. (2004). The varieties of capitalism paradigm: Not enough variety? *Socio-Economic Review, 2*, 87–108.

Almeida, R., Anazawa, L., Menezes Filho, N., & Vasconcellos, L. (2015). *Policy research Working Paper 7246.* Retrieved from investing in technical & vocational education and training: Does it yield large economic returns in Brazil? Retrieved from http://documents.worldbank.org/curated/pt/465981468181787054/pdf/WPS7246.pdf

Almfraji, M. A., Almsafir, M. K., & Yao, I. (2014). Economic growth and foreign direct investment inflows: The case of Qatar. *Procedia-Social and Behavioral Science, 109*, 1040–1045.

ALTRATEC. (2012). *Formación en el Sistema Dual.* Retrieved from http://www.altratec.mx/organizacion.html

Amable, B. (2003). *The diversity of modern capitalism*. Oxford University Press.

Amable, B., Demmou, L., & Gatti, D. (2011). The effect of employment protection and product market regulation on labour market performance: Substitution or complementarity? *Applied Economics, 43*, 449–464.

Amblard, F., Ferrand, N., & Hill, D. R. (2001). How a conceptual framework can help to design models following decreasing abstraction. In *13th SCS-European Simulation Symposium* (pp. 843–847).

M. Kappler, *Western Multinational Corporations in Latin America*, Contributions to Economics, https://doi.org/10.1007/978-3-030-93805-5

Anckar, C. (2008). On the applicability of the most similar systems design and the most different systems design in comparative research. *International Journal of Social Research Methodology, 2008*, 389–401.
Anderson, G. W. (2000). *Multinational corporations and tacit knowledge: Determination of entry mode and impact of entry*. In Paper presented at the 7th Convention of the East Asian Economics Association.
Andonova, V., & Losada-Otálora, M. (2018). *Multilatinas: Strategies for internationalisation*. Cambridge University Press.
Aoki, M. (2001). *Toward a comparative insitutional analysis*. The MIT Press.
Aoki, M. (2010). *Corporations in evolving dinversity*. Oxford Universtiy Press.
Aragón, E. (2019). nopoor: Working Paper n° 74. *Increasing employability of young people through policy changes in educational systems: The Mexican Model of Dual Formation*. Retrieved from Increasing employability of young people through Policy changes in Educational Systems: The Mexican Model of Dual Formation.
Artega García, A., Sierra Romero, S., & Flores Lima, R. (2010). The vocational training system in Mexico: Characteristics and actors, strenghts and weaknesses. In I. G. Bosch & J. Charest (Eds.), *Vocational training. International perspectives (Routledge studies in employment and work relations in context)* (Vol. 4, pp. 187–213). Routledge.
Assunção, J., & Gonzaga, G. (2010). *Educação Profissional no Brasil: Inserção e Retorno*. SENAI-DN.
Astorga, P. (2010). A century of economic growth in Latin America. *Journal of Development Economics, 92*, 232–243.
Bacha, E., & Feinberg, R. (1985). The World bank and structural adjustment in Latin America. In *Texto para discussão, No. 100, Pontifícia Universidade Católica doRio de Janeiro (PUC-Rio)*, pp. 2–28.
Balasubramanyam, V. N., Salisu, M., & Sapsford, D. (1996). Foreign direct investment and growth in EP and IS countries. *The Economic Journal, 106*, 92–105.
Bardasi, E., Beegle, K., Dillon, A., & Serneels, P. (2010, January). Do labor statistics depend on how and to whom the questions are asked. *Policy Research Working Paper 5192*, pp. 1–56.
Bartram, T., Boyle, B., Stanton, P., Burgess, J., & McDonnell, A. (2015). Multinational companies and industrial relations: A research agenda for the 21st century. *Journal of Industrial Relations, 57*(2), 127–145.
Battaglia, M. P., Link, M. W., Frankel, M. R., Osborn, L., & Mokdad, A. H. (2008). An evaluation of respondent selection methods for household mail surveys. *Public Opinion Quarterly, 72*(3), 459–469.
Benson, J. K. (1977). Organizations: A dialectic view. *Administrative Science Quarterly, 22*, 1–21.
Berg, A., Ostry, J. D., & Zettelmeyer, J. (2012). What makes growth sustained? *Journal of Development Economics, 98*, 149–166.
BiBB. (2017). *Ausbildungsordnungen und wie sie entstehen*. Bundesinstitut für Berufsbildung.
BiBB. (2018). *Imove*. Retrieved from Mexiko und Deutschland vertiefen Zusammenarbeit in Berufsbildung https://www.imove-germany.de/de/alle_news.htm?content-url=/cps/rde/xchg/imove_projekt_de_2020/hs.xsl/Mexiko-und-Deutschland-vertiefen-Zusammenarbeit-in-Berufsbildung.htm
Biglaiser, G. (2002). The internationalization of Chicago's economics in Latin America. *Economic Development and Cultural Change, 50*(2), 269–286.
Birkinshaw, J., & Hood, N. (1998). Multinational subsidiary evolution: Capability and charter change in foreign-owned subsidiary companies. *The Academy of Management Review, 23*, 773–795.
Bisberg, I., & Théret, B. (2015). *Variedades del capitalismo en américa Latina: los casos de México, Brasil*. El Colegio de México.
Bizberg, I. (2014a). Tipos de Capitalismo en América Latina. In I. Bizberg (Ed.), *Variedades de Capitalismo en América Latina: los Casos de México, Brasil, Argentina y Chile* (pp. 41–94). El Colegio de México.

Bizberg, I. (2014b). *Variedades de Capitalismo en América Latina: los Casos de México, Brasil, Argentina y Chile*. El Colegio de México.

Bizberg, I., & Théret, B. (2014). Introducción. In I. Bizberg (Ed.), *Variedades de Capitalismo en América Latina: los Casos de México, Brasil, Argentina y Chile* (pp. 11–39). El Colegio de México.

Bizberg, I., & Théret, B. (2015). *Variedades del capitalismo en América Latina: los casos de México, Brasil, Argentina y Chile*. El Colegio de México.

Blackman, A., Batz, M., & Evans, D. (2004). Maquiladoras, air pollution, and human health in Ciudad Juaréz and El Paso. In *Ressources for the future, Discussion paper*, pp. 3–18.

Blank, F. (2016). Unemployment and pensions protection in Europe: The changing role of social partners. In *OSE Paper Series, Research Paper No. 29*.

Blomquist, W., & deLeon, P. (2011). The design and promise of the institutional analysis and development framework. *The Policy Studies Journal, 39*(1), 1–6.

Blomström, M., Kokko, A., & Zejan, M. (2000). *Foreign direct investment: Firm and host country strategies*. Macmillan Press.

Blomström, M., & Lipsey, R. E. (1989). The export performance of US and Swedish multinationals. *Review of Income and Wealth, 35*(3), 245–264.

Blomström, M., & Lipsey, R. R. (1991). Firm size and foreign operations of multinationals. *Scandinavian Journal of Economics, 93*(1), 101–107.

Blonigen, B. A. (2005). A review of the empirical literature on FDI determinants. *Atlantic Economic Journal, 33*, 383–403.

BMBF. (2010). *Marktstudie Brasilien: für den Export beruflicher Aus- und Weiterbildung*. iMove beim Bundesinstitut für Berufsbildung (BIBB).

BMBF. (2017). *Bundesministerium für Bildung und Forschung (BMBF), Referat Grundsatzfragen der beruflichen Aus- und Weiterbildung*. Retrieved from Duale Berufsausbildung sichtbar gemacht https://www.freie-berufe.de/wordpress/wp-content/uploads/2017/09/BMBF_Duale_Berufsausbildung.pdf

BMBF. (2018). *Berufsbildungsbericht 2018*. Bundesministerium für Bildung und Forschung (BMBF) Referat Grundsatzfragen der beruflichen Aus und Weiterbildung.

BMWi. (2019). *Assoziierungsabkommen zwischen der EU und den MERCOSUR-Staaten*. Retrieved from https://www.bmwi.de/Redaktion/DE/Artikel/Aussenwirtschaft/assoziierungsabkommen-zwischen-der-eu-und-den-mercosur-staaten.html

Bockmann, J. (2019). Democratic socialism in Chile and Peru: Revisiting the "Chicago Boys" as the origin of neoliberalism. *Comparative Studies in Society and History, 61*(3), 654–679.

Bodemer, K. (2008). *Del "viejo" Cepalismo a la crítica de la globalización Cambio y continuidad en el debate sobre las estrategias de desarrollo en América Latina*. Retrieved from http://www.redalyc.org/home.oa, http://www.redalyc.org/pdf/774/77411616001.pdf

Boessen, A. C. (2008). *The politics of European Union health policy-making: An actor-centred institutionalist analysis*. Datawyse/Universitaire Pers Maastricht.

Bond, P. (2008). South Africa's "developmental state" distraction. *Mediations, 24*(1), 8–27.

Borensztein, E., De Gregoria, J., & Lee, J. (1998). How does foreign direct investment affect economic growth? *Journal of International Economics, 45*(1), 115–135.

Boris, D. (2009). *Lateinamerikas Politische Ökonomie: Aufbruch aus historischen Abhängigkeiten im 21. Jahrhundert*. VSA Verlag.

Bosch. (2018a). *Bosch in Brazil*. Retrieved from https://www.bosch-presse.de/pressportal/de/en/bosch-in-brazil-162240.html

Bosch. (2018b). *Factsheet: Bosch in Mexico*. Retrieved from https://www.bosch-presse.de/pressportal/de/en/press-release-146373.html

Bovaird, T. (2007). Beyond engagement and participation: User and community coproduction of public services. *Public Administration Review, 67*, 846–860.

Boxenbaum, E. (2006). Corporate social responsibility as institutional hybrids. *Journal of Business Strategies, 23*, 45–63.

Boxenbaum, E., & Jonsson, S. (2017). Isomorphism, diffusion and decoupling: Concept evolution and theoretical challenges. In R. Greenwood, C. Oliver, T. B. Lawrence, & R. E. Meyer (Eds.), *The SAGE handbook of organizational institutionalism* (pp. 77–101). Sage.

Boyer, R. (2005). *How and why capitalisms differ*. MPIfG Discussion Paper 05/4.

Braig, M. (2011). Hinterhof der USA? Eine Beziehungsgeschichte. *Politik und Zeitgeschichte Heft, 40–42*, 36–42.

Bresser-Pereira, L. C. (2012). Five models of capitalism. *Brazilian Journal of Political Economy, 32*(1), 21–32.

Brewster, C., Wood, G., & Brookes, M. (2008). Similarity, isomorphism or duality? Recent survey evidence on the human resource management policies of multinational corporations. *British Journal of Management, 19*, 320–342.

Brookes, M., Brewster, C., & Wood, G. (2017, 2017). Are MNCs norm entrepreneurs or followers? The changing relationship between host country institutions and MNC HRM practices. *The International Journal of Human Resource Management*, 1690–1711.

Brosius, A., van Elsas, E., & de Vreese, C. H. (2020). Trust in context: National heuristics and survey context effects on political trust in the European Union. *European Union Politics*.

Bruinshoofd, A. (2016). *Institutional quality and economic performance*. Rabo Research/Economic Research.

Buckley, P. J., & Casson, M. C. (1976). *The future of the multinational enterprise*. Macmillan.

Buckley, P. J., & Casson, M. C. (2009, 2009). The internalisation theory of the multinational enterprise: A review of the progress of a research agenda after 30 years. *Journal of International Business Studies*, 1–18.

Buckley, P. J., & Casson, M. (2010a). *The multinational enterprise revisited*. Palgrave Macmillan.

Buckley, P. J., & Casson, M. (2010b). *The multinational enterprise revisited: The essential Buckley and Casson*. Palgrave Macmillan.

Buckley, P. J., Clegg, J., & Wang, C. (2006). Inward foreign direct investment and host country productivty: Evidence from China electronics industry. *Transnational Corporations, 15*(1), 13–37.

Buckley, P. J., & Pearce, R. D. (1979). Overseas production and exporting by the world's leading enterprises. *Journal of International Business Studies, 10*(1), 9–20.

Burns, J., & Nielsen, K. (2006). How do embedded agents engage in institutional change? *Journal of Economic Issues, 40*(2), 449–456.

Busch, K. (2010). *World economic crisis and the welfare state: Possible solutions to reduce economic and social imbalances in the world economy, Europe and Germany*. Friedrich Ebert Stiftung.

Busemeyer, M. R. (2009, 7). Asset specificity, institutional complementarities and the variety of skill regimes in coordinated market economies. *Socio-Economic Review*, 375–406.

Bushouse, B. K. (2011). Governance structures: Using IAD to understand variation in service delivery for club goods with information asymmetry. *The Policy Studies Journal, 39*(1), 105–119.

Cáceres-Reebs, D., & Schneider, U. (2020). *Vocational education and training in Mexico - How the country has tropicalised the dual model*. Retrieved from https://www.bibb.de/en/22624.php

Cadena, A., Remes, J., Grosman, N., & de Oliveira, A. (2017). *McKinsey Global Institute: Where will Latin America's growth come from?* McKinsey& Company.

calculator.net. (2019). *Sample size calculator*. Retrieved from https://www.calculator.net/sample-size-calculator.html

Câmara dos Deputados. (2020). *Biblioteca Digital*. Retrieved from LDB Lei de diretrizes e bases da educação nacional: Lei n° 9.394, de 20 de dezembro de 1996, que estabelece as diretrizes e bases da educação nacional http://bd.camara.leg.br/bd/handle/bdcamara/19339

CAMEXA. (2019). *Análisis Sectorial y Regional: Modelo Mexicano de Formación Dual*. CAMEXA.

CAMEXA. (2020). *Die deutsche duale Berufsausbildung in Mexiko*. Retrieved from https://mexiko.ahk.de/dual/deutsche-duale-berufsausbildung

Cantwell, J., Dunning, J. H., & Lundan, S. M. (2010). An evolutionary approach to understanding international business activity: The co-evolution of MNCs and the institutional environment. *Journal of International Business Studies, 41*, 567–586.
Cardoso, F. H., & Faletto, E. (1979). *Dependency and development in Latin America*. University of California Press.
Carney, M., Gedajlovic, E., & Yang, X. (2009). Varieties of Asian capitalism: Toward an institutional theory of Asian enterprise. *Asia Pacific Journal of Management, 2009*, 361–380.
Casper, S. (2009). Can new technology firms succeed incoordinated market economies? A response to Herrmann and Lange. *Socio-Economic Review, 2009*, 209–215.
Central Intelligence Agency. (2019, January 10). *The World Factbook*. Retrieved from https://www.cia.gov/library/publications/the-world-factbook/rankorder/2172rank.html
Centro Alemán de Información para Latinoamérica. (2015). *El CEDUAL expande sus operaciones en Puebla, México*. Retrieved from https://alemaniaparati.diplo.de/mxdz-es/aktuelles/cedualexpansionpuebla/1087570
CEPAL. (2015). *National Programme for access to technical education and employment-PRONATEC (Programa Nacional de Acesso ao Ensino Técnico e Emprego) (2011-)*. Retrieved from https://dds.cepal.org/bpsnc/programme?id=80
Chandler, A. (1974). *The visible hand*. Harvard University Press.
Chang, S.-J., Chung, J., & Moon, J. J. (2013, March). When do wholly owned subsidiaries perform better than joint ventures? *Strategic Management Journal, 34*(3), 317–337.
Chankseliani, M., & Anuar, A. M. (2019). Cross-country comparison of engagement in apprenticeships: A conceptual analysis of incentives for individuals and firms. *International Journal for Research in Vocational Education and Training, 2019*, 261–283.
Chao, J., Rinaudo, E. K., & Uhlaner, R. (2014, January). mckinsey.com. Retrieved from Avoiding blind spots in your next joint venture https://www.mckinsey.com/~/media/McKinsey/Business%20Functions/Strategy%20and%20Corporate%20Finance/Our%20Insights/Avoiding%20blind%20spots%20in%20your%20next%20joint%20venture/Avoiding%20blind%20spots%20in%20your%20next%20joint%20venture.ashx
Chicago Tribune. (2015). *Key automotive investments in Mexico*. Retrieved from https://www.chicagotribune.com/business/ct-mexican-auto-plants-0711-biz-20150710-story.html
Choe, J. I. (2003). Do foreign direct investment and gross domestic investment promote economic growth? *Review of Development Economics, 2003*, 44–57.
Choi, J. J., & Dow, S. (2008). *Institutional approach to global corporate governance: Business systems and beyond* (Vol. 9). Emerald Group Publishing.
Christophers, B. (2015). The limits to financialization. *Dialogues in Human Geography, 5*(2), 183–200.
Clark, E., & Geppert, M. (2010). Subsidiary integration as identity constructionand institution building: A political sensemaking approach. *Journal of Management Studies, 48*(2), 395–416.
Clark, E., & Geppert, M. (2011). Subsidiary integration as identity construction and institution building: A political sensemaking approach. *Journal of Management Studies, 48*(2), 395–416.
Clark, K., & Lengnick-Hall, M. L. (2012). MNC practice transfer: Institutional theory, strategic opportunities and subsidiary HR configuration. *The International Journal of Human Resource Management, 23*(18), 3813–3837.
CNI. (2014). *Portrait of Brazilian population: Professional education*. CNI.
Coase, R. (1937). The nature of the firm. *Economica, 4*, 386–405.
Coase, R. H. (1992). The institutional structure of production. *University of Chicago Law Occasional Paper, 28*, 1–16.
Cohen, J. (1988). *Statistical power analysis for the behavioral sciences* (2nd ed.). Lawrence Erlbaum Associates.
Cohen, J. (1992). A power primer. *Psychological Bulletin, 112*(1), 155–159.
Cohen, S. D. (2007). *Multinational corporations and foreign direct investment: Avoiding simplicity, embracing complexity*. Oxford University Press.

Cole, D. H. (2013). The varieties of comparative institutional analysis. *Articles by Maurer Faculty, Paper 834*.

Colégio Humboldt. (2020). *Duale Berufsbildung*. Retrieved from Berufsbildung https://www.humboldt.com.br/de/berufsbildung/

Coleman, J. (1974). *Power and the structure of society*. W. W. Norton & Company.

Confederação Nacional da Indústria. (2014). *Pesquisa CNI-IBOPE: Retratos da Sociedade Brasileira: Saude publica*. CNI.

Conklin, D. (2013, March 7). *Harvard Business Review*. Retrieved May 22, 2017, from Hugo Chavez Was No Outlier https://hbr.org/2013/03/hugo-chavez-was-no-outlier

Cooke, W. N. (2008). Multinational companies and global human resource strategy. In P. Boxall, J. Purcell, & P. Wright (Eds.), *The Oxford handbook of human resource management*. Oxford University Press.

Coolidge, F. L. (2012). *Statistics: A gentle introduction*. Sage.

Corak, M. (2013). Income inequality, equality of opportunity, and intergenerational mobility. *Journal of Economic Perspectives, 27*(3), 79–102.

CRANET. (2015). *Strategic human resource management*. Retrieved October 05, 2017, from https://hrpepper.de/cranet/studie/

Crouch, C., Schröder, M., & Voelzkow, H. (2009). Regional and sectoral varieties of capitalism. *Economy and Society, 2009*, 654–678.

Crouch, C., Streeck, W., Boyer, R., Amable, B., Hall, P. A., & Jackson, G. (2005). Dialogue on 'Institutional complementarity and political economy'. *Socio-Economic Review, 3*, 359–382.

Cusack, T. R., Iversen, T., & Rehm, P. (2006). Risks at work: The demand and supply sides of government redistribution. *Oxford Review of Economic Policy, 22*, 365–389.

Cypher, J. M. (2018). From structuralism to neoliberal depredation and beyond: Economic transformations and labor policies in Latin America, 1950–2016. *Latin American Perspectives, 45*(1), 24–46.

da Silva Filho, L. A. (2016). Labour market and turnover in the industrial employment in the Brazilian Northeast region. *Investigación Económica, LXXV*(295), 203–230.

Dacin, M. T., Ventresca, M. J., & Beal, B. D. (1999). The embeddedness of organizations: Dialogue & directions. *Journal of Management, 25*, 317–356.

Dang, D. A. (2013). How foreign direct investment promote institutional quality: Evidence from Vietnam. *Journal of Comparative Economics, 41*, 1054–1072.

Dasgupta, B. (1997). SAP: Issues and conditionalities: A global review. *Economic and Political Weekly, 1997*, 1091–1104.

Daude, C., & Stein, E. (2007, November). The quality of institutions and foreign direct investment. *Economics & Politics, 19*, 317–344.

David, M., & Sutton, C. (2004). *Social research: The basics*. Sage.

Davis, G. F., & Kim, S. (2015). Financialization of the economy. *Annual Review of Sociology, 41*, 203–221.

de Jong, G., & Van Vo, D. (2010). The impact of the institutional environment on the autonomy of MNCs' subsidiaries. *Problems and Perspectives in Management, 8*(2), 53–63.

De Mello, L. R. (1999). Foreign direct investment-led growth: Evidence from time series and panel data. *Oxford Economic Papers, 51*, 133–151.

De Meur, G., & Berg-Schlosser, D. (1994). Comparing political systems: Establishing similarities and dissimilarities. *European Journal of Political Research, 26*, 193–219.

de Rivero, O. (2001). *The myth of development: Nony-viable economies of the 21st century*. Zed Books.

Deeg, R., & Hardie, I. (2016). What is patient capital and who supplies it? *Socio-Economic Review, 14*(4), 627–645.

Deeg, R., & Jackson, G. (2007). Towards a more dynamic theory of capitalist variety. *Socio-Economic Review, 5*, 149–179.

DellaPosta, D., Nee, V., & Opper, S. (2017). Endogenous dynamics of institutional change. *Rationality and Society, 29*(I), 5–48.

Demir, F. (2016). Effects of FDI flows on institutional development: Does it matter where the investors are from? *World Development, 78*, 341–359.

Dequech, D. (2006). The new institutional economics and the theory of behaviour under uncertainty. *Journal of Economic Behavior & Organization, 59*, 109–131.

Detomasi, D. (2015). The multinational corporation as a political actor: 'Varieties of capitalism' revisited. *Journal of Business Ethics, 3*, 685–700.

DGB. (2019, April 5). *DGB.Index Gute Arbeit*. Retrieved from https://index-gute-arbeit.dgb.de/

Dias, D. A., Marques, C. R., & Martins, F. (2012). Labour cost-cutting strategies: Microeconomic evidence from survey data. *Economic Bulleting, 2012*, 37–55.

Diekmann, A. (1995). *Empirische Sozialforschung. Grundlagen, Methoden, Anwendungen*. Reinbek.

Dijkstra, A. G. (2000). Trade liberalization and industrial development on Latin America. *World Development, 28*, 1567–1582.

DiMaggio, P. (1988). Interest and agency in institutional theory. In L. Zucker (Ed.), *Institutional patterns and organizations: Culture and environment* (pp. 3–21). Ballinger Publishing.

DiMaggio, P. (1991). Social structure, institutions, and cultural goods: The case of the U.S. In I. P. Bourdieu & J. Coleman (Eds.), *Social theory for a changing society*. Westview Press.

DiMaggio, P. J., & Powell, W. W. (1983a, April). The iron cage revisited: Institutional isomorphism and collective rationality in organizational fields. *American Sociological Association, 48*(2), 147–160.

DiMaggio, P., & Powell, W. W. (1983b). The iron cage revisited: Institutional isomorphism and collective rationality in organization fields. *American Sociological Review, 48*, 147–160.

Doner, R. F., & Schneider, B. R. (2000). Business associations and economic development: Why some associations contribute more than others. *Business and Politics, 2*(3), 261–288.

Dornbach, S. (2016). *Berufsbildung in Brasilien*. Ribeiro do Espinho Fachmedien Berlin.

Dos Santos, T. (1971). The structure of dependence. In K. T. Fann & D. C. Hodges (Eds.), *Readings in U.S. imperialism* (p. 226). Porter Sargent.

dos Santos Mayer, B. (2016). *Volkswagen führt mit der AHK São Paulo duale Ausbildung für Mechatroniker in Brasilien ein*. Retrieved from Kooperation international https://www.kooperation-international.de/aktuelles/nachrichten/detail/info/volkswagen-fuehrt-mit-der-ahk-sao-paulo-duale-ausbildung-fuer-mechatroniker-in-brasilien-ein/

Doz, Y. L., & Prahalad, C. K. (1991). Managing DMNCs: A search for a new paradigm. *Strategic Management Journal, 12*, 145–164.

Drahokoupil, J., & Myant, M. (2010). Varieties of capitalism, varieties of vulnerabilities: Financial crisis and its impact on welfare states in Eastern Europe and the Commonwealth of Independent States. *Historical Social Research/Historische Sozialforschung, 35*(2), 266–295.

Dunn, O. J. (1964). Multiple comparisons using rank sums. *Technometrics, 6*, 241–252.

Dunning, J. (1979). Toward an eclectic theory of international production: Some empirical tests. *Journal of International Business Studies, 11*, 9–31.

Dunning, J. H. (1993). Internationalizing Porter's diamond. *Management International Review, 33*, 7–15.

Dunning, J. H. (2009). Location and the multinational enterprise: A neglected factor? *Journal of International Business Studies, 40*(1), 5–19.

Dunning, J. H., & Rugman, A. M. (1985). The influence of Hymer's dissertation on the theory of foreign direct investment. *American Economic Review, 75*, 228–232.

Dunning, J. H., Suhk Pak, Y., & Beldona, S. (2007). Foreign ownership strategies of UK and US international franchisors: An exploratory application of Dunning's envelope paradigm. *International Business Review, 16*(5), 531–548.

Dutt, P., & Traca, D. (2010). With whom do you trade? Defensive innovation and the skill-bias. *Canadian Journal of Economics, 43*(4), 1198–1221.

DW. (2016). *Formación profesional dual: la experiencia mexicana*. Retrieved from https://alemaniaparati.diplo.de/mxdz-es/aktuelles/dwformaciondualbalance/1077542

Easterly, W. (2000). *Policy research working paper: The middle class consensus and economic development*. The World Bank.

Easterly, W. (2007). Inequality does cause underdevelopment: Insights from a new instrument. *Journal of Development Economics, 84*, 755–776.

Ebenau, M. (2012). Varieties of capitalism or dependency? A critique of the VoC approach for Latin America. *Competition and Change, 16(3)*, 206–223.

ECLAC. (2018, April). *repositotio.cepal.org*. Retrieved from https://repositorio.cepal.org/bitstream/handle/11362/43423/1/S1800258_en.pdf

ECLAC/ILO. (2013, May). *CEPAL*. Retrieved from The employment situation in Latin America and the Caribbean https://repositorio.cepal.org/bitstream/handle/11362/37580/1/ECLAC-ILO-Bulletin8_en.pdf

Economic Commission for Latin America and the Caribbean (ECLAC). (2015). *Foreign direct investment in Latin America and the Caribbean*. LC/G.2641-P.

Edwards, T., Almond, P., Clark, I., Colling, T., & Ferner, A. (2005). Reverse diffusion in US multinationals: Barriers from the American Business system. *Journal of Management Studies, 42*, 1261–1286.

Edwards, J. R., & Cable, D. M. (2009). The value of value congruence. *Journal of Applied Psychology, 94*, 654–677.

Edwards, P., Edwards, T., Ferner, A., Marginson, P., & Tregaskis, O. (2007). *Employment practices of MNCs in organisational context: A large-scale survey*. Retrieved from University of Warwick http://www2.warwick.ac.uk/fac/soc/wbs/projects/mncemployment/conference_papers/full_report_july.pdf

Edwards, T., & Ferner, A. (2004). Multinationals, reverse diffusion and national business systems. *Management International Review, 44*(1), 49–79.

El Alaoui, A. (2012). When Europe hits home: How Europeanization triggers the conflict of capitalism in the German system of corporate control. In *Claremont-UC Undergraduate Research Conference on the European Union*.

Elbling, V. (n.d.). *La Iniciativa Alemana de Formación Dual en México*. Retrieved from https://mexiko.diplo.de/blob/875018/d3801d26df8bb017bb778b35b3abcc3a/flyer-formaci%25C3%25B3n-dual-data.pdf

Ellguth, P., & Kohaut, S. (2017). *wsi mitteilungen 4/2017: Tarifbindung und betriebliche Interessenvertretung: Ergebnisse aus dem IAB-Betriebspanel 2016*. Retrieved from https://www.boeckler.de/data/wsimit_2017_04_ellguth.pdf

Erramilli, M. K. (1990). Entry mode choice in service industries. *International Marketing Review, 7*(5), 50–62.

Erramilli, M. K., Agarwal, S., & Dev, C. S. (2002). Choice between non-equity entry modes: An organizational capability perspective. *Journal of International Business Studies, 33*(2), 223–242.

European Commision. (2012). *Comunicación de la Comisión al Parlamento Europeo, alconsejo, al Comité Económico y Social Europeo y al Comité de las Regiones – Un nuevo concepto de educación: invertir en las competencias para lograd mejores resultados socioeconómicos*. Retrieved from https://eur-lex.europa.eu/legal-content/ES/TXT/PDF/?uri=CELEX:52012DC0669&from=EN

European Parliament. (2019). *The trade pillar of the EU-Mercosur Association Agreement*. Retrieved from http://www.europarl.europa.eu/RegData/etudes/BRIE/2019/640138/EPRS_BRI(2019)640138_EN.pdf

Eurostat. (2019). *Real labour productivity per person employed - annual data*. Retrieved from https://ec.europa.eu/eurostat/web/products-datasets/product?code=tipsna70

Evans, P. B. (1979). *Dependent development: The alliance of multinational, state, and local capital in Brazil*. Princeton University Press.

Fabro, G., & Aixalá, J. (2013). Do the models of institutional quality differ according to the income level of the countries? The case of the low-income countries. *Review of Public Economics, 206*, 11–26.

FAO. (2019, February 5). *fao.org*. Retrieved from http://www.fao.org/3/w5973e/w5973e0b.htm

FARLEX. (2019, May 4). *The Free Dictionary*. Retrieved from https://www.thefreedictionary.com/human+capital

Farndale, E., Brewster, C., & Poutsma, E. (2008). Coordinated vs. liberal market HRM: The impact of institutionalization on multinational firms. *The International Journal of Human ResourceManagement, 26*, 2004–2023.

Fenton-O'Creevy, M., Gooderham, P., & Nordhaug, O. (2007). Human resource management in US subsidiaries in Europe and Australia: Centralisation or autonomy? *Journal of International Business Studies, 17*, 151–166.

Ferguson, C. J. (2009). An effect size primer: A guide for clinicians and researchers. *Professional Psychology: Research and Practice, 40*(5), 532–538.

Ferner, A., Almond, P., & Colling, T. (2005). Institutional theory and the cross-national transfer of employment policy: The case of 'workforce diversity' in US multinationals. *Journal of International Business Studies, 36*(3), 304–321.

Ferner, A., Edwards, T., & Tempel, A. (2011). Power, institutions and the cross-national tranfer of employment practices in multinationals. *Human Relations, 65*, 163–187.

Ferrari, C. A. (2016). *Capitalismo: Crisis, cambios, y evolución en el siglo XXI.* Retrieved from Pontificia Universidad Javeriana https://www.javeriana.edu.co/documents/16113/9477233/N+1+Capitalismo+crisis+cambios+y+evoluci%C3%B3n+en+el+sXXI+%28WEB%29.pdf/939499f0-2d3f-4e87-ac23-6215fbc2fccc

Ferraz, R. L. (2018). *bibliotecadigital.fgv.br*. Retrieved from Operations decisions and the influence of host-country institutions: An exploratory study under the Paraguayan 'Maquila regime'. Retrieved from https://bibliotecadigital.fgv.br/dspace/bitstream/handle/10438/27235/20190322.%20Disserta%c3%a7%c3%a3o%20Renan%20Lucas%20Ferraz_FINAL%20BIBLIOTECA.pdf?sequence=4&isAllowed=y

Fischer, W. (2002). *Tue Gutes und rede darüber: Erfolgreiche Öffentlichkeitsarbeit für Non-Profit-Organisationen.* Orell Füssli Verlag.

Fleckenstein, T., & Lee, S. C. (2017). The politics of labor market reform in coordinated welfare capitalism: Comparing Sweden, Germany, and South Korea. *World Politics, 69*(1), 144–183.

Fleury, A., Leme Fleury, M. T., & Glufke Reis, G. (2010). El camino se hace al andar: La trayectoria des la multinacionales brasilenas. *Universia Business Review, 25*, 34–55.

Flick, U. (2011). *Introducing research methodology*. Rowohlt Verlag.

Flick, U., von Kardorff, E., & Steinke, I. (2005). *Qualitative Forschung: Ein Handbuch*. Rowohlt-Taschenbuch-Verlag.

Fligstein, N., & Zhang, J. (2011). A new agenda for research on the trajectory of Chinese capitalism. *Management and Organization Review, 7*, 39–62.

Forsgren, M., Holm, U., & Johanson, J. (2005). *Managing the embedded multinational: A business network view*. Edward Elgar.

Forsgren, M., & Johanson, J. (2010). A dialogue about the Uppsala model of internationalization. In U. Andersson & U. Holm (Eds.), *Managing the contemporary multinational: The role of headquarters* (pp. 283–304). Edward Elgar Publishing.

Fortanier, F. (2007, August). Foreign direct investment and host country economic growth: Does the investor's country of origin play a role? *Transnational Corporations, 16*(2), 41–76.

Fortwengel, J., & Jackson, G. (2016). Legitimizing the apprenticeship practice in a distant environment: Institutional entrepreneurship through inter-organizational networks. *Journal of World Business, 51*, 895–909.

Fox, J. (2008). *Applied regression analysis and generalized linear models* (2nd ed.). Sage.

Fox, J. (2016). *Applied Regression analysis and generalized linear models* (3rd ed.). Sage.

Frank, A. G. (1966). The development of underdevelopment. *Monthly Review, 18*. https://doi.org/10.14452/MR-018-04-1966-08_3

Frank, A. G. (2009). *Capitalism and underdevelopment in Latin America: Historical studies of Chile and Brazil*. Monthly Review Press.

Franz, T. (2017, May 4). *lse.ac.uk*. Retrieved from Latin America's productivity problems can only be overcome by incentivising, underwriting, and enforcing technological investment https://blogs.lse.ac.uk/latamcaribbean/2017/05/04/latin-americas-productivity-problems-can-only-be-overcome-by-incentivising-underwriting-and-enforcing-technological-investment/

Friedland, R., & Alford, R. R. (1991). Bringing society back. In I. W. W. Powell & P. J. DiMaggio (Eds.), *Symbols, practices, and institutional contradictions. The new institutionalism in organizational analysis* (pp. 232–263). University of Chicago Press.

Friel, D. (2011). Forging a comparative institutional advantage in Argentina: Implications for theory and praxis. *Human Relations., 64*(4), 553–572.

Frumkin, P., & Galaskiewicz, J. (2004). Institutional isomorphism and public sector organizations. *Journal of Public Administration Research and Theory, 14*(3), 283–307.

Fuchs, M., Schamp, E. W., & Wiemann, J. (2016). Duale Aus-und Fortbildung goes global? Zur Internationalisierung von Wissen in der industriellen Fertigung durch global-lokale Qualifizierungsstrategien multinationaler Unternehmen. *Geographische Zeitschrift, 104*(3), 140–157.

Fukuyama, F. (1992). *The end of history and the last man*. Penguin Group.

Fulton, L. (2020). *National industrial relations, an update*. Labour Research Department and ETUI (online publication). Retrieved from http://www.worker-participation.eu/National-Industrial-Relations

Furtado, C. (1965). *Development and stagnation in Latin America: A structuralist approach*. Social Science Institute.

Furubotn, E., & Richter, R. (2005). The new insititutional economics applied to markets, firms, and the state: General remarks. In *Institutions and economic theory: the contribution of the new institutional economics* (pp. 291–312). University of Michigan Press.

Galaskiewicz, J., & Wasserman, S. (1989). Mimetic processes within an interorganizational field: An empirical test. *Administrative Science Quarterly, 34*(3), 454–479.

Gardiner, L., Summers, E., & Raftl, G. (2013). By invitation only? In S. R. Whittle & R. C. Stevens (Eds.), *Changing organizations from within*. Routledge.

Garud, R., Hardy, C., & Maguire, S. (2007). Institutional entrepreneurship as embedded agency: An introduction to the special issue. *Organization Studies, 2007*, 957–969.

Georg, W. (2005). Vergleichende Berufsbildungsforschung. In F. Rauner (Ed.), *Handbuch Berufsbildungsforschung* (pp. 186–192). Bertelsmann.

Geppert, M., & Dörrenbacher, C. (2011). *Politics and power in the multinational corporation: The role of institutions, interests and identities*. Cambridge University Press.

Geppert, M., Matten, D., & Walgenbach, P. (2006). Transnational institution building and the multinational corporation: An emerging field of research. *Human Relations, 59*, 1451–1465.

Geppert, M., Matten, D., & Walgenbach, P. (2007). Transnational institution building and the multinational corporation: An emerging field of research. *Human Relations, 59*(11), 1451–1465.

Geppert, M., & Williams, K. (2006). Global, national and local practices in multinational corporations: Towards a sociopolitical framework. *The International Journal of Human Resource Management, 17*, 49–69.

Geppert, M., Williams, K., & Matten, D. (2003). The social construction of contextual rationalities in MNCs: An Anglo-German comparison of subsidiary choice. *Journal of Management Studies, 40*(3), 617–641.

Gereffi, G., Bamber, P., & Fernandez-Stark, K. (2016). *Promoting decent work in global supply chains in Latin America and the Caribbean*. ILO.

Gessler, M. (2017). Educational transfer as transformation: A case study about the emergence and implementation of dual apprenticeship structures in a German automotove transplant in the United States. *Vocations and Learning, 10*, 71–99.

Gessler, M., Fuchs, M., & Pilz, M. (2019). *Konzepte und Wirkungen des Transfers Dualer Berufsausbildung*. Springer VS.

Ghoshal, S., & Bartlett, C. A. (1990). The multinational corporation as an interorganizational network. *The Academy of Management Review, 15*, 603–625.

Ghoshal, S., & Westney, D. E. (1993). *Organization theory and the multinational corporation*. St. Martin's Press.

Giddens, A. (1984). Elements of the theory of structuration. In A. Giddens (Ed.), *The constitution of society: Outline of the theory of structuration* (pp. 1–28). University of California Press.

Gignac, G. E., & Szodorai, E. T. (2016). Effect size guidelines for individual differences researchers. *Personality and Individual Differences, 102*, 74–78.

Gilpin, R., & Gilpin, J. M. (2000). *The challenge of global capitalism: The world economy in the 21st century*. Princeton University Press.

GIZ. (2019). *GIZ program for strengthening the Mexican Model of Dual Vocational Education and Training (MMFD)*.

Glassman, J., & Carmody, P. (2001). Structural adjustment in East and Southeast Asia: Lessons learned from Latin America. *Geoforum, 32*, 77–90.

Glennerster, H., & Lieberman, R. C. (2011). Hidden convergence: Toward a historical comparison of U.S. and U.K. health policy. *Journal of Health Politics, Policy and Law, 36*, 5–31.

Glogowska, M. (2011). Paradigms, pragmatism and possibilities: Mixed-methods research in speech and language therapy. *International Journal of Language & Communication Disorders, 46*, 251–260.

Gobierno del Estado de México. (2018). *CONALEPMEX*. Retrieved from https://www.conalepmex.edu.mx/educacion-conalep/modelo-educacion-dual.html

Goodin, R., March, J., & Olsen, J. (2011). The logic of appropriateness. In *The Oxford handbook of political science*. Oxford University Press. Retrieved from https://www.oxfordhandbooks.com/view/10.1093/oxfordhb/9780199604456.001.0001/oxfordhb-9780199604456-e-024

Gore, C. (2000). The rise and fall of the Washington consensus as a paradigm for developing countries. *World Development, 28*(5), 789–804.

Graf, L., Powell, J., Fortwengel, J., & Bernhard, N. (2014). *Duale Studiengänge im globalen Kontext: Internationalisierung in Deutschland und Transfer nach Brasilien, Frankreich, Katar, Mexiko und in die USA*. Deutscher Akademischer Austauschdienst (DAAD).

Granovetter, M. (1985, November). Economic action and social structure: The problem of embeddedness. *American Journal of Sociology, 91*(3), 481–510.

Guillén, M. F., & García-Canal, E. (2009, March). The American model of the multinational firm and the "new" multinationals from emerging economies. *Academy of Management Perspectives, 23*(2), 23–35.

Gulati, C., Lin, Y.-X., Mishra, S., & Rayner, J. (2002). *From Adam Smith to Michael Porter: Evolution of competitiveness theory*. Mainland Press.

Hadwiger, F. (2015). Global framework agreements: Achieving decent work in global supply chains? *International Journal of Labour Research, 7*, 75–94.

Halcomb, E. J., & Hickman, L. (2015). Mixed methods research. *Nursing Standards: Promoting Excellence in Nursing Care, 29*(32), 41–47.

Hall, P. A. (2010). Historical institutionalism in rationalist and sociological perspective. In J. Mahoney & K. Thelen (Eds.), *Explaining institutional change* (pp. 204–223). Cambridge University Press.

Hall, D. (2012). *Re-municipalising municipal services in Europe. A report commissioned by EPSU to Public*. Services International Research Unit (PSIRU).

Hall, P. A., & Gingerich, D. W. (2004). Varieties of capitalism and institutional complementarities in the macroeconomy: An empirical analysis. *MPIfG Discussion Paper 04/5*.

Hall, P. A., & Gingerich, D. W. (2009). Varieties of capitalism and institutional complementarities in the political economy. *British Journal of Political Science, 39*(3), 449–482.

Hall, P. A., & Soskice, D. (2001). *Varieties of capitalism: The institutional foundations of comparative advantage*. Oxford University Press.

Hall, P. A., & Taylor, R. C. (1996). Political science and the three new institutionalisms. *Political Studies, XLIV*, 936–957.

Hall, P. A., & Thelen, K. (2009). Institutional change in varieties of capitalism. Socio-Economic Review, 7 pp. 7-34.
Hamilton, D. (1962, July). Why is institutional economics not institutional? *The American Journal of Economics and Sociology, 21*, 309–317.
Hansen, H., & Rand, J. (2006). On the causal links between FDI and growth in developing countries. *The World Economy, 29*, 21–41.
Hanson, M. (2001). Institutional theory and educational change. *Educational Administration Quarterly, 37*(5), 637–661.
Hardy, C., & Maguire, S. (2007). Institutional entrepreneurship. In I. R. Greenwood, C. Oliver, K. Sahlin-Andersson, & R. Suddaby (Eds.), *Handbook of organizational institutionalism*. Sage.
Häusermann, S. (2010). Solidarity with whom? Why organised labour is losing ground in continental pension politics. *European Journal of Political Research, 49*, 223–256.
Heidenreich, M. (2012a). The social embeddedness of multinational companies: A literature review. *Socio-Economic Review, 10*, 549–579.
Heidenreich, M. (2012b, July 1). The social embeddness of multinational companies: A literature review. *Socio-Economic Review, 10*(3), 549–579.
Hejazi, W., & Pauly, P. (2003). Motivations for FDI and domestic capital formation. *Journal of International Business Studies, 34*, 282–289.
Herranz, D. (2018, May 14). *World Economic Forum*. Retrieved from It's time to tackle the informal economy problem in Latin America https://www.weforum.org/agenda/2018/03/it-s-time-to-tackle-informal-economy-problem-latin-america/
Herrigel, G. (1996). Crisis in German decentralized production. *European Urban and Regional Studies, 3*, 33–52.
Herzberg, F. (1966). *Work and the nature of man*. World Publishing.
Hilbe, J. M. (2016). *Practical guide to logistic regression*. CRC Press.
Hill, C. (2000). *International business - Competing in the global marketplace*. University of Washington.
Hodgson, G. M. (2006, March). What are institutions? *Journal of Economic Issues, XL*(1), 1–25.
Hoelscher, M. (2012). Spielarten des Kapitalismus und Kompetenzen. *Kölner Zeitschrift für Soziologie und Sozialpsychologie, 64*, 479–505.
Hoenen, A. K., & Kostova, T. (2015). Utilizing the broader agency perspective for studying headquarters–subsidiary relations in multinational companies. *Journal of International Business Studies, 46*, 104–113.
Hollingsworth, J. R., & Boyer, R. (1997). *Contemporary capitalism: The embeddedness of institutions*. Cambridge University Press.
Hölscher, M. (2012). Spielarten des Kapitalismus und Kompetenzen von Hochschulabsolventinnen und-absolventen: Eine komparative empirische Analyse. *Kölner Zeitschrift für Soziologie und Sozialpsychologie, 64*, 479–505.
Hopf, C. (1995). Qualitative Interviews in der Sozialforschung. Ein Überblick. In I. U. Flick, E. V. Kardorff, H. Keupp, L. V. Rosenstiel, & S. Wolff (Eds.), *Handbuch qualitative Sozialforschung. Grundlagen, Konzepte, Methoden und Anwendungen* (2nd ed., pp. 177–182). Psychologie-Verlags-Union.
Höpner, M. (2009). "Spielarten des Kapitalismus" als Schule der vergleichenden Staatstätigkeitsforschung. *Zeitschrift für Vergleichende Politikwissenschaft, 3*(2), 303–327.
Horn, J. L. (1965). A rationale and test for the number of factors in factor analysis. *Psychometrika, 30*(2), 179–185.
Howell, D. C. (2010). *Statistical methods for psychology* (7th ed.). Cengage Learning.
Huntington, S. P. (1968). *Political order in changing societies*. Yale University Press.
Hymer, S. H. (1976). *The international operations of national firms: A study of direct foreign investment. Unpublished 1960 PhD thesis*. MIT Press.
IDB. (2003). *Good jobs wanted: Labor markets in Latin America*. The Johns Hopkins University Press.
IDB. (2004). *Good jobs wanted: Labor markets in Latin America*. Johns Hopkins University Press.

ILO. (2008). *Vocational training and productivity. Montevideo: ILO/Cinterfor*. Retrieved from ILO https://www.oitcinterfor.org/sites/default/files/file_publicacion/trazos37_eng.pdf

ILO. (2014). *Poverty, inequality and employment in Chile*. International Labour Office.

ILO. (2015a). *Global wage report 2014/15: Wages and income inequality*. PRODOC.

ILO. (2015b). *Global wage report 2014/15: Wages and income inequality*. International Labour Office.

ILO. (2016). *Global wage report 2016/17: Wage inequality in the workplace*. International Labour Office.

ILO. (2017). *Unemployment protection: A good practices guideand training package*. International Labour Organization.

ILO. (2017b). *Labour relations and collective bargaining*. Retrieved from https://www.ilo.org/wcmsp5/groups/public/%2D%2D-ed_protect/%2D%2D-protrav/%2D%2D-travail/documents/publication/wcms_409422.pdf

ILO. (2019, April 6). *Decent work*. Retrieved from https://www.ilo.org/global/topics/decent-work/lang%2D%2Den/index.htm

IMF. (2003). *World economic outlook: Growth and institutions*. International Monetary Fund.

IMF. (2007). *imf.org*. Retrieved May 31, 2017, from Latin America: Productivity Is Lagging https://www.imf.org/external/pubs/ft/weo/2007/01/c2/FIG 2_7.pdf

IMF. (2017, April). *World Economic Outlook database*. Retrieved from https://www.imf.org/external/pubs/ft/weo/2017/01/weodata/weorept.aspx?pr.x=43&pr.y=10&sy=2017&ey=2022&scsm=1&ssd=1&sort=country&ds=.&br=1&c=336%2C213%2C218%2C223%2C228%2C288%2C233%2C293%2C248%2C366%2C298%2C299&s=NGDPD%2CPPPGDP%2CPPPPC&grp=0&a=

IMF. (2019). *IMF DataMapper*. Retrieved from https://www.imf.org/external/datamapper/NGDPD@WEO/OEMDC/ADVEC/WEOWORLD

Immergut, E. M. (2006). Historical-institutionalism in political science and the problem of change. In A. Wimmer & R. Kössler (Eds.), *Understanding change* (pp. 237–259). Palgrave Macmillan.

iMove. (2012). *Developing skills for employability with German partners*. iMOVEat the Federal Institute for Vocational Education and Training (BIBB).

INEP. (2019). *Instituto Nacional de Estudos e Pesquisas Educacionais Anísio Teixeira*. Retrieved from Censo Escolar http://portal.inep.gov.br/censo-escolar

International Labour Organisation. (2012). *ilo.org*. Retrieved from International institutite for labour studies https://www.ilo.org/inst

Iqbal, B. A., Rahman, M. N., & Hassan, M. (2016). MNCs and their role and contribution in Latin American countries. *Transnational Corporations Review, 8*(2), 151–164.

Ivankova, N. V., Creswell, J. W., & Stick, S. L. (2006). Using mixed-methods sequential explanatory design: From theory to practice. *Field Methods, 18*(1), 3–20.

Iversen, T., & Soskice, D. (2001). An asset theory of social policy preferences. *American Political Science Review, 95*, 875–893.

Iversen, T., & Soskice, D. (2006). Electoral institutions, parties and the politics of class: Why some democracies distribute more than others. *American Political Science Review, 100*(2), 165–181.

Jackson, G. (2010). Actors and institutions. In G. Morgan, J. L. Campbell, C. Crouch, O. K. Pedersen, & R. Whitley (Eds.), *The Oxford handbook of comparative institutional analysis* (pp. 63–87). Oxford University Press.

Jackson, G., & Deeg, R. (2006). *How many varieties of capitalism? Comparing the comparative institutional analyses of capitalsit diversity*. MPIfG Discussion Paper.

Jackson, G., & Deeg, R. (2008). Comparing capitalisms: Understanding institutional diversity and its implications for international business. *Journal of International Business Studies, 39*, 540–561.

Jackson, G., & Rathert, N. (2017). Private governance as regulatory substitute or complement? A comparative institutional approach to csr adoption by multinational corporations. *Research in the Sociology of Organizations, 49*, 445–478.

Jafar, B. (2015). *Why trickle-down economics won't eliminate poverty*. Retrieved from World Economic Forum https://www.weforum.org/agenda/2015/10/why-trickle-down-economics-wont-eliminate-poverty/?utm_source=Cambridge%20Judge%20Business%20School&utm_medium=email&utm_campaign=6342300_Media%20summary%2030%20October%202015&dm_i=HVY,3RXR0,EFFS53,DLMYN,1

Janert, J. (2017). *Erfolgsmodell duale Ausbildung*. Retrieved from https://www.deutschland.de/de/topic/wissen/erfolgsmodell-duale-ausbildung

Javorcik, B. S., & Spatareanu, M. (2011a). Does it matter where you come from? Vertical spillovers from foreign direct investment and the origin of investors. *Journal of Development Economics, 96*, 126–138.

Javorcik, B. S., & Spatareanu, M. (2011b). Does it matter where you come from? Vertical spillovers from foreign direct investment and the origin of investors. *Journal of Development Economics, 96*, 126–138.

Jencks, C. (2002). Does inequality matter? *Daedalus, 131*(1), 49–65.

Johanson, M. (2016). *BBC*. Retrieved from There's a mass expat exodus from Brazil https://www.bbc.com/worklife/article/20160729-theres-a-mass-expat-exodus-from-brazil

Johanson, J., & Vahlne, J.-E. (1977). The internationalization process of the firm: A model of knowledge development and increasing foreign market commitments. *Journal of International Business Studies, 8*(1), 23–32.

Johanson, J., & Vahlne, J.-E. (2009). The Uppsala internationalization process model revisited: From liability of foreignness to liability of outsidership. *Journal of International Business Studies, 40*(9), 1411–1431.

Jürgens, U., & Krzywdzinski, M. (2016). *New worlds of work: Varieties of work in car factories in the BRIC countries*. Oxford University Press.

Kang, N. (2006). A critique of the "varieties of capitalism" approach. In *No. 45-2006 ICCSR Research Paper Series*.

Kauer, M. (2015). *Unpublished Dissertation: The status (quo) of VET in Brazil: An empirical study about its function, meaning and impingements from the perspective of former dual system apprentices*. Retrieved from https://opendata.uni-halle.de/bitstream/1981185920/11937/1/Dissertation%20-%20Marcelo%20Kauer%20%28184027%29.pdf

Kaulihowa, T., & Adjasi, C. (2018). FDI and welfare dynamics in Africa. *Thunderbird International Business Review, 60*(3), 313–328.

Kay, C. (2005). Celso Furtado: Pioneer of structuralist development theory. *Development and Change, 36*(6), 1201–1207.

Kellogg, K. C. (2009). Operating room: Relational spaces and microinstitutional change in surgery. *American Journal of Sociology, 115*, 657–711.

Kemp, M. (1961). Foreign investment and national advantage. *Economic Record, 28*, 56–62.

Keppel, G., & Wickens, T. D. (n.d.). *Design and analysis: A researcher's handbook* (4th ed.). Prentice-Hall.

Kersan-Skabic, I. (2013). *Institutional development as a determinant of FDI attractiveness in Southeast Europe*.

Kettl, D. F. (2006). Is the worst yet to come? *The Annals of the American Academy of Political and Social Science, 604*(1), 273–287.

Khanna, T., Palepu, K., & Bullock, R. J. (2010). *Winning in emerging markets: A road map for strategy and execution*. Harvard Business Press Book.

Kim, S., & Park, C. (2008). The influence of multinational corporations on institutional diffusion in emerging markets: Evidence from hiring the disabled in Korea. *Seoul Journal of Business, 14*, 4–30.

Klassen, A. C., Creswell, J., Plano Clark, V. L., Clegg Smith, C., & Meissner, H. I. (2012). Best practices in mixed methods for quality of life research. *Quality of Life Research, 21*, 377–380.

Kluike, M., & Pull, K. (2013). Similar, but still different: How US multinational companies in Germany and Switzerland use host-country training and skill practices. *Industrial Relations Journal, 44*(5–6), 495–513.

Knight, J. (1992). *Institutions and social conflict*. Cambridge University Press.

Knoema. (2019). *Total economy database: Output, labor, and labor productivity, 1950-2018*. Retrieved from https://knoema.de/TEDOLLPCD2018Nov/total-economy-database-output-labor-and-labor-productivity-1950-2018?country=1000750-argentina

Koene, B., & Ansari, S. (2011). Institutional change and the multinational change agent: A study of the temporary staffing industry in Spain. *Journal of Organizational Change Management, 24*, 511–531.

Kogut, B. (2001). Multinational corporations. In I. N. J. Smelser & P. B. Baltes (Eds.), *International Encyclopedia of social & behavioral sciences* (pp. 10197–10204). Pergamon Press.

Kokko, A. (1996). Productivity spillovers from competition between local firms and foreign affiliates. *Journal of International Development, 8*, 517–530.

Korzeniewicz, R. P. (2003). Reviewed work(s): Models of capitalism: Lessons for Latin America by Evelyne Huber. *Perspectives on Politics, 1*(4), 812–813.

Kostova, T., Marano, V., & Tallmann, S. (2015). Headquarters–subsidiary relationships in MNCs: Fifty years of evolving research. *Journal of World Business, 51*, 176–184.

Kostova, T., Nell, P. C., & Hoenen, A. K. (2018). Understanding agency problems in headquarters-subsidiary relationships in multinational corporations: A contextualized model. *Journal of Management, 44*, 2611–2637.

Kostova, T., & Roth, K. (2002). Adoption of an organizational practice by subsidiaries of multinational corporations: Institutional and relational effects. *Academy of Management Journal, 45*, 215–233.

Kostova, T., Roth, K., & Dacin, M. T. (2008, October). Institutional theory in the study of multinational corporations: A critique and new directions. *The Academy of Management Review, 33*(4), 994–1006.

Kostova, T., & Zaheer, S. (1999). Organizational legitimacy under conditions of complexity: The case of the multinational enterprise. *Academy of Management Review, 24*(1), 64–81.

Kowalski, P., Brüge, M., Sztajerowska, M., & Egeland, M. (2013). *State-owned enterprises: Trade effects and policy implications*. Retrieved from ECD Trade Policy Papers, No. 147, OECD Publishing. https://doi.org/10.1787/5k4869ckqk7l-en

Kristof, A. L. (1996). Person-organization fit: An integrative review of its conceptualizations, measurements, and implications. *Personnel Psychology, 49*, 1–49.

Kromrey, H., Roose, J., & Strübing, J. (2016). *Empirische Sozialforschung*. UVK Verlagsgesellschaft mbh.

Krouwel, A., & Abts, K. (2007). Varieties of Euroscepticism and populist mobilization: Transforming attitudes from Mild Euroscepticism to Harsh Eurocynicism. *Acta Politica, 42*, 252–270.

Krzywdzinski, J., & Jürgens, U. (2019). Transfer deutscher und japanischer Ansätze der Facharbeiter-ausbildung an die BRIC-Standorte: Volkswagen und Toyota im Vergleich. In M. Gessler, M. Fuchs, & M. Pilz (Eds.), *Konzepte und Wirkungen des Transfers Dualer Berufsausbildung* (pp. 281–320). Springer VS.

Kuckartz, U. (2005). *Einführung in die computer-gestützte Analyse qualitativer Daten*. VS Verlag für Sozialwissenschaften.

Kurtishi-Kastrati, S. (2013). The effects of foreign direct investments for host country's economy. *European Journal of Interdisciplinary Studies, 5*(1), 26–38.

Kuznetsov, A., & Jacob, M. (2015). Convergence versus divergence: Testing varieties of capitalism on the globalization of buiness practices. In I. S. Marinova (Ed.), *Institutional impacts on firm internationalization* (pp. 12–39). Palgrave Macmillan.

Kwok, C. C., & Tadesse, S. (2006). The MNC as an agent of change for host-country institutions: FDI and corruption. *Journal of International Business Studies, 7*, 767–785.

Laerd Statistics. (2015). *Simple linear regression using SPSS Statistics*. Retrieved from Statistical tutorials and software guides https://statistics.laerd.com/

Laerd Statistics. (2015b). *Ordinal logistic regression using SPSS statistics. Statistical tutorials and software guides*. Retrieved from https://statistics.laerd.com/

Laerd Statistics. (2015c). *Independent-samples t-test using SPSS statistics. Statistical tutorials and software guides.* Retrieved from https://statistics.laerd.com/premium/spss/istt/independent-t-test-in-spss-24.php

Laerd Statistics. (2015d). *Kruskal-Wallis H test using SPSS statistics. Statistical tutorials and software guides.* Retrieved from https://statistics.laerd.com/premium/spss/kwht/kruskal-wallis-test-in-spss-19.php

Laerd Statistics. (2017). *Binomial logistic regression using SPSS Statistics.* Retrieved from Statistical tutorials and software guides https://statistics.laerd.com/

Laerd Statistics. (2017b). *One-way ANOVA using SPSS statistics. Statistical tutorials and software guides.* Retrieved from https://statistics.laerd.com/premium/spss/owa/one-way-anova-in-spss-28.php

Laerd Statistics. (2017c). *Chi-square test of homogeneity (2 x C) using SPSS statistics. Statistical tutorials and software guides.* Retrieved from https://statistics.laerd.com/premium/spss/cstoh2xc/chi-square-test-of-homogeneity-2xc-in-spss-22.php

Lalonde, C. (2007). The potential contribution of the field of organizational development to crisis management. *Journal of Contingencies and Crisis Management, 15*, 95–104.

LaMarche, C. (2015). *I Z A World of labor.* Retrieved from https://wol.iza.org/uploads/articles/183/pdfs/collective-bargaining-in-developing-countries.pdf

Larson, M. S. (1977). *The rise of professionalism: A sociological analysis.* University of California Press.

Lawernce, T. B. (1999). Institutional strategy. *Journal of Management, 25*, 161–187.

Lawrence, T. B., Hardy, C., & Phillips, N. (2002). Institutional effects of interorganizational collaboration: The emergence of proto-institutions. *The Academy of Management Journal, 45*, 281–290.

Lawrence, T., Suddaby, R., & Leca, B. (2011). Institutional work: Refocusing institutional studies of organization. *Journal of Management Inquiry, 20*, 52–58.

Leca, B., Battilana, J., & Boxenbaum, E. (2009). Agency and institutions: A review on institutional entrepreneurship. *The Academy of Management Annals, 2009*, 2–51.

Lee, J. H., & Gaur, A. S. (2013). Managing multi-business firms: A comparison between Korean chaebols and diversified U.S. firms. *Journal of World Business, 48*, 443–454.

Lenzner, T., Neuert, C., & Wanda, O. (2015). *GESIS survey guidelines - Kognitives pretesting.* GESIS – Leibniz-Institut für Sozialwissenschaften.

Leon, P. (2010). *Address to 'miners from the frontiers' conference Macquarie Connections–Macquarie Capital (Europe) Ltd, London.* Retrieved from https://www.moneyweb.co.za/mw/action/media/downloadFile

Levi, M. (1990). A logic of institutional change. In K. Schweers, K. Cook, & M. Levi (Eds.), *The limits of rationality* (pp. 402–418). Universtiy of Chicago Press.

Levi, M. (1998). A state of trust. In V. Braithwaite & M. Levi (Eds.), *Trust and governance* (pp. 77–101). Russell Sage Foundation.

Levy, D. L. (2008). Political contestation in global production networks. *Academy of Management Review., 33*(4), 943–962.

Levy, D., & Scully, M. (2007). The institutional entrepreneur as modern Prince: The strategic face of power in contested fields. *Organization Studies, 28*, 971–991.

Lexas. (2019). *LaenderDaten.* Retrieved from https://www.laenderdaten.de/indizes/hdi.aspx

Lindenberg, S. (1992). The method of decreasing abstraction. In T. Fararo (Ed.), *Rational choice theory: Advocacy and critique* (pp. 3–20). Sage.

Lipsey, R. E. (2004). Home- and host-country effects of foreign direct investment. In R. E. Baldwin & L. A. Winters (Eds.), *Challenges to globalisation: Analzying the economics* (pp. 333–382). University of Chicago Press.

Long, C., Yang, J., & Zhang, J. (2015). Institutional impact of foreign direct investment in China. *World Development, 66*, 31–48.

López-Fogués, A., Rosado, R., Valiente, O., Fuentes, H., & Aragón, E. (2018). *Pilot evaluation of the Mexican model of dual TVET in the State of Mexico*. Retrieved from http://eprints.gla.ac.uk/159540/7/159540.pdf

Luo, Y. (2007). Are joint venture partners more opportunistic in a more volatile environment? *Strategic Management Journal, 28*, 39–60.

Lyon, F., Möllering, G., & Saunders, M. N. (2011). Introduction: The variety of methods for the multi-faceted phenomenon of trust. In F. Lyon, G. Möllering, & M. N. Saunder (Eds.), *Handbook of research methods on trust* (pp. 1–18). Edward Elgar.

Machado-da-Silva, C. L., Guarido Filho, E. R., & Rossoni, L. (2006). Organizational fields and the structuration perspective: Analytical possibilities. *Brazilian Administration Review, 3*, 32–56.

Maguire, S., Hardy, C., & Lawrence, T. B. (n.d.). Institutional entrepreneurship in emerging fields: HIV/AIDS treatment advocacy in Canada. *Academy of Management Journal, 47*, 657–679.

Mahoney, J., & Thelen, K. (2010). A theory of gradual institutional change. In J. Mahoney & K. Thelen (Eds.), *Explaining institutional change* (pp. 1–37). Cambridge University Press.

Mankiw, N. G., & Taylor, M. P. (2018). *Grundzüge der Volkswirtschaftslehre*. Schäffer-Poeschel Verlag Stuttgart.

March, J. G., & Olsen, J. P. (2004). *The logic of appropriateness*. Retrieved from Centre for European Studies https://www.researchgate.net/publication/5014575_The_Logic_of_Appropriateness/link/55d2f0c808aec1b0429f03e4/download

March, J. G., & Olsen, J. P. (2009). The logic of appropriateness. In R. E. Gooding (Ed.), *The Oxford handbook of political science* (pp. 478–497). Oxford University Press.

Marino, P., Soares, R., De Luca, M., & de Vasconcelos, A. (2016). Global governance indicators: How they relate to the socioeconomic indicators of the BRICS countries. *Revista Administrativa Pública, 50*(5), 721–743.

Marinova, S. (2015). Institutions and international business. In I. S. Marinova (Ed.), *Institutional impacts on firm internalization* (pp. 1–11). Palgrave Macmillan.

Martinelli, A. (1998). Contemporary capitalism: The embeddedness of institutions. *American Journal of Sociology, 104*(1), 233–235.

Mattes, J. (2013). The regional embeddness of multinational companies: A critical perspective. *European Planning Studies, 21*(4), 433–451.

Maudsley, G. (2011). Mixing it but not mixed-up: Mixed methods research in medical education (a critical narrative review). *Medical Teacher, 33*(2), 92–104.

Maurer, A. (2012). "Social embeddedness" viewed from an institutional perspective, revision of a core principle of new economic sociology with special regard to Max Weber. *Polish Sociological Review, 180*, 475–496.

Maxwell, S. E., Delaney, H. D., & Kelley, K. (2017). *Designing experiments and analyzing data: A model comparison perspective* (3rd ed.). CRC Press.

Mayntz, R., & Scharpf, F. W. (1995). Der Ansatz des akteurzentrierten Institutionalismus. In R. Mayntz & F. W. Scharpf (Eds.), *Gesellschaftliche Selbstregelung und politische Steuerung* (pp. 39–73). Campus Verlag.

Mayntz, R., & Scharpf, F. W. (1999). Der Ansatz des akteruzentrierten Institutionalismus. In I. R. Mayntz & F. W. Scharpf (Eds.), *Gesellschaftliche Selbstregelung und Steuerung* (pp. 39–72). Campus.

Mayring, P. (2014). *SSOAR*. Retrieved from Qualitative content analysis: theoretical foundation, basicprocedures and software solution http://nbn-resolving.de/urn:nbn:de:0168-ssoar-395173

McEvoy, P., & Richards, D. (2006). A critical realist rationale for using a combination of quantitative and qualitative methods. *Journal of Research in Nursing*, 66–78.

McGinnis, M. D. (2011). An introduction to IAD and the language of the Ostrom workshop: A simple guide to a complex framework for the analysis of institutions and their development. *Policy Studies Journal, 39*(1), 169–183.

Menard, S. (2010). *Logistic regression: From introductory to advanced concepts and applications*. Sage.

Ménard, C., & Shirley, M. M. (2014). The contribution of Douglass North to New institutional economics. In S. Galani & I. Sened (Eds.), *Institutions, property rights and economic growth: The legacy of Douglass North* (pp. 11–29). Cambridge University Press.
Meyer, K. E., Mudambi, R., & Narula, R. (2011). Multinational enterprises and local contexts: The opportunities and challenges of multiple embeddedness. *Journal of Management Studies, 48*(2), 235–252.
Meyer, W. J., & Rowan, B. (1977). Institutionalized organizations: Formal structure as myth and ceremony. *American Journal of Sociology, 83*(2), 340–363.
Micheel, H.-G. (2010). *Quantitative empirische Sozialforschung*. Ernst Reinhardt Verlag.
Ministério da Educação. (2018). *Secretaria de Educação Profissional e Tecnológica*. Retrieved from http://portal.mec.gov.br/setec/legisla_tecnico_parecer1699.pdf
Mitchell, M. C. (2010). An institutional perspective of the MNC as a social change agent: The case of environmentalism. *Journal of Global Responsibility, 1(2)*, 382–398.
Moe, T. M. (1995). The politics of structural choice: Toward a theory of public bureaucracy. In O. E. Williamson (Ed.), *Organization theory: From Chester Barnard to the present and beyond* (pp. 116–153). Oxford University Press.
Moreno-Brid, J. C., & Ros, J. (2009). *Development and growth in the Mexican economy*. Oxford University Press.
Morgan, G., & Kristensen, P. H. (2006). The contested space of multinationals: Varieties of institutionalism, varieties of capitalism. *Human Relations, 59*, 1467–1490.
Mourshed, M., Farrell, D., & Barton, D. (2013). *Educação para o Trabalho: Desenhando um Sistema que Funcione*. McKinsey Center for Government.
Muravyev, A. (2014). *Employment protection legislation in transition and emerging markets*. IZA World of Labor.
Murillo, M. V. (2001). *Labor unions, partisan coalitions, and market reforms in Latin America*. Cambridge University Press.
Myles, J. (2002). How to design a liberal welfare state: A comparison of Canada and the United States. In E. Huber (Ed.), *Models of capitalism: Lessons for Latin America* (pp. 339–366). The Pennsylvania State University Press.
Naím, M. (1994). Latin America: The second stage of reform. *Journal of Democracy, 5(4)*, 32–48.
Neeser, R., & Camargo, L. (2017, May 17). *Brazil: Unions struggle after labor reform*. Retrieved from https://www.shrm.org/resourcesandtools/legal-and-compliance/employment-law/pages/global-brazil-unions-after-labor-reform.aspx
Negrín, A., & Pérez, A. V. (n.d.). México y Alemania: una agenda a futuro. *Revista Mexicana de Política Exterior, 105*, 135–154.
Nielsen, L. (2011). *Classifications of countries based on their level of development: How it is done and how it could be done*. International Monetary Fund.
Nigussie, Z., Tsunekawa, A., Haregeweyn, N., Adgo, E., Cochrane, L., Floquet, A., & Abele, S. (2018). Applying Ostrom's institutional analysis and development framework to soil and water conservation activities in north-western Ethiopia. *Land Use Policy, 71*, 1–10.
Nölke, A. (2010). A "BRIC"-variety of capitalism and social inequality: The case of Brazil. *Revista de Estudos e Pesquisas sobre as Américas, 4*(1), 1–14.
Nölke, A. (2013, August 15). *linksnet.de*. Retrieved from https://www.linksnet.de/sites/default/files/pdf/130-131_14_noelke_0.pdf
Nölke, A. (2018). Dependent versus state-permeated capitalism: Two basic options for emerging markets. *International Journal of Management and Economics, 54*(4), 269–282.
Nölke, A., & Perry, J. (2007). The power of transnational private governance: Financialization and the IASB. *Business and Politics, 9*(3), 1–25.
Nölke, A., & Vliegenhart, A. (2009, October). Enlarging the varieties of capitalism: The emergence of dependent market economies in East Central Europe. *World Politics, 61*(4), 670–702.
Norman, G. (2010). Likert scales, levels of measurement and the "laws" of statistics. *Advances in Health Sciences Education, 15*(5), 625–632.

North, D. (1991a). *Institutions, institutional change and economic development*. Cambridge University Press.

North, D. C. (1991b). Institutions. *Journal of Economic Perspectives, 5*(1), 97–112.

North, D. C. (1992). Institutions and economic theory. *The American Economist, 36*(1), 3–6.

Northern Arizona University. (2020). Retrieved from http://oak.ucc.nau.edu/homepage/. http://oak.ucc.nau.edu/rh232/courses/EPS625/Handouts/One-Way%20ANOVA/ANOVA%20-%20Example%20-%20Welch%20and%20G-H%20-%20Key.pdf

Norus, J. (1997). The role of personal and professional networks in the process of technological transformation. *American Behavioral Scientist, 40*(4), 514–522.

nube. (2020). *Núcleo Brasileiro de Estágios*. Retrieved from https://www.nube.com.br/cota-aprendiz

Nye, J. (2011). Taking institutions seriously: Rethinking the political economy of development in the Philippines. *Asian Development Review, 28*(1), 1–21.

NYU. (2019). *Country default spreads and risk premiums*. Retrieved from http://pages.stern.nyu.edu/~adamodar/New_Home_Page/datafile/ctryprem.html

O'Cathain, A. (2009). Reporting results. In S. Andres & E. Halcomb (Eds.), *Mixed methods research for nursing and the health sciences*. Blackwell Publishing.

O'Leary, Z. (2010). *The essential guide to doing your research project*. Sage.

O'Leary, Z. (2019). *The essential guide to doing your research project*. Sage.

Oakerson, R. J., & Parks, R. B. (2011). The study of local public economies: Multi-organizational, multi-level institutional analysis and development. *The Policy Studies Journal, 39*(1), 147–167.

Ocampo, J. A. (2004). La América Latina y La Economía Mundial en El Largo Siglo XX. *El Trimestre Económico, LXXI*(284), 725–786.

OECD. (2006, February 16). *Glossary of statistical terms*. Retrieved from https://stats.oecd.org/glossary/detail.asp?ID=4842

OECD. (2011). *The call for innovative and open government: An overview of national initiatives*. OECD Publishing.

OECD. (2013). *PISA 2012 Ergebnisse im Fokus: Was 15-Jährige wissen und wie sie dieses Wissen einsetzen können*. .

OECD. (2014). *All on board: Making inclusive growth happen*. .

OECD. (2016). *oecd.org*. Retrieved May 30, 2017, from FDI stocks https://data.oecd.org/fdi/fdi-stocks.htm

OECD. (2017). *Education in Chile, Reviews of national policies for education*. OECD Publishing.

OECD. (2018a, September 18–19). *OECD*. Retrieved from Latin American and Caribbean Competition Forum-Session I: Informal Economy in Latin America and the Caribbean: Implications for Competition Policy: https://one.oecd.org/document/DAF/COMP/LACF(2018)4/en/pdf

OECD. (2018b). *OECD economic surveys Brazil*. OECD.

OECD. (2018c). *OECD economic surveys Chile*. OECD.

OECD. (2019). *FDI Regulatory Restrictiveness Index*. Retrieved from https://www.oecd.org/investment/fdiindex.htm

OECD. (2019a). *FDI Regulatory Restrictiveness Index*. Retrieved from https://www.oecd.org/investment/fdiindex.htm

OECD. (2019b). *OECD economic surveys Argentina*. OECD.

OECD. (2019c). *OECD economic surveys Colombia*. OECD.

OECD. (2019d). *OECD productivity statistics*. Retrieved from GDP per capita and productivity growth https://data.oecd.org/lprdty/gdp-per-hour-worked.htm

Oliva, B. T. (2014). *Três ensaios de economia da educação*. Fundação Getúlio Vargas.

Oliver, C. (1991). Strategic respones to institutional processes. *Academy of Management Review, 16*(1), 145–179.

Olofsdotter, K. (1998). Foreign direct investment, country capabilities and economic growth. *Weltwirtschaftliches Archiv, 134*(3), 534–547.

Osland, G. E., Taylor, C. R., & Zou, S. (2001). Selecting international modes of entry and expansion. *Marketing Intelligence & Planning, 19*(3), 153–161.

Ostrom, E. (1990). *Governing the commons: The evolution of institutions for collective action.* Cambridge University Press.
Ostrom, E. (1996). Crossing the great divide: Coproduction, synergy, and development. *World Development, 24*(6), 1073–1087.
Ostrom, E. (2005). *Understanding institutional diversity*. Princeton University Press.
Ostrom, E. (2009a, March 4). *Biographical. Nobel Prize.org*. Retrieved from Nobel Media AB 2019 https://www.nobelprize.org/prizes/economic-sciences/2009/ostrom/biographical/
Ostrom, E. (2009b, December 8). *nobelprize.org*. Retrieved from Beyond Markets and states: Polycentric Governance of Complex Economic Systems: Prize Lecture by Elinor Ostrom https://www.nobelprize.org/uploads/2018/06/ostrom_lecture.pdf
Ostrom, E. (2010a). Analyzing collective action. *International Association of Agricultural Economist, 41*, 155–166.
Ostrom, E. (2010b). Institutional analysis and development: Elements of the framework in historical perspective. In C. Crothers (Ed.), *Historical developments and theoretical approaches in sociology* (Vol. II, pp. 261–288). Eolss Publishers.
Ostrom, E. (2011). Background on the institutional analysis and development framework. *The Policy Studies Journal, 39*, 7–27.
Otero-Iglesias, M., & Vermeiren, M. (2015). China's state-permeated market economy and its constraints to the internationalization of the renminbi. *International Politics, 52*(6), 684–703.
Otto, F. (2014). *audi.com.* Retrieved from Audi México: Inaugurado nuevo Centro de Especialización https://www.audi.com.mx/dam/nemo/mx/compania/media-center/noticias/pdf/141021_centro-de-especializacion.pdf
Padayachee, V. (2013). Introducing varieties of capitalism into the South African debate: Uses and limits. *Transformation: Critical Perspectives on Southern Africa, Number, 81*(82), 5–32.
Page, R. (2018). *ARBEITSPAPIER Nummer 313: Co-determination in Germany –A beginner's guide*. Hans Böckler Stiftung.
Pagel, H., Ranke, K., Hempel, F., & Köhler, J. (2014). *The use of the concept "global south" in social science & humanities*. Globaler Süden/Global South: Kritische Perspektiven. Institut für Asien- & Afrikawissenschaften, Humboldt-Universität zu Berlin.
Palley, T. I. (2013). *Financialization: The economics of finance capital domination*. Palgrave Macmillan.
Pancaldi, F. (2012, September). The turn to real actors: Achievements and challenges for actor-centered institutionalism in the comparative political economy. *La Metodologia dei Giovani Politologi in Italia,* pp. 1-28.
Pargendler, M. (2012). The unintended consequences of state ownership. *Theoretical Inquiries in Law,13*(2), 503–523. Retrieved from Social Science Research Network.
Patil, V. H., Singh, S. N., Mishra, S., & Donavan, D. T. (2008). *Parallel analysis engine to aid determining number of factors to retain [Computer software].* Retrieved from http://smishra.faculty.ku.edu/parallelengine.htm
Patil, V. H., Singh, S. N., Mishra, S., & Donavan, D. T. (2017). *Parallel analysis engine to aid in determining number of factors to retain using R [Computer software].* Retrieved from https://analytics.gonzaga.edu/parallelengine/
Pauly, L. W. (2000). *The myth of the global corporation*. European Union Center of California.
Pauly, L. W., & Reich, S. (1997). National structures and multinational corporate behavior: Enduring differences in the age of globalization. *International Organization, 51*, 1–30.
Paunescu, M., & Schneider, M. (2004). Wettbewerbsfähigkeit und Dynamik institutioneller Standortbedingungen: Ein empirischer Test des "Varieties-of-Capitalism"-Ansatzes. *Schmollers Jahrbuch, 124*, 31–59.
Paunescu, M., & Schneider, M. R. (2012a). Changing varieties of capitalism and revealed comparative advantages from 1990 to 2005: A test of the Hall and Soskice claims. *Socio-Economic Review, 1*, 731–753.

Paunescu, M., & Schneider, M. R. (2012b). Changing varieties of capitalism and revealed comparative advantages from 1990 to 2005: A test of the Hall and Soskice claims. *Socio-Economic Review, 1*, 731–753.

Peck, J., & Zhang, J. (2013). A variety of capitalism ... with Chinese characteristics? *Journal of Economic Geography, 13*, 357–396.

Pere, E. (2015). The impact of good governance in the economic development of Western Balkan countries. *European Journal of Government and Economics, 4(1)*, 25–45.

Pessoa, J. P., & Van Reenen, J. (2013). *Wage growth and productivity growth: The myth and reality of 'decoupling'*. Retrieved from CentrePiece Autumn 2013 http://cep.lse.ac.uk/pubs/download/cp401.pdf

Philips, N. W., & Tracey, P. (2009a). Institutional theory and the MNC. *The Academy of Management Review, 2009*, 169–173.

Philips, N., & Tracey, P. (2009b). Insitutitonal theory and the MNC. *The Academy of Management Review, 34*(1), 169–171.

Pieczynski, D. (2016). *radford*. Retrieved from Employee Turnover Slows in Brazil, Even as the Tech Sector Remains an Economic Bright Spot https://radford.aon.com/insights/articles/2016/employee-turnover-slows-in-brazil

Popal, P. (2019). *Small to medium sized enterprises and corporate social responsibility: The role of international networks*. Routledge.

Pope, R. A. (2002). Why small firms export: Another look. *Journal of Small Business Management, 40*(1), 17–26.

Porst, R. (2014). *Fragebogen*. VS Verlag für Sozialwissenschaften.

Portelo Souza, A., Lima, L., Arabage, A., Camargo, J., de Lucena, T., & Soares, S. (2015, June). *Inter-American Development Bank*. Retrieved from https://publications.iadb.org/publications/english/document/Vocational-Education-and-Training-in-Brazil-Knowledge-Sharing-Forum-on-Development-Experiences-Comparative-Experiences-of-Korea-and-Latin-America-and-the-Caribbean.pdf

Porter, M. E. (1990). *The competitive advantage of nations*. Free Press.

Poteete, A. R., Janssen, M. A., & Ostrom, E. (2010). *Working together: Collective action, the commons, and multiple methods in practice*. Princeton University Press.

Powell, W. W., & Colyvas, J. A. (2008). Microfoundations of institutional theory. In R. Greenwood, C. Oliver, K. Sahlin, & R. Suddaby (Eds.), *The SAGE handbook of organizational institutionalism* (pp. 276–298). Sage.

Powell, W. W., & DiMaggio, P. J. (1991). *The new institutionalism in organizational analysis*. University of Chicago Press.

Praça, S. (2009). *Preference formation and institutional change*. Retrieved from brazilian political science review http://socialsciences.scielo.org/pdf/s_bpsr/v4nse/a04.pdf

Presidência da República. (2000). *LEI No 10.097, DE 19 DE DEZEMBRO DE 2000*. Retrieved from https://www.planalto.gov.br/ccivil_03/Leis/L10097.htm

Presidência da República. (2016). *DECRETO N° 8.637, DE 15 DE JANEIRO DE 2016*. Retrieved from http://www.planalto.gov.br/ccivil_03/_ato2015-2018/2016/decreto/D8637.htm

Presidencia de la Nación. (1992a). *Ministerio de Justicia y Derechos Humanos*. Retrieved from http://servicios.infoleg.gob.ar/infolegInternet/anexos/0-4999/497/norma.htm

Presidencia de la Nación. (1992b). *Ministerio de Justicia y Derechos Humanos*. Retrieved from Información Legislativa http://servicios.infoleg.gob.ar/infolegInternet/anexos/0-4999/497/norma.htm

Priddat, B. P. (2015). *Fakultät für Wirtschaftswissenschaft Universität Witten/Herdecke*. Retrieved from Die Zeit der Institutionen.Geschichte und Theoriegeschichte der Institutionenökonomie https://www.uni-wh.de/fileadmin/user_upload/04_W/03_Forschung/Discussion_Papers/31_Priddat.pdf

Pries, L. (2000). Globalisierung und Wandelinternationaler Unternehmen. *Kölner Zeitschrift für Soziologie und Sozialpsychologie, 52*, 670–695.

Prüfer, P., & Rexroth, M. (2000). www.gesis.org. Retrieved from Zwei-Phasen-Pretesting: https://www.gesis.org/fileadmin/upload/forschung/publikationen/gesis_reihen/zuma_arbeitsberichte/00_08.pdf

Prüfer, P., & Rexroth, M. (2005). *Kognitive interviews.* ZUMA How-to-Reihe, 15.

Pudelko, M., & Harzing, A.-W. (2007). Country-of-origin, localization, or dominance effect? An empirical investigation of HRM practices in foreign subsidiaries. *Human Resource Management, 46*, 535–559.

Radaelli, C., Dente, B., & Dossi, S. (2012). Recasting institutionalism: Institutional analysis and public policy. *European Political Science, 11*, 1–14.

Radin, B. (2006). *Challenging the performance movement: Accountability, complexity, and democratic values.* Georgetown University Press.

Raheem, N. (2014). Using the institutional analysis and development (IAD) framework to analyze the acequias of El Río de las Gallinas, New Mexico. *The Social Science Journal, 51*, 447–454.

Raheem, N. (2019). Using the institutional analysis and development (IAD) framework to analyze the acequias of El Río de las Gallinas, New Mexico. *The Social Science Journal, 51*, 447–454.

Rao, H., Morrill, C., & Zald, M. N. (2000). Power plays: How socialmovements and collectiveaction create neworganizational forms. *Research in Organizational Behaviour, 2000*, 239–282.

Redding, G. (2005). The thick description and comparison of societal systems of capitalism. *Journal of International Business Studies, 36*, 123–155.

Richmond, P. (2020). *European integration and labour market institutions: A varieties of capitalism perspective.* Retrieved from Birkbeck Politics Occasional Paper 3/2020 https://eprints.bbk.ac.uk/31241/1/31241.pdf

Riordan, M. H., & Williamson, O. E. (1985). Asset specificity and economic organization. *International Journal of Industrial Organization, 3*, 365–378.

Root, F. R. (1994). *Entry strategies for international markets.* Lexington Books.

Rosenzweig, P. M., & Singh, J. V. (1991). Organizational environments and the multinational enterprise. *The Academy of Management Review, 27*, 340–361.

Roth, K., & Kostova, T. (2003). Organizational coping with institutional upheaval in transition economies. *Journal of World Business, 38*, 314–330.

Roy, A., Shah, M., & Sharma, R. (2017, April). Need for foreign investment. *Journal of Accounting, Finance & Marketing Technology, 1*(1), 18–21.

Royo, S. (2009). Varieties of capitalism for Latin America? *Jean Monnet/Robert Schuman Paper Series, 9*(12), 2–23.

Rugman, A. M. (1981). *Inside the multinationals: The economics of internal markets.* Colombia University Press.

Rugman, A., & Verbeke, A. (2008). Internalization theory and its impact on the field of international business. In J. Boddewyn (Ed.), *International business scholarship: AIB fellows on the first 50 years and beyond. Research in global strategic management* (Vol. 14, pp. 155–174). Emerald.

Rugman, A., & Verbeke, A. Internalization theory and its impact on the field of international business. In J. Boddewyn (Ed.), *International business scholarship: AIB fellows on the first 50 years and beyond. Research in global strategic management* (Vol. 14, pp. 155–174). Emerald.

Ruigrok, W., & van Tulder, R. (1995). *The logic of international restructuring.* Routledge.

Ruiz-Velasco Sánchez, E., & Bárcenas López, J. (2019). *Edutecnología y Aprendizaje 4.0.* Sociedad Mexicana de Computación en lad Educación A.C.

Rutherford, A. (2011). *ANOVA and ANCOVA: A GLM approach* (2nd ed.). Wiley.

Sako, M. (2005). Does embeddedness imply limits to within country diversity? *British Journal of Industrial Relations, 43*(4), 585–592.

Salazar-Xirinachs, J. M. (2015, May 7). *weforum.org.* Retrieved May 31, 2017, from World Economic Forum https://www.weforum.org/agenda/2015/05/6-ways-latin-america-can-close-its-skills-gap/

Sampaio de Freitas, C. A., & de Aquino Guimarães, T. (2007). Isomorphism, institutionalization and legitimacy: Operational auditing at the court of auditors. *Brazilian Administration Review, 4*, 35–50.

Sawyer, W. C. (2010). Institutional quality and economic growth in Latin America. *Global Economy Journal, 10*(4), 1850214.

Sayer, A. (2000). Contemporary capitalism: The embeddedness of institutions by J. Rogers Hollingsworth and Robert Boyer. *Work, Employment & Society, 14*(3), 600–602.

Scania. (2020). *Scania*. Retrieved from https://www.volkswagenag.com/de/brands-and-models/scania.html

Scharpf, F. W. (1997). *Games real actors play: Actor-centered institutionalism in policy research*. Westview Press.

Scharpf, F. (2000). Institutions in comparative policy research. *Comparative Political Studies, 33*(6–7), 762–790.

Schneider, B. R. (2004). *Business politics and the state in 20th-century Latin America*. Cambridge University Press.

Schneider, B. R. (2009, August). Hierarchical market economies and varieties of capitalism in Latin America. *Journal of Latin American Studies, 41*(3), 553–575.

Schneider, B. R. (2013). *Hierarchical capitalism in Latin America: Business, labor, and the challenges of equitable development*. Cambridge University Press.

Schneider, B. R., & Karcher, S. (2010). Complementarities and continuities in the political economy of labour markets in Latin America. *Socio-Economic Review, 8*(4), 623–651.

Schneider, M. R., Schulze-Bentrop, C., & Paunescu, M. (2010). Mapping the institutional capital of high-techfirms: A fuzzy-set analysis of capitalist variety and export performance. *Journal of International Business Studies, 41*, 246–266.

Schneider, B. R., & Soskice, D. (2009). Inequality in developed countries and Latin America: Coordinated, liberal and hierarchical systems. *Economy and Society, 38*(1), 17–52.

Scholz, J. T., & Pinney, N. (1995). Duty, fear, and tax compliance: The Heuristic basis of citizenship behavior. *American Journal of Political Science, 39*(2), 490–512.

Schoonenboom, J., & Johnson, R. B. (2017). How to construct a mixed methods research design. *Kolner Zeitschrift für Soziologie und Sozialpsychologie, 2017*, 107–131.

Schröder, M. (2014). *Varianten des Kapitalismus: Die Unterschiede liberaler und koordinierter Marktwirtschaften*. Springer VS.

Schuler. (2020). *Centro de especialización cedual*. Retrieved from https://www.schulergroup.com/minor/mx/training_center/index.html

Scott, R. W. (2010). Reflections: The past and future of research on institutions and institutional change. *Journal of Change Management, 10*(1), 5–21.

Sehnbruch, K. (2006). *The Chilean Labor Market: A key to understanding Latin American labor markets*. Palgrave Macmillan.

Sehnbruch, K. (2016). Unemployment insurance or individual savings accounts: Can Chile's new scheme serve as a model for other developing countries? *International Social Security Review, 59*(1), 27–48.

Seo, M.-G., & Creed, D. W. (2002). Institutional contradictions, praxis, and institutional change: A Dialectical perspective. *The Academy of Management Review, 27*(2), 222–247.

SEP. (2014). *Modelo Mexicano de Formación Dual*. Retrieved from https://www.gob.mx/sep/acciones-y-programas/modelo-mexicano-de-formacion-dual

Sheahan, J. (2002). Alternative models of capitalism in Latin America. In E. Huber (Ed.), *Models of capitalism: Lessons for Latin America* (pp. 25–52). The Pennsylvania State University Press.

Sherman, A. J. (2011). *Franchising & licensing: Two powerful ways to grow your business in any economy*. AMA.

Silva, J., Almeida, R., & Strokova, V. (2015). *Sustaining employment and wage gains in Brazil*. World Bank Group.

Simons, L., & Lathlean, J. (2010). Mixed methods. In K. Gerrish & A. Lacey (Eds.), *The Research Process in Nursing* (6th ed.). Wiley-Blackwell.

Sirra, V. (2020). *GeeksforGeeks*. Retrieved from https://www.geeksforgeeks.org/ml-feature-scaling-part-2/
Smets, M., Aristidou, A., & Whittington, R. (2017). Towards a practice-driven institutionalism. In R. Greenwood, C. Oliver, T. B. Lawrence, & R. Meyer (Eds.), *The Sage handbook of organizational institutionalism* (2nd ed., pp. 384–411). Sage.
Smets, M., Morris, T., & Greenwood, R. (2012a). From practice to field: A multilevel model of practice-driven institutional change. *The Academy of Management Journal, 55*(4), 877–904.
Smets, M., Morris, T., & Greenwood, R. (2012b). From practice to field: A multilevel model of practice-driven institutional change. *The Academy of Management Journal, 55*, 877–904.
Smets, M., & Reihlen, M. (2012). Institutional entrepreneurship: A literature review and analysis of the maturing consulting field: Discussion Paper #6. *Leuphana Discussion Paper Series*, pp. 1–37.
Smith, A. (1776). *An inquiry into the nature and causes of the wealth of nations*. Oxford University Press.
socioeco. (2019, May 15). *Sitio de recursos de la economía social y solidaria*. Retrieved from Programa de Economia del Trabajo (PET) http://www.socioeco.org/bdf_organisme-302_es.html#type_PUB_plusieurs
Solow, R. M. (1956). A contribution to the theory of economic growth. *Quarterly Journal of Economics, 70*, 65–94.
SP. (2020). saopauolo.sp.gov.br. Retrieved from https://www.saopaulo.sp.gov.br/orgaos-e-entidades/governador
Statistics Solutions. (2020a). *Can an ordinal Likert Scale be a continuous variable?* Retrieved from https://www.statisticssolutions.com/can-an-ordinal-likert-scale-be-a-continuous-variable/
Statistics Solutions. (2020b). *Missing values in data*. Retrieved from https://www.statisticssolutions.com/missing-values-in-data/
Storz, C., Amable, B., Casper, S., & Lechevalier, S. (2013). Bringing Asia into the comparative capitalism perspective. *Socio-Economic Review, 11*, 217–232.
Streeck, W. (2009). *Reforming capitalism: Institutional change in the German political economy*. Oxford University Press.
Streeck, W., & Thelen, K. (2005). *Beyond continutiy: Institutional change in advanced political economies*. Oxford University Press.
Suchanek, A. (2004). Ökonomische Unternehmensethik. In V. Arnold (Ed.), *Wirtschaftsethische Perspektiven VII* (pp. 79–101). Springer.
Suchanek, A. (2008). *Discussion paper NR.2008-3: Business ethics and the golden rule*. Wittenberg-Zentrum für Globale Ethik e.V.
Suchanek, A. (2010). Die Verantwortung von Unternehmen in der Gesellschaft. In I. S. Braun (Ed.), *Gesellschaftliches Engagement von Unternehmen. Der deutsche Weg im internationalen Kontext* (pp. 37–49). VS Verlag.
Südzucker AG. (2019). *Annual Report 2018/19 Südzucker AG*. Retrieved from https://www.suedzucker.de/sites/default/files/2019-12/2018-19_Annual_Report.pdf
Swidler, A. (1979). *Organization Without Authority: Dilemmas of Social Control of Free Schools*. Harvard University Press.
Tashakkori, A., & Teddlie, C. (2008). Introduction to mixed method and mixed model studies in the social and behavioral science. In V. L. Plano-Clar & J. W. Creswell (Eds.), *The mixed methods reader* (pp. 7–26). Springer.
Tempel, A., Edwards, T., Ferner, A., Muller-Carmen, M., & Wächter, H. (2006, November 1). Subsidiary responses to institutional duality: Collective representation practices of US multinationals in Britain and Germany. *Human Relations, 59*(11), 1543–1570.
Terrell, S. R. (2012). Mixed-methods research methodologies. *The Qualitative Report, 17*(1), 254–280.
The Economic Times. (2018). economictimes.com. Retrieved from https://economictimes.indiatimes.com/definition/gross-domestic-product

The Economic Times. (2020). *Definition of 'gross domestic product'*. Retrieved from https://economictimes.indiatimes.com/definition/gross-domestic-product

The Financial Times. (2017a). *FDI intelligence*. FT.

The Financial Times. (2017b, May). *fDi Intelligence from the Financial Times Ltd.* Retrieved from https://www.fdimarkets.com/

The Financial Times Ltd. (2017). *fDi Intelligence*.

The Law Dictionary. (2019, February 5). *The Law dictionary: Featuring Black's law dictionary free online legal dictionary* (2nd ed). Retrieved from https://thelawdictionary.org/multinational-corporation-mnc/

The World Bank. (2011). worldbank.org. Retrieved from http://web.worldbank.org/WBSITE/EXTERNAL/DATASTATISTIC/0,,contentMDK:20420458~menuPK:64909257~pagePK:64909151~piPK:64909148~theSitePK:6950074,00.html

The World Bank. (2017a, May). *worldbank.org*. Retrieved May 30, 2017, from http://data.worldbank.org/indicator/NY.GDP.PCAP.CD?end=2015&locations=AR-CO-BR-CL&start=1985

The World Bank. (2017b, May 26). *worldbank.org*. Retrieved May 31, 2017, from GINI Index (World Bank Estimate) http://data.worldbank.org/indicator/SI.POV.GINI

The World Bank. (2018a, October 15). *GINI index (World Bank estimate)*. Retrieved from https://data.worldbank.org/indicator/SI.POV.GINI

The World Bank. (2018b). *iccmoot.com*. Retrieved from http://iccmoot.com/wp-content/uploads/2017/07/World-Bank-List-of-Economies.pdf

The World Bank. (2019). *World Bank Statistics*. Retrieved from https://data.worldbank.org/indicator/SI.POV.GINI?end=2017&locations=DE-GB-US-FR-OE&start=1995&view=chart

The World Bank. (2020). *CHAPTER 6: Ease of doing business score and ease of doing business ranking*. Retrieved from https://openknowledge.worldbank.org/bitstream/handle/10986/32436/9781464814402_Ch06.pdf

Thelen, K. (2001). Varieties of labor politics in the developed democracies. In P. A. Hall & D. Soskice (Eds.), *Varieties of capitalism: The institutional foundations of comparative advantage* (pp. 71–103). Oxford University Press.

Thelen, K. (2012). Varieties of capitalism: Trajectories of liberalization and the new politics of social solidarity. *Annual Review of Political Science, 15*, 137–159.

Thelen, K., & Busemeyer, M. R. (2008). *From collectivism towards segmentalism: Institutional change in German vocational training*. MPIfG Discussion Paper.

Thomas, H., & Turnbull, P. (2018). From horizontal to vertical labour governance: The International Labour Organization (ILO) and decent work in global supply chains. *Human Relations, 71*, 536–559.

Thornton, P. H., & Ocasio, W. (2008). Institutional logics. In R. Greenwood, C. Oliver, K. Sahlin, & R. Suddaby (Eds.), *The Sage handbook of organizational institutionalism* (pp. 99–129). Sage.

Tilly, C. (1989). *Big structures, large processes, huge comparisons*. Russell Sage Foundation.

Tolbert, P. S., & Zucker, L. G. (1996). The institutionalization of institutional theory. In S. Clegg, C. Hardy, & W. Nord (Eds.), *Handbook of organization studies* (pp. 175–190). Sage.

Trading Economics. (2017, May). *tradingeconomics.com*. Retrieved May 30, 2017, from https://tradingeconomics.com/commodity/crude-oil

Trading Economics. (2019). *Brazil productivity*. Retrieved from https://tradingeconomics.com/brazil/productivity

Treib, O. (2003). Die Umsetzung von EU-Richtlinien im Zeichen der Parteipolitik: Eine akteurzentrierte Antwort auf die Misfit-These. *Politische Vierteljahresschrift, 44*(4), 506–528.

Tuominen, E. (2015). Reversal of the Kuznets curve: Study on the inequality-development relation using top income shares data. *WIDER Working Paper, No. 2015/036, ISBN 978-92-9230-921-3, The United Nations University World Institute for Development Economics Research (UNU-WIDER).*

Tuynman, J. (n.d.). *University of Southern California*. Retrieved from Working Paper: Can Liberal and Hierarchical Economies Implement the German Model of Vocational Training? https://dornsife.usc.edu/assets/sites/793/docs/Tuynman_DualModelAbroad.pdf

Ullrich, K. (2016). *KfW research: South America after the commodity boom - productivity worries are back*. KFW.

UN Secretary-General Ban Ki-moon. (2014, February 20). *United Nations Secretary-General*. Retrieved from Secretary-General's message for the World Day of Social Justice https://www.un.org/sg/en/content/sg/statement/2014-02-20/secretary-generals-message-world-day-social-justice-scroll-down

UNCTAD. (2006). *Investment policy review Colombia.*. Retrieved from https://unctad.org/en/Docs/iteipc200511_en.pdf

UNCTAD. (2016a). *unctad.org*. Retrieved May 30, 2017, from World Investment Report 2016: Annex Tables http://unctad.org/en/Pages/DIAE/World%20Investment%20Report/Annex-Tables.aspx

UNCTAD. (2016b). *unctad.org*. Retrieved May 30, 2017, from World Investment Report 2016: Annex Tables http://unctad.org/en/Pages/DIAE/World%20Investment%20Report/Annex-Tables.aspx

UNCTAD. (2016c). *World investment report 2016*. United Nations Publications.

UNCTAD. (2017). *United Nations conference on trade and development: Properity for all*. Retrieved May 25, 2017, from http://unctad.org/en/Pages/DIAE/Foreign-Direct-Investment-(FDI).aspx

UNCTAD. (2018a, November). *United Nations Confrence on Trade and Development*. Retrieved from https://unctad.org/en/Pages/DIAE/World%20Investment%20Report/Country-Fact-Sheets.aspx

UNCTAD. (2018b). *World investment report 2018*. United Nations.

UNCTAD. (2019a). *Investment policy hub*. Retrieved from https://investmentpolicy.unctad.org/international-investment-agreements/countries/8/argentina

UNCTAD. (2019b). *World investment report 2019*. Retrieved from unctad.org https://unctad.org/en/Pages/DIAE/World%20Investment%20Report/Annex-Tables.aspx

UNCTAD STAT. (2019). *United Nations Conference on Trade and Development*. Retrieved from https://unctadstat.unctad.org/wds/TableViewer/tableView.aspx

UNESCO. (2016). *Brazil*. Retrieved from http://www.unesco.org/new/en/gefi/partnerships/gefi-champion-countries/brazil/

United Nations. (2018a, December 15). *Economic Analysis & Policy Division*. Retrieved from https://www.un.org/development/desa/dpad/least-developed-country-category.html

United Nations. (2018b). *United Nations Development Programme Human Development Index (HDI)*. Retrieved from http://hdr.undp.org/en/content/human-development-index-hdi

United Nations. (2019). *DESA/Population Division*. Retrieved from https://population.un.org/wpp/, https://population.un.org/wpp/

Uwazie, I. U., Igwemma, A. A., & Uka, F. I. (2015). Contributions of Andre Gunder Frank to the theory of development and underdevelopment: Implications on Nigeria's development situation. *Journal of Economics and Sustainable Development, 6*(18), 27–38.

van Lieshout, H. A. (2008). *Different hands. Markets for intermediate skills in Germany, the U.S. and the Netherlands*.

Van Ryzin, G. G. (2006). Testing the expectancy disconfirmation model of citizen satisfaction with local government. *Journal of Public Administration Research and Theory, 16*, 599–611.

vetnet. (2020). *German chambers worldwide network (AHK) for cooperative, work-based Vocational Education & Training*. Retrieved from Bundesministerium für Bildung und Forschung https://www.berufsbildung-international.de/de/projekte-und-kooperationslaender-strategieprojekte-vetnet.html

VETnet. (n.d.). *Elf Länder, ein Ziel: Erfolg durch berufliche Bildung*. Retrieved from https://mexiko.ahk.de/fileadmin/AHK_Mexiko/Dokumente/vetnet-deutsch.pdf

Viehmann, S. M. (2017). *Formação Dual e sua aplicação no Brasil*. Retrieved from http://www.brasilalemanhanews.com.br/formacao/formacao-dual-e-sua-aplicacao-no-brasil/?doing_wp_cron=1592298898.9241828918457031250000

Voith. (2019a). *A stepping stone for your dream career*. Retrieved from http://www.voith.com/corp-en/careers___students.html

Voith. (2019b). *Summer 1964 - summer 2014: 50 years of Voith in Brazil*. Retrieved from http://www.voith.com/corp-en/sala-de-imprensa__press-releases-77217_59346.html

Volkswagen Group. (2020a). *Volkswagen Group Academy Mexico*. Retrieved from http://www.vwi.com.mx/auditors.html

Volkswagen Group. (2020b). *Volkswagen de México*. Retrieved from https://www.vw.com.mx/es.html

Vora, D., Kostova, T., & Roth, K. (2007). Roles of subsidiary managers in multinational corporations: The effect of dual organizational identification. *Management International Review, 47*, 595–620.

Wach, K. (2014). Market entry modes for international businesses. In E. Horská (Ed.), *International marketing: Within and beyond Visegrad Borders, Edition 1, Chapter 7* (pp. 135–147). Wydawnictwo Episeteme.

Wadhwa, K., & Reddy, S. (2011). Foreign direct investment into developing Asian Countries: The role of market seeking, resource seeking and efficiency seeking factors. *International Journal of Business and Management, 6*(11), 219–226.

Walker, J. T., Brewster, C., & Wood, G. (2014). Diversity between and within varieties of capitalism: Transnational survey evidence. *Industrial and Corporate Change, 23(2)*, 493–533.

Walker, K., Schlosser, F., & Deephouse, D. L. (2014, March 5). Organizational ingenuity and the paradox of embedded agency: The Case of the Embryonic Ontario Solar Energy Industry. *Organization Studies, 2014*, 613–634.

Walter, A., & Zhang, X. (2012). *East Asian capitalism: Diversity, continuity, and change*. Oxford University Press.

Weinert, F. (2018). The role of trust in political systems. A philosophical perspective. *Open Political Science, 1*, 7–15.

Weinstein, B. (1997). *For social peace in Brazil: Industrialists and the remaking of the working class in São Paulo, 1920-1964*. University of North Carolina Press.

Weisberg, S. (2014). *Applied linear regression* (4th ed.). Wiley.

Weiss, S. (2016). *Vorreiter in Mexiko – die VW-Akademie*. Retrieved from https://www.deutschland.de/de/topic/wissen/bildung-lernen/vorreiter-in-mexiko-die-vw-akademie

Welch, L. S., & Luostarinen, R. (1988). Internationalization: Evolution of a concept. *Journal of General Management, 14*(2), 34–55.

Westervelt, E. (2012). *The secret to Germany's low youth unemployment*. Retrieved from https://www.npr.org/2012/04/04/149927290/the-secret-to-germanys-low-youth-unemployment

Weyland, K. (1999). Neoliberal populism in Latin America and Eastern Europe. *Comparative Politics, 31*(4), 379–401.

Whalley, J., & Weisbrod, A. (2012). The contribution of Chinese FDI to Africa's pre crisis growth surge. *Global Economy Journal, 12*(4), 1–28.

White, H. (1992). *Identity and control: A structural theory of social integration*. Princeton University Press.

Whitley, R. (1998). Internationalization and varieties of capitalism: The limited effects of cross-national coordination of economic activities on the nature of business systems. *Review of International Political Economy, 5*, 445–481.

Whitley, R., & Kristensen, P. H. (1996). *The changing European firm*. Routledge.

Whittington, R. (1992). Putting giddens into action: Social systems and managerial agency. *Journal of Management Studies, 29*(6), 693–712.

Wiemann, K. (2018). *Mexiko. Internationales Handbuch der Berufsbildung, Band 49*. Bundesinstitut für Berufsbildung.
Wiemann, J., & Fuchs, M. (2018). The export of Germany's "secret of success" dual technical VET: MNCs and multiscalar stakeholders changing the skill formation system in Mexico. *Cambridge Journal or Regions, Economy and Society, 11*(2), 373–386.
Wiemann, K., & Pilz, M. (2017). Berufliche Ausbildung durch mexikanische und deutsche Unternehmen in Mexiko - ein Home-International-Vergleich. *Journal für International und Interkulturell Vergleichende Erziehungswissenschaft, 23*(2), 217–245.
Williamson, O. E. (1973). Markets and hierarchies: Some elementary considerations. *The American Economic Review, 63*, 316–325.
Williamson, O. (1985). *The economic institutions of capitalism: Firms, markets, relational contracting*. Free Press.
Williamson, O. (1993). Calculativeness, trust and economic organization. *Journal of Law and Economics, 36*, 453–486.
Williamson, O. E. (1995). Transaction costs economics and organization theory. In I. O. E. Williamson (Ed.), *Organization theory: From Chester Barnard to the present and beyond* (pp. 207–256). Oxford University Press.
Williamson, O. E. (2000). The new institutional economics: Taking stock, looking ahead. *Journal of Economic Literature, 3*, 595–613.
Witt, M. A., & Redding, G. (2013a). Asian business systems: Institutional comparison, clusters and implications for varieties of capitalism and business systems theory. *Socio-Economic Review, 11*(2), 265–300.
Witt, M., & Redding, G. (2013b). Asian business systems: Institutional comparison, clusters and implications for varieties of capitalism and business systems theory. *Socio-Economic Review, 11*(2), 217–232.
Woll, C., & Jacquot, S. (2010). Using Europe: Strategic action in multi-level politics. *Comparative European Politics, 8*, 110–126.
Wooten, M., & Hoffman, A. J. (2016). Organizational Fields: Past, Present and Future. In R. Greenwood, C. Oliver, K. Sahlin, & R. Suddaby (Eds.), *The SAGE handbook of organizational institutionalism* (pp. 130–148). Sage.
World Bank. (2017a, May). *worldbank.org*. Retrieved May 30, 2017, from http://data.worldbank.org/indicator/NY.GDP.PCAP.CD?end=2015&locations=AR-CO-BR-CL&start=1985
World Bank. (2017b, May 26). *worldbank.org*. Retrieved May 31, 2017, from GINI Index (World Bank Estimate) http://data.worldbank.org/indicator/SI.POV.GINI
World Bank. (2017c). *doingbusiness.org*. Retrieved June 2, 2017, from About doing business: Doing business 2017 http://www.doingbusiness.org/~/media/WBG/DoingBusiness/Documents/Annual-Reports/English/DB17-Chapters/DB17-About-Doing-Business.pdf
World Population Review. (2019). *Education rankings by country 2019*. Retrieved from http://worldpopulationreview.com/countries/education-rankings-by-country/
WTO. (2019). *World Trade Organization*. Retrieved from Members and Observers: https://www.wto.org/english/thewto_e/whatis_e/tif_e/org6_e.htm
Wuensch, L. (2012). *East Carolina University*. Retrieved from Pairwise comparisons http://core.ecu.edu/psyc/wuenschk/stathelp/Pairwise.htm.
Xu, D., & Shenkar, O. (2002). Institutional distance and the multinational enterprise. *The Academy of Management Review, 27*(4), 608–618.
Yan, A., & Luo, Y. (2015). *International joint ventures: Theory and practice*. CRC Press.
Yildirim, A., & Gökalp, M. F. (2016). Institutions and economic performace: A review on the developing countries. *Procedia Economics and Finance, 38*, 347–359.

Zaheer, S. (1995). Overcoming the liablity of foreignness. *Academy of Management Journal, 38*(2), 341–363.

Zajac, E. J., & Kraatz, M. S. (1993). A diametric forces model of strategic change: Assessing the antecedents and consequences of restructuring the higher education industry. *Strategic Management Journal, 14*, 83–102.

Zander, I., & Sölvell, Ö. (2004). Cross-border innovation in the modern multinational: Three dilemmas. In M. G. Serapio & T. Hayashi (Eds.), *Research in international business* (Vol. 8, pp. 13–40). Elsevier.

Zhang, X., & Whitley, R. (2013). Changing macro-structural varieties of East Asian capitalism. *Socio-Economic Review, 11*(2), 301–336.

The manufacturer's authorised representative in the EU is Springer Nature Customer Service Centre GmbH, Europaplatz 3, 69115 Heidelberg, Germany. If you have any concerns regarding our products, please contact ProductSafety@springernature.com

Printed and bound by CPI Group (UK) Ltd, Croydon, CR0 4YY
30/09/2026
02225493-0016